THE DELL CROSSWORD DICTIONARY

COMPILED BY KATHLEEN RAFFERTY, EDITOR-IN-CHIEF
OF DELL CROSSWORD PUZZLE MAGAZINES AND BOOKS

GALAHAD BOOKS • NEW YORK CITY

ABOUT THIS BOOK

Looking for an "Assam silkworm"? Cannot remember the name of a "Brazilian coin"? Do not know a "Candlenut tree"? You will with the aid of this book.

The purpose of this dictionary is to give puzzlers the pleasure of completing, down to the last three-letter word, every crossword they begin. It is meant to eliminate the frustration of filling in "all but a few" of those final puzzle squares. Here is a complete 384-page reference book, including the exclusive cross-referenced Word-Finder, to be used by puzzle solvers to find all those little-known, but much-used, cross-word words.

The Dell Crossword Dictionary is the result of many years of exhaustive research and was prepared by the editor of the famous Dell Crossword publications, all leaders in the puzzle world.

Kathleen Rafferty
Compiler and Editor

TABLE OF CONTENTS

CROSSWORD DEFINITIONS
WITH ANSWER WORDS
page 6 to page 186

All the important crossword puzzle words are listed alphabetically by definition.

Look under group headings for these special word listings:

SPECIAL SECTION
READY REFERENCE WORD LISTS

THE WORD-FINDER
starts page 218

Every essential two-, three- and four-letter word in the English language. Cross-referenced to Definition pages for utmost aid to solving. You can complete unfinished puzzle words with this section.

ABBREVIATIONS USED IN THIS BOOK

abbr. .... abbreviation
Abyssin. .... Abyssinia(n)
Afgh. .... Afghanistan
Afr. .... Africa(n)
Am. .... American
Arab. .... Arabia(n)
Arch. .... Architecture
A.-S. .... Anglo-Saxon
Austr. .... Austria(n)
Austral. .... Australia(n)
Babyl. .... Babylonian
Bibl. .... Biblical
biol. .... biology
bot. .... botany; botanical
Braz. .... Brazil(ian)
Cent. Am. ... Central America(n)
Chin. .... Chinese
comb. form .... combining form
Dan. .... Danish
Du. .... Dutch
Du. E. Ind. ... Dutch East Indies
E. .... East
Egyp. .... Egypt(ian)
E. Ind. .... East Indies
Eng. .... England; English
Eur., Europ. .... Europe(an)
fort. .... fortification
Fr. .... France; French
geol. ...... geology; geological
geom. .... geometry
Ger. .... German(y)
Goth. .... Gothic
govt. .... government
Gr. .... Greek
Hebr. .... Hebrew
Her. .... heraldry
Himal. .... Himalayan
Holl. .... Holland
Ind. .... India(n)
Indo-Chin. .... Indo-Chinese
Ir. .... Ireland; Irish
Is. .... Island

Ital. .... Italian; Italy
Jap. .... Japan(ese)
Lat. .... Latin
math. .... mathematics
med. .... medical
Medit. .... Mediterranean
Mex. .... Mexican; Mexico
milit. .... military
Min. .... Minor
mus. .... music; musical
myth. .. mythological; mythology
N., No. .... North
naut. .... nautical
N. Hebr. .... New Hebrides
N. T. .... New Testament
N. Z. .... New Zealand
Nor. .... Norway; Norwegian
O. Eng. .... Old English
P. I. .... Philippine Islands
P. R. .... Puerto Rico
Pacif. .... Pacific
Pers. .... Persian
pert. .... pertaining
pharm. .... pharmacy
philos. .... philosophical
poet. .... poetry
Polyn. .... Polynesia(n)
Port. ...... Portugal; Portuguese
Pruss. .... Prussian
R. C. .... Roman Catholic
Rom. .... Roman
Russ. .... Russian
S. .... South
S. Afr. .... South Africa(n)
Scot. .... Scottish
Sp. .... Spanish
Teut. .... Teutonic
Turk. .... Turkey; Turkish
W. .... West
W. Ind. .... West Indian
WW .... World War
zool. .... zoology

4

DEFINITIONS
SECTION

CROSSWORD DEFINITIONS
AND ANSWERS

HOW TO USE THIS SECTION:

Here are crossword DEFINITIONS, arranged alphabetically.

Look up the DEFINITION of a crossword word, and you will find, in bold-face type, the word you want.

There are two kinds of crossword definitions. One is the almost unvarying definition: "Bitter vetch" or "Vetch" is used to define ERS. If you look in this dictionary under "B" for "bitter vetch" or under "V" for "vetch" you will find it there.

The other kind of definition, far more common, is the more varied definition where the puzzle-maker can choose from among many descriptive words when he defines a puzzle word: "India nurse," "Oriental nurse," "Oriental maid," "Oriental nursemaid" are all used in crossword puzzles as definitions for AMAH. For efficiency's sake, crossword words with varying definitions are listed here under the ESSENTIAL definition word. In the case of AMAH, the listing is under "nurse," "maid," and "nursemaid".

So, if you don't find your wanted word under the first word of the definition given, look for it under the other words of the definition.

The length of a word is important to crossword solvers, and so, when a definition fits two or more words the words are arranged according to length. For example: adage .... SAW, MAXIM, PROVERB.

Remember to use also the efficiently-arranged reference word lists in the SPECIAL SECTION, beginning on page 187.

5

A

a Aaron's brother .... MOSES
Aaron's sister .... MIRIAM
Aaron's miracle worker ... ROD
Aaron's son, oldest .... NADAB
abaca .... LINAGA
abaca, top-quality ..... LUPIS
Abadan's land .... IRAN
abalone shell money
             ULLO, UHLLO
abandon   MAROON, DISCARD
abandoned .... DERELICT
abate .... EBB, LESSEN
abatement .... LETUP
abbess .... AMMA
abbey: Sp. .... ABADIA
abbot: Lat. .... ABBAS
abbreviations
       PTA, SRO, NATO (1949
            pact)
abdominal .... VENTRAL
Abel's brother .... CAIN
abhor   HATE, DETEST, LOATHE
Abie's girl .... ROSE
Abijah's son .... ASA
ability ...... POWER, TALENT
abject .... BASE
b abode, blissful .... EDEN
abode of dead .. HADES, SHEOL
abode of dead: Egypt.
           AALU, AARU
abound .... TEEM
abounding .... RIFE
about .. OF, RE, ANENT, CIRCA
about: Lat. .... CIRCITER
above ..... O'ER, OVER, UPON
abrade .... RUB, CHAFE
Abraham's birthplace ..... UR
Abraham's brother
        HARAN, NAHOR
Abraham's father ..... TERAH
Abraham's nephew .... LOT
Abraham's son
      ISAAC, ISHMAEL
Abraham's wife . SARAH, SARAI
abrasive .... EMERY
abrogate .... ANNUL
abrupt flexure .... GENU
Absalom's cousin ..... AMASA
Absalom's sister ...... TAMAR
abscond ...... ELOPE, LEVANT
absence, license for .... EXEAT
absent ..... OFF, OUT, AWAY,
             GONE
absolute .... UTTER, PLENARY
absolve sins .... SHRIVE

c absorbed .... RAPT
abstruse .... ESOTERIC
abundance, in .... GALORE
abundant .... RIFE, AMPLE
abuse: India .... GALI, GALEE
abuse ... VIOLATE, MISTREAT
abusive, be .... REVILE
abusive charges .... MUD
abut .... ADJOIN, BORDER
abyss .... GULF, HOLE, CHASM
Abyssinian ..... KAFA, KAFFA
Abyssin. fly .... ZIMB
Abyssin. grain .... TEFF
Abyssin. Hamite . AFAR, AGAO,
           BEJA, AFARA
Abyssin. language ...... SAHO
Abyssin. mountain wolf
           KABERU
Abyssin. ruler's title ... NEGUS
Abyssin. ox .. GALLA, SANGA,
           SANGU
Abyssin. Semitic dialect
         GEEZ, GHESE
Abyssin. tree .... .KOSO
Abyssin. tribesman ..... SHOA
Abyssin. vizier .... RAS
accent .... TONE
accent, Irish .. BLAS, BROGUE
d access .... ENTREE
accommodate .... LEND
"— accompli" .... FAIT
according to . ALA, AUX, ALLA
accost .... HAIL, GREET
account entry ...ITEM, DEBIT,
            CREDIT
accumulate .... AMASS,
       HOARD, ACCRUE
accumulation .... FUND
accustomed ..... USED, WONT,
           ENURED
acetic acid ester .... ACETATE
acetone derivative ... ACETOL
acetylene .... ETHIN, ETHINE
Achilles' adviser ...... NESTOR
Achilles' father .... PELEUS
Achilles' mother ...... THETIS
Achilles' slayer .... PARIS
acid, kind of .. AMINO, BORIC
acid radical .... ACYL, ACETYL
acidity .... ACOR
acknowledge .... OWN
acknowledge frankly .. AVOW
acorns, dried .... CAMATA
acoustics apparatus ... SIRENE
acquainted .... VERSANT
acquiesce .... ASSENT

a acquiesce, fully ..... ACCEDE
acquire .... WIN, GAIN, REAP
acrobat of India .... NAT
Acropolis of Thebes .. CADMEA
across: comb. form
TRAN, TRANS
acrostic, Hebrew .... AGLA
act ..... DEED, FEAT, EMOTE
act: Lat. ...... ACTU, ACTUS
action, put into .... ACTUATE
action word .... VERB
active ... SPRY, AGILE, BRISK,
LIVELY, NIMBLE
actor .... HISTRIO, HISTRION
actor's group .... TROUPE
actor's hint .... CUE
actor's valet .... DRESSER
actual .... REAL, TRUE
actual being .... ESSE
actuality .... FACT
adage .... SAW, MAXIM,
PROVERB
Adam's ale .... WATER
Adam's 1st mate: legend
LILITH
Adam's grandson .... ENOS
Adam's son . ABEL, CAIN, SETH
adapt .... FIT
adept .... ACE
add on .... AFFIX, ANNEX,
ATTACH
b adder, common .... ASP
additions .... ADDENDA
addition, bill's .... RIDER
adequate .... DUE, FULL,
AMPLE, EQUAL
adhere .... CLING, STICK,
CLEAVE
adherent .... IST
adhesive .. GUM, GLUE, PASTE
ADJECTIVE ENDING, see SUF-
FIX, ADJECTIVE
adjust ...... FIX, SET, ADAPT,
ATTUNE, ORIENT
adjutant .... AIDE
adjutant bird .... ARGALA,
HURGILA, MARABOU
admonish .... WARN, EXHORT,
REPROVE
admonisher .... MONITOR
adolescence .... TEENS,
YOUTH, NONAGE
adopted son of Mohammed . ALI
Adriana's servant ...... LUCE
adroit ...... READY, HABILE,
SKILLFUL
adulterate .. DEBASE, DEFILE,
DENATURE
advance guard .... VAN
advantage .... USE, GAIN,
PROFIT, BENEFIT

c adventitious lung sound .. RALE
adventure ...... GEST, GESTE
adviser, woman .... EGERIA
Aeëtes' daughter ..... MEDEA
Aegir's wife .... RAN
Aeneas' wife .... CREUSA
Aeneid author VERGIL, VIRGIL
Aesir ... TIU, TYR, ULL, FREY,
LOKE, LOKI, ODIN, THOR,
VALE, VALI, DONAR,
FREYA, BRAGI, WODEN,
BALDER
affectionate ... FOND, WARM,
LOVING, TENDER
affirm .. AVER, POSIT, ASSERT
affirmative .... AY, AYE,
YEA, YES
affirmative vote .... AY, AYE,
YEA, YES
afflict ...... TRY, VEX, PAIN,
DISTRESS
affluence ...... EASE, RICHES,
WEALTH
affray .... BRAWL, FIGHT,
MELEE
Afghan prince .. AMIR, AMEER
Afghan title .... KHAN
afresh .... ANEW
d afraid: obsolete .... REDDE
AFRICAN .... see also SOUTH
AFRICAN and AFRICAN in
SPECIAL SECTION
AFRICAN ANTELOPE
see ANTELOPE
Afr. bass .... IYO
Afr. bustard .... KORI
Afr. cotton garment .... TOBE
Afr. disease .... NENTA
Afr. worm .... LOA
Afr. grass, millet-like .. FUNDI
Afr. hornbill .... TOCK
Afr. plant .... ALOE
Afr. scrub .... BITO
Afr. soldier .... ASKARI
Afr. squirrel .... XERUS
Afr. stockade .... BOMA
Afr. tableland .... KAROO
Afrikaans ...... TAAL, BOERS
aft .... ABAFT, ASTERN
after awhile .... ANON
aftermath .... ROWEN
afterpart of ship's keel
SKAG, SKEG
afterpiece, comic ..... EXODE
aftersong .... EPODE
again .... ENCORE
against .... CON, ANTI,
CONTRA, VERSUS
agalloch wood .. AGAR, ALOE,
GAROO
Agamemnon's son .... ORESTES

7

a
agate stone .... ACHATE
age .... EON, ERA, AERA,
RIPEN, PERIOD
aged .... OLD, ANILE, SENILE
agave fiber .... ISTLE
agency, depression-era .. N R A
agency, govt. ... E C A, F H A
agency, wage, price .... E S A
agency, ration-book .... O P A
agency, World-War II .. O P A
agent .... DOER, FACTOR,
FACIENT
agents acted through .. MEDIA
aggregate . SUM, MASS, TOTAL
agitate .... STIR
agitation ...... STIR, DITHER,
TUMULT
agitation, be in state of SEETHE
agnomen .... NAME
agree ..... GIBE, JIBE, TALLY,
ASSENT, CONCUR
agreeable: old Eng. ... AMENE
agreeableness of letters EUTONY
agreement ...... MISE, PACT,
CONCORD, ENTENTE
agriculture goddess .... CERES,
VACUNA, DEMETER
Agrippina's son .... NERO
Ahasuerus' minister .. HAMAN

b
ahead . ON, BEFORE, FORWARD
Ahiam's father .... SACAR
aid ... ABET, ASSIST, SUCCOR,
FURTHER
aim ...... END, GOAL, ASPIRE
aims, with the same ... AKIN
air .. AER, ARIA, MIEN, TUNE
air apparatus ...... AERATOR
air current, ascending THERMAL
air, fill with .... AERATE
air, fresh .... OZONE
air passage ...... FLUE, VENT
air spirit .... SYLPH
air, upper .... ETHER, AETHER
aircraft, motorless .... GLIDER
airplane .... JET, AERO
airplane: Fr. .... AVION
airport marker .... PYLON
airport, Paris .... ORLY
airship . AERO, BLIMP, PLANE
airy .... LIGHT, ETHEREAL
ait .... ISLE
Ajax, tale about ...... MYTH
Ajax's father ...... TELAMON
akin .... SIB
alang grass .... LALANG
alarm . SCARE, SIREN, AROUSE
alas! .. ACH, HEU, OCH, OIME
alas: Irish .. OHONE, OCHONE
alas: poetic .... AY
Alaska glacier .... MUIR

c
ALBANIAN see COINS, TRIBES,
GAZETTEER in SPECIAL
SECTION
Albanian dialect .. GEG, CHAM,
GHEG, TOSK
albatross, sooty ...... NELLY
alchitran .... TAR, PITCH
alcohol radical .... AL
alcohol, solid . STERIN, STEROL
alcoholic drink .... GIN, RUM,
RHUM
Alcott heroine ...... JO, AMY,
MEG, BETH
alcove .... BOWER, RECESS
alder tree: Scot .... ARN
ale mug .... TOBY
ale, sour .... ALEGAR
alewife fish .... POMPANO
ALEUTIAN see TRIBES, GAZET-
TEER in SPECIAL SECTION
Alexandrian theologian . ARIUS
Alexander victory
ISSUS, ARBELA
alfalfa .... LUCERN, LUCERNE
Alfonso's queen .... ENA
alga .... NORI
alga, one-cell .... DIATOM
algae genus, fan-shaped
PADINA
algarroba tree ...... CALDEN

d
Algerian governor .... DEY
ALGERIA—see SPECIAL SEC-
TION
ALGONQUIN .... see Page 192
Ali Baba's word ...... SESAME
Ali, caliph descendants .. ALIDS
Alien in Hebrew territory .. GER
alienate ... WEAN, ESTRANGE
align ... TRUE, ALINE, RANGE
alkali ..... LYE, REH, USAR
alkaline solution .... LYE
alkaloid .. CAFFEIN, CAFFEINE
alkaloid, calabar bean
ESERINE
all: Lat. .... TOTO
all religions, believer in
OMNIST
all right .... OKAY, OKEH
allanite .... CERINE
allay .... CALM, ASSUAGE,
RELIEVE
alleged force .... OD
allegory, religious ... PARABLE
Allepo native .... SYRIAN
alleviate .... EASE, ALLAY,
LESSEN
alley .... MIB, MIG
alliance ..... UNION, LEAGUE
alliance, Western ...... NATO
alligator .... LAGARTO

8

a
alligator pear ..... AVOCADO
alligator, S.A. ...... CAIMAN,
CAYMAN
allot .... METE, GRANT,
ASSIGN, PORTION
allotment .... QUOTA, RATION
allow .... LET
allowance TARE, TRET, RATION
alloy .... MOKUM, OROIDE
alloy, aluminum ...... DURAL
alloy, copper .... BRASS
alloy, copper-tin ...... BRONZE
alloy, gold-silver: Egyp. . ASEM
alloy, lead-tin .. CALIN, TERNE
alloy, non-ferrous ...... TULA
alloy, yellow .... AICH
allspice .... PIMENTO
allure .... TICE, TOLE,
TEMPT, ENTICE
allusion .... HINT
almond emulsion ..... ORGEAT
almost .... ANEAR
alms box or chest ...... ARCA
aloe .... AGAVE
aloe derivative .... ALOIN
aloes product .... ALOIN
alone, on stage .. SOLA, SOLUS
along .... ON, BESIDE
alp .... PEAK

b
alpaca .... PACO
alphabet letter, old .... RUNE
Alps, Austro-It.
TIROL, TYROL, TIROLO
Alps, one of .... BLANC
Alps pass .... CENIS
Alps, river rising in .. RHONE
Altar constellation ...... ARA
altar end of church .... APSE
altar screen .... REREDOS
altar shelf . GRADIN, RETABLE
altar side curtain .... RIDDEL
altar top .... MENSA
alternate .... ROTATE
alternative ...... OR, EITHER
alumni .... GRADS
always ... AY, AYE, EER, EVER
amadou .... PUNK
amass ...... HOARD, GATHER
amateur TIRO, TYRO, NOVICE
Amazon cetacean ...... INIA
Amazon tributary .. APA, ICA
ambary .... DA
ambary hemp .... NALITA
ambassador .. ENVOY, LEGATE
amber fish
RUNNER, MEDREGAL
Amen-Ra's wife .... MUT
amend ALTER, EMEND, REVISE
amendment, document . RIDER
amends, make .... ATONE
ament .... CHAT

c
Am. artist ..... WEST, HICKS,
HOMER, MARIN, PEALE, BEN-
TON, COPLEY, INNESS, COR-
BINO, ALBRIGHT
AMERICAN INDIAN ...... see
INDIANS, Page 192
Am. aloe fiber .... PITA, PITO
Am. author . ADE, POE, AMES,
BAUM,   HARTE,   WYLIE,
YERBY, CORWIN, FERBER,
HERSEY, KANTOR, MORLEY
Am. author, illustrator ... PYLE
Am. capitalist .... ASTOR
Am. caricaturist .. REA, NAST
Am. dramatist . AKINS, BARRY,
ODETS, CROUSE
Am. editor .... BOK
Am. educator .... MANN
Am. explorer . BYRD, FREMONT
Am. general
LEE, OTIS, GREENE
Am. humorist ...... ADE, NYE,
COBB, NASH, ROGERS
Am. jurist .... TANEY
Am. inventor ... IVES, MORSE,
TESLA, EDISON
American: Mex. ..... GRINGO
Am. nature writer BEEBE, SETON
Am. nighthawk .... PISK
AM. PAINTER see AM. ARTIST

d
Am. patriot ...... HALE, OTIS,
ALLEN, REVERE
Am. philanthropist ...... RIIS
Am. philosopher ..... EDMAN
Am. pianist
ARRAU, DUCHIN, LEVANT
Am. poet . POE, AUDEN, BENET,
FROST, GUEST, RILEY,
STEIN, MILLAY
Am. poetess ... STEIN, LOWELL
Am. sculptor .... CALDER
AM. SINGER ... see SOPRANO
Am. statesman
CLAY, BARUCH, DULLES
Am. suffragist .... CATT
Am. surgeon .... PARRAN
AM. WRITER see AM. AUTHOR
AMERIND (means any American
Indian) See pages 192, 193
amide, pert. to .... AMIC
a mine: Corn. .... BAL
ammonia compound .. AMIN,
AMIDE, AMINE
ammoniac plant ...... OSHAC
ammunition . SHOT, SHRAPNEL
ammunition, short for: . AMMO,
AMMU
ammunition wagon ... CAISSON
among ...... IN, MID, AMID
amorously, stare .. LEER, OGLE
amount assessed ...... RATAL

Amount

a amount staked in gambling
MISE
amuse .... DIVERT
ampere .... WEBER
amphibian
FROG, TOAD, ANURAN
amphibian, order HYLA, ANURA
amphitheater .... ARENA
amphitheater, natural . CIRQUE
amplification factor ...... MU
amulet .... CHARM, PERIAPT
analyze .... ASSAY, DISSECT
analyze grammatically . PARSE
ancestor of Irish .... IR, ITH,
MIL, MILED
ancestor of man, Hindu . MANU
ancestral spirit, P. I. .. ANITO
ancestral .... AVITAL
ancestral spirits LARES, MANES
anchor ..... FIX, TIE, MOOR,
KEDGE
anchor part .... FLUKE
anchor, small, light ... KEDGE
anchor tackle .... CAT
ancient Asiatic .... MEDE
ancient Briton .... CELT
ancient Chinese .... SERES
anchovy sauce .... ALEC
ancient city, Asia Minor MYRA,
NICAEA
ancient country ...... GAUL
Ancient Egyp. kingdom SENNAR
ancient flute .... TIBIA
ancient Greece division AETOLIA
ancient invader, India
SAKA, SACAE
b ancient people of Gaul .. REMI
ancient Persian .... MEDE
ancient Persian money .. DARIC
ancient philosophy .... YOGA
ancient race .... MEDES
ancient Slav
VEND, WEND, VENED
ancient times .... ELD, YORE
ancient tribe of Britons . ICENI
ancient weight .... MINA
and .. TOO, ALSO, PLUS, WITH
and: Lat. .... ET
and not .... NOR
and so on: abbr. .... ETC.
Andes cold higher region.PUNA
Andes grass .... ICHU
Andes mountain .... SORATA
andiron .... DOG
"Andronicus,—" ...... TITUS
anecdotage or anecdotes
ANA, TALES
anent .... RE, ABOUT, BESIDE
anent, close — .... TO
anesthetic ...... GAS, ETHER
Angel of Death ...... AZRAEL
angel, Pers. .... MAH

c anger .... IRE, RAGE
RILE, CHOLER
anger, fit of .. PIQUE, TEMPER
angle, 57 degrees .... RADIAN
angle of leaf and axis ... AXIL
angle of leafstalk ...... AXIL
angle of stem, pert. to . AXILE
Anglo-Saxon "G" . YOK, YOGH
A.-S. god of peace ...... ING
A.-S. lord's man THANE, THEGN
A.-S. king .... INE
A.-S. money (coin) ...... ORA
A.-S. slave .... ESNE
A.-S. warrior .. THANE, THEGN
Angora goat .... CHAMAL
angry .... HOT, MAD,
SORE, IRATE
animal, Afr. .. CIVET, GENET,
POTTO, ZEBRA, GENETTE
animal, ant-eating . ECHIDNA
animal, aquatic . SEAL, OTTER,
WHALE, DUGONG,
WALRUS, MANATEE
animal, arboreal .... TARSIER
animal, Austral. .... ECHIDNA
animal, badgerlike, Java
TELEDU
animal body .... SOMA
animal, draft ......OX, OXEN
d animal, fabulous .... DRAGON
animal, giraffelike .... OKAPI
animal, India .... DHOLE
animal, Madagascar
FOSSA, FOUSSA
animals of area ..... FAUNA
animal-plant life ...... BIOTA
animal, Peru .... ALPACA
animal, sea .... SEAL, CORAL,
WHALE, WALRUS,
DUGONG, MANATEE
animal, S. Afr. ...... ZORIL
animal, S. Am. . APARA, COATI
animal trail .... RUN, SLOT,
SPUR, SPOOR
animating principle .... SOUL
ankle TALUS, TARSI, TARSUS
ankle, pert. to ...... TARSAL
Annamese measure ..... TAO
ANNAMESE..see also ANNAM
in SPECIAL SECTION
Annapolis student PLEB, PLEBE
anneal ... TEMPER, TOUGHEN
annex .... ADD, ELL,
WING, ATTACH
annatto seeds: Sp. .. ACHIOTE
annihilate DESTROY, DISCREATE
ANNIVERSARY . see WEDDING
announce .... HERALD
annoy .. IRK, TRY, VEX, RILE,
PEEVE, TEASE, BOTHER,
MOLEST, PESTER, DIS-
TURB

10

a annual, as winds .... ETESIAN
   annuity, form of .... TONTINE
   annul .... UNDO, VOID,
             CANCEL, REVOKE
   annular die .... DOD
   annulet: Her. .... VIRE
   anoint ... OIL, ANELE, ENELE
   another ... NEW, ADDITIONAL
   ant .... EMMET, PISMIRE
   antarctic bird ...... PENGUIN
   antarctic icebreaker .... ATKA
   antecedent . PRIOR, ANCESTOR
   antelope, Afr. .... GNU, KOB,
      BISA, GUIB, KOBA, KUDU,
      ORYX, POKU, PUKU, TORA,
      ADDAX, ELAND, ORIBI,
      RHEBOK
   antelope, Afr., large .. IMPALA
   antelope, Afr., small .. DUIKER
   antelope, Ind.
      SASIN, NILGAI, NILGAU
   antelope, Siberian ..... SAIGA
   antelope, tawny .... ORIBI
   antenna HORN, PALP, AERIAL
                        FEELER
   antenna, with nodose
                      NODICORN
   anthracite, inferior ..... CULM
   anti-aircraft shells ..... FLAK
   anti-tank gun .... PIAT
b antic ... DIDO, CAPER, PRANK
   antique red color .. CHAUDRON
   antiseptic .... EUPAD, EUSOL,
      IODIN, SALOL, CRESOL,
      IODINE
   antiseptic, mercury
             EGOL, METAPHEN
   antitoxin ...... SERA, SERUM
   antler point .... SNAG, TINE,
                        PRONG
   antler, unbranched ...... DAG
   antlers, stag's .... ATTIRE
   "Anthony and Cleopatra" char-
      acter .... IRAS
   anvil .... INCUS, TEEST
   anxiety .... CARE
   any: dialect .... ONI
   any one .... AN
   aoudad .... ARUI
   apathy ... ENNUI, DOLDRUMS
   ape .... long-tailed ... ORANG
   ape, long-tailed, India ... KRA
   appelation ... NAME, TITLE
   APERTURE . see also OPENING
   aperture .... GAP, HOLE,
             SLOT, VENT, ORIFICE
   apex, at the .... APICAL
   aphasia, motor .... ALALIA
   aphorism .. SAW, RULE, SUTRA
   Aphrodite .... VENUS

c Aphrodite, got apple from
                         PARIS
   Aphrodite, love of ... ADONIS
   Aphrodite's mother .... DIONE
   Aphrodite's son .... EROS
   apocopate .... ELIDE
   Apocrypha, book from . ESDRAS
   Apollo's instrument ..... BOW,
                    LUTE, LYRE
   Apollo's mother LETO, LATONA
   Apollo's sister
             DIANA, ARTEMIS
   Apollo's son .... ION
   Apollo's twin .... ARTEMIS
   Apollo's vale, sacred ... TEMPE
   apoplexy, plant .... ESCA
   Apostle (12) .... JOHN, JUDE
      (THADDEUS), JAMES, JUDAS,
      PETER (SIMON PETER), SI-
      MON, ANDREW, PHILIP,
      THOMAS (DIDYMUS), MAT-
      THEW (LEVI), MATTHIAS,
      BARTHOLOMEW
   Apostle, Capernaum MATTHEW
   Apostles, teaching of . DIDACHE
   apparent ..... OVERT, PLAIN,
                      EVIDENT
   apparition .. SPECTER, SPECTRE
   appear .... LOOK, LOOM, SEEM
   appearance . AIR, MIEN, GUISE
d appease ...... CALM, ALLAY
                      PLACATE
   appellation ..... NAME, TITLE
   append .... ADD, AFFIX,
                      ATTACH
   appendage, caudal ..... TAIL
   appetizer . CANAPE, APERITIF
   apple ... POME, TREE, FRUIT,
                        PIPPIN
   apple acid .... MALIC
   apple seed .... PIP
   apple tree .... SORB
   apple tree genus ...... MALUS
   apple, winter .... ESOPUS
   apples, crushed .... POMACE
   apple-like fruit .... POME
   appoint .. SET, NAME, CHOOSE
   apportion DEAL, METE, ALLOT
   appraise RATE, VALUE, ASSESS
   apprise ...... ADVISE, NOTIFY
   approach ...... NEAR, ANEAR,
                       ACCESS
   appropriate, ... APT, FIT, MEET
   appropriate, not INAPT, UNFIT
   apricot, Jap. .... UME
   apricot, Korean . ANSU, ANZU
   apricots .... MEBOS
   apropos .... PAT, FITTING
   apteryx .... KIWI
   aptitude ..... FLAIR, ABILITY

a aptitude, natural
　　　　　　FLAIR, TALENT
aquamarine .... **BERYL**
AQUATIC . see SEA or MARINE
Arab ....**GAMIN, SEMITE**
Arab cloak, sleeveless .... **ABA**
Arab drink ...... **BOSA, BOZA**
　　　　　　　　BOZAH
Arab name .... **ALI**
Arab's state of bliss ..... **KEF**
Arabia, people of ..... **OMANI**
ARABIAN . see ARAB, ARABIA,
　　　　　　SPECIAL SECTION
Arabian chief . **SAYID, SAYYID**
Arabian chieftain **AMIR, EMIR,**
　　　　　　　AMEER, EMEER
Arabian chieftain's domain
　　　　　　　　EMIRATE
Arabian cloth .... **ABA**
Arabian district .... **TEMA**
Arabian garment .... **ABA**
Arabian jasmine .... **BELA**
Arabian judge .... **CADI**
"Arabian Nights" dervish . **AGIB**
Arabian noble .. **AMIR, EMIR,**
　　　　　　　AMEER, EMEER
Arabian nomadic tribesman
　　　　　　　　　SLEB
Arabian sailboat .. see VESSEL,
　　　　　　　　　ARAB
Arabian sleeveless garment **ABA**
b Arabian tambourine
　　　　TAAR, DAIRA, DAIRE
Arabic jinni, evil
　　AFRIT, AFREET, AFRITE
Arabic letter . **GAF, KAF, MIM,**
　　　　WAW, ALIF, DHAL
Arabic script .... **NESKI**
Arabic surname .... **SAAD**
arachnid . **MITE, TICK, SPIDER**
Arawakan language .... **TAINO**
arbitrator ... **UMPIRE, REFEREE**
arboreal .... **DENDRAL**
arc .... **LINE, CURVE**
arch of heaven .... **COPE**
arch, pointed .... **OGIVE**
archaeology, mound ..... **TERP**
archangel .... **URIEL**
archbishop .... **PRIMATE**
archbishop, Canterbury **BECKET**
archer in Eng. ballad
　　　　　　CLIM, CLYM
archetype ... **MODEL, PATTERN**
archfiend .... **SATAN**
architect's drawing ..... **EPURE**
architecture, school of
　　　　　　　BAUHAUS
architecture, type
　　　　　DORIC, IONIC
ARCTIC ..... see GAZETTEER
Arctic . **NORTH, POLAR, FRIGID**

c arctic air force base .... **THULE**
arctic dog .... **SAMOYED**
arctic gull genus ...... **XEMA**
arctic plain .... **TUNDRA**
Arden .... **FOREST**
ardor ... **ELAN, ZEAL, FERVOR**
area measure .. **RADII, RADIUS**
area, small .... **AREOLA**
areca .... **BETEL**
arena .... **FIELD**
Ares' mother .... **ENYO**
Ares' sister .... **ERIS**
ares, 10 .... **DECARE**
Argonaut ... **JASON, ACASTUS**
Argonauts' leader ...... **JASON**
Argonauts' ship .... **ARGO**
argument .... **AGON,**
　　　　　DEBATE, HASSLE
arhat .... **LOHAN**
aria ...... **AIR, SOLO, SONG,**
　　　　　　TUNE, MELODY
arias .... **SOLI**
aridity, having .... **XERIC**
arikara .... **REE**
arise .... **REBEL, ACCRUE,**
　　　　　　　　APPEAR
arista .... **AWN**
Arizona aborigine ...... **HOPI**
ARIZONA INDIAN see page 192
d **ARIZONA** ... see also SPECIAL
　　　　　　　　SECTION
Ark, porter of: Bible ..... **BEN**
Ark's landing place .. **ARARAT**
arm .... **LIMB, TENTACLE**
arm, movable with verniers
　　　　　　　ALIDADE
arm of sea . **BAY, FIRTH, FRITH**
armadillo ...... **APAR, APARA**
armadillo, Braz. . **TATU, TATOU**
armadillo, giant . **TATU, TATOU**
armadillo, large 12-banded
　　　　　　　TATOUAY
armadillo, 6-banded .. **PELUDO**
armadillo, small .. **PEBA, PEVA**
armadillo, 3-banded .... **APAR,**
　APARA, MATACO, MATICO
armed band .... **POSSE**
armed galley of old Northmen
　　　　　　　　　AESC
ARMOR .... see also SPECIAL
　　　　　SECTION, page 194
armor bearer .... **ARMIGER**
armor, body .... **CUIRASS**
armor, chain .... **MAIL**
armor, horse .. **BARD, BARDE**
armor, leg .... **JAMB, JAMBE**
armor, leg below knee **GREAVE**
armor, lower body ..... **CULET**

a armor part .... LORICA
armor part, throat ... GORGET
armor, skirt .... TACE, TASSE,
TASSET
armor, thigh ... CUISH, TUILE,
CUISSE, TUILLE
armpit .... ALA
army .... HOST, TROOPS
army group .... CADRE
army provisioner ...... SUTLER
aroid, an .... ARAD, ARUM
aromatic herb
DILL, MINT, SAGE
aromatic herb, carrot genus
CARUM
aromatic herb-plant .... NARD
aromatic seed
CUMIN, CUMMIN
aromatic seed, plant ... ANISE
aromatic substance ... BALSAM
aromatic weed .... TANSY
around .... CIRCA
arouse .... FIRE, STIR, PIQUE
arpeggio .... ROULADE
arquebus support .... CROC
arraign ..... ACCUSE, INDICT
arrange ...... FIX, SET, FILE,
DISPOSE
arrangement: comb. form . TAX,
TAXI, TAXO, TAXEO, TAXIS
b arrangement, pert. to..TACTIC
array .. DECK, ORDER, ATTIRE
arrest .... NAB, HALT
arrest writ .... CAPIAS
arris .... PIEN
arrow .... BOLT, DART
arrow, body of .... STELE
arrow, fit string to ..... NOCK
arrow, spinning .... VIRE
arrow wood .... WAHOO
arrowroot .... PIA, ARARU
arroyo .... HONDO
art: Lat. .... ARS
art style .... DADA, GENRE
Artemis . UPIS, DELIA, PHOEBE
Artemis' twin .... APOLLO
Artemis' victim .... ORION
artery, largest .... AORTA
artery of neck .... CAROTID
artful .... SLY, WILY
arthritis aid ACTH, CORTISONE
Arthur's foster brother ... KAY
Arthurian lady
ENID, ELAIN, ELAINE
article .... AN, THE, ITEM
article, Fr. ...... LA, LE, DES,
LES, UNE
article, Ger. .... DAS, DER
article, Sp. ... EL, LA, LAS, LOS
articulated joint ...... HINGE
artifice ... RUSE, WILE, TRICK

c artificial language .... RO, IDO
ARTIST .... see also PAINTER
and under Country
of each artist
artist, primitive .... MOSES
artless .... NAIVE
arum family plant TARO, CALLA
arum plant ..... ARAD, AROID
Aryan .... MEDE, SLAV
as .. QUA, LIKE, SINCE, WHILE
as far as .... TO
as it stands: mus. .... STA
as written: mus. .... STA
asafetida .... HING
asbestos .... ABISTON
ascent .... UPGO, CLIMB
ascetic, ancient .... ESSENE
asceticism, Hindu ...... YOGA
ash, fruit, seed ..... SAMARA
ash key .... SAMARA
ashy pale .... LIVID
ASIA .. see also SPECIAL SEC-
TION
Asia Minor district, old IONIA
Asia Minor region, pert. to
EOLIC, AEOLIC
Asia native, S.E. ...... SHAN
Asiatic ancient people .. SERES
d Asiatic country .. see page 210
Asiatic cow .... ZO, ZOH
Asiatic evergreen .... BAGO
Asiatic fowl .... SAT
Asiatic gangster .... DACOIT
Asiatic sardine .... LOUR
Asiatic shrub .... TEA, TCHE
Asiatic tree .... ACLE,
ASAK, ASOK, ASOKA
"— asinorum" .... PONS
askew .... WRY, AGEE,
ALOP, AWRY
aspect ... SIDE, FACET, PHASE
asperse .... SLANDER
aspire .... HOPE
ass, wild
KULAN, ONAGER, QUAGGA
assail .... BESET, ATTACK
ASSAM ..... see also SPECIAL
SECTION, Page 191
Assam hill tribe .... AKA
Assam mongol .... NAGA
Assam silkworm .... ERI, ERIA
Assam tribe, Naga Hills
AO, NAGA
assault .... ONSET, STORM
assault, prolonged ...... SIEGE
assayer .... TESTER
assaying cup .... CUPEL
assemble .... MEET, MUSTER,
COLLECT

a assembly .... DIET, SYNOD
SESSION, GATHERING
assembly, A.-S. GEMOT, GEMOTE
assembly, China, Hawaii .. HUI
assembly, Dutch .... RAAD
assent, solemn .... AMEN
assert .... AVER, POSIT, STATE
assert formally .... ALLEGATE
assess .... TAX, LEVY, VALUE
assessment RATE, SCOT, RATAL
asseverate .... AVER
assignor of property ... CEDENT
assimilate .. ABSORB, DIGEST
assistance AID, HELP, SUPPORT
assistant .... AIDE
associate .. ALLY, COLLEAGUE
association, trade GILD, GUILD
assuage .... MITIGATE
ASSYRIAN .. see also SPECIAL
SECTION, Page 198
Assyrian king .... PUL
Assyrian queen, myth.
SEMIRAMIS
asterisk .... STAR
astern ..... AFT, BAFT, ABAFT
astringent .... ALUM, STYPTIC
astringent, black ...... KATH
astringent fruit .... SLOE
astrologer of India .... JOSHI

b astronomical .... URANIC
astron. luminous "cloud"
NEBULA
Aswan, ancient .... SYENE
asylum ...... HAVEN, REFUGE
at all .... ANY
at any time .... EVER
at odds .... OUT
at the home of: Fr. ..... CHEZ
Atahualpa, king ...... INCA
atap palm .... NIPA
atelier .... STUDIO
Athamas' wife .... INO
Athena ... PALLAS, MINERVA
Athena, appellation, title . ALEA
Athena, possession of ... EGIS
Athenian .... ATTIC
Athenian bronze coin CHALCUS
Athenian demagogue ... CLEON
Athens, last king of .. CODRUS
athlete, famous ...... THORPE
a-tiptoe .... ATIP
atmospheric pressure, of BARIC
at no time: poet. ...... NEER
atoll's pool .... LAGOON
atom part .... PROTON
atomic machine
BETATRON, RHEOTRON
atomic physicist .. BOHR, RABI,
UREY, FERMI, PAULI,
COMPTON, MEITNER
MILLIKAN

c atomic submarine .... SKATE,
SARGO, TRITON, NAUTILUS
atone for .... REDEEM
attach .... ADD, FIX, TIE,
APPEND
attack .... BESET, ONSET
attack, mock .... FEINT
attar .... OTTO
attempt .... TRY, STAB, ESSAY
attendant, hunter's
GILLY, GILLIE
attention ... EAR, CARE, HEED
attest ..... VOUCH, CERTIFY
attic .... LOFT, GARRET
Attica resident .... METIC
Attila .... ATLI, ETZEL
attitudinize .... POSE
attribute .. IMPUTE, ASCRIBE
attune .... KEY, ACCORD
auction .... SALE
audience ...... EAR, HEARING
auditory ...... OTIC, AURAL
auger .... BORE, BORER
augment .... EKE
augur .... BODE, PORTEND
augury ..... OMEN, PORTENT
auk genus .. ALCA, ALLE, URIA
auk, little ... ROTCH, ROTCHE
aura, pert. to .... AURIC

d aureola .... HALO
auric acid salt ...... AURATE
auricle .... EAR
auricular ...... OTIC, EARED
aurochs .. TUR, URUS, AURUS
aurora .... EOS, DAWN
auspices .... EGIS, AEGIS
Australasian harrier-hawk
KAHU
Australasian shrub genus
HOYA
AUSTRALIA . see also SPECIAL
SECTION
Australian boomerang .. KILEY
Austral. food .... KAI
Austral. gum tree
KARI, TUART
Austral. hut .... MIAM, MIMI
Austral. marsupial
TAIT, KOALA
Austral. scaly-finned fish
MADO
Austral. tree, timber .. PENDA
Austrian folk dance .. DREHER
Austr. violinist .... MORINI
author .... PARENT
author, boys' .. ALGER, HENTY
author, nature stories .. SETON
authoritative .... MAGISTRAL
author unknown: abbr. ... ANON

a authority, name as **CITE, QUOTE**
auto, old .. **JALOPY, JALOPPY**
automaton .... **ROBOT**
automaton: Jew. legend **GOLEM**
automobile "shoe" . **TIRE, TYRE**
ave .... **HAIL**
avena .... **OAT**
avenger: Hebr. .... **GOEL**
average .... **PAR, MEAN,
          NORM, USUAL, MEDIAL**
averse .... **LOTH, LOATH**
Avesta division
          YASNA, GATHAS, YASHTS
avid .... **KEEN, EAGER**
avifauna .... **ORNIS**
avocado, Mex. .... **COYO**
avoid .... **SHUN, ESCHEW**

c avouch .... **AVER, ASSERT**
away .... **OFF, GONE, ABSENT**
aweather, opposed to .... **ALEE**
aweto .... **WERI**
awkward .... **INEPT**
awkward fellow .... **LOUT**
awn .... **ARISTA**
awned .... **ARISTATE**
awry .... **AGEE, AJEE, AGLEY**
axilla .... **ALA**
axilla, pert. to .... **ALAR**
axillary .... **ALAR**
axis deer .... **CHITAL**
Aztec god, sowing ...... **XIPE**
Aztec "Noah" (hero) ... **NATA**
Aztec "Noah's" wife .. **NANA**
Aztec spear .... **ATLATL**

B

babbler: Scot. .... **HAVEREL**
Babism, founder .... **BAB**
babul tree pods .... **GARAD**
baby animal: Fr. .... **TOTO**
baby carriage .... **PRAM**
b **BABYLONIAN GODS, DEITY,**
          see also GODS and also SPE-
          CIAL SECTION on page 198
Babylonian abode of dead
          ARALU
Babylonian city .... **IS**
Babylonian chief gods ... **EA,
          ANU, BEL, HEA, ENKI**
Babylonian chief goddess
          ISTAR, ISHTAR
Babylonian chief priest of
          shrine .... **EN**
Babylonian division .... **SUMER**
Babylonian hero ...... **ETANA**
Babylonian lunar cycle
          SAROS
Babylonian neighbor
          ELAMITE
Babylonian numeral .... **SAROS**
Babylonian priestess .. **ENTUM**
Babylonian purgatory .. **ARALU**
Bacchanals' cry .... **EVOE**
bacchante .... **MAENAD**
Bacchus' follower ...... **SATYR**
Bacchus' son .... **COMUS**
back .. **AID, AFT, FRO, ABET,
          HIND, REAR, SPONSOR**
back, call .... **REVOKE**
back door .... **POSTERN**
back, flow .... **EBB, RECEDE**
back, lying on ...... **SUPINE**
back of neck .... **NAPE**
back, pert. to ...... **DORSAL**

back, take .... **RETRACT**
back, thrust .... **REPEL**
back, toward .... **RETRAL**
back: Zool.   **NOTA, NOTUM**
d backbone ...... **CHINE, SPINE**
bacteria-free .... **ASEPTIC**
bacteriologist's wire ..... **OESE**
bacteriostatic subst. . **CITRININ**
badge, Jap. .... **MON**
badger .... **DAS, BAIT**
badgerlike animal
          PAHMI, RATEL
badgers, Old World .... **MELES**
baffle .... **FOIL, POSE, ELUDE**
bag .... **SAC**
bag net .... **FYKE**
bagatelle .... **TRIFLE**
bagpipe, hole in .... **LILL**
bagpipe sound .... **SKIRL**
bailiff, old Eng. .... **REEVE**
baize fabric .... **DOMETT**
baker bird .... **HORNERO**
baking chamber ... **OST, KILN,
          OAST, OVEN**
baking pit .... **IMU**
balance .. **REST, POISE, SCALE**
balance, sentence ... **PARISON**
Balance, The .... **LIBRA**
balancing weight ... **BALLAST**
Balder's killer **LOK, LOKE, LOKI**
Balder's wife .... **NANNA**
baldness .... **ACOMIA**
Balkan .... **SERB**
ball, low .... **LINER**
ball, to hit
          LOB, BUNT, SWAT

15

Ball

a ball, yarn thread ...... **CLEW**
ballad .... **LAY, DERRY**
ballet jump .... **JETE**
ballet skirt .... **TUTU**
ballet turn .... **FOUETTE**
balloon basket **CAR, NACELLE**
ball-rope missile
            BOLA, BOLAS
balm of Gilead ..... **BALSAM**
balsalike wood .... **BONGO**
balsam .... **FIR, TOLU, RESIN**
Balt .... **ESTH**
BALTIC ... see also SPECIAL
    SECTION
Baltic Finn .... **VOD**
Baltimore stove .... **LATROBE**
Balto-Slav .... **LETT**
Baluchistan tribe .... **REKI**
Baluchistan tribesman .. **MARI**
"Bambi" author ...... **SALTEN**
bamboo .... **REED**
bamboo shoots, pickled **ACHAR**
Bana's daughter: Hindu **USHA**
banal .... **STALE, TRITE**
banana genus .... **MUSA**
banana, kind of .. **PLANTAIN**
banana, Polyn. .... **FEI**
band .... **BELT, TAPE,**
         STRIP, FILLET
band: Arch. .. **FACIA, FASCIA**
band, muscle, nerve .. **TAENIA**
band, narrow .. **STRIA, STRIAE**
bandage ...... **STUPE, TAENIA**
bandicoot .... **RAT**
b bandmaster, Am. ..... **SOUSA**
banish ..... **EXILE, RELEGATE**
bank .... **RELY, DEPEND**
bank, of a river ... **RIPARIAN**
bank, river .... **RIPA**
banker, India .. **SARAF, SHROFF**
banner .... **FLAG,**
    ENSIGN, BANDEROLE
banter ... **CHAFF, PERSIFLAGE**
BANTU see also TRIBES in
    SPECIAL SECTION, Page 191
Bantu .... **KAFIR, KAFFIR**
Bantu, Congo ... **RUA, WARUA**
Bantu language .... **ILA**
Bantu nation .... **GOGO**
Bantu-speaking tribe
    RAVI, RORI, PONDO
Bantu tribesman ..... **DUALA**
baobab, dried .... **LALO**
baobab leaves, powdered . **LALO**
baptism font .... **LAVER**
baptismal basin .... **FONT**
bar .... **RAIL, INGOT,**
    HINDER, STRIPE
bar legally .... **ESTOP**
bar, supporting .... **FID**
barb, feather .... **HARL, HERL**

c Barbados native .... **BIM**
barbarian .... **HUN, GOTH**
Barbary ape .... **MAGOT**
barber ..... **SHAVER, TONSOR**
bard, Goth. .... **RUNER**
bare ..... **BALD, MERE, NUDE**
bargain .... **DEAL, PALTER**
bargain: Dutch .... **KOOP**
barge .... **HOY**
bark .... **BAY, YAP, YIP**
bark, bitter .. **NIEPA, NIOTA**
bark, inner .... **CORTEX**
bark, lime tree .. **BAST, BASTE**
bark, medicinal .... **COTO**
bark, paper mulberry .. **TAPA**
bark, pert. to ..... **CORTICAL**
bark remover .... **ROSSER**
bark, rough exterior .... **ROSS**
barking .... **LATRANT**
barn owl genus .... **TYTO**
barometric line ...... **ISOBAR**
barony, Jap. .... **HAN**
barracuda, small **SPET, SENNET**
barrelmaker .... **COOPER**
barrel slat .... **STAVE**
barren land .... **USAR**
Barrie character ...... **ALICE**
barrow, Russ. .... **KURGAN**
base .... **LOW, VILE**
base, architectural
    SOCLE, PLINTH
d base, attached by .... **SESSILE**
baseball position: abbr. .... **LF,**
    RF, SS
Bashan, king of .... **OG**
bashful .... **COY, SHY, TIMID**
basilica, Rome ..... **LATERAN**
basin: Geol. .... **TALA**
basis of argument ... **PREMISE**
basket .... **KISH, CABAS,**
    PANIER, PANNIER
basket, coarse .... **SKEP**
basket, Eng. ...... **PED, CAUL**
basket, fish ... **WEEL, CRAIL,**
    CREEL, WICKER
basket grass, Mex. ..... **OTATE**
basket, large .... **HAMPER**
basket strip .... **RAND**
basketball player ..... **CAGER**
basketry rod .... **OSIER**
Basra native .... **IRAQI**
bass, Europ. .... **BRASSE**
basswood .... **LINDEN**
bast fiber .... **RAMIE**
bat .... **RACKET**
batfish .... **DIABLO**
bathe .... **LAVE**
bathing-suit .... **MAILLOT**
baths, Roman ..... **THERMAE**
Bathsheba's husband
    URIA, URIAH

a baton .... ROD
batrachian .... FROG, TOAD
batter .... RAM
battering machine .... RAM
battery plate .... GRID
battle, Am. Rev. ... CONCORD
battle area .... SECTOR
battle, Arthur's last .. CAMLAN
battle ax ... TWIBIL, TWIBILL
battle, Civil War, Tenn. SHILOH
battle cry, Irish .. ABU, ABOO
battle, Eng.-Fr. CRECY, CRESSY
battle formation ...... HERSE
battle, Franco-Pruss. .. SEDAN
battle, 100 Years War
            CRECY, CRESSY
"Battle Hymn of Republic"
    author .... HOWE
battle, WWI .. MARNE, SOMME,
            YPRES, VERDUN
battlefield .... ARENA
bauble .... BEAD
bay .... COVE, BIGHT, INLET
bay, Orkney, Shetland ... VOE
bay tree .... LAUREL
bay window .... ORIEL
bazaar .... FAIR
be foolishly overfond ... DOAT,
            DOTE
be silent: music ...... TACET
b be still .... SH, HUSH, QUIET
beach .... SHORE, STRAND
beach cabin .... CABANA
beads, prayer .... ROSARY
beak .... NEB, NIB, BILL
beam, supporting
        TEMPLET, TEMPLATE
bean .... SOY, URD, LIMA
bean, E. Ind. .... URD
bean, field .... PINTO
bean, green .... HARICOT
bean, poisonous ... CALABAR
bean, S. Am. .... TONKA
bean tree .... CAROB
bear .. STAND, YIELD, ENDURE
Bear constellation ...... URSA
bear, nymph changed to
            CALLISTO
bear, Austral. .... KOALA
bear witness .. VOUCH, ATTEST
beard of grain .. AWN, ARISTA
bearded seal .... MAKLUK
bearer, Ind. .... SINDAR
bearing .... MIEN, ORLE
bearing plate .... GIB
bear's-ear .... ARICULA
beast of burden .... ASS,
        BURRO, LLAMA
beat .... WIN, CANE, DRUB,
        FLAP, POMMEL, PULSE
beat about: naut. ...... BUSK

c beater, mortar .... RAB
beauty, goddess of: Hindu
    SRI, SHRI, SHREE, LAKSHMI
beauty, Greek .... LAIS
beaver .... CASTOR
beaver skin .... PLEW
beche-de-mer ...... TREPANG
beckon .... NOD
bed .... KIP, PALLET
bed of dry stream .... DONGA
bed of press, handle .. ROUNCE
bed: slang .... DOSS
Bedouin headband cord .. AGAL
bee, honey, genus .... APIS
bee house ..... APIARY, HIVE
bee, male .... DRONE
bee tree .... LINDEN
bees, pert. to .... APIAN
bee's pollen brush ..... SCOPA
beech tree genus ...... FAGUS
beechnuts .... MAST
beefwood: Polyn. ...... TOA,
        TOOA, BELAH
beehive, straw .... SKEP
Beehive State .. see page 209
beer ...... ALE, BOCK, LAGER
beer, Afr. millet ..... POMBE
beer ingredient .. HOPS, MALT
beer mug .... STEIN
beer, P. I. rice ..... PANGASI
d beet variety .... CHARD
Beethoven's birthplace . BONN
beetle .... DOR, ELATER
beetle, burrowing ...... BORER
beetle, click .... ELATER
beetle, fruit-loving .... BORER
beetle genus, ground .. AMARA
beetle, ground .... CARAB
beetle, sacred Egyp. .. SCARAB
beetle, wood .... SAWYER
befall .... HAP
before .... ERE, PRE,
            ANTERIOR
before: obs. .... ERER
before: naut. .... AFORE
beget .... EAN, SIRE
"Beggar's Opera" dramatist
            GAY
beginner .... TIRO, TYRO,
        NOVICE, NEOPHYTE
beginning .... GERM, ONSET,
        ORIGIN, INITIAL
beginning .... NASCENCY
behave toward .... TREAT
behind .... AFT, AREAR,
            ASTERN
behold ..... LO, ECCE, VOILA
behoove .... DOW
beige .... ECRU
being .... ENS, ENTITY

a being, abstract **ENS, ESSE, ENTIA**
being, essential .... **ENS**
Bela, son of .... **IRI**
beleaguerment .... **SIEGE**
Belem .... **PARA**
belief .... **CREED,**
FAITH, TENET
believe .... **TROW,**
CREDO, CREDIT
believer in god of reason **DEIST**
bell, alarm .... **TOCSIN**
bell, sacring .... **SQUILLA**
bell tower .... **BELFRY,**
CAMPANILE
bell's tongue .... **CLAPPER**
bellbird, N.Z. .... **MAKO**
bellowing .... **AROAR**
below: nautical .... **ALOW**
belt .... **CEST, SASH**
belt, sword .... **BALDRIC,**
BAWDRIC, BALDRICK
ben .... **BENE**
bench ...... **EXEDRA, SETTLE**
bench, judge's .. see JUDGE'S
BENCH
bench in a galley ..... **BANK**
bend .... **SNY, FLEX, GENU,**
STOOP, FLEXURE
benediction .... **BENISON**
benefactor .... **PATRON**
beneficiary: Law ...... **USES**
b benefit .... **BOON, AVAIL**
Bengal native .... **KOL**
Bengal singer .... **BAUL**
Benjamin's first born .. **BELA**
bent .... **PRONATE**
bequeath .... **WILL**
bequest .... **DOWER**
Berber .... **RIFF**
Bermuda arrowroot
ARARU, ARARAO
Bermuda grass .. **DOOB, DOUB**
berserk .... **AMOK, AMUCK**
beseech .... **PRAY,**
OBTEST, ENTREAT
beside .... **BY**
besides .. **TOO, YET, ALSO, ELSE**
bestow .... **AWARD,**
CONFER, IMPART
bets, fail to pay
WELCH, WELSH
betel leaf ...... **BUYO, PAUN**
betel nut .... **SERI, SIRI,**
BONGA, SIRIH
betel palm .. **ARECA, PINANG**
betel pepper ..... **IKMO, ITMO**
Bethuel's son .... **LABAN**
betoken .... **DENOTE**
betroth .... **AFFY**
between: prefix .... **INTER**
Bevan's nickname .... **NYE**

c bevel .... **BEZEL, SLANT**
bevel out .... **REAM**
bevel ship timber ..... **SNAPE**
bevel to join .. **MITER, MITRE**
BEVERAGE ... see also DRINK
beverage .... **ADE, ALE,**
TEA, BEER
beverage, curdled .... **POSSET**
beverage, hot wine .... **NEGUS**
beverage, Polyn.
KAVA, KAWA
beverage, S. Am. .... **MATE**
bewitch .... **HEX, SPELL**
beyond: comb. form .. **ULTRA**
Bhutan pine .... **KAIL**
biased person .... **BIGOT**
BIBLICAL .. see also SPECIAL
SECTION
Biblical city .... **DAN,**
BABEL, EKRON
Biblical character .. **ARA, IRA,**
ERI, ARAN, ATER, ONAN
Biblical country . **EDOM, ENON**
SEBA, SHEBA
Biblical driver .... **JEHU**
Biblical judge .... **ELI,**
ELON, GIDEON, SAMSON
Biblical king **OG, ASA, AGAG,**
AHAB, ELAH, OMRI, SAUL,
HEROD, NADAB
d Biblical kingdom ...... **ELAM,**
MOAB, SAMARIA
Biblical land .... **NOD**
Biblical lion .... **ARI**
BIBLICAL MEASURE ...... see
HEBREW MEASURE
BIBLICAL MOUNT see Page 197
Biblical name .... **ED, ER, IRI,**
ONO, REI, TOI, ABIA, ADER,
ANER, ANIM, ASOM, DARA,
ENOS, IRAD, IVAH, REBA,
ABIAM, AHIRA, AMASA,
ASEAS
Biblical name for part of Arabia
SHEBA
Biblical ornaments ..... **URIM**
Biblical priest, high ...... **ELI,**
AARON, ANNAS
Biblical region .. **ARAM, EDAR**
Biblical ruler .... **IRA**
Biblical sacred objects .. **URIM**
Biblical serpent .. **NEHUSHTAN**
Biblical son .... **HAM**
Biblical spy .... **CALEB**
Biblical tower .... **EDAR**
Biblical town in Samaria **ENON**
BIBLICAL TRIBE .... see
Page 197
Biblical weed .... **TARE**
Biblical well; spring . **AIN, ESEK**
Biblical wild ox .... **REEM**

a Biblical witch's home .. ENDOR
Biblical woman RAHAB, LEAH
Biblical word .. SELAH, MENE
Biblical word of reproach RACA
bicarbonate .... SODA
bice blue .... AZURITE
bicker .... CAVIL
bicycle for two ...... TANDEM
biddy .... HEN
"— bien" .... TRES
big casino .... TEN
bile .... GALL
bill .... DUN, NEB, BEAK
bill of fare ..... MENU, CARTE
bill, part of .... CERE
billiard shot .. CAROM, MASSE
billow .... SEA, WAVE
bind .... TAPE, SWATH
biography ..... LIFE, MEMOIR
biological .. BIOTIC, BIOTICAL
biological reproductive body
.... GAMETE
biotic community ..... BIOME
bird .... CLEE, COCK, CROW,
   DOVE, FINK, GLED, HUIA,
   IIWI, JACU, KALA, KIWI,
   KOEL, KORA, KUKU, KYAH,
   LARK, LOON, LORO, LORY,
   LOUN, LOWA, LULU, LUPE,
   MAKO, MAMO, MIRO,
   MOHO, MORO, MYNA,
b NENE, PAPE, PEHO, PISK,
   RAIL, RAYA, ROOK, RUFF,
   RURU, RYPE, SKUA, SMEE,
   SMEW, SORA, STIB, SWAN,
   TEAL, TERN, TOCK, TOCO,
   TODY, UTUM, WAEG,
   WREN, YENI, YUTU,
   DRAKE, ROBIN, SERIN, EL-
   ANET, SHRIKE, SISKIN,
bird, Am. .... TOWHEE
bird, Arctic .. BRANT, FULMAR
bird, Austral. .... EMU, KOEL,
   COOEE, COOEY
bird, black ANI, ROOK, RAVEN
bird, blue .... JAY
bird, C. & S. Am. ...... COIN,
   CONDOR, CONDORES
bird cry .... CAW, COO
bird, diving ...... AUK, LOON,
   LOUN, SMEW
bird, ducklike .... COOT
bird, extinct .... MOA,
   DODO, MAMO
bird, Europ. .... GLEDE, TEREK
bird genus ...... CRAX, RHEA
bird, gull-like .... TERN
BIRD, HAWAIIAN .... see
   HAWAIIAN BIRD
bird house .... COTE
bird, hunting .... FALCON

c bird, India .... SARUS
   SHAMA, ARGALA
bird, laughing .... LOON
bird life .... ORNIS
bird, long-legged
   AGAMI, STILT
bird, marsh .... RAIL,
   SORA, BITTERN
bird, mythical .... ROC
bird, national .... EAGLE
bird nest collector .. OOLOGIST
bird of prey ...... ERN, ERNE,
   HAWK, KITE, EAGLE,
   CORMORANT
bird, orange .... ORIOLE
bird order ..... PICI, RASORES
bird, oscine .. CHAT, ORIOLE
BIRD, OSTRICHLIKE ...... see
   OSTRICHLIKE BIRD
bird, Persian .... BULBUL
BIRD, SEA ..... see SEA BIRD
bird, shore RAIL, SORA, SNIPE,
   WADER, AVOCET, PLOVER
bird, small .... TIT, PIPIT
bird, small brown ...... WREN
BIRD, S. AM. .... see
   S. AMER. BIRD
bird, swimming .. LOON, GREBE
bird, talking .. MYNA, MYNAH
d bird, tropical ..... ANI, ANO,
   TROGON, JACAMAR
bird, U. S.
   COLIN, VEERY, TANAGER
BIRD, WADING .... see
   ..WADING BIRD
bird, wading, Afr.
   UMBER, UMBRETTE
bird, water see WADING BIRD
BIRD, WEB-FOOTED .... see
   WEB-FOOTED BIRD
bird, W. Ind. .... TODY
bird, white-plumed .... EGRET
bird, white-tailed .. ERN, ERNE
birds .... AVES
bird's beak .... NEB, NIB
bird's cry .... CAW, WEET
birds of region .... ORNIS
birds' route .... FLYWAY
biretta .... CAP
birth, by .... NEE
birth, of one's .... NATAL
birthmark
   MOLE, NEVUS, NAEVUS
birthplace, Apollo, Diana DELOS
birthplace, Constantine's
   NIS, NISH
birthplace, Mohammed's MECCA
birthplace, Muses, Orpheus
   PIERIA

a birthstone .... Jan., **GARNET;**
Feb., **AMETHYST;** March,
JASPER, AQUAMARINE,
BLOODSTONE; April, **DIA-**
MOND; May, **AGATE, EM-**
ERALD; June, **PEARL,**
MOONSTONE; July, **ONYX,**
RUBY; Aug., **CARNELIAN,**
SARDONYX, PERIDOT;
Sept., **SAPPHIRE;** Oct.,
OPAL; Nov., **TOPAZ;** Dec.,
TURQUOISE, ZIRCON
birthwort, Europ. .. **CLEMATITE**
bishop .... **PRELATE**
bishop of Róme .... **POPE**
bishopric .... **SEE**
bishop's attendant ... **VERGER**
bishop's hat
HURA, MITER, MITRE
bishop's office .... **LAWN**
bishop's seat ...... **SEE, APSE**
bishop's title, East ..... **ABBA**
bite .... **CHAM, MORSEL**
bite upon .... **GNAW**
biting .... **ACERB, ACRID**
bitter .... **ACERB, ACRID**
bitter almonds compound
AMARINE
bitter drug .... **ALOE**
bitter vetch .... **ERS**
b bittern .... **HERON**
bivalve .... **CLAM, MUSSEL**
bivalve genus .... **PINNA**
bizarre .... **OUTRE**
black .... **JET, EBON, INKY,**
RAVEN, SABLE, TARRY,
NIGRINE
black and blue .... **LIVID**
black buck .... **SASIN**
black gum tree genus **NYSSA**
black haw .... **SLOE**
black kelpie .... **BARB**
black nightshade .... **DUSCLE**
Black Sea arm ... **AZOF, AZOV**
blackbird
ANI, MERL, MERLE, RAVEN
blackbird, Europ.
OSSEL, OUSEL, OUZEL
blackbird: variant ...... **ANO**
blacken .... **INK, SOOT**
black-fin snapper .... **SESI**
blackfish .... **TAUTOG**
Blackmore heroine .... **LORNA**
blacksnake .... **RACER**
blacksmith's block .... **ANVIL**
blackthorn fruit .... **SLOE**
blackwood, India .... **BITI**
blade .... **OAR**
Blake's symbolic figure .. **ZOA**
Blake's symbolic figures **ZOAS**
blanch .... **ETIOLATE**

c blanket, cloak-like .. **PONCHO**
blanket, coarse wool .. **COTTA**
blanket, horse .... **MANTA**
blanket, Sp.-Am. ...... **SERAPE**
blast furnace, stone in .. **TYMP**
blaubok, S. Afr. .... **ETAAC**
blaze star .... **NOVA**
bleach .... **CHLORE**
bleaching vat .... **KEIR, KIER**
bleak .... **RAW**
blesbok .... **NUNNI**
bless .... **SAIN**
bless: Yiddish .... **BENSH**
blessing
BOON, GRACE, BENEFICE
blight .... **NIP**
blight of drought, India **SOKA**
blind, as hawks .... **SEEL**
blind dolphin .... **SUSU**
blind god, Teut. **HOTH, HODER**
blind impulse to ruin ... **ATE**
blindness .... **CECITY**
blister .. **BLEB, BULLA, BULLAE**
block, small arch
DENTEL, DENTIL
block, wood .... **NOG**
blockhead .... **ASS, DOLT**
blood factor .... **RH**
blood, lack of red
ANEMIA, ANAEMIA
d blood of gods .... **ICHOR**
blood, part of .... **SERUM**
blood, pert. to ...... **HEMAL,**
HEMIC, HAEMAL, HAEMIC
blood vessel .... **VEIN**
blood vessel, main .... **AORTA**
blood, watery part of
SERA, SERUM
blood sucker .... **LEECH**
blood-sucking parasite .. **TICK**
blouse, long .... **TUNIC**
blow..... **COUP, CRIG, ONER,**
SWAT, WAFT
blubber, piece of ..... **LIPPER**
blubber, to strip ..... **FLENSE**
blue .... **CADET, PERSE,**
SMALT, COBALT
blue-dye yielding herb **WOAD**
blue dyestuff .... **WOAD**
"Blue Eagle" .... **NRA**
blue-footed petrel ...... **TITI**
blue grass (genus) ...... **POA**
blue grape anthocyanin
ENIN, OENIN
blue gray
CHING, MERLE, SLATE
blue, greenish .... **BICE,**
SAXE, TEAL, EMAIL
blue mineral .... **IOLITE**
blue-pencil .... **EDIT**
blue pointer shark ..... **MAKO**

a   blue pine .... LIM
Bluebeard's wife ..... FATIMA
bluebonnet .... LUPINE
bluff .... CRUSTY
bluish-white metal ...... ZINC
blunder .... ERR
blunt .... DULL
blushing .... ROSY
boa, ringed .... ABOMA
boast .... BRAG, VAUNT
boastful air .... PARADO
BOAT . see also SHIP, CANOE,
     GALLEY, VESSEL,
boat .... ARK, TUB, PUNT
boat, assault .... LST
boat, Ceylon, India
     DONI, DHONI
boat, collapsible
     FALTBOAT, FOLDBOAT
boat, dispatch .... AVISO
boat, E. Ind. .... DONI, DHONI
boat, Egypt .... BARIS
boat, Eskimo .. BIDAR, CAYAK,
     KAYAK, UMIAK, OOMIAC,
     OOMIAK, UMIACK
boat, fishing
     TROW, DOGGER, CORACLE
boat, fishing, North Sea COBLE
boat, flat-bottomed
     SCOW, BARGE
b   boat, freight .... LIGHTER
boat front ...... BOW, PROW
boat, Ind. landing .. MASOOLA
boat, landing .... LCI, LST
boat, Levantine .... BUM
boat, light .... WHERRY
boat, mail .... PACKET
boat, Malay .... PAHI, PRAH,
     PRAO, PRAU, PROA,
     PRAHU, PRAHO
boat, Manila Harbor .. BILALO
boat, military ..... PONTOON
boat, Nile 2-masted .. SANDAL
boat, P. I. .. BANCA, BANKA
boat, racing .. SCULL, SHELL
boat, river
     BARGE, FERRY, PACKET
boat, river, Chin. ... SAMPAN
boat, small .... DORY
boat, 3-oar .... RANDAN
boat, used on Tigris
     GUFA, KUFA
boat, with decks cut
     RASEE, RAZEE
bob bait for fish .... DIB
bobbin .. PIRN, REEL, SPOOL
bobbins, frame for .... CREEL
bobwhite .... COLIN
Boche .... HUN
bodice, India .... CHOLI
bodily motion, pert. to GESTIC

c   body .... SOMA, LICHAM
body, heavenly . STAR, COMET
body of laws .... CODE
body of men .... FORCE
body of persons ...... CORPS
body of retainers .... RETINUE
body of writing .... TEXT
body, part of
     THORAX, THORACES
body, pert. to SOMAL, SOMATIC
body, trunk of .. TORSE, TORSO
body: zool. .... SOMA
Boer general .... BOTHA
bog. FEN, MIRE, QUAG, MARSH
boggy .... FENNY
boil .... STEW, SEETHE
boil down .... DECOCT
boiled rice without salt: P. I.
     CANIN
boiler, disk for hole in .. SPUT
"Bolero" composer .... RAVEL
boll weevil .... PICUDO
Bolshevik leader ...... LENIN
bolt .... SCREEN
bomb, defective .... DUD
bombardment, short, intense
     RAFALE
bombast .... ELA
bombastic TURGID, OROTUND
Bombyx .... ERI
d   bond .... NEXUS
bond-stone .... PERPEND
bondman ...... SERF, VASSAL
bonds, chem. with 2 double
     DIENE
bone .... OS
bone, ankle TALUS, ASTRAGAL
bone, arm .... ULNA
bone, arm, pert. to ... ULNAR
bone, breast
     STERNA, STERNAL, STERNUM
bone, ear ..... ANVIL, INCUS
bone: Greek .... OSTE
bone, leg .... FEMUR,
     TIBIA, FIBULA, TIBIAE
bone, pelvic, hip ...... ILIUM
bone, pert. to .... OSTEAL
bone scraper .... XYSTER
bone, skull .... VOMER
bones .... OSSA
bones, dorsal .... ILIA
bones, end of spine .. SACRA
bones, hip .... ILIA
bonnet monkey ZATI, MUNGA
bonnyclabber .... SKYR
bony .... OSTEAL
book .... MO, TOME, PRIMER
book, case for FOREL, FORREL
book, largest .... FOLIO
book, manuscript
     CODEX, CODICES

a book, map .... **ATLAS**
book, Bible .. see SPECIAL SEC-
TION, Page 196
book of devotions .... **MISSAL**
book of feasts, Catholic **ORDO**
book of hours .. **HORA, HORAE**
book palm, tree .... **TARA**
book, The .... **BIBLE**
books, Bible .... **GOSPEL**
bookbinding style ...... **YAPP**
bookkeeping entry
DEBIT, CREDIT
booklet .... **BROCHURE**
boor **OAF, CLOD, LOUT, CHURL**
boot, Eskimo .... **KAMIK**
booth .... **STALL**
booth, Oriental market
SUQ, SOOK, SOUK
bootlace .... **LACET**
booty ..... **LOOT, PELF, SWAG**
booty, take .... **REAVE**
borax, crude .... **TINCAL**
border ...... **HEM, RIM, EDGE,**
RAND, SIDE, MARGE
border on .... **ABUT**
bore .... **TIRE, EAGRE,**
WEARY, CALIBER
borecole .... **KAIL, KALE**
boredom .... **ENNUI**
boric acid salts ...... **BORATE**
b born .... **NEE**
born, being .... **NASCENT**
born: old Eng. .... **NATE**
Bornean squirrel shrew
PENTAIL
Borneo native .. **DYAK, DAYAK**
boron, pert. to .... **BORIC**
borough .... **BURG**
borrowed stock: Irish law **DAER**
bosh .... **ROT, POOH**
boss .... **STUD**
boss on shield .... **UMBO**
Bostonian .... **HUBBITE**
botanical suffix ...... **ACEAE**
botanist .... **MENDEL**
botch .... **FLUB, MESS**
both ears, involving use of
BINAURAL
bother ... **ADO, FUSS, TODO,**
TEASE, MOLEST, PESTER
bo-tree .... **PIPAL**
bottle, glass water .. **CARAFE**
bottle, oil, vinegar
CRUET, FLASK
bottomless pit .... **ABADDON**
boundary ...... **LINE, MERE,**
METE, LIMIT
boundaries, mark off
DEMARCATE
bounder .... **CAD**
bounding line .... **SIDE**

c bounds .... **AMBIT**
bouquet .... **AROMA**
bovine .... **OX, COW**
bovine, male .... **STEER**
bow of ship .... **PROW**
bow, low Oriental
SALAM, SALAAM
bow-shaped .... **ARCATE**
bower .... **ARBOR**
bowfin .... **AMIA**
bowl: cricket .... **YARK**
bowling term .... **SPARE**
bowstring hemp **IFE, PANGANE**
box .... **BIN, BINN, CASE,**
CIST, SPAR, CHEST
box, ecclesiastic .... **ARCA**
box canyon: Sp. ...... **CAJON**
box, metal .... **CANISTER**
box opener .... **PANDORA**
box, papyrus rolls, Rom.
CAPSA
box, sacred, ancient Rom. **CIST**
box sleigh .... **PUNG**
boxing glove, Rom. .... **CESTUS**
boxing term .... **KO, TKO**
BOY'S NAME .. see MAN'S
NAME
boy ... **BUB, BUD, LAD, TAD**
boys in blue .... **ELI'S**
B.P.O.E. member .... **ELK**
d brace .... **PAIR, TRUSS**
braced aback: nautical **ABOX**
bracing .... **TONIC**
brag .... **BOAST, VAUNT**
Brahman rule .. **SUTRA, SUTTA**
Brahmany bull .... **ZEBU**
braid ... **PLAT, PLAIT, QUEUE**
braid, kind of .... **LACET**
brain canal-passage .... **ITER**
brain, layer in .... **OBEX**
brain opening .... **LURA, PYLA**
brain part .... **PIA**
brain: P. I. .... **UTAC**
brain ridges .... **GYRI**
brain tissue .... **TELA**
brain ventricle opening **PYLA**
branch .... **ARM, LIMB, RAMI,**
RAME, RAMUS, SPRIG
branch-like **RAMOSE, RAMOUS**
branchia .... **GILL**
branch of learning ...... **ART**
brass, man of .. **TALOS, TALUS**
brassart .... **BRACER**
"Brave Bulls" author .... **LEA**
brawl .... **MELEE, FRACAS**
BRAZIL ..... see also SPECIAL
SECTION
Brazil drink .... **ASSAI**
Brazil red .... **ROSET**
Brazil dance .... **SAMBA**
Brazil heron .... **SOCO**

22

a Brazil Negro .... MINA
Brazil plant ..... YAGE, YAJE
Brazil rubber tree ULE, HULE
Brazil tree ...... APA, ANDA
Brazil capital .... RIO
breach .... GAP
bread, hard-baked ...... RUSK
bread crumbs, dish with
.... PANADA
breadfruit: P. I. .... RIMA
breadfruit: P. R. ... CASTANA
bread-tree seeds .... DIKA
break .... SNAP
break in .... STAVE
breakers .... SURF
breakwater ...... MOLE, PIER
breastbone, of ...... STERNAL
breastplate .... URIM
breastwork .... PARAPET
breastplate, Gr.
.... THORAX, THORACES
breath of life .... PRANA
breathed .... SPIRATE
breathing, harsh
.... RALE, STRIDOR
breech-cloth, Polyn. .. MALO
breeches: Scot. .... TREWS
breed .... REAR, RAISE
Bremen's river ...... WESER
breviary .. PORTAS, PORTASS
b brewer's ferment .. LOB, LOBB
brewer's vat .... TUN
brewing .... MALTING
brewing, one
.... GAAL, GAIL, GYLE
bribe .... SOP
brick carrier .... HOD
brick, sun-dried .... ADOBE
bricklayer .... MASON
bricklayer's helper ...... CAD
bridal wreath .... SPIREA
bridge .... SPAN
bridge, floating .... PONTOON
bridge, maneuver ..... FINESSE
bridge, Mississippi ...... EADS
bridge part TRESSEL, TRESTLE
brief .... SHORT, TERSE
brigand .... LATRON
Brigham Young U. site PROVO
bright .... APT, NITID
bright colored fish
.... BOCE, OPAH, WRASSE
bright: music .... ANIME
brilliance .... ECLAT, ORIENCY
brilliant group .... PLEIAD
bring forth .... EAN
bring on oneself ...... INCUR
bring together ...... COMPILE
bring up .... REAR, RAISE
brisk: music .... ALLEGRO
bristle .... SETA

c bristles .... SETAE
bristle, pert. to .... SETAL
bristly .... SETOSE
Britain's ancient inhabitant
.... PICT
BRITISH .. also see ENGLISH
British conservative ..... TORY
British king, legendary .. LUD,
BELI, BRAN, BRUT, LUDD,
NUDD
Britisher, early .... PICT
Brittany; city, ancient ...... IS
broach .... RIMER
broad band: Her. .... FESS
broadbill, E. Ind. .... RAYA
broadbill duck .... SCAUP
broken glass to remelt .. CALX
broken seed coats ...... BRAN
broken spike of grain .. CHOB
broken stone, etc. ... RUBBLE
Bronte heroine .... EYRE
bronze, Rom. money ..... AES
brood ...... SET, NIDE, COVEY
brook, small ...... RUN, RILL
broom of twigs .... BESOM
broom-corn millet
.... HIRSE, KADIKANE
brother .. FRA, FRIAR, FRATER
brought up .... BRED
brow of hill; Scot. .... SNAB
d brown ..... TAN, SEAR, SEPIA,
UMBER, BISTER, RUSSET,
SIENNA, SORREL
brown kiwi .... ROA
brown, pale .... ECRU
brown, red-yellow ..... PABLO
brown, yellowish dull ... DRAB
brown-skinned race ... MALAY
brown sugar .... PANELA
browned .... RISSOLE
brownie ..... NIS, NIX, NISSE
Browning poem, girl in PIPPA
browse .... GRAZE
Brünnhilde's mother .... ERDA
brushwood .... TINET, TINNET
brusque ...... BLUNT, TERSE
Brythonic .... CORNISH
Brythonic sea god ...... LER
bubble .... BLEB
buck, 4th year .... SORE
Buddha .... FO
Buddha, Jap. AMIDA, AMITA
Buddha's foe .... MARA
Buddha's mother .... MAYA
Buddha's tree .... PIPAL
Buddhist angel ..... DEVA
Buddhist language .... PALI
Buddhist church in Jap. .. TERA
Buddhist monastery, Jap. TERA
Buddhist Mongol ...... ELEUT
Buddhist monk .... BO, LAMA

23

a Buddhist pillar .... **LAT**
Buddhist monument .. **STUPA**
Buddhist novice ...... **GOYIN**
Buddhist priest .... **LAMA**
Buddhist relic .... **STUPA**
Buddhist sacred city .. **LASSA**
Buddhist sacred dialect **PALI**
Buddhist sacred mountain **OMEI**
Buddhist saint **LOHAN, ARHAT**
Buddhist scripture **SUTRA, SUTTA**
Buddhist sect, Jap. ..... **ZEN**
Buddhist shrine **TOPE, STUPA,**
DAGABA, DAGOBA, DAG-
HOBA, DHAGOBA
Buddhist spirit of evil .. **MARA**
buds, pickled .... **CAPERS**
buffalo, India

ARNA, ARNI, ARNEE
buffalo pea .... **VETCH**
buffalo, water, P. I. **CARABAO**
buffet .... **SLAP, SMITE, TOSS**
buffoon .. **FOOL, MIME, ZANY,**
CLOWN, MUMMER, JESTER
bug .... **BEETLE**
bugaboo: S. Afr. **GOGA, GOGO**
bugle call
TATOO, TATTOO, TANTARA
bugle note .... **TIRALEE**
build .... **REAR, ERECT**
builder .... **ERECTOR**
b builder, jetty-dam ...... **EADS**
building site .... **LOT**
building wing .... **ELL, ANNEX**
bulb, edible .... **SEGO**
bulb, Indian food
CAMAS, CAMASS, CAMMAS
bulb-like stem .... **CORM**
BULGARIAN .. see also **SPE-**
CIAL SECTION
Bulgarian czar .... **BORIS**
bulge, as eyes .... **BUG**
bulk .... **MASS**
bull, girl carried off on **EUROPA**
bull, sacred Egyp. .... **APIS**
bullet, size of
CALIBER, CALIBRE
bullet sound ...... **ZIP, PHIT,**
PHUT, PIFF
bullfight .... **CORRIDA**
bullfight cry .... **OLE**
bullfighter on foot .. **TORERO**
bullfighter's queue .... **COLETA**
bullfinch, Eng. .... **ALP**
bully .... **HECTOR**
bulrush .... **TULE**
Bulwer-Lytton heroine .. **IONE**
bumblebee .... **DOR**
bumpkin .... **LOUT**
bunch .... **TUFT, WISP**
bunch grass .... **STIPA**
bundle .... **BALE, PACK**

c bundle, small .... **PACKET**
bundle, twig, stick .... **FAGOT**
bundling machine ...... **BALER**
bungle .... **BOTCH**
bunting .. **ESTAMIN, ETAMINE,**
ORTOLAN, ESTAMENE
bunting bird .... **CIRL**
buoy, Eng. .... **DAN**
buoy, kind of . **CAN, NUN, NUT,**
BELL, SPAR, WHISTLING
buoyancy .... **FLOTAGE**
burbot .... **LING**
burbot genus .... **LOTA, LOTE**
Burchell's zebra .... **DAUW**
burden ... **LADE, LOAD, ONUS**
burden bearer .... **ATLAS**
burglar .... **YEGG**
burial place, Polyn. ..... **AHU**
BURMA .. see also **SPECIAL**
SECTION
Burma Buddhist (native) **MON**
Burma chief .... **BO, BOH**
Burmese capital, ancient **AVA**
Burmese demon (devil) .. **NAT**
Burmese gibbon .... **LAR**
Burmese governor **WUN, WOON**
Burmese hill-dweller ..... **LAI**
Burmese hills .... **NAGA**
Burmese knife .. **DAH, DHAO**
Burmese language .. **WA, PEGU**
d Burmese mongoloid ...... **LAI**
Burmese native (s) **WA,LAI,WAS**
Burmese premier .... **UNU**
Burmese 3-string viol .. **TURR**
Burmese wood sprite .... **NAT**
burn incense .... **CENSE**
burn .... **ASH, CHAR, SERE**
Burnett, Frances, heroine **SARA**
burning bush .... **WAHOO**
burning, malicious .... **ARSON**
burnish .... **RUB**
burrowing animal **MOLE, RATEL**
burst asunder .... **SPLIT**
burst forth .... **ERUPT**
bury .... **INTER, INHUME**
bush or bushy clump .... **TOD**
bushel, fourth of .... **PECK**
Bushmen .... **SAN, SAAN**
bushy .... **DUMOSE**
business .... **TRADE**
business cartel .... **TRUST**
"Bus Stop" author ..... **INGE**
bustard genus .... **OTIS**
bustle .... **ADO, TODO**
bustle about .... **FISK**
busy, to be .... **HUM**
but .... **YET, ONLY, STILL**
butcher's hook .... **GAMBREL**
butter, illipe .... **MAHUA**
butter, India ..... **GHI, GHEE**
butter, liquid ..... **GHI, GHEE**

butter tree .... SHEA
butter tub .... FIRKIN
butterbur .... OXWORT
butterfly .... IO, SATYR
butterfly, large .... IDALIA
butterfly-lily .... SEGO
button .... STUD
button, part of .... SHANK
buyer .... VENDEE
buyer: Law .... EMPTOR

buzzard .... BUTEO
buzzing sound .. WHIR, WHIZ
by .... AT, PER, PAST,
.... ALONG, BESIDE
by birth .... NEE
by hand, bred .... CADE
by means of .... PER
bygone .... AGO
Byron poem .... LARA
Byzantine capital .... NICAEA

C

C, mark under .... CEDILLA
caama .... ASSE
cab, Near East .... ARABA
cabal .... PLOT
cabbage .... COLE, KAIL,
.... KALE, KEAL
cabbage type .... SAVOY
cabin, main .... SALOON
cabinet, open, bric-a-brac
.... ETAGERE
cactus fruit, edible ... COCHAL
cactus, genus .... CEREUS
cactus-like .... CACTOID
caddis fly worm ..... CADEW
Caddoan Indian .... REE
cadet .... LAD
Cadmus' daughter .... INO
Caen's river .... ORNE
Caesar's conspirator-slayer
CASCA, BRUTUS, CASSIUS
cafe .... CABARET
caffein in tea
THEIN, THEINA, THEINE
caffein-rich nut .. COLA, KOLA
cage .... MEW
Cain's brother .... ABEL
Cain's land .... NOD
Cain's son .... ENOCH
Cain's wife, Byron poem
.... ADAH
cake, rich ... TORTE, TORTEN
cake, small ..... BUN, BUNN
calabar bean alkaloid
ESERIN, ESERINE
calamity ..... WOE, DISASTER
calcium oxide .... LIME
calf of leg, pert. to ... SURAL
calf's cry .... BLAT
caliber .... BORE, DIAMETER
calico colors, mix ..... TEER
calico horse .. PINTO, PIEBALD
calico-printing method .. LAPIS
California army base .... ORD
Calif. fish ...... RENA, REINA
Calif. fort .... ORD

Calif. herb .... AMOLE
Calif. motto .... EUREKA
Calif. shrub, berry ..... SALAL
Calif. wine valley .... NAPA
Caliph .... ALI, IMAM
call .. CRY, DUB, DIAL, NAME,
ROUSE, WAKEN, MUSTER
call for hogs .... SOOK
call forth .. EVOKE, SUMMON,
ELICIT, EVOCATE
call, to attract attention
HEY, PST, HIST, PIST
calling ... METIER, VOCATION
Calliope's sister .... ERATO
calm ...... LAY, COOL, LULL,
QUIET, STILL, PLACID, SE-
RENE, SMOOTH, SOOTHE
calorie ..... THERM, THERME
calumniate .... MALIGN
calumny .... SLANDER
Calvinists, Scotch .. BEREANS
calyx leaf .... SEPAL
cam .... TAPPET
cambric .... PERCALE
cambric grass .... RAMIE
CAME .... see COME
camel: Anglo-Ind. .... OONT
camel hair cloth .... ABA
camel hair robe .... ABA
camel-like animal ..... LLAMA
Camelot lady .... ENID
cameo stone .... ONYX
camera platform ..... DOLLY
Cameroons tribe .... ABO
"Camille" author .... DUMAS
camlet .... PONCHO
camp, fortified ...... TABOR
camp, pert. to ...... CASTRAL
camphor, kind of ..... ALANT
campus, restrict. to Eng. GATED
Canaanite month .... BUL
Canada goose ...... OUTARDE
canal bank .... BERM, BERME
canal betw. N. and Balt. Seas
KIEL

25

a
canary yellow ...... **MELINE**
canasta play .... **MELD**
cancel .. **DELE, ANNUL, ERASE**
candid .... **OPEN, FRANK**
candidates list .. **LEET, SLATE**
candle ..... **DIP, TEST, TAPER**
candle holder
SCONCE, GIRANDOLE
candle wick .. **SNAST, SNASTE**
candlenut tree .... **AMA**
candlenut tree fiber ..... **AEA**
cane ... **RATTAN, MALACCA**
Canio's wife "I Pagliacci"
NEDDA
canister, tea, alloy for .. **CALIN**
canna plant .... **ACHIRA**
cannabis .... **HEMP**
cannon .... **MORTAR**
cannon, old
MOYENNE, ROBINET
CANOE .. see also BOAT
canoe, Afr. .. **BONGO, BUNGO**
canoe, Hawaii ...... **WAAPA**
canoe, Malabar ...... **TONEE**
canoe, Malay (South Seas) outrigger ..... **PAHI, PRAH,
PRAO, PRAU, PROA,
PRAHO, PRAHU**
canoe, Maori .... **WAKA**
b
canoe, P. I. .. **BANCA, BANKA**
canon .... **LAW, RULE**
canonical hour .. **SEXT** (noon),
**LAUDS, NONES, PRIME,
MATINS, TIERCE**
canopy **COPE, SHADE, TESTER**
cant **TIP, TILT, SLANG, CAREEN**
cant-hook .... **PEAVY, PEEVY,
PEAVEY, PEEVEY**
cantankerous command. . **SCAT**
cantata, pastoral .. **SERENATA**
canticle, Scripture ...... **ODE**
"Cantique de Noel" composer
ADAM
CANTON .. see the country in
SPECIAL SECTION
canvas .. **DUCK, TUKE, SAILS**
canvas, piece of .... **TARP**
canvas shelter .... **TENT**
canyon mouth .... **ABRA**
canyon, small .... **CANADA**
CAP .. see HEADGEAR
capable .... **ABLE**
cape .... **NES, RAS,
NASE, NAZE, NESS**
cape, early .... **COPE**
cape, fur .... **PALATINE**
Cape Horn native .... **ONA**
cape, Pope's .. **FANON, ORALE**
Cape Verde native ..... **SERER**
Capek creature .... **ROBOT**

c
caper .... **DIDO, LEAP, ANTIC**
CAPITAL .. see SPECIAL SEC-
TION
caprice **WHIM, FANCY, VAGARY**
captain, fiction .... **AHAB**
captain, Nile ...... **RAIS, REIS**
capture **BAG, NAB, NET, SEIZE**
car .... **SEDAN**
car, last **CABOOSE, CAMBOOSE**
car, old make .... **REO**
caracal .... **LYNX**
Caradoc .... **BALA**
caravan .... **CAFILA**
caravansary
CHAN, KHAN, SERAI
caravel, Columbus **NINA, PINTA**
carbolic acid .... **PHENOL**
carbon, powdery .... **SOOT**
CARD .. see also GAME, CARD
card .. **ACE, PAM, SIX, TEN,
TWO, FOUR, JACK, KING,
NINE, TREY, KNAVE,
POSTAL**
card game like bridge .. **VINT**
card game, 3-handed ... **SKAT**
card game, old ...... **TAROT**
card game, Sp. .... **OMBER,
OMBRE**
card holding .... **TENACE**
card in euchre .... **BOWER**
card, playing
TAROC, TAROT, TAROCCO
d
card wool ...... **TUM, TEASE**
cards, highest ...... **HONORS**
care for .... **RECK, TEND**
care, heavy .... **CARK**
careen ...... **TIP, LIST, TILT**
caress .... **PET**
cargo .... **LOAD, PORTAGE**
cargo, put on .... **LADE, LOAD**
"Carmen" composer .... **BIZET**
carnation .... **PINK**
carnelian .... **SARD**
carnivore, Afr. .... **RATEL**
carol .... **NOEL, SING**
carol singer .... **WAIT**
carom .... **RICOCHET**
carousal **ORGY, BINGE, SPREE**
carouse .... **REVEL**
carp .... **ID, CAVIL**
carp, Jap. .... **KOI**
carp, red-eyed .... **RUD, RUDD**
carpet, Afgh...**HERAT, HERATI**
carpet, Caucasian **BAKU, KUBA**
carpet, India .... **AGRA**
carpet, Pers. ... **KALI, SENNA**
carriage .. **GIG, MIEN, POISE,
CALASH, LANDAU, CARIOLE**
carriage: Fr. .... **FIACRE**
carriage, India .... **EKKA**
carriage, Java, Oriental **SADO**

26

a carried away .... RAPT
carrier, of Orient .... HAMAL
Carroll heroine .... ALICE
carrot-family plant .... ANISE
carrot-like herb genus .. MEUM
carrot ridges .... JUGA
carry ...... LUG, BEAR, TOTE
carry across water .... FERRY
carry on (a war) ...... WAGE
cart, heavy .... DRAY
carte .... MENU
Carthage, of .... PUNIC
Carthage queen .... DIDO
cartograph .... MAP
cartoonist
    ARNO, CAPP, NAST, KIRBY
carve in itaglio ...... INCISE
case, grammatical .... DATIVE
case of explosives .... PETARD
case, toilet, small
         ETUI, ETWEE
casing, bore-hole ...... LINER
cask .. KEG, TUB, TUN, BUTT,
  CADE, TIERCE, PUNCHEON
cassava .. AIPI, JUCA, YUCA
cassia leaves .... SENNA
cast, founded .. FUSIL, FUSILE
cast metal mass .. PIG, INGOT
cast off MOLT, SHED, MOULT
b caste AHIR, BICE, GOLA, JATI
caste, agricultural ...... MEO
caste, gardener .... MALI
caste, low KOLI, KULI, PARIAH
caste, Tamil merchant
          CHETTY
caster ...... CRUET, ROLLER
casting mold .... DIE
castor-oil bean poison .. RICIN
castor-oil plant .... KIKI
Castor's killer .... IDAS
Castor's mother .... LEDA
cat .... ANGORA
cat, Afr.
    CIVET, GENET, GENETTE
cat, Am.
    PUMA, COUGAR, OCELET
cat cry .. MEW, MIAU, MIAW,
    MIAOU, MIAOW, MIAUL
cat genus .... FELIS
cat-headed goddess, Egypt BAST
cat, spotted
    PARD, MARGAY, OCELET
cat, tailless .... MANX
catalogue ..... LIST, RECORD
catamaran ...... BOAT, RAFT
catapult .... ONAGER
cataract .... FALLS
catch .... NAB, HAUL, HOOK,
    SNAG, TRAP, DETENT
catchword ..... CUE, SLOGAN

c catechu-like resin ...... KINO
category .... GENRE, SPECIES
cater ...... PANDER, PURVEY
caterpillar .... LARVA
caterpillar hair .... SETA
caterpillar, N. Z. .... WERI
catfish, Egypt ...... DOCMAC
catfish, S. Am. .... DORAD
cathedral .... MINSTER
cathedral city, Eng. ..... ELY
cathedral, famous .. CHARTRES
cathedral passage ..... SLYPE
cathedral, Russian .... SOBOR
Catholic, Greek UNIAT, UNIATA
Catholic tribunal ...... ROTA
catkin ..... AMENT, AMENTA
catnip .... NEP
catspaw DUPE, TOOL, STOOGE
cattail ...... TULE, MATREED
cattail India, narrow .. REREE
cattail, N. Z. .... RAUPO
cattle, breed of .... DEVON
cattle dealer .... DROVER
cattle genus .... BOS
cattle stealing, crime of
        ABIGEAT
CAUCASIAN .... see
    CAUCASUS NATIVE
Caucasian bharal ...... TUR
Caucasian goat .... TUR, TEHR
Caucasian ibex .... ZAC
d Caucasian language
        ANDI, AVAR
Caucasion Moslem
        LAZ, LAZZI
Caucasian race in China
        LOLO, NOSU
Caucasus native
     SVAN, SVANE, OSSET
caucho tree .... ULE
caudal appendage ...... TAIL
caulk lightly .... CHINSE
cause ...... CAUSA, REASON
caustic ... LYE, LIME, ACRID,
    ERODENT, MORDANT
caustic poison ...... PHENOL
cauterize .... SEAR
cautery plant .... MOXA
cautious WARE, WARY, CHARY
"Cavalleria Rusticana" heroine
        LOLA
cavalryman .... ULAN, UHLAN
cavalryman, Turk., Alg.
     SPAHI, SPAHEE
cave: archaic .... ANTRE
cave explorer .... SPELUNKER
cave: poet. .... GROT
cavern .. CAVE, GROT, GROTTO
caviar .... ROE, IKRA
caviar fish .... SHAD, STERLET
cavil .... CARP, OBJECT

Cavity

cavity .... ATRIA, ANTRA, SINUS, ANTRUM
cavity, ear, nose .... ANTRUM
cavity, in a rock .. VUG, VOOG, VUGG, VUGH, GEODE
cavy .... APEREA
cease! .... HALT, AVAST
Cecrops' daughter ...... HERSE
cedar, E. Ind. ...... DEODAR
Celebes ox .... ANOA
celebrated .... EMINENT
celery-like plant .... UDO
cella .... NAOS
cellulose acetate .... ACETOSE
cellulose: comb. form .. CELLO
Celt .... ERSE, GAEL
Celt, legendary IR, ITH, MILED
Celtic ... ERSE, MANX, WELSH
Celtic church early center IONA
Celtic dart .... COLP
Celtic god .... TARANIS
Celtic goddess
ANA, ANU, DANA, DANU
Celtic mother of gods
ANA, ANU, DANA, DANU
Celtic name meaning black
DHU
Celtic Neptune .... LER
Celtic paradise ..... AVALON
Celtic sea god .... LER
Celtic sun god .... LUG, LUGH
cement..LUTE, PUTTY, SOLDER
cement well lining .... STEEN
cenobite .... MONK
censure.BLAME, CHIDE, SLATE
center .... HUB, CORE, FOCI, FOCUS, HEART
center, away from .... DISTAL
center, toward ...... ENTAD
centerpiece .... EPERGNE
centesimal unit..GRAD, GRADE
centesimi, 100 .... LIRA
centipede: Tahiti ...... VERI
central .... MID, FOCAL
Cent. Am. gum tree
TUNO, TUNU
Cent. Am. tree .... EBO, EBOE
central line .... AXIS
central points .... FOCI
century plant .... AGAVE
century plant fiber..PITA, PITO
cere .... WAX
cereal .... FARINA
cereal grain .... OAT, RYE
cereal grass ...... OAT, RYE, WHEAT, MILLET
cereal grass, E. Ind. ... MAND, RAGI, RAGGI, RAGGEE

cereal grass genus ... SECALE
cereal plant: obs. ...... RIE
cereal spike ...... COB, EAR
ceremonial .chamber .... KIVA
Ceres' mother .... OPS
certificate, money ..... SCRIP
cerulean blue COELIN, COELINE
cervine animal .... DEER
cesspool .... SUMP
cetacean . ORC, WHALE, NAR-WAL, NARWHAL, PORPOISE
cetacean, dolphinlike, genus
INIA
Ceylon ape .... MAHA
Ceylon foot soldier ..... PEON
Ceylon governor .... DISAWA
Ceylon moss .... AGAR
Ceylon native
VEDDA, VEDDAH, WEDDAH
Ceylon sandstone ...... PAAR
Ceylon trading vessel .. DONI
chafe RUB, FRET, FROT, GALL
chaff .... BANTER
chaffinch ..... CHINK, SPINK
chain .... CATENA
chain, nautical .... TYE
chainlike .... CATENATE
chair .... SEDAN
chair part ...... RUNG, SPLAT
chaise .... GIG
chalcedony .... ONYX, AGATE
chalcedony, red .... SARD
Chaldean astron. cycle .. SAROS
Chaldean city .... UR
chalice
AMA, AMULA, CALIX, GRAIL
chalice veil .... AER
chalky silicate .... TALC
challenge .. DARE, DEFY, CAGE
chamber .... ROOM, CAMERA
chamber, pert. to ... CAMERAL
champagne, Marne .... AY
chance .... HAP, LOT, LUCK
chances, excess of ..... ODDS
chanced upon .... MET
chancel part .... BEMA
chancel screen .... JUBE
chancel seat .. SEDILE, SEDILIA
change .... FLUX, VARY, ALTER, AMEND
change appearance .. OBVERT
change direction CANT, KANT, TACK, TURN, VEER
change: music .... MUTA
channel .... GAT, MEDIA, STRIA, MEDIUM, STRIAL
Channel Island .... SARK
channel marker .... BUOY
channels .... MEDIA

a chant .... INTONE
chanticleer .... COCK
chantry .... CHAPEL
chaos .... NU, NUN
chaos, Babyl. .... APSU
chaos, Egypt. .... NU, NUN
chaos, Maori myth .... KORE
Chaos' son .... EREBUS
chap: S. Afr. .... KEREL
chapel, private .... ORATORY
chapel, sailor's ...... BETHEL
chaperon: Sp. DUENA, DUENNA
chaplain .... PADRE
chaplet .. ANADEM, WREATH
chapped .... KIBY
character .... NATURE
characteristic .... TRAIT
charcoal: Pharm. ...... CARBO
charge .... FEE, COST,
DEBIT, INDICT
charge solemnly ..... ADJURE
charged particle .... ION
charger .... STEED
chariot, ancient Briton
ESSED, ESSEDA, ESSEDE
chariot race site ...... CIRCUS
chariot, religious RATH, RATHA
charity .... ALMS
Charlemagne, race subdued by
AVARS
b Charlemagne's father ... PEPIN
Charlotte —, dessert .. RUSSE
charm .... JUJU,
SPELL, AMULET, GRIGRI
Charon, payment for .. OBOL
Charon, river of .... STYX
chart .... MAP
Charybdis, rock opp. .. SCYLLA
chasm GAP, ABYSS, CANYON
chaste .... PURE, VESTAL
chat, friendly .... COSE, COZE
Chateaubriand heroine, novel
ATALA
chatelaine bag .... ETUI
chatter GAB, GAS, YAP, PRATE
chatterbox .... PIET
cheat .... RENIG, RENEGE
cheat .... BAM,
CON, FOB, FUB, GIP, GYP,
BILK, MUMP, COZEN, SHARP
cheaters: slang ..... GLASSES
check ...... NIP, TAB, REIN,
STEM, BRAKE, STUNT
checking block .... SPRAG
cheek .... GENA, JOLE, JOWL
"cheek"..GALL, BRASS, NERVE
cheek, pert. to ...... MALAR
cheek-bone .... MALAR
cheer .... OLE, RAH,
BRAVO, ELATE, ENCORE
cheer pine .... CHIR

c cheer up .... LIVEN
cheerless .... SAD, DRAB
cheese ...... EDAM, STILTON
cheese, Dutch .... EDAM
cheese, hard brown .. MYSOST
cheese, soft .... BRIE
cheesy .... CASEOUS
cheetah, Ind. . YOUSE, YOUZE
chela .... CLAW
Chemical compound ... IMID,
AMIDE, AMINE, IMIDE,
IMINE, ESTER
CHEMICAL ELEMENT .... see
SPECIAL SECTION
chemical ending OL, INE, ENOL
chemical prefix .... ACI, OXA,
AMIDO, AMINO
chemical salt .... SAL, ESTER,
NITRE, BORATE
CHEMICAL SUFFIX .. see SUF-
FIX, CHEMICAL
chemical unit .... TITER
chemist's pot .... ALUDEL
cherish ... FOSTER, TREASURE
cherry .... GEAN
cherry red .... CERISE
chess piece .... MAN
chess term,—passant ..... EN
chessman ..... KING, PAWN,
ROOK, QUEEN, BISHOP,
d CASTLE, KNIGHT
chest, acacia wood ...... ARK
chest, antique .... CIST, KIST
chest, sacred ARK, ARCA, CIST
chest sound .... RALE
chestnut, Eur. ...... MARRON
chestnut, Polyn. ...... RATA
chevrotain . NAPU, MEMINNA
chew ..... BITE, CHAM, GNAW
chew, leaf to .... COCA
chewink .... TOWHEE
Chibcha chief's title .... ZIPA
chick-pea .... GRAM
chicken snake .... BOBA
chide SCOLD, BERATE, REPROVE
chief ... ARCH, HEAD, MAIN
chief, Afr. tribe .... KAID
chief, Am. Ind. ...... SACHEM
chief: Chinook .... TYEE
chief deity, Panopolis .... MIN
chief in Italy .... DUCE
chief, India .... SIRDAR
Chief Justice 1921-30 ... TAFT
Chief Justice 1941-46 .. STONE
chief, Moslem .... RAIS, REIS
chief officer, India .. DEWAN,
DIWAN
chief Norse god ...... ODIN,
WODAN, WODEN, WOTAN
chief, Pres. .... MIR
child .... TIKE, TYKE

Child

a
child of streets..ARAB, GAMIN
"Child of the Sun" ..... INCA
child, pert. to .... FILIAL
child: Scot. .... BAIRN
child: Tagalog, P. I. .... BATA
Chilean proletariat ..... ROTO
Chilean timber tree ..... PELU
Chilean volcano ..... ANTUCO
chill .... ICE, AGUE
chills and fever
          AGUE, MALARIA
chimney: dialect .... LUM
chimney pipe .... FLUE
chin .... MENTA, MENTUM
China .... CATHAY
China blue .... NIKKO
China grass .... BON
Chinese .. SERES, SERIC, SINIC
Chinese aborigine . YAO, MANS
Chin. aboriginal population
    division .... MIAO
Chin. are .... MU
Chin. boat .... JUNK
Chin. brick bed .... K'ANG
Chin. Causasian tribesman LOLO
Chin. characters in Jap. . MANA
Chin. club .... TONG
CHIN. COIN .. see also COINS
              Page 190
Chin., coin, bronze LI
b
Chin., coin, early .... PU
Chin. Communist .. MAO, CHOU
Chin. cult .... JOSS
Chin. department .... FU
Chin. dialect .... WU
Chin. division .... MIAO
Chin. dynasty . HAN, KIN, SUI,
    WEI, YIN, CH'IN, CHOU,
    HSIA, T'ANG, MING, SUNG,
    TS'IN, YUAN
Chin. factory .... HONG
Chin. feudal state .... WEI
Chin. flute .... TCHE
Chin. god .... GHOS, JOSS
Chin. govt. section
          HIEN, HSIEN
Chin. guild .... HUI
Chin. idol .... GHOS, JOSS
Chin. instrument, stringed . KIN
Chin. kingdom, old
          WU, SHU, WEI
CHIN. MEASURE.see also pages
          188, 189
Chin. measure of length . TSUN
Chin. mile LI
Chin. monetary unit .... YUAN
CHIN, MONEY see also page 190
Chin. negative principle ... YIN
Chin. noodles .... MEIN
Chin. official .. KUAN, KWAN
Chin. philos. principle.LI, YANG

c
Chin. plant .... UDO
Chin. pottery .... CHUN,
          KUAN, MING, TING
Chin. ruler .. YAO, YAU, YAOU
Chin. secret society ..... TONG
Chin. shop: Du. E. Ind. .. TOKO
Chin. silk .... PONGEE
Chin. wax, wax insect .. PELA
Chin. wormwood ...... MOXA
Chin. yellow .... SIL
chinin .... COYO
chink ...... RIFT, RIMA, RIME
chink-like .. RIMAL, RIMATE
chinky ...... RIMAL, RIMOSE,
          RIMOUS
chip .... NICK
chip of stone .. SPALL, GALLET
chipmunk .... HACKEE
chirp CHEEP, TWEET, TWITTER
chisel, primitive .... CELT
chisel, very broad .... TOOLER
chocolate powder ..... PINOLE
chocolate source ..... CACAO
choice .... CREAM, ELITE,
          PRIME, SELECT
choke up .... DAM, CLOG
choler .... IRE, BILE, RAGE
choose .... OPT, ELECT
chop ... AXE, CUT, HEW, LOP
chop fine .... MINCE
d
chopped .... HEWN
choral music
          MOTET, CANTATA
chord, 3 tones .... TRINE
chore .... JOB, CHARE
Chosen .... COREA, KOREA
Christ's thorn .. NABK, NUBK
Christmas .... NOEL, YULE
Christmas crib .... CRECHE
chromosome .... IDANT
chronicle .... ANNAL, ANNALS
chrysalis .... PUPA
chrysanthemum .. MUM, KIKU
chub, Europ. .... CHEVIN
chunk .... GOBBET
church .... FANE
church bench .... PEW
church, body of ...... NAVE
church calendar .... ORDO
church contribution .... TITHE
church council .... SYNOD
church court .... ROTA
church dignitary.POPE, BISHOP,
          PRELATE, CARDINAL
church dish .... PATEN
church, India .... SAMAJ
church living .... BENEFICE
church maintenance, canon's
          PREBEND
church officer .... ELDER

a church official
SEXTON, VERGER
church part ..... APSE, BEMA,
NAVE, ALTAR
church, Pope's ..... LATERAN
church porch .... PARVIS
church property .... GLEBE
church reader .... LECTOR
church recess .... APSE
church, Scot. .... KIRK, KURK
church vessel .. AMA, PIX, PYX
churchman .... PRELATE
churl. CEORL, VILLAIN, VILLEIN
churl: var. .... CARLE
churn plunger .... DASHER
cibol .... ONION
cicatrix .... SCAR
cigar .... CLARO, SMOKE,
CORONA, CHEROOT
cigar, cheap ... STOGY, STOGIE
cigarette, medicinal ... CUBEB
cigarfish .... SCAD
cincture .... BELT
cinnamon, kind of .... CASSIA
cion .... GRAFT
cipher .... ZERO, OUGHT
cipher system .... CODE
Circe's home .... AEAEA
circle .... CIRC, CIRQUE,
RONDURE
b circle of light ... HALO, NIMB
circle, part of .... ARC
circle segment .... SECTOR
circuit .... LAP, TOUR,
AMBIT, ORBIT
circuit judge, court ...... EYRE
circular motion .... GYRE
circular plate ...... DISC, DISK
circular turn .... LOOP
circular saw .... EDGER
cirque, geol. .... CWM
cistern .... BAC, VAT
citation .... CITAL
cite .... QUOTE, ADDUCE
citron ...... ETROG, CEDRAT,
ETHROG
citrus fruit ....LIME,
LEMON, ORANGE,
SHADOCK, SHADDOCK
CITY .. see also TOWN and
GAZETTEER
city, ancient, Asia Min. . MYRA,
TYRE, SARDES, SARDIS
city, ancient Thessalian
LARISSA
city: Gr. .... POLIS
City of a Hundred Towers PAVIA
City of Bridges ...... BRUGES
City of God .... HEAVEN
City of Kings .... LIMA
City of Lights .... PARIS

c City of Luxury ...... SYBARIS
City of Masts .... LONDON
City of Rams .... CANTON
City of Refuge ...... MEDINA
City of Saints .... MONTREAL
City of the Prophet .. MEDINA
City of the Seven Hills .. ROME
City of the Violet Crown
ATHENS
City of Victory .... CAIRO
city, pert. to .. CIVIC, URBAN
city, Philistines' ...... EKRON
city political division ... WARD
civet, Chinese .... RASSE
civet, Indian .... ZIBET
civet, Java .... DEDES
civet, Madagascar .... FOSSA,
FOUSSA
civetlike cat . GENET, GENETTE
civic goddess, Gr. ..... ALEA
Civil War commander ..... LEE,
POPE, GRANT, EWELL,
MEADE, SCOTT, SYKES,
HOOKER, CUSTER, FOR-
REST, JACKSON
civil wrong or injury .... TORT
claim ...... ASSERT, DEMAND
clam genus .... MYA
clam, giant .... CHAMA
clam, razor .... SOLEN
clamor .... DIN, NOISE
d clamp .... VICE, VISE
clan ...... GEN, SEPT, TRIBE
clan chieftain successor. TANIST
clan division: Gr. .... OBE
clan, Gr. .... GENOS
clan, head of .... ALDER
clarinet socket .... BIRN
clash .... JAR, COLLIDE
clasp . HASP, ENFOLD, INFOLD
clasp for a cope ...... MORSE
class .... ILK, CASTE, GENUS,
GENERA, SPECIES
class leader, Eng. .... DUX
class, lowest Jap. ..... HEIMIN
class, scientific
GENUS, GENERA
classic tongue .... LATIN
classification .... RATING
classification method . SYSTEM
classify .. RANK, RATE, SORT,
TYPE, GRADE
claw .... NAIL, TALON,
UNGUIS, UNGUES
claw, crustacean's
CHELA, CHELAE
claw ornament .... GRIFF
claw: zool. .... UNCI, UNCUS
clay ..... BOLE, ARGIL, LOESS
clay, baked .... TILE

a clay bed .... **GAULT**
clay, building: Sp.
　　　　ADOBE, TAPIA
clay-covered .... **LUTOSE**
clay, friable .... **BOLE**
clay layer ..... **SLOAM, SLOOM**
clay, melting pot ..... **TASCO**
clay mineral .... **NACRITE**
clay molding plate ...... **DOD**
clay pigeon shooting ... **SKEET**
clay pipe .... **TD**
clay plug .... **BOTT**
clay, porcelain ...... **KAOLIN**
clay, potter's .... **ARGIL**
clayey .... **BOLAR**
clayey soil.**BOLE, MALM, MARL**
cleansing agent ...... **BORAX**
clear.**NET, RID, LUCID, LIMPID,**
　　AUDIBLE, TRANSPARENT
clear, as anchor .... **AWEIGH**
clear of charges ...... **ACQUIT**
clearing of land, Eng. ... **SART**
cleave ... **REND, RIVE, CLING**
cleaving tool .... **FROE**
cleft ...... **REFT, RIFT, RIMA**
Clemenceau's nickname . **TIGRE**
clement .... **MILD**
Cleopatra's attendant ... **IRAS**
Cleopatra's handmaid ... **IRAS**
b Cleopatra's needle ... **OBELISK**
Cleopatra's serpent .... **ASP**
clergyman .... **ABBE, CANON,**
　　VICAR, CURATE, PRIEST,
　　RECTOR
cleric, Fr. .... **ABBE**
clerical cap .... **BIRETTA**
clerical, not .... **LAIC, LAICAL**
clever .... **APT, HABILE**
click beetle ...... **DOR, DORR,**
　　ELATER
climb .... **GRIMP, SCALE**
climbing plant ..... **IVY, VINE,**
　　LIANA, LIANE
cling .... **STICK, ADHERE**
clingfish .... **TESTAR**
clinging, for .... **TENENT**
Clio, sister of .... **ERATO**
clip . **CUT, MOW, SNIP, SHEAR**
clique .... **SET**
CLOAK .... see also GARMENT
cloak ... **ABA, WRAP, CAPOT,**
　　CAPOTE, MANTLE
cloak, Ind. .... **CHOGA**
cloak, Rom. . **SAGUM, ABOLLA,**
　　ABOLLAE
cloak, woman's ..... **DOLMAN**
clock, ship-form .... **NEF**
clog-like shoe .... **PATTEN**
cloister .... **MONASTERY**
"Cloister-Hearth" author.**READE**

c close eyes of .... **SEEL**
close, keep .... **HUG**
close: musical .... **CODA**
close to . **AT, BY, NEAR, ANEAR**
close, to fit ..... **FAY, FADGE**
closed, as wings .... **PLIE**
closing measure, music .. **CODA**
CLOTH .... see also SILK,
　　COTTON, FABRIC
cloth, bark .... **TAPA**
cloth, figured old ..... **TAPET**
cloth measure .... **ELL**
cloth, old wool ..... **CHEYNEY**
cloth, stout .... **BRIN**
cloth strip, India .... **PATA**
cloth used in mourning . **CRAPE**
cloth, wrapping .... **TILLOT**
clothe .... **GIRD, VEST, ENDUE**
clothes moth .... **TINEA**
clothespress, old Dutch ... **KAS**
clothing .. **DUDS, GARB, GEAR,**
　　TOGS, RAIMENT
cloud .... **SMUR, CIRRI,**
　　NUBIA, CIRRUS
cloud dragon, Vedic ...... **AHI**
cloud, luminous ..... **NIMBUS**
clouds, broken .... **RACK**
clouds, wind-driven.**RACK, SCUD**
cloudberry .... **MOLKA**
cloudy .... **DULL, LOWERY**
d clout .... **HIT, SWAT**
cloven-footed ...... **FISSIPED**
clover .... **HUBAM,**
　　ALSIKE, MELILOT
clown .... **APER, GOFF, ZANY**
clown, Shakesperean . **LAVACHE**
cloy .... **PALL, SATE, ACCLOY**
club member, Gr. .... **ERANIST**
club, women's .... **ZONTA**
clubfoot ... **TALIPED, TALIPES**
clumsily, handle . **PAW, BOTCH**
clumsy .... **INEPT, OAFISH**
cluster .... **NEP, TUFT**
cluster, grape .... **RACEME**
cluster pine .... **PINASTER**
coach dog ...... **DALMATIAN**
coach, Eastern .... **ARABA**
coagulate ...... **GEL, CLOT**
coal dust ...... **COOM, SMUT**
coal, heat-treated ...... **COKE**
coal, live .... **EMBER**
coal, size of .. **EGG, NUT, PEA**
coal refuse .... **CULM**
coal scuttle .... **HOD**
coalfish .... **CUDDY**
coalition .... **UNION, MERGER**
coarse .... **GROSS**
coarse sugar, E. Ind. .... **RAAB**
coast bird .... **GULL, TERN**
coast dweller ...... **ORARIAN**
coastal range, India .... **GHAT**

a COAT ..... see also GARMENT
coat .... LAYER
coat, animal .... PELAGE
coat, Arab .... ABA
coat, soldier's .... TUNIC
coat with alloy .... TERNE
cob .... SWAN
cobbler .... SUTOR
cobra ... HAJE, NAGA, MAMBA
cobra genus ..... NAIA, NAJA
cocaine source ... COCA, CUCA
cockatoo, Austral. .... GALAH
cockatoo, palm .. ARA, ARARA
cockboat .... COG
cockpit .... ARENA
coconut, dried .... COPRA
coconut fiber .... COIR, KOIR,
              KYAR, COIRE
coconut, Ind. .... NARGIL
coconut palm, P. I. ..... NIOG
cocoon insect .... PUPA
cocoon, silkworm .... CLEW
cod genus .... GADUS
cod, pert. to .... GADOID
cod, young ... . SCROD
code .... LAW, CIPHER
codfish, Eur. .... POOR
coffee ... RIO, JAVA, MOCHA
coffee-chocolate flavor.MOCHA
coffer-dam, Egypt .... SADD
b coffin stand .... BIER
cognizant .... AWARE
cognomen ... NAME, EPITHET
cohere .... BIND
coil .... WIND, TWINE
          TWIST, WREATHE
COIN ...... see also SPECIAL
          SECTION, Page 190
coin .... RIN, YEN, SPECIE
coin, cut edges of .... NIG
coin, edging .... REEDING
coin, gold .... LEV
coin, mill .... NURL
coin money .... MINT
coin, pewter .... TRA
coin, reverse side ...... VERSO
coin, silver .... SCEAT
coin tester, Orient
          SARAF, SHROFF
coin, tin .... TRA
coincide .... JIBE, AGREE
colander .... SIEVE
cold .... ALGID, GELID
cold, producing .... ALGIFIC
cold tableland, Andes ... PUNA
collar .. ETON, FICHU, GORGET
collar, clerical .... RABAT,
          RABATO, REBATO
collar, deep .... BERTHA
collar, wheel-shaped .... RUFF
collect ...... AMASS, GARNER

c collection .... ANA, SET
collection .... SORTITE
collection, motley ...... RAFT
collection of facts ...... ANA
collection of sayings .... ANA
COLLEGE DEGREE . see DEGREE
college, Iowa .... COE
college, N.J., East Orange
                  UPSALA
college official .... DEAN
college quadrangle ..... QUAD
colloquialism .... IDIOM
colonists greeting to Ind. NETOP
colonize .... SETTLE
colonizer .... OECIST
colonnade .... STOA
colony, Eng. ...... CAROLINA
colony, Fr. .... ALGERIA
color .... DYE, HUE, TINT
color .. ASH, BAY, RED, TAN,
     BLUE, FAON, FAWN, GRAY,
     GREY, HOPI, JADE, LIME,
     NAVY, NILE, PINK, PUCE,
     ROSE, SAXE, AMBER, BEIGE,
     CORAL, CREAM, EBONY,
     HENNA, IVORY, MAUVE,
     MOCHA, SEPIA, UMBER,
     CERISE, CITRON, COBALT,
     MAROON, RESEDA, SEVRES,
     SIENNA, SORREL, CAR-
     MINE, CELESTE, CITRINE,
     MAGENTA
d color brown sugar ... CARAIBE
color changer, photo ... TONER
color, neutral .. GREGE, GREIGE
color, purplish-brown ... PUCE
color, slightly .... TINT, TINGE
color, stripe of .... PLAGA
color, terrapin .... FEUILLE
Colorado park .... ESTES
coloring agent .... RUDDLE
coloring matter in fustic.MORIN
colorless .... DRAB
colorless alkaloid ...... ESERIN
colorless oil .... CETANE
columbite, variety of.DIANITE
Columbus' birthplace .. GENOA
Columbus' city sailed from
                  PALOS
Columbus' ship .. NINA, PINTA
column, Buddhist-Hindu, building
                  LAT
column, Gr. ..... DORIC, IONIC
column, memorial .... LAT
column, twisted . TORSE, TORSO
columns, arranged in TABULAR
coma .... TRANCE
comb horse .... CURRY
comb wool ...... CARD, TEASE
combat, field, place of . ARENA
combat, knight's ...... JOUST

33

Combat

combat, scene of ..... ARENA
combination .. UNION, CARTEL
combination, card .... TENACE
COMBINING FORMS:
above .... SUR
air ...... AER, AERI, AERO
all .... PAN, OMNI
ass .... ONO
bad .... MAL
bee .... API
beyond .... SUR
black .... MELA
blood .... HEMO
body ...... SOMA, SOMATO
bone .... OSTEO
both .... AMBI
boundary .... ORI
bread .... ARTO
bristle .... SETI
cetacean .... CETO
Chinese .... SINO
communications .... TEL
contemporary .... NEO
daybreak .... EO
dry .... XER
ear .... OTO, AURI
earth .... GEO
egg .... OO, OVI
eight .... OCT, OCTO
equal .... ISO, PARI
eye .... OCULO
far .... TEL, TELE
fat ... SEBI, STEAT, STEATO
fearful .... DINO
feast day .... MAS
female .... GYNE
firm .... STEREO
five .... PENTA
follower .... IST
food .... SITO
foot ...... PED, PEDI, PEDO
four-parted .... TETRA
fruit .... CARPO
gas .... AER, AERO
gate .... PYLE
glade .... NEMO
gland .... ADEN
gray .... POLIO
great .... MEGA
gums .... ULO
hair .... PIL, PILI
half .... DEMI, SEMI
heat ..... THERM, THERMO
hundred ..... CENTI, HECTO
idea .... IDEO
ill .... MAL
individual .... IDIO
inner .... ENTO
in zoology .... EAE
late, latest .... NEO
line .... STICH

many .... POLY
medicine .... IATRO
middle .... MEDI
milk .... LACT, LACTO
monster .... TERAT
mountain .... ORO
mouth ...... STOM, STOMO
moving .... KINO
narrow .... STENO
neck types .... DERA
needle .... ACU
nerve .... NEURO
new .... NEO
nine .... ENNE, ENNEA
nose .... NASI
not .... UN, NON
numerical .... UNI
numerous .... MULTI
oil .... OLEO
one .... UNI, MONO
on this side .... CIS
other .... HETER
outside .... ECTO
peculiar .... IDIO
power .... DYNA
powerful .... MEGA
quality .... ACY
recent .... NEO, CENE
reversal .... ALLO
ribbon .... TENE
round .... GYRO
sad .... TRAGI
seeds .... CARPO
seizure of illness .... AGRA
self .... AUT, AUTO
shoulder .... OMO
small .... STENO
solid .... STEREO
speak .... LALO
star .... ASTRO
stone .... LITH
strange .... XENO
sun .... HELIO
ten .... DECA
thin .... SERO
third .... TRIT
thread .... NEMA
threefold, thrice ...... TER
tooth .... ODONT
touch .... TAC
thought .... IDEO
thousand .... MILLE
up .... ANO
vapor .... ATMO
various ...... VARI, VARIO
watery .... SERO
white .... ALBO
whole .... TOTO
wind .... ANEMO
within .... ENT, ESO,
ENDO, ENSO, ENTO

a
without .... ECT
wood .... XYLO
worker .... ERGATE
come.ENSUE, ACCRUE, ARRIVE
come back .... RECUR
come forth .... ISSUE,
EMERGE, EMERSE
come forth from .. JET, GUSH,
SPEW, EMANATE
comedian's foil .... STOOGE
comedy .... FARCE
"Comedy of Errors" servant
LUCE
comfort .... EASE, SOLACE
comfortable .... COSH, SNUG
comforter .... SCARF
command .... BID, FIAT,
ORDER, DICTATE
command: archaic ..... HEST
command to horse
GEE, HAW, HUP
commander, Egypt .. SIRDAR
commander, Moslem
AGA, AGHA
commander, fortress CAID, QAID
commentary: Hebrew .... BIUR
commission, milit. ..... BREVET
commodity .... WARE, STAPLE
common ... VULGAR, GENERAL
common brant .... QUINK

b
common: Hawaiian ..... NOA
common man .... PLEB
commonplace .. BANAL, TRITE
commotion . ADO, STIR, TO-DO
commune, Dutch, Holland EDE
COMMUNE see its country in
GAZETTEER
communion cup .... AMA
communion dish .... PATEN
communion service ..... MASS
communion table ...... ALTAR
compact ...... DENSE, SOLID
companion .... PAL, MATE
comparative conjunction . THAN
comparative suffix ending . ER
compass point .... NE, SE, SW,
ENE, ESE, NNE, NNW, SSE,
SSW, WNW, WSW
compass point, mariner's RHUMB
compassion ...... PITY, RUTH
compel .... MAKE, FORCE,
COERCE
compendium .... SYLLABUS
compensate .... PAY
compensation, N. Z. ...... UTU
competent .... ABLE
complain .... FRET, FUSS,
GRIPE, REPINE
complainant .... RELATOR
complete ...... TOTAL, UTTER,
ENTIRE, PLENARY

c
completely .... ALL, QUITE
completely occupy ... ENGROSS
complication ..... NODE, NODI
comply .... OBEY, YIELD
composer, Am. . NEVIN, SOUSA,
FOSTER, COPLAND
composer, Eng. ...... ARNE,
ELGAR, COATES
composer, Fr. ... LALO, AUBER
BIZET, IBERT, RAVEL
composer, Ger. .... ABT, BACH,
WEBER
composer, Roum. ..... ENESCO
COMPOSITION.see also MUSIC
composition ... ESSAY, THEME
composition, mus. ...... OPUS,
ETUDE, MOTET, RONDO,
SUITE, SONATA, CON-
CERTO, FANTASIA
composition of selections.CENTO
composition, operatic .. SCENA
composition, sacred ... MOTET
compositor .... TYPO
compound, organic .... AMIDE
compound with oxygen . OXIDE
comrade-in-arms .... ALLY
concave .... DISHED
conceal: law .... ELOIN
concealed ..... INNER, PERDU
concealed obstacle ...... SNAG
concede .... ADMIT,
GRANT, YIELD

d
conceive .... IDEATE
concern .... CARE
concerning .... RE. INRE,
ABOUT, ANENT
conch .... SHELL
conciliate .... ATONE
conciliatory gift .... SOP
concise .. BRIEF, SHORT, TERSE
concluding passage music CODA
concoct .... BREW
concrete mixer .... PAVER
concur .. JIBE, AGREE, ASSENT
condescend .... DEIGN, STOOP
condiment .... SALT,
CURRY, SPICE
condition .. IF, STATE, STATUS
condition in agreement PROVISO
conduct .... LEAD, GUIDE
conductor .... MAESTRO
conductor's stick ..... BATON
conduit . MAIN, DRAIN, SEWER
cone ...... STROBIL, STROBILE
cone of silver .... PINA
confection .... COMFIT
confection, nut .... PRALINE
confederate .... ALLY
Confederate soldier ...... REB
confederation .... LEAGUE
conference .... PALAVER

a
confess .... AVOW, ADMIT
confession of faith .... CREDO
confidence .... FAITH, TRUST
confidences .... SECRETS
confident .... RELIANT
confidential .... ESOTERIC
confine ...... BOX, HEM, PEN,
CAGE, CRAMP
confined .... PENT
confront .... MEET
confused, make .... ADDLE
confusion .... BABEL
congealed dew .... RIME
conger .... EEL
congregate .. MEET, GATHER
conical mass of thread ... COP
coniferous tree ..... FIR, YEW,
PINE, CEDAR, SPRUCE
conjunction .... OR, AND,
BUT, NOR
connect ... JOIN, LINK, UNITE
connecting strip of land
ISTHMUS
connection
NEXUS, CORRELATION
connective .... AND, NOR
connective tissue ..... FASCIA
connubial .... MARITAL
conquer .... MASTER
conqueror, Mex.

b
CORTES, CORTEZ
Conrad's "Victory" heroine
LENA
conscript .... DRAFT
consecrate .... BLESS
consecrated .... OBLATE
consequence .... OUTCOME
conservative .... TORY
consider .... DEEM, RATE,
TREAT, REGARD
consonant, hard ...... FORTIS
consonant, unaspirated .. LENE
conspire .... PLOT
Constantine VIII's daughter. ZOE
constellation ...... ARA, LEO,
APUS, ARGO, LYNX, LYRA,
PAVO, URSA, VELA, ARIES,
CANIS, CETUS, DRACO,
LIBRA, MENSA, ORION,
VIRGO, AQUILA, GEMINI,
PISCES, TAURUS
constellation, Altar ...... ARA
constellation, Aquila ... EAGLE
constellation, Ara ..... ALTAR
constellation, Aries ..... RAM
constellation, Balance .. LIBRA
constellation, Bear ...... URSA
constellation, Bull ... TAURUS
constellation, Crab ... CANCER
constellation, Crane ..... GRUS
constellation, Crow ... CORVUS

c
constellation, Dog .... CANIS
constellation, Dragon .. DRACO
constellation, Hunter ... ORION
constellation, Lion .... LEO
constellation near South Pole
APUS
constellation, northern .... LEO
constellation, Peacock ... PAVO
constellation, Ram ..... ARIES
constellation, Southern ... ARA,
APUS, ARGO, GRUS, PAVO,
VELA, INDUS
constellation's main star .. COR
constitution supporter .CARTIST
constrictor ..... BOA, ABOMA
constructor .... ERECTOR
consume: obs. .... ETE
container .... BOX, CAN, TIN,
TUB, VAT, URN, CASE
containing ore .... ORY
contempt, exclamation of.PISH
contempt, look of ..... SNEER
contend .... VIE, COPE,
DEAL, COMPETE
contest .... AGON, BOUT
continent: abbr. ..... NA, SA,
AFR, EUR
continue .... LAST,
ENDURE, RESUME
contort . WARP, GNARL, TWIST

d
contradict ..... DENY, REBUT,
NEGATE
contrition .... REMORSE
contrive .... MAKE, DEVISE
control .... STEER
controversial .... ERISTIC
controversy .... DEBATE
conundrum .. ENIGMA, RIDDLE
convert to Judaism ...... GER
conveyance of estate .. DEMISE
convoy .... ESCORT
cony .. DAS, DAMAN, GANAM
cook in cream .... SHIR, SHIRR
cooking odor .... NIDOR
cooking pot .... OLLA
cooky .... SNAP
cool .... ICE
coolie woman .... CHANGAR
Cooper novel .... PILOT
copal .... ANIME
copper .... CENT
Copperfield, Mrs. ..... DORA
copse .... HOLT, COPPICE
Coptic bishop .... ANBA
copy .... APE, MODEL, ECTYPE
copy, court record ... ESTREAT
coral .... POLYP
cord .... LINE, RAIP,
ROPE, WELT
cord, hat of Bedouin .... AGAL
cord, Hawaii .... AEA

a cordage fiber . DA, COIR, ERUC,
      FERU, HEMP, IMBE, JUTE,
      RHEA, ABACA, SISAL
   cordage tree .... SIDA
   Cordelia's father .... LEAR
   "Cordiale, —" ...... ENTENTE
   core ...... AME, PITH, HEART
   core, casting mold .... NOWEL
   core material of earth ... NIFE
   core to fashion metal ... AME
   core, wooden .... AME
   cork .... SPILE
   Cork County port .... COBH
   cork, extract of .... CERIN
   cork, flat .... SHIVE
   cork helmet ..... TOPI, TOPEE
   corkwood .... BALSA
   corm .... BULB
   corn crake bird .... RAIL
   corn crake genus .... CREX
   corn, hulled .... HOMINY
   corn, India ... RAGEE, RAGGEE
   corn lily .... IXIA
   corn meal .... MASA
   cornbread .... PONE
   corner ... NOOK, TREE, ANGLE
   cornerstone .... COIN, COYN,
         COIGN, QUOIN, COIGNE
   cornice support ...... ANCON
b Cornish prefix: town .... TRE
   Cornish prefix in names . LAN,
                           ROS
   cornu .... HORN
   Cornwall mine .... BAL
   corolla part .... PETAL
   corona ... AUREOLA, AUREOLE
   coronach, Scot. .... DIRGE
   coronation stone ...... SCONE
   corpulent .... OBESE
   corral: Sp. .... ATAJO
   correct .. OKEH, TRUE, AMEND,
         EMEND, REVISE
   correct behaviour, Chin. ... LI
   correlative .... OR, NOR
   correspond JIBE, AGREE, TALLY
   corridor .... HALL
   corrie .... CWM
   corrode .... EAT, RUST, ERODE
   corrupt ...... TAINT, VENAL,
                        VITIATE
   corrupt with money .... BRIBE
   corsair .... PIRATE
   corset bone .... BUSK
   cortege .... RETINUE
   corundum .... EMERY
   cos lettuce .... ROMAINE
   Cos, pert. to .... COAN
   cosmic cycle .... EON
   cosmic order: Vedic ..... RITA
   Cossack .... TATAR
   Cossack chief ...... ATAMAN

c Cossack headman ... HETMAN
   Cossack regiment . POLK, PULK
   cosset .... PET
   costa .... RIB
   coterie .... SET
   cottage, Ind. .... BARI
   cotton batting .... BATT
   cotton, Bengal .... ADATI
   cotton, Egypt .... SAK, PIMA,
                         SAKEL
   cotton fabric ... JEAN, LAWN,
         LENO, DENIM, SURAT,
         MADRAS
   cotton fabric, corded.CANTOON
   cotton machine .... GIN
   cotton, matted .... BATT
   cotton tree .... SIMAL
   cottonwood, Texas .... ALAMO
   couch .... LAIR
   cougar ..... PUMA, PANTHER
   council .... SOVIET
   council, ecclesiastical . SYNOD
   council, king's .... WITAN
   "Council of —" ...... TRENT
   counsel .... REDE
   counselor .... MENTOR
   count .... ENUMERATE
   count, Ger. .... GRAF
   counter .... BAR
   counter, in cards ...... MILLE
d countercurrent .... EDDY
   countermand .... REVOKE
   counterpart .... LIKE
   countersink .... REAM
   counting frame ...... ABACUS
   COUNTRY see also GAZETTEER,
         beginning on Page 210
   country, ancient .... ELAM
   country, ancient, Asia Min., Gr.
         EOLIS, AEOLIA, AEOLIS
   country, ancient, Bib. .. SHEBA
   country, ancient Greek ... ELIS
   country bumpkin
         RUBE, YOKEL, RUSTIC
   country: law .... PAIS
   COUNTY.see also GAZETTEER,
         beginning on Page 210
   county: Dan. .... AMT
   county: Eng. .... SHIRE
   county: Nor. .... AMT, FYLKE
   county: Swed. .... LAN
   couple .... TWO, PAIR
   courage .... METTLE
   courier .. ESTAFET, ESTAFETTE
   course .... WAY, ROAD,
                    TACK, ROUTE
   course, complete ...... CYCLE
   course, meal . SALAD, ENTREE
   course, part of ..... LAP, LEG
   court .... AREA

a court action .... SUIT
court, A.-S. .. GEMOT, GEMOTE
court, church .... ROTA
court cry .... OYES, OYEZ
court hearing .... OYER
court, inner .... PATIO
court, Jap. ...... DARI, DAIRO
court, old English .... LEET
court order .... ARRET
court panel .... JURY
court, pert. to church .. ROTAL
court proceeding ...... TRIAL
courtly .... AULIC
courtship strut, grouse's .. LAK
courtway .... AREA
courtyard .... PATIO
Covenant, — of the .... ARK
cover inner surface ..... LINE
covering .. TEGMEN, TEGUMEN
covey .... BEVY, BROOD
cow .... BOSSY, BOVINE
cow house .... BYRE
cows .... KINE, BOSSIES
coward .... CRAVEN
cowboy garment ...... CHAPS
cowboy, S. Am. ..... GAUCHO
cowfish .... RAY, TORO
cowl .... HOOD
cowlike .... COUS
coxcomb .... FOP

b coy .... ARCH
coyotillo .... MARGARITA
coypu .... NUTRIA
cozy .... HOMY, SNUG
cozy place ..... DEN, NEST
crab-eating mongoose .. URVA
crab, front of .... METOPE
crack . SNAP, CHINK, CREVICE
crackling .... CREPITANT
crackpot .... NUT
craft .... ART, TRADE
craftsman .... ARTISAN
crafty ...... SLY, FOXY, WILY
craggy hill .... TOR
cramp .... KINK
crane arm .... GIB, JIB
crane genus .... GRUS
crane, India .... SARUS
crane, pert. to ...... GRUINE
crane, ship's .... DAVIT
cranelike bird ...... CHUNGA
cranelike bird, S. Amer.
.... SERIEMA
cranial nerve ... VAGI, VAGUS
cravat .... TIE
crave . ASK, BEG, LONG, DESIRE
craw .... MAW, CROP
crayon .... CHALK, PASTEL
craze .... FAD, MANIA
crazy .... LOCO, LUNY, WILD

c cream .... ELITE
credit transfer system .. GIRO
creed ...... CREDO, NICENE
creek .... RIA, KILL
creek: N.Y. .... VLEI
creeper .... IVY
creeping .. REPENT, REPTANT
Cremona .... AMATI
crescent moon's point ... CUSP
crescent-shaped ..... LUNATE
crescent-shaped figure .. LUNE
crescent-shaped mark . LUNULA
crest . TOP, COMB, PEAK, TUFT
crest, sharp rugged mountain
.... ARETE
crested as birds ..... PILEATE
Cretan princess .... ARIADNE
Cretan spikenard .... PHU
CRETE . see SPECIAL SECTION
crevice ... CREVAS, CREVASSE
crew .... MEN, GANG,
TEAM, EIGHT
cribbage pin or score .... PEG
cribbage term .... NOB, NOBS
cricket .... GRIG
cricket, ball in .... EDGER
cricket, field parts ONS, OFFS
cricket, run in .... BYE
cricket term OVER, TICE, YORK

d crime, Eccl. .... SIMONY
Crimean river .... ALMA
criminal .... FELON
crimp .... CURL, GOFFER
crimson ..... RED, CARMINE
crippled ...... HALT, LAME
criticize .... SLATE
criticize in a small way
CARP, CAVIL
crocodile, India ...... GAVIAL
crocodile-head god, Egyp.
SOBK, SEBEK
crocus .... IRID
crocus bulb .... CORM
Croesus' land .... LYDIA
crony .... PAL, CHUM, BUDDY
crony: old Eng. .... EME
crooked .... AGEE, AWRY
crooner, early .... VALLEE
crop .... MAW, CRAW
crop, spring, India ...... RABI
cross ...... IRATE, TRAVERSE
cross, church .... ROOD
cross-examine .... GRILL
cross of life, Egypt .... ANKH
cross oneself .... SAIN
cross out .... DELETE
cross-stroke .... SERIF
cross timber, ship ..... SPALE
crossbeam ..... TRAVE, TREVE
crossbill genus .... LOXIA
crossbow .... RODD

a crossing, fence .... STILE
crosspiece . BAR, RUNG, CLEAT
crosspiece, vehicle ... EVENER
crossthreads ..... WEFT, WOOF
crosswise .... THWART
crossword champion, former
COOPER
crow .. ROOK, CRAKE, CORVUS
crow: Eng. .... BRAN
crow, Guam .... AGA
crow, kind of .... DAW
crowd, common ... MOB, RUCK
crowd together .. HERD, SERRY
crowded .... SERRIED
crown .... CAP, PATE,
TIARA, DIADEM
crown colony, Brit.
ADEN, BAHAMAS
crown of Osiris or Egypt .. ATEF
crown: poetic .... TIAR
crown, Pope's triple TIAR, TIARA
crucial point .... CRUX, PIVOT
crucible .... CRUSET
crucifix .... ROOD
crude . RAW, ROUGH, COARSE
crude metal .... ORE
crude sugar-molasses MELADA
cruel person .... SADIST
cruet .... AMA, CASTER

b cruising .... ASEA
crumbled easily ..... FRIABLE
Crusader's foe ...... SARACEN
Crusader's headquarters . ACRE
crush .... MASH, SUBDUE
crustacean .... CRAB, ISOPOD,
SHRIMP, LOBSTER
crustacean order, one of
DECAPOD
cry .... HO, HOA, SOB, HOWL,
WAIL, WEEP, LAMENT
cry, Austral. ... COOEE, COOEY
cry for silence, court
OYES, OYEZ
crystal-clear .... PELLUCID
ctenophores, no tentacle .NUDA
Cuban dance .... CONGA
Cuban rodent .... PILORI
Cuban secret police ... PORRA
Cuban timber tree ..... CUYA
cubic decimeter .... LITER
cubic measure .. CORD, STERE
cubic meter .... STERE
cubicle .... CELL
cubitus .... ULNA
Cuchulain's wife . EMER, EIMER
cuckoo, black, keel-billed ANI
cuckoo, Oriental .. COEL, KOEL
cuckoopint .... ARUM
cucumber .... CUKE, PEPO
cud .... QUID, RUMEN

c cudgel .... BAT, CLUB, DRUB,
BASTE, STAVE, STICK
cue .... HINT
cue, music .... PRESA
cuff fastener .... TAB
cuirass .... LORICA
cull .... SORT
culmination ..... ACME, APEX
cultivate land .... HOE, PLOW,
TILL, HARROW
cultivation method, Bengal
JUM, JOOM
cultivation, soil .... TILTH
culture medium .... AGAR
cunning ... ART, CUTE, FOXY,
WILY, DEDAL, CALLID,
DAEDAL
cup .... CRUSE
cup, assaying .... CUPEL
cup, ceremonial .... AMA
cup, gem cutting .... DOP
cup stand of metal .... ZARF
cup to hold gem .... DOP
cupbearer .... SAKI
cupbearer of gods ...... HEBE
cupboard .... AMBRY, CLOSET
Cupid .... AMOR, EROS
Cupid's title .... DAN
cupola .... DOME
cur .... MUT, MUTT

d curare .... URALI, OORALI
curassow .... MITU
curassow genus .... CRAX
curdling powder ..... RENNET
cure-all .... ELIXIR, PANACEA
cure by salting .... CORN
cure with salt grass ..... DUN
curfew .... BELL
curios .... VIRTU
curl COIL, FRIZ, WIND, FRIZZ
curl of hair ...... FEAK, TRESS,
RINGLET
curling, mark aimed at ... TEE
currant genus .... RIBES
current .... AC, DC, EDDY,
RIFE, TIDE, STREAM
curt ...... BRUSK, BRUSQUE
curve .... ARC, BOW, ESS,
ARCH, BEND, SINUS
curve in a stream . HOEK, HOOK
curve, plane .... ELLIPSE,
PARABOLA
curve, sigmoid or double .. ESS
curved handle .... BOOL
curved in .. ADUNC, CONCAVE
curved out .... CONVEX
curved plank, vessel's .... SNY
Cush, son of .... SEBA
cushion ...... PAD, HASSOCK
custard .... FLAN
custard apple ...... ANNONA

a custard cake .... ECLAIR
custard dish .... FLAN
custody .... CHARGE
custom .... LAW, WONT,
        HABIT, USAGE
custom, India .... DASTUR
custom: Lat. .... RITUS
custom: obs. .... URE
customer .... PATRON
customs .... MORES
cut . HEW, LOP, MOW, DOCK,
  GASH, HACK, KERF, REAP,
  SLIT, SNEE, SNIP, TRIM,
  SEVER, SHEAR, SLIVE,
  CLEAVE, TREPAN
cut down .... FELL
cut edges of coins .... NIG
cut of meat .... LOIN
cut off ... DOCK, SNIP, ELIDE
cut off, as mane ..... ROACH
cut out .... EXCISE
cut: Shakespeare ...... SLISH
cut vertically
    SCARP, ESCARP, ESCARPE
cutter .... SLED
cutting .... SECANT, INCISAL

c cutting tool .. AX, ADZ, AXE,
    HOB, SAW, SAX, SYE, ADZE
cuttlefish ...... SEPIA, SQUID
cuttlefish fluid .... INK
Cyclades, one of, see GAZET-
               TEER
cycle, astronomical ..... SAROS
cyclorama .... CYKE
cylinder, moving ...... PISTON
cylindrical .... TERETE
cyma .... GOLA
cyma recta or reversa ... OGEE
cymbal, Orient .... ZEL
cymbals, India .... TAL
Cymbeline's daughter . IMOGEN
Cymric deity
    GWYN, LLEU, LLEW
Cymry .... WELSH
cypher system .... CODE
cyprinoid fish .... ID, IDE,
            CARP, CHUB
Cyrus' daughter ..... ATOSSA
cyst .... WEN
Czar .... IVAN, FEDOR
Czech .... SLAV
Czech, Eastern .... ZIPS

D

b Dadaist .... ERNST
dado, pedestal ...... SOLIDUM
Daedalus' son .... ICARUS
dagger .. DIRK, SNEE, BODKIN
dagger, ancient . SKEAN, SKENE
dagger, Ir. DHU, SKENE, SKEAN
dagger, Malay .... CRIS, KRIS,
    CREES, KREES, CREESE,
            KREESE
dagger: obs. .... SNEE
dagger, thin .... STILETTO
Dahomey Negro .. FON, FONG
daily .... DIURNAL
dais .... ESTRADE
daisy . MOON, OXEYE, SHASTA
Dallas school .... SMU
dam .... WAER, WEIR
dam, Egypt ...... SADD, SUDD
dam site .... ASWAN
damage . MAR, HARM, IMPAIR
Damascus river ...... ABANA
damp .... DANK
damselfish .... PINTANO
dance .... HOP, JIG, REEL,
    GALOP, GAVOT, POLKA,
    TANGO, RUMBA, REDOWA,
    RHUMBA, GAVOTTA, GA-
    VOTTE
dance, country . REEL, ALTHEA
dance, Gr. .... HORMOS
dance, Israeli .... HORA

d dance, lively ..... JIG, REEL,
    GALOP, POLKA, BOLERO
dance, old Eng. ...... MORRIS
dance, Sp. ... TANGO, BOLERO
dance, stately, old
   PAVAN, MINUET, PAVANE
dance step ..... PAS, CHASSE,
           GLISSADE
dancer .... KELLY, SHAWN,
    BOLGER, ZORINA, ASTAIRE
dancing girl, Egypt .... ALMA,
        ALME, ALMEH
dancing girl, Jap. ...... GEISHA
dandy FOP, DUDE, JAKE, TOFF
DANISH ... see also DENMARK
    in SPECIAL SECTION
Danish astronomer .... BRAHE
Dan. borough (in Eng.) .. BORG
Dan. chieftain ... JARL, YARL
Dan. division, territorial . AMT
Dan. fjord .... ISE
Dan. king ..... CNUT, KNUT,
           CANUTE
Dan. measure .... ALEN
Dan. money ..... ORA, ORAS
Dan. physicist .... BOHR
Dan. speech sound ...... STOD
dank .... WET
Dante's patron .... SCALA
Danube city ..... ULM, LINZ
Danube, old name of ... ISTER

a Danube tributary
INN, OLT, ISAR, PRUT
daring .... BOLD, NERVE
dark .... MIRKY, MURKY
dark horse .... ZAIN
dark rock .... CHERT
dark wood .... TEAK, EBONY
darkness .... MIRK, MURK
darling: Ir. . ROON, ACUSHLA,
ASTHORE
darnel .... TARE
dart along .... FLIT
"Das Rheingold" role ... ERDA
dash .... ELAN
date, pert. to .... DATAL
date plum .... SAPOTE
date, Roman .... IDES, NONES
"David Copperfield" character
DORA, HEEP, DARTLE
David's captain .... JOAB
David's commander ... AMASA
David's daughter ..... TAMAR
David's father .... JESSE
David's nephew ...... AMASA
David's ruler, one of ..... IRA
David's son .... SOLOMON
David's wife .... MICHAL
dawn .... DEW, EOS, AURORA
dawn, pert. to .... EOAN
day, Hebr. .... YOM
b day, Rom. .... IDES, NONES
day-breeze, It. .... ORA
days: Lat. .... DIES
day's march .... ETAPE
daybreak .... DAWN
dazing larks, device for DARE
deacon's stole ...... ORARION
dead ... FLAT, AMORT, INERT
dead, abode of . HADES, SHEOL
dead, region of: Egypt AMENTI
dead trees .... DRIKI
deadly ...... FATAL, LETHAL
deadly carrot .... DRIAS
deadly sins, 7 ENVY, LUST, AN-
GER, PRIDE, SLOTH, GLUT-
TONY, COVETOUSNESS
dealer .... MONGER
dealer, cloth
DRAPER, MERCER
dean ...... DOYEN, DOYENNE
dearth .... WANT
death .... MORT, DEMISE
death deity: Rom. ...... MORS
death note on hunter's horn
MORT
death notice .... OBIT
death rattle .... RALE
debate—debatable
AGON, MOOT
debauchee ...... RAKE, ROUE
debris, rocky .... SCREE

c decade .... TEN
decamp ...... ELOPE, LEVANT
decay, dental .... CARIES
decay tree ..... CONK, KONK
deceit .... SHAM, WILE,
FRAUD, GUILE
deceive .. BILK, DUPE, FOOL,
GULL, TRICK, ILLUDE
decelerate .... RETARD
deception HOAX, STRATAGEM
decide: Rom. law .... CERN
decimal unit .... TEN
deck, ship's .... POOP
decks, cut away . RASEE, RAZEE
declaim .... RANT, RAVE,
ORATE, RECITE
declaration in whist .... MISERE
declare .... AVER, AVOW,
STATE, AVOUCH
declare, in cards .... MELD
decline .... EBB, SINK,
WANE, REFUSE
declivity ...... SCARP, SLOPE
declivity in menage .. CALADE
decorate .... DECK, ADORN
decorated letter .... FAC
decorated wall part .... DADO
decorous ..... STAID, DEMURE
decoy .... LURE, PLANT
decrease .... EBB, WANE,
LESSEN, RECEDE
d decree .... ACT, FIAT,
CANON, EDICT, ORDAIN
decree, Fr. law .... ARRET
decree, Moslem .... IRADE
decree, Rom. law .... DECRETE
decree, Russian .... UKASE
deduce .... INFER
deed .... GEST, GESTE
deeds .... ACTA
deer, Asia ...... AHU, KAKAR,
SAMBAR, SAMBUR,
SAMBHAR, SAMBHUR
deer, barking .... KAKAR
deer, Chile, Andes ..... PUDU
deer, female . DOE, ROE, HIND
deer genus, E. Ind. ..... RUSA
deer, India .... AXIS
deer, Jap. .... SIKA
deer, Kashmir ...... HANGUL
deer, red .... ROE, HART
deer, S. Am. .... GEMUL,
GUEMAL, GUEMUL
deer, spotted .... CHITAL
deer, Tibet .... SHOU
deer track .... SLOT
deerlet .... NAPUS
deerlike .... CERVINE
defamation .... LIBEL
defeat, chess .... MATE
defeat utterly ... BEST, ROUT

a
defect, weaving .... SCOB
defendant's plea .... NOLO
deference .... RESPECT
defraud .... GYP, BILK,
          GULL, CHEAT
defy .... DARE
degrade ...... ABASE, LOWER,
          DEBASE
degrading .... MENIAL
degree .... GRADE, STAGE
degree .. (dental) DDS, DDSC;
     (engineer) CE, EE; (divin-
     ity) DD; (science) BSC;
     (arts) BA, MA, MFA; (law)
     LLB, LLD
degree, extreme .... NTH
degree taken, Cambridge
          INCEPTOR
degrees, angle of 57.30.RADIAN
deified sky, Rom. ..... CAELUS
DEITY . see also GOD, GODDESS
     and SPECIAL SECTION
deity .... GOD
deity, Buddhist ... DEV, DEVA
deity, Hindu ...... DEV, DEVA
deity, Jap. .. AMIDA, AMITA
deity, primeval .... TITAN
deity, Sumerian .... ABU
deity, Syrian .... EL

b
delay . WAIT, DETAIN, LINGER
delay, law .... MORA, MORAE
delicacy .... FINESSE
delight .... REVEL
delusion: Buddhism .... MOHA
demand . NEED, CLAIM, INSIST
demeanor .... AIR
Demeter's daughter CORA, KORE
demigod .... HERO
demolish .... RASE, RAZE
demon .... IMP, DEVIL, FIEND
demon, Arab, Moslem, Oriental
     JIN, JINN, GENIE,
     GENII, JINNI, JINNEE
demon, Hindu . ASURA, DAITYA
demon, sun-swallowing, Hindu
     myth .... RAHU
demon, Zoroastrian
          DEV; DIV, DEVA
demonstrative pronoun
     THAT, THIS, WHOM
den ...... DIVE, LAIR, HAUNT
denary .... TEN
denial .... NO, NAY
DENMARK .. see also DANISH
     and SPECIAL SECTION
denomination .... SECT
denote .... MEAN, SHOW,
          INDICATE
denoting unfit ships in Lloyd's
     registry .... AE

c
dense . **CRASS, THICK, STUPID**
density .... DORD
dental tool .... SCALER
deny .... NEGATE
depart ..... BEGONE, DECAMP
depart fast VAMOSE, VAMOOSE
depart: Lat. .... VADE
departed ... GONE, LEFT, WENT
department, Chin. .. FU, FOO
departure .... EXODUS
dependent .... MINION
depict .... DRAW, PAINT,
          DESCRIBE
deplore .... LAMENT
deposit, alluvial DELTA, GEEST
deposit, clayey .... MARL
deposit, geyser .... SINTER
deposit, mineral .... LODE
deposit, river
     ALLUVIA, ALLUVIUM
deposit, wine cask ... TARTAR
depressed .... SAD
depression ...... DENT, FOVEA
deprivation .... LOSS
deprived .... REFT
depute .... SEND
deputy ...... AGENT, VICAR
derby .... BOWLER
deride .... GIBE, JIBE
derrick .... CRANE, STEEVE

d
dervish, "Arab. Nights" . AGIB
dervish, Moslem ...... SADITE
descendant .... SON, CION
descendant, Fatima's
     SAID, SEID, SAYID
descendants, male line .. GENS
descent, deep .... SCARP
descriptive term ..... EPITHET
desert dweller .... EREMITE
desert, Mongolia .... GOBI
desert plant .... AGAVE
deserter .... RAT
deserve .... EARN, MERIT
design .... AIM
desire .... YEN, URGE,
          WANT, WISH
desire eagerly .... ASPIRE
desirous .... FAIN
desolate ...... LORN, BLEAK
despoil .... RUIN
despot .. CZAR, TSAR, TZAR,
     TYRANT, DICTATOR
dessert .... ICE, PIE, MOUSSE,
          TRIFLE
destiny . DOOM, FATE, KARMA
destroy .... RASE, RAZE,
          DECIMATE
destruction .... RUIN
detach .... WEAN
detachable button ...... STUD
detail .... ITEM

a detain **CHECK, DELAY, ARREST**
detecting device ...... **SONAR**
detective .... **TEC, DICK**
detent .... **PAWL**
determination .... **WILL**
determine .... **FIX, DECIDE,
RESOLVE**
detest .... **HATE, LOATHE**
dethrone .... **DEPOSE**
detonator .... **CAP**
"— deum" .... **TE**
devaluate .... **DEBASE**
developed compound animal
ZOON
Devi .... **UMA**
deviate ... **ERR, YAW, DIVERGE**
deviation .... **LAPSE**
deviation from course .... **YAW**
devil .. **DEMON, DEUCE, SATAN**
devil: Gypsy .... **BENG**
devil, Moslem
SHAITAN, SHEITAN
devil, Russian folklore .. **CHORT**
devil worship ...... **SATANISM**
devilfish .... **MANTA**
Devon river .... **EXE**
devotee .... **FAN, IST**
devotion, nine-day .. **NOVENA**
devoutness .... **PIETY**
dewberry .... **MAYES**
b dewy .... **RORAL, RORIC**
dexterity .... **ART**
dexterous .... **CLEVER**
diadem .... **TIARA**
diagonal .... **BIAS**
DIALECT . see also LANGUAGE
dialect . **IDIOM, LINGO, PATOIS**
dialect, Chin. .... **CANTON**
dialect, Ethiopic .... **TIGRE**
dialect, Gr. .... **DORIC, IONIC**
diamond corner .... **BASE**
diamond fragments ..... **BORT**
diamond holder .... **DOP**
diamond, impure industrial **BORT**
diamond, perfect ... **PARAGON**
diamonds, low quality ... **BORT**
Diana .... **ARTEMIS**
Diana's grove .... **NEMUS**
Diana's mother ...... **LATONA**
diaphanous ..... **THIN, SHEER**
diaphragm, pert. to .. **PHRENIC**
diatonic note .... **MI**
diatribe .. **SCREED, HARANGUE**
dibble .... **DAP, DIB**
Dickens character .. **PIP, TIM,
DORA, GAMP, HEEP,
FAGIN, DORRIT**
Dickens' pseudonym ...... **BOZ**
"Die Fledermaus" girl .. **ADELE**
die for making drain pipe . **DOD**
die, gambling .. **TAT, TESSERA**

c "Dies —," "Day of Wrath" **IRAE**
diet .... **BANT, FARE**
differ ...... **VARY, DISAGREE**
difference between solar and
lunar year .... **EPACT**
different ..... **OTHER, DIVERS**
difficulty .... **RUB, KNOT**
dig ...... **GRUB, PION, DELVE**
digest .... **PANDECT**
digit, foot .... **TOE**
digraph **AE, EA, OA, OE, SH, TH**
dike .... **LEVEE**
dilation .... **ECTASIA**
dilatory ...... **SLOW, TARDY,
REMISS**
dilemma .... **FIX**
dill herb .... **ANET**
dilute .... **THIN, WATER**
dim, become .. **BLEAR, DARKLE**
diminish .... **EBB, BATE, SINK,
WANE, ABATE, TAPER**
diminish front: military **PLOY**
dingle ..... **DALE, DELL, GLEN**
dining room, ancient ... **OECUS**
diocese center .... **SEE**
Dioscuri .... **ANAX**
dip .... **DAP, DIB, DOPP,
DUNK, LADE**
dip out .... **BAIL**
diplomacy .... **TACT**
d diplomat .... **ENVOY, CONSUL,
ATTACHE**
diphthong ..... **AE, IA, OA, UO**
Dipper constellation ..... **URSA**
direct .... **AIM, LEAD**
direct attention .... **REFER**
direct steering of boat .. **CONN**
dirge .... **LINOS, LINUS**
dirigible .... **BLIMP**
dirk .... **SNY, SNEE**
dirty lock .... **FRIB**
disable .... **LAME, MAIM**
disagreeable .... **ILL**
disappear gradually . **EVANESCE**
disavow ...... **DENY, RECANT**
disbeliever .... **ATHEIST**
disburse ...... **SPEND, EXPEND**
discard . **DROP, SCRAP, REJECT**
discernment .... **TACT**
discharge .... **EMIT, FIRE,
SACK, SHOOT**
discharged .... **SHOT**
disciple .... **APOSTLE**
disciple: India .... **CHELA**
disciplinarian ..... **MARTINET**
disclaim .... **DENY**
disclose .... **BARE, REVEAL**
discolored ...... **DOTY, LIVID**
disconcert ..... **FAZE, ABASH**
discourse .. **HOMILY, DESCANT**
discourse, art of ... **RHETORIC**

discover . SEE, SPY, ESPY, FIND
discriminate .... SECERN
discuss ...... TREAT, DEBATE
discussion group ...... FORUM
disease ..... MAL, POX, HIVES
disease, Afr. .... NENTA
disease cause .... VIRUS
disease, diver's .... BENDS
disease, fowl ...... PIP, ROUP,
PEROSIS
disease, fungus .... ERGOT
disease, grape-vine
ESCA, ERINOSE
disease, plant ... SMUT, SCALD
disease, skin .... ECZEMA
disease spreader
VECTOR, CARRIER
disease, tropical .... SPRUE
disembark .... LAND
disembodied spirit: Chin.
KUEI, KWEI
disencumber .... RID
disengage .... FREE
disfigure .... MAR, DEFACE
disgrace .... SCANDAL
disguise .... MASK
disgust, word of .... AW
DISH .... also see VESSEL
dish .... PLATE
dish, Hawaiian .... POI
dish, highly seasoned
OLIO, OLLA
dish, hominy .... POSOLE
dish, Hungarian .... GOULASH
dish, It. .... RAVIOLI
dish, main .... ENTREE
dish, meat .... STEW, RAGOUT
dish, Mex. .. TAMAL, TAMALE,
TAMALI
dish, stemmed ..... COMPOTE
dishearten .... DAUNT, DETER
dishonor .... SHAME, VIOLATE
dishonorable .... BASE
disinclined .... AVERSE
disinfectant . CRESOL, PHENOL,
CRESSOL, CRESSYL
disk, ice hockey ...... PUCK
disk, like a .. DISCAL, DISCOID
disk, metal .... PATEN
dislocate .... LUXATE
dismal .... DREAR
dismantle .... STRIP
dismay .... APPAL, DAUNT
dismiss .... DEMIT, FIRE
dismounted .... ALIT
disorder .... MESS, DERAY,
CLUTTER
disorderly flight .... ROUT
disparaging .... SNIDE
disparaging remark ..... SLUR
dispatch .... SEND, HASTE

dispatch boat .... AVISO
dispelled .... GONE
display .... AIR, SHEW, SHOW,
ARRAY, EVINCE
display proudly
VAUNT, OSTENT
displease .... VEX, MIFF,
ANGER, ANNOY
disposed .... PRONE
disposition .... MOOD, TEMPER
dispossess .... OUST, EVICT
disprove .... REFUTE
disputable .... MOOT
dissertation ... THESES, THESIS
dissolute person .. RAKE, ROUE
dissonant .... ATONAL
distance, at-from a . OFF, AFAR
distant ... FAR, YON, REMOTE
distilling vessel .... MATRASS
distinctive air ... AURA, MIEN,
CACHET
distracted .... DISTRAIT
distraint: old Eng. law .. NAAM
distribute .. DEAL, DOLE, METE
DISTRICT .... see also REGION
district .... AREA, ZONE
district, old Eng. court
SOC, SOKE
disturb .... ROIL, MOLEST
disturbance ...... ROW, RIOT
ditch .... FOSS, RINE,
FOSSE, TRENCH
ditch, castle .... MOAT
ditch, fort. .... RELAIS
ditch millet .... HUREEK
ditto .... SAME
divan .... SOFA
dive .... DEN, HEADER
dive bomber .... STUKA
diverge .... DEVIATE
divers .... SEVERAL
divest .... STRIP, DEPRIVE
divide .... PART, SHARE
divide for study ..... DISSECT
divided .... REFT, SPLIT
divider .... MERIST
dividing wall, membrance, parti-
tion ...... SEPTA, SEPTUM
divination by lots: Lat.
SORS, SORTES
"Divine Comedy" author DANTE
divine favor .... GRACE
divine law: Rom. .... FAS
divine revelation TORA, TORAH
divine utterance ..... ORACLE
divinity .... DEITY
divorce bill, Jewish law
GET, GETT
divorce, Moslem ...... TALAK
"— dixit" .... IPSE
dizziness, pert. to ..... DINIC

44

a docile .... TAME
dockyard barge .... LUMP
doctor ..... INTERN, INTERNE
Dr. Brown's dog hero .... RAB
Dr. Jekyll's other self .. HYDE
doctrinaire .... ISMY
doctrine .. ISM, DOGMA, TENET
documents, box for .. HANAPER
dodder .... AMIL
dodo genus .... DIDUS
doe .... HIND
doe, young .... TAG, TEG
dog, ... CANIS, CANINE
dog ...... POM, CHOW, PEKE,
   BASSET, POODLE, SPANIEL
dog, chops of .... FLEWS
dog-faced ape .... AANI
dog-fisher .... OTTER
DOG, GUN see DOG, HUNTING
dog, Hungarian PULI, KUVASZ
dog, hunting (bird) ... ALAN,
   ALAND, ALANT, BASSET,
   BEAGLE, SETTER, COURSER,
   HARRIER, POINTER
dog, John Brown's ...... RAB
dog, large .... ALAN
dog, "Odyssey" .... ARGOS
dog salmon .... KETA
dog, small-toy ..... POM, PUG,
                          PEKE
b dog snapper, fish ...... JOCU
dog, Sputnik's .... LAIKA
dog star .... SEPT, SOPT,
   SEPTI, SIRIUS
dog, tropical .... ALCO
dog, Welsh .... CORGI
dog, wild, Austral. ...... DINGO
dog, wild, India ...... DHOLE
doge, office of ...... DOGATE
dogfish .... SHARK
dogma .... TENET
dogwood ...... OSIER, CORNEL
dole .... METE
dolphin fish .... DORADO
dolphin genus .... INIA
dolphin-like cetacean .... INIA
dolt .... ASS, OAF, CLOD,
               LOUT, DUNCE
domain ..... BOURN, REALM,
   BOURNE, DEMENE, ESTATE,
   DEMESNE
dome .... CUPOLA
dome-shaped .... DOMOID
Domesday Book money ... ORA
domestic .... MAID, LOCAL
domestic animal .... ASS, CAT,
   COW, DOG, HOG, PIG,
   RAM, SOW, MULE
domestic slave .... ESNE
domesticated .... TAME
dominion .... REALM, EMPERY

c domino .... MASK
Don Juan's mother ...... INEZ
donkey .... ASS, MOKE,
   BURRO, NEDDY
doom .... CONDEMN, DESTINE
doom palm, Afr. .... DUM
door .... PORTAL
door: Lat. .... JANUA
door part ...... JAMB, SASH,
   SILL, LINTEL
door section .... PANEL
doorkeeper, Masonic .... TILER
dorado, color .... CUIR
Doric frieze slab ...... METOPE
dormant ..... ASLEEP, LATENT
dormouse .... LOIR
dormouse, garden ...... LEROT
dormouse genus .... GLIS
dorsal .... NOTAL
dote .... DRIVEL
dots, paint with ..... STIPPLE
dotted with figures ...... SEME
double . DUAL, TWIN, BINATE
double cocoon .... DUPION
double dagger .... DIESIS
double, Egypt .... KA
double salt .... ALUM
double tooth .... MOLAR
doubletree .... EVENER
d dovkie ...... ROTCH, ROTGE,
                      ROTCHE
Dovyalis .... ABERIA
dowel ..... PIN, COAG, COAK
dower, pert. to .... DOTAL
dower property .... DOS
down ...... FUZZ, PILE, EIDER
down, facing.PRONE, PRONATE
down quilt .... DUVET
"downunder" native clan .. ATI
downward, curve ...... DEFLEX
dowry .... DOS, DOT
drag ... LUG, TUG, HAUL, SNIG
dragnet .... TRAWL
dragon, like a ... DRACONTINE
dragon of darkness, Bibl. RAHAB
drain . SAP, DEPLETE, VITIATE
drain .... SUMP, SEWER
dram, small .... NIP
DRAMA .... see also PLAY
Dravidian KOTA, MALE, NAIR,
   TODA, TULU, TAMIL
draw ...... TIE, TOW, LIMN,
   PULL, DEPICT
draw forth .... EDUCE
draw from .... DERIVE
draw out . EDUCE, ATTENUATE
draw tight: naut. .... FRAP
drawing curve .... SPLINE
drawing room .... SALON
dreadful .... DIRE
dream, day .... REVERIE

45

Dream

a
"Dream Girl" playwright . RICE
dregs .... FAEX, LEES,
DROSS, SEDIMENT
drench .... SOUSE, TOUSE
drenched .... WET, DEWED
DRESS .... see also GARMENT
dress .... GARB, CLOTHE,
ACCOUTER
dress, as stone ...... DAB, NIG
dress feathers .... PREEN
dress leather ...... DUB, TAN
dress up .... TOG, PREEN
dressed .... CLAD
dressing wounds, material for
LINT, LINTS
dried berry: Sp. .... PASA
dried up .... SERE
drift .... TREND
drill .... BORE, TRAIN
drilling rod .... BAR, BIT
DRINK .... see also BEVERAGE
drink .... GULP, SWIG,
QUAFF, IMBIBE
drink, Christmas NOG, WASSAIL
drink, fermented ...... MEAD
drink, honey .... MEAD
drink, hot .... TODDY
drink, hot milk .... POSSET
drink of gods .... NECTAR
drink of liquor .. NIP, BRACER

b
drink, old honey ...... MORAT
drink, palm .... NIPA
drink, rum-gin .... BUMBO
drink slowly .... SIP, SUP
drink, small ...... NIP, PEG,
DRAM, SLUG
drink to excess .. TOPE, BOUSE
drink, whiskey ...... STINGER
drinking bowl .... MAZER
drinking cup, Gr. .... HOLMOS
drinking vessel .... CUP, MUG,
TIG, TYG, JORUM,
STEIN, TANKARD
drive ..... RIDE, URGE, IMPEL
drive away ..... SHOO, DISPEL
drive back
ROUT, REPEL, REPULSE
drive in .... TAMP
drivel .... DROOL, SLAVER
driver, fast reckless ..... JEHU
drizzle .. MIST, SMUR, SMURR
droll .... ODD
dromedary, female .... DELUL
dromedary, swift .... MEHARI
drone .... BEE, DOR, HUM
droop .... LOP, SAG, WILT
drooping .... ALOP
drop ...... DRIB, FALL, SINK,
GUTTA, GLOBULE
drop a fish line or bait .. DAP
drop, one .... MINIM

c
drop: Prov. Eng. ..... SIE, SYE
dropsy .... EDEMA
dross .. SLAG, SPRUE, SCORIA
drought-tolerant plant .. GUAR
drove .... HERD, RODE
drove of horses .... ATAJO
drowse .... NOD
drudge ... MOIL, TOIL, LABOR
drug ..... DOPE, SINA, ALOES,
OPIATE, DILANTIN
drug, Hippocrates' .... MECON
drugged bliss .... KEF
drum-call to arms .... RAPPEL
drum roll, reveille .... DIAN
drum, small . TABOR, TABOUR,
TABRET
drum, W. Ind. .... GUMBY
drumbeat .... DUB, TATOO,
TATTOO
drunkard .... SOT, SOAK,
SOUSE, TOPER
dry .... SEC, ARID, SERE
dry, as wine .... SEC
dry bed of river .... WADI
dry goods dealer ..... DRAPER
dub .... NAME, KNIGHT
duck .... ANAS, SMEE,
TEAL, PEKIN

d
duck, Arctic .... EIDER
duck, breed of .... ROUEN
duck, diving .... SMEW
duck eggs, Chin. ...... PIDAN
duck, fresh water .... TEAL
duck genus .. AEX, AIX, ANAS
duck, like a .... ANATINE
duck lure .... DECOY
duck, male .... DRAKE
duck, Muscovy .... PATO
duck, pintail .... SMEE
duck, ring-necked ...... DOGY
duck, river ..... TEAL, EIDER,
SHOVELER
duck, sea ...... COOT, SCAUP
duck, sea, northern ... SCOTER
duck-shooting boat ..... SKAG
duck to cook: Fr. .. CANETON
duct: anat. .... VAS, VASA
dude .... FOP, DANDY
due, India .... HAK, HAKH
duet .... DUI, DUO
dugout canoe BANCA, PIROGUE
dugout, India . DONGA, DUNGA
duke's dominion ...... DUCHY
dulcimer .... CITOLE
dulcimer, Oriental ..... SANTIR
dull . DRY, DUN, DRAB, LOGY,
BLUNT, PROSY, BORING
dull color .. DUN, MAT, DRAB,
MATTE, TERNE
dull in finish .... MAT, MATTE

dull silk fabric .... **GROS**
dullard .... **BOOR**
Dumas hero
ATHOS, ARAMIS, PORTHOS
dummy whist .... **MORT**
dung beetle .... **DOR**
dunlin bird .... **STIB**
dupe .... **USE, FOOL**
duration measure .... **TIME**
dusk .... **EVE**
dusky .... **DIM, DARK, SWART**
dusty: Scot. .... **MOTTY**
DUTCH see also NETHERLANDS,
SPECIAL SECTION
Dutch: bit .... **DOIT**
cupboard .... **KAS**
donkey .... **EZEL**
"mister" .... **HEER**
out .... **UIT**
woman .... **FROW**
Dutch cheese .... **EDAM**
Dutch commune .... **EDE**
Dutch early geographer .. **AA**
Dutch fishing boat .. **DOGGER**
Dutch measure, old ..... **AAM**
Dutch meter .... **EL**
Dutch minor coin .... **DOIT**
Dutch news agency, old **ANETA**
Dutch painter
LIS, HALS, LELY, STEEN
Dutch two-masted vessel **KOFF**
duty .... **CHORE, TARIFF**
dwarf .. **RUNT, STUNT, TROLL**

dwarf cattle, S. Am.
NATA, NIATA
dwell ...... **BIDE, LIVE, ABIDE**
dwelling .... **ABODE**
dwindle .... **PETER**
Dyak knife .... **PARANG**
Dyak, sea .... **IBAN**
dye base .... **ANILINE**
dye, blue .... **WOAD**
dye, blue-red .... **ORSELLE**
dye gum .... **KINO**
dye, indigo .... **ANIL**
dye, lichen
ARCHIL, ORCHAL, ORCHIL
dye plant .... **ANIL**
dye, red **AAL, ANATO, AURIN,
EOSIN, ANATTA, ANATTO,
AURINE, EOSINE, ANNAT-
TA, ANNATTO, ANNOTTO,
ARNATTO**
dye, red, poisonous
AURIN, AURINE
dye stuff .. **EOSINE, MADDER**
dye, yellow .... **WELD,
WOLD, WOALD**
dyeing apparatus ...... **AGER**
dyeing reagent .... **ALTERANT**
dyestuff from lichens .. **LITMUS**
dyewood tree .... **TUI**
dynamite inventor .... **NOBEL**
DYNASTY see CHIN. DYNASTY
dynasty, first Chin. ...... **HSIA**
dynasty, It. .... **SAVOY**

E

eager .. **AGOG, AVID, ARDENT**
eagle .... **ERN, ERNE**
eagle, Bible .... **GIER**
eagle, tried to mount to heaven
on .... **ETANA**
eagle, sea .... **ERN, ERNE**
eagle's nest
AERY, EYRY, AERIE, EYRIE
eaglestone ... **ETITE, AETITES**
ear .... **LUG, HANDLE**
ear canal .... **SCALA**
ear cavity .... **UTRICLE**
ear doctor .... **AURIST**
ear inflamation .... **OTITIS**
ear of wheat: archeol.
SPICA, SPICAE
ear, pert. to .... **OTIC, AURAL**
ear, prominence **TRAGI, TRAGUS**
ear shell .. **ORMER, ABALONE**
ear stone .. **OTOLITE, OTOLITH**
earache ... **OTALGY, OTALGIA**
eared seal .... **OTARY**

early Britisher .... **PICT**
early Christian priest ... **ARIUS**
earnest
ARDENT, INTENT, SINCERE
earnest money: law .... **ARRA,
ARLES, ARRHA**
earth .... **GEO**
earth deposit in rocks .. **GUHR**
earth: dial. .... **ERD**
earth god, Egypt. **GEB, KEB, SEB**
earth goddess ..... **GE, ERDA,
GAEA, GAIA**
earth goddess, Khonds' .. **TARI**
earth goddess, Rom.
CERES, TERRA
earth, kind of .... **LOAM**
earth, pert. to .... **GEAL**
earth's surface, made on
EPIGENE
earthenware maker ... **POTTER**
earthly .... **TERRENE**
earthquake .. **SEISM, TEMBLOR**

a earthquake, pert. to .. SEISMIC
earthquake, shock of .TREMOR
earthwork, Rom. ...... AGGER
East .. ASIA, LEVANT, ORIENT
E. African native ... SOMALI
E. Afr. spiritual power .. NGAI
E. Indian animal .... TARSIER
E. Ind. dye tree ...... DHAK
E. Ind. fruit DURIAN, DURION
E. Ind. grass .... KASA
E. Ind. herb .... PIA, SESAME
E. Ind. herb root CHAY, CHOY
E. Ind. palm .... NIPA
E. Ind. plant .. JUTE, SESAME
E. Ind. shrubby herb .... SOLA
E. Ind. tanning tree .. AMLA,
                         AMLI
E. Ind. term of address SAHIB
E. Ind. timber tree..ACH, SAJ,
        SAL, SAIN, SAUL, TEAK
E. Ind. tree, large ..... SIRIS
E. Ind. vine ..... AMIL, GILO,
          ODAL, ODEL, SOMA
E. Ind. vine, milky ..... SOMA
E. Ind. weight .... TOLA
E. Ind. wood, strong, heavy ENG
E. Ind. woody vine ODAL, GILO
East Indies .... INDONESIA
east wind .... EURUS
east wind's opposite .... AFER
Easter ...... PASCH, PASCHA

b Eastern .... ORTIVE
Eastern Catholic ...... UNIAT
Eastern Church doxology DOXA
Eastern European ...... SLAV
Eastern garment .... SARI
Eastern name ..... ALI, ABOU
Eastern title ...... AGA, RAS
Eastern Turkey tribesman KURD
easy .... SOFT
easy gait .... LOPE
easy job SNAP,CINCH,SINECURE
eat away .... ERODE
eat voraciously
        RAVEN, RAVIN, RAVINE
eaten away .... EROSE
eating away CAUSTIC, ERODENT
eccentric person .... GINK
eccentric piece, rotating .. CAM
ecclesiastic .... PRELATE
ECCLESIASTICAL see CHURCH
eclipse .... DIM
eclipse demon, Hindu
              KETU, RAHU
ecru .... BEIGE
Ecuadorian extinct Indians CARA
edentate genus .... MANIS
edge .... HEM, LIP, RIM,
        ARRIS, BRINK, MARGE
edged unevenly .... EROSE
edging .... PICOT

c edging, make .... TAT
edible fungus .... CEPE
edible root ...... OCA, YAM,
      TARO, CASAVA, CASSAVA
edible shoot, Jap. .... UDO
edict .... LAW, FIAT, DECREE
Edinburgh: poet ...... EDINA
edit .... REVISE, REDACT
editorial "I" .... WE
Edom district .... TEMAN
Edomite .... OMAR
Edomite city .... PAU
Edomite duke UZ, ARAN, IRAM
Edomite king, ruler ..... BELA
educated .... BRED, LETTERED
educator, Am. .... MANN
educe .... EVOKE, ELICIT
Edward Bradley's pseudo. BEDE
eel, marine .... CONGER
eel: old Eng. .... ELE
eel-shaped amphibian ... OLM
eel, S. Am. .... CARAPO
eel, young .... ELVER
eelworm .... NEMA
Eghbal's land .... IRAN
effervescent, to make . AERATE
effigy .... IDOL
effluvium ... MIASM, MIASMA
effort .... DINT, ASSAY,
              NISUS, TRIAL

d effusive .... GUSHING
eft .... EVET, NEWT
egg .... OVUM
egg dish .. OMELET, OMELETTE
egg drink ...... NOG, NOGG
egg, insect .... NIT
egg-shaped
   OOID, OVAL, OVATE, OVOID
egg-shaped ornaments ... OVA
egg white, raw .... GLAIR
eggs .... OVA, ROE
ego .... SELF
Egypt, pert. to ...... COPTIC
Egyptian bird .... IBIS
Egyp. Christian .... COPT
Egyp. city, ancient SAIS, THEBES
Egyp. cobra .... HAJE
Egyp. crown .... ATEF
Egyp. dog-headed ape, deity
                      AANI
Egyp. gateway .... PYLON
Egyp. god of creation ... PTAH
EGYPTIAN GODS — GODDESSES
      —DEITY see also GODS and
      SPECIAL SECTION
Egyp. guard .... GHAFIR
Egyp. heaven
   AALU, AARU, IALU, YARU
Egyp. immortal heart AB, HATI
Egyp. king .. MENES, RAMESES
Egyp. lute .... NABLA

a Egyp. nationalist party . WAFD
Egyp. precious alloy .... ASEM
Egyp. primeval chaos ..... NU
Egyp. queen of gods .... SATI
Egyp. sacred bird .. BENU, IBIS
Egyp. sacred bull .... APIS
Egyp. season .... AHET
Egyp. tambourine ...... RIKK
Egyp. thorn .... KIKAR
Egyp. writing surfaces PAPYRI
eh?: obs. ....ANAN
eight days after feast .. UTAS
eight, group of
OCTAD, OCTET, OCTAVE
eight, set of .... OGDOAD
eighth day of feast .... UTAS
eighth day, on ...... OCTAN
eighth note .... UNCA
Eire legislature .... DAIL
ejaculation, mystic ...... OM
eject ...... EMIT, OUST, SPEW
elaborate .... ORNATE
Elam, capital of .... SUSA
eland .... IMPOFO
elanet .... KITE
elasmobranch fish RAY, SHARK
Elbe, river to ...... EGER, ISER
Elbe tributary .... EGER, ISER
elbow .... ANCON
elder .... SENIOR
b elder son of Zeus ...... ARES
elder statesmen, Jap. ... GENRO
eldest: law ...... AINE, EIGNE
electric catfish .... RAAD
electric force .... ELOD
electric force unit ...... VOLT
electric reluctance unit .. REL
electric unit .. ES, AMP, MHO,
OHM, REL, PERM, FARAD,
HENRY, AMPERE
electrified particle ...... ION
electrode .. ANODE, CATHODE
electromagnet .... RELAY
electron tube
TRIODE, KLYSTRON
elegance .... GRACE
elegant .... FINE, POSH
elegist .... POET
elegy .... NENIA
ELEMENT, non-metallic and metallic, gaseous on page 195
elemi .... ANIME
element, radioactive of URANIC
elephant goad .... ANKUS
elephant: India .... HATHI
elephant's cry .... BARR
elephant's ear .... TARO
elevated ground MESA, RIDEAU
elevation of mind .. ANAGOGE
elevator: Brit. .... LIFT

c elf .... SPRITE
elf, Egypt. .... OUPHE
elfin .... FEY
Elia .... LAMB
elicit .... EDUCE
elide .... DELE, OMIT
Elija .... ELIAS
eliminate ... DELETE, REMOVE
Elizabeth I, name for ORIANA
elk, Am. .... WAPITI
elk, Europ. .... MOOSE
elk, Europ. genus ...... ALCES
elliptical ...... OVAL, OVOID
elm .... ULM, ULME
elm fruit seed ...... SAMARA
elongated .... PROLATE
else .... OTHER
elude .... DODGE, EVADE
elver .... EEL
emaciation .... TABES, MACIES
emanation .... AURA
emanation, star .... BLAS
embankment ... DAM, BUND,
DIKE, DYKE, DIGUE, LEVEE
embellish
GILD, ADORN, DECORATE
embellished .... ORNATE
ember .... ASH, COAL
emblem ... INSIGNE, INSIGNIA
d emblem of authority .... MACE
emblem of U.S. .... EAGLE
embrace
HUG, CLASP, ENARM, INARM
embrocation .... LINIMENT
embroidery frame
TABORET, TABOURET
emend .... EDIT
emerald .... BERYL, SMARAGD
emerge RISE, ISSUE, EMANATE
emetic .... IPECAC
eminent .... NOTED
emit .... REEK, EXUDE
emmer .... SPELT
emmet .... ANT
Emperor of Russia
CZAR, TSAR, TZAR
emphasis .... ACCENT, STRESS
empire .... REALM
employ .... USE, HIRE, PLACE
employed for wine, meas. AAM
employees .... PERSONNEL
employer .... BOSS, USER
employment .... PLACE
emporium ...... MART, STORE
Empress, Byzant. ...... IRENE
Empress, Russian ... CZARINA,
TSARINA, TZARINA
empty .... VOID, INANE,
DEPLETE
emulate .... RIVAL
enamel ware .... LIMOGES

a enchantress .... **CIRCE, MEDEA**
encircle .... **ORB, GIRD, GIRT, RING, EMBAY**
encircled
   GIRT, RINGED, SURROUNDED
encircling band .... **ZONE**
enclose .... **MEW**
enclosure .... **MEW, PEN, REE, STY, CORRAL**
enclosure, cattle ..... **ATAJO**
enclosure: Sp. Am. .... **CANCHA**
encomium .... **ELOGE**
encompass .. **GIRD, GIRT, RING**
encompassed by .... **AMID**
encore .... **BIS**
encounter .... **MEET**
encourage .... **ABET**
end **TIP, FINIS, LIMIT, OMEGA**
end: music .... **FINE**
end result .... **PRODUCT**
end, tending to an ..... **TELIC**
endeavor .. **TRY, ESSAY, NISUS**
ENDING ... see also SUFFIX or
   type of ending
ending, comparative . **IER, IOR**
ENDING, NOUN see SUFFIX,
   NOUN ENDING
ending, plural .... **EN, ES**
ending, superlative ...... **EST**
endow ...... **DOWER, INVEST**
b endue .... **ENDOW**
endure .... **BEAR, LAST, WEAR**
endure: dial. .... **BIDE**
energy .... **PEP, VIM, ZIP, POWER, VIGOR, VIGOUR**
energy, potential ...... **ERGAL**
energy unit **ERG, RAD, ERGON**
enfeeble **WEAKEN, DEBILITATE**
engage **HIRE, ENTER, CHARTER**
engender .... **BEGET, BREED, PROMOTE, GENERATE**
engine, donkey .... **YARDER**
engine of war .... **RAM**
engine part .... **STATOR**
engine, rotary .... **TURBINE**
engineer, Am. .... **EADS**
engineer, military .... **SAPPER**
English actor .... **EVANS**
Eng. actress .... (Nell) **GWYN, TERRY, NEAGLE**
Eng. architect .... **WREN**
Eng. author .... **MORE, WEST, ARLEN, BACON, CAINE, DEFOE, DORAN, ELIOT, HARDY, READE, SHUTE, WAUGH, WELLS, AMBLER, AUSTEN, BARRIE, BELLOC, BRONTE, ORWELL, STERNE**
Eng. car .... **ROVER**
Eng. cathedral city **ELY, YORK**
Eng. city, historic **COVENTRY**

c Eng. college ... **ETON, BALIOL**
ENG. COMPOSER
   see COMPOSER, ENG.
Eng. country festival .... **ALE**
Eng. dramatist
   SHAW, PEELE, DRYDEN
Eng. emblem .... **ROSE**
Eng. essayist .... **SALA, STEELE**
Eng. explorer ... **ROSS, CABOT**
Eng. historian .... **BEDE**
Eng. king
   BRAN, CNUT, KNUT, CANUTE
Eng. monk ..... **BEDE, BAEDA**
Eng. murderer .... **ARAM**
Eng. musician .... **ARNE**
ENG. NOVELIST .... see ENG.
   AUTHOR
Eng. painter .... **OPIE, ORPEN**
Eng. philosopher ...... **HUME, JOAD, BACON, SPENCER**
Eng. playwright .... **SHAW**
Eng. poet ..... **GRAY, AUDEN, BLAKE, BYRON, CAREW, DONNE, ELIOT**
Eng. queen ..... **ANNE, MARY**
Eng. rebel leader, 1450 .. **CADE**
Eng. royal house **YORK, TUDOR**
Eng. scholar, schoolmaster
   ARAM
Eng. school, boys' ...... **ETON**
Eng. sculptor .... **EPSTEIN**
d Eng. spa .... **BATH, MARGATE**
Eng. spy .... **ANDRE**
Eng. statesman ... **EDEN, PITT**
Eng. theologian ...... **ALCUIN**
Eng. woman politician .. **ASTOR**
ENG. WRITER ..... see ENG.
   AUTHOR and ENG. ESSAYIST
engraver ... **CHASER, ETCHER, GRAVER**
engraver, famous .. **PYE, DORE**
engraver's tool .... **BURIN**
engrossed .... **RAPT**
enigma .... **RIDDLE**
enlarge
   DILATE, EXPAND, INCREASE
enlarge a hole .... **REAM**
enlarging, as chimneys .. **EVASE**
enmity .... **ANIMUS**
Enoch's father .... **CAIN**
enough .... **ENOW**
enrol .... **ENTER, ENLIST**
ensign .... **FLAG**
ensnare .... **NET, WEB**
entangle .... **MAT, MESH**
enter .... **ENROL**
entertain
   AMUSE, DIVERT, REGALE
enthusiasm
   ELAN, ARDOR, VERVE, SPIRIT
enthusiastic .... **RABID**

a entice .... BAIT, LURE,
    TOLE, TEMPT, ALLURE
enticement .... TICE
entire man .... EGO
entity .... ENS, ENTIA
entomb .... INURN
entrance
    ADIT, DOOR, GATE, PORTAL
entrance halls .... ATRIA
entreat .... PRAY, PLEAD
entreaty .... PLEA
entry, separate .... ITEM
entwine
    WEAVE, ENLACE, WREATHE
enumerate .... COUNT
envelop WRAP, ENFOLD, INFOLD
environment .... MILIEU
envoy .... LEGATE
envy .... COVET
enzyme .... ASE, LOTASE,
    RENNIN, MALTASE
eon .... OLAM
ephah, 1/10 .... OMER
epic poetry .... EPOS, EPOPEE
epoch .... ERA
epochal .... ERAL
epode .... POEM
eponymous ancestor .... EBER
equal IS, ARE, TIE, EVEN, PEER
equality .... PAR, PARITY

b equally .... AS
equilibrium .... POISE
equine .... HORSE
equip .... FIT, RIG
equitable ... JUST, IMPARTIAL
equivalence .... PAR
equivocate .... EVADE
era .... EPOCH
eradicate .... ERASE, UPROOT
eral .... EPOCHAL
erase .... DELE, DELETE
erect .... REAR, RAISE
ergo .... HENCE
Eris' brother .... ARES
ermine, summer .... STOAT
Eros .... CUPID
errand boy .... PAGE
error, publication ...... TYPO,
    ERRATA, ERRATE, ERRATUM
Esau .... EDOM
Esau's brother .... JACOB
Esau's father-in-law ... ELON
Esau's grandson .... OMAR
Esau's home .... SEIR
Esau's wife .... ADAH
escape .. LAM, ELUDE, EVADE
eschew .... SHUN
escutcheon band .... FESS
Esdra's angel .... URIEL
eskers .... OSAR
Eskimo .... ITA

c Eskimo boat
    KIAK, KYAK, KAYAK
Eskimo boot .... MUKLUK
Eskimo coat
    PARKA, NETCHA, TEMIAK
Eskimo curlew .... FUTE
Eskimo house
    IGLU, IGLOE, IGLOO, IGLOU
Eskimo settlement ..... ETAH
Eskimo summer hut .... TOPEK
Eskimos of Asia YUIT, INNUIT
esoteric .... INNER
espy .... SEE, SPY
esquire .... ARMIGER
essay ... TRY, TEST, ATTEMPT
essay, scholarly
    THESIS, TREATISE
essence: Hindu religion .. RASA
essence, rose .... ATTAR
essential oils fluid ..... NEROL
essential part .... CORE, PITH
"— est" (that is) .... ID
establish .... BASE, FOUND
established value .... PAR
estate, landed, large .. MANOR
estate manager .... STEWARD
estate, not held by feudal ten-
    ure ALOD, ALLOD, ALODIUM
esteem .... HONOR,
    PRIZE, ADMIRE, HONOUR

d ester, hydriodic acid ... IODIDE
ester, liquid .... ACETIN
ester, oleic acid ..... OLEATE
estimate .... RATE, APPRAISE
Estonian .... ESTH
estuary .... RIA
estuary, Brazil .... PARA
estuary, S. Am. .... PLATA
Eternal City .... ROME
eternity ..... AGE, EON, OLAM
ether compound .... ESTER
ethereal .... AERY, AERIAL
ETHIOPIA see also ABYSSINIA
Ethiopia .... CUSH
Ethiopian title .... RAS
Ethiopic .... GEEZ
ethos, opposed to .... PATHOS
Etruscan god .... LAR
Etruscan Juno .... UNI
Etruscan Minerva .... MENFRA
Etruscan title, peer LAR, LARS
eucalyptus secretion
    LAAP, LARP, LERP
eucalyptus tree .... YATE
Eucharist case ...... PIX, PYX
Eucharist cloth
    FANO, FANON, FANUM
Eucharist spoon .... LABIS
Eucharist wafer .... HOST
eulogy .... ELOGE
euphorbia .... SPURGE

a Eurasian dock plant .. **PARELLE**
eureka red .... **PUCE**
Euripides heroine ..... **MEDEA**
EUROPEAN see also specific
word, as FISH, ANIMAL,
etc.
European .... **POLE, SLAV**
Eur. colorful fish ..... **BOCE**
EUROP. FISH .. see FISH, EUR.
European, in Moslem East
FRANGI
Europ. iris .... **ORRIS**
Europ. kite ..... **GLED, GLEDE**
Europ. porgy .... **PARGO**
Eurytus' daughter ...... **IOLE**
evade
SHUN, DODGE, ELUDE, SHIRK
evaluate .... **RATE, ASSESS**
Evangelist ...... **LUKE, MARK**
Evans, Mary Ann .... **ELIOT**
Eve's grandson .... **ENOS**
even ..... **EEN, LEVEL, PLANE**
even if .... **THO**
evening party .... **SOIREE**
evening prayer .... **VESPER**
eventual lot .... **FATE**
ever .... **EER**
evergreen .... **FIR, YEW, PINE,**
CAROB, CEDAR, OLIVE,
SAVIN, LAUREL, SABINE,
b **SAVINE, SPRUCE**
evergreen, bean ...... **CAROB**
evergreen genus
OLAX, ABIES, CATHA
evergreen, red-berry
YEW, WHORT
evergreen, tropical .. **CALABA**
everlasting ... **ETERN, ETERNE**
evict .... **OUST**
evident **CLEAR, PLAIN, PATENT**
evil .... **MAL**
evil god, Egypt. ... **SET, SETH**
evil intent: law .... **DOLUS**
evil spirit, Haiti **BAKA, BOKO**
evil spirit, Hindu ..... **ASURA**
evolve .... **EDUCE**
ewe, old .... **CRONE**
exact **BLEED, DEMAND, EXTORT**
exacerbate .... **IRE**
exact point .... **TEE**
examine ..... **PRY, SPY, SCAN**
excavate .. **DIG, PION, DREDGE**
excavation for extracting ore
STOPE
excavation, mine .. **PIT, STOPE**
exceed .... **TOP**
exceedingly: music .....**TRES**
excellence .... **VIRTU**
excellent .... **AONE**
except .... **BUT, SAVE**
excess ...... **LUXUS, NIMIETY**

c excess, fill to ... **GLUT, SATE**
excess of solar year ... **EPACT**
exchange medium, Chin. **SYCEE**
exchange premium, discount
AGIO
exchequer .... **FISC, FISK**
excite .... **ELATE, ROUSE**
excited .... **AGOG, MANIC**
excitement, public
FUROR, FURORE
exclamation .. **AH, EH, HA, HI,**
MY, OH, OW, UM, ACH,
AHA, AUH, BAH, BAW, FIE,
FOH, GRR, HAH, HAW,
HAY, HEM, HEP, HEU, HEY,
HIC, HIP, HOI, HOY, HUH,
OHO, OUF, PAH, PEW, POH,
PUE, SOH, TCH, TCK, TUT,
UGH, WEE, WHY, WOW,
YAH, YOI, YOW, ALAS,
PHEW, ALACK
exclamation, Fr. .... **HEIN**
exclamation, Ger. ..... **HOCH**
exclamation, Ir. ...... **ADAD,**
AHEY, ARAH, ARRA, ARRO,
BOOH, EHEU, OCHONE
exclude ... **BAR, OMIT, DEBAR**
exclusive .... **SOLE**
exclusive set .... **ELECT, ELITE**
exclusively .... **ONLY**
d excoriate .... **ABRADE**
excrete from skin ...... **EGEST**
excuse .. **PLEA, ALIBI, REMIT**
excuse, court **ESSOIN, ESSOINE**
execrated ..... **CURST, SWORE**
exemplar ... **MODEL, PATTERN**
exhaust
SAP, TIRE, SPEND, DEPLETE
exhausted .... **EFFETE**
exhibits leaping ..... **SALTATE**
exigency .... **NEED**
exist .... **LIVE**
exist .. all forms of verb "BE"
exist, beginning to .. **NASCENT**
existence .... **ENS, ESSE**
existentialist leader ... **SARTRE**
existing **ALIVE, BEING, EXTANT**
exit .. **LEAVE, DEPART, EGRESS**
expand ..... **DILATE, DISTEND**
expanse .... **SEA**
expatriate .... **EXILE**
expectation .... **HOPE**
expedite .... **HURRY, HASTEN**
expedition .. **SAFARI, SUFFARI**
expert ... **ACE, ONER, ADEPT**
expiate .... **ATONE**
explain .... **DEFINE**
explode
POP, DETONATE, FULMINATE
exploit
DEED, FEAT, GEST, GESTE

explosive
CAP, TNT, GAINE, TONITE
explosive sound ... POP, CHUG
expose .... AIR, DISPLAY
expression, elegant . ATTICISM
expression, local .... IDIOM
expressionless ..... WOODEN
expunge DELE, ERASE, DELETE
extend
JUT, LIE, REACH, BEETLE
extend the front ..... DEPLOY
extensive .... AMPLE
extent .... AREA
external .... EXOTERIC
external covering.HIDE, HUSK,
PEEL, PELT, RIND, SKIN
extinct wild ox .... URUS
extirpate .. ROOT, ERADICATE
extort .... BLEED, EXACT
extra .... ODD, SPARE
extra leaf .... INSERT
extra, theatrical .... SUPE
extract DRAW, ELICIT, EVULSE
extraneous .... EXOTIC
extraordinary person, thing
ONER

extravagance .... ELA
extreme .... ULTRA
extreme unction, give
ANELE, ENELE
exudate, plant
GUM, LAC, RESIN
exude ..... EMIT, OOZE, REEK
exult .... ELATE
eye .... ORB, SEE, OGLE
eye cosmetic ... KOHL, KUHL
eye inflammation STY, IRITIS
eye, inner coat ...... RETINA
eye, layer .... UVEA
eye of bean .... HILA, HILUM
eye of insect .... STEMMA
eye, part of the .... IRIS,
UVEA, CORNEA, RETINA
eye, pert. to .... OPTIC
eye socket .... ORBIT
eye, symbolic .... UTA
eye-worm, Afr. .... LOA
eyelash .... CILIA, CILIUM
eyes: old Eng. .... NIE
eyestalk .... STIPE
eyewink ...... LOOK, GLANCE
eyot .... ISLE, ISLET

F

Fabian .... SHAW
fable .... APOLOG, APOLOGUE
fable writer .... ESOP, AESOP
fabled bird .... ROC, RUKH
"Fables in Slang" author ADE
fabric .... REP, ACCA, BAFT,
DRAB, DUCK, IKAT,
LAWN, LENO, MOFF, REPP,
SILK, SUSI, TAPA, TUKE,
CRAPE, CREPE, MOIRE,
NINON, ORLON, RAYON,
CANVAS, COVERT, MAN-
TUA, MOHAIR
farbic, Angora ..... CAMLET,
MOHAIR
fabric, coarse cotton .. SURAT
fabric, coarse wool
TAMIN, TAMINE
fabric, corded REP, REPP, PIQUE
fabric, cotton ... LENO, MULL,
DENIM, MANTA, SCRIM,
CALICO, CRETON, NAN-
KIN, PENANG, NANKEEN,
CRETONNE
fabric, curtain ... NET, SCRIM
fabric, felt-like .... BAIZE
fabric, fig'd DAMASK, PAISLEY
fabric from remnants MUNGO
fabric, Ind. .. SHELA, SHELAH

fabric, knitted .... TRICOT
fabric, light wool ... ALPACA
fabric, lustrous POPLIN, SATEEN
fabric, mourning ALMA, CRAPE
fabric, net .. TULLE, MALINE
fabric, plaid . MAUD, TARTAN
fabric, printed BATIK, BATTIK
FABRIC, RIBBED
see RIBBED FABRIC
fabric, satin .. PEKIN, ETOILE
fabric, satiny
SATINET, SATINETTE
fabric, sheer .... GAUZE,
BEMBERG, ORGANZA
fabric, short nap .... RAS
fabric, silk .... SURAH,
PONGEE, SAMITE, TOBINE
fabric, silk, gold, medieval ACCA
fabric, silk, thick ...... GROS
fabric, stiff .... WIGAN
fabric stretcher
TENTER, STENTER
fabric, striped .. SUSI, DOREA,
DORIA, DOOREA, MADRAS
fabric, thick .... DRAB
fabric, twilled .... REP
fabric, upholstery .. BROCATEL,
BROCATALL, BROCATELL
BROCATELLE

a
fabric, velvet-like .... **PANNE**
fabric, voile-like ...... **ETAMINE**
fabric, wool .. **SERGE, TAMIN, TAMIS, MERINO, TAMINE, TAMINY, TAMISE, TAMMIN, ESTAMIN, ETAMINE, STAMMEL, ESTAMINE**
fabric, worsted ...... **ETAMINE**
fabricate .... **MAKE**
fabulist .... **ESOP, AESOP**
fabulous bird ..... **ROC, RUKH**
face **MAP, MUG, PHIZ, FACADE**
face with stone ...... **REVET**
facet of gem .. **BEZEL, BEZIL, CULET, COLLET**
facile .... **EASY**
facing glacier .... **STOSS**
fact .... **DATUM**
fact, by the: law ..... **FACTO**
facts .... **DATA**
faction .. **SECT, SIDE, CABAL**
factor .... **GENE**
factory .... **PLANT**
faculty .... **SENSE**
fade ...... **DIE, DIM, WITHER**
"Faerie Queene" iron man **TALUS**
"Faerie Queene" lady .... **UNA**
failure .... **DUD, FLOP**
fainting: med. ...... **SYNCOPE**

b
fair . **BAZAR, FERIA, BAZAAR KERMIS, KIRMES**
fair **JUST, CLEAR, IMPARTIAL**
fair-haired .. **BLOND, BLONDE**
fair-lead, naut. .... **WAPP**
fairy .. **ELF, FAY, PERI, SPRITE**
fairy fort .... **LIS, LISS**
fairy king .... **OBERON**
fairy queen ... **MAB, TITANIA**
fairy, Serbo-Croat **VILA, VILY**
fairylike creature ...... **PERI**
faith, article of ...... **TENET**
faith, pert. to .... **PISTIC**
faithful .... **LEAL, TRUE, STANCH, STAUNCH**
falcon ...... **SACER, SAKER, LANNER, MERLIN, SAKERET**
falcon, Asia **LAGGAR, LUGGAR**
falcon genus .... **FALCO**
falcon-headed god **MENT, MENTU**
falcon, Ind. **SHAHIN, SHAHEEN**
falcon of sea ...... **ERN, ERNE**
falconer's bait .... **LURE**
fall **DROP, PLAP, PLOP, SPILL**
fall back .... **RETREAT**
fallacy ...... **IDOLA, IDOLUM**
fallow-deer, female ...... **TEG**
false excuse .... **SUBTERFUGE**
false friend .. **IAGO, TRAITOR**
false fruit of rose .... **HIP**

c
false god .... **IDOL**
Falstaff's follower ...... **NYM**
fame .... **ECLAT, KUDOS, RENOWN, REPUTE**
famed .... **NOTED**
familiar .... **VERSANT**
familiar saying .... **SAW, TAG**
family, Florentine .... **MEDICI**
family, Genoese ...... **DORIA**
family: Scot. .... **ILK**
famous .... **NOTED**
fan .... **ROOTER**
fan palm genus ...... **INODES**
fan's stick .... **BRIN**
fanatical .... **RABID**
fancy ... **IDEA, WHIM, IDEATE**
fanfare .... **TANTARA, TANTARO, TANTARARA**
fanning device **PUNKA, PUNKAH**
fare .... **DIET**
farewell ... **AVE, VALE, ADIEU**
farinaceous .... **MEALY**
farinaceous food **SAGO, SALEP**
farm group .... **GRANGE**
farm, small, Sp. Am. **CHACRA**
farm, Sw. small leased .. **TORP**
farm: Swedish .... **TORP**
farm, tenant .... **CROFT**
farmer ..... **KULAK, GRANGER**

d
farmyard, S. Afr. ...... **WERF**
Faroe Is. wind .... **OE**
Faroe judge .... **FOUD**
Farouk's father .... **FUAD**
fashion .... **FORM, MODE, MOLD, MODEL, STYLE**
fasten ... **BOLT, LOCK, NAIL, SEAL, SNIB, TACK, RIVET**
fasten: naut **BELAY, BATTEN**
fastener .... **NUT, PIN, BRAD, CLIP, HASP, NAIL, SNAP, STUD, CLASP, RIVET, CLEVIS, COTTER**
fastener, wire .... **STAPLE**
fastener, naut. .... **BITT**
fastener, wood **FID, NOG, PEG, PIN**
fastening .... **LATCH**
fastidious .... **NICE**
fasting month .... **RAMADAN**
fasting period .... **LENT**
fat **LARD, LIPA, SUET, OBESE**
fat, animal .. **ADEPS, TALLOW**
fat: comb. form **STEAT, STEATO**
fat, liquid part ...... **ELAIN, OLEIN, ELAINE, OLEINE**
fat, natural .... **ESTER**
fat, of .... **SEBAIC**
fat, solid part **STEARIN, STEARINE**
fatal ...... **FUNEST, LETHAL**

a fate .... **LOT, DOOM, KISMET**
Fates, Gr. & Rom. .... **MOIRA,
MORTA, PARCA, CLOTHO,
DECUMA, MOIRAI, PAR-
CAE, ATROPOS, LACHESIS**
fateful .... **DIRE**
father .... **SIRE, BEGET**
father: Arab. .... **ABU, ABOU**
father: Hebr. .... **ABBA**
father of modern engraving **PYE**
father's side, kinship on
AGNAT, AGNATE
fathom .... **PROBE, SOUND**
fatigue .. **FAG, TIRE, WEARY**
Fatima's huband .... **ALI**
fatty .... **ADIPOSE**
fatty gland secretion **SEBUM**
fatuous .... **INANE**
faucet ... **TAP, COCK, SPIGOT**
fault find ...... **CARP, CAVIL**
faultfinder .. **MOMUS, CAVILER**
faulty .... **BAD**
faux pas ...... **ERROR, GAFFE**
favor .... **BOON**
favorable vote .. **AY, AYE, YES**
favorite .... **PET, IDOL**
fawn color .... **FAON**
fawning favorite .... **MINION**
fear .... **PHOBIA**
fearful .... **TREPID**

b feast .... **REGALE**
feast day: comb. form .... **MAS**
feather **PENNA, PINNA, PLUME**
feather grass .... **STIPA**
feather palms .... **EJOO, IROK**
feather: zool. .... **PLUMA**
feathers, cast .... **MEW**
feathers of o-o .... **HULU**
feathered scarf .... **BOA**
feeble .. **PUNY, WEAK, DEBILE**
feel .... **SENSE**
feel one's way .... **GROPE**
feeler **PALP, PALPI, ANTENNA**
feet, having .... **PEDATE**
feet, pert. to **PEDAL, PEDARY**
feign .... **ACT, SHAM**
feline .... **CAT, PUMA**
felis leo .... **LION**
fellow ..... **GUY, LAD, BOZO,
CHAP, DICK, CHAPPY,
CHAPPIE**
felt ...... **GROPED, SENSATE**
female animal, parent
DAM, DOE
female camel .... **NAGA**
female disciple at Joppa
DORCAS
female insect .... **GYNE**
fence of shrubs .... **HEDGE**
fence of stakes .... **PALISADE**
fence step .... **STILE**

c fence, sunken, hidden
AHA, HAHA
fence to restrain cattle .. **OXER**
fencer's cry .. **HAI, HAY, SASA**
fencing dummy .... **PEL**
fencing position **CARTE, SIXTE,
QUARTE, QUINTE, TIERCE,
SECONDE, SEPTIME**
fencing sword ...... **EPEE, FOIL**
fencing term .... **TOUCHE**
fencing thrust ...... **LUNGE,
PUNTO, REMISE, RIPOST,
RIPOSTE, REPRISE**
fend .... **WARD**
fennel: P. I. .... **ANIS**
"Ferdinand the Bull" author
LEAF
feria, pert. to .... **FERIAL**
ferment .... **YEAST**
ferment: med. .... **ZYME**
fermented milk dessert **LACTO**
fern, climbing, P. I. .... **NITO**
fern, Polyn., edible .... **TARA**
fern root, N. Z. .... **ROI**
fern "seed" .... **SPORE**
fern species .... **WEKI**
fern spore ...... **SORI, SORUS**
Ferrara ducal family .... **ESTE**
ferrum .... **IRON**
ferryboat .... **BAC**

d ferryboat, Afr. .... **PONT**
fertilizer ..... **MARL, GUANO**
fervent .... **ARDENT**
fervor ... **ZEAL, ZEST, ARDOR**
fester .... **RANKLE**
festival .... **ALE, FAIR, FETE,
GALA, FERIA, FIESTA, KER-
MIS, KIRMES**
festival, Creek Indian .. **BUSK**
festival, Gr.
AGON, DELIA, HALOA
fetid .... **OLID, RANK**
fetish ...... **OBI, JUJU, OBIA,
ZEME, ZEMI, CHARM,
OBEAH, GRIGRI**
fetish, P. I. .... **ANITO**
fetter .... **GYVE, IRON**
feud, opposed to ...... **ALOD,
ALLOD, ALODIUM, ALLODIUM**
feudal benefice .... **FEU**
feudal estate **FEOD, FEUD, FIEF**
feudal land .... **BENEFICE**
feudal service, form of **AVERA**
feudal tax
TAILAGE, TALLAGE, TAILLAGE
feudal tenant .... **VASSAL**
fever, intermittent
AGUE, TERTIAN
feverish .... **FEBRILE**
fez .... **TARBUSH,
TARBOOSH, TARBOUCHE**

a fiber .... JUTE, PITA,
RAFFIA, STAPLE, THREAD
fiber, bark
TAPA, OLONA, TERAP
fiber, coarse .... ADAD
fiber, cordage .... DA, COIR,
FERU, HEMP, IMBE, JUTE,
RHEA, ABACA, SISAL
fiber from palm .... ERUC
fiber, hat or basket .... DATIL
fiber knot .... NEP
fiber plant
ISTLE, IXTLE, IXLE, RAMIE
fiber plant, Brazil .... CAROA
fiber plant, E. Ind. SANA, SUNN
fiber, textile .... SABA
fiber, tropical
IXLE, ISTLE, IXTLE
fiber, woody .... BAST, BASTE
fictional submarine character
NEMO
fiddle, medieval .... GIGA
fiddler crab genus ...... UCA
field LEA, ACRE, WONG, CROFT
field deity ...... PAN, FAUN
field, enclosed: law ..... AGER
field, stubble .... ROWEN
fifth segment crustacean
CARPOS
b fig marigold, Afr. ..... SAMH
figs, Smyrna .. ELEME, ELEMI
fight
CLEM, FRAY, MELEE, AFFRAY
figurative use of word .. TROPE
figure .... SOLID
figure, equal angles
ISAGON, ISOGON
figure, 4-sided .... TETRAGON
figure, geom. .... SECTOR
figure of speech
TROPE, SIMILE, METAPHOR
figure, oval .... ELLIPSE
figure, 10-sided .... DECAGON
figwort .... MULLEIN
Fiji chestnut .... RATA
Fiji tree .... BURI
filament .... FIBER, HAIR
filament, flax ... HARL, HARLE
filament, plant
ELATER, THREAD
filch .... STEAL
file .... ROW
file, coarse .... RASP
file, three-square single-cut
CARLET
filled to capacity
SATED, REPLETE
fillet, architectural ORLE, ORLO
fillet, narrow heraldic
ORLE, ORLO, LISTEL
fillet, shaft's ..... ORLE, ORLO

c fillip .... SNAP
film, old green ..... PATINA
filthy .... VILE
filthy lucre .... PELF
finale: music .... CODA
finally: Fr. .... ENFIN
finback whale .... GRASO
finch .. MORO, LINNET, SISKIN
finch, Europ.
TARIN, TERIN, SERIN
finch, S. Afr. .... FINK
find fault ...... CARP, CAVIL
fine, as a line .... LEGER
fine, punish by ...... AMERCE
fine, record of ...... ESTREAT
finesse .... ART, SKILL
Fingal's kingdom .... MORVEN
finger .... DIGIT
finger cymbals ... CASTANETS
finger, 5th PINKIE, MINIMUS
finger inflammation ... FELON
finger nail half-moon
LUNULA, LUNULE
fingerless glove .... MIT, MITT
fingerprint pattern .... WHORL
finial ornament, slender .. EPI
finisher .... EDGER, ENDER
finishing tool .... REAMER
FINLAND, FINNISH
see also SPECIAL SECTION
d Finland .... SUOMI
Finn in Ingria ..... VOT, VOTE
Finns .... SUOMI
Finnish god .... JUMALA
Finnish poetry .... RUNES
Finnish steam bath ... SAUNA
fire basket .... CRESSET
fire bullet .... TRACER
fire god .... VULCAN
fire god, Hindu .. AGNI, AKAL,
CIVA, DEVA, KAMA, SIVA
fire in heart: Buddhism RAGA
fire opal: Fr. ...... GIRASOL
fire, sacrificial, Hindu .. AGNI
fire worshipper PARSI, PARSEE
firearm . GUN, RIFLE, MAUSER,
PISTOL, CARBINE, REVOLVER
firecracker .... PETARD
fired clay .... TILE
firedog .... ANDIRON
fireplace
GRATE, INGLE, HEARTH
fireplace side shelf .... HOB
firewood bundle BARIN, FAGOT
firewood, Tex. .... LENA
firework .... GERB
firm FAST, STANCH, STAUNCH
firm: Hawaii .... HUI
firmament .... SKY
firn .... NEVE
firs, true .... ABIES

a first **PRIME, INITIAL, ORIGINAL**
first American-born white
   child .... **DARE**
first appearance ...... **DEBUT**
first born: law .... **EIGNE**
first fruits of a benefice
               ANNATES
first miracle site ...... **CANA**
first mortal, Hindu ..... **YAMA**
first part in duet ..... **PRIMO**
first principles .... **ABCS**
first-rate .... **ACE**
firth: Scot. .... **KYLE**
fish .. **ANGLE, TRAWL, TROLL,**
fish ..... **ID, EEL, IDE, CARP,**
   DACE, HAKE, HIKU, JOCU,
   LIJA, LING, MADO, MASU,
   OPAH, ORFE, PEGA, PETO,
   PIKE, POGY, ROUD, RUDD,
   SCAD, SCUP, SESI, SHAD,
   SIER, SKIL, SOLE, SPET,
   TOPE, TUNA, ULUA, PAR-
   GO, POWAN, POWEN,
   ROACH, SKATE, CONGER,
   MULLET, SABALO, TOMCOD
fish, ancient .. **ELOPS, ELLOPS**
fish, Atlant. **TAUTOG, ESCOLAR**
fish, boneless .. **FILET, FILLET**
fish, bony .... **CARP, TELEOST**
fish, butterfly .... **PARU**
b fish by trolling .... **DRAIL**
fish, Calif. surf .... **SPRAT**
fish, carplike
    RUD, DACE, ROUD, RUDD
fish cleaner .... **SCALER**
fish, climbing ...... **ANABAS**
fish, cod-like **CUSK, HAKE, LING**
fish, colorful
   BOCE, OPAH, WRASSE
fish, Congo .... **LULU**
fish, Cuban .... **DIABLO**
fish, cyprinoid
   ID, IDE, ORF, ORFE
fish, edible .... **SPRAT**
fish eggs .... **ROE**
fish, Egypt. .... **SAIDE**
fish, elongated **EEL, GAR, PIKE**
fish, Europ. .. **ID, BOCE, DACE,**
   BREAM, SPRAT, UMBER,
   BARBEL, BRASSE, PLAICE,
   SENNET, WRASSE
fish, flat .. **DAB, RAY, SOLE,**
   BRILL, FLUKE, FLOUNDER
fish, Florida .... **TARPON**
fish, food .. **COD, CERO, HAAK,**
   HAIK, HAKE, LING, SHAD,
   TUNA, TUNNY, SARDINE
fish, food: Ind. .... **HILSA**
fish, fresh water
   IDE, BASS, DACE, ESOX
fish from boat .... **TROLL**

c fish, game .... **BASS,**
   MARLIN, TARPON, TARPUN
fish, gobeylike .... **DRAGONET**
fish, Gr. Lakes .. **CISCO, PERCH**
fish, Hawaiian .... **AKU**
fish, herringlike .... **SHAD**
fish, hook for **GIG, GAFF, DRAIL**
fish, lancet .... **SERRA**
fish line ...... **SNELL, TRAWL**
fish line cork .... **BOB**
fish, linglike .... **COD**
fish, long-nosed .... **GAR**
fish, mackerellike
   CERO, TUNNY, TINKER
fish, many .... **SHOAL**
fish, marine **BONITO, TARPON**
fish measure .... **MEASE**
fish, Medit. .... **NONNAT**
fish, nest-building .... **ACARA**
fish net
   SEINE, TRAWL, SPILLER
fish, N. Z. .... **IHI**
fish, No. Pacif. .... **INCONNU**
fish, parasitic .... **REMORA**
fish, perch-like ...... **DARTER**
fish, Pers. myth .... **MAH**
fish pickle .... **ALEC**
fish, piece of ... **FILET, FILLET**
fish, pikelike .... **GAR**
d fish-pitching prong . **PEW, GAFF**
fish-poison tree .... **BITO**
fish, predatory .... **GAR**
fish, river .... **BLAY**
fish, Russian .... **STERLET**
fish sauce .... **ALEC, GARUM**
fish sign .... **PISCES**
fish, silvery .... **MULLET**
fish, small .. **ID, IDE, DARTER**
fish, snouted .... **SAURY**
fish, S. Am. ...... **ARAPAIMA**
fish, sparoid .... **SAR, SARGO**
fish, spiny ..... **GOBY, PERCH**
fish, sucking .... **REMORA**
fish, trap .... **WEEL, WEIR**
fish, tropical
   SARGO, ROBALO, SALEMA
fish, warm sea
   GUASA, GROUPER
fish, W. Ind.
   BOGA, CERO, TESTAR
fish whisker .... **BARBEL**
fish with moving line .. **TROLL**
fish with net .. **SEINE, TRAWL**
fish, young .... **FRY**
fisherman's hut, Orkney
   SKEO, SKIO
fishhook line-leader ... **SNELL**
fishhook part .... **BARB**
fishing expedition: Scot. **DRAVE**
fishing grounds, Shetlands **HAAF**

fissure .... **RENT,
RIFT, RIMA, RIME, CLEFT**
fissures, full of **RIMOSE, RIMOUS**
fist .... **NEAF**
fit .. **APT, RIPE, SUIT, ADAPT**
fit for cultivation .... **ARABLE**
fit for human consumption
POTABLE
fit of sulks .... **HUFF**
five-dollar bill .... **VEE**
five-franc piece .... **ECU**
five, group of .... **PENTAD**
five in cards .... **PEDRO**
fix or fixed .... **SET**
fixed charge .... **FEE**
fixed income person .. **RENTIER**
fixed payment .... **KIST**
flaccid .... **LIMP**
flag. **JACK, ENSIGN, BANDEROLE**
flag, flower, blue .... **IRIS**
flag, military .... **GUIDON**
flag, pirate .... **ROGER**
flag, small
BANNERET, BANNERETTE
flagellants .... **ALBI**
flag's corner .... **CANTON**
flank .... **SIDE**
flank: dialect .... **LEER**
flannel .... **LANA**
flap .... **TAB, LOMA**
flap, as sails .... **SLAT**
flare .... **FUSEE, FUZEE**
flaring edge .. **LIP, FLANGE**
flashed lightning ... **LEVINED**
flask, drinking ..... **CANTEEN**
flat .... **EVEN, LEVEL, PLANE**
flat-bottomed boat
ARK, DORY, PUNT, SCOW
flat, music ...... **MOL, MOLLE**
flatfish ..... **DAB, RAY, SOLE,
BRILL, FLUKE, FLOUNDER**
flatten out .... **CLAP**
flattened .. **OBLATE, PLANATE**
flatter .... **PALP**
flattery .... **PALAVER**
flavor .... **LACE, TANG,
AROMA, SAPOR, SEASON**
flavoring plant .. **HERB, LEEK,
MINT, ANISE, BASIL**
flavoring root ...... **LICORICE**
flax fiber .... **TOW**
flax, like .... **TOWY**
flax, prepare .... **RET**
flee .... **LAM, BOLT**
fleece .... **FELL, WOOL**
fleece, poorest .... **ABB**
fleet .... **NAVY**
fleet, esp. Span.
ARMADA, ARMADO, ARMATA
fleet, merchant ...... **ARGOSY**
fleur-de-lis .... **LIS, LYS, LISS**

fleur-de-lis, obs. ...... **LUCE**
flexible .... **LITHE**
flexible wood: dial. ..... **EDDER**
flight ...... **HEGIRA, HEJIRA**
flight of ducks .... **SKEIN**
flight organ .... **WING**
flight, pert. to .... **AERO**
flightless bird
EMU, KIWI, WEKA, PENGUIN
flip .... **SNAP**
flit .... **FLY, GAD**
float
BUOY, RAFT, SWIM, WAFT
floating .... **NATANT**
floating vegetation on Nile
SADD, SUDD
floating wreckage .. **FLOTSAM**
flock of quail .... **BEVY**
flock of swans .... **BANK**
flock, pert. to .... **GREGAL**
flock, small .... **COVEY**
flog
BEAT, LASH, WHIP, SWINGE
flood .... **SEA, EAGRE,
SPATE, FRESHET, TORRENT**
floodgate ..... **CLOW, SLUICE**
flora and fauna .... **BIOTA**
floral leaf .... **BRACT, SEPAL**
Florentine family ..... **MEDICI**
Florida tree .... **MABI**
flounder
DAB, SOLE, FLUKE, PLAICE
flour sieve .... **BOLTER**
flour, unsorted Ind. **ATA, ATTA**
flourish, music ...... **ROULADE**
flourishing: dialect ..... **FRIM**
flow .... **RUN, FLUX**
flow out .... **EMIT, SPILL**
flow, to stop
STANCH, STAUNCH
flower cluster
CYME, ANADEM, RACEME
flower extract
ATAR, OTTO, ATTAR, OTTAR
flower, fall
ASTER, COSMOS, SALVIA
flower, field .... **GOWAN**
flower, genus of .... **ROSA**
flower-goddess, Norse **NANNA**
flower-goddess, Rom. .. **FLORA**
flower leaf ... **BRACT, SEPAL**
flower, Oriental ...... **LOTUS**
flower part .... **PETAL,
SEPAL, CARPEL, SPADIX**
flower, showy .... **CALLA**
flower spike .... **AMENT**
flowering plant .... **ARUM**
fluctuate .... **WAVER**
fluent .... **GLIB**
fluff, yarn .... **LINT**

a fluid, aeriform .... GAS
fluid, medical ... SERA, SERUM
fluid, serous .... SERA, SERUM
fluidity unit .... RHE
flume .... SHUTE, SLUICE
flushed .... RED
flute, ancient Gr. .. HEMIOPE
flute, India ... BIN, MATALAN
flute, small .... FIFE
flutter .. FLAP, WAVE, HOVER
fly GNAT, SOAR, WING, AVIATE
fly agaric .... AMANITA
fly aloft .... SOAR
fly, artificial
  HARL, HERL, CAHILL, CLARET
fly, kind of .... BOT
fly, small ...... GNAT, MIDGE
fly, S. Afr. .... TSETSE
flycatcher
  TODY, ALDER, PEWEE, PHOEBE
flying .... VOLANT, VOLITANT
"Flying Dutchman" saver SENTA
flying fox .... KALONG
flying lemur .... COLUGO
flying, of .... AERO
flying saucer .... UFO
foam .... SUD, SUDS
focus .... CONCENTRATE
fodder pit .... SILO
fodder storage place .... SILO
b fodder, to store ...... ENSILE,
  ENSILO, ENSILAGE, ENSILATE
fog .... MIST
fog horn .... SIRENE
fog: old Eng. .... RAG
foist .... FOB, PALM
fold .... LAP, PLY, PLIE,
  RUGA, PLEAT, CREASE
fold of skin .... PLICA
folds, arrange in ...... DRAPE
folded .... PLICATE
folio .... PAGE
folk dance, Slavic ...... KOLO
folklore being .... TROLL
folkway .... MOS
folkways .... MORES
follow .... DOG, TAIL,
  ENSUE, TRACE, SHADOW
follow suit, not RENIG, RENEGE
follower .. IST, ITE, ADHERENT
foment .... ABET
fondle .... PET, CARESS
fondness: Ir. .... GRA
font .... LAVER, STOUP
food .... FARE, MEAT,
  MANNA, ALIMENT, PABULUM
food bit .... ORT
food, farinaceous ...... SAGO
food for animals .... FORAGE
food forbidden Israelites TEREFA

c food, Hawaii .... POI
food: Maori, N. Z. ...... KAI
food of gods
  AMRITA, AMREETA, AMBROSIA
food: Polyn. .... KAI
food, provide .... CATER
food, soft invalid's ...... PAP
foods, choice .... CATES
fool..ASS, DOLT, GABY, RACA,
  SIMP, IDIOT, NINNY
fool's bauble ...... MAROTTE
fool's gold .... PYRITE
foolish .. DAFT, ZANY, INANE,
  SILLY, HARISH, ASININE
foot, animal's ..... PAD, PAW
foot, Chin. .... CHEK
foot, Gr. poet. .... IONIC
foot, having .... PEDATE
foot part, horse's .. PASTERN
foot, poet. ... IAMB, IAMBIC,
  IAMBUS, ANAPEST, ANAPAEST
foot soldier .... PEON
foot soldier, Ir. KERN, KERNE
foot, two-syllable
  SPONDEE, TROCHEE
foot, verse .... IAMB,
  DACTYL, ANAPEST, ANAPAEST
football position: abbr. .. FB,
  HB, LE, LT, QB, RE, RT
d footless .... APOD, APODAL
footless animal APOD, APODE
footless animal genus .. APODA
footlike .... PEDATE
footlike part .... PES
footpad .... WHYO
footstalk, leaf .... STRIG
footstool HASSOCK, OTTOMAN
for .... PRO
for example .... EG
for fear that .... LEST
for shame .... FIE
forage plant .. GUAR, ALSIKE,
  LUCERN, ALFALFA, LUCERNE
foramen .... PORE
foray .... RAID
forbidden
  TABU, TABOO, BANNED
Forbidden City .... LASSA
forbidding .... STERN
force ... VIS, DINT, DRIVE,
  IMPEL, POWER, ENERGY,
  VIOLENCE
force, alleged
  OD, BIOD, ELOD, ODYL
force, hypothetical .... OD
force, unit of .... DYNE
force, with .... AMAIN
foreboding .... OMEN
forefather .... SIRE
forefoot .... PUD
forefront .... VAN

a forehead, of the .... **METOPIC**
forehead strap .... **TUMP**
foreign in origin ...... **EXOTIC**
foreign trade discount .. **AGIO**
foreigner: Hawaii ..... **HAOLE**
foreigners' quarter, Constanti-
 nople .... **PERA**
foremost part
 BOW, VAN, FRONT
foremost segment, insect's
 ACRON
foreordain .... **DESTINE**
foreshadow .... **BODE**
forest: Brazil .... **MATTA**
forest clearing .... **GLADE**
forest: obsolete .... **WOLD**
forest ox .... **ANOA**
forest partly inundated **GAPO**
forest, pert. to
 SILVAN, SYLVAN, NEMORAL
forest, P. I. .... **GUBAT**
forest warden ...... **RANGER**
forestall .... **AVERT, PREVENT**
foretell .... **AUGUR, INSEE**
foreteller .... **SEER**
foretoken .... **OMEN**
forever .... **AY, AYE**
forever: Maori .... **AKE**
forever: poet. **ETERN, ETERNE**
forfeit .... **LOSE, LAPSE**

b forfeits, Jap. .... **KEN**
forgetfulness fruit .... **LOTUS**
forgetfulness water ... **LETHE**
forgive .... **REMIT**
forgiving .... **CLEMENT**
forgo .... **WAIVE**
form a network .... **PLEX**
form: Buddhism .... **RUPA**
form into line **ALIGN, ALINE**
form, pert. to .... **MODAL**
form, philos. .... **EIDOS**
formal choice .... **VOTE**
formation, military .. **ECHELON**
former .... **ERST**
former ruler **CZAR, TSAR, TZAR**
formerly .... **NEE, ERST, ONCE**
formerly: pref. .... **EX**
formic acid source ...... **ANT**
formicid .... **ANT**
formula .... **LAW**
forsaken .... **LORN**
fort ...... **DIX, ORD, REDAN,**
 CITADEL, REDOUBT, RAVELIN
fort, N. Z. .... **PA, PAH**
forth .... **OUT**
forth, issuing ..... **EMANANT**
forthwith .... **NOW**
fortification
 REDAN, RAVELIN, REDOUBT

c fortification, ditchside
 SCARP, ESCARP, ESCARPE
fortification, felled trees
 ABATIS
fortification, slope .... **TALUS**
fortified place ...... **LIS, LISS**
fortify .... **ARM, MAN**
fortunate (India) .... **SRI**
fortune: Gypsy .... **BAHI**
forty days fast ...... **CARENE**
forty: Gr. .... **MU**
forward .... **ON, AHEAD**
fossil, mollusk .... **DOLITE**
fossil resin .... **RETINITE**
fossil worm track ... **NEREITE**
foul smelling
 OLID, FETID, REEKY
found .... **BASE**
found, thing .... **TROVE**
foundation .. **BED, BASE, BASIS**
fountain .... **FONS**
four, group of ...... **TETRAD**
four-inch measure ...... **HAND**
fourth calif (caliph) .... **ALI**
fourth estate .... **PRESS**
fowl .... **HEN, CAPON, POULT**
fowl's gizzard, etc. .... **GIBLET**
fox .... **TOD**
fox, Afr. .... **FENNEC**
fox hunter's coat .... **PINK**

d fox, S. Afr. .... **ASSE, CAAMA**
"Fra Diavolo" composer **AUBER**
fraction ..... **PART, DECIMAL**
fragment, pottery
 SHARD, SHERD, SHEARD
fragments .... **ANA, ORTS**
fragrant .... **OLENT**
frame, supporting
 TRESSEL, TRESTLE
framework .... **TRUSS**
France .... **GAUL**
franchise .... **CHARTER**
Franciscan .... **MINORITE**
frank .... **OPEN, HONEST**
Franks, pert. to .... **SALIC**
frankincense ...... **OLIBANUM**
Frankish law .... **SALIC**
Frankish peasant .. **LITI, LITUS**
fraud .... **SHAM**
fraught .... **LADEN**
fray .... **MELEE**
free .... **RID, GRATIS**
free-for-all .... **FRAY, MELEE**
free from discount ..... **NET**
free from knots: obs. .. **ENODE**
freebooter .... **PIRATE**
freedman, Kentish law .. **LAET**
freehold land, Turkey .. **MULK**
freeman ...... **CEORL, THANE**
freight-boat .... **ARK**

a freight car .... GONDOLA
FRENCH WORDS: (accent marks
omitted throughout)
    according to ..... ALA, AUX
    after .... APRES
    again .... ENCORE
    airplane .... AVION
    alas .... HELAS
    all .... TOUT
    among .... ENTRE
    and .... ET
    angel .... ANGE
    annuity .... RENTE
    arm .... BRAS
    article .... LA, LE, DE,
      (plural) DES, LAS, LES, UNE
    at the home of ..... CHEZ
    aunt .... TANTE
    baby .... BEBE
    bacon .... LARD
    back .... DOS
    ball .... BAL
    bang! .... PAN
    bath .... BAIN
    beach .... PLAGE
    beast .... BETE
    before .... AVANT
    being .... ETRE
    bench .... BANC

b between .... ENTRE
    beware .... GARE
    bitter .... AMER
    black .... NOIR, NOIRE
    blue .... BLEU
    bread crumbs ...... PANURE
    bridge .... PONT
    business house .... CIE
    but .... MAIS
    cabbage .... CHOU
    cake .... GATEAU
    carefully groomed .. SOIGNE
    carriage .... FIACRE
    charmed .... RAVI
    chicken .... POULE
    child .... ENFANT
    clear .... NET
    climax, theatre .... CLOY
    cloth .... DRAP
    cloud .... NUAGE
    coarse cloth .... BURE
    connective .... ET
    cowardly .... LACHE
    cup .... TASSE
    dance, formal .... BAL
    dare .... OSER
    daughter .... FILLE
    deal .... DONNE
    dear .... CHER, CHERI
    deed .... FAIT
    defy .... DEFI

c department .... see SPECIAL
      SECTION, GAZETTEER
    depot .... GARE
    detective force .... SURETE
    devil .... DIABLE
    dirty .... SALE
    donkey .... ANE
    down with .... ABAS
    dream .... REVE
    duck to cook .... CANETON
    dugout .... ABRI
    duke .... DUC
    dungeon .... CACHOT
    ear of grain .... EPI
    east .... EST
    egg .... OEUF
    elegance .... LUXE
    enamel .... EMAIL
    equal .... PAREIL
    evening .... SOIR
    exaggerated .... OUTRE
    exclamation .... HEIN
    exist .... ETRE
    fabric .... RAS, DRAP
    father .... PERE
    fear .... PEUR
    finally .... ENFIN
    fingering .... DOIGTE
    fire .... FEU

d five .... CINQ
    for .... CAR
    friend .... AMI, AMIE
    froth .... BAVE
    full .... PLEIN
    game .... JEU, JEUX
    gift .... CADEAU
    god .... DIEU
    golden .... DORE
    good .... BON
    good-bye ADIEU, AU REVOIR
    grain ear .... EPI
    gray .... GRIS
    gravy .... JUS
    grimace .... MOUE
    ground .... TERRE
    half-mask .... LOUP
    hall .... SALLE
    handle .... ANSE
    head .... TETE
    health .... SANTE
    here ICI
    hill .... PUY
    his .... SES
    house .... MAISON
    hunting match .... TIR
    husband .... MARI
    idea .... IDEE

(French words continued on
pages 62 and 63)

French

FRENCH:

impetuosity	ELAN
in	DANS
income, annual	RENTE
is	EST
island	ILE
kind	SORTE
king	ROI
lamb	AGNEAU
land	TERRE
laugh	RIRE
laughter	RISEE
law	LOI, DROIT
leather	CUIR
lift	LEVE
lily	LIS
little	PEU
lively	VIF
lodging place	GITE
low	BAS
maid	BONNE
mail	POSTE
mask, half	LOUP
material	DRAP
May	MAI
meat dish	SALMI
milk	LAIT
mine	AMOI
mother	MERE
mountain	MONT
museum	MUSEE
nail	CLOU
name	NOM
near	PRES
network	RESEAU
night	NUIT
no	NON
nose	NEZ
nothing	RIEN
number, one	UNE
nursemaid	BONNE
of	DE
one	UNE
our	NOS, NOUS
out	HORS
outbreak	EMEUTE
over	SUR
oyster farm	PARC
petticoat	JUPE, COTTE
picnic spot	BOIS
pinion	AILE
poem	DIT
pork	SALE
pout	MOUE
preposition	DES
pretty	JOLI, JOLIE
pronoun	CES, ILS, MES, TOI, UNE, ELLE
queen	REINE
quickly	VITE

rabbit	LAPIN
railway station	GARE
read	LIRE
rear	ARRIERE
reception	ACCUEIL
rent	LOUER
river	RIVIERE
roast	ROTI
royal edict	ARRET
saint: abbr.	STE
salt	SEL
salted	SALE
school	ECOLE, LYCEE
scow	ACON
sea	MER
security	RENTE
senior	AINE
servant	BONNE
she	ELLE
sheath	ETUI
sheep	MOUTON
shelter	ABRI
shine	LUSTRE
shooting match	TIR
sickness	MAL
silk	SOIE
situated	SISE
small	PETIT
smitten	EPRISE
soldier	POILU
some	DES
son	FILS
soul	AME
spirit	AME
star	ETOILE
state	ETAT
stocking	BAS
storm	ORAGE
summer	ETE
superior quality	LUXE
superfluous	DETROP
surnamed	DIT
sweetmeat	DRAGEE
that	CE, CET, QUE, QUI, CELA
thee	TE
there!	VOILA
they	ILS
thirty	TRENTE
this	CE
thou	TOI
to be	ETRE
to go	ALLER
to love	AIMER
too much	TROP
under	SOUS
upon	SUR
us	NOUS
verb	ETRE
verse	RONDEL

a FRENCH:

very	TRES
vineyard	CRU
wall	MUR
water	EAU
wave	ONDE
weapon	ARME
well	BIEN
wine	VIN
wine, delicacy of	SEVE
wine-plant	CEP
with	AVEC
with the	AU
without	SANS
wing	AILE
wood	BOIS
yesterday	HIER
you	TOI
your	VOTRE

Fr., annuity	RENTE
Fr. art group	FAUVES
Fr. artist	DORE, DUFY, GROS, COROT, DEGAS, MANET, MONET, BRAQUE, DERAIN, RENOIR, CHAGALL, CHIRICO, MATISSE, UTRILLO
Fr. artist cult	DADA
b Fr. author	SUE, GIDE, HUGO, LOTI, ZOLA, CAMUS, DUMAS, RENAN, STAEL, VERNE, RACINE, SARTRE, COCTEAU
Fr. Calvinist	CALAS
Fr. chalk	TALC
Fr. coin, old	SOU
Fr. commercial company	CIE
FR. COMPOSER	see COMPOSER, FR.
Fr. dramatist	RACINE
Fr. ecclesiastic city	SENS
Fr. explorer	CARTIER
Fr. fort, battle of Verdun	VAUX
Fr. general	FOCH, HOCHE GAMELIN
Fr.-Ger. river basin	SAAR
Fr. guerillas	MAQUIS
Fr. Guiana tribesman	BONI
Fr. historical area	ANJOU
Fr. honeysuckle	SULLA
Fr. illustrator	DORE
Fr. island	ILE
Fr. lace-making town	CLUNY
Fr. marshal	NEY, MURAT
FR. NOVELIST see FR. AUTHOR	
FR. PAINTER see FR. ARTIST	
Fr. philosopher	COMTE
Fr. premier, former	LAVAL
Fr. priest	ABBE, PERE
Fr. protectorate	TUNIS
Fr. psychologist	BINET

c

Fr. Revolution month	NIVOSE, FLOREAL, PRAIRAL, VENTOSE, BRUMAIRE, FERVIDOR, FRIMAIRE, MESSIDOR, PLUVIOSE, THERMIDOR
Fr. revolutionist	MARAT
Fr. sculptor	RODIN
Fr. security	RENTE
Fr. singer	PIAF, SABLON
Fr. soprano	PONS, CALVE
Fr. statesman	COTY
FR. WRITER .. see FR. AUTHOR	
Frenchman	GAUL
frenzied	AMOK
frequently	OFT
fresh	NEW, SPICK
fresh supply	RELAY
freshet	FLOOD, SPATE
freshwater worm	NAID, NAIS
fretted	EROSE
Frey's wife	GERD
friar	FRA, MONK
friar, mendicant	SERVITE
friend: law	AMY
friends	KITH
Friendly Islands	TONGA
friendship	AMITY
frigate bird, Hawaiian	IWA
Frigg's brother-in-law	VE
Frigg's husband	ODIN
d fright	FUNK, PANIC
frighten	FLEY, ALARM, SCARE
frill, neck	RUFF, JABOT
fringe of curls	FRISETTE
fringe: zool.	LOMA
frisk	PLAY, ROMP
frisky	PEART
FROCK see GARMENT	
frog	TOAD
frog genus	RANA
frogs, order of	ANURA
frogs, pert. to	RANINE
frolic	LARK, PLAY, ROMP, CAPER, SPORT, SPREE
from head to foot	CAP-A-PIE
from: Lat.	DE
from: prefix	AB
front	VAN, FORE, FACADE
front page weather box	EAR
front, to extend	DEPLOY
frontier post	FORT
frontiersman	BOONE, CARSON
frost	ICE, HOAR, RIME
frosty	RIMY
froth	FOAM, SPUME
frothlike	SPUMY, YEASTY
frown	LOUR, GLOOM, LOWER, SCOWL, GLOWER
frugal	CHARY
fruit	BERRY, OLIVE
fruit, Afr.	PECEGO

Fruit

a
fruit, aggregate ..... ETAERIO
fruit decay .... BLET
fruit dish
   COMPOTE, COMPOTIER
fruitdots, fern .... SORI, SORUS
fruit, dry .... ACHENE
fruit, fleshy ...... PEAR, PEPO
fruit, hard-shelled NUT, GOURD
fruit, India .... BEL
fruit-jelly .... RHOB
fruit, lemonlike ..... CITRON
fruit of maple .... SAMARA
fruit pigeon, Polyn. ..... LUPE
fruit, plumlike .... SLOE
fruit, pulpy ..... UVA, DRUPE
fruit shrub, E. Ind. .... CUBEB
fruit, small, 1-seeded
  AKENE, ACHENE, ACHENIUM
fruit, southern .... PAPAW
fruit squeezer ...... REAMER
fruit, tropical .. DATE, MANGO
fruit, vine .... MELON
fruit, yellow tropical
  PAPAW, PAPAYA, PAWPAW
fruiting spike .... EAR
frustrate ... SCOTCH, THWART
fry lightly .... SAUTE
Fuegan Indian .... ONA
fuel   LOG, COAL, COKE, PEAT
fuel ship .... OILER, TANKER
fuel, turf .... PEAT, PEET
fugue theme .... DUX
fulcrum, oar .... THOLE
full .... PLENARY
full and clear ..... OROTUND
fullness .... PLENUM
fulmar .... NELLY, MALDUCK
fume .... REEK, SMOKE

c
fun .... SPORT
function ...... GO, USE, WORK
function, trig. ... SINE, COSINE
fundamental
   BASIC, ELEMENTAL
funeral bell KNELL, MORTBELL
funeral music .... DIRGE
funeral notice .... OBIT
funeral oration .... ELOGE
funeral pile .... PYRE
funeral song .... NENIA
fungi, tissue in .... TRAMA
fungus .... AGARIC
fungus, edible
  MOREL, MORIL, TRUFFLE
fungus, white-spored AMANITA
fur ...... SEAL, VAIR, GENET
  MARTEN, NUTRIA, MINIVER
fur cape .... PELERINE
fur: Her. PEAN, VAIR, VAIRE
furbelow ...... FRILL, RUFFLE
Furies, Gr. .... ERINYS
ERINNYS, ERINYES, ERINNYES
Furies, one of
 ALECTO, MEGAERA, TISIPHONE
Furies, Rom. .... DIRAE
furlongs, eight .... MILE
furnish crew .... MAN
furnish with .... ENDOW
furnishings, mode of .. DECOR
furrows, with RIVOSE, RUTTED
further .... AID, YET
furtive .... SLY, SNEAKY
fury .... IRE
furze ...... WHIN, WHUN,
  GORSE, GORST, GORSTE
fuse partly .... FRIT
fuss .... ADO, TO-DO

b
gabl .... TARO
Gad, son of .... ARELI
gadget .... GISMO
Gael .... SCOT
Gaelic .. ERSE, CELTIC, KELTIC
Gaelic poem .... DUAN
Gaelic sea god .... LER
gaff .... SPAR
gain .... GET, WIN, EARN
gait .. LOPE, CANTER, GALLOP
gait, horse's ..... PACE, RACK
Galahad's mother ..... ELAINE
Galatea's beloved ..... ACIS
Galilee town .... CANA
galla ox ...... SANGA, SANGU
gallery, art .... SALON
gallery: hist. .... ALURE

d
gallery, open .... LOGGIA
gallery protecting troops
   ECOUTE
galley, armed, old Northmen's
   AESC
galley, fast
  DROMON, DROMOND
galley, 1 oar bank   UNIREME
galley, 2 oar banks .. BIREME
galley, 3 oar banks TRIREME
gallop, rapid .... TANTIVY
gallop slowly .... LOPE
Galsworthy heroine .... IRENE
Galway Bay, isles in .... ARAN
gamble .... GAME
gambling place .... CASINO

a gambol .... DIDO, CAPER
game ... LOTO, BINGO, LOTTO
game, Basque .... PELOTA
game, board ... CHESS, HALMA
game, card .... LU, LOO, NAP,
    PAM, PUT, FARO, CINCH,
    MACAO, MONTE, OMBER,
    OMBRE, STUSS, TAROT,
    WHIST, BASSET, CASINO,
    ECARTÉ, ROUNCE, CA-
    NASTA
game, child's .... TAG
game, dice .... LUDO
game, follow .... STALK
game, gambling
    FARO, PICO, STUSS
game, Hawaii .... HEI
game, Ind. guessing .. CANUTE
game, It. guessing .... MORA
game of skill .... POOL, CHESS
game piece ... MAN, DOMINO
gamecock .... STAG
gamekeeper .... RANGER
gaming cube .... DIE, DICE
Ganges boat .... PUTELI
gangplank .... RAMP
gangster .. MUG, THUG, WHYO
gannet, common ...... SOLAN
gannet genus .... SULA
gap .... HIATUS, LACUNA
gap in hedge
b   MUSE, MEUSE, MUSET
gar fish .... SNOOK
garland .... LEI, ANADEM
GARMENT . see COAT, BLOUSE
garment .... ROBE
garment, Arab .... ABA
garment, bishop's
    CHIMAR, CHIMER, CHIMERE
garment, church ...... COTTA
GARMENT, CLERICAL OR EC-
    CLESIASTIC, see GARMENT,
    PRIESTLY
garment, fitted .... REEFER
garment, India, Hindu .. SARI,
    SAREE, BANIAN, BANYAN
GARMENT, LITURGICAL
    see GARMENT, PRIESTLY
garment, loose .CAMIS, CAMUS,
    CYMAR, SIMAR, CAMISE
garment, Malay ..... SARONG
garment, Moslem ...... IZAR
garment, N. Afr. .... HAIK
garment, Old Ir. .... INAR
garment, outer
    CAPOTE, PALETOT
garment, Polyn. ...... PAREU
garment, priestly .. ALB, COPE,
    AMICE, EPHOD, STOLE
garment, rain .... PONCHO
garment, scarflike .... TIPPET

c garment, Turk. .... DOLMAN
garment, woman's
    BODICE, MANTUA
garnishment .... LIEN
garret .... ATTIC
garter snake genus ..... ELAPS
gas .... FUEL, NEON
gas apparatus ...... AERATOR
gas, charge with ..... AERATE
gas, colorless .... OXAN
gas, inert .... ARGON, XENON
gas, radioactive
    RADON, NITON
GASEOUS ELEMENT
    see ELEMENTS, SPECIAL
    SECTION, Page 195
gaseous sky "cloud" . NEBULA
GASTROPOD see also MOLLUSK
gastropod ...... WELK, WILK,
    WHELK, LIMPET
gastropod, Haliotis .. ABALONE
gate .... PORTAL
gate, water .... SLUICE
gateway .... PYLON
gateway, Buddhist temple
    TORAN, TORANA
gateway, Pers. .... DAR
gateway, Shinto temple . TORII
gather .... AMASS, GLEAN,
    GARNER, MUSTER
gather, as grouse .... LEK
d gather in bundles .... SHEAVE
gathers, put in
    SHER, SHIR, SHIRR
gaunt .... SPARE
Gawain's father .... LOT
gazelle .... ARIEL
gazelle, Afr. .. ADMI, DAMA,
    MOHR, KORIN, MHORR
gazelle, Asia .... AHU
gazelle, black-tailed ..... GOA
gazelle, Pers. .... CORA
gazelle, Sudan .... DAMA
gazelle, Tibetan .... GOA
gear .... CAM
gear tooth .... COG
gear wheel, smallest .. PINION
Geb's consort .... NUT
Gelderland city .... EDE
gelid .... ICY, COLD
GEM .... see also STONE
gem ..... JADE, ONYX, OPAL,
    RUBY, SARD, AGATE, PEARL,
    STONE, GARNET, SPINEL,
    EMERALD, PERIDOT
gem-bearing earth, Burma BYON
gem, carved .... CAMEO
gem facet ..... BEZEL, BEZIL,
    CULET, COLLET
gem weight .... CARAT
Gemini's mortal half .. CASTOR

Gender

a
gender, a .... NEUTER
genealogy .... TREE
GENERAL, CIVIL WAR
    see CIVIL WAR COMMANDER
general, Morocco .... KAID
general Sitting Bull defeated
                         CUSTER
generation .... AGE
Genesis matriarch ...... SARAI
genie, Egypt. .... HAPI
genip tree .... LANA
genipap wood .... LANA
gentle . MILD, TAME, TENDER
gentle breeze .... AURA
gentle heat .... TEPOR
genuflect .... KNEEL
GENUS . see PLANT or
              ANIMAL named
genus of plants .... ARUM
geode VUG, VOOG, VUGG, VUGH
geological division . LIAS, LYAS
geol. epoch BALA, ECCA, LIAS,
        MUAV, ERIAN, UINTA,
        PLIOCENE
geol. formation ..... TERRAIN,
        TERRANE, TERRENE
geol. period .... DYAS,
        EOCENE, MIOCENE
geol. stage ...... RISS, ACHEN
geol. vein angle .... HADE

b
geometric ratio .... SINE
geometric solid
        CONE, CUBE, PRISM
geometrical lines ...... LOCI,
        LOCUS, SECANT
geometry rule ...... THEOREM
geometry term .... VERSOR
geophagy .... PICA
George Sand novel ..... LELIA
Geraint's wife .... ENID
geranium lake color . NACARAT
germ .. BUG, VIRUS, MICROBE
germ-free ASEPTIC, ANTISEPTIC
germs, produced by ... SEPTIC
GERMAN . see also TEUTONIC
GERMAN WORDS: (umlauts
omitted throughout)
    "A" .... EIN
    above .... UBER
    again .... UBER
    alas .... ACH
    article ...... DAS, DER, EIN
    ass .... ESEL
    beer .... BIER
    blood .... BLUT
    conjunction .... UND
    count .... GRAF
    donkey .... ESEL
    dumpling .... KNODEL
    eat .... ESSEN

c
eight .... ACHT
evening .... ABEND
everything .... ALLES
exclamation .... HOCH
four .... VIER
gentleman .. HERR, HERREN
hall .... AULA, SAAL
heaven .... HIMMEL
hunter .... JAGER
"I" .... ICH
ice .... EIS
iron .... EISEN
is .... IST
it .... ES
league (s) .... BUND, BUNDE
love .... LIEBE
mister .... HERR
nation .... VOLK
never .... NIE
new .... NEUE
no .... NEIN
noble .... EDEL
old .... ALT
one .... EIN, EINE
out of .... AUS
pronoun .... ICH
people .... VOLK
school hall .... AULA
softly .... LEISE

d
song .... LIED
spirit .... GEIST
state .... STAAT
steel .... STAHL
temperament ...... GEMUT
than .... ALS
the .... DAS, DER
three .... DREI
thunder .... DONNER
title .... VON, PRINZ
town .... STADT
us .... UNS
very .... SEHR
with .... MIT
without .... OHNE
yes .... JA
you .... SIE
your ...... IHR, DEIN, EUER

German .... BOCHE
Ger. admiral .... SPEE
Ger. bacteriologist ...... KOCH
Ger. camp, war ...... STALAG
GER. COMPOSER
        see COMPOSER, GER.
Ger.-Czech region ... SUDETEN
Ger. district, old .... GAU
Ger. dive bomber ...... STUKA
Ger. emperor .... OTTO
Ger. highway ..... AUTOBAHN
Ger. John .... HANS

a Ger. king .... OTTO
Ger. landscape painter .. ROOS
Ger. name prefix .... VON
Ger. philosopher . KANT, HEGEL
Ger. physicist .. OHM, ERMAN
Ger. president .... EBERT
Ger. princely family ..... WELF
Ger. theologian .... ARND
Ger. title .. VON, GRAF, PRINZ
Ger. tribal region
GAU, GAUE, GAUS
Germanic deity .... DONAR
Germanic letter .... RUNE
gesture dance, Samoa; Fiji SIVA
get out! . SCAT, SHOO, SCRAM
ghastly .... LURID
ghost .... HANT, SPOOK,
SPECTER, SPECTRE
ghost, India .... BHUT
ghost-town state: abbrev.: UT
giant .... TITAN
giant, frightful .... OGRE
giant, Hindu myth ..... BANA
giant, killed by Apollo .. OTUS
giant, Norse, Scand. myth YMER,
YMIR, JOTUM, MIMIR
giant, Rom. .... CACA
giant, 1000-armed, Hindu BANA
giants, Bibl. .... ANAK, EMIM
gibbon, Malay .... LAR
gift, receiver of .... DONEE
gig .... NAPPER
b gigantic person .... TITAN
"Gil —" LeSage novel .. BLAS
Gilead's descendant .... ULAM
Gilgit language, Kashmir SHINA
gills, four .... PINT
gilt .... DORE
gin .... TRAP
gingerbread tree .... DUM
ginkgo tree .... ICHO
GIPSY .... see GYPSY
giraffe-like animal .... OKAPI
girasol .... OPAL
girder .... TRUSS
girdle .... OBI, CEST, SASH
girl .... SIS, CHIT,
DAME, SKIRT
GIRL'S NAME
see WOMAN'S NAME
girth, saddle .... CINCH
gist .... NUB, PITH
give: law .... REMISE
give reluctantly ..... GRUDGE
give up .. CEDE, WAIVE, YIELD
give up wholly ...... DEVOTE
give way .... YIELD
glacial hill .... PAHA
glacial ice block, pinnacle SERAC
glacial ridge ... AS, OS, ASAR,
KAME, OSAR, ESCAR,
ESKAR, ESKER

c glacial snow field FIRN, NEVE
glacial stage .... WURM
glacier chasm
CREVAS, CREVASSE
glacier, facing a .... STOSS
gladiolus .... IRID
gladly .... FAIN
gland ... PINEAL, THYROID
gland, edible .... NOIX
glass .... LENS
glass, blue .... SMALT
glass bubble .... BLEB
glass defect .... TEAR
glass, flatten .... PLATTEN
glass furnace mouth .. BOCCA
glass ingredient ...... SILICON
glass-like material ... PLASS
glass maker .... GLAZIER
glass, molten .... PARISON
glass, partly fused FRIT, FRITT
glass, transparent ..... UVIOL
glass vial .. AMPULE, AMPOULE
glassmaker's oven . LEER, LEHR
glasswort .... KALI
glassy .... HYALINE
glazier's tack .... BRAD
gleam .... GLINT
glide .... SKIM, SLIP,
SKATE, SLIDE
d glittering piece ..... SPANGLE
globe .... ORB, SPHERE
global .... ROUND, SPHERAL
gloom ...... MIRK, MURK
gloomy ...... DARK, DOUR,
DREAR, DREARY
"Gloomy Dean" .... INGE
glossy-surfaced ...... GLACE
glottal stop: Dan. .... STOD
glove leather ..... KID, NAPA,
MOCHA, SUEDE
glove shape, unstitched TRANK
glowing .... CANDENT
glucoside, root .... GEIN
glut ... SATE, GORGE, SATIATE
gnarl .... NUR, KNUR, NURR
gnat, small .... MIDGE
gnome .... NIS, GREMLIN
go .... WEND
go astray .... ABERRATE
go astray slightly .... ERR
go back .... REVERT
go forth .... FARE
go hence: Lat. .... VADE
go on! ...... GARN, SCAT
go shufflingly .. MOSY, MOSEY
goad .... PROD, SPUR, INCITE
goal .... AIM, END
goat, Alpine mountain .. IBEX
goat antelope .... GORAL
goat, Asian .... JAGLA

a
goat, genus .... CAPRIA
goat god .... PAN
goat, wild .. TUR, IBEX, TAHR,
TAIR, TEHR, THAR
goatsucker .... POTOO
gob .... TAR
Gobi Desert .... SHAMO
goblet .... HANAP
goblin .... POOK, PUCA, PUCK
goblin, Egypt .... OUPHE
goblin, Norse NIS,NISSE,KOBOLD
goby, small .... MAPO
GOD . see also DEITY, and see
also SPECIAL SECTION
god, Babyl. EA, ABU, ANU, BEL
GOD, CHIEF see CHIEF NORSE
GOD, also BABYLONIAN
CHIEF GOD
god: Chin. .... SHEN
god: Hebrew .... EL
god: Jap .... KAMI
god: Lat. .... DEUS
god of alcoholic drinks, SIRIS
god of Arcadia .... PAN
GOD OF CHAOS ... see CHAOS
god of darkness—evil, Egyp.
SET, SETH
god of dead, Hindu .... YAMA
god of dead, Rom. .... ORCUS

b
god of discord, Norse
LOK, LOKE, LOKI
god of earth, Babyl. .. DAGAN
GOD OF EARTH, Egyptian
see EARTH GOD
god of evil: Egyp. ... SET, SETH
god of evil, to ward off BES,BESA
god of fertility, Norse ... FREY
god of fields, flocks, forest
PAN, FAUN
god of fire ... AGNI, VULCAN
god of Hades ..... DIS, PLUTO
god of harvests ...... CRONUS
god of light, Norse
BALDR, BALDER, BALDUR
god of love, Gr. .... EROS
god of love, Rom. AMOR, CUPID
god of love, Vedic .... BHAGA
god of mirth .. COMUS, KOMOS
god (goddess) of mischief . ATE
god of michief, Norse
LOK, LOKE, LOKI
GOD OF MOON see MOON GOD
god of music .... APOLLO
god of north wind ... BOREAS
god of pleasure ..... BES, BESA
god of procreation, Egyp. MIN
god of prosperity, Teutonic FREY
god of revelry, Gr. ... COMUS,
KOMOS
god of ridicule .... MOMUS
GOD OF SEA .... see SEA GOD
GOD OF SKY .... see SKY GOD

c
God of Southeast Wind: Gr.
EURUS
GOD OF STORMS
see STORM GOD
GOD OF SUN .... see SUN GOD
god of thunder THOR, DONAR
god of Tuesday TIU, TIW, TYR
GOD OF UNDERWORLD
see UNDERWORLD GOD
god of war, Assyrian
ASUR, ASSUR
god of war, Babyl. . IRA, IRRA
god of war, Gr. .... ARES
god of war, Norse
TY, TYR, TYRR
god of war, Rom. .... MARS
god of war, Teut. .... ER
god of wind, Norse ... VAYU
god of wind, storm, Babylonian
ZU, ADAD, ADDA, ADDU
god of winds, Gr. ..... AEOLUS
god of wisdom, Babyl.
NABU, NEBO
god of wisdom, Norse .. ODIN
god of youth .... APOLLO
god skilled with bow, Norse ULL
god, Sumerian .... ABU
god, unknown, Hindu ..... KA
gods, Chief Teut., Norse AESIR
gods: Lat. .... DI

d
gods, mother of .... RHEA
gods, mother of: Ir. ANA, ANU
GODS, QUEEN OF
see QUEEN OF GODS
gods, the .... DEI, DII
GODDESS see also SPECIAL SECT.
GODDESS, CHIEF see BABY-
LONIAN CHIEF GODDESS
goddess, cow-headed ..... ISIS
goddess: Latin .... DEA
GODDESS, MOTHER
see MOTHER GODDESS
goddess of agriculture
CERES, DEMETER
goddess of art or science . MUSE
goddess of astronomy URANIA
goddess of beauty: Norse FREYA
goddess of betrothal, Norse VOR
goddess of chase .DIAN, DIANA
goddess of crops, Rom. ANNONA
goddess of dawn, Gr. ..... EOS
goddess of dawn, Rom.
AURORA
goddess of dawn, Vedic .. USAS
goddess of dead ... HEL, HELA
goddess of deep, Babyl. . NINA
goddess of destiny, Norse
URD, URTH
goddess of destruction ... ARA
goddess of discord .. ATE, ERIS
goddess of earth, Teut. . ERDA

goddess of earth ... **GE, ERDA, GAEA, GAIA, TARI**
goddess of earth: Rom. **CERES, TERRA**
goddess of faith, Rom. . **FIDES**
goddess of fate, Rom. **NONA, PARCA**
goddess of fate, Teutonic **NORN**
goddess of fertility **ASTARTE**
goddess of fertility, Anatolian **MA**
goddess of field, Rom. . **FAUNA**
goddess of flowers, Gr. **CHLORIS**
goddess of flowers, Norse **NANNA**
goddess of flowers, Rom. **FLORA**
goddess of grain **CERES, DEMETER**
goddess of harvest ...... **OPS**
goddess of harvest, Attica **CARPO**
goddess of healing ...... **EIR**
goddess of hearth ..... **VESTA**
goddess of heavens, Egyp. . **NUT**
goddess of hope .... **SPES**
goddess of hunt . **DIAN, DIANA**
goddess of infatuation .. **ATE**
goddess of justice . **MA, MAAT**
goddess of love ...... **VENUS, ASTARTE, APHRODITE**
goddess of love, Babylonian **ISTAR, ISHTAR**
goddess of love, Norse **FREYA, FREYJA**
goddess of magic .... **HECATE**
GODDESS OF MATERNITY see MATERNITY GODDESS
goddess of mischief .... **ATE**
GODDESS OF MOON see MOON GODDESS
goddess of nature **CYBELE, ARTEMIS**
GODDESS OF NIGHT, NORSE see NIGHT, NORSE
goddess of night: Rom. **NOX, NYX**
goddess of peace **IRENE, EIRENE**
goddess of plenty .... **OPS**
goddess of prosperity: Rom. **SALUS**
goddess of retribution .... **ATE**
goddess of retribution, Gr. **ARA**
goddess of revenge .. **NEMESIS**
GODDESS OF SEA see SEA GODDESS
goddess of seasons .... **HORAE**
goddess of splendor, Hindu **UMA**
goddess of truth, Egypt **MA, MAAT**
GODDESS OF UNDERWORLD see UNDERWORLD GODDESS

goddess of vegetation .. **CORA, KORE, CERES**
goddess of vengeance .... **ARA**
goddess of victory ...... **NIKE**
goddess of volcanoes, Hawaii **PELE**
goddess of war, Gr. .... **ENYO**
goddess of wisdom **ATHENA, PALLAS**
goddess of woods ...... **DIAN, DIANA, ARTEMIS**
goddess of youth .... **HEBE**
goddess, Queen .. **HERA, JUNO**
goddesses of destiny ... **FATES**
goddesses of fate, Gr. **MOERAE**
goddesses of fate, Norse **NORNS**
Goethe drama .... **FAUST**
Goethe heroine ...... **MIGNON**
golconda .... **MINE**
gold .... **AU, CYME, GILT**
gold alloy, ancient ..... **ASEM**
Gold Coast Negro .... **GA**
Gold Coast tong. **CHI, TWI, TSHI**
gold-colored metal . **ORMOLU**
gold, cover with .... **GILD**
gold deposit .... **PLACER**
gold district-field, Afr. .. **RAND**
gold: Her. .... **OR**
gold, mosaic .... **ORMOLU**
gold, pert. to .... **AURIC**
golden .... **AUREATE**
Golden Fleece keeper .. **AEETES**
Golden Fleece seeker .. **JASON**
golden in color .. **DORE, DURRY**
golden oriole .... **PIROL**
golden oriole, Eur. .... **LORIOT**
golden-touch king ..... **MIDAS**
golf attendant .. **CADY, CADDY**
golf club ...... **IRON, CLEEK, MASHIE, PUTTER**
golf club, part .... **TOE**
golf club socket .... **HOSEL**
golf hole .... **CUP**
golf pro .... **SNEAD**
golf score .... **PAR**
golf stroke-shot .. **PUT, BAFF, CHIP, LOFT, PUTT, DRIVE, SCLAFF**
golf term ..... **LIE, PAR, TEE**
golfer .... **TEER**
gomuti .... **ARENGA**
gondolier's song **BARCAROLE, BARCAROLLE**
gone .... **OUT, AWAY**
gone by .... **AGO, PAST, YORE**
gonfalon .... **BANNER**
good-bye: Fr. **ADIEU, AU REVOIR**
good digestion ..... **EUPEPSIA**
good health, in .... **PEART**
"Good King" .... **HAL**
good news **EVANGEL, EVANGILE**

Good

a "Good Queen Bess," name for ORIANA
good: Tagalog .... MABUTI
goods .... WARES
goods in sea .... JETSAM
goods sunk at sea
LAGAN, LIGAN
goose barnacle genus .. LEPAS
goose cry ...... HONK, YANG
goose genus .... ANSER
goose, male .... GANDER
goose, sea .... SOLAN
goose, wild .... BRANT
gooseberry .... FABES
gopher tortoise ... MUNGOFA
gorge .... GLUT, CHASM,
FLUME, RAVINE
Gorgons, one of ...... MEDUSA
gorse ... WHIN, WHUN, FURZE
goshawk genus . ASTUR, BUTEO
gospel ... EVANGEL, EVANGILE
gossamer .... WEB
gossip .... EME
gossip: India .... GUP
Gottfried's sister .... ELSA
gourd fruit .... PEPO
gourd rattle .... MARACA
gourmet .... EPICURE
gout of knee ...... GONAGRA
government .... STATE
b government control .... REGIE
STATISM
governor .... REGENT
governor, Mecca
SHERIF, SHEREEF
governor, Persia ..... SATRAP
governor, Turkish .... BEY
GOWN .... see GARMENT
grace .... ADORN
Graces' mother .... AEGLE
Graces, The . AGLAIA, THALIA
graceful .... GAINLY
grackle .... DAW, MINA,
MYNA, MYNAH
grade .... RANK, RATE,
SORT, STEP
gradient .... SLOPE
Graf —, ship .... SPEE
graft .... CION, SCION
grafted: Her. .... ENTE
Grail, Holy, finder of .... BORS
grain .... OAT, RYE, SEED,
WALE, SPELT, MILLET
grain beetle .... CADELLE
grain, chaff of .... BRAN
grain, coarse .... SAMP
grain given Romans . ANNONA
grain, sorghum, Ind., .. DARI,
DORA, DURR, MILO, CHENA,
DARRA, DARSO, DURRA,
DHURRA, DOURAH, HEGARI

c grain, sorghum, U. S. FETERITA
grain, stalks of ...... HAULM
grain to grind ...... GRIST
gram molecule .... MOL
grammatically, describe . PARSE
grampus .... ORC
granary, India
GOLA, GUNJ, GUNGE
grandparental .... AVAL
grandson, Adam's, Eve's. . ENOS
grant .... CEDE, MISE, REMISE
grant, India, Hindu .... ENAM
grant of rights
PATENT, CHARTER
granular snow .... FIRN, NEVE
grape .... UVA, MUSCAT,
CATAWBA, CONCORD
grape conserve .... UVATE
grape disease .... ESCA
grape genus .... VITIS
grape jelly .... SAPA
grape juice DIBS, MUST, STUM
grape juice sirup .... SAPA
grape-like .. UVA, UVAL, UVIC
grape-like fruit .... UVA
grape refuse .... MARC
grape, white .... MALAGA
grapefruit .. POMELO, PUMELO
graphite .... KISH
grasp .... SEIZE
d grass .... POA, REED, DARNEL
grass, Andes .... ICHU
grass, blue .... POA
grass, coarse .... REED, SEDGE
grass genus ...... AIRA, COIX,
AVENA, STIPA
grass, kind of .... RIE
grass, marsh .... REED
SEDGE, FESCUE
grass, N. Afr. .... ALFA
grass, pasture .... GRAMA
grass rope: Sp. .... SOGA
grass, rope-making
MUNG, MUNJ
grass, sour .... SORREL
grass stem .... CULM
grass tuft .... HASSOCK
grass, yard, wire .... POA
grasshopper .... GRIG
grassland
SAVANNA, SAVANNAH
grassland, S. Afr. ..... VELDT
grasslands, Western ... RANGE
grate ...... JAR, RASP, GRIDE
gratify . SATE, ARRIDE, PLEASE
grating . GRID, GRILL, GRILLE
gratuitous .... FREE
gratuity .... FEE, TIP
gratuity, customer ..... PILON
grave .... SOBER

70

a gravestone, Gr. & Rom. **STELA, STELE, STELAE, STELAI**
graving tool .... **STYLET**
Gray, botanist .... **ASA**
gray .... **OLD, HOAR, ASHEN, SLATE**
gray kingbird .... **PIPIRI**
gray, mole .... **TAUPE**
gray parrot .... **JAKO**
gray plaid, gray shawl .. **MAUD**
grayish-brown ... **DUN, TAUPE**
graze .... **AGIST, BROWSE**
grease ... **OIL, LARD, AXUNGE**
great barracuda ..... **PICUDA**
Great Barrier Island, N. Z. **OTEA**
"Great Emancipator" .... **ABE**
great: Gypsy .... **BARO**
greater .... **MORE, MAJOR**
Greece, ancient name . **HELLAS**
Greece, modern .... **ELLAS**
greedy .... **AVID**
Greek Letters, Numbers:
Greek A, One .... **ALPHA**
Greek B, Two .... **BETA**
Greek D, Four .... **DELTA**
Greek E, Eight .... **ETA**
Greek I, Ten .... **IOTA**
Greek M, Forty .... **MU**
b Greek N, Fifty .... **NU**
Greek O, 800 .... **OMEGA**
Greek P, Eighty .... **PI**
Greek R, 100 .... **RHO**
Greek T, 300 .... **TAU**
Greek Z, Seven .... **ZETA**
Greek 90 .... **KOPPA**
Greek 900 .... **SAMPI**
Gr. ancient .... **ATTIC**
Gr. assembly .... **AGORA**
Gr. athletic contest ...... **AGON**
Gr. authors .... **ZENO, AESOP, HOMER, PLATO, TIMON, HESIOD, PINDAR, SAPPHO, STRABO, THALES, PLUTARCH**
Gr. city, ancient **ELIS, SPARTA**
Gr. city, word for ..... **POLIS**
Gr. colony, ancient ... **IONIA**
Gr. column ... **DORIC, IONIC**
Gr. commonalty ...... **DEMOS**
Gr. community .... **DEME**
Gr. dialect ..... **EOLIC, AEOLIC**
Gr. district, ancient ... **ATTICA**
Gr. drama .... **MIME**
Gr. festival city .... **NEMEA**
Gr. galley **TRIREME, UNIREME**
Gr. garment .... **CHITON**
Gr. ghost .... **KER**
GREEK GODS, GODDESSES . see SPECIAL SECTION and see GODS, GODDESSES
Gr. hero ...... **AJAX, JASON**

c Gr. historian .... **CTESIAS**
Gr. January .... **GAMELION**
Gr. legendary hero ...... **IDAS**
Gr. market place ..... **AGORA**
Gr. meeting place of voters **PNYX**
Gr. musical term .. **MESE, NETE**
Gr. myth flier .... **ICARUS**
Gr. native .... **CRETAN**
Gr. patriarch .... **ARIUS**
Gr. philosopher **PLATO, THALES**
Gr. poet ..... **ARION, HOMER, PINDAR**
Gr. poetess ... **SAPHO, SAPPHO**
Gr. poetry, simple ..... **DORIC**
Gr. priest .... **MYST**
Gr. princess .... **IRENE**
Gr. province .... **NOME**
Gr. resistance group ..... **EDES**
Gr. rose .... **CAMPION**
Gr. sculptor .... **PHIDIAS**
Gr. shield .... **PELTA**
Gr. slave .... **PENEST**
Gr. statesman ..... **ARISTIDES**
Gr. temple .... **NAOS**
Gr. theologian .... **ARIUS**
Gr. township-commune .. **DEME**
Gr. underground .... **ELAS**
Gr. vase .... **PELIKE**
d Gr. weight, old .. **MNA, MINA**
green ..... **NILE, VERD, VERT, OLIVE, RESEDA**
green chalcedony ..... **JASPER**
green cheese .... **SAPSAGO**
green chrysolite ..... **PERIDOT**
green copper arsenate . **ERINITE**
green fly .... **APHID**
green: Her. .... **VERT**
Green Mountain hero ... **ALLEN**
green parrot: P. I. .... **CAGIT**
green stone ... **JADE, PERIDOT**
greenish yellow **OLIVE, RESEDA**
Greenland Eskimo .... **ITA**
Greenland geol. div. .... **KOME**
Greenland settlement, town, base ..... **ETAH**
Greenland's colonizer ... **ERIC**
greeting .. **AVE, HAIL, SALUTE**
gridiron .... **GRILL**
grief .... **DOLOR, DOLOUR**
griffon genus .... **GYPS**
grimalkin .... **CAT**
grinding .... **MOLAR**
grindstone, Indian ..... **MANO**
grit .... **SAND**
grivet .... **WAAG**
grivet monkey .... **TOTA**
grommet, naut. ..... **BECKET**
groom, India . **SAIS, SICE, SYCE**
groove .... **RUT, SCARF**

a groove, pilaster **STRIA, STRIAE**
grooved ..... **LIRATE, STRIATE**
grope .... **FEEL**
gross .... **CRASS**
ground grain .... **MEAL**
ground wheat-husk ..... **BRAN**
groundhog .... **MARMOT**
group .... **BAND, BODY,
CREW, TEAM**
group, animal ..... **NID, NYE,
HERD, NIDE, COVEY,
DROVE, CLUTCH**
grouper .... **MERO**
grouse .... **PTARMIGAN**
grouse, red: Scot. . **MUIRFOWL**
grove, small-tree ...... **COPSE**
grow .... **WAX, RAISE**
grow together ...... **ACCRETE**
growing out .... **ENATE**
growl .... **YAR, GNAR,
YARR, SNARL**
growth, skin .... **WEN**
grub .... **LARVA**
grudge .... **SPITE**
gruel, maize .... **ATOLE**
gruesome .. **GRISLY, MACABRE**
guarantees .... **SURETIES**

b guard .... **SENTRY**
guard, as door .... **TILE**
guardhouse .... **BRIG**
guardian, alert
ARGUS, CERBERUS
Guatemala fruit .... **ANAY**
guava .... **ARACA**
Gudrun's husband
ATLI, SIGURD
Guenon monkey .... **MONA**
guest house .... **INN**
Guiana tree .... **MORA**
guide .... **LEAD, PILOT, STEER**
guiding .... **POLAR**
guiding rule .... **MOTTO**
Guido's note .... **UT, ELA**
guild, merchants' ..... **HANSE**
guillemot ...... **COOT, MURR,
MURRE**
guilty .... **NOCENT**
guinea fowl's young ..... **KEET**
guinea pig .... **CAVY**
gulch: Sp. .... **ARROYO**
GULF, ... also see GAZETTEER
gulf, Ionia sea .... **ARTA**
gulf, Medit. .... **TUNIS**

c gull ..... **MEW, SKUA, TERN,
WAEG, XEMA**
gull, fork-tailed .... **XEMA**
gull genus ...... **LARI, XEMA**
gulls, of, like .... **LARINE**
gullet .... **MAW, CRAW**
gullible person .. **DUPE, GULL**
"Gulliver's Travels," men
YAHOOS
gully: Afr. .... **DONGA**
gulp .... **SWIG**
gum .... **RESIN, BALATA**
gum arabic
ACACIA, ACACIN, ACACINE
gum, astringent .... **KINO**
gum resin .... **ELEMI, LOBAN,
MYRRH**
gum resin, aromatic ... **MYRRH**
gum, Somaliland ..... **MATTI**
gums .... **ULA**
gumbo ... **OCRA, OKRA, OKRO**
gumbo limbo tree ... **GOMART**
gun .... **GAT**
gun, British .... **STEN**
gun fire, burst of ..... **SALVO**
gun, Ger. .... **BERTHA**

d gun, kind of .... **BREN**
gun lock catch .... **SEAR**
gun, P. I. .... **BARIL**
gun, slang ..... **ROD, HEATER
ROSCOE**
gun: S. Afr. ..... **ROER, ROHR**
gunny cloth .... **TAT**
gusto .... **ZEST**
gutta mixture .... **SOH**
gutta, Sumatra .... **SIAK**
guy-rope .. **STAT, STAY, VANG**
gym feat .... **KIP**
gymnast .... **TURNER**
gypsum, kind of . **YESO, GESSO,
YESSO, SELENITE**
gypsy .... **ROM, CALE, CALO,
ROAMER, ROMANY**
gypsy boy .... **ROM**
gypsy gentleman .... **RYE**
gypsy girl .... **CHAI**
gypsy husband .... **ROM**
gypsy lady .... **RANI**
gypsy married woman .. **ROMI**
gypsy: Sp. .... **GITANO**
gypsy tent, camp .... **TAN**
gypsy village .... **GAV**
gypsy word .... **LAY**
gypsy word for paper, book .**LIL**

H

H .... AITCH
habit .... RUT, WONT, USAGE
habitat plant form ..... ECAD
habitation .... ABODE
habituate ..... ENURE, INURE
habituated .... USED
hackney coach, Fr. .... FIACRE
hackneyed .... STALE, TRITE
Hades ... DIS, ORCUS, PLUTO,
        SHEOL, TARTARUS
Hades: Old Eng. .... ADES
Hades, place before .. EREBUS
Hades river
     STYX, LETHE, ACHERON
hag .... CRONE
haggard .... DRAWN
Haggard, H. Rider, novel .. SHE
hail .... AVE, GREET
hail: naut. .... AVAST
hair, arrange .... COIF
hair, caterpillar .... SETA
hair coat .... MELOTE
hair-do, old .... TETE
hair dressing .... POMADE
hair, false . RAT, WIG, TOUPEE
hair, head of .... CRINE
hair, knot of .. BUN, CHIGNON
hair, lock of .... CURL, TRESS
hair net .... SNOOD
hair, remove .... EPILATE
hair, rigid .... SETA
hair, rough, matted .... SHAG
hair shirt .... CILICE
hair, standing .... ROACH
hair unguent .... POMADE
hairless: Sp. Am. ...... PELON
hairlike process
        CILIA, CILIUM
hairy . PILAR, COMOSE, PILOSE
Haiti bandit .... CACO
Halcyone's husband .... CEYX
half .... MOIETY
half-boot .... PAC
half-breed ... MESTEE, MUSTEE
half-caste .... METIS
half-moon figure .... LUNE
half-way .... MID
halfway house .... INN
halfpenny: Brit. .... MAG
hall: Ger. ...... AULA, SAAL
hallow .... BLESS
halo .... NIMB, CORONA,
   NIMBUS, AUREOLA, AUREOLE
halt .... LAME, STOP
halting place, troops' .. ETAPE
Hamilton's party .... FEDERAL

Hamite .... SOMAL, BERBER,
              SOMALI
Hamitic language AGAO, AGAU
hamlet ... BURG, DORP, TOWN
Hamlet's castle .... ELSINORE
hammer .... KEVEL
hammer head part ...... PEEN
hammer, heavy .... MAUL
hammer, large .... SLEDGE
hammer, lead .... MADGE
hammer, tilt .... OLIVER
hamper ..... CRAMP, FETTER,
              TRAMMEL
Ham's son .... CUSH
hand .... PUD, NEAF, MANUS
hand, pert. to .... CHIRAL
hand, whist .... TENACE
handbill .... LEAF
handcuff .... MANACLE
handle .... EAR, LUG, PAW,
         ANSA, HILT, KNOB,
         HELVE, TREAT
handle, bench plane .... TOTE
handle, having ...... ANSATE
handle roughly ... PAW, MAUL
handle, scythe .... SNATH,
    SNEAD, SNEED, SNATHE
handstone for grinding . MANO
handwriting .... SCRIPT
handwriting on the wall . MENE,
    MENE, TEKEL, UPHARSIN
hang .... DRAPE, DROOP,
         HOVER, IMPEND
hank of twine .... RAN
Hannibal's defeat ...... ZAMA
Hannibal's victory .. CANNAE
happen ...... OCCUR, BEFALL,
         BETIDE, CHANCE
happening .... EVENT
happiness god, Jap.
         EBISU, HOTEI
harangue .... ORATE,
         TIRADE, DIATRIBE
Haran's son .... LOT
harass .... NAG, BESET
harbinger .... HERALD
harbor .... BAY, COVE,
         PORT, HAVEN
hard cash .... SPECIE
harden .... GEL, SET
    ENURE, INURE, INDURATE
hardship .... TRIAL
hardtack .... PANTILE
hardwood .... ASH, OAK
Hardy novel heroine ..... TESS
hare: dialect .... WAT

73

a hare, genus .... **LEPUS**
hare, young, 1 year .. **LEVERET**
harem ... **ZENANA, SERAGLIO**
harem room .... **ODA**
harlot of Jericho, Bibl. . **RAHAB**
harm .**BANE, DAMAGE, INJURE**
harm: old Eng. .... **DERE**
harm: poetic .... **BALE**
harmful .... **NOCENT**
harmonize .... **ATTUNE**
harmony .. **UNISON, CONCORD**
harp, ancient .... **TRIGON**
Harp constellation ...... **LYRA**
harp guitar key .... **DITAL**
harp, kind of .... **EOLIC**
harp, Nubian .... **NANGA**
harpy, Gr. myth .... **AELLO**
harquebus projection .... **CROC**
harrow .... **DRAG**
harsh to taste .... **ACERB**
hartebeeste ..... **ASSE, TORA,**
CAAMA, KAAMA
harvest .... **REAP**
harvest festival, Rom. . **OPALIA**
harvest goddess .... **OPS**
harvest, India ... **RABI, RABBI**
has not: Old Eng. .... **NAS**
hashish .... **BHANG**
hasty pudding .... **SEPON**
HAT .... see HEADGEAR
b hat: Anglo-Ir. .... **CAUBEEN**
hat plant .... **SOLA**
hat, straw .. **MILAN, PANAMA**
hatchet, archeol. .... **HACHE**
hatchet, stone .... **MOGO**
hatred .... **ODIUM, AVERSION**
hatred: Buddhism ...... **DOSA**
hatter's mallet .... **BEATER**
haul tight, naut. .. **BOUSE, TRICE**
haunt, low .. **DEN, DIVE, NEST**
hautboy .... **OBOE**
haven .... **LEE**
having buttery account:
Oxford .... **BATTEL**
having holes, as cheese **EYEY**
having true luster when uncut
NAIF
haw!: P.I. .... **MANO**
haw, as cattle .... **HOI**
Hawaiian bird .. **IO, O-O, IIWI**
Hawaiian bird, extinct . **MAMO**
Hawaiian bird, red-tailed **KOAE**
Hawaiian blueberry ... **OHELO**
Hawaiian chant .... **MELE**
Hawaiian cloth .. **TAPA, KAPA**
Hawaiian cudweed ... **ENAENA**
Hawaiian dance .... **HULA**
Hawaiian farewell, greeting
ALOHA
Hawaiian feather cloak . **MAMO**
Hawaiian fern .... **HEII**

c Hawaiian floral emblem **LEHUA**
Hawaiian food .... **POI**
Hawaiian food-game fish .**ULUA**
Hawaiian garland .... **LEI**
Hawaiian god .... **KANE**
Hawaiian goddess, fire .. **PELE**
Hawaiian goose .... **NENE**
Hawaiian gooseberry .... **POHA**
Hawaiian governor, 1st . **DOLE**
Hawaiian grass .... **HILO**
Hawaiian hawk .... **IO**
Hawaiian herb .... **HOLA**
Hawaiian loincloth .... **MALO**
Hawaiian musical instrument
PUA
Hawaiian porch .... **LANAI**
Hawaiian president, 1st .. **DOLE**
Hawaiian royal chief ... **ALII**
Hawaiian shrub .... **AKIA**
Hawaiian staple .... **POI**
Hawaiian starch .... **APII**
Hawaiian timber tree ... **OHIA**
Hawaiian tree
KOA, AULU, ALANI, ILIAHI
Hawaiian tree, dark .... **AALII**
Hawaiian tree fern ..... **PULU**
Hawaiian vine .... **IE**
Hawaiian volcano goddess.**PELE**
Hawaiian windstorm .... **KONA**
hawk .... **KITE**
d hawk, falconry .... **BATER**
hawk, fish .... **OSPREY**
hawk genus .... **BUTEO**
hawk-head god, Egypt . **HORUS**
hawk, India .... **SHIKRA**
hawk-like bird .... **KITE**
hawk, Scot. .... **ALLAN**
hawk, young ..... **BRANCHER**
hawks .... **IOS**
hawk's cage .... **MEW**
hawk's leash .... **LUNE**
hawthorn .... **MAY**
hawthorn berry .... **HAW**
hay, spread to dry .... **TED**
haystack .... **RICK**
hazard .... **DARE, RISK, PERIL**
hazardous .... **CHANCY**
haze: Old Eng. .... **HASE**
hazelnut .... **FILBERT**
hazy, make ..... **DIM, BEDIM**
"he remains": Lat. ... **MANET**
head ..... **NOB, LEAD, PATE,**
POLL, TETE, CAPUT, CHIEF,
CAPITA, LEADER, NODDLE,
NOODLE
head covering .... **CAP, HAT,**
TAM, HOOD, VEIL, BERET
head covering, fleecy .. **NUBIA**
head, crown of .... **PATE**
head, having round ... **RETUSE**
head, membrane covering **CAUL**

a head, Moslem .... RAIS, REIS
head of Benjamin's clan .. IRI
head, shaved .... TONSURE
head: slang .... NOGGIN
head wrap .... NUBIA, SHAWL
headband, Gr. .... TAENIA
HEADDRESS
          see also HEADGEAR
headdress, bishop's
          MITER, MITRE
headgear, brimless ..... TOQUE
headgear, clerical
          BERETTA, BIRETTA
headgear, dervish .... TAJ
headgear, kind of ... PANAMA
headgear, military .... SHAKO
headgear, Moslem .. TARBUSH,
    TARBOOCH, TARBOOSH,
          TARBOUCHE
headgear, poetic .... TIAR
headgear, priest's
          BERETTA, BIRETTA
headgear, tropics
    TOPI, TERAI, TOPEE
headgear, Turk. .... FEZ
headland .. RAS, CAPE, NASE,
          NESS, NOZE
headless: Her. .... ETETE
headstrong .... RASH
healing goddess .... EIR
health, in good .... FIT

b health-drinking word
    SALUD, PROSIT
health resort .... SPA
heap ...... PILE, RAFF, RAFT
hear ye! .... OYES, OYEZ
hearing: law .... OYER
hearken .. HEAR, HEED, LIST,
          ATTEND, LISTEN
heart .... COR, CORE
heart auricle . ATRIA, ATRIUM
heart contraction .... SYSTOLE
heart, immortal, Egyp. .... AB
heart trouble .... ANGINA
heartleaf .... MEDIC
heartless ... CRUEL, SARDONIC
heat .... WARM, CALOR
heated to whiteness .CANDENT
heath .... MOOR
heath genus .... ERICA
heathen .... PAGAN
heathen god .... IDOL
heather .... LING, ERICA
heating apparatus, vessel .ETNA
heave upward .... SCEND
heaven .. SION, ZION, URANO
heaven, eagle-borne flier to
          ETANA
heaven personified: Babyl.. ANU
heavens, pert. to .... URANIC
heavenly .... EDENIC

c heavenly being .... ANGEL
    SERAPH, SERAPHIM
heavenly Jerusalem SION, ZION
heavy blow .... ONER
HEBREW see also JEWISH
          and BIBLICAL
Hebr. Bible books .... NEBIIM
Hebr. Bible pronunciation aid
    GRI, KRI, KERE, KERI,
    QERE, QERI, QUERI
Hebr. drum .... TOPH
Hebr. dry measure .. CAB, KAB
Hebr. lyre .... ASOR
Hebr. measure .... KOR, EPHA,
          OMER, EPHAH
Hebr. precept .... TORA
HEBREW PROPHETS . see
    SPECIAL SECTION, Page 196
Hebr. proselyte .... GER
Hebr. reclaimer .... GOEL
Hebr. teacher ...... RAB, REB
Hebr. universe .... OLAM
Hebrews' ancestor, legend
          EBER
Hector's mother ..... HECUBA
hedge plant .... PRIVET
hedgerow: Eng. .... REW
heed .... HEAR, MIND,
          OBEY, RECK
heel .... CAD, CALX
d height .... STATURE
heir .... SON, SCION,
    HERITOR, LEGATEE
held, able to be .... TENABLE
Helen: It. .... ELENA
Helen of Troy's mother . LEDA
Helen's lover .... PARIS
helical .... SPIRAL
Helios .... SUN
hell .... HADES, SHEOL
Hellespont swimmer . LEANDER
helm position .... ALEE
helmet, light .... SALLET
helmet, medieval
          ARMET, HEAUME
helmet, Rom. .... GALEA
helmet-shaped ...... GALEATE
helmet-shaped part ... GALEA
helmsman .... PILOT
Heloise's husband ... ABELARD
help .. AID, ABET, BACK, TIDE,
    ASSIST, SUCCOR, SUCCOUR
helper .... AIDE
Helvetic .... SWISS
hem in .... BESET
hemp .... TOW, RINE, RAMIE
hemp, Afr. .... IFE
hemp, India .... KEF, BANG,
    KEEF, KEIF, KIEF, BHANG,
    DAGGA, RAMIE
hemp, Manila .... ABACA

a
hemp narcotic ...... **CHARAS**
hemp shrub, India
  PUA, POOA, POOAH
hen .... **LAYER**
hen harrier, Europ. .... **FALLER**
hence .... **SO, OFF, AWAY**
Hengist's brother ..... **HORSA**
Henry IV birthplace ...... **PAU**
"Henry IV" character ... **PETO**
"Henry V" knave ...... **NYM**
"Henry VI" character ... **IDEN**
hep .... **ONTO**
her: obs. .... **HIR**
Hera's son .... **ARES**
herald .... **USHER**
HERALDIC TERMS . see also
  SPECIAL SECTION, Page 194
herald's coat .... **TABARD**
heraldic bearing **ORLE, FILLET**
heraldic cross .... **PATEE**
heraldic wreath .... **ORLE**
herb ..... **RUE, LEEK, MINT,**
  MOLY, WORT, ANISE, TANSY,
  YARROW, OREGANO
herb, aromatic **BASIL, DITTANY**
herb, bitter ...... **RUE, ALOE**
herb, carrot family .... **ANISE**
herb eve .... **IVA**
herb, fabulous **MOLY, PANACE**
herb, forage .... **SULLA**

b
herb genus .... **ABFA**
  GEUM, RUTA, ALETRIS
herb, medicinal .. **ALOE, SENNA**
herb of grace .... **RUE**
herb, snake-charm .... **MUNGO**
herb with aromatic root .**NONDO**
herb, wooly .... **POLY**
Hercules' captive .... **IOLE**
Hercules, monster slain by
  HYDRA
Hercules' mother .. **ALCMENE**
herd .... **DROVE**
herd of horses .... **CAVIYA**
herd of whales .... **GAM, POD**
herdsman, Swiss .... **SENN**
hereditary right .... **UDAL**
hereditary factor .. **GEN, GENE**
heretic, 4th cent.
  ARIAN, ARIUS
heretofore .... **ERENOW**
Hermes' mother .... **MAIA**
Hermes' son .... **PAN**
hermit . **EREMITE, ANCHORITE**
hero, legendary .... **PALADIN**
Hero's love .... **LEANDER**
heroic .... **EPIC, EPICAL**
heroic poem **EPIC, EPOS, WORK**
heroic song .... **EDDA**
heron .... **EGRET**
heron brood, flock .... **SEDGE**
heron, kind of ...... **BITTERN**

c
herring .... **ALEC, BRIT, SILL**
herring, grayback ..... **CISCO**
herring keg .... **CADE**
herring small Eur. ...... **SPRAT**
hesitate
  DEMUR, FALTER, TEETER
hesitation syllable .... **ER, UM**
Hesperides, one of .... **AEGLE**
Heyward, Du Bose, heroine.**BESS**
Hezekiah's mother .... **ABI**
hiatus .... **GAP, LACUNA**
hickory tree ...... **SHELLBARK**
hidden ..... **INNER, ARCANE,**
  COVERT, LATENT
hide .... **VEIL, CACHE**
hide of beast ..... **FELL, SKIN**
hide, thongs of .... **RIEM**
hide, undressed .... **KIP**
hides, Russian leather ... **JUFTI**
hiding in .... **PERDU**
high in pitch: mus. ...... **ALT**
high on scale .... **ELA**
high priest ...... **ELI, AARON,**
  ANNAS
highest note .... **ELA**
highest point .. **APEX, ZENITH**
highway .... **ITER, PIKE**
highway, Alaska-Canada **ALCAN**
highwayman .. **PAD, LADRONE**
hike .... **TRAMP**

d
hill .... **TOR**
hill, broad .... **LOMA, LOMITA**
hill dweller, Ceylon .... **TODA**
hill dweller, India ..... **DOGRA**
hill, flat-topped .... **MESA**
hill fort: Ir. .... **RATH**
hill, isolated .... **BUTTE**
hill, pointed .... **TOR**
hill, Rome
  CAELIAN, PALATINE
hill, S. Afr. ...... **KOP, BULT**
hill: Turk. .... **DAGH**
hillock .... **TUMP**
hillside: Scot. .... **BRAE**
hilltop .... **KNAP**
hilt, sword .... **HAFT, HANDLE**
Himalayan animal .... **PANDA**
Himal. broadmouth ..... **RAYA**
Himal. ibex .... **KYL**
Himal. monkshood ...... **ATIS**
Himal. mountain .... **API**
Himal. wild goat . **KRAS, TAHR,**
  TAIR, THAR
hind ...... **ROE, BACK, REAR**
hinder by fear .... **DETER**
hindrance .... **BAR, LET**
Hindu age, cycle .... **YUGA**
Hindu ancestor .... **MANU**
Hindu ascetic .... **JOGI,**
  YATI, YOGI, FAKIR,
  SADHU, FAKEER

a Hindu bible .... **VEDA**
Hindu charitable gift ... **ENAM**
Hindu cymbal .... **TAL**
Hindu deity .... **DEVA, RAMA,
SIVA, SHIVA**
HINDU DEITY . see also GOD
and see SPECIAL SECTION
Hindu divorce law ..... **TALAK**
Hindu female slave ..... **DASI**
Hindu festival .... **HOLI**
Hindu festival, religious . **PUJA**
Hindu gentlemen **BABU, BABOO**
HINDU GODS .... see SPECIAL
SECTION, Page 200, and
also GOD
Hindu guitar .... **BINA,
VINA, SITAR**
Hindu holy man .... **SADH**
Hindu laws, giver of ... **MANU**
Hindu legendary hero ... **NALA**
Hindu life energy .... **JIVA**
Hindu, low caste .... **KORI**
Hindu magic .... **MAYA**
Hindu mantra .... **OM**
Hindu mendicant ...... **NAGA**
Hindu monastery ...... **MATH**
Hindu "Olympus" ...... **MERU**
Hindu philosophy ...... **YOGA**
Hindu poet .... **TAGORE**
Hindu prince
RAJA, RANA, RAJAH
b Hindu progenitor, myth **MANU**
Hindu queen .... **RANI, RANEE**
Hindu religious adherent
JAIN, JAINA
Hindu rites .... **ACHARA**
Hindu sacred literature .. **VEDA**
Hindu sacred word .... **OM**
Hindu scripture ...... **AGAMA**
Hindu scriptures, pert. to **VEDIC**
Hindu sect, one of **SEIK, SIKH**
Hindu teacher .... **GURU**
Hindu temple .... **DEUL**
Hindu term of respect **SAHIB**
Hindu title .... **AYA, SRI**
Hindu trader
BANIAN, BANYAN
Hindu unknown god ...... **KA**
Hindu, unorthodox .... **JAINA**
Hindu widow, suicide .. **SUTTEE**
Hindu woman's garment
SARI, SAREE
Hindu word .... **OM**
Hindu writings .... **VEDA**
Hinduism, elixir
AMRITA, AMREETA
Hindustani .... **URDU**
hinge, kind of .... **BUTT**
hint .... **TIP, CLEW, POINTER**
hip .... **COXA, ILIA, ILIAC**
hipbone, of the .... **ILIAC**

c Hippocrates' birthplace ... **KOS**
Hippodrome .... **ARENA**
hire
LET, RENT, ENGAGE, CHARTER
hired carriage .... **HACK**
hired labor: S. Afr. ..... **TOGT**
history .... **LORE**
hitherto .... **YET**
Hittites ancestor .... **HETH**
hive for bees .... **SKEP**
hives .... **UREDO**
hoard .... **AMASS, STORE**
hoarder .... **MISER**
hoarfrost .... **RIME**
hoarfrost: Eng. .... **RAG**
hoary .... **OLD, GRAY**
hoax .... **RUSE, CANARD**
hobgoblin ..... **PUCK, SPRITE**
hock, horse's ...... **GAMBREL**
hockey ball .... **ORR**
hodgepodge ..... **MESS, OLIO**
hog cholera .... **ROUGET**
hog deer .... **AXIS**
hog, female .... **GILT**
hog plum, W. Ind. **AMRA, JOBO**
hog, wild .... **BOAR, PECCARY**
hog's heart, liver, etc. **HASLET**
Hogan, golfer .... **BEN**
hoist .... **HEAVE**
hold, as in war .... **INTERN**
d hold back .... **DETER**
hold fast: naut. ...... **BELAY**
holding .... **TENURE**
holding device .. **VISE, TONGS**
hole for molten metal .. **SPRUE**
hole in embankment .... **GIME**
hole in mold .... **GEAT**
hole-in-one .... **ACE**
holidays, Roman .... **FERIA**
HOLLAND see NETHERLANDS
SPECIAL SECTION
hollow .... **DENT, HOWE**
holly .... **HOLM, ILEX**
holly, U. S. .... **ASSI,
YAPON, YUPON, YAUPON**
holm oak .... **ILEX**
"Holy Hill," Gr. .... **ATHOS**
Holy Land city .... **DAN**
holy orders, give .... **ORDAIN**
holy water font .... **STOUP**
homage .... **HONOR**
home .... **ABODE**
home of gods, Norse .. **ASGARD**
"Home Sweet Home" author
PAYNE
homeopath school-founder
HERING
Homer's epic .... **ODYSSEY**
hominy, Indian coarse .. **SAMP**
honey .... **MEL**
honey-badger .... **RATEL**

a honey buzzard .... PERN
honey drink .. MEAD, MORAT
honey eater bird
　　　IAO, MOHO, MANUAO
honeybee .... DESERET
honeycomb, like a ... FAVOSE
honor .... EXALT, REVERE
honorarium .... TIP
honorary commission .. BREVET
Honshu bay .... ISE
Honshu port .... KOBE
hooded garment ...... PARKA
hoodoo .... JINX, JYNX
hoof ...... UNGUES, UNGUIS
hook, bent into ..... HAMATE
hook, double curve .... ESS
hook, engine .... GAB
hook for pot .... CLEEK
hook money .... LARI, LARIN
hooks .... HAMI
hookah .... NARGILE
hooked .... HAMUS,
　　HAMATE, HAMOSE, FALCATE
Hoover Dam lake ...... MEAD
hop-picker's basket ...... BIN
hope goddess, Rom. ..... SPES
hop plant .... LUPULUS
hopscotch stone ...... PEEVER
Horae, one of .... DIKE,
　　　　EIRENE, EUNOMIA
Horeb .... SINAI
b horizontal stripe .... BAR
horizontal timber ..... LINTEL
horn .... CORNU
horn, crescent-moon ..... CUSP
horn, Hebr. SHOFAR, SHOPHAR
horn quicksilver ..... CALOMEL
horn-shaped structure .. CORNU
horn sounded for kill .. MORT
horn tissue, bit of ..... SCUR
horneblende .... EDENITE
hornless, Eng. dial. ...... NOT
hornless stag .... POLLARD
hors d'oeuvre .... CANAPE
horse .. BAY, COB, NAG, ARAB,
　　MARE, MERE, ROAN,
　　MOUNT, STEED, EQUINE,
　　JENNET
horse, Austral. .... WALER
horse, Barbary native ... BARB
horse blanket .... MANTA
horse breed .... MORGAN
horse, brown
　　　BAY, ROAN, SORREL
horse color BAY, ROAN, SORREL
horse dealer, Eng. .... COPER
horse, disease of .... SPAVIN
horse, draft .... SHIRE
horse genus .... EQUUS
horse: gypsy .. GRI, GRY, GRAS
horse-mackerel .... SCAD

c horse-man, myth ... CENTAUR
horse, piebald .... PINTO
horse, race .... PACER
horse-radish, fruit of ... BEN
horse, saddle .... MOUNT
horse, small .... GENET,
　　GENNET, JENNET, GENETTE
horse, Sp. Am. ...... CABALLO
horse, swift .. ARAB, COURSER
horse, talking, Gr. .... ARION
horse, war .... CHARGER
horse, white-flecked ... ROAN
horse, wild Asiatic ... TARPAN
horse, young ..... COLT, FOAL
horses, goddess of ..... EPONA
horse's sideways tread ... VOLT
horsehair .... SETON
horsemanship, art of MANEGE
horseshoe gripper ...... CALK
horseshoeing stall
　　　　TRAVE, TREVE
Horus' mother .... ISIS
Hosea's wife .... GOMER
host .... ARMY, HORDE
hostelry .... INN
hot air chamber .... OVEN
hot iron to sear ..... CAUTER
hot spring, eruptive .. GEYSER
Hottentot .... NAMA
hourly .... HORAL
d house ROOF, VILLA, COTTAGE
house, like a .... DOMAL
house, mud, Afr. ..... TEMBE
house urn: Rom. ... CAPANNA
housefly genus ..... MUSCA
housefly genus, lesser FANNIA
household MENAGE, MAINPOST
household god .... LAR, LARES
howl .... ULULATE
howling monkey MONO, ARABA
hub .. NAVE, BOSTON, CENTER
hubbub .. ADO, STIR, TUMULT
hue .... COLOR, TINGE
huge .... VAST, ENORM
Huguenot leader ..... ADRETS
hull .... POD, HUSK
humble .... ABASE
hummingbird
　　　AVA, TOPAZ, COLIBRI
humorist .... WIT
humpback salmon
　　　　HADDO, HOLIA
Humphreys, Mrs. (pseudo.)
　　　　　　　RITA
hundred .... CENTUM
hundredweight ...... CENTAL
Hungarian dog .... PULI
Hungarian hero .... NAGY
Hungarian king .... BELA
Hungarian people ... MAGYAR
Hungarian pianist ... SANDOR

a Hungarian playwright **MOLNAR**
Hungarian violinist .... **AUER**
Huns, king of
        ATLI, ETZEL, ATTILA
hunt, Ind. .... **SHIKAR**
hunter ...... **ORION, NIMROD**
hunter, India .... **SHIKARI**
hunting cry .. **HO, YOI, TOHO,
    HALLOO, YOICKS, TALLY-
    HO**
hunting hat .... **TERAI**
hunting hound .... **ALAN**
huntress .... **ATALANTA**
huntsman .... **JAGER**
HUNTSMAN'S CRY see HUNT-
    ING CRY
hup: army .... **ONE**
hurdy-gurdy ..... **LIRA, ROTA**
hurry .... **HIE, HASTEN**
hurt .... **MAR, ACHE, LESION**

c hurt: old Eng. .... **DERE**
hurtful .... **MALEFIC**
husband's brother ...... **LEVIR**
hush .... **SH, HSH**
husk, cereal .... **BRAN**
hut, India .... **BARI**
hut, Mex. .... **JACAL**
hydrate, as lime ..... **SLAKE**
hydraulic pump .... **RAM**
hydrocarbon . **TOLAN, ETHANE,
    OCTANE, RETENE, TERPENE**
hydrogen compound ... **IMINE**
hydrogen isotope ... **PROTIUM**
hymn .... **ODE**
hymn of praise ..... **ANTHEM**
hypnotic state ...... **TRANCE**
hypothetical force
        OD, BIOD, ELOD, ODYL
hypothetical force of ... **ODIC**
hyson .... **TEA**

I

b I .... **EGO**
"I have found it" .... **EUREKA**
"I love": Lat. .... **AMO**
Iago's wife .... **EMILIA**
Iberians .... **IBERI, IBERES**
ibex .... **KYL, TUR, KAIL**
Ibsen character ... **ASE, NORA**
ice block, glacial ...... **SERAC**
ice mass .... **BERG, FLOE**
ice, slushy ...... **SISH, LOLLY**
iced .... **GLACE**
Iceland epic, literature, tales
        EDDA
Icelandic narrative ..... **SAGA**
icy .... **GELID**
"id —" (that is) .... **EST**
idea, Plato .... **EIDOS**
ideal .... **UTOPIAN**
ideal republic, imaginary
        OCEANA
ideal state .... **UTOPIA**
identical .... **ONE, SAME**
ideology .... **ISM**
idiocy .... **ANOESIA**
idiot .... **AMENT, CRETIN**
idle .... **OTIANT, OTIOSE**
idle, to be ...... **LAZE, LOAF**
idol: archaic .... **PAGOD**
idol: philos. .... **EIDOLON**
idolatrous .... **PAGAN**
ids, pert. to .... **IDIC**
Idumaea .... **EDOM**
if ever .... **ONCE**
if not .... **ELSE**
ignoble .... **BASE**

d Ignominy .... **SHAME**
ignorance, Hindu philos. **TAMAS**
ignorant .. **STUPID, UNAWARE**
ignore .... **ELIDE**
Igorot's neighbor tribesman **ATA**
ill .... **EVIL**
ill-will .... **SPITE, RANCOR**
illumination unit .... **LUX**
illusion .... **CHIMERA**
illusory riches .... **MINE**
image .... **IDOL,
    IDOLON, IDOLUM, EIDOLON**
image, pert. to ...... **ICONIC**
image, religious .. **ICON, IKON**
imagine: arch. .... **WIS**
imbecile .... **AMENT,
        ANILE, CRETIN**
imbibe .... **SIP, GULP, DRINK**
imitate ... **APE, MIME, MIMIC**
imitation .... **MIMESIS**
imitation gems .... **PASTE**
immature seed .... **OVULE**
immature: zool. ..... **NEANIC**
immeasurable ..... **BOUNDLESS**
immediately ..... **NOW, ANON**
immense .... **VAST**
immerse .. **DIP, DUNK, DOUSE**
immigrant, Greek ..... **METIC**
immunizing substance
    SERUM, HAPTEN, HAPTENE
imou pine .... **RIMU**
impair .. **MAR, DAMAGE, SPOIL**
impart .... **GIVE, LEND**
impartial .... **EVEN**
impede ...... **ESTOP, HAMPER**
impel .... **URGE**

a
impertinent ..... **PERT, SAUCY**
IMPLEMENT ... see also **TOOL**
implement, pounding .. **PESTLE**
implement to skid logs .. **TODE**
implied .... **TACIT**
import .... **SENSE**
important, critically ... **VITAL**
importune .... **URGE**
impose .... **LAY**
impost .... **TAX**
imposture .... **SHAM**
impoverish .... **IMPOOR**
impressionist painter .. **DEGAS**
    MANET, MONET, RENOIR
imprison .... **IMMURE**
improve .... **AMEND**
improvise music .... **VAMP**
impudence .... **LIP,**
    BRASS, CHEEK, NERVE
impure metal product .. **MATTE**
in addition .. **TOO, ALSO, YET**
in agreement .... **UNITED**
in disagreement .... **OUT**
in half, in — .... **TWO**
"in medias —" .... **RES**
in name only ...... **NOMINAL**
in same place .... **IBID**
in so far as .... **QUA**
in the know .... **AWARE**
in the matter of .... **INRE**
in the past .... **OVER**

b
in the very near future..**ANON**
in unison .... **ONE**
in very truth .... **AMEN**
inability to hear ..... **ASONIA**
inactive .... **INERT**
inadequate .... **SCANT**
inborn .... **NATIVE**
incarnation, Hindu .... **RAMA,**
    AVATAR
incense ingredient
    GUM, SPICE, STACTE
incense receptacle, Rom.**ACERRA**
incense, Somali .... **MATTI**
incentive .... **GOAD, MOTIVE**
incessantly .... **EVER**
inch, .001 of .... **MIL**
incidentally .... **OBITER**
incinerate .... **CREMATE**
incite ..... **EGG, PROD, URGE,**
    IMPEL, SET ON, SUBORN
inciter .... **EGGER**
inclination .... **BENT**
incline .. **TEND, SLOPE, TREND**
inclined .... **APT, PRONE**
inclined way .... **RAMP**
income, annual, Fr. ..... **RENTE**
incompletely .... **SEMI**
inconsiderable ..... **NOMINAL**
increase .... **WAX, RISE**
incrustation .... **SCAB**

c
incursion, predatory .... **RAID**
indeed: Ir. ...... **ARU, AROO**
indentation
    CRENA, CRENAE, CRENELET
index mark .... **FIST**
INDIA, INDIAN ... see also
    SPECIAL SECTION and see
    also HINDU
India farmer .... **MEO**
India minstrel .... **BHAT**
India native chief .... **SIRDAR**
India native servant ... **MATY**
India: poet. .... **IND**
India, swamp belt of .. **TERAI**
INDIAN .. see also page 192
Indian .... **SAC**
INDIAN, ALGONQUIN .... see
    page 192
Indian, Arawak ...... **ARAUA**
Indian, Arikara .... **REE**
Indian, Athapasca ..... **TAKU**
Indian buzzard .... **TESA**
Indian corn .... **MAIZE**
Indian corn: N. Z. ... **KANGA**
Indian elk .... **SAMBAR**
Indian farmer, Fla. .. **CALUSA**
Indian in Chaco .... **TOBA**
Indian mahogany tree .. **TOON**
Indian mulberry **AL, AAL, ACH**
Indian of Jalisco ...... **CORA**
Indian of Keresan .... **SIA**
Indian of Mex., scattered **CORA**

d
Indian ox .... **ZEBU**
Indian, Panamint .... **KOSO**
INDIAN, PLAINS . see page 193
Indian race .... **JAT**
Indian shell currency
    ULO, UHLLO
INDIAN, SIOUAN see page 193
Indian, S. Peru ..... **CHANCA**
INDIAN TREE.see TREE, INDIA
Indian, warlike ...... **APACHE**
Indian weight ..... **SER, TOLA**
Indian, whaler .... **HOH**
Indian yellow .... **PURI,**
    PIURI, PURREE
Indicating succession **ORDINAL**
indict .... **ARRAIGN**
indifferent to pain
    STOIC, STOICAL
indigo plant .... **ANIL**
indistinct, make ...... **BEDIM**
indite .... **PEN, WRITE**
individual .... **ONE, SELF**
Indo-Chin. native **LAO,MRU,TAI**
Indo-Chin. tribe **TAI,LAOS,SHAN**
Indo-Chin. tribes ...... **MOI**
Indo-European **ARYA, ARYAN**
Indo-Malayan animal .. **NAPU**
indolent ...... **OTIOSE, SUPINE**
Indonesian ..... **ATA, NESIOT**

a

Induce .... **LEAD**
Indus tribesman .... **GOR**
ineffectual .... **VAIN**
inelastic .... **LIMP**
inert .... **SUPINE**
infatuation .... **ATE**
infertile moor .... **LANDE**
infinity .... **OLAM**
infirm .... **ANILE, SENILE**
inflamed, be .... **RANKLE**
inflammable liquid .. **ACETONE**
inflammation: med. .. **ANGINA**
inflexible .... **IRON, RIGID**
inflict .... **DEAL, IMPOSE**
inflorescence **RACEME, SPADIX**
inflorescence, racemose **AMENT**
influence .... **AFFECT**
informer: slang .... **NARK**
infusion .... **TEA**
ingenuous .... **NAIVE**
inhabitant .... **ITE**
inhabitant of a town ..... **CIT**
inheritance .... **ENTAIL**
inheritor .... **LEGATEE**
initiate ... **OPEN, BEGIN, START**
initiate, Gr. ... **EPOPT, EPOPTA**
injure ... **MAR, HARM, MAIM**
injury ...... **LESION, TRAUMA**
inlaid .... **MOSAIC**
inlaid decoration .... **BUHL**

b

inlet .. **ARM, BAY, RIA, FIORD**
inlet: Dutch .... **ZEE**
inlet, Orkneys .... **VOE**
inn .... **KHAN,**
    HOSTEL, POSADA, HOSPICE
Inn, "Canterbury Tales" **TABARD**
inn, Oriental .... **SERAI**
inn, Turkish .... **IMARET**
inner .... **ENTAL**
inner meaning .. **CORE, HEART**
inner parlor: Scot. ...... **BEN**
innkeeper **PADRONE, BONIFACE**
insect ... **ANT, BEE, BUG, DOR,**
    FLY, FLEA, GNAT, MITE,
    APHID, CADEW, EMESA,
    BEETLE, CADDIS, CICADA,
    CICALA, MANTIS
insect, adult .... **IMAGO**
insect body
    THORAX, THORACES
Insect, immature ...... **PUPA,**
    LARVA, INSTAR
insect mature .... **IMAGO**
insect order .... **DIPTERA**
insect, plant sucking .. **APHID**
insect, ruinous **APHID, BORER**
insertion mark .... **CARET**
inset .... **PANEL**
insidious .... **SLY**
insincere talk .... **CANT**
insipid, become .... **PALL**

c

insist .... **URGE, PRESS**
inspire .... **IMBUE**
install .... **INSTATE**
instance .... **CASE**
instant .... **MO, TRICE**
instar .. **PUPA, IMAGO, LARVA**
instigate .. **EGG, ABET, INCITE**
instruct ...... **BRIEF, EDUCATE**
INSTRUMENT .. see also **MUS-
    ICAL INSTRUMENT**
instrument, Afr. reed
    GORA, GORAH, GOURA
instrument, Chin. ancient **KIN**
instrument, Hebr. ... **TIMBREL**
instrument, India ..... **RUANA**
instrument, Jap. ..... **SAMISEN**
instrument, lutelike **BANDORE**
instrument, lyrelike ... **KISSAR**
instrument, math. ..... **SECTOR**
instrument, medieval .. **ROCTA**
instrument, naut.
    PELORUS, SEXTANT
instrument, Sp. .... **CASTANET**
instrument, stringed ... **LYRE,**
    NABLA, REBAB, REBEC,
    SAROD, SITAR, VIOLA,
    **CITHER, CITHARA, CITH-
    ERN, CITTERN, GITTERN**
instrument, surveying **TRANSIT**
instrumentality **MEDIA, MEDIUM**

d

insulate .... **ISLE**
insult .... **CAG**
insurgent .... **REBEL**
intact .... **WHOLE**
intellect .... **MIND,**
    NOUS, MAHAT, REASON
Inter. .... **BURY, INHUME**
intercharged ..... **PERMUTED**
interdict .... **BAN**
interferometer ...... **ETALON**
interior, ancient temple **CELLA**
interjection for silence .... **TST**
interlace .... **WEAVE**
interlock .... **LINK**
international language **RO, IDO**
inter. money unit .... **BANCOR**
international pact ... **ENTENTE**
interpret .... **REDE**
intersect .... **MEET**
interstice, small
    AREOLA, AREOLE
interstices, with .... **AREOLAR**
intervening: law ...... **MESNE**
interweave .. **TWINE, RADDLE**
intimidate **AWE, COW, DAUNT**
intone .... **CHANT**
intoxicant: India ...... **SOMA**
intoxicated .... **SOSH**
intricate .... **DEDAL, DAEDAL,**
    GORDIAN

a Intrigue .... **CABAL**
Introduce
BROACH, INSERT, PRESENT
Introducer of jetties for deepen-
ing .... **EADS**
Inundation .... **SPATE**
inveigle ...... **LURE, ENTICE**
inventor, claim of rights **PATENT**
inventor, elevator .... **OTIS**
inventor, sewing machine **HOWE**
inventor, steam engine **WATT**
invest ...... **ENDOW, ENDUE,
INDUE, CLOTHE, ORDAIN**
invested .... **CLAD**
investigate .... **PROBE**
investigator .... **TRACER**
invite .... **ASK, BID**
involve **ENTAIL, ENTRAMMEL**
Io butterfly .... **KIHO**
iodine source .... **KELP**
ion, negative .... **ANION**
ion, positive .... **CATION**
Ionian city .... **TEOS**
iota .... **JOT, MITE**
Iowa college town ...... **AMES**
ipecac source .... **EVEA**
IRAN .. see also **PERSIAN**
Iran, former part of .... **ELAM**
Iranian .... **TAT, KURD**

b Iranian Turk .... **SART**
irascible .... **TESTY**
irate .... **MAD**
Ireland .... **EIRE, ERIN**
Ireland, old name ..... **IERNE**
Ireland personified .... **IRENA**
iridescent gem .... **OPAL**
iris .... **FLAG**
Iris, Florentine, European **ORRIS**
iris, layer of .... **UVEA**
iris, of a layer .... **UVEAL**
iris root .... **ORRIS**
IRISH .. see also **IRELAND**
Irish .... **ERSE**
Ir. alphabet, early
OGAM, OGUM
Ir. ancestor **IR, MIL, ITH, MILED**
Ir. assembly .... **DAIL**
Ir. church .... **KIL**
Ir. city, ancient .... **TARA**
Ir. clan, ancient .... **SEPT**
Ir. competitive meet .... **FEIS**
Ir. crowning stone, — Fail **LIA**
Ir. dramatist .... **SYNGE**
Ir. exclamation .... **ARU,
AROO, ARRA, WHIST, WURRA**
Ir. fairies .... **SHEE**
Ir. family .... **CINEL**
Ir. Free State .... **EIRE**
Irish-Gaelic .... **ERSE**
Ir. goddess, battle **BADB, BODB**

c **IR. GODS' MOTHER see page 200**
Ir. kings' home .... **TARA**
Ir. law, tribe .... **CINEL**
Ir. lower house parliament **DAIL**
Ir. nobleman .... **AIRE**
Ir. poet
AE, COLUM, MOORE, YEATS
Ir. rebel group .... **IRA**
Ir. tribe .... **SIOL**
Ir. writing .... **OGAM, OGHAM**
Irishman .. **AIRE, CELT, MICK**
iron disulfide .... **PYRITE**
iron, pert. to .... **FERRIC**
ironwood ...... **ACLE, COLIMA**
irony .... **SATIRE**
Iroquoian .... **ERIE**
Iroquois demon .... **OTKON**
irrational number ...... **SURD**
irregularity .... **JOG**
irrigation ditch **FLUME, SLUICE**
irritate .... **VEX, GALL, RILE,
NETTLE, RANKLE**
Isaac's son **EDOM, ESAU, JACOB**
Ishmael .... **PARIAH**
Ishmael, son of ...... **DUMAH**
Ishmael's mother ..... **HAGAR**
isinglass .... **MICA**
Isis, husband of .... **OSIRIS**
ISLAM .... see **MOSLEM**

d island ... **OE, AIT, CAY, KAY,
KEY, EYOT, HOLM, ILOT,
ISLE, ATOLL, ISLET, ISLOT**
ISLAND, AEGEAN .... see
GAZETTEER
island, Argyll .... **IONA**
island, coral .... **ATOLL**
island, Dodecanese . **COO, KOS,
CASO, LERO, SIMI**
island, Great Barrier ..... **OTEA**
island, Gr. (fine marble) **PAROS**
island, Gr., pert. to ... **CRETAN**
island, inhabiting an . **NESIOTE**
ISLAND, INNER HEBRIDES
see **HEBRIDES GAZETTEER**
island, Ionian .... **ZANTE**
island, Micronesia ... **PONAPE**
island near Ireland ..... **ARAN**
island, near Italy ...... **CAPRI**
island off Scotland .... **IONA,
ARRAN**
island, Riga Gulf ...... **OESEL**
island, river **AIT, EYOT, HOLM**
island, South Seas ..... **ARU,
TAITI, TAHITI, OTAHEITE**
island, west of Sumatra .. **NIAS**
islands, Gulf of Bothnia **ALAND**
islands, Irish .... **ARAN**
islands, off Timor ...... **LETI**
Isle of Man, pert. to ... **MANX**
islet .... **AIT, CAY, HOLM**
isolate .... **ENISLE**

Israel .... JACOB
ISRAEL, KING OF ... see KING
 OF ISRAEL
ISRAELITE .. see also HEBREW
 and BIBLICAL
ISRAELITE JUDGE ...... see
 BIBLICAL JUDGE
ISRAELITE KING .. see KING
 OF ISRAEL
Israelite tribe .... DAN
Israelites .... SION, ZION
issue.EMIT, EMERGE, EMANATE
isthmus .... NECK
istle fiber .... PITA, PITO
it proceeds: music .... VA
ITALIAN WORDS: (accent marks
omitted throughout)
 arts .... ARTES
 article .... LA
 canal (s) CANALE, CANALI
 chest .... CASSO
 custom house ..... DOGANA
 day-breeze .... ORA
 dear .... CARA, CARO
 dough .... PASTA
 drink .... BEVERE
 enough .... BASTA
 evening .... SERA
 enthusiasm .... ESTRO
 feast .... FESTINO
 field .... CAMPO
 food .... PASTO
 from beginning .... DACAPO
 gentleman .... SER
 goodby .... ADDIO
 gondola cabin ...... FELZE
 hamlet .... CASAL, CASALE
 hair .... PELO
 hand .... MANO
 harbor .... PORTO
 harp .... ARPA
 hatred .... ODIO
 Helen .... ELENA
 holiday .... FESTA, FESTE
 host .... OSTE
 Italy .... ITALIA
 judge .... PODESTA
 lady .... DONNA, SIGNORA
 lake .... LAGO
 little .... POCO
 love .... AMORE
 lover .... AMOROSO
 mother .... MADRE
 mountain peak ...... CIMA
 nine .... NOVE
 ninth .... NONO

 one .... UNO
 paste .... PASTA
 peak .... CIMA
 pronoun .... MIA
 right .... DESTRO
 Rome .... ROMA
 sign .... SEGNO
 somebody .... UNO
 street .... CALLE
 three .... TRE
 time .... TEMPO
 tour .... GIRO
 town ...... CASAL, CASALE
 you .... TU
 voice .... VOCE
 well .... BENE
 with .... CON

Italian actress .... DUSE
It., ancient
 ITALI, OSCAN, SABINE
It. astronomer ...... GALILEO
It. author .... SILONE
It. car .... FIAT
It. cathedral city .... MILAN
It. commune .... ESTE
It. composer .... BOITO,
 GUIDO, VERDI, ROSSINI
It. day breeze .... ORA
It. family .... ESTE,
 CENCI, DORIA, MEDICI
It. family royal name ... ESTE
It. gambling game ..... MORA
It. gentleman .... SER
It. guessing game ..... MORA
It. lady ..... DONA, SIGNORA
It. millet ...... BUDA, MOHA
It. painter .... RENI,
 LIPPI, VINCI, ANDREA,
 CRESPI, GIOTTO
It. poet
 DANTE, TASSO, ARIOSTO
It. resort .... LIDO
It. rice dish .... RISOTTO
It.: Rome .... ROMA
It. sculptor .... LEONI
It. singer .... AMATO
It. title, early .... SER
It. university city BARI, PADUA
It. violin maker ...... AMATI
It. wine .... ASTI
Italy .... ITALIA
itch .... PSORA
itemize .... LIST
ivory nut .... ANTA, TAGUA
ivy crowned .... HEDERATED
ivy thicket .... TOD

J

a jack in cribbage .... NOB
jack-in-the-pulpit ARAD, AROID
jack tree .... JACA
jackal, Afr. .... THOS
jackal, India .... KOLA
jackal, N. Afr. .... DIEB
jackdaw .... DAW
jackdaw: Scot. .... KAE
JACKET .. see also GARMENT
jacket .. ETON, JUPE, BOLERO
jacket, armor .... ACTON
jacket, Malay .... BAJU
Jackson heroine .. . RAMONA
Jacob's brother .. EDOM, ESAU
Jacob's son..DAN, GAD, ASER,
LEVI, ASHER
Jacob's twin brother .... ESAU
Jacob's wife .. LEAH, RACHEL
jaeger gull ..... SKUA, ALLAN
jagged line .... ZAG, ZIG
jai alai .... PELOTA
Jamashid .... YIMA
James II daughter ..... ANNE
Janizaries, Chief of ...... DEY
JAPANESE: . see also SPECIAL
SECTION
Jap. aborigine ... AINO, AINU
Jap. admiral .... ITO
b Jap.-Am. .... ISSEI,
KIBEI, NISEI, SANSEI
Jap. army reserve ...... HOJU
Jap. army second line ... KOBI
Jap. art of self-defense JUDO
Jap. badge, family ...... MON
Jap. badge, imperial KIRIMON
Jap. beer, rice .... SAKE, SAKI
Jap. beverage .... SAKE
Jap. box, girdle .... INRO
Jap. bush clover ...... HAGI
Jap. cedar .... SUGI
Jap. celery-like vegetable UDO
Jap. cherry .... FUJI
Jap. clogs .... GETA
Jap. deer .... SIKA
Jap. drama ..... NO, KABUKI
Jap. emperor's title ... TENNO
Jap. festival .... BON
Jap. fish .... TAI, FUGU
Jap. food, seaweed
KOBU, KOMBU
Jap. gods .... KAMI
Jap. happiness god
EBISU, HOTEI
Jap. harp .... KOTO
Jap. herb, stout .... UDO

c Jap. immigrant .... ISSEI
Jap. mile measure .... RI
Jap. monastery .... TERA
Jap. national park ..... ASO
Jap. naval station ..... KURE
Jap. news agency ... DOMEI
Jap. nobleman .... KUGE
Jap. outcast
ETA, YETA, RONIN
Jap. outer garment
MINO, HAORI, KIMONO
Jap. parliament .... DIET
Jap. perfecture .... FU
Jap. persimmon .... KAKI
Jap. plant .... UDO
Jap. plane .... ZERO
Jap. primitive ... AINO, AINU
Jap. province, old ... ISE, KAI
Jap. receptacle .... INRO
Jap. salad plant .... UDO
Jap. salmon .... MASU
Jap. sash, kimono .... OBI
Jap. school of painting KANO
Jap. ship name .... MARU
Jap. sock .... TABI
Jap. statesman .... ITO
Jap. straw cape .... MINO
Jap. sword .. CATAN, CATTAN
d Jap. vegetable ... UDO, GOBO
Jap. verse .... UTA
Jap. village .... MURA
Jap. volcano .... FUJI
Jap. writing .... KANA
Japheth, son of ...... GOMER
jar ...... EWER, OLLA, CRUSE
jar ring .... LUTE
jar, wide-mouthed ...... OLLA
jargon CANT, ARGOT, PATOIS
Jason's father .... AESON
Jason's 2d wife ..... CREUSA
Jason's ship .... ARGO
Jason's wife .... MEDEA
jaunty .... PERK
Java plum: P. I. ..... DUHAT
Javanese carriage ...... SADO
Javanese language KAVI, KAWI
Javanese poison tree ... UPAS
javelin, Afr. ASSAGAI, ASSEGAI
javelin game .. JERID, JEREED
javelin, Rom. .... PILUM
jeer .... GIBE, SCOFF
jeer at ...... TAUNT, DERIDE
Jehoshaphat, father of ... ASA
Jehovah .... GOD
Jehovah: Hebr. .... JAH,
JAVE, JAVEH, YAHWEH

84

jejune .. **DRY, ARID, BARREN**
jelly base .... **PECTIN**
jelly fruit .... **GUAVA**
jelly, meat .... **ASPIC**
jeopardize .... **ENDANGER**
Jericho, land opposite .. **MOAB**
jersey, woollen ..... **SINGLET**
Jerusalem, ancient name **SALEM**
Jerusalem: poet. ...... **ARIEL**
jest .... **JAPE**
jester .... **MIME, BUFFOON**
jet, U.S. .... **SABRE, SCORPION**
Jether, son of .... **ARA**
jetty .... **MOLE**
Jew .... **SEMITE**
JEWEL ...... see GEM, STONE
jewelry setting .... **PAVE**
jewels, adorn with ..... **BEGEM**
JEWISH .. see also HEBREW
Jewish ascetic ...... **ESSENE**
Jewish benediction ... **SHEMA**
Jewish bride .... **KALLAH**
Jewish ceremony **SEDAR, SEDER**
Jewish feast of tabernacles
                    SUCCOTH
Jewish festival **PURIM, SEDER**
Jewish law, body of .. **TALMUD**
Jewish marriage contract
                    KETUBA
Jewish offering ..... **CORBAN**
Jewish prayer book . **MAHZOR**
Jewish scholar .... **RAB**
Jewish sect, ancient .. **ESSENES**
Jewish teacher ... **REB, RABBI**
Jewish title of honor
                  RAB, GAON
Jezebel's husband ..... **AHAB**
Joan of Arc's victory **ORLEANS**
Job's-tears .... **COIX**
jog .... **TROT, NUDGE**
John: Gaelic, Scot. **IAN, EOAN**
John: Ir. .... **EOIN, SEAN**
John: Russ. .... **IVAN**
johnny-cake .... **PONE**
Johnson, Dr., hero .. **RASSELAS**
join ..... **LINK, PAIR, SEAM,**
    WELD, YOKE, MERGE,
    UNITE, ATTACH
join corners ... **MITER, MITRE**
join wood .... **RABBET**
joining bar .... **YOKE**
joint **HIP, KNEE, NODE, HINGE**
joint part **TENON, MORTISE**
joke with **KID, RIB, JAPE, JOSH**
joker .... **WAG, WIT**
Jordan city, ancient region
                    PETRA
Joseph's father .... **JACOB**
Joseph's nephew .... **TOLA**

Joshua tree .... **YUCCA**
Joshua's father .... **NUN**
jostle .... **JOG, ELBOW**
jot .... **IOTA, TITTLE**
journey .... **ITER, RIDE, TOUR,**
    TREK, TRIP, TRAVEL
journey in circuit .... **EYRE**
joy ...... **DELIGHT, RAPTURE**
joyous .... **GLAD**
Judah, city in ... **ADAR, ENAM**
Judah's son ...... **ER, ONAN**
Judaism scriptures
            TORA, TORAH
judge .. **DEEM, RATE, ARBITER**
JUDGE, BIB. ... see BIBLICAL
                    JUDGE
judge in Hades ...... **MINOS**
judge of dead, Egypt ... **OSIRIS**
judge's bench .... **BANC**
judge's chamber .... **CAMERA**
judges' rule, Israel **KRITARCHY**
judgment, Fr. law ..... **ARRET**
JUDICIAL see also LEGAL, LAW
judicial assembly ..... **COURT**
jug, large beer ..... **RANTER**
jug shaped like man ... **TOBY**
jug, wide-mouthed .... **EWER**
juice .... **SAP**
juice, thickened .... **RHOB**
jujitsu .... **JUDO**
jujube .... **BER, ELB**
Jules Verne character ... **NEMO**
Juliet's betrothed ...... **PARIS**
Juliet's father, family **CAPULET**
jumble .... **PI, PIE, MESS**
jump: music .... **SALTO**
jumping disease, Malay **LATA**
jumping rodent ..... **JERBOA**
juncture, line of .... **SEAM**
June bug .... **DOR**
Jungfrau's site .... **ALPS**
jungle clearing .... **MILPA**
juniper .... **GORSE,**
    SAVIN, SABINE, SAVINE
juniper, Europ. .... **CADE**
juniper tree, Bibl. **EZEL, RETEM**
Jupiter .... **JOVE**
Jupiter's moon, inner ..... **IO**
Jupiter's wife .... **HERA, JUNO**
jurisdiction .... **VENUE**
jurisdiction, old Eng. **SOC, SOKE**
jurisprudence .... **LAW**
jury list .... **PANEL**
jury, writ summoning **VENIRE**
just .... **MORAL**
justice, goddess of . **MA, MAAT**
jute .... **DESI**
Jutlander .... **DANE**
jutting rock .... **TOR**
juxtaposition, place in **APPOSE**
jynx .... **SPELL**

K

Kaffir language .... XOSA
Kaffir tribe .... ZULU
Kaffir war club .... KIRI
Kaffir warrior .... IMPI
Kalmuck ..... ELEUT, ELEUTH
Kandh language .... KUI
kangaroo, male ...... BOOMER
kangaroo, young .... JOEY
Katmandu's country ... NEPAL
kava .... AVA
kava bowl .... TANOA
Kaw .... AKHA
Keats poem-1820 .... LAMIA
keel .... CAREEN
keel, at right angle to ABEAM
keel block wedge ... TEMPLET
keel, having no ...... RATITE
keel, kind of .... FIN
keel, part of .... SKEG
keel-shaped part
            CARINA, CARINAE
keen ACUTE, SHARP, ASTUTE
keep account of .... TAB
keepsake .... TOKEN
keeve .... KIVER
Kentucky coffee tree . CHICOT
Kentucky college ..... BEREA
kerchief .... MADRAS
kernel .... NUT
ketch, Levant .... SAIC
ketone, liquid ...... ACETONE
ketone, oily .... CARONE
kettledrum .. NAKER, ATABAL,
    ATTABAL, TIMPANI, TIM-
    PANO, TYMPANO
key .... ISLE
key fruit .... SAMARA
key notch .... WARD
key part .... BIT
key-shaped ...... URDE, URDY
keyed up .... AGOG
Khedive's estate ...... DAIRA
kid, undressed .... SUEDE
kidney .... NEER
kidney bean .... BON
kidneys, pert. to ..... RENAL
killer whale .... ORCA
kiln ...... OST, OAST, OVEN
kiloliter .... STERE
kind
    ILK, SORT, GENRE, SPECIES
kind: Gr. .... GENOS
kindle: dialect .... TIND
kindly .... BENIGN
kindness .... LENITY
kindred .... SIB

king .... REX, REY, REGES
king —, cartoon character
                        AROO
King Alfred's city: abbr. .. LON
king, Amalekite .... AGAG
King Arthur's abode
AVALON, AVALLON, CAMELOT
King Arthur's burial place
        AVALON, AVALLON
King Arthur's court CAMELOT
King Arthur's father .. UTHER
King Arthur's fool .. DAGONET
King Arthur's lance ... RON
King Arthur's mother IGERNA,
    IGERNE, YGERNE, IGRAINE
King Arthur's queen
    GUINEVER, GUINEVERE
KING, BIBLICAL .... see
            BIBLICAL KING
King Ethelred "The —"
                    UNREADY
king, Gr. .... MINOS
King Gradlon's capital .... IS
king, Hebrew .... HEROD
king, Midianite .... REBA
king, mythical .... MIDAS
king of beasts .... LION
King of Colchis' daughter
                        MEDEA
king of Crete .... MINOS
king of elves ...... ERLKING
king of gods, Egypt
        AMEN, AMON, AMUN
king of Greece, ancient MINOS
king of Israel ... AHAB, ELAH,
        OMRI, SAUL, NADAB
king of Jews .... HEROD
king of Judah ... ASA, AHAZ,
        AMON, UZZIAH
king of Judea .... HEROD
king of Naples ...... MURAT
king of Persia .... CYRUS
king of Sodom .... BERA
king, pert. to ...... REGNAL
king, Phrygian .... MIDAS
king, rich .... CROESUS
king, Spartan AGIS, LEONIDAS
king, Teut. Visigoth .. ALARIC
king's bodyguard ..... THANE
king's yellow ..... ORPIMENT
KINGDOM ..see also COUNTRY
kingdom, ancient ...... MOAB
KINGDOM, BIB. .. see page 197
kingfish .... HAKU, OPAH
kinkajou .... POTTO
kinship, Moslem law ... NASAB
Kipling hero .... KIM

86

a kismet .... FATE
kiss .... BUSS, SMACK
kitchen, ship's ...... GALLEY
kitchen tool
      CORER, RICER, GRATER
kite, bird
      GLED, GLEDE, ELANET
kittiwake gull, Shetlands WAEG
kitty, feed the .... ANTE
kiwi .... ROA
knave .... ROGUE
knave, in cribbage ..... NOBS
knave of clubs .... PAM
knead .... ELT
knead, in massage .... PETRIE
knee: Lat. .... GENU
kneecap ... ROTULA, PATELLA
KNIFE .. see also DAGGER
knife .... CHIV, STAB,
      MACHETE, MACHETTE
knife, Burmese .... DAH, DOW
knife dealer .... CUTLER
knife, Eskimo .... ULU
knife, large ...... SNY, SNEE
knife, loop-cutting
      TREVAT, TRIVAT, TRIVET
knife, P. I. .... BOLO
knife, single-edge .... BOWIE
knife, surgical .... SCALPEL
knight SIR, RITTER, TEMPLAR
knight, heroic ...... PALADIN
knight, make .... DUB
knight, medieval ...... BEVIS
knight's mantel ..... TABARD

c knight's wife .... DAME
knitting stitch .... PURL
knob: anat. .... CAPUT
knobbed .... TOROSE
knoblike .... NODAL
knobkerrie .... KIRI
knockout .... KO, KAYO
knot ..... MILE, NODE, NODI,
      SNAG, GNARL, KNURL,
      NODUS
knot, fiber .... NOIL, NOYL
knot in wood .... BURL,
      KNAR, KNOR, KNUR, NURL
knot, insecure ..... GRANNY
knot lace .... TAT, TATT
knot, like a .... NODAL
knot of thread .... BURL
knots, fiber .... NEP
knots, having .... NODED
know .... KEN, WIST
knowledge .... KEN, LORE
knowledge, pert. to .. GNOSTIC
knowledge, pure ..... NOESIS
known as milo maize, grain
      MILO
knucklebones, sheep ... DOLOS
kobold .... NIS, NISSE
Kol dialect .... HO
kopecks, 100 .... RUBLE
Koran chapter .... SURA
Koran interpreters .... ULEMA
Korea .... CHOSEN
Korean president ..... RHEE
Korean soldier .... ROK
Kronos' wife .... RHEA
kurrajong tree .... CALOOL

L

b "La Boheme" heroine ... MIMI
Laban, daughter of .... LEAH
label .... TAG, PASTER
LABOR GROUP ... see UNION
laborer, China . COOLY, COOLIE
laborer, India .... TOTY
Labrador tea .... LEDUM
labyrinth .... MAZE
lac .... RESIN
lace .... BEAT, LASH
lace, barred GRILLE, GRILLEE
lace, Fr. ... CLUNY, ALENCON
lace, gold, silver .... ORRIS
lace, metal tip of
      AGLET, AIGLET
lace, square hole ...... FILET
lacerate .... RIP, TEAR
laceration .... RIP, TEAR
lack .... NEED, WANT
lack of power .... ATONY

d Laconian clan group ..... OBE
Laconian subdivision ..... OBE
ladder, scale fort wall with
      SCALADE, SCALADO, ES-
      CALADE, ESCALADO
ladderlike .... SCALAR
lady, India .... BIBI
"Lady of the Lake" outlaw DHU
ladylove, in poetry .... DELIA
lagoon .... LIMAN
lake .... MERE
lake, Afr. salt .. SHAT, SHOTT
lake, Blue Nile source .. TANA
Lake Erie battle officer PERRY
Lake, Great (5) ERIE, HURON,
      ONTARIO, MICHIGAN, SU-
      PERIOR
lake, mountain .... TARN
lake near Galilee sea .. MEROM
lake, resort .... TAHOE

a
lake: Scot. .... LOCH
Lake Tahoe trout ...... POGY
lake whitefish .... POLLAN
lama, head .... DALAI
lamb .... EAN, EWE, YEAN
lamb, holy .... AGNUS
lamb: Lat. .... AGNI, AGNUS
lamb, young .... COSSET
Lamb's pen name ...... ELIA
Lamech, ancestor of ... CAIN
Lamech's son
    NOAH, JABAL, JUBAL
lament .... KEEN, WAIL,
   WEEP, GRIEVE, PLAINT
lamentation .... LINOS
lamp black .... SOOT
lamprey .... EEL
lance head .... MORNE
lance, mythical .... RON
lance rest, breastplate FAUCRE
lance, short .... DART
Lancelot's beloved ... ELAINE
lancer, Ger. ... ULAN, UHLAN
lancewood .... CIGUA
land, absolute property ALOD,
ALLOD, ALODIUM, ALLODIUM
land amid water .. ISLE, ISLET
land breeze .... TERRAL
land, church's .... GLEBE

b
land held in fee simple
    ODAL, UDAL
land: law .... SOLUM
LAND MEASURE .. see also
   AREA in SPECIAL SECTION
land measure
   AR, ARE, ROD, ACRE, ROOD
land ownership, pert. to ODAL
land snail genus ...:. CERION
land spring .... LAVANT
land, tilled, plowed: Sp.
   ARADA, ARADO
land under tenure: Scot. ... FEU
landing place ..... KEY, PIER,
   QUAI, QUAY, LEVEE
landing place, India
   GAUT, GHAT
landing ship .... LST
landmark .... COPA
landmark: Sp. .... SENAL
lands .... ACRES
language, Aramaic ... SYRIAC
language, Assam .... AO, AKA
language, dead ...... LATIN
language, early It. ..... OSCAN
language, Egypt. ..... COPTIC
language, Finnish ..... UGRIC
language form, peculiarity
   IDIOM
language, Gilgit ...... SHINA
language, Hittite ...... PALA
language, Indic .... HINDI

c
language, Indo-Chin. .... AO,
WA, AKA, ANU, LAI, LAO,
MRO, MRU, PWO, SAK,
AHOM, AKHA, AMOY,
BODO, GARO, KAMI, NAGA,
RONG, SGAU, SHAN
language, Ir. .. CELTIC, KELTIC
language, Kandh .... KUI
language, Kashmir .... SHINA
language, Mossi .... MO, MOLE
language, N. Afr. .... BERBER
language of Bible days
   ARAMAIC
language, P. I.
   TAGAL, TAGALOG
language, Scot. CELTIC, KELTIC
language, Semitic .... ARABIC
language, Siberian
   ENISEI, YENISEI
language, S. Afr. ...... TAAL
language, Sudanic MO, MOLE
language, synthetic .. RO, IDO
language, Welsh CELTIC,KELTIC
languages, E. Europ. ... UGRIC
languish .... FLAG, PINE
languor, drug-induced
   KEF, KAIF, KIFF
langur .... MAHA
lantern feast .... BON

d
Laomedon's father ...... ILUS
Laomedon's son
   PRIAM, TITHONUS
Laos aborigine ... KHA, YUN
lapel .... REVER
lapidate .... STONE
Lapp's sledge ... PULK, PULKA
larboard .... APORT
larch TAMARAC, TAMARACK
large amount .... SCAD
lariat .... LAZO, ROPE,
   LASSO, REATA, RIATA
lariat, metal eye of
   HONDA, HONDO, HONDOO
larva .... GRUB
larva of fly ...... BOT, BOTT
lash .... TIE, WHIP
lasso
   ROPE, REATA, RIATA, LARIAT
last .... FINAL, OMEGA
last but one .... PENULT
"Last Days of Pompeii" character .... IONE
last Imam .... MAHDI
last section .... FINALE
Last Supper picture .... CENA
Last Supper room .. CENACLE
latching: naut. .... LASKET
late ... NEW, TARDY, RECENT
late, one at school ..... SERO
lateen-rigged boat ..... DOW,
   DHOW, SETEE, MISTIC

a latent .... DORMANT
   lateral .... SIDE
   lath .... SLAT
   LATIN .... see also ROMAN
   LATIN:
     abbot .... ABBAS
     above ..... SUPER, SUPRA
     about .... CIRCITER
     across .... TRANS
     act .... ACTU, ACTUS
     after .... POST
     aged .... AET (abbr.)
     all .... TOTO
     alone .... SOLO, SOLUS
     and .... ET
     and others .... ETAL (abbr.)
     around .... CIRCUM
     art .... ARS
     backward .... RETRO
     before .... ANTE
     behold .... ECCE
     being .... ESSE
     believe, I .... CREDO
     beneath .... INERA
     bird .... AVIS
     book .... LIBER
     blessed .... BEATA
     bronze .... AES
     but .... SED
     cattle .... PECORA

b   country .... RUS, RURIS
     cup .... CALIX
     custom .... RITUS
     day .... DIEM
     days .... DIES
     depart! .... VADE
     divination by lots .... SORS,
                          SORTES
     door .... JANUA
     earth .... TERRA
     egg .... OVUM
     eight .... OCTO
     error .... LAPSUS
     event .... REI
     evil .... MALA, MALUM
     fate .... NONA
     field .... AGER
     fields .... AGRI
     fire .... IGNIS
     first .... PRIMUS
     fish .... PISCES
     force .... VIS
     from .... DE
     go! .... VADE
     god .... DEUS
     goddess .... DEA
     gods .... DI
     gold .... AURUM
     good ...... BONUM, BONUS
     grandfather .... AVUS
     he .... ILLE

c he remains .... MANET
   he was .... ERAT
   head .... CAPUT
   high .... ALTA
   himself .... IPSE
   I love .... AMO
   in so far as .... QUA
   is .... EST
   itself .... IPSO
   ivory .... EBUR
   journey .... ITER
   knee .... GENU
   lamb .... AGNI, AGNUS
   land .... AGER
   learned .... DOCTUS
   life .... VITA, ANIMA
   lo .... ECCE
   man .... VIR
   mass .... MISSA
   mine .... MEUM
   more than .... SUPER
   mountain .... MONS
   name .... NOMEN
   nose, of the .... NAS
   not .... NON
   observe .... NOTA
   offense ..... MALA, MALUM

d once .... SEMEL
   or .... AUT
   other .... ALIA
   over .... SUPER
   pardon .... VENIA
   palm .... VOLA
   part .... PARS
   partly .... PARTIM
   peace .... PAX
   pin .... ACUS
   pledge .... VAS
   possessive .... SUA
   power .... VIS
   pronoun .... SUA
   property .... BONA
   quickly .... CITO
   rate .... RATA
   religious law .... FAS
   right .... DEXTER
   same .... IDEM
   scarcely VIX
   see .... VIDE
   side .... LATUS
   table .... MENSA
   tail .... CAUDA
   that is .... "ID EST"
   that one .... ILLE
   the same .... IDEM
   thing .... RES

a **LATIN**(continued from page 89)

this one .... HIC, HAEC
thus .... SIC
throat .... GULA
to be .... ESSE
to use .... UTOR
tooth .... DENS
toward .... AD
twice .... BIS
under .... SUB
unless .... NISI
vein .... VENA
voice .... VOX
water .... AQUA
we .... NOS
well .... BENE
where .... UBI
within .... INTRA
without .... SINE
wool .... LANA
wrong ...... MALA, MALUM

Latvia, native of .... LETT
laugh .... FLEER
laugh, able to .... RISIBLE
laughing .... RIANT
laughing, pert. to .. GELASTIC
laurel .... BAY, DAPHNE
b laurel bark, medicinal .. COTO
lava .... AA, LATITE, SCORIA
lava, rough .... AA
lavender, Eur. .... ASPIC
lavish affection .... DOTE
law
    JURE, RULE, CANON, EDICT
law, abstract .... JUS
law, D. E. Ind. .... ADAT
law excluding women from
    reign .... SALIC
law of Moses .. TORA, TORAH
law, Rom. .... JUS, LEX
lawful .... LEGAL, LICIT
lawgiver, Gr.
    DRACO, MINOS, SOLON
lawgiver, Hebr. .... MOSES
lawmaker .... SOLON
lawyer .... LEGIST
lawyers' patron saint ... IVES
lay .... PUT, DITTY
layer .... PLY,
    LAMINA, STRATA, STRATUM
layer of a plant ..... PROVINE
layer, wood .... VENEER
layman .... LAIC
lazar .... LEPER
lazy .... OTIOSE
lead-colored .... LIVID
lead: music PRESA, PRECENT
lead, ore .... GALENA

c lead, pellets of .... SHOT
lead, pencil .... GRAPHITE
lead sulphide, native GALENA
lead telluride ...... ALTAITE
lead, white .... CERUSE
leaden color, having ... LIVID
leader, fishing .... SNELL
leader of movement .... VAN
leader, Rom. .... DUX
leaf appendage ...... STIPEL
leaf-cutting ant ...... ATTA
leaf division .... LOBE
leaf, fern .... FROND
leaf, flower .... BRACT, SEPAL
leaf-miner beetle ..... HISPA
leaf of book .... FOLIO
leaf vein .... RIB
league, Ger. .... BUND
league, trading .... HANSE
Leah's father .... LABAN
Leah's son .... LEVI
lean .. CANT, GAUNT, SPARE
lean-to .... SHED
Leander's love .... HERO
"Leaning Tower" city .... PISA
leap LUNGE, VAULT, CURVET
leap: music .... SALTO
leap: Scot. LOUP, LOWP, STEND
leaping .... SALTANT
learned .. ERUDITE, LETTERED
d learning .... LORE
learning, man of
    SAGE, PEDANT, SAVANT
Lear's daughter ...... REGAN
Lear's faithful follower KENT
least bit .... RAP
leather bottle .... MATARA
leather flask, Gr. ...... OLPE
leather, glove
    KID, NAPA, MOCHA, SUEDE
leather, kind of ... ELK, BOCK
leather, prepare—make into
    TAN, TAW
leather, soft
    NAPA, ALUTA, SUEDE
leather thong, hawk's .. BRAIL
leatherfish .... LIJA
"leatherneck" .... MARINE
leave
    GO, QUIT, EXEAT, DEPART
leave destitute ...... STRAND
leave of absence, school EXEAT
leave-taking .... CONGE
leaves, having: Her. .. POINTE
leaven .... YEAST
leaving .... ORT
leavings .... DREGS, RESIDUE
Lebanese port, old .... TYRE
ledge, fort .... BERM, BERME
ledger entry
    ITEM, DEBIT, CREDIT

a
lee, opposed to .... STOSS
leeangle .. LEAWILL, LEEWILL
leer .... OGLE
Leeward Island .... NEVIS
left: comb. form ...... LEVO
left-hand .... LEVO
left-hand page ... VO, VERSO
left, to turn .... HAW
leftover .... ORT
leg, covering, ancient PEDULE
leg, front of .... SHIN
leg joint, animal .... HOCK
leg-like part .... CRUS
leg of mutton, lamb .. GIGOT
leg, part of .... SHIN, SHANK
leg, pert. to calf of ... SURAL
legal action suit .. RES, CASE
legal claim .... LIEN
legal delays .... MORAE
legal injury .... TORT
legal job .... CASE
legal matter .... RES
legal offense .. DELIT, DELICT
legal order .... WRIT
legal paper .... DEED
legal profession ... BAR, LAW
legal prosecution .... SUIT
legend ... MYTH, SAGA, TALE
legion division, Rom. COHORT
legislate .... ENACT

b
legislative assembly, Afr. RAAS
legislator ... SOLON, SENATOR
legislature ... DIET, SENATE
legislature: Sp. ...... CORTES
legume ..... PEA, POD, BEAN
leisure .... REST, OTIUM
lemur .... MAKI, INDRI,
    LORIS, AYE-AYE, SEMIAPE
lemur, Afr. .... GALAGO
lemur, Asia, Ceylon LORI, LORIS
lemur, Ceylonese .... LORI
lemur, flying .... COLUGO
lemur, ruffed .... VARI
lemuroid .... POTTO
lengthily, address .. PERORATE
Leningrad's river .... NEVA
lens, hand .... READER
lentil .... ERVUM
leopard .... PARD
Leporidae, one of the ... HARE
leprosy .... LEPRA
Lepus genus, one of ..... HARE
lerp .... LAAP
Lesbos, poet of .... ARION
"Les Etats —" .... UNIS
less .... MINUS
lessen BATE, ABATE, MITIGATE
let HIRE, RENT, LEASE, PERMIT
let bait drop .... DAP
let it stand! .... STA, STET

c
let up .... ABATE
lethal .... FATAL
lethargy
    COMA, STUPOR, TORPOR
letter .. AR (18), EF (6), EM
    (13), EN (14), EX (24),
    WY (25), BEE (2), CEE
    (3), DEE (4), ESS (19),
    GEE (7), JAY (10), PEE
    (16), TEE (20), VEE (22),
    WYE (25), ZED (26), ZEE
    (26), AITCH (8)
letter, according to .. LITERAL
letter, Ang.-Sax. .. EDH, ETH
letter, early Gr. .... SAN
LETTER, GR. and NUMBER . see
    also GREEK LETTER
letter, Gr. .. MU, NU, PI, XI,
    CHI, ETA, PHI, PSI, RHO,
    TAU, BETA, IOTA, ZETA,
    ALPHA, DELTA, GAMMA,
    KAPPA, OMEGA, SIGMA,
    THETA, LAMBDA, EPSILON,
    OMICRON, UPSILON
letter, Hebr. HE (5), PE (17),
    AIN (16), MEM (13),
    NUN (14), SIN (21), TAV
    (22), TAW (22), VAU
    (16), WAW (16), ALEF
    (11), AYIN (16), BETH
    (2), CAPH (11), ELEF (1),

d
    KAPH (11), KOPH (19),
    QOPH (19), RESH (20),
    SADE (18), SHIN (21),
    TETH (9), YODH, (10),
    ALEPH (13), GIMEL (3),
    LAMED (12), DALETH (4),
    LAMEDH (12)
letter of resignation .. DEMIT
letters, sloping ...... ITALICS
lettuce, kind of COS, ROMAINE
Levantine ketch .... SAIC
levee .... DIKE, DYKE
level EVEN, RASE, RAZE, PLANE
leveling slip .... SHIM
lever .... PRY, PEVY, PEAVY,
    PEEVY, PEAVEY, PEEVEY,
    TAPPET
levy .... TAX, CESS, IMPOST
Lew Wallace hero .... HUR
Lhasa holy man .... LAMA
Lhasa's country .... TIBET
liability .... DEBT
liana .... CIPO
liang .... TAEL
liar .... ANANIAS
Liberian native .... VAI, VEI
Liberian tribes .. GI, KRA, KRU
license: slang .... READER
lichen .... MOSS
lichen genus USNEA, EVERNIA

a
lichen, kind **PARELLA, PARELLE**
lie in wait .... **LURK**
Liege, town near .... **ANS**
liegeman .... **VASSAL**
lieu .... **STEAD**
life .... **BIOS, BIOTA**
life: Lat. ...... **VITA, ANIMA**
life, of .... **VITAL**
life principle .... **PRANA**
life principle, Hindu .. **ATMAN**
life prolonger .... **ELIXIR**
life, relating to
BIOTIC, BIOTICAL
life tenant .... **LIVIER**
lifeless **AMORT, AZOIC, INERT**
lifetime .... **AGE**
lifted with effort ...... **HOVE**
ligament .... **BOND**
light .... **LAMP, KLEIG,**
KLEIG, TAPER, ILLUME
light and fine, as lines .. **LEGER**
light as a line .... **LEGER**
light bulb filler ...... **ARGON**
light, circle of
HALO, NIMB, NIMBUS
light intensity unit ...... **PYR**
light, kind of .... **ARC**
light ring .... **CORONA**
light, science of ...... **OPTICS**
light, sun's **AUREOLA, AUREOLE**

b
light unit **PYR, LUMEN, HEFNER**
lighter, lamp .... **SPILL**
lighter, make .... **LEAVEN**
lighthouse .... **PHAROS**
lightning: poet. .... **LEVIN**
ligulate .... **LORATE**
like .... **AS, AKIN**
likely .... **APT**
likeness ...... **ICON, IMAGE**
likewise not .... **NOR**
lily .... **LIS, LYS, ALOE,**
ARUM, SEGO, CALLA
lily family plant ..... **CAMAS**
CAMASS, CAMMAS
lily genus .... **ALOE**
lily genus, plantain .... **HOSTA**
Lily Maid of Astolat
ELAIN, ELAINE
lily, palm .... **TI**
limb ...... **ARM, LEG, MANUS**
limber .... **LITHE**
lime, to hydrate ..... **SLAKE**
lime tree .... **TEIL, TEYL**
limestone, grainy ..... **OOLITE**
limestone, Irish .... **CALP**
limestone, soft **MALM, CHALK**
limicoline bird **SNIPE, PLOVER**
limit .... **TERM, BOURN,**
STENT, STINT, BOURNE
limn.......... **DRAW, PAINT**
Lindbergh's book .... **WE**

c
linden .... **LIN, TEIL, TEYL**
line .... **ROW, RANK**
line, cutting .... **SECANT**
line, fine, on type letter **CERIF,**
SERIF, CERIPH
line, fishing .... **SNELL**
line, in a .... **AROW**
line, intersecting ... **SECANT**
line inside of .... **CEIL**
line, math. .... **VECTOR**
line, naut. . **EARING, MARLINE**
line not forming angle **AGONE**
line on a letter .... **SERIF**
line, pert. to .... **LINEAR**
line, thin ..... **STRIA, STRIAE**
line, waiting ..... **CUE, QUEUE**
line with stone **STEAN, STEENE**
lines, marked with
RULED, STRIATE, STRIATED
lines, telescope-lens .. **RETICLE**
linen .... **CREA**
linen, fine ..... **LAWN, TOILE**
linen, household, table **NAPERY**
linen, one caring for royal
NAPERER
linen tape, braid ...... **INKLE**
linger .... **WAIT, TARRY**
lingo .... **ARGOT**
lingua .... **GLOSSA**
liniment .... **ARNICA**

d
link .... **YOKE, CATENATE**
links connected ..... **CATENAE**
linnet ...... **TWITE, LENARD**
lion .... **LEO, SIMBA**
lion group .... **PRIDE**
lion killed by Hercules **NEMEAN**
lion of God .... **ALI**
lionet .... **CUB**
lips, pert. to .... **LABIAL**
liqueur .... **CREME, NOYAU**
liqueur, sweet .... **GENEPI**
liquid element
BROMIN, BROMINE
liquid, made ... **FUSIL, FUSILE**
liquid, without ..... **ANEROID**
liquor .. **GIN, RUM, RYE, GROG**
liquor, malt .... **ALE, PORTER**
liquor, oriental ...... **ARRACK**
liquor, P. I. .... **VINO**
liquor, Russian **VODKA, VODKI**
liquor, sugar-cane
TAFIA, TAFFIA
Lisbon's river .... **TAGUS**
lissome .... **SVELTE**
list .... **ROTA, SLATE,**
ROSTER, CATALOG, CATALOGUE
list of persons
ROTA, PANEL, ROSTER
list, one of a .... **ITEM**
listen .... **HARK, HEAR**
listless, be .... **MOPE**

a listlessness .. ENNUI, APATHY
liter, Dutch .... AAM, KAN
literary collection .... ANA
literary extracts
     ANALECTA, ANALECTS
literary master ...... STYLIST
literary scraps, bits ANA, NOTES
literate .. LEARNED, LETTERED
lithograph .... CHROMO
Lithuanian .... BALT, LETT
litter, E. Ind. .. DOOLI, DOOLY,
     DOOLEE, DOOLEY, DOOLIE
"Little Boy Blue" poet .. FIELD
little casino .... TWO
little chief hare .... PIKA
little: music .... POCO
liturgy .... RITE
live .... all forms of verb "BE"
live oak, Calif. ...... ENCINA
lively .... PERT, BRISK, PEART
lively, make .... PERK
lively: music
     VIVO, DESTO, ANIMATO
lively person .... GRIG
lively song .... LILT
liver .... HEPAR
liver, pert. to .... HEPATIC
liverwort genus .... RICCIA
b livid .... BLAE
living in currents ...... LOTIC
Livonian LIV
lixivium .... LYE, LEACH
lizard .. GILA, GECKO, GUANA,
     SKINK, VARAN, IGUANA
lizard, Am. .... ANOLE, ANOLI
lizard, beaded .... GILA
lizard, changeable CHAMELEON
lizard genus .... UTA, AGAMA
lizard, large .. GILA, MONITOR
lizard, old world ...... SEPS
lizard, small ..... EFT, GECKO
lizard, starred .... AGAMA
lizard, tropical ...... AGAMA
lizardlike .... SAURIAN
llamalike animal ..... ALPACA
load .... LADE, ONUS
loadstone .... MAGNET
loaf, small: dial. .... BAP
loam .... LOESS
loam, India .... REGUR
loath .... AVERSE
loathe .... ABHOR
lobster box .... CAR
local .... TOPICAL
locale .... SITE
locality .... AREA,
     LOCUS, VENEW, VENUE
location ... SITE, SPOT, PLACE
lock .... CURL, TRESS

c locks, Panama Canal .. GATUN
lockjaw ... TETANUS, TRISMUS
locust .... ACACIA,
     CICADA, CICALA
locust, N. Z. .... WETA
lodge, soldier's .... BILLET
lofty dwelling .... AERIE
log birling contest .... ROLEO
log drive, escape work on SNIB
log, spin floating ...... BIRL
log splitter .... WEDGE
logarithm unit .... BEL
loge .... STALL
logger's implement ... PEAVY,
         PEAVEY
logic, omission of step in
     proof .... SALTUS
logician .... DIALECTOR
Lohengrin's wife .... ELSA
Loire, city on .... BLOIS
loiter .... LAG
Loki's daughter .... HEL, HELA
Loki's son .... NARE
Loki's wife .... SIGYN
London district .... SOHO
long .... YEN, PINE,
     CRAVE, YEARN, ASPIRE
long ago .... ELD, YORE
long journey .. TREK, ODYSSEY
d long line (fishing) with hooks
         TROT
long live! .... VIVA, VIVE
long-suffering .... MEEK
look .... LO, SEE
look after ...... MIND, TEND
look askance .... LEER
look at .... EYE, SCAN, VIEW
look here! .... HIST
look narrowly PEEK, PEEP, PEER
look slyly .... LEER, OGLE
loom, heddles of ...... CAAM
loom, lever in .... LAM
loon genus .... GAVIA
loon, kind of .... DIVER
loop, edging .... PICOT
loophole .... MUSE, MEUSE
looplike structure, anat. ANSA
loose .... LAX
loose coat PALETOT, MANTEVIL
loose robe .... SIMAR
loosen .... UNDO, UNTIE
lop ... SNED, PRUNE, SNATHE
lopsided .... ALOP, ALIST
loquat tree .... BIWA
Lord High Executioner in
     "Mikado" .... KOKO
Lord: Jacobite Church ... MAR
lord, Oriental .... KHAN
lord, Pers. .... KAAN,
     KAUN, KAWN, KHAN
lord, privileged .... PALATINE

a   lord, Scot. .... **LAIRD**
lore, Norse .... **RUNE**
lorica .... **CUIRASS**
"Lorna Doone" character **RIDD**
lose .... **AMIT**
"Lost Chord" finale .... **AMEN**
lot .... **FATE**
Lotan's father .... **SEIR**
Lot's birthplace .... **UR**
Lot's father .... **HARAN**
Lot's son .... **MOAB**
lottery prize .... **TERN**
lotus enzyme .... **LOTASE**
Lotus: poet .... **LOTE**
lotus tree .... **SADR**
loud: music .... **FORTE**
loud-voiced one .... **STENTOR**
loudness, measurement unit
               PHON
loudspeaker for high sound
           TWEETER
loudspeaker for low sound
          WOOFER
Louis XVI's nickname .. **VETO**
Louisiana county ..... **PARISH**

b   Louisiana native ..... **CREOLE**
lounge .... **LOAF, LOLL**
love . **JO, GRA, ADORE, AMOUR**
love: Anglo-Irish ...... **GRA**
love apple .... **TOMATO**
love feast .... **AGAPE**
love god
LOVE GOD . see **GOD OF LOVE**
LOVE GODDESS . see **GODDESS**
          OF LOVE
love, inflame with
     ENAMOR, ENAMOUR
love knot .... **AMORET**
love to excess ... **DOAT, DOTE**
lover .... **ROMEO**
"Love's Labour's Lost" constable
               DULL
loving
  FOND, AMATIVE, AMATORY
low .... **MOO, BASE**
low caste Hindu .. **PASI, TELI**
low caste Indian .... **DOM,**
           MAL, GADDI
Lowell, poetess .... **AMY**
lower **ABASE, DEBASE, NETHER**
lower: arch. .... **VAIL**
lower jaw, bird's ...... **MALA**
lower world gods, Rom. **MANES**
lowest deck .... **ORLOP**
lowest part of base ... **PLINTH**

c   lowest point .... **NADIR**
loyal .... **LEAL,**
   TRUE, STANCH, STAUNCH
loyalist .... **TORY**
lozenge ..... **PASTIL, ROTULA**
  TROCHE, PASTILE, PASTILLE
loyalty fulfilling religious
    obligations: Rom. . **PIETAS**
Lubeck, pert. to .... **LUBS**
lucerne .... **MEDIC, ALFALFA**
luck: Ir. .... **CESS**
luck, pert. to ..... **ALEATORY**
lucky stroke .... **FLUKE**
lugubrious .... **SAD**
lukewarm .... **TEPID**
lumber along ...... **LOB, LOBB**
Lumber State .... see page 208
lumberman .... **SAWYER**
lumberman's boot .... **PAC**
lumberman's boots
         PACS, OVERS
lumberman's hook ..... **PEVY,**
  PEAVY, PEEVY, PEAVEY,
  PEEVEY
luminaire .... **LAMP**
luminary .... **STAR**

d   lump .... **NUB, WAD,**
    CLOT, NODE, SWAD
lunar crater .... **LINNE**
lunar god, Phrygian ..... **MEN**
luncheon .... **TIFFIN**
lurch .... **CAREEN**
lure .... **BAIT, DECOY**
luster .... **GLOSS, SHEEN**
lusterless .. **DIM, MAT, MATTE**
lustrous .... **NITID**
lute, Oriental .... **TAR**
luxuriant .... **LUSH, RANK**
luxuriate .... **BASK**
Luzon native .... **ATA, ITA,**
    AETA, ATTA, TAGAL,
    TAGALA
Luzon negrito .... **ATA,**
   AETA, ITA, ATTA
Luzon pagan .... **ITALON**
Lynette's knight .... **GARETH**
lynx, Afr. .... **SYAGUSH**
lynx, Pers. .... **CARACAL**
lyrebird genus ...... **MENURA**
lyric .... **ODE, MELIC**
lyric Muse .... **ERATO**
Lytton heroine .... **IONE**

94

M

a macaque Indian **BRUH, RHESUS**
macaw .... **ARA, ARARA**
macaw, Braz.
    ARA, ARARA, MARACAN
mace-bearer .... **BEADLE**
macerate .... **RET, STEEP**
machine, finishing .... **EDGER**
machine, grain cleaner **AWNER**
machine gun .... **BREN, STEN**
machine, hummeling .. **AWNER**
machine, ore-dressing **VANNER**
machine part
    CAM, PAWL, TAPPET
machine, rubber .. **EXTRUDER**
mackerel net .... **SPILLER**
mackerel, young .... **SPIKE**
Madagascar mammal .. **LEMUR**
Madagascar native .... **HOVA**
madam .... **MUM, MAAM**
madder ..... **RUBIA, MUNJEET**
madder, common Eu. **GARANCE**
madder shrub genus ... **EVEA**
madness .... **MANIA**
mafura tree .... **ROKA**
maggot .... **LARVA**
Magi, one of .... **GASPAR**
magic .... **RUNE**
magic: Hindustan **JADU, JADOO**
magic, pert. to .... **GOETIC**
b magic stone .... **AGATE**
magic: W. Ind. .... **OBEAH**
magician .... **MAGE,**
    MAGI, MAGUS, MERLIN
magistrate, Athens **ARCHON**
magistrate, It. .... **DOGE**
magistrate, Rom. ...... **EDILE,**
    AEDILE, CONSUL, PRETOR
magnate ... **MOGUL, TYCOON**
magnifying glass .... **LENS**
Magog, ruler of .... **GOG**
magpie .. **MAG, PIE, MAGG,**
    PIET, PIOT, PYAT, PYET,
    NINUT, PIANET
magpie genus .... **PICA**
mah-jongg piece .... **TILE**
mahatma
    ARAHT, ARHAT, ARAHAT
mahogany pine ...... **TOTARA**
mahogany, Sp. .... **CAOBA**
mahogany streak .... **ROE**
mahogany tree, Ind. ... **TOON**
MAHOMET .. see **MOHAMMED**
MAHOMETAN ... see **MOSLEM**
maid .... **LASS, BONNE**
maid, lady's .... **ABIGAIL**
maid-of-all-work ..... **SLAVEY**
maid, Oriental
    AMA, IYA, AMAH, EYAH
maiden .... **DAMSEL**

c maiden name, signifying..**NEE**
maiden of myth .... **IO**
mail .... **POST, SEND**
mail, coat of . **BRINIE, BYRNIE**
mail, India **DAK, DAUK, DAWK**
main point ... **NUB, GIST, PITH**
maintain.**AVER, HOLD, ASSERT**
maize .... **CORN**
maize bread .... **PIKI**
maize genus .... **ZEA**
major: music .... **DUR**
major third: Gr. mus. .. **DITONE**
make .... **RENDER**
make as one: obs. ...... **UNE**
make evident .... **EVINCE**
make fast: naut. ...... **BELAY**
make good by action . **REDEEM**
make happy .... **ELATE**
make public: Old Eng. **DELATE**
Makua .... **KUA**
malarial fever .... **AGUE**
malarial poison
    MIASM, MIASMA
Malay apple .... **KAWIKA**
Malay canoe
    PRAH, PRAO, PRAU, PROA
Malay chief or headman.**DATO,**
    DATU, DATTO
d Malay dagger ... **CRIS, KRIS,**
  CREES, KREES, CREESE, KREESE
Malay lanseh tree ..... **DUKU**
Malay law .... **ADAT**
Malay lugger .... **TOUP**
malay negrito ..... **ATA, ITA**
Malay nerve ailment ... **LATA**
MALAY OUTRIGGER see MALAY
  CANOE
Malay title of respect .. **TUAN**
Malay ungulate ...... **TAPIR**
Malay verse form ... **PANTUN**
Malay vessel
    PRAH, PRAO, PRAU, PROA
Malay, word meaning dark **AETA**
Malayan ape .... **LAR**
male cat .... **GIB, TOM**
male figure, used as support
    ATLAS, TELAMON
male swan .... **COB**
malefic .... **EVIL**
malic acid, fruit with
    ATTA, APPLE, GRAPE
malign .... **REVILE**
malignant .... **EVIL**
malignant spirit ... **KER, KERES**
malleable ..... **SOFT, DUCTILE**
mallet .... **MALL, GAVEL**
malt drink, pert. to .... **ALY**
malt infusion .... **WORT**
maltreat .... **ABUSE**

a MAMMAL .. see also ANIMAL
mammal, sea aquatic .. SEAL,
    OTTER, WHALE, DUGONG,
    MANATEE
mammoth .... GIANT
man-eating monster ... LAMIA
man, handsome ...... ADONIS
man, rich .... CROESUS
man's name .. ELI, GUY, IAN,
    IRA, JOB, LEE, RAY, REX,
    ADAM, ALAN, AMOS,
    BRAM, CARL, DANA, DION,
    EBEN, EMIL, ENOS, ERIC,
    EVAN, EZRA, HANS, HUGH,
    HUGO, IVAN, JOEL, JOHN,
    JOSE, JUAN, JUDE, KARL,
    KNUT, LEON, LUKE, MARC,
    MARK, NEIL, NOEL, OTTO,
    OWEN, PAUL, SEAN, SETH,
    TEIG, BASIL, CALEB,
    CLARE, ENOCH, HIRAM,
    HOMER, SERGE, STEVE,
    TERRY, DEXTER, GASPAR,
    GEORGE, OLIVER, SAMSON,
    STEVEN, WARREN
man's nickname. AL, ABE, ALF,
    BEN, BOB, DON, GUS, JIM,
    JOE, KIT, LEW, LON, LOU,
    MAC, MAT, MAX, MOE,
    NED, PAT, ROB, SAM, SID,
b SIM, TED, TOM, ABIE,
    ALGY, ANDY, BART, BERT,
    BILL, BONY, DAVE, DAVY,
    DICK, DODE, FRED, GENE,
    JACK, JAKE, JOCK, JOEY,
    MART, MIKE, MOSE, NOLL,
    PETE, PHIL, RUBE, TOBY,
    TONY, WALT, ZACH, ZEKE
manageable .... YARE
manager .... GERENT
Manasseh, city of ...... ANER
Manasseh, son of ..... AMON
mandarin's home
            YAMEN, YAMUN
manducate .... EAT
maned .... JUBATE
manger .... CRIB, CRECHE
mangle .... MAUL
mango, P. I. ...... CARABAO
mania .... CRAZE
manifest .... SHOW,
        OVERT, ATTEST, EVINCE
manifestation .... AURA
manifestation of god of lower
    world .... SERAPIS
maniple FANO, FANON, FANUM
manner
        AIR, WAY, MIEN, MODE
manner of walking ..... GAIT
manners .... MORES
manor .... DEMENE, DEMESNE

c mantis crab .... SQUILLA
mantle .... CAPE
manual training, Swed. . SLOID,
            SLOYD
manuao .... IAO
Manxman .... GAEL
many .... MAINT
many-colored
        PIED, PINTO, MOTLEY
many-colored stone ... AGATE
Maori tattooing .... MOKO
Maori village ... KAIK, KAIKA
Maori wages .... UTU
Maori war club MERE, MARREE
Maori war-club wood ... RATA
map .... PLAT
map in a map .... INSET
maple fruit, seed .... SAMARA
maple genus .... ACER
maple tree tap .... SPILE
mar .... DEFACE
marabou .... ARGALA
marble MIB, MIG, TAW, MIGG,
        AGATE, AGGIE, MARMOR,
        MEALIE, SHOOTER
marble, Belgian RANCE, RANSE
marble, choice   ALAY, ALLEY
marble, It. .... CARRARA
marble, Rom. .... CIPOLIN
d marble, white .... DOLOMITE
marbles, game at ...... TAW
March King .... SOUSA
mare: Gypsy .... GRASNI
margin .... RIM, EDGE, MARGE
marginal reading, Hebrew
    Bible .... KRI
margosa tree .... NIM, NEEM
Marie Wilson, character played
    by .... IRMA
MARINE .. see also SEA
marine annelid .... LURG
marine fish, E. Ind. ... DORAB
marine measure, Jap. ..... RI
marine snail
        WELK, WILK, WHELK
marine snail genus ... NERITA
marine turtle genus..CARETTA
marine worm .... SYLLID
marionette maker ...... SARG
mark .... STIGMA, STIGMATA
mark, diacritic TILDE, MACRON
mark of omission ..... CARET
mark, reference
        OBELI, OBELUS, OBELISK
mark, short vowel .... BREVE
marked with spots: bot. NOTATE
marker, Gr. & Rom. .... STELA,
        STELE, STELAE, STELAI

a market .... **MART, SELL,**
        VEND, RIALTO
market: India .... **PASAR**
market, Oriental
        SUQ, SOOK, SOUK
market place **BAZAR, BAZAAR**
market place, Gr. .... **AGORA**
marksman .... **AIMER**
marmalade tree
        MAMEY, SAPOTE
marmoset .... **MICO**
marmoset, S. Am. .. **TAMARIN**
"Marner, — " Eliot novel **SILAS**
marriage, absence of .. **AGAMY**
marriage notice **BAN, BANNS**
marriage portion, pert. to
        DOTAL
marriage portion: Scot.
        DOS, DOTE
marriage settlement
  DOS, DOT, DOWRY, DOWERY
marriage vows .... **TROTH**
marriageable .... **NUBILE**
marrow .... **PITH**
marry .... **WED, WIVE**
Mars .... **ARES**
Mars' outer satellite .. **DEIMOS**
Mars, pert. to .... **AREAN**
"Marseillaise" author ... **LISLE**

b marsh .... **BOG, FEN,**
      SLUE, LIMAN, SWALE
marsh elder .... **IVA**
marsh fever .... **HELODES**
marsh gas .... **METHANE**
marsh hen .... **RAIL**
marsh mallow .... **ALTEA**
marsh marigold .... **CAPER**
marsh plant
    REED, SEDGE, FESCUE
marshal, Waterloo .... **NEY**
marshy . **PALUDAL, PALUDINE**
marsupial, arboreal
    COALA, KOALA, POSSUM
marten .... **SOBOL**
martyr, 1st Christian . **STEPHEN**
marvel .... **MIRACLE**
Mascagni heroine .... **LOLA**
MASCULINE
    see also MALE, MAN'S
mashy .... **IRON**
masjid ...... **MOSK, MOSQUE**
mask, half .... **DOMINO**
mask topknot, Gr. ..... **ONKOS**
masons' pickax ...... **GURLET**
masquerade cloak .... **DOMINO**
mass ...... **GOB, WAD, BULK**
mass book .... **MISSAL**
mass meeting .... **RALLY**
mass, pert. to .... **MISSATICAL**
mass, rounded .... **BOLUS**
mast .... **SPAR**

c mast: obs. .... **SPIR**
mast, support .... **BIBB**
mast, wood for .... **POON**
master: archaic .... **DAN**
master, India
    MIAN, SAHEB, SAHIB
master, pert. to .... **HERILE**
master, S. Afr. .... **BAAS**
master-stroke .... **COUP**
mastic tree .... **ACOMA**
masticate ...... **CHAW, CHEW**
mat, ornamental ...... **DOILY**
match, friction . **FUSEE, FUZEE**
match, wax .... **VESTA**
matchmaker .... **EROS**
MATERIAL ... see also FABRIC
maternity goddess, Egypt . **APET**
matgrass .... **NARD**
math quantity .**SINE, OPERAND**
math ratio, quantity .. **PI, SINE**
math term, hyperbolic function
    COSH, SECH, SINH, TANH
matter: law .... **RES**
matter-of-fact ...... **LITERAL**
matter: philos. .... **HYLE**
mattress case .... **TICK**
mature ..... **AGE, RIPE, RIPEN**
mature reproductive cell
    GAMETE

d maul .... **MALLET**
Mau Mau territory .... **KENYA**
Mauna — .... **LOA**
mausoleum, at Agra ..... **TAJ**
maw: dialect .... **MAA**
maxilla .... **JAW, MALA**
maxim . **SAW, ADAGE, AXIOM,**
    GNOME, MOTTO, SAYING
maxwell per ampere turn . **PERM**
May 1, Celtic ...... **BELTANE**
May fly .... **DUN**
MAYAN . see MAYAN INDIAN,
    page 192
Mayan year .... **HAAB**
Mayan year-end days .. **UAYEB**
mayor, Sp. . **ALCADE, ALCALDE**
meadow .... **LEA, MEAD**
meadow barley .... **RIE**
meadow grass genus ..... **POA**
meadow mouse .... **VOLE**
meadow saxifrage ..... **SESELI**
meadowsweet **SPIREA, SPIRAEA**
meager .... **SCANT,**
    LENTEN, SCANTY
meal .... **REPAST**
meal, boiled .... **MUSH**
meal, fine .... **FARINA**
meal, grain .. **PINOLA, PINOLE**
meal, Indian, Hindu **ATA, ATTA**
meal, light .... **BEVER**

a meaning .... **SENSE, PURPORT**
meantime .... **INTERIM**
MEASURE ... Area, Liquid, Dry
Length, Distance
see SPECIAL SECTION
measure ...... **EM, EN, GAGE,
METE, PACE, GAUGE**
MEASURE, BIB. .. see HEBREW
MEASURE
measure, Chin. length .... **LI**
"Measure for Measure"
character .... **ANGELO**
MEASURE, DRY, BIB. .... see
HEBREW DRY MEASURE
measure, Jap. distance ... **RI**
measure of distance, Ang.-Ind.
COSS
measure of spirits .... **PEG**
measure, old Arab ...... **SAA**
measure, old length ...... **ELL**
measure, poetry .... **SCAN**
measure, square .... **AR, ARE**
meat, cut of ...... **HAM, RIB,
CHOP, LOIN, FILET,
STEAK, FILLET**
meat on skewer ...... **CABOB,
KABOB, KEBAB**
meat roll, fried ...... **RISSOLE**
Mecca pilgrim garb .... **IHRAM**
Mecca shrine .... **CAABA,**

b **KAABA, KAABEH**
Mecca, trip to .... **HADJ**
mechanical man ...... **ROBOT**
mechanical part .... **CAM**
mechanics, branch of . **STATICS**
mechanics of motion
DYNAMICS
meddle ...... **PRY, TAMPER**
Medea's father .... **AEETES**
median line of valve ... **RAPHE**
medical .... **IATRIC**
medical fluid .... **SERUM**
medicinal capsule .... **CACHET**
medicinal fruit shrub ... **ALEM**
medicinal gum .... **KINO**
medicinal herb .... **ALOE,
IPECAC, BONESET**
medicinal plant .... **ALOE**
medicinal plant, leaves **SENNA**
medicinal tablet ..... **TROCHE**
medicine man ...... **SHAMAN**
medicine man, S. Am.
PEAI, PIAY
medieval lyric .... **ALBA**
medieval society **GILD, GUILD**
medieval tale, poem . **LAI, LAY**
Medina Arab .... **AUS**
MEDITERRANEAN .... see also
GAZETTEER
Mediterranean, East of.**LEVANT**
Medit. grass .... **DISS**

c Medit. herb genus ...... **AMMI**
Medit. island: It. .... **RODI**
Medit. resort .... **NICE**
medlar .... **MESPIL**
medley .... **OLIO**
Medusa's slayer ..... **PERSEUS**
meet .... **SIT**
meeting ..... **TRYST, SESSION**
meeting, political .... **CAUCUS**
megapode .... **MALEO**
melancholy . **SAD, BLUE, DREAR**
melancholy: poet. ..... **DOLOR**
mellow .... **AGE, RIPE**
melodic .... **ARIOSE**
melodious .... **ARIOSO**
melody .... **AIR, ARIA,
TUNE, MELOS**
melon .... **PEPO, CASABA**
melt together ..... **FUSE, FUZE**
melted .... **MOLTEN**
membership .... **SEAT**
membrane ...... **WEB, TELA,
VELA, VELUM**
memento .... **RELIC**
memorabilia .... **ANA**
memorandum .... **CHIT, NOTE**
memorial post, Indian .. **TOTEM**
memory, pert. to
MNESIC, MNEMONIC
Memphis chief god .... **PTAH**

d Memphis street, famous.**BEALE**
men .... **SONS**
mendacious person ...... **LIAR**
mender, chief .... **TINKER**
mendicant, Mos.
FAKIR, FAKEER
Menelaus' wife .... **HELEN**
menhaden fish .... **POGY**
menhaden, young ... **SARDINE**
Mennonite .... **AMISH**
Menotti heroine .... **AMELIA**
men's party .... **STAG**
mental .... **PHRENIC**
mental deficiency ... **AMENTIA**
mental deficient **IDIOT, MORON**
mention .... **CITE**
Mercator ...... **MAP, CHART**
mercenary . **VENAL, HIRELING**
merchandise .... **WARES**
merchant .... **TRADER**
merchant: India .... **SETH**
"Merchant of Venice" heiress
PORTIA
merchant ship .... **ARGOSY**
merchant vessel, Gr. . **HOLCAD**
Mercury, Gr. .... **HERMES**
Mercury's wand ... **CADUCEUS**
mercy, show .... **SPARE**
mere .... **SIMPLE**
merely .... **ONLY**

merganser duck **SMEW, GARBILL**
merge .... **MELD**
merit .... **EARN**
merriment .... **GLEE**
merry-go-round ... **CAROUSAL,
CAROUSEL, CARROUSAL**
"Merry Widow" composer **LEHAR**
"Merry Wives" character
PISTOL
mesh .... **NET, WEB**
Mesopotamia ..... **IRAK, IRAQ**
Mesopotamian boat **GUFA, KUFA**
Mesopotamian city ..... **URFA**
mesquite bean flour ... **PINOLE**
mess, to make a ...... **BOTCH**
mestizo .... **METIS**
metal .... **TIN, MONEL**

metal alloy .... **BRASS,
MONEL, BRONZE**
metal, bar of .... **INGOT**
metal bar on house door . **RISP**
metal casting .... **PIG, INGOT**
metal, coat with .**PLATE, TERNE**
metal-decorating art .. **NIELLO**
metal disk .... **MEDAL**
metal dross .... **SLAG**
metal filings .... **LEMEL**
metal fissure .... **LODE**
metal leaf .... **FOIL**
metal mixture .... **ALLOY**
metal refuse .... **SCORIA**
metal spacer: print. ..... **SLUG**
metal suit .... **MAIL**
metal sulfide, impure . **MATTE**
metal, white .... **TIN**
metallic rock .... **ORE**
metalware, lacquered .... **TOLE**
metalwork, god of .. **VULCAN**
metarabic acid ..... **CERASIN**
meteor .... **LEONID**
meteor, exploding
BOLIS, BOLIDE
meter, Dutch .... **EL**
meter, one-millionth .. **MICRON**
meters, 100 sq. ...... **AR, ARE**
metheglin .... **MEAD**
method ...... **PLAN, ORDER**
Methuselah's grandson .. **NOAH**
methyl-phenol
CRESOL, CRESSOL
metric measure ..... **AR, ARE,
GRAM, KILO, LITER, METER,
STERE, DECARE, HECTARE**
metric "quart" .... **LITER**
metrical beat .... **ICTUS**
metrical unit .... **MORA**
metropolitan .... **URBAN**
mew .... **GULL**
mew, cat's .... **MIAU, MIAW,
MIAOU, MIAUL**

Mexican dollar .... **PESO**
Mex. mush .... **ATOLE**
Mex. painter .... **RIVERA**
Mex. persimmon .... **CHAPOTE**
Mex. plant .... **JALAP**
Mex. president ...... **ALEMAN,
CALLES, MADERO**
Mex. resin tree .... **DRAGO**
Mex. rodent .... **TUCAN**
Mex. slave .... **PEON**
Mex. spiny tree ...... **RETAMA**
Mex. timber tree ...... **ABETO**
Mex. wind instrument . **CLARIN**
mezzanine .... **ENTRESOL**
miasma .... **MALARIA**
mica, kind of .... **BIOTITE**
mica of muscovite ...... **TALC**
microbe .... **GERM**
microspores .... **POLLEN**
middle .... **MESAL,
MESNE, MEDIAN**
middle, in the ...... **ATWEEN**
middle, toward .... **MESAD**
middling .... **SOSO**
Midgard Serpent slayer .. **THOR**
midge .... **GNAT**
midship, off .... **ABEAM**
"Midsummer Night's Dream"
character .. **PUCK, SNUG**
midwife: India .... **DHAI**
MID-EAST land .. **IRAK, IRAQ**
mien .... **AIR**
might .... **POWER**
mignonette ... **GREEN, RESEDA**
migrate .... **TREK**
migratory worker
OKIE, ARKIE
Mikado's court . **DAIRI, DAIRO**
Milanion's wife ... **ATALANTA**
Milan's "Met" ..... **LA SCALA**
mild ...... **SHY, MEEK, SOFT,
BLAND, GENTLE**
mildness .... **LENITY**
mile: naut. .... **KNOT**
mile, part of, Burma ... **DHA**
Miled, son of .... **IR, ITH, EBER**
milestone .... **STELE**
milfoil .... **YARROW**
military award .... **DSO**
military cap .... **KEPI**
military command ... **AT EASE**
military group . **CADRE, CORPS**
military maneuvers .. **TACTICS**
milk, coagulated ...... **CURD**
milk coagulator ..... **RENNIN**
milk, curdled .... **CLABBER**
milk, part of **SERUM, LACTOSE**
milk, pert. to .... **LACTIC**
milk: pharm. .... **LAC**
milk protein .... **CASEINE**

a milk, watery part of .... WHEY
milkfish .... AWA, SABALO
Milky Way .... GALAXY
mill .... QUERN
MILLET
    see also GRAIN SORGHUM
millet, India JOAR,JUAR,CHENA
millimeter, 1000th part MICRON
millstone support .... RYND
millwheel board .... LADE
millwheel bucket .... AWE
Milton, masque by .... COMUS
Milton rebel angel ..... ARIEL
mime .... APER
mimic ...... APE, APER, MIME
mimicking, practice of . APISM
mimosa .... ACACIA
minced oath .. GAD, GED, GEE,
    LUD, DRAT, EGAD, HECK,
    OONS, SWOW, MAFEY,
    MACKINS
mind .... CARE, TEND
mind, opposite of: Hindu
    ATTA, ATMAN
mind: philos. .... NOUS
Mindanao native, Indonesian
    ATA, AETA, MORO
mine ceiling .... ASTEL
mine entrance .... ADIT
mine narrow veins ..... RESUE
b mine passage .... STULM
mine roof support .... NOG
mine shaft drain pit .... SUMP
mine step .... LOB
mineral, alkaline ..... TRONA
mineral, blue .... IOLITE
mineral group ...... URANITE
mineral group, pert. to . SALIC
mineral, hard SPINEL, SPINELLE
mineral, lustrous .... SPAR
mineral, raw, native ..... ORE
mineral salt .... ALUM
mineral, soft .... TALC
mineral spring .... SPA
mineral tar .... BREA
mineral, transparent ... MICA
mineral used gun-powder NITER
Minerva .... ATHENA
minim .... DROP
mining refuse .... ATTLE
mining road .... BORD
mining tool ..... GAD, BEELE
minister, Moslem VIZIR, VIZIER
minister (to) .... CATER
mink, Amer. .... VISON
minority, legal ...... NONAGE
Minos' daughter .... ARIADNE
Minotaur's slayer .... THESEUS
minstrel .... RIMER
minstrel, medieval ... GOLIARD
minstrel, Norse . SCALD, SKALD

c mint .... COIN
mint, Europ. ... CLARE, CLARY,
    CLARRY, HYSSOP, DITTANY
mint genus .... MENTHA
mint herb .... SAGE
mints, the .... NEPETA
minus .... LESS
minute .... WEE, TINY, SMALL
mira .... STAR
miracle, scene of first .. CANA
mirage .... SERAB
miscellany .... ANA
mischief .... HOB
mischievous spirit ...... PUCK
misconceive .... ERR
Mishnah section . ABOT, ABOTH
Mishnah section festivals .MOED
misinterpret .... ERR
mislay .... LOSE
misplay .... ERROR
misrepresent .... BELIE
Miss Dombey's suitor .. TOOTS
missile .... DART, SNARK
missile, guided ... JUNO, NIKE,
    THOR, ATLAS, TITAN,
    BOMARC, JUPITER, PERSH-
    ING, REGULUS, REDSTONE,
    BOLD ORION,MINUTEMAN
mist .... HAZE, SMUR, MISLE
mist: Eng. .... RAG
d mistake, stupid .... BONER
mistakes .... ERRATA
mistakes, make .... ERR
mite .... ACARI, ATOMY,
    ACARID, ACARUS
mite genus .. ACARI, ACARUS
mite, tick, order of
    ACARIDA, ACARINA
mitigate . EASE, ABATE, ALLAY
mix .... STIR, ADDLE. KNEAD
mixture .... OLIO
mixture, mineral .... MAGMA
Moab city, chief .... UR
Moab king .... MESHA
Moabites, Bibl. .... EMIM
moat .... FOSS, FOSSE
"Moby Dick" pursuer .. AHAB
moccasin .... PAC
mock ..... GIBE, JIBE, FLEER,
    TAUNT, DERIDE
mock blow .... FEINT
mock orange ...... SYRINGA
mockingbird genus .... MIMUS
model, perfect ..... PARAGON
moderate .... BATE,
    ABATE, LESSEN
modernist .... NEO
modest .... SHY, DEMURE
modify .... VARY, ALTER,
    EMEND, TEMPER
Mogul emperor ...... AKBAR

MOHAMMEDAN .. see MOSLEM
Mohammedanism ...... ISLAM
Mohammed's adopted son . ALI
Mohammed's birthplace .MECCA
Mohammed's daughter .FATIMA
Mohammed's descendant
   SAID, SEID, SAYID
Mohammed's son-in-law .. ALI
Mohammed's supporters .ANSAR
Mohammed's title .... ALI
Mohammed's tomb city MEDINA
Mohammed's uncle .... ABBAS
Mohammed's wife ..... AISHA
Mohawk, city on .... UTICA
Mohicans, last of the .. UNCAS
moiety .... HALF
moist .... WET, DAMP, DANK,
  DEWY, UVID, HUMID
moist spot, rock-ledge .... SIPE
moisten ... DAMPEN, IMBRUE
moisture, having medium MESIC
mojarra fish .... PATAO
molasses .. TREACLE, TRIACLE
molasses, rum made from
    TAFIA
mold .... MUST
mold, hole in casting .GIT, GEAT
molded clay .... PUG
molding .. CYMA, GULA, OGEE,
  TORUS, REGLET, REEDING
molding, concave
   CONGE, SCOTIA
molding, convex
  OVOLO, TORUS, ASTRAGAL
molding, curved . CYMA, OGEE
molding, edge of . ARIS, ARRIS
molding, flat .... FILLET
molding, rounded TORI, TORUS
molding, S-shaped ...... OGEE
molding, square ...... LISTEL
moldings, quarter-round .OVOLI
moldy .... MUSTY
mole .... NEVUS, NAEVUS
mole cricket, S. Am. . CHANGA
mole genus .... TALPA
molecule part .... ION
molelike mammal ... DESMAN
MOLLUSK.see also GASTROPOD
mollusk ...... CLAM, CHITON,
  MUSSEL, ABALONE
mollusk, bivalve ..... SCALLOP
mollusk, chamber-shelled
   NAUTILUS
mollusk, gastropod
  SNAIL, ABALONE
mollusk genus ARCA, MUREX,
  OLIVA, ANOMIA
mollusk, largest ...... CHAMA
mollusk's rasp organ .. RADULA
molt .... MEW, SHED

molten rock ... LAVA, MAGMA
moment ..... MO, JIFF, TRICE
Monaco, pert. to
  MONACAN, MONEGASQUE
monad .... ATOM, UNIT
monastery .... MANDRA
monastery church .. MINSTER
MONEY . see also SPECIAL
   SECTION COINS
money ... CASH, CUSH, GELT
money, Amer. Ind. .. WAMPUM
money, bronze .... AES
money certificate .BOND, SCRIP
money, copper .... AES
money: dialect .... SPENSE
money, early Eng. .... ORA
money drawer .... TILL
money exchange fee .... AGIO
money, fishhook . LARI, LARIN
money, medieval .... ORA
money of account .... ORA
money, piece of .... COIN
money premium .... AGIO
money, put in .... INVEST
money reserve .... FUND
money, shell . SEWAN, SEAWAN
money, trade unit .... UNITAS
moneylender .... USURER
moneylender, Ind. .. MAHAJAN
Mongol ... HU, ELEUT, TATAR,
  ELEUTH, TARTAR
Mongol dynasty .... YUAN
Mongol warrior .... TATAR
Mongolian tent .... YURT
Mongoloid .... TURK, DURBAN
Mongoloid in Indo-China .SHAN
mongrel .... CUR, MUTT
monitor lizard .... URAN
monk .. FRA, FRIAR, CENOBITE
monk, Buddhist ...... ARAHT,
  ARHAT, ARAHAT
monk, Eng. ...... BEDA, BEDE
monk, Gr. Church ... CALOYER
monk, head .... ABBOT
monk settlement.SCETE, SKETE
monk's hood .... COWL
monk's title ..... FRA, ABBOT
monkey .... APE, LAR, SAI,
  SIME, SIMIAN, MARMOSET
monkey, Afr. .... MONA,
  WAAG, GRIVET
monkey, Asia .... LANGUR
monkey, capuchin .... SAI
monkey, Chin. .... DOUC
monkey genus .... CEBUS
monkey, guenon ...... NISNAS
monkey, howling ...... ARABA
monkey, P. I. .... MACHIN
monkey puzzle .... PINON
monkey, red, Afr. ..... PATAS
monkey, small .... LEMUR

a monkey, S. Am. .. **SAKI, TITI, ACARI, ARABA, SAJOU, TETEE, PINCHE, SAGUIN, SAMIRI, SAIMIRI, SAPAJOU**
monkey, spider, genus.**QUATA, ATELES, COAITA**
monkshood .... **ATIS, ATEES, ACONITE**
monolith .... **MENHIR**
monopoly ..... **TRUST, CARTEL**
monosaccharide .... **OSE**
Mons, language of ...... **PEGU**
monster .. **GOUL, GOWL, OGRE**
monster, Gr. myth .. **CHIMERA**
monster, half-man-bull
MINOTAUR
monster: med. ...... **TERAS**
monster, 100 eyes ..... **ARGUS**
monster slain by Hercules
HYDRA
month, Egypt. .... **AHET, APAP, TYBI**
month, first day, Rom.
CALENDS, KALENDS
month, Hindu .... **ASIN, JETH, KUAR, MAGH**
month, in last .... **ULTIMO**
month, Jewish ancient ..... **AB** (11th), **BUL** (8th), **ZIF**
b (8th), **ABIB** (7th), **ADAR** (6th), **ELUL** (12th), **IYAR**, (8th), **NISAN** (7th), **SEBAT** (5th), **SIVAN** (9th), **TEBET** (4th), **TIZRI** (1st), **TEBETH** (4th), **TISHRI** (1st)
month, Moslem ...... **RABIA, RAJAB, SAFAR, SHABAN, RAMADAN**
month, Nisan .... **ABIB**
monument, stone.**LECH, CAIRN, DOLMEN, CROMLECH**
moon . **LUNA, DIANA, PHOEBE**
moon, age at beginning of calendar year ..... **EPACT**
moon angel .... **MAH**
moon flower .... **ACHETE**
moon god, Babyl. .. **SIN, ENZU**
moon goddess ...... **ASTARTE**
moon goddess, Gr. .... **SELENA, SELENE, ARTEMIS**
moon goddess, Rom. ... **LUNA, DIAN, DIANA**
moon nearest earth, point
PERIGEE
moon valley ..... **RILL, RILLE**
moor grass .... **NARD**
moorhen .... **GORHEN**
Moorish .... **MORISCAN**
moose genus .... **ALCES**
mop .... **SWAB, SWOB**

c Mogul, one of .... **HOPI**
morals overseer ...... **CENSOR**
morass .... **QUAG, MARSH**
moray .... **EEL**
Mordecai, enemy of .. **HAMAN**
more .... **PLUS**
more! ...... **BIS, PIU, ENCORE**
more than enough ...... **TOO, EXTRA, EXCESS**
More's island .... **UTOPIA**
morepork, N. Z. .. **PEHO, RURU**
morindin dye .... **AL**
moringa seed .... **BEN**
morning glory ..... **IPOMEA**
morning music ...... **AUBADE**
morning: P. I. .... **UMAGA**
morning prayer ...... **MATINS**
morning song .... **MATIN**
Moro .... **SULU, LANAO**
Moro chief **DATO, DATU, DATTO**
Moro mantle .... **JABUL**
Moroccan Berber ...... **RIFF**
Moroccan land, public .. **GISH**
Moroccan native .... **MOOR**
moron .... **AMENT, IDIOT**
morose ... **BLUE, GLUM, GRUM**
morsel .... **ORT**
mortar implement .... **PESTLE**
d mortar ingredient ...... **LIME**
mortar mixer ... . **RAB**
mortar tray .... **HOD**
mortise insert .... **TENON**
Mosaic law .... **TORA, TORAH**
mosaic piece .... **TESSERA**
Moselle, river to .... **SAAR**
Moses, law given to here
SINA, SINAI
Moses' brother .... **AARON**
Moses' death mountain .. **NEBO**
Moses' father-in-law .. **JETHRO**
Moses' spy in Canaan .. **CALEB**
MOSLEM ..... see also MECCA
Moslem .... **TURK**
Moslem ablution before prayer
WIDU, WUDU, WUZU
Moslem, Afr. .... **MOOR**
Moslem beggar .**FAKIR, FAKEER**
Moslem bible .... **KORAN**
Moslem call to prayer
ADAN, AZAN
Moslem chief .... **AGA, IMAM, DATTO**
Moslem chief gold coin.**DINAR**
Moslem converts ..... **ANSAR**
Moslem deity ... **JANN, ALLAH**
Moslem demon .. **JANN, EBLIS**
Moslem Easter .... **EED**
Moslem fast ...... **RAMADAN**
Moslem festival ...... **BAIRAM**

a Moslem fiat .... **IRADE**
Moslem fourth Caliph .... **ALI**
Moslem grant of property
WAKF, WAQF, WUKF
Moslem guide .... **PIR**
Moslem holy city ..... **MECCA**
Moslem holy man
IMAM, IMAUM
Moslem, hostile to Crusaders
SARACEN
Moslem in Turkestan ... **SALAR**
Moslem judge .. **CADI, CAZI,**
CAZY, KADI, KAZI, KAZY
Moslem leader . **IMAM, IMAUM**
Moslem marriage. **MOTA, MUTA**
Moslem marriage settlement
MAHR
MOSLEM MORO ... see **MORO**
CHIEF
Moslem mystic .... **SUFI**
Moslem name .... **ALI**
Moslem Negroids .... **MABA**
Moslem noble .... **AMIR, EMIR,**
AMEER, EMEER
Moslem, N. W. India ... **SWAT**
Moslem official .... **AGA**
Moslem, orthodox ..... **HANIF**
Moslem, P.I. .... **MORO**
Moslem potentate .... **AGA**
Moslem prayer .... **SALAT**
Moslem prayer place ... **IDGAH**
Moslem priest . **IMAM, IMAUM**
b Moslem prince ... **AMIR, EMIR,**
AMEER, EMEER
Moslem principle .... **IJMA**
Moslem pulpit ...... **MIMBAR**
Moslem reformer .... **WAHABI**
Moslem religion .... **ISLAM**
Moslem religious college
ULEMA
Moslem ruler .... **HAKIM**
Moslem saber ...... **SCIMITAR**
Moslem saint .... **PIR**
Moslem school ..... **MADRASA**
Moslem spirit ... **JINN, JINNI**
Moslem spiritual guide ... **PIR**
Moslem teacher .. **ALIM, COJA**
Moslem temple. **MOSK, MOSQUE**
Moslem theologians ... **ULEMA**
Moslem title .... **AGA, RAIS,**
REIS, SEID, SIDI, SYED,
SYUD, CALIF, SAYID,
SEYID, CALIPH
Moslem tunic .. **JAMA, JAMAH**
Moslem weight .... **ROTL**
Moslem woman's dress .. **IZAR**
Moslems, Sunnite .... **SART**
Moslemized Bulgarian . **POMAK**
mosque .... **MASJID**
mosque, central .... **JAMI**
mosque, Jerusalem .... **OMAR**
mosque student .... **SOFTA**

c mosquito, genus, yellow-fever
AEDES
mossbunker fish .... **POGY**
moss of Ceylon .... **AGAR**
moth .... **IO, LUNA,**
EGGER, TINEA
moth, clearwing, genus . **SESIA**
moth, clothes .... **TINEA**
moth, green .... **LUNA**
mother goddess; Baby. . **ERUA**
mother goddesses. Hindu **MATRIS**
mother of Arthur .... **IGRAINE**
mother of gods .... **RHEA**
MOTHER OF IRISH GODS .. see
page 200
mother-of-pearl .... **NACRE**
mother-of-pearl shell. **ABALONE**
mother turned to stone . **NIOBE**
mother's side, related on
ENATE, ENATIC
mother's side, relation on
ENATE, ENATION
motherless calf .. **DOGY, DOGIE**
motion, producing .... **MOTILE**
motionless ..... **INERT, STILL**
motive ...... **CAUSE, REASON**
motmot, S. Am. ..... **HOUTOU**
motor part .... **ROTOR**
mottled .... **PIED, PINTO**
d mottled, as wood ...... **ROEY**
MOULDING .... see **MOLDING**
mound ...... **TUMP, BARROW**
mound, Polyn. .... **AHU**
Mount of Olives ...... **OLIVET**
mountain, Alps .... **BLANC**
mountain ash .. **SORB, ROWAN**
mountain, Asia Minor ..... **IDA**
mountain, Bibl. .. **HOR, NEBO,**
SEIR, SINA, HOREB,
SINAI, ARARAT
(see others on page 197)
mountain chain .... **SIERRA**
mountain climbing staff .**PITON**
mountain crest .... **ARETE**
mountain, Crete .... **IDA**
mountain, Edom .... **HOR**
mountain, fabled Hindu . **MERU**
mountain, famous .... **IDA**
mountain, Gr. ...... **HELICON**
mountain in Thessaly ... **OSSA**
mountain lion .... **PUMA**
mountain mint .... **BASIL**
mountain, Moab .... **NEBO**
mountain pass .... **COL**
mountain pass, Alps **CENIS**
mountain pass, India
GAUT, GHAT
mountain peak .... **ALP**
mountain pool .... **TARN**
mountain recess .... **CWM**
mountain ridge .... **ARETE**

a mountain ridge, Port. .. **SERRA**
mountain, 2nd highest N.A.
   LOGAN
mountain sickness **PUNA, VETA**
mountain spinach ..... **ORACH**
mountain spur .... **ARETE**
mountains, Asia .... **ALTAI**
mountains, myth ... **KAF, QAF**
mourn .... **WEEP,**
   GRIEVE, LAMENT
mournful .... **SAD, DIRE**
mourning band .... **CRAPE**
mouse .... **VOLE**
mouse, field .... **VOLE**
mouse genus .... **MUS**
mousebird ..... **COLY, SHRIKE**
mouth .... **OS, ORA**
mouth, away from .... **ABORAL**
mouth open .... **AGAPE**
mouth, river .... **DELTA**
mouth, tidal river ...... **FRITH**
mouth, toward .... **ORAD**
mouthful .... **SIP, SUP**
mouthlike orifice ...... **STOMA**
mouthpiece ..... **REED, BOCAL**
move .... **STIR, AFFECT**
move a camera .... **PAN**
move back ..... **EBB, RECEDE**
move to and fro
   WAG, FLAP, SWAY
b movement: biol. .... **TAXIS**
movement, capable of . **MOTILE**
movement: music ...... **MOTO**
movement,with:music **CONMOTO**
movie: Sp. .... **CINE**
moving part .... **ROTOR**
mow, barn's .... **LOFT**
mow of hay .... **GOAF**
mowed strip .... **SWATH**
Mowgli's bear friend ... **BALU,**
   BALOO
Mozambique native ...... **YAO**
muck .... **MIRE**
mud .... **MIRE, MURGEON**
mud deposit .... **SILT**
mud, slimy .... **OOZE**
mud, stick in .... **MIRE**
mud, viscous .... **SLIME**
mud, volcano .... **SALSE**
muddle .... **MESS, ADDLE**
muddy .... **ROIL**
muffin .... **GEM**
mug .... **STEIN, NOGGIN**
mug, small .... **TOBY**
mugger .... **GOA**
mulatto .... **METIS**
mulberry bark cloth .... **TAPA**
mulberry genus ...... **MORUS**
mulberry, India ...... **AL, AAL**
mulct .... **FINE, AMERCE**
mullet, red .... **SUR**

c multiform .... **DIVERSE**
multiplicand: math. . **FACIEND**
multiplier: math. .... **FACIENT**
multitude .... **HOST, HORDE**
mum .... **ALE**
munch .... **CHAMP**
mundane .... **TERRENE**
Munich's river .... **ISAR**
municipal officer, Sp. . **ALCADE,**
   ALCAID, ALCAIDE,
   ALCAYDE
muntjac deer . **KAKAR, RATWA**
murder by suffocation . **BURKE**
murder fine, Scot. .... **CRO**
murderer, first .... **CAIN**
murmuring sound
   CURR, PURL, PURR
Musci, plant of .... **MOSS**
muscle .... **THEW, SINEW**
muscle coordination, lack of
   ATAXIA
muscle, deep, pert. to
   SCALENE
muscle, kind of
   ERECTOR, LEVATOR
muscle, like .... **MYOID**
muscle, round, rolling .. **TERES**
muscle, stretching .... **TENSOR**
muscles .... **BRAWN**
d muscular action, irregular
   ATAXIA
muscular spasm .... **TIC**
Muse, chief .... **CALLIOPE**
muse in reverie .... **REVE**
Muse of astronomy ... **URANIA**
Muse of comedy ..... **THALIA**
Muse of dancing .**TERPSICHORE**
Muse of history .... **CLIO**
Muse of lyric poetry
   CLIO, ERATO
Muse of music ...... **EUTERPE**
Muse of poetry .... **ERATO**
Muse of sacred lyric
   POLYMNIA
Muse of tragedy . **MELPOMENE**
Muses, 9 .... **PIERIDES**
Muses' region .... **AONIA**
Muses, The .... **NINE**
musette .... **OBOE**
museum head ...... **CURATOR**
mush .... **ATOLE, SEPON**
mushroom .... **MOREL, MORIL**
mushroom cap .... **PILEUS**
music: as written .... **STA**
music character .... **DOT,**
   CLEF, REST
music drama .... **OPERA**
music for nine .... **NONET**
music for three .... **TRIO**
music for two .... **DUET**
music from the sign: abbr. . **DS**

a music hall .... ODEA,
　　　　ODEON, ODEUM
music interval ...... TRITONE
music: it proceeds .... VA
music lines .... STAFF
music piece
　　SERENATA, SERENATE
music, sacred
　　CHORAL, CHORALE
music symbols, old ... NEUME
MUSICAL .... see also MUSIC
musical beat .... TAKT
musical composition, India
　　　　RAGA
musical direction . STA, TACET
musical instrument ..... ASOR,
　DRUM, FIFE, GIGA, HARP,
　HORN, LUTE, LYRE, OBOE,
　PIPE, REED, TCHE, TUBA,
　TURR, VINA, VIOL, CELLO,
　RAPPEL, SPINET, CLAVIER,
　HELICON, OCARINA
musical sign .. DOT, CLEF, REST
musical study .... ETUDE
musical work .... OPUS
musician, 11th century . GUIDO

c musket ball, India ...... GOLI
Musketeer .... ATHOS,
　　　ARAMIS, PORTHOS
mussel, fresh-water ..... UNIO
must .... STUM
mustache monkey ... MOUSTOC
mustard family plant ... CRESS
musteline animal
　　OTTER, RATEL
mustiness .... FUST
mutilate .... MAIM
muttonbird .... OII
muttonfish .... SAMA
"My Name is —" ..... ARAM
mysteries .... ARCANA
mysterious .... OCCULT
mystery .... RUNE
mystic word, Hindu ...... OM
mystic writing .... RUNE
mythical land ...... LEMURIA
mythical stream .... STYX
mythical submerged island
　　ATLANTIS
mythical warrior .... ARES
MYTHOLOGY .... see SPECIAL
　SECTION, Page 198

N

b nab .... GRAB, ARREST
Nabal's wife: Bibl. .... ABIGAIL
NaCl .... SALT
nahoor sheep .... SNA
nail .... CLAW, TALON,
　　UNGUES, UNGUIS
nail, hooked .... TENTER
nail, mining, surveying .. SPAD
nail, thin .... BRAD
nail with aperture ...... SPAD
nails, 100 lbs. .... KEG
namaycush .... TOGUE
NAME .... see also MAN'S
　NAME, WOMAN'S NAME
name .... DUB, TERM, CLEPE,
　NOMEN, TITLE, ENTITLE
name: Dan. .... NAAM
name plate, shop's .... FACIA
named ... Y-CLEPT, Y-CLEPED
namely .... VIZ
Naomi, name claimed by MARA
Naomi's daughter-in-law . RUTH
naos .... CELLA
nap, coarse, long .... SHAG
nap-raising device ... TEASEL,
　TEASLE, TEAZEL, TEAZLE
nap-raising machine ...... GIG
nap, to raise .... TEASE
napoleon, game like ..... PAM

d Napoleon's brother-in-law
　　MURAT
Napoleon's isle .... ELBA
Napoleon's marshal general NEY
Napoleonic victory .JENA, LODI
Narcissus, nymph who loved
　　ECHO
narcotic .... DOPE, DRUG,
　　HEROIN, OPIATE
narcotic, India . BANG, BHANG
narcotic plant .... DUTRA
narcotic shrub
　　KAT, KAAT, KHAT
narcotic shrub, S. Am.
　　COCA, CUCA
narrate .... TELL
narrow ...... LINEAL, STRAIT
nasal .... RHINAL
Nata's wife: myth ..... NANA
nation: Ger. .... VOLK
nation, pert. to ...... STATAL
NATIVE .... see TRIBES in
　SPECIAL SECTION, Page 191
native ... ITE, RAW, NATAL,
　ENDEMIC, INDIGENE
natural luster, having ... NAIF
natural talent . DOWER, FLAIR
nature ...... OUSIA, ESSENCE
nature goddess ...... CYBELE

Nature

a
nature principal: Hindu . GUNA
nature spirit .... NAT
nature story writer ..... SETON
nautical .... MARINE
nautical cry
AHOY, OHOY, AVAST
Navaho hut .... HOGAN
naval hero .... PERRY
navy jail .... BRIG
near . AT, NIGH, ABOUT, CLOSE
Near East native . ARAB, TURK
Near East river valley .. WADI
near the ear .... PAROTIC
near to .... BY, ON
nearest .... NEXT
nearsighted person .... MYOPE
nearsightedness ..... MYOPIA
neat ...... TIDY, TOSH, TRIG,
TRIM, SPRUCE
neat cattle .... NOWT
neatly .... FEATLY
necessitate .... ENTAIL
neck, nape of .... NUCHA
necklace ..... BEADS, RIVIERE
neckline shape
VEE, BOAT, CREW
neckpiece ...... ASCOT, STOLE
neckpiece, feather ...... BOA
neckpiece, woman's .... FICHU
NECKTIE .... see TIE

b
need .... WANT, REQUIRE
needle .... PROD, BODKIN
needle bug .... NEPA
needle case .... ETUI
needle-shaped ...... ACUATE,
ACERATE
needlefish .... GAR
needlelike bristle .... ACICULA
negative .... NE, NO, NAY,
NON, NOT
negative pole ...... CATHODE
neglect .... OMIT
neglected school subject:
abbr. .... LAT.
negligent .... LAX
negotiate .... TREAT
negrito . ATA, ATI, ITA, AETA,
ATTA
NEGRO .... see also TRIBES in
SPECIAL SECTION
Negro dance .... JUBA
Negro: India .... HUBSHI
NEGRO TRIBE .... see SPECIAL
SECTION
Nelson's victory site ..... NILE
nematocyst .... CNIDA
nemesis .... BANE
Nepal Mongoloid .... RAIS
Nepal native .... KHA
Nepal people .... RAIS
nephew .... NEPOTE

c
nephew, Fijian .... VASU
Neptune .... LER
Neptune's spear ..... TRIDENT
nerve cell .... NEURON
nerve-cell process ...... AXON
nerve layers, brain ..... ALVEI
nervous .... EDGY
nervous disease ...... CHOREA
nest .... NID, NIDE,
NIDI, NIDUS
nest, eagle's .... AERY, AERIE,
EYRY, EYRIE
nested boxes .... INRO
nestling .... EYAS
net .... CLEAR
net, fishing .... SEINE,
STENT, TRAWL
net of hair-lines ..... RETICLE
NETHERLANDS
see SPECIAL SECTION
netlike .... RETIARY
nettle family .. RAMIE, RAMEE
network .... WEB, MESH,
RETE, RETIA
neuroglia .... GLIA
neve .... FIRN
— Nevis, Gt. Brit. peak .. BEN
new .... NOVEL, RECENT
New Caledonia bird .... KAGU
New England state: abbr. .. RI

d
New Guinea area ..... PAPUA
New Guinea tribesman . KARON
New Guinea victory .... GONA
New Guinea wild hog .... BENE
New Jerusalem foundation
JASPER
new, lover of .... NEO
new star .... NOVA
new wine .... MUST
New York harbor isle .... ELLIS
New Zealand aborigine .. ATI
N.Z. bird .... HUIA, KAKI,
PEHO, RURU
N.Z. clan .... ATI
N.Z. evergreen .... TAWA
N.Z. fruit pigeon ...... KUKU
N.Z. laburnum .... GOAI
N.Z. mollusk .... PIPI
N.Z. native .... MAORI
N.Z. native fort ..... PA, PAH
N.Z. parson bird ...... KOKO
N.Z. plant .... KARO
N.Z. rail bird .... WEKA
N.Z. scabbard fish ...... HIKU
N.Z. shrub .... KARO
N.Z. shrub, poisonous .. TUTU
N.Z. subtribe .... HAPU
N.Z. timber tree . GOAI, HINO,
MIRO, PELU, RATA, RIMU,
HINAU, HINOU, KAURI,
KAURY, TOTARA

106

N.Z. tree ... **AKE, KOPI, NAIO, PUKA, TORO**
N.Z. tree, lightwood ... **WHAU**
N.Z. tribe .... **ATI**
N.Z. wages .... **UTU**
N.Z. wood hen .... **WEKA**
news agency, Eng. ... **REUTERS**
news agency, Europ. ... **ANETA**
news agency, Jap. ..... **DOMEI**
news agency, Rus. Soviet . **TASS**
news paragraph .... **ITEM**
newspaper service ...... **AP, UP, INS, UPI, REUTERS**
newspapers .... **PRESS**
newt ..... **EFT, EVET, TRITON**
nibble ... **GNAW, KNAB, KNAP**
niche .... **RECESS**
Nichols' hero .... **ABIE**
Nick Charles' dog .... **ASTA**
Nick Charles' wife ...... **NORA**
nickel steel alloy ...... **INVAR**
nicotine acid .... **NIACIN**
nictitate .... **WINK**
Niger delta native .... **IJO**
NIGERIA
 see SPECIAL SECTION
Nigerian Negro ..... **ARO, IBO**
Nigerian tribe .... **EDO**
NIGERIAN TRIBE OR PEOPLE
 see also SPECIAL SECTION
 page 191

niggard .... **MISER**
nigh .... **NEAR**
night, Norse ..... **NATT, NOTT**
nightingale, Pers. .... **BULBUL**
nightjar .... **POTOO**
nightmare demon, Teut. .**MARA**
nightmare, the ...... **INCUBUS**
nightshade, black
 MOREL, MORIL
Nile, as god .... **HAPI**
Nile island .... **RODA**
Nile native .... **NILOT**
Nile sailboat .... **CANGIA**
Nile valley depression ... **KORE**
Nile, waste matter on
 SADD, SUDD
Nilotic Negro ...... **JUR, LUO, LWO, SUK**
nimble .... **SPRY, AGILE**
nimbus .... **HALO, NIMB**
nimrod .... **HUNTER**
nine-angled polygon .**NONAGON**
nine, based on ..... **NONARY**
nine, group of ..... **ENNEAD**
nine inches .... **SPAN**
nine, music for .... **NONET**
Nineveh's founder ..... **NINUS**
ninth day, every ...... **NONAN**
ninth: mus. .... **NONA**
niton .... **RADON**

nitrogen .... **AZO, AZOTE**
Noah, pert. to .... **NOETIC**
Noah's landing ..... **ARARAT**
Noah's 1st son .... **SEM, SHEM**
Noah's 2nd son .... **HAM**
Nobel prize, literature '04
 MISTRAL
Nobel prize, science .... **UREY**
noble, nobleman .. **DUKE, EARL, LORD, PEER, BARON, COUNT**
noble: Ger. .... **GRAF, RITTER**
NOBLEMAN ...... see **NOBLE**
nobleman, Jap .... **KAMI**
nocturnal mammal **BAT, LEMUR**
nod .... **BOW, BECK**
Nod, west of .... **EDEN**
nodding .... **NUTANT**
noddy tern: Hawaii ..... **NOIO**
node .... **KNOB, KNOT, KNUR, NODUS**
"— noire" .... **BETE**
nomad .... **ARAB, SCENITE**
Nome in Greece .... **ELIS**
nomenclature .... **NAME**
nominal value .... **PAR**
nominate .... **NAME**
non-gypsy: Romany ..... **GAJO**
non-Jew .... **GOI, GOY**
non-Moslem of Turkey or
 Ottoman Empire **RAIA, RAYA**
non-professional ... **LAY, LAIC**
non-union worker .... **SCAB**
nonchalant .... **COOL**
none: dialect .... **NIN**
nonsense . **PISH, POOH, HOOEY**
nonsense creature ...... **GOOP**
noodles: Yiddish **FARFEL, FERFEL**
nook, sheltered .... **COVE**
noose .... **LOOP**
Norn, one of **URD, URTH, WYRD**
Norse "Adam" .... **ASKR**
Norse bard .... **SCALD, SKALD**
Norse chieftain .. **JARL, YARL**
Norse epic .... **EDDA**
Norse explorer ..... **ERIC, LEIF**
NORSE GOD or GODDESSES
 see also GODS and GODDESSES
 and see also SPECIAL SEC-
 TION Page 200
Norse gods .... **VANS, AESIR, VANIR**
Norse letter .... **RUNE**
Norse myth. hero **EGIL, EGILL**
Norse myth. king ...... **ATLI**
Norse myth. "Life" force **LIF**
Norse myth. woman .... **IDUN**
Norse neighbor .... **FINN**
Norse poetry .... **RUNES**
Norse prose .... **EDDA**
Norse sea goddess ...... **RAN**
Norseman ..... **DANE, SWEDE**

a North African .... BERBER
N. Afr. outer garment .. HAIK
North Carolina college .. ELON
North Carolinian .... TARHEEL
North Caucasian language
        UDI, AVAR, UDIC, UDISH
North, Mrs. of fiction . PAMELA
North Sea fishing boat . COBLE
North Sea, river into ELBE, TEES
North Star .... POLARIS
North Syrian deity .... EL
northern .... BOREAL
northern Scandinavian ... LAPP
northern tribe, China ..... HU
northernmost land ..... THULE
Northumberland river ... TYNE
Norway coin .... ORE
Norway territorial division.AMT
Norwegian author ... HAMSUN
Norwegian composer .... GRIEG
Norwegian county AMT, FYLKE
Norwegian saint ...... OLAF
nose .... CONK, NASI,
            NASUS, SNOOP
nose, having large ... NASUTE
nose, having snub ...... SIMOUS
nose openings .. NARES, NARIS
nose, snub .... PUG
nostrils .... NARES, NARIS
b nostrils, of .... NARIC,
            NARIAL, NARINE
"— Nostrum," Mediterranean
                    MARE
not at home .... OUT
not ever: poet. .... NEER
not genuine .... TIN
not in style ...... OUT, PASSE
not long ago .... LATELY
not moving ... INERT, STATIC
not one .... NARY, NONE
not so great .... LESS, FEWER,
                SMALLER
notch ... KERF, NICK, NOCK,
            CRENA, CRENAE
notched .. SERRATE, SERRATED
note .... CHIT, MEMO
note, double, whole .... BREVE
note, Guido's .... UT, ELA
note, Guido's low ..... GAMUT
note, half .... MINIM
note, high, highest .... ELA
note, marginal
            POSTIL, APOSTIL
note: music .. DI, DO, FA, FI,
    LA, LE, LI, ME, MI, RA, RE,
    RI, SE, SI, SO, TE, TI, SOL
note, old Gr. musical .... NETE
note, old musical .... ELA
NOTE, SCALE ...... see NOTE:
                MUSIC
notes, furnish with . ANNOTATE

c notes in Guido's scale .. ELAMI
nothing . NIL, NIX, NUL, NULL,
            ZERO, NIHIL
notion .... BEE, IDEA
notion, capricious ..... WHIM
notional .... IDEAL
notorious .... ARRANT
Nott's son .... DAG
notwithstanding .... YET
nought .... ZERO, NULL
NOUN ENDING
            see SUFFIX, noun
noun form .... CASE
noun suffix of condition .. ATE
noun with only 2 cases. DIPTOTE
nourish .... FEED, FOSTER
nourishment ...... PABULUM
Nova Scotia .... ACADIA
novel, advocate of .... NEO
novel by A. France ..... THAIS
novelty .... FAD
novice .... TIRO, TYRO
now: dial. .... NOO
noxious .... MIASMIC
Nubian .... NUBA
nucha .... NAPE
nuclear element ...... PROTON
nudge .... POKE
nuisance .... PEST
nullify .... NEGATE
d nullify, legally .... VOID
number, describable by .SCALAR
number under 10 ...... DIGIT
number, whole ...... INTEGER
numbered: Bib. .... MENE
numerous .. MANY, MULTIPLE
nun, Franciscan .... CLARE
nun, head .... ABBESS
nun's dress .... HABIT
nunbird .... MONASE
nuque .... NAPE
nurse, Oriental, India .. AMA,
    IYA, AMAH, AYAH, EYAH
nurse, Slavic .... BABA
nursemaid: Fr. .... BONNE
nut ...... COLA, KOLA, LICHI,
        ALMOND, CASHEW,
        LICHEE, LITCHI
nut, beverage .... COLA, KOLA
nut, hickory .... PECAN
nut, pert. to .... NUCAL
nut, P. I. .... PILI
nut, pine .... PINON
nut, stimulating .... BETEL
nut tree, Afr. .... COLA, KOLA
nuts for food .... MAST
nuthatch genus .... SITTA
nutlike drupe .... TRYMA
nutmeg husk .... MACE
nutria .... COYPU

a nutriment ... **FOOD, ALIMENT**
nutritive .... **ALIBLE**
nymph .... **MAIA, LARVA**
nymph, fountain ...... **EGERIA**
nymph, laurel .... **DAPHNE**
nymph, Moslem .... **HOURI**

c nymph, mountain ..... **OREAD**
nymph, ocean ...... **OCEANID**
nymph, water . **NAIAD, NEREID**
nymph, wood . **DRYAD, NAPEA,**
NAPAEA, HAMADRYAD
Nyx's daughter .... **ERIS**

O, plural .... **OES**
oaf .... **LOUT**
oak, Calif. .... **ENCINA**
oak, dried fruit of ... **CAMATA**
oak, evergreen .... **HOLM**
oak moss .... **EVERNIA**
oak, Turkey .... **CERRIS**
oakum, seal with .... **CALK**
oar .... **ROW, BLADE, PROPEL**
oar at stern .... **SCULL**
oasis, N. Afr. ... **WADI, WADY**
oat genus .... **AVENA**
oats as rent .... **AVENAGE**
oath, knight's .... **EGAD**
oath, old-fashioned . **ODS, EGAD**
oath, say under ...... **DEPOSE**
obeisance, Oriental
BOW, SALAAM
b obey .... **HEED, MIND**
object ... **AIM, CAVIL, DEMUR**
object of art .... **CURIO**
objection, petty .... **CAVIL**
objective .... **AIM, GOAL**
obligation .... **TIE, DEBT**
DUTY, ONUS
oblique .... **CANT, BEVEL,**
SLANT, SLOPE
obliterate .... **ERASE, EFFACE**
obliteration .... **RASURE**
oblivion ..... **LETHE, LIMBO**
oblivion stream .... **LETHE**
obscure ..... **DIM, FOG, DARK**
BEDIM, CLOUD
obscure, render ...... **DARKLE**
observe .. **SEE, NOTE, BEHOLD,**
REMARK, CELEBRATE
obstinate .... **SET, HARD**
obstruction, petty .... **CAVIL,**
obtain .... **GET**
obvious ...... **OPEN, PATENT**
obvious, not . **SUBTLE, SUBTILE**
occasional .... **ODD**
Occident .... **WEST**
occipital protuberances ... **INIA**
occultism .... **CABALA**
occupant .... **TENANT**
occupation .... **TRADE**
occupy .... **USE, FILL**
occurrence .... **EVENT**

ocean's rise, fall ...... **TIDE**
oceanic .... **PELAGIC**
oceanic tunicate .... **SALP**
ocher, black ..... **WAD, WADD**
octave, designating high ... **ALT**
octave of church feast ... **UTAS**
octopus .... **POULPE**
octoroon **METIS, MESTEE, MUSTEE**
odd-job man .... **JOEY**
Odin . **WODAN, WODEN, WOTAN**
Odin's brother ...... **VE, VILI**
Odin's granddaughter . **NANNA**
Odin's son ... **TY, TYR, THOR,**
TYRR, VALE, VALI
Odin's wife .... **RIND**
odor .... **AROMA, SCENT**
ODYSSEUS ... see also ULYSSES
d Odysseus' companion . **ELPENOR**
Odysseus' friend ..... **MENTOR**
Odyssey beggar .... **IRUS**
Odyssey singer .... **SIREN**
Oedipus' father .... **LAIUS**
Oedipus' mother .... **JOCASTA**
of speed of sound ...... **SONIC**
of the age: abbr. .... **AET**
off .... **AWAY**
offend .... **CAG**
offense .... **CRIME**
offense: law .. **MALA, MALUM**
offer .... **BID, TENDER**
offered up .... **OBLATE**
offhand .... **CASUAL**
office, ecclesiastic .. **MATINS**
office, priest's ...... **MATINS**
office, R. C. curia
DATARY, DATARIA
officer, church ...... **BEADLE**
officer, court: Scot. .... **MACER**
officer, municipal: Scot. **BAILIE**
officer, Rom. .... **LICTOR**
officer, synagogue .... **PARNAS**
officer, university
DEAN, BEADLE, BURSAR
official, Moslem .... **HAJIB**
official, Rom.
EDILE, AEDILE, TRIBUNE
official, subordinate .. **SATRAP**
official, weights ...... **SEALER**
offspring .... **SONS, HEIRS**

Ogygian

a ogygian .... AGED
Ohio college town .... ADA
oil .... FAT, LARD, LUBE, ATTAR, OLEUM
oil beetle .... MELOE
oil bottle ..... CRUCE, CRUET, CRUSE, CRUIZE
oil, cruet .... AMPULLA
oil, edible .... ACEITE
oil, orange .... NEROLI
oil, pert. to .... OLEIC
oil, rub with .... ANOINT
oil-yielding Chinese tree . TUNG
oil-yielding tree ... EBO, EBOE
oilfish .... ESCOLAR
oilstone .... HONE
oily ketone .... IRONE
ointment .... BALM, NARD, SALVE, CERATE, POMADE
Ojibway secret order
MEDA, MIDE
O.K. .... ROGER
okra .... GOMBO, GUMBO
old .... AGED, ANILE, SENILE
"Old Curiosity Shop" girl . NELL
old English army .... FYRD
old Eng. gold piece ..... RYAL
old Eng. rune .... WEN, WYN
old Greek coin .... OBOL
old Irish coin .... RAP
old Persian money .... DARIC
OLD TESTAMENT see BIBLICAL and SPECIAL SECTION
Old Testament objects ... URIM
b Old Test. people . PHUD, PHUT
old person .... DOTARD
old Sp. gold coin ...... DOBLA
old times .... ELD, YORE
old-womanish .... ANILE
oleaginous .... OILY
oleander genus .... NERIUM
oleic acid salt ...... OLEATE
oleoresin .... ANIME, ELEMI, BALSAM
olive fly genus .... DACUS
olive genus .... OLEA
olive, inferior .... MORON
olive, stuffed .... PIMOLA
Oliver's nickname ...... NOLL
Olympian deity-god-goddess
ARES, HERA, APOLLO, ATHENA, HERMES, ARTEMIS, DEMETER
Olympus, mountain near . OSSA
Olympus queen .... HERA
Olympus, region by .... PIERIA
omen .... BODE, PRESAGE
omission, vowel ...... ELISION
omit .... DELE, PASS, SKIP
omit in pronunciation .. ELIDE

c omitted, having part
ELLIPTIC, ELLIPTICAL
onager .... ASS
once: dial. .... ANES
one .... AIN, UNIT
one-base hit .... SINGLE
one behind other .. TANDEM
one-eighth Troy ounce .. DRAM
one-eyed giant ..... CYCLOPS
one-horse carriage ..... SHAY
one hundred sq. meters AR, ARE
one hundred thousand rupees
LAKH
one, music by .... SOLI, SOLO
one-spot .... ACE
one thousand .... MIL
one-year record .... ANNAL
O'Neill heroine .... ANNA
onion .... CEPA
onion, Welsh .... CIBOL
onionlike plant .. CIVE, LEEK, CHIVE, SHALLOT, ESCHALOT
only .... MERE, SAVE, SOLE
onward .... AHEAD, FORTH
onyx, Mex. .... TECALI
oorial .... SHA
ooze .... LEAK, SEEP, SEIP, SIPE, SYPE, EXUDE
open ...... AJAR, OVERT, BROACH, PATENT, UNWRAP
d open court .... AREA
open plain .... VEGA
opening .... GAP, HOLE, RIFT, SLOT, VENT, HIATUS
opening, long ... RIMA, SLOT
opening, mouthlike
STOMA, STOMATA
opening, slit-like .... RIMA
opening, small .... PORE
opera ... AIDA, BORIS, ORFEO
opera, Beethoven .... FIDELIO
opera, Bizet .... CARMEN
opera composer, modern
BRITTEN, MENOTTI
opera, Gounod .... FAUST
opera hat .... GIBUS
opera heroine ... AIDA, ELSA, MIMI, SENTA, ISOLDE
opera house, Milan .... SCALA
opera, Massenet
MANON, THAIS
opera, Puccini .... TOSCA
opera scene .... SCENA
opera singer .... MELBA
opera soprano, star.ALDA, PONS
BORI, RISE, RAISA, STEBER
opera star .... DIVA
opera, Verdi ... AIDA, ERNANI
opera, Wagner .... RIENZI
operate .... RUN, MANAGE
operetta composer ..... FRIML

110

a opium poppy seed ...... MAW
opossum, S. Am. ...... QUICA
opponent .. FOE, ANTI, RIVAL
opportune .... TIMELY
opportunity .... CHANCE
oppose .... IMPUGN
opposed, one .... ANTI
opposed to solo .... TUTTI
opposite extremities ... POLES
opposite .... REVERSE
Ops' daughter .... CERES
Ops' husband .... SATURN
optical glass .... LENS
optical illusion ...... MIRAGE
optical instrument lines RETICLE
optimistic .... ROSY, ROSEATE
oracle, Apollo's .... DELOS
oracle, Gr. .. DELPHI, DELPHOI
oral .... PAROL
orange-red stone .... SARD
orange tincture, Her. .. TENNE
orangutan, Malay ...... MIAS
orarion .... STOLE
orator .... OTIS, RHETOR
orb of day .... SUN
orbit point .... APSIS, APOGEE
orchid genus .... DISA
orchid leaves for tea
                  FAAM, FAHAM
orchid tuber .... SALEP
b ordain .... DECREE
order .... BID, FIAT,
          ARRAY, EDICT, DECREE
order, one of Catholic. MARIST
order, put in .... TIDY, SETTLE
orderliness .... SYSTEM
ordinance .... LAW
ordnance piece ...... MORTAR
ore deposit ...... LODE, MINE
ore of iron .... OCHER, OCHRE
ore receptacle ...... MORTAR
organ .... EAR, EYE
organ of algae .... PROCARP
organ part .... STOP
organ pipe .... REED
organ pipe, displayed MONTRE
organ prelude .... VERSET
organ, seed-bearing .... PISTIL
organ stop REED,SEXT,DOLCAN,
         CELESTE, MELODIA
organism, 1-cell
          AMEBA, AMOEBA
organism, simple
          MONAD, MONAS
organization .... SETUP
orgy .... REVEL
Orient .... EAST
Oriental .... ASIAN, TATAR
Oriental dwelling .... DAR

c Oriental lute .... TAR
Oriental nursemaid .... AMA,
     IYA, AMAH, AYAH, EYAH
Oriental plane tree .. CHINAR
Oriental porgy .... TAI
Oriental potentate ...... AGA
Oriental sailing ship ... DHOW
Oriental servant ..... HAMAL
Oriental ship captain .... RAS
Oriental weight .... ROTL
orifice. PORE, STOMA, OSTIOLE
orifices, sponge ...... OSCULA
origin .... SEED
original .... NEW
original sin .... ADAM
originate ARISE, START, CREATE
Orinoco tributary .... ARO
oriole, golden .... LORIOT
ornament .... FRET
ornament, curly ..... SCROLL
ornament in relief ... EMBOSS
ornament, spire .... EPI
ornamental border .... DADO
ornamental grass ... EULALIA
ornamental nailhead .... STUD
Orpheus' destination ... HADES
Orpheus' instrument ..... LYRE
orris .... IRIS
orris-root ketone, oil ... IRONE
oscillate .... WAVE
osier .... WITHE
d Osiris' brother .... SET
Osiris' wife, sister .... ISIS
ostentation .... POMP
ostracism ..... TABU, TABOO
ostrich, Am. .... RHEA
ostrich-like bird
          EMU, EMEU, RATITE
Otaheite apple .... HEVI
Othello was one .... MOOR
Othello's lieutenant, foe IAGO
otherwise .... ELSE
otic .... AURAL
otologist .... AURIST
otter brown, color ... LOUTRE
otter genus .... LUTRA
Ottoman .... TURK
Ottoman court .... PORTE
Ottoman official ...... PASHA
"Our Mutual Friend," ballad-
     seller in .... WEGG
oust .... EJECT, EVICT
out .... AWAY, FORTH
out-and-out .... ARRANT
out: Dutch .... UIT
out of style .... PASSE
out of the way .... ASIDE
outbreak, unruly ...... RIOT
outburst, sudden ...... SPATE
outcast

     LEPER, PARIAH, ISHMAEL

a outcome, final .... **UPSHOT**
outcry .... **CLAMOR**
outer .... **ECTAL**
outer portion of earth ... **SIAL**
outfit .. **KIT, RIG, GEAR, SUIT**
outfit, queer .... **GETUP**
outlet .... **VENT**
outline .... **PERIMETER**
outlook .... **VISTA**
outmoded .... **PASSE**
OUTRIGGER see **MALAY CANOE**
outward .... **ECTAD**
ova .... **EGGS**
oval ... **ELLIPTIC, ELLIPTICAL**
oven .... **KILN, OAST**
oven, annealing .. **LEER, LEHR**
oven, Polyn. native ..... **UMU**
over .... **ATOP, ABOVE,**
AGAIN, ENDED, ACROSS
over-nice .... **FINICAL**
overnice person .... **PRIG**
over: poet. .... **OER**
over there ..... **YON, YONDER**
overact .... **EMOTE**
overcoat ... **ULSTER, PALETOT**
overdue payment ..... **ARREAR**
overflow .... **DEBORD**
overfond, be ..... **DOAT, DOTE**
overjoy .... **ELATE**
overlay .... **CEIL**
overripe grain ...... **BRITE**
overseer, ranch: Sp. Am.
CAPORAL
overshadow .... **DOMINATE**
overshoe
GOLOE, GALOSH, GALOSHE
overskirt .. **PANIER, PANNIER**
overspreading mass ..... **PALL**

c overt .... **OPEN, FRANK**
overwhelm .... **DELUGE**
overwhelming amount .... **SEA**
Ovid's "— Amatoria" .... **ARS**
ovule .... **SEED**
ovum .... **EGG**
owala tree .... **BOBO**
owl, barn, Samoa ...... **LULU**
owl, eagle .. **BUBO, KATOGLE**
owl, horned .... **BUBO**
owl, S. Asia .... **UTUM**
owl's cry .... **HOOT**
own up to .... **AVOW**
ownership, of land, old law
ODAL, UDAL
ox, extinct wild .... **URUS**
ox, forest .... **ANOA**
ox, long-haired .... **YAK**
ox of Caesar's time .... **URUS**
ox, wild .... **ANOA**
ox, wild: India .... **GAUR**
GOUR, ZEBU, GAYAL
oxalis, S. Amer. .... **OCA**
oxen .... **KINE**
oxhide strap ..... **REIM, RIEM**
oxide .... **CALX**
oxidize .... **RUST**
oxygen compound **OXID, OXIDE**
oxygen, form of ..... **OZONE**
oxygen radical ...... **OXYL**
oyster bed material
CULCH, CUTCH, CULTCH
oyster drill .... **BORER**
oyster farm: Fr. .... **PARC**
oyster, young .... **SPAT**
oysterfish .... **TAUTOG**
Ozarks, town west of in Okla.
ADA
Oz books author ...... **BAUM**

P

b pace .... **RATE, STEP**
pachisi, kind of .... **LUDO**
pachyderm .... **ELEPHANT**
Pacific aroid food plant **TARO**
Pacific Island cloth ..... **TAPA**
Pacific pine .... **HALA**
Pacific shrub .... **SALAL**
pacify
CALM, SOOTHE, PLACATE
pack .... **WAD, STOW**
pack animal .... **ASS,**
BURRO, LLAMA, SUMPTER
pack horse .... **SUMPTER**
pack down ...... **RAM, TAMP**
package, India ...... **ROBBIN**
package of spun silk .. **MOCHE**
pad .... **TABLET**

d padded jacket under armor
ACTON
padnag .... **TROT, AMBLE**
Padua, town near ...... **ESTE**
pagan god .... **IDOL**
page, "Love's Labor Lost" **MOTH**
page number .... **FOLIO**
pageantry .... **POMP**
"Pagliacci" character .. **CANIO**
"Pagliacci" heroine ... **NEDDA**
pagoda, Chinese ..... **TA, TAA**
pagoda ornament ... **EPI, TEE**
paid notice .... **AD**
pail .... **SKEEL**
pain, dull .... **ACHE**
pain reliever **OPIATE, ANODYNE**
paint, face .... **FARD, ROUGE**

pain-killer alkaloid source **COCA**
painted bunting: Creole .. **PAPE**
PAINTER .. see also ARTIST
  and country of each artist
painter, modernist
  KLEE, MIRO, ERNST
painting style .... **GENRE**
painting, wall .... **MURAL**
pair .... **DUO, DIAD,**
  DUAD, DYAD, MATE
pair of horses ... **SPAN, TEAM**
pairing .... **MATING**
palanquin .... **JAUN**
palanquin bearer ..... **HAMAL**
palanquin, Jap. .... **KAGO**
palatable, very .... **SAPID**
pale ....•....... **WAN, ASHY,**
  ASHEN, PASTY
pale color .... **PASTEL**
pale-colored .... **MEALY**
Palestine in Jewish use **ERETS**
palisade: fort. .... **RIMER**
Pallas .... **ATHENA**
pallid .... **WAN, PALE**
palm ...... **TI, COCO, TALA,**
  TALIPAT, TALIPOT, TALI-
  PUT
palm, Afr. .... **DUM**
palm, Asia .... **ARENG, BETEL**
palm, betel .... **ARECA**
palm, book .... **TARA**
palm, Brazil .... **ASSAI**
palm, climbing .... **RATTAN**
palm cockatoo .... **ARARA**
palm, dwarf genus ..... **SABAL**
palm fiber **DOH, TAL, RAFFIA**
palm fiber, S. Amer. **DATIL**
palm genus .... **ARECA**
palm genus, Asia ... **ARENGA**
palm juice, fermented .. **SURA**
palm leaf
  OLA, OLE, OLAY, OLLA
palm-leaf mat .•........ **YAPA**
palm lily .... **TI**
palm, liquor ..... **BENO, BINO**
palm, N. Z. .... **NIKAU**
palm, nipa ..... **ATAP, ATTAP**
palm off .... **FOB, FOIST**
palm, palmyra leaf ..... **OLA,**
  OLE, OLLA, OLAY
palm sago, Malay ... **GOMUTI**
palm sap .... **TODDY**
palm starch .... **SAGO**
palm, W. Ind. **GRIGRI, GRUGRU**
palmetto ...•....... **SABAL**
palmyra leaf .... **OLA, OLE,**
  OLAY, OLLA
palmyra palm .... **BRAB**
palp .... **FEELER**
palpitation .... **PALMUS**

pamper .... **COSHER, COSSET**
pamphlet .... **TRACT**
panacea .... **ELIXIR**
Panama gum tree (`A, YAYA`
Panama, old name ... **DARIEN**
Panama tree, large .. **CATIVO**
Panay negrito .... **ATI**
panda .... **WAH, BEAR**
panel .... **PANE**
panel of jurors ...... **VENIRE**
pang .... **THROE**
pangolin .... **MANIS**
panic .... **FEAR, FUNK**
pannier .... **DOSSER**
Panopolis, chief god of .. **MIN,**
  KHEM
pant .... **GASP**
pantry .... **AMBRY, LARDER,**
  SPENCE, BUTTERY
— Paulo, Brazil .... **SAO**
papal cape ... **FANO, FANON,**
  FANUM, ORALE, PHANO,
  FANNEL
papal church .... **LATERAN**
papal collar .. **FANO, FANON,**
  FANUM, ORALE, PHANO,
  FANNEL
papal court ...... **SEE, CURIA**
papal fanon .... **ORALE**
papal letter .... **BULL, BULLA**
papal scarf .... **ORALE**
papal veil .... **FANO, FANON,**
  FANUM, ORALE, PHANO,
  FANNEL
papal vestment .... **FANO,**
  FANON, FANUM, ORALE,
  PHANO, FANNEL
paper folded once ..... **FOLIO**
paper, imperfect, poor
  CASSE, CASSIE, RETREE
paper, lighting .... **SPILL**
paper measure .. **REAM, QUIRE**
paper mulberry .... **KOZO**
paper mulberry bark .... **TAPA**
paper size
  DEMY, POTT, OCTAVO
paper, thin crisp ...... **PELURE**
par, 2 under .... **EAGLE**
Para, Brazil, capital .. **BELEM**
parade .... **MARCH, STRUT**
paradise .... **EDEN**
paradise, Buddhist ...... **JODO**
paradise, like .... **EDENIC**
"Paradise Lost" angel .. **ARIEL**
paragraph .... **ITEM**
parallelogram .... **RHOMB**
paralysis .... **PARESIS**
parapet, solid portion of **MERLON**
parasite .... **LEECH**

113

a parasite in blood .... TRYP
parasitic insect MITE, ACARID
parasitic plant MOSS, DODDER
paravane .... OTTER
Parcae .... FATES
Parcae, one of
NONA, MORTA, DECUMA
parcel of land .... LOT, PLAT
parchment, book
FOREL, FORREL
pardon .... REMIT, CONDONE
pardon, general .... AMNESTY
pare .... PEEL
Paris art exhibit ...... SALON
Paris, first bishop of
DENIS, DENYS
Paris section .... PASSY
Paris subway .... METRO
Paris thug .... APACHE
Paris' father .... PRIAM
Paris' wife .... OENONE
parish head .... RECTOR
parley .... PALAVER
Parliament report .. HANSARD
parol .... ORAL
paroxysm .... FIT, SPASM
parrot
KEA, LORY, VASA, VAZA
parrot, Brazil ... ARA, ARARA
parrot-fish
b LORO, LAUIA, SCARID
parrot, hawk .... HIA
parrot, monk .... LORO
parrot, N. Z. large KEA, KAKA
parrot, P. I., green .... CAGIT
parrot, sheep-killing .... KEA
parrot's bill, part of .... CERE
parrotlike .... ARINE
parry .... FEND, EVADE
Parsi priest .... MOBED
Parsi scripture .... AVESTA
parsley camphor .... APIOL
parsley, plant kin to
ANISE, CELERY
parson bird
POE, TUE, TUI, KOKO
parsonage .... MANSE
part .... ROLE, SOME, PIECE,
BREAK, SEVER, SHARE,
CLEAVE, ELEMENT
part, Greek play
EXODE, EXODOS
part of church .... BEMA
NAVE, AISLE, ALTAR
part of horse's foot .. PASTERN
part of speech .. NOUN, VERB
parted .... PARTITE
participle ending .... ING
parti-colored .... PIED, PINTO

c parti-colored horse
ROAN, CALICO
particle ...... ACE, BIT, ION,
JOT, ATOM, IOTA, DROP,
MITE, MOTE, GRAIN,
SHRED, TITTLE
particle, electrically charged
ION
particle in cosmic rays MESON
particle of chaff ...... PALEA
particle, small
JOT, ATOM, IOTA, MOTE
particular .... ITEM
Partlet .... HEN, BIDDY
partnership: Hawaii HUI, HOEY
partridge call ... JUCK, JUKE
partridge, sand ...... SEESEE
partridge, snow ...... LERWA
party .... SECT
parvenu .... UPSTART
pasha .... DEY
pass .... HAND, ELAPSE
pass a rope through ... REEVE
pass between peaks ..... COL
pass by .... BYGO
pass on .... RELAY
pass over ... OMIT, SKIP, ELIDE
pass through .... REEVE
pass through mountains .. COL,
DEFILE
passable .... SOSO
d passage .... GUT, ITER,
CANAL, TRANSIT
passage, bastion .... POSTERN
passage, covered .... ARCADE
passage: hist. .... ALURE
passage: music TUTTI, STRETTA
passage out ..... EXIT, EGRESS
passageway ADIT, HALL, AISLE
Passover ..... PASCH, PASCHA
Passover meal SEDAR, SEDER
passport endorsement VISA, VISE
past AGO, GONE, OVER, AGONE
paste .... STRASS
pasteboard .... CARD
pasted-up art work .. COLLAGE
pastel .... TINT
pastoral .... IDYLLIC
pastoral place ...... ARCADIA
pastoral poem .. IDYL, IDYLL
pastoral staff .. PEDA, PEDUM
pastry
PIE, FLAN, TART, ECLAIR
pasture .... LEA
pasture: N. Eng. .... ING
pasture, to .... AGIST
pasty .... DOUGHY
pat .... DAB, TAP
pat, very .... APT
Patagonian cavy .... MARA
patchwork, literary .... CENTO

a patella .... ROTULA
paten .... ARCA, ARCAE
patent from monarch .. BERAT
path: Anglo-Ir. ..... CASAUN
path: math. .... LOCUS
path of planet .... ORBIT
pathos, false .... BATHOS
patriarch Jacob .... ISRAEL
patriarch's title .... NASI
patron .... CLIENT
patron saint of France
　　　　　　DENIS, DENYS
patronage ...... EGIS, AEGIS
pattern .... NORM, TYPE,
　IDEAL, MODEL, PARAGON
pattern, large square DAMIER
Paul, Apostle .... SAUL
Paul's birthplace ..... TARSUS
paulownia tree .... KIRI
pause .... REST
pause: poet. & music
　SELAH, CESURA, CAESURA
paver .... TUP
paver's mallet .... TUP
pavilion .... TENT
paving stone .... FLAG, SETT
paw .... PUD, FOOT
pawl .... DETENT
b pawn .... HOCK
Pawnee Indian rite .... HAKO
Pawnee tribes .... CHAUI
pay .... ANTE, WAGE, REMIT
pay dirt .... ORE
pay, fixed .... STIPEND
pay for another ...... TREAT
pay homage: feudal law
　　　　　　　　ATTORN
pay one's part .... ANTE
pay out .... SPEND
payable .... DUE
paymaster, India ...... BUXY
payment back .... REBATE
payment for a bride, S. Afr.
　　　　　　　　LOBOLA
payment for death, feudal CRO
payment for homicide ... ERIC
payment, press for ...... DUN
payment to owner: Fr. law CENS
pea .... LEGUME
peace .... PAX
peace god, Anglo-Saxon .. ING
peace of mind .... REST
peaceful ... IRENE, IRENICAL
peach, clingstone ...... PAVY
peacock .... MAO, PAVO
peacock blue .... PAON
peacock butterfly .... IO
peacock fish .... WRASSE
peacock genus .... PAVO
peacock: Kipling .... MAO

c peak ...... ALP, TOR, ACME,
　APEX, PITON, ZENITH
peak: Scot. .... BEN
peanut ...... MANI, GOOBER
pear, autumn .... BOSC
pear cider .... PERRY
pearl blue color ...... METAL
Pearl Buck heroine ..... OLAN
pearl, imitation ...... OLIVET
pearl millet ... BAJRA, BAJRI
pearlweeds .... SAGINA
peasant.CARL, CEORL, CHURL
peasant, India .... RYOT
peasant, Scot.
　　　　COTTAR, COTTER
peat .... TURF
peat spade .... SLADE
pecan tree .... NOGAL
peccary, collared ..... JAVALI
peck .... DAB, NIP, KNIP
pedal .... TREADLE
peddle ... HAWK, SELL, VEND
peddle: Eng. .... TRANT
pedestal .... GAINE
pedestal part .. DADO, PLINTH
peduncle, plant .... SCAPE
peel . BARK, PARE, RIND, SKIN
peep-show .... RAREE
PEER .... see also NOBLE
peer .... PEEK, PEEP
d Peer Gynt's mother ..... ASE
peevish .... PETULANT
peg .... KNAG
peg, golf .... TEE
peg, wooden
　NOG, TRENAIL, TREENAIL
Pegu ironwood .... ACLE
Peleg's son .... REU
pellucid ...... CLEAR, LIMPID
pelma .... SOLE
pelota court .... FRONTON
pelt ...... FELL, SKIN, STONE
pelvic bone, pert. to .... ILIAC
pelvic bones .... ILIA
pen name, Dickens ..... BOZ
pen name, G. Russell ...... AE
pen name, Lamb .... ELIA
pen point .... NEB, NIB
pen-text .... RONDE
penman, Yutang .... LIN
penalty .... FINE
pendulum weight .... BOB
Penelope's father .... ICARIUS
penetrate
　GORE, ENTER, PERMEATE
penitential season ..... LENT
penmanship .... HAND
pennies .... PENCE
Pennsylvania sect ..... AMISH
Pentateuch .... TORA, TORAH

115

People

PEOPLE .. see also TRIBES in
  SPECIAL SECTION
people .... MEN, FOLK,
  ONES, RACE, DEMOS
people, ancient Asian ... SERES
people: Ger. .... VOLK
people: Ir. .... DAOINE
people, Nigerian . BENI, BENIN
people: Sp. .... GENTE
people, spirit of ...... ETHOS
people, the .... DEMOS
pepper, climbing ...... BETEL
pepper, garden .... PIMIENTO
pepper plant, Borneo .... ARA
pepper shrub
  AVA, CAVA, KAVA, KAWA
pepper vine .... BETEL
Pequod's captain ...... AHAB
"per —" ..... DIEM, ANNUM
perceive .. SEE, SENSE, DESCRY
perception . EAR, TACT, SENSE
perch .... SIT, ROOST
perch genus .... PERCA
perchlike fish .... DARTER
percolate .. OOZE, SEEP, LEACH
peregrine .... ALIEN
perenially shifting sands region
  AREG
perfect .... IDEAL, MODEL
perforate ...... BORE, DRILL,
  PUNCH, RIDDLE
perform .... RENDER
performer
  DOER, ACTOR, ARTISTE
perfume
  ATAR, OTTO, AROMA, ATTAR
perfume base .... MUSK
perfume with incense .. CENSE
perfumed pad .... SACHET
Pericles' consort .... ASPASIA
periphery ... RIM, PERIMETER
period .... DOT
period, time
  AGE, EON, ERA, STAGE
periodic as Med. winds ETESIAN
permit .. LET, ALLOW, LICENSE
permission .... LEAVE
pernicious, something .... PEST
perplex
  BAFFLE, CONFUSE, BEWILDER
Persephone ..... CORA, KORE
Persephone's husband
  HADES, PLUTO
Persia .... IRAN
Persian .... IRANI
Persian coin, ancient .. DARIC
Pers. demigod .... YIMA
Pers. elf .... PERI
Pers. enameled tile ..... KASI
Pers. fairy .... PERI
Pers. governor, old ... SATRAP
Pers. headdress, ancient TIARA

Pers. lord ..... KAAN, KHAN
Pers. mystic .... SUFI
Pers. native .... LUR
Pers. poet .... OMAR
Pers. potentate .... SHAH
Pers. priestly caste ..... MAGI
Pers. province, ancient . ELAM
Pers. race, tribesman LUR,KURD
Pers. rug .. SENNA, HAMADAN
Pers. ruler .... SHAH
Pers. ruler of dead ..... YIMA
Pers. sect .... BABI
Pers. sprite .... PERI
PERS. TITLE .... see TITLE,
  PERSIAN
Pers. tribe member ..... LUR
Pers. weight .... SER
persimmon, E. Ind. GAB, GAUB
person of mixed blood
  METIS, MESTIZO
person, overnice .... PRIG
personage .... NIBS
personification of folly ... ATE
personification of light: Polyn.
  AO
personnel .... STAFF
perspiration .. SUDOR, SWEAT
perspire .... EGEST, SWEAT
pert girl .... CHIT, MINX
pertaining to the chin MENTAL
pertinent .... APT, PAT
perturb .... DERANGE,
  DISTURB, AGITATE, TROUBLE
PERU INDIAN .. see page 193
peruse ..... CON, READ, SCAN
peruser .... CONNER
Peruvian fertility goddess MAMA
Peruvian plant .... OCA
pervade .... PERMEATE
pester .... ANNOY, TEASE
pestle .... PILUM
pestle vessel .... MORTAR
pet .... CADE
pet lamb ...... CADE, COSSET
"Peter Pan" dog ...... NANA
"Peter Pan" pirate ...... SMEE
petiole .... STIPE
Petrarch's love .... LAURA
petrol .... GAS
peyote .... MESCAL
phantoms .... EIDOLA
Pharaoh .... RAMESES
Pharaoh after Rameses I .. SETI
phase .... FACET, STAGE
pheasant brood NID, NYE, NIDE
pheasant, Himal. . CHIR, CHEER
pheasant, India ...... MONAL
Phidias statue .... ATHENA
philippic .... TIRADE
PHILIPPINE ISLANDS
  see also SPECIAL SECTION

a Philippine Islands attendant
.... **ALILA**
P.I. bast fiber ...... **CASTULI**
P.I. cedar .... **CALANTAS**
P.I. chief **DATO, DATU, DATTO**
P.I. DWARF see P. I. NEGRITO
P.I. dyewood tree
.... **TUI, IPIL, TUWI**
P.I. food .... **POI, SABA**
P.I. fort .... **COTA, KOTA**
P.I. grass ...... **BOHO, BOJO**
P.I. lighter .... **CASCO**
P.I. lizard .... **IBID, IBIT**
P.I. Moslem .... **MORO**
P.I. negrito, native, dwarf
.... **ATA, ATI, ITA,**
.... **AETA, ATTA**
P.I. palm wine ... **BENO, BINO**
P.I. peasant .... **TAO**
P.I. poisonous tree .... **LIGAS**
P.I. rice ...... **PAGA, MACAN**
P.I. sash .... **TAPIS**
P.I. servant .... **ALILA**
P.I. shrub, rope **NABO, ANABO**
P.I. skirt .... **SAYA**
P.I. tree .... **DAO, IBA, TUA,**
TUI, BOGO, DITA, IFIL,
IPIL, YPIL
P.I. warrior .... **MORO**
Philistine city .... **GATH,**
.... **GAZA, EKRON**

b Philistine deity, principal **DAGON**
philosopher's stone .... **ELIXIR**
philosophical element ... **RECT**
philosophical theory **MONISM**
philosophy, pert. to Gr. **ELEATIC**
phloem .... **BAST**
phoebe .... **PEWEE, PEWIT**
Phoebus .... **SOL, SUN**
Phoenician city .... **TYRE**
Phoenician goddess .. **ASTARTE**
Phoenician port .... **SIDON**
Phoenician princess .. **EUROPA**
phonetic notation system
.... **ROMIC**
phonetical sound .... **PALATAL**
phosphate of lime ... **APATITE**
photo-developing powder **METOL**
photography solution ... **HYPO**
Phrygian god .... **ATTIS**
Phrygian lunar god ..... **MEN**
physical ... **SOMAL, SOMATIC**
physician ... **GALEN, MEDIC**
physician's group .... **AMA**
physician's symbol **CADUCEUS**
physicist, Am. .... **EINSTEIN**
physicist, Eng. .... **BOYLE**
physicist, Fr. .... **CURIE**
physicist, Nobel prize-winner
1944 .... **RABI**
physiological individual .. **BION**

c piano, upright ...... **CLAVIAL**
pick, miner's: Eng.
.... **MANDREL, MANDRIL**
pick out .... **CULL, GLEAN**
picket .... **PALE**
pickled bamboo shoots **ACHAR**
pickled meat .... **SOUSE**
pickling fluid .... **BRINE**
pickling herb .... **DILL**
pickpocket .... **DIP**
"Picnic" author .... **INGE**
picture ... **DRAW, PORTRAIT**
picture border .... **MAT**
picture, composite .. **MONTAGE**
picturesque .... **SCENIC**
pie, meat, small .... **PASTY**
piebald .... **PINTO**
piebald pony ... **PIED, PINTO**
piece of eight .... **REALS**
piece out .... **EKE**
piece, thin .... **SLAT**
pier .... **KEY, DOCK,**
.... **MOLE, QUAI, QUAY**
pier, architectural ..... **ANTA**
pier support .... **PILE, PILING**
pierce ... **GORE, STAB, SPEAR**
pig. **HOG, SOW, SHOAT, SHOTE**
pig, wild .... **BOAR**
pig, young .... **ELT, GRICE**
pigs .... **SUS**

d pigs' feet .... **PETTITOES**
pigs, litter of .... **FARROW**
pigs, red .... **DUROC**
pigeon ... **NUN, BARB, DOVE,**
.... **POUTER, ROLLER**
pigeon hawk .... **MERLIN**
pigeon pea. **DAL, TUR, GANDUL**
piglike animal ..... **PECCARY**
pigment, blue-green ..... **BICE**
pigment, brown .... **SEPIA**
pigment, brown, from soot
.... **BISTER, BISTRE**
pigment, deep blue .... **SMALT**
pigment, red .... **LAKE**
pigment test crystalline **DOPA**
pigment, without .... **ALBINO**
pigmentation, lack of
.... **ACHROMA**
pigtail .... **CUE, QUEUE**
pike, full grown . **LUCE, LUCET**
pike, walleyed .... **DORE**
pilaster .... **ANTA**
pilchard .. **FUMADO, SARDINE**
pilchard-like fish ...... **SPRAT**
pile ...... **NAP, HEAP, SPILE**
pile driver .... **OLIVER**
pile driver ram .... **TUP**
pile of hay .... **RICK, STACK**
pilfer .... **STEAL**
pilgrim .... **PALMER**

117

a
pilgrimage city .... MECCA
pilgrimage to Mecca .... HADJ
pill, large .... BOLUS
pillage .... LOOT, SACK, STEAL
pillage .... RAPINE
pillar, as of ore .... JAMB
pillar, Hindu .... LAT
pillar, resembling ..... STELAR
pillar, tapering ...... OBELISK
pillow .... BOLSTER
pilot .... GUIDE, STEER
pimento or —spice ..... ALL
pin .... BROOCH
pin, firing .... TIGE
pin, gunwale .... THOLE
pin, machine .... COTTER
pin, metal .... RIVET
pin, pivot .... PINTLE
pin, rifle firing .... TIGE
pin, Roman .... ACUS
pin, small, very LILL
pin, splicing .... FID
pin, wooden .. FID, NOG, PEG,
          COAG, COAK, DOWEL
pin wrench .... SPANNER
pinafore .... TIER
pincer claw .... CHELA
pinch .... NIP
pinched with cold ..... URLED
Pindar work .... ODE

b
pine-cone, like a ...... PINEAL
pine, Mex. .... OCOTE, PINON
pine, Scot. .... RIGA
pine, textile screw
              ARA, PANDAN
pineapple NANA, PINA, ANANA
pineapple genus .... PUYA
pinfeather .... PEN
pinion .... WING
pink .... DAMASK
pinnacle .... TOP, APEX
pinnacle, ice .... SERAC
pinniped .... SEAL
pinochle score, term
              DIX, MELD
pint, half .... CUP
pintado fish .... SIER
pintail .... SMEE
pinworm .. ASCARID, ASCARIS
pious Biblical Jew ..... TOBIT
pipe .... TUBE, RISER
pipe, Irish .... DUDEEN
pipe joint, fitting .... TEE
pipe, pastoral .... REED
pipe, tobacco
       BRIAR, BRIER, DUDEEN
pipe, water.HOOKAH, NARGILE
pipe with socket ends
              HUB, HUBB
pipelike .... TUBATE
pique .... PEEVE

c
pirate ...... ROVER, CORSAIR
pirate in War of 1812 LAFITTE
pismire .... ANT, EMMET
pistil part .... CARPEL
pistol .... DAG, DAGG,
          MAUSER, SIDEARM
pistol: slang .... HEATER
pit ..... HOLE, ABYSS, STONE
pit for roots, Maori ..... RUA
pit: medical .... FOSSA
pit, small .. FOVEA, LACUNA
pitch .... KEY, TAR, TONE
pitcher .... JUG, EWER
pitcher's false move .... BALK
pith .... NUB, GIST
pith helmet .... TOPI, TOPEE
pithy .... TERSE
pithy plant .... SOLA
pitiful quality ...... PATHOS
pittance .... DOLE
pitted .... FOVEATE
pity .... RUTH
placard .... POSTER
place ...... SET, LIEU, LOCI,
       SPOT, LOCUS, STEAD, LO-
       CALE
place before .... APPOSE
place, camping .... ETAPE
place case is tried .... VENUE
place in office again .. RESEAT

d
place, in relation .... POSIT
place, market .... FORUM
place of shelter .. GITE, HAVEN
placid .... CALM, SERENE
plagiarize .... STEAL
plague .... PEST, TEASE
plain, arctic .... TUNDRA
plain, Argentine ...... PAMPA
plain, Asia .... CHOL
plain, Palestine .... ONO
plain, Russia .... STEPPE
plain, S. Am. .... LLANO
plain, treeless ...... SAVANNA
plain, treeless Arctic TUNDRA
plain, upland .. WOLD, WEALD
Plains Indian .... see page 193
plainly woven .... UNI
plait .... PLY, BRAID
plan .... PLOT, INTEND
plane, Fr. .... SPAD
plane, Ger. .... STUKA
plane, Jap. .... ZERO
plane part .... FLAP,
          NOSE, TAIL, WING
plane, Russ. fighter ...... MIG
planets (in order of distance from
   sun) MERCURY (1), VE-
   NUS (2), EARTH (3),
   MARS (4), JUPITER (5),
   SATURN (6), URANUS (7),
   NEPTUNE (8), PLUTO (9)

a planets in distance from Earth
  (closest first)

1—VENUS	5—SATURN
2—MARS	6—URANUS
3—MERCURY	7—NEPTUNE
4—JUPITER	8—PLUTO

planets in size
  (largest first)

1—JUPITER	6—VENUS
2—SATURN	7—PLUTO
3—NEPTUNE	8—MARS
4—URANUS	9—MERCURY
5—EARTH	

planetarium .... ORRERY
planetary aspect CUSP, TRINE
plank's curve on ship ..... SNY
plant .... SOW, SEED
plant, bayonet .... DATIL
plant broom .... SPART
plant, bulb
       CAMAS, CAMASS, CAMMAS
plant cutter bird ..... RARA
plant cutting .. SLIP, PHYTON
plant disease .... RUST, SMUT
plant joined to another GRAFT
plant life .... FLORA
PLANT, LILY ...... see LILY
plant, lily-like
       CAMAS, CAMASS, CAMMAS
plant louse .... APHID
plant, male .... MAS
b plant, medicinal, S. Am.
       ALOE, SENNA, IPECAC
plant modified by environment
  to abnormal development
       ECAD
plant, mustard family
       KALE, CRESS
plant organ .... LEAF
plant pod .... BOLL
plant, poisonous .... LOCO
plant, sea-bottom ... ENALID
plant stem: bot. ..... CAULIS
plant stem tissue ...... PITH
plant used as soap ... AMOLE
plants of area .... FLORA
plantain lily genus ..... HOSTA
plantation, osier .... HOLT
planter .... SEEDER
plaster .... SMEAR
plaster, artist's painting. GESSO
plaster of Paris .... GESSO
plastic .... LUCITE
plate, battery .... GRID
plate, Eucharist .... PATEN
plate, reptile's .... SCUTE
plate to hurl .... DISCUS
plateau .... MESA
plateau, Andes .... PUNA
platform ...... DAIS, STAGE
platform, ancient ...... BEMA

c platform, mine shaft
       SOLLAR, SOLLER
platinum, of .... OSMIC
platinum wire loop ..... OESE
Plato's "Idea" ... EIDE, EIDOS
play .... DRAMA
play on words .... PUN
play, part of ..... ACT, SCENE
play unskillfully ...... STRUM
player .... ACTOR
playing card, old It. ... TAROT
playwright .... INGE
plea, to end: law .... ABATER
plead .... SUE, ENTREAT
pleading: law .... OYER
please .... SUIT
pleasing .... NICE
pleasure god, Egypt. . BES, BESA
pledge .... VOW,
       GAGE, OATH, PAWN,
       TROTH, ENGAGE
pledge, Rom. law .... VAS
plexus .... RETE, RETIA
pliable .... WAXY
pliant .... LITHE
plinth .... ORLO, SOCLE
plot .... LOT,
       PLAT, CABAL, CONSPIRE
plow, cutter COLTER, COULTER
d plow part .... SHETH, SHEATH
plow, sole of .... SHARE
plowed field .... ERD, ARADA
plug .... BUNG,
       CORK, SPILE, STOPPER
plum .... GAGE, SLOE
plume ..EGRET, PREEN, AIGRET
plummet .... FATHOM
plump child .... FUB
plunder .... ROB, LOOT, PREY,
       SACK, BOOTY, RAVEN,
       RAVIN, REAVE, PILFER,
       RAPINE, RAVAGE, RAVINE
plunder ruthlessly ... MARAUD
plunge .... DIVE, DOUSE
plural ending .... EN, ES
plus .... AND
Pluto .... DIS, HADES, ORCUS
Pluto's mother-in-law DEMETER
pneumonia, kind of .... LOBAR
Po tributary .... ADDA
pochard .... SMEE
pocket billiards .... POOL
pocket gopher, Mex. .... TUZA
pod, cotton .... BOLL
pods for tanning .... PIPI
Poe poem .... RAVEN
poem .... ODE, ELEGY, EPODE
poem division, or part . CANTO
poem, 8 line .... TRIOLET

a poem, long heroic .. EPIC, EPOS
poem, love .... SONNET
poem, lyric ...... ODE, EPODE
poem, mournful .... ELEGY
poem, of a .... ODIC
poem, old Fr. .... DIT
poem, sacred .... PSALM
poet .... BARD, ODIST
poet, A.-S. .... SCOP
poet, Bengal .... TAGORE
poet, blind, epic ..... HOMER
poet, lyric .... ODIST
poet, Norse ... SCALD, SKALD
poet, poor .... RIMER
poetry .... EPOS, POESY
poetry, early .... RUNE
poetry, Finnish .... RUNES
poetry, mournful, pert. to
ELEGIAC
poetry, Norse god of
BRAGE, BRAGI
poi, source of .... TARO
point END, TIP, BARB, PUNTO
point in moon's orbit nearest
earth .... PERIGEE
point of curve .... NODE
point of land .... SPIT
point of moon .... CUSP
point of view .... ANGLE
b point on mariner's compass
RUMB
point on tooth's crown .. CUSP
point, tennis or golf .... ACE
point won .... GOAL
pointed ..... SHARP, ACUATE
pointed arch .... OGEE
pointed end .... CUSP
pointed missile DART, SPEAR
pointed remark .... BARB
pointed staff .... PIKE
pointer .... WAND
pointless .... INANE
poison .... BANE, TAINT
poison, arrow ... INEE, UPAS,
URALI, URARE, URARI,
CURARE, CURARI
poison, hemlock ..... CONINE
poison, India BISH, BISK, BIKH
poisonous protein RICIN, RICINE
poisonous weed .... LOCO
poke ..... JAB, PROD, NUDGE
poker stake ...... POT, ANTE
pokeweed ..... POCAN, SCOKE
Polar explorer .... BYRD
pole .... MAST
pole, Gaelic games
CABER, CABIR
Pole .... SLAV
pole, naut. .... MAST, SPRIT
pole to handle fish .... PEW
pole to pole, from AXAL, AXIAL

c polecat, Cape ZORIL, ZORILLA
police line .... CORDON
policeman ...... COP, PEELER
policeman, state .... TROOPER
policeman, S. Afr. ...... ZARP
polish .... RUB, WAX,
SHINE, LEVIGATE
POLISH ... see also POLAND
SPECIAL SECTION
Polish assembly ... SEIM, SEJM
Polish cake .... BABA
Polish general ... BOR, ANDERS
Polish title of address
PAN, PANI
polished .... SHINY, SLEEK,
URBANE, ELEGANT
polisher .... EMERY
polishing material
RABAT, ROUGE
polite CIVIL
political booty .... GRAFT
pollack fish .... SEY
pollen brush .. SCOPA, SCOPAE
Pollux or Castor .... ANAX
Pollux' mother .... LEDA
Pollux' twin .... CASTOR
polo stick .... MALLET
Polynesian .... MAORI
Polyn. "Adam" .... TIKI
Polyn. chestnut .... RATA
d Polyn. cloth .... TAPA
Polyn. dance .... SIVA
Polyn. deity, demon
AKUA, ATUA
Polyn. drink .... AVA
Polyn. for nature's power MANA
Polyn. god .... ATEO
Polyn. god of forest .... TANE
Polyn. herb .... PIA
Polyn. hero .... MAUI
Polyn. island group ... SAMOA
Polyn. languages
MAORI, MAHORI
Polyn. lily .... TI
Polyn. stone heap .... AHU
pome .... APPLE
"Pomp and Circumstance" Composer .... ELGAR
pompous .... TURGID
pond ... MERE, POOL, LOCHAN
ponder .... MUSE, PORE
pontiff .... POPE
pony .... CAVY
pony, student's .... CRIB
pool .... MERE, TARN,
LAGOON, PUDDLE
pool: Scot. .... DIB, CARR,
LINN, LLYN
poon tree DILO, DOMBA, KEENA
poor .... NEEDY
poor joe .... HERON

a poor player .... DUB
poorly ILL
POPE .. see also PAPAL
Pope ... JOHN, PIUS, ADRIAN
Pope, English .... ADRIAN
Pope John XXIII first name
ANGELO
Pope John XXIII last name
RONCALLI
Pope Pius XI .... RATTI
Pope Pius XII ...... PACELLI
POPE'S CAPE, COLLAR ... see
PAPAL CAPE, COLLAR
Pope's triple crown TIAR, TIARA
poplar .... ALAMO, ASPEN
poplar, white ... ABELE, ASPEN
poppy red .... GRANATE
poppy seed .... MAW
populace, the .... DEMOS
popular girl .... BELLE
porcelain
CHINA, SEVRES, LIMOGES
porcelain, ancient .... MURRA
porcelain, Chin. ...... JU, KO
porcelain, Eng. .... SPODE
porch .... ANTA, STOOP,
VERANDA, VERANDAH
porch, Gr. .... STOA
porch, Hawaiian ...... LANAI
b porch swing .... GLIDER
porcupine anteater .. ECHIDNA
porcupine, Canada .... URSON
pore .... PORUS, STOMA,
OSTIOLE, STOMATA
porgy .... SCUP
porgy, Europ. .... PARGO
porgy genus .... PAGRUS
porgy, Jap. (Oriental) .... TAI
porkfish .... SISI
porous rock ..... TUFA, TUFF
porpoise .... DOLPHIN
porridge .... POB, BROSE
porridge, corn meal ..... SAMP
porridge: Sp. Am. ..... ATOLE
Porsena of Clusium ..... LARS
PORT .. see also SPECIAL SEC-
TION — GAZETTEER

port .... HAVEN
port, banana, Hondurus .. TELA
port, Black Sea ...... ODESSA
Port Moresby land ... PAPUA
port of Rome .... OSTIA
port opp. Gibraltar .... CEUTA
port, South Seas .... APIA
port, Suez .... SAID
port wine city .... OPORTO
portable chair .... SEDAN
portal .... DOOR, GATE
portend BODE, AUGUR, PRESAGE

c portent .... OMEN, SIGN
porter, Orient
HAMAL, HAMMAL
Portia's waiting woman NERISSA
portico .... STOA
portion . PART, SOME, SEGMENT
portion out DOLE, METE, ALLOT
portray .... DRAW,
LIMN, DEPICT, DELINEATE
Portuguese coin .... REI
Port. colony, India ...... GOA
Port. folk tune .... FADO
Port. lady .... DONA
Port. man .... DOM
Port. navigator .... GAMA
Port. title ..... DOM, DONNA
pose .... SIT
Poseidon .... NEPTUNE
Poseidon's son .... TRITON
posited .... SET
position ...... SITUS, STATUS
position without work SINECURE
positive .... THETIC
positive pole, terminal ANODE
possession, landed .... ESTATE
possum .... COON
possum, comic-strip ..... POGO
post .... MAIL, SEND
post-hole digger (slick) ...LOY
d postpone .... DEFER
postulate .... POSIT
posture .... STANCE
pot .... OLLA
pot, chem. .... ALUDEL
pot, earthen .... CRUSE
pot herb .... WORT
pot, India LOTA, LOTO, LOTAH
pot liquor .... BREWIS
pot metal .... POTIN
potassium .... KALITE
potassium chloride .. MURIATE
potassium nitrate
NITER, GROUGH
potation, small .... DRAM
potato .... SPUD
potato, sweet .. YAM, BATATA
pother .... ADO
potpourri .... OLIO
potter's blade .... PALLET
pottery fragment .... SHARD
pottery, pert. to .... CERAMIC
pouch .... SAC
pouch-shaped ...... SACCATE
poultry .... HENS, BIRDS
poultry disease .... PIP, ROUP
pounce .... SWOOP
pound .... TUND
pound down ...... RAM, TAMP
pour .... RAIN, TEEM
pour off gently ...... DECANT

a pour out .... LIBATE
poverty .... NEED, WANT
powder, astringent .... BORAL
powder, mineral ingredient
.... TALC
powder of aloes .... PICRA
powdered pumice .... TALC
power .. DINT, MANA, FORCE
practical joke .... HOAX
practice .... HABIT
practice exercise, musical ETUDE
praise LAUD, EXTOL, EXTOLL
prance .... CAPER
prank .... DIDO, CAPER
prate .... GAB, YAP
prate: India ..... BUKH, BUKK
pray: Yiddish .... DAVEN
prayer AVE, BEAD, BENE, PLEA,
CREDO, MATIN, ORISON
prayer form .... LITANY
prayer, 9-day ...... NOVENA
prayer-rug, Hindu ..... ASANA
prayer stick, Am. Ind.
BAHO, PAHO, PAJO
prayers, deacon's
ECTENE, EKTENE
prayerbook
ORDO, PORTAS, PORTASS
praying figure .... ORANT
preacher, Gospel .... EVANGEL
b precepts .... DICTA
precipice, Hawaii .... PALI
precipitous .... STEEP
preclude ...... AVERT, DEBAR
preconceive .... IDEATE
predicament .... SCRAPE
predicate
BASE, FOUND, AFFIRM
predict
AUGUR, FORECAST, FORETELL
predisposed .... PRONE
preen .... PLUME, PRINK
preface .... PROEM
prefecture, Jap. .... KEN
PREFIX:
about .... PERI
above .... HYPER
across .... DIA, TRANS
again .... RE
against .... ANTI
ahead .... PRE
an .... AE
apart .... DIS
away .... DE, DI, APO
back .... ANA
backward .... RETRO
bad .... MAL
badly .... MIS
beauty .... CALLI
before ..... OB, PRE, ANTE
blood .... HAEM, HEMO

c both .... AMBI
CHEMICALS .. see page 29
common .... PRE
distant .... TEL, TELE
double .... DI
down .... DE, CATA
eight ... OCT, OCTA, OCTO
equal .... ISO
far .... TEL, TELE
faulty .... MIS
fire .... PYR
former, formerly ...... EX
four .... TETRA
from .... EC
half ..... DEMI, HEMI, SEMI
ill .... MIS
mountain .... ORO
negative .... IR, NON
new .... NEO
not ... IL, IM, IR, UN, NON
not fully .... SEMI
numerical .... UNI
of atmospheric pressure BARO
of the stars .... ASTRO
on this side .... CIS
one .... UNI
out of .... EC, EX
d outer ..... ECT, EXO, ECTO
outer skin .... EPI
outside .... ECT, EXO
over .... EPI, SUPER,
SUPRA, SUPERB
partly .... SEMI
people .... DEMO
pray .... ORA
recent .... NEO
same .... ISO, EQUI, HOMO
separation .... DIS
single .... MONO
ten .... DEC, DECA
thousand .... KILO
three .... TER, TRI
thrice .... TER, TRIS
threefold .... TRI
through .... DIA, PER
to .... AP
together .... COM
town .... TRE
turning .... ROTO
twice .... BI
two .... DI, DUA
twofold .... DI
under .... SUB
upon .... EPI
upward .... ANA, ANO
with .... SYN
within .... ENDO
wrong .... MIS

a
prehistoric implement ... **CELT**
prehistoric mound ...... **TERP**
prejudice .... **BIAS**
prelate, high .... **PRIMATE**
prelude .... **PROEM**
premium, exchange ..... **AGIO**
prepare .... **FIT, GIRD,**
MAKE, ADAPT, EQUIP
prepare for publication .. **EDIT**
prepared opium
CHANDU, CHANDOO
preposition ...... **AT, IN, ON,**
UP, INTO
presage
OMEN, HERALD, PORTEND
prescribed .... **THETIC**
prescribed quantity ..... **DOSE**
present .. **GIFT, GIVE, DONATE**
present, be .... **ATTEND**
present in brief .... **SUM**
presently.**ANON, ENOW, SOON**
preserve .... **CAN, JAM, KEEP,**
SAVE, PROTECT, MAINTAIN
preserve in brine .. **CORN, SALT**
Presidential nickname ... **ABE,**
CAL, IKE, TEDDY
press together .... **SERRY**
pressure .... **DURESS**
pressure unit .. **BARAD, BARIE**
pretend .. **FAKE, SHAM, FEIGN**

b
pretense .... **SHAM**
pretensions .... **AIRS**
pretentious .... **SIDY**
prevail .... **WIN**
prevail on .... **INDUCE**
prevalent .... **RIFE**
prevent ... **DETER, PRECLUDE**
prevent by law .... **ESTOP**
prey .... **RAVIN**
prey upon
RAVEN, RAVIN, RAVINE
Priam's son
PARIS, HECTOR, HEKTOR
price .... **RATE**
price of transportation .. **FARE**
prickle .... **SETA**
prickles .... **SETAE**
prickly pear
TUNA, NOPAL, CACTUS
prickly plant ... **BRIAR, BRIER,**
NETTLE
prickly seed coat .. **BUR, BURR**
pride .... **PLUME**
PRIEST .. see also CLERGYMAN
priest
FRA, ABBE, CURE, PADRE
priest, Celtic .... **DRUID**
priest, Gr. .... **MYST**

c
PRIEST, HIGH, see HIGH PRIEST
priest in "Iliad" .... **CALCHAS**
priest, Mongol ...... **SHAMAN**
priest, Moro **SARIP, PANDITA**
priestess, Gr. .... **AUGE**
priestess, Rom. ...... **VESTAL**
priesthood, Rom. ...... **SALII**
priestly caste ... **MAGI, MAGUS**
prima donna .... **DIVA**
PRIMA DONNA ...... see also
OPERA SOPRANO
prime minister: Brit. ... **EDEN,**
PEEL
primeval .... **OLD,**
EARLY, PRIMAL, PRISTINE
prince, Abyssin. .... **RAS**
prince, Arabian .. **EMIR, SAYID,**
SAYYID, SHERIF, SHEREEF
prince, India
RAJA, RANA, RAJAH
prince of Argos ...... **DANAE**
Prince of Darkness .... **SATAN**
prince, Oriental .... **KHAN**
prince, Persian .. **AMIR, AMEER**
prince, petty .... **SATRAP**
prince, Slavic .... **KNEZ**
Prince Val's father ... **AGUAR**
princeling .... **SATRAP**
princely .... **ROYAL**
princess, Gr. myth ...... **IOLE**
princess, India .. **RANI, RANEE**

d
principal .... **TOP, ARCH**
MAIN, CHIEF
principal commodity .. **STAPLE**
principle, accepted
AXIOM, PRANA, TENET
print .... **STAMP**
print measure .... **EM, EN**
printer, 1st colonial .... **DAYE**
printer's direction ...... **STET**
printer's mark .... **DELE**
printer's mistake
TYPO, ERRATUM
printer's mistakes .... **ERRATA**
printing plate .... **STEREO**
printing roller .... **PLATEN**
prison.**JUG, GAOL, JAIL, QUOD**
prison sentence .... **RAP**
prison spy .... **MOUTON**
privation .... **LOSS**
privilege, commercial .. **OCTROI**
prize .... **PRY, AWARD**
pro .... **FOR**
"— pro nobis" .... **ORA**
probe, medical .... **STYLET**
problem .... **POSER**
proboscis .... **SNOUT**
proboscis monkey ...... **KAHA**
proceed ... **WEND, ADVANCE**
proceedings .... **ACTA**

a procession .... TRAIN, PARADE, MOTORCADE
proclaim .... CRY, VOICE, HERALD, DECLARE
prod .... URGE
produce .... BEGET, YIELD CREATE, INWORK, GENERATE
produce as an effect ... BEGET
produced, quantity ..... YIELD
producing cold ...... ALGIFIC
production, artistic .. FACTURE
profane .... VIOLATE
profane, Hawaiian .... NOA
profession ART, CAREER, METIER
professional, not LAIC, LAICAL
profit ... GAIN, VAIL, AVAIL
profit, to yield .... NET
profits, taker of: law . PERNOR
profitable ...... FAT, USEFUL
profound .... DEEP
"— profundis" .... DE
progenitor ..... SIRE, PARENT
progeny .... ISSUE
prohibit .... BAN, BAR, VETO, DEBAR, ESTOP
prohibition BAN, VETO, EMBARGO
Prohibition, against ...... WET
project ...... JUT, IDEA, PLAN
b projectile .... MISSILE
projecting edge RIM, FLANGE
projecting piece ARM, RIM, TENON, FLANGE
projecting rim .... FLANGE
projecting tooth .... SNAG
projection . EAR, BARB, PRONG
projection, fireplace.HOB, HOBB
projection, jagged SNAG, TOOTH
projection, studlike .... KNOP
promenade .... MALL
promise .... WORD
promise to pay .... IOU, NOTE
"Promised Land" fountain AIN
promontory ..... CAPE, NASE, NAZE, NESS
promontory, Orkneys .... NOUP
promontory, rocky ...... TOR
promote .... FOSTER
prompt .... CUE, YARE
prone .... APT, FLAT
prong .... TINE, TOOTH
pronghorn .... CABREE, CABRET, CABRIE, CABRIT
pronoun .. IT, ME, US, WE, YE, HER, HIM, ONE, SHE, THAT, THIS, THEE, THEM, THEY, THOU, THESE, THOSE

c pronoun, possessive . MY, HER, HIS, ITS, OUR, HERS, MINE, OURS, YOUR
pronounce indistinctly ... SLUR
pronounce strongly .... STRESS
pronouncement DICTA, DICTUM
proof, corrected ...... REVISE
proof, printer's .... GALLEY
proofreader's mark DELE, STET, CARET
prop .... HOLD, STAY, BRACE, BOLSTER, SUSTAIN
propeller .... OAR
proper .... DUE, FIT
properly .... FEATLY
property, hold on .... LIEN
property, India .... DHAN
property, item of ASSET, CHATTEL
property, landed ...... ESTATE
property owned absolutely ALOD, ALLOD, ALODIUM, ALLODIUM
property, receiver of .. ALIENEE
prophesy .... FORETELL
prophet .... SEER, AUGUR, PREDICTOR, FORETELLER
PROPHETS, BIBLICAL ..... see SPECIAL SECTION
prophets .... VATES
d prophetic ... VATIC, VATICAL
proportion .... RATIO
proportionally assess PRORATE
proposition THESES, THESIS, PREMISE
proposition, logic ..... LEMMA
proposition: math. .. THEOREM
prosecutor .... SUER
prosecutor: abbr. .... DA
proselyte to Judaism .... GER
"— prosequi," .... NOLLE
Proserpina ...... CORA, KORE
prospect .... VISTA
prosperity .... WEAL
prosperity god, Teut. .... FREY
Prospero's servant ..... ARIEL
prostrate .... PRONE, REPENT
protagonist .... HERO
protected .... HOUSED
protection .... EGIS, AEGIS
protection right, Old Eng. MUND
protective building .... REDAN
protective influence EGIS, AEGIS
Protestant denomination: abbr. ME, PE, BAP, PRESB
prototype .... IDEAL
protozoan order .... LOBOSA
protuberance ..... JAG, NUB, HUMP, KNOB, KNOT, NODE, WART, KNURL, TORUS

124

a protuberant .... **TOROSE**
prove: law .... **DERAIGN**
proverb .... **SAW, ADAGE,**
AXIOM, MAXIM, SAYING
provide ...... **ENDOW, ENDUE**
provided .... **IF**
provided that .... **SO**
province, Rom. .... **DACIA**
provisional clause ... **PROVISO**
proviso .... **CLAUSE**
provoke............ **IRE, RILE,**
ANGER, ANNOY
prow .... **BOW, STEM**
prune: prov. Eng. ...... **SNED**
pruning knife .... **DHAW**
Prussian spa, town ...... **EMS**
pry .... **NOSE, LEVER, SNOOP**
Psalm, 51st .... **MISERERE**
Psalmist .... **DAVID**
Psalms, selection of .. **HALLEL**
Psalms, word in .... **SELAH**
pseudonym ...... **NOM, ALIAS**
pseudonym of Louise Del La
Ramee .... **OUIDA**
psyche .... **SOUL**
psychiatrist
JUNG, ADLER, FREUD
Ptah, embodiment of ... **APIS**
ptarmigan .... **RYPE**
b pteropod genus ...... **CLIONE**
pua hemp ....:...... **POOA**
public .... **OPEN, OVERT**
public: Chin. .... **KUNG**
public esteem .... **REPUTE**
public, make ... **AIR, DELATE**
public vehicle .... **BUS, TAXI**
publication, style of . **FORMAT**
publish .... **ISSUE, PRINT**
publish illegally ...... **PIRATE**
Puccini heroine .... **MIMI**
puck, hockey .... **RUBBER**
pudding.......... **DUFF, SAGO**
pueblo dweller .... **HOPI**
Pueblo Indian ... **HOPI, ZUNI,**
KERES, MOQUI, TANOA
Pueblo sacred chamber .. **KIVA**
Pueblo, Tanoan .... **HANO**
Puerto Rican plant ...... **APIO**
puff up .... **ELATE**
puffbird, Brazil .... **DREAMER**
puffbird genus ..... **MONASA**
puffer fish .... **TAMBOR**
Pulitzer poet .... **FROST**
pull .. **TOW, TUG, DRAG, HALE**
pull with nautical tackle **BOUSE**
pulley .... **SHEAVE**
pulp, fruit .... **POMACE**
pulpit .... **AMBO, BEMA**
pulpy mass left in cider **POMACE**
pulverize .... **MICRONIZE**

c pump handle .... **SWIPE**
pumpkin .... **PEPO**
punch .... **JAB**
"Punch and Judy" dog .. **TOBY**
punch, engraver's .. **MATTOIR**
punctuation mark. **DASH, COLON**
pungent .. **TEZ, SPICY, TANGY**
punish by fine ...... **AMERCE**
punishment .... **FERULE**
punishment, of .... **PENAL**
punitive .... **PENAL**
Punjab native .... **JAT**
punk .... **AMADOU**
pupa .... **INSTAR**
pupil of eye .... **GLENE**
puppet .... **DOLL**
puppet, famous **JUDY, PUNCH**
puppeteer, famous ...... **SARG**
pure sirup .... **CLAIRCE**
pure thought .... **NOESIS**
purification, ancient Roman
LUSTRUM
purloin .... **STEAL**
purple
MAUVE, MODENA, TYRIAN
purple dye source .... **MUREX**
purple medic
LUCERN, ALFALFA, LUCERNE
purple ragwort ...... **JACOBY**
purple seaweed . **SION, LAVER**
d purport, general ...... **TENOR**
purpose .... **AIM, END,**
GOAL, SAKE, INTENT
purposive .... **TELIC**
purse net .... **SEINE**
pursy .... **STOUT**
push up .... **BOOST**
put aside .... **DAFF**
put away .... **STORE**
put back .... **REPLACE**
put forth .... **EXERT**
put in bank .... **DEPOSIT**
put off .... **DEFER**
put out .... **OUST, EJECT**
put up .... **ANTE**
puzzle .... **POSER,**
REBUS, BAFFLE, ACROSTIC
puzzles .... **CRUCES**
Pygmalion's statue .. **GALATEA**
pygmy .... **ATOMY**
pygmy people, Congo
AKKA, ACHUAS
pygmy people, Equatorial Africa
BATWA, ABONGO, OBONGO
Pylos, kin of .... **NESTOR**
Pyramus, lover of .... **THISBE**
pyromaniac .... **FIREBUG**
Pythias' friend .... **DAMON**
python .... **BOA**

Q

a

qua .... AS
"— qua non" .... SINE
quack IMPOSTOR, CHARLATAN
quack medicine .... NOSTRUM
quadrant .... ARC
quadrate .... SQUARE
"quae —" which see .... VIDE
quaff .... DRINK
quail .... COLIN, COWER
quake .... SHAKE,
SHIVER, TREMOR, TREMBLE
Quaker .... FRIEND
Quaker Poet .... WHITTIER
quaking .... TREPID
qualify .... FIT, ADAPT,
EQUIP, PREPARE
qualified .... FIT, ABLE
quality .... CALIBER, CALIBRE
quantity, indeterminate . SOME
quantity: math.
SCALER, VECTOR

b

quarrel .... ROW, FEUD,
SPAT, TIFF
quarter of a year: Scot. RAITH
quartz .../....... JASPER
quartz, green .... PRASE
quartz, translucent ... PRASE
quash: law .... CASSARE
quaternion .... TETRAD
quay .... LEVEE
Quebec, district, town ... LEVIS
Quebec's patron saint .. ANNE
Queen .... CLEO
queen: Moslem BEGUM, BEEGUM
queen of gods, Egypt. ... SATI
queen of gods, Rom. ... HERA,
JUNO
Queen of Italy .... ELENA
Queen of Ithaca ... PENELOPE
Queen of Roumania ... MARIE
Queen of Scots .... MARY
Queen of Spain, last ..... ENA
queen, "Romeo and Juliet"
MAB

c

queenly .... REGAL, REGINAL
Queensland hemp plant
SIDA
Queensland tribe .... GOA
quell .... CALM, CRUSH
quench .... SLAKE
quench steel ..... AUSTEMPER
quern .... MILL
query .... ASK
queue .... LINE
question .... ASK, GRILL
question, hard .... POSER
quetzal .... TROGON
quibble .... CAVIL, EVADE
quick .... FAST, AGILE,
ALIVE, RAPID
quick: music .... TOSTO
quicken ... HASTEN, ENLIVEN
quickly .... CITO, APACE,
PRESTO, PRONTO
quickly, move
SCAT, SCUD, SKITE
quicksilver ...... HEAUTARIT
quid .... CUD

d

"quid — quo," equivalent . PRO
quiescent LATENT, DORMANT
quiet .... CALM, LULL,
STILL, SMOOTH
quiet! .... SH, PST, TST
quilkin .... FROG, TOAD
quill .... PEN, SPINE
quill feathers REMEX, REMIGES
quill for winding silk ..... COP
quilt .... EIDER, COVER
quince, Bengal .... BEL, BHEL
quinine .... KINA
quintessence ... PITH, ELIXIR
quirt, cowboy's ...... ROMAL
quit .... CEASE, LEAVE
quite .... ALL
quivering ... ASPEN, TREMOR
"quod — demonstrandum"
ERAT
"Quo Vadis" tyrant character
NERO
quoits, mark of .... MOT
quote .... CITE

R

Ra, consort of .... MUT
Ra, son of .... SU, SHU
rabbi, law-teaching ... AMORA
rabbit cage .... HUTCH
rabbit, Europ. . CONY, CONEY
rabbit, female .... DOE
rabbit fur .... LAPIN
rabbit home .... WARREN
rabbit, small swamp .. TAPETI
rabbit, So. Am. .... TAPETI
rabble .... MOB
rabies .... LYSSA
raccoon-like mammal .. COATI
RACE .. see also TRIBES in
    SPECIAL SECTION
race, boat .... REGATTA
race, kind of .... RELAY
race, short .... SPRINT
race-track .... OVAL
race-track circuit ...... LAP
race-track tipster ...... TOUT
races, pert. to ...... ETHNIC
Rachel's father .... LABAN
racing boat .... GIG
racket, game .... PELOTA
radar screen .... SCOPE
radiate .... EMANATE
radical .... RED
radicle .... STEMLET
radio advertiser .... SPONSOR
radio bulletin ..... NEWSCAST
radio-guided bomb ..... AZON
radio wave ..... MICROWAVE
radio wire .... LITZ
radio-TV awards ..... EMMIES
radioactive counter .. GEIGER
radioactive element ... NITON
radioactive ray .... GAMMA
radium discoverer ...... CURIE
radium emanation .... NITON
radius, pert. to ...... RADIAL
radon .... NITON
raft, kind of ... CATAMARAN
raft, Maori .... MOKI
rag doll .... MOPPET
rage .... RAMP, RANT,
    RESE, STORM
ragged person: Sp. ...... ROTO
raging monster, Bibl. .. RAHAB
ragout, game .... SALMI
ragweed genus .... IVA
raid .... FORAY, INROAD
raid, soldier's .... COMMANDO
rail at .... REVILE
rail bird SORA, WEKA, CRAKE
railing .... PARAPET

railroad bridge ...... TRESSEL,
    TRESTLE
railroad light .... FLARE
railroad signal
    TRIMMER, SEMAPHORE
railroad tie .... SLEEPER
railroad timber .... TIE
railway station: Fr. ..... GARE
rain after sunset ...... SEREIN
rain, fine .... MISLE
rain forest .... SELVA
rain gauge .... UDOMETER
rain serpent, Hindu .... NAGA
rain spout: Scot. ...... RONE
rain tree .... SAMAN
rainbow .... ARC, IRIS
rainbow goddess .... IRIS
rainbow, pert. to ..... IRIDAL
raincoat .... PONCHO
rainy .... WET
raise . REAR, BREED, ELEVATE
raised .... BRED
raisin: Sp. .... PASA
raising device .... JACK
Rajah's lady ... RANI, RANEE
rake ...... ROUE, LOTHARIO
rake with gunfire .. ENFILADE
ram . TUP, BUTT, TAMP, ARIES
ram, male .... TUP
ram-headed god, Egypt
    AMEN, AMON, AMUN
Ramachandra, wife of .. SITA
ramble .... GAD, ROVE
Ramee, de la, penname . OUIDA
rammed earth building material
    PISE
rampart ...... AGGER, VALLUM
range .... AREA, GAMUT,
    SCOPE, SIERRA
Rangoon's state .... PEGU
rank .... ROW, RATE, DEGREE
ranks, press in .... SERRY
rankle .... FESTER
ransom .... REDEEM
rapeseed ..... COLSA, COLZA
rapid, more: music .. STRETTA,
    STRETTE, STRETTI, STRETTO
rapids, river .... SOO
rapidly .... APACE
rapier .... BILBO
rare earth element ... ERBIUM
rascal .... IMP, ROGUE
rase .... INCISE
rasorial .... GNAWING
rasp .... FILE, GRATE

127

a raspberry, variety . BLACKCAP
rasse .... CIVET
rat .... DESERTER
rat, Ceylon, India . BANDICOOT
rat hare .... PIKA
rate .... ESTIMATE
rate, relative .... AT
ratify .... SEAL
ratio .... RATE
RATIO: MATH see MATH, RATIO
rational .... SANE
rational integer .... NORM
rational principle ...... LOGOS
rationalize .... THOB
ratite bird ...... CASSOWARY
rattan .... CANE
rattlesnake
      RATTLER, CROTALUS
rave .... RANT
"Raven" author .... POE
"Raven" character .... LENORE
ravine
    GAP, DALE, VALE, GORGE
ravine, Afr. .... WADI, WADY
ravine, Arabia .. WADI, WADY
rawboned .... LEAN
rawboned animal ...... SCRAG
ray fish .... SKATE
rays, like .... RADIAL
rayon ... ACETATE, CELANESE
b raze .... DEVASTATE
razor-billed auk
    ALCA, MURR, MURRE
reach across .... SPAN
react .... RESPOND
read, inability to ..... ALEXIA
read metrically .... SCAN
read publically ...... PRELECT
reader, first .... PRIMER
reading desk .... AMBO
reading substituted: Bibl.
    KERE, KERI
ready: dialect .... YARE
ready-made tie .... TECK
real being, pert. to .... ONTAL
real thing .... MCCOY
reality .... FACT
realm .... DOMAIN
reamer .... BROACH
rear ... ERECT, RAISE, ARRIERE
rear, to the
    AFT, ABAFT, ASTERN
rearhorse .... MANTIS
rearing of horse ...... PESADE
reason .... NOUS
reason, deprive of ... DEMENT
reasoning .... LOGIC
reasoning, deductive .. APRIORI
reata
    LAZO, ROPE, LASSO, LARIAT

c rebec of India .... SAROD
Rebecca's hairy son ..... ESAU
rebound .. CAROM, RICOCHET
rebuff .... SLAP, SNUB
rebuke
    CHIDE, SCOLD, REPROVE
recalcitrant .... RENITENT
recant .... RETRACT
recede .... EBB
recent
    NEO, NEW, LATE, NEOTERIC
receptacle .... BIN, BOX,
      TRAY, VESSEL
reception, a.m. .... LEVEE
reception: Fr. .... ACCUEIL
reception, India ...... DURBAR
recess .... APSE, ALCOVE
recess, wall .... NICHE
recipient .... DONEE
recite metrically .... SCAN
reckon .... ARET, COUNT
reckoning .... TALLY
reclaim .... REDEEM
recline .... LOLL
recluse ...... ASCETIC, EREMITE,
    ANCHORET, ANCHORITE
recoil .... SHY, RESILE
recommit .... REMAND
recompense .. PAY, FEES, MEED
reconnaissance RECCO, RECON
d reconnoiter .... SCOUT
reconstruct .... REMODEL
record .. TAB, NOTE, ENROL,
    ENTER, ENTRY, REGISTER
record of investigation REPORT
record, ship's .... LOG
record, year's .... ANNAL
records .... ANNALS
recorded proceedings ... ACTA
recording device .... TAPE
records, one who ..... NOTER
recourse, have .... REFER
recover strength ...... RALLY
recovery, legal .... TROVER
recruit .... BOOT
rectifier, current ...... DIODE
rectify ...... AMEND, EMEND
recurring pattern ..... CYCLE
red .... CARMINE,
    MAGENTA, NACARAT
red, Brazil .... ROSET
red cedar .... SAVIN, SAVINE
red circle: Her. .... GUZE
red currant .... RISSEL
red deer .... ELAPHINE
red dye root ... CHAY, CHOY
red garden flower .... CANNA
red: Her. .... GULES
red horse .... BAY, ROAN
red ocher .... KEEL, KIEL,
    TIVER, RADDLE, RUDDLE

red pigment .... ROSET,
ASTACIN, ASTACENE
red pine .... RIMU
red planet .... MARS
red powder, India .... ABIR
red, painter's .... ROSET
Red River Rebellion leader
RIEL
red: Sp. .... ROJO
red squirrel ...... CHICKAREE
red swine .... DUROC
red, Venetian .... SIENA
red-yellow color .... ALOMA
redact .... EDIT
redbreast .... ROBIN
redcap .... PORTER
reddish yellow .... SUDAN
redeem .... RANSOM
redshank .... CLEE
reduce .... PARE, DEMOTE
reduce sail .... REEF
reduce taxes .... DERATE
reebok .... PEELE
reedbuck .... NAGOR
reek .... FUG, FUME
reef .... SHOAL
reel, fishing-rod .... PIRN
refer .... PERTAIN
refer to repeatedly ..... HARP
refined grace ...... ELEGANCE
reflection .... GLARE
refracting device .... LENS
refractor, light .... PRISM
refrain .... FORBEAR
refrain in songs .. FALA, LALA,
DERRY, LUDDEN
refrigerant .... FREON
refuge ...... HAVEN, SHELTER
refugee .... EMIGREE
refuse .... DENY
refuse .... ORT, DROSS,
SCUM, OFFAL, TRASH
refuse, bit of .... SCRAP
refuse, flax .... POB
refuse: law .... RECUSE
refuse, metal . DROSS, SCORIA
refuse, wool .... COT
refute .... REBUT, DISPROVE
regale .... FETE
regard ...... ESTEEM, RESPECT
regarding .... RE, ANENT
regenerate .... RENEW
regiment's framework .. CADRE
REGION .... see also DISTRICT
region .... CLIME, SECTOR
region, Afr. .. CONGO, NUBIA
region, Boeotia ...... AONIA
region, Cent. Afr.
SUDAN, SOUDAN
region, Fr. .... ALSACE

region, Gr. .... DORIC
region, Indo-China ..... LAOS
region, pert. to .... AREAL
register .... ENROL,
ENROLL, RECORD
reiterate .... REPEAT
regret .... RUE, DEPLORE
reign: India .... RAJ
reign, pert. to .... REGNAL
reigning .... REGNANT
reigning beauty .... BELLE
reimbursed .... PAID
reindeer .... CARIBOU
reindeer, Santa's .... DASHER,
DONDER, BLITZEN,
PRANCER
reinstate .... REVEST
reject .... SPURN, REPULSE
relate .... TELL,
RECITE, NARRATE
related .... AKIN, TOLD,
COGNATE, GERMANE
related by blood .... SIB
related on mother's side ENATE
relation .... SIB
relative. SIB, SIS, AUNT, NIECE
relative amount ...... RATION
relative pronoun .... WHO,
THAT, WHAT
relative speed .... TEMPO
relatives .... KIN
relatives, favoring .. NEPOTAL
relax .... EASE
relaxing of state tensions
DETENTE
relay of horses ..... REMUDA
release .... LOOSE
release: law .... REMISE
release, phonetic .... DETENTE
relevant .... GERMANE
reliable .... HONEST
relief, — .... BAS
relief .... DOLE
relieve .... EASE, ALLAY
relieve: Scot. .... LISS
religieuse .... NUN
religion .... FAITH
religion, Jap. .... SHINTO
religious art, work of .. PIETA
religious brother .... FRA,
MONK, FRIAR
religious festival ..... EASTER
religious festival, India .. MELA
religious law, Rom. ..... FAS
religious laywoman .. BEGUINE
religious opinion .... DOXY
religious order, one in . OBLATE
religious sayings ...... LOGIA
relinquish .... CEDE,
WAIVE, YIELD

a reliquary .... APSE, ARCA,
ARCAE, CHEST
relish .... GUSTO
reluctant ..... LOATH, AVERSE
rely .... TRUST
remain .... BIDE, STAY
remainder .... REST
remaining .... OVER
remark, witty .... MOT, SALLY
remiss .... LAX
remit .... SEND
remnant .... END, SHRED
remora fish . PEGA, LOOTSMAN
remove .. DELE, DOFF, DELETE
remove interior .... GUT
remove: law .... ELOIN,
ELOIGN, ELOIGNE
remunerate .... PAY
rend ...... RIP, TEAR, WREST
render fat .... TRY
rendezvous .... TRYST
renegade .... APOSTATE
renounce .... ABNEGATE
renovated hat ..... MOLOKER
renown .... FAME, NOTE,
EMINENCE, PRESTIGE
rent .... LET, HIRE, TEAR,
TORN, LEASE
rent, old Eng. law .... TAC
renter .... LESSEE
b repair ..... DARN, MEND
repartee .... RIPOST, RIPOSTE
repast .... MEAL
repay .... REQUITE
repay in kind .... RETALIATE
repeat .... ECHO, ITERATE
repeat: music .... BIS
repeat performance .. ENCORE
repeat sign: music ..... SEGNO
repeat tiresomely .. DIN, DING
repeated phrase ..... REPRISE
repeatedly hit ...... POMMEL
repetition .... ROTE
replete .... FULL
report, small .... POP
repose .... EASE, REST
representation .... IDOL
representative .... AGENT
reproach ..... BLAME, TAUNT
reproach, old term ..... RACA
reproductive body .. GAMETE
reproductive cell ...... SPORE
reptile, pert. to ..... SAURIAN
repulse .... REPEL
reputation .... NAME, REPUTE
repute .... CHARACTER
request .... PLEA
rescind .... REPEAL
resentment .... IRE
reserve supply .... STORE

c residence ..... HOME, ABODE
residence, ecclesiastical . MANSE
resident of .... ITE
resign .... QUIT, DEMIT
resin ..... GUM, LAC, ANIME,
COPAL, ELEMI, JALAP,
MYRRH, BALSAM, MASTIC
resin, fossil . AMBER, GLESSITE
resin, fragrant .... ELEMI
resist .... OPPOSE
resist authority .... REBEL
resisting pressure ... RENITENT
resistor, current ... RHEOSTAT
resort .... SPA
resort, Fr. .... PAU,
NICE, CANNES
resources .... FUND,
MEANS, ASSETS
respect .... ESTEEM
respond .... REACT
rest .... SIT, EASE, REPOSE
rest, lay at .... REPOSE
restaurant, small ..... BISTRO
resthouse ...... CHAN, KHAN
resting .... ABED
restive .... BALKY
restore .... RENEW
restrain .. CURB, REIN, DETER,
STINT, TETHER
d restrict .... LIMIT
retaliate .... REPAY
retain .... HOLD, KEEP
retaliation .... TALION
retinue .... SUITE, TRAIN
retort, quick . RIPOST, RIPOSTE
retract .... RECANT
retreat .... RECEDE
retreat, cosy . DEN, NEST, NOOK
retribution .... NEMESIS
retribution, get .... VENGE
retrograde .... RECEDE
return ...... RECUR, RESTORE
return a profit .... PAY
return blow .... TIT
return on investment .. YIELD
returning .... REDIENT
reunion, hold a .... REUNE
reveille, call to .... DIAN
revelry, cry of .... EVOE
revelry, drunken .... ORGY
revenue, church: Scot. ANNAT
reverberate .... ECHO
reverberating ...... REBOANT
revere ...... HONOR, HONOUR
reverence .... AWE
reversed in order .. CONVERSE
reversion to type .... ATAVISM

revert to state (land) ...... ESCHEAT
revise .... EDIT, AMEND
revive wine .... STUM
revoke legacy, grant .. ADEEM
Revolution hero . HALE, ALLEN
revolutions per minute .. REVS
revolve . SPIN, TURN, ROTATE
revolve: logging .... BIRL
revolver.GAT, GUN, ROD, COLT
reward .... MEED
rhebok .... PEELE
Rhine city .... MAINZ
Rhine tributary .... AAR
rhinoceros beetle ...... UANG
rhinoceros, black
BORELE, NASICORN
rhinoceros: obs.
ABADA, ABATH
Rhone tributary ...... SAONE
rhythm .... TIME, METER,
METRE, CADENCE
rhythmical accent ...... BEAT
rhythmical swing .... LILT
rib .... COSTA
rib, pert. to .... COSTAL
rib, woman from .... EVE
ribs, with .... COSTATE
ribbed fabric ..... REP, CORD,
REPP, PIQUÉ
ribbon, badge ...... CORDON
ribbon: comb. form ..... TENE
ribbonfish .... GUAPENA
rice .... PADI, PADDY
rice dish ...... PILAU, PILAW
rice field, Java .... PADI
rice grass, P.I. .... BARIT
rice in husk .... PALAY
rice paste, Jap. .... AME
rice polishings .... DARAC
rich man .... MIDAS,
NABOB, NAWAB
rich silk cloth .... CAFFA
riches .... PELF
rid .... FREE
riddle .... ENIGMA
ridge .... ARETE,
SPINE, MOUNTAIN
ridge, camp's .... RIDEAU
ridge, glacial, sandy ...... OS,
OSAR, ESKER, OESAR
ridge on cloth .... WALE
ridge on skin .... WELT
ridge, stony .... RAND
ridges, rounded .... GYRI
ridged area, Balkan ..... BILO
ridicule .... GUY, MOCK,
RAZZ, DERIDE
ridicule personified, Gr.
MOMUS

riding academy ..... MANEGE
riding dress .... HABIT
rifle .... KRAG, MINIE,
GARAND, CARBINE
rifle ball .... MINIE
rifleman, Ger. .... JAGER
right conduct, Buddhist ... TAO
right conduct: Taoism ..... TE
right hand: music .... DM
right-hand page .. RO, RECTO
right: law .... DROIT
right, pert. to .... DEXTER
right to speak .... SAY
right, turn .... GEE
rights, of ...... JURAL, UDAL
Rigoletto's daughter ... GILDA
rigorous ...... HARSH, STERN,
STRICT, SEVERE, AUSTERE
rim ...... LIP, EDGE, FLANGE
rim of wheel .. FELLY, FELLOE
"Rime cold giant" . YMER, YMIR
ring ...... PEAL, TOLL, KNELL
ring, boxing .... ARENA
ring for reins . TERRET, TERRIT
ring, gun carriage ..... LUNET
ring, harness pad
TERRET, TERRIT
ring, lamp condensing ... CRIC
ring, little .... ANNULET
ring, naut. .... GROMMET
ring of light .... HALO, NIMB,
NIMBUS, AUREOLA,
AUREOLE
"Ring of the Nibelung" goddess
ERDA
"Ring of the Nibelung" smith
MIME
ring out .... PEAL
ring, part of .... CHATON
ring, rubber jar .... LUTE
ring, seal .... SIGNET
ring-shaped ...... CIRCINATE
ring-shaped piece ..... QUOIT
ring, stone of .... CHATON
ringlet .... CURL, TRESS
ringworm ..... TINEA, TETTER
ripening agent .... AGER
ripple ...... LAP, RIFF, WAVE
rise above .... TOWER
rise aloft .... TOWER
rise: old Eng. .... RIS
risible .... GELASTIC
rites, religious .... SACRA
ritual .... RITE
RIVER . see also GAZETTEER in
SPECIAL SECTION
river .... RIO
river, Balmoral Castle's ... DEE
river bank .... RIPA
river bank, growing by
RIPARIAN

131

River

a river-bank stair, Ind.
          GAUT, GHAT
river bed, dry, Afr.
          WADI, WADY
river between Europe and Asia
          KARA
river, Bremen's .... **WESER**
river Caesar crossed . **RUBICON**
river, Dutch Meuse ..... **MAAS**
river in Baltic .... **ODER**
river in Essex .... **CAM**
river in Orleans .... **LOIRE**
river in Petrograd ...... **NEVA**
river into Moselle ...... **SAAR**
river into Rhone ...... **SAONE**
river islet .... **AIT**
river, "Kubla Khan" .... **ALPH**
river, Munich's .... **ISAR**
river mouth ..... **LADE, DELTA**
river nymph .... **NAIS**
river to the Humber
          OUSE, TRENT
River of Woe ..... **ACHERON**
river, Southwest .... **PECOS**
river: Sp. .... **RIO**
river: Tagalog .... **ILOG**
river to Medit. .... **EBRO**
river valley .... **STRATH**
rivulet .... **RILL**
road .... **VIA, PATH,
          ITER, AGGER**
b road: Roman .... **ITER**
road: Gypsy .... **DRUN**
roadhouse .... **INN**
roam .... **GAD, ROVE**
roast .... **CALCINE**
roasted meat strip .... **CABOB**
roasting rod .... **SPIT**
rob .... **REAVE, DESPOIL**
Rob Roy .... **CANOE**
robber .... **THIEF**
ROBE ..... see also GARMENT
robe .... **MANTLE**
robe to ankles .... **TALAR**
"Roberta" composer .... **KERN**
robot drama .... **RUR**
rock aggregate .... **AUGE**
rock, basic igneous ..... **SIMA**
rock cavity ..... **VOOG, VUGG,
          VUGH, GEODE**
rock, dangerous ...... **SCYLLA**
rock, dark .... **BASALT**
rock, fine grained ...... **TRAP**
rock, flintlike .... **CHERT**
rock, granitoid **DUNITE, GNEISS**
rock, hard .... **WHIN**
rock, jutting .... **TOR**
rock, laminated ...... **SHALE
          SLATE, GNEISS**
rock, melted .... **LAVA**
rock, mica-bearing ... **DOMITE**

c rock, projecting ... **TOR, CRAG**
rock, rugged .... **CRAG**
rock snake .... **PYTHON**
rock whiting genus ..... **ODAX**
rock-wren .... **TURCO**
ROCKET .. see under MISSILE,
          GUIDED
rocket's goal .... **MOON**
rockfish ... **RASHER, TAMBOR**
rockfish, Calif. .. **RENA, REINA**
rockweed .... **FUCI, FUCUS**
Rocky Mt. peak .... **ESTES**
Rocky Mt. range
          TETON, UINTA
rocky peak, eminence,
     pinnacle .... **TOR**
rod ... **POLE, WAND, BATON,
          PERCH, STAFF**
rod, barbecue .... **SPIT**
rod, basketry .... **OSIER**
rod, billiard .... **CUE**
rod, chastening ...... **FERULE**
rodent .... **RAT, HARE**
rodent genus .... **MUS**
rodent, rabbit-like ...... **PIKA**
rodent, S. Am. .. **CAVY, DEGU,
          PACA, COYPU, AGOUTI**
rodent, W. Ind. .... **HUTIA**
Rhoderick Dhu .... **SCOT**
rogue .... **PICARO**
roguish .... **SLY, ARCH**
d roister .... **REVEL**
Roland's destroyer ...... **GAN,
          GANO, GANELON**
roll and heave .... **TOSS**
roll of bread: dialect. .... **BAP**
roll of cloth .... **BOLT**
roll of paper .... **SCROLL**
roll up .... **FURL**
romaine .... **COS**
ROMAN GODS
          see SPECIAL SECTION
Rom. assembly ...... **COMITIA**
Rom. authors ..... **CATO, LIVY,
          OVID, LUCAN, NEPOS,
          PLINY, CICERO, HOR-
          ACE, SENECA, SILIUS,
          VERGIL, SALLUST**
Rom. barracks
          CANABA, CANNABA
Rom. box .... **CAPSA**
Rom. boxing glove ... **CESTUS**
Rom. bronze .... **AES**
Rom. brooch .... **FIBULA**
Rom. building .... **INSULA**
Rom. cap .... **PILEUS**
Rom. cavalry body
          TURM, TURMA
Rom. circus post .... **META**
Rom. clan ..... **GENS, GENTES**
Rom. cloak ... **TOGA, ABOLLA**

a Rom. coin, ancient ..... SEMIS, DINDER
Rom. coins .... AS, AES, ASSES, SOLIDUS
Rom. Curia court ...... ROTA
Rom. date ...... IDES, NONES
Rom. dictator .... SULLA
Rom. dish .... LANX
Rom. emperor .... NERO, OTHO, TITUS
Rom. farce .... EXODE
Rom. galley ..... TRIREME, UNIREME
Rom. gaming cube ..... TALUS
Rom. garment .. TOGA, STOLA, TUNIC, PLANETA
Rom. goal post in racing . META
Rom. highway ..... VIA, ITER
Rom. historian ... LIVY, NEPOS
Rom. judge .... EDILE, AEDILE
Rom. law control ..... MANUS
Rom. legendary king ... NUMA
Rom. liquid measure .... URNA
Rom. list ...... ALBE, ALBUM
Rom. magistrate or official
    EDILE, AEDILE, ARCHON, CONSUL, PRETOR, TRIBUNE
Rom. market ... FORA, FORUM
Rom. meal .... CENA
b Rom. money, copper ..... AES
Rom. numerals 1-I, 5-V, 10-X, 50-L, 100-C, 500-D, 1000-M
ROMAN OFFICIAL
    see ROMAN MAGISTRATE
Rom. patriot .... CATO
Rom. philosopher
    CATO, SENECA
Rom. platter .... LANX
Rom. pledge .... VAS
Rom. poet ..... OVID, LUCAN, HORACE, VERGIL, VIRGIL
Rom. pound .... AS
Rom. province .... DACIA
Rom. public games ...... LUDI
Rom. public lands ...... AGER
Rom. religious festivals . VOTA
Rom. road .... VIA, ITER
Rom. robe .... TOGA
Rom. room, principal
    ATRIA, ATRIUM
Rom. scroll .... STEMMA
Rom. statesman .... CATO
Rom. sword .... FALX
Rom. vessel .... PATERA
Rom. war garb .... SAGUM
Rom. weight .... AS

c Rom. well-curb ...... PUTEAL
Rom. writer .... MACER
romance, tale of . GEST, GESTE
ROMANIA .... see RUMANIA
Rome, a founder of ... REMUS
Rome's cathedral church
    LATERAN
Rome's conqueror ..... ALARIC
Rome's river .... TIBER
Romulus' twin .... REMUS
rood .... CROSS
roof .... MANSARD
roof edge .... EAVE
roof of mouth .... PALATE
roof of mouth, pert. to
    PALATAL
roof ornament .... EPI
roof, rounded . DOME, CUPOLA
roof, rounded like a ... DOMAL
roof, truncated .... HIP
roofing piece ...... RAG, TILE
roofing slate .... TILE
roofing timber .... PURLIN
rook's cry .... CAWK
room, Eng. college supply
    BUTTERY
room, snug .... DEN
room, rooms .... SPACE, SUITE
room, architecture ..... OECUS
room for household goods,
    linen, etc. . EWRY, EWERY
d room, main, Rom.
    ATRIA, ATRIUM
room, mineshaft . PLAT, PLATT
room, Rom. .... ALA
roomy .... WIDE
roost .... PERCH
rooster .... COCK
root ...... RADIX, RADICES
root, drug-yielding ..... JALAP
root, edible ..... OCA, TARO, CASSAVA
root, tree used for sewing
    WATAP
root, word .... ETYM
rootlet .... RADICEL, RADICLE
rootstock, edible .... TARO
rootstock, fern (Maori) ... ROI
rootstock, fragrant ..... ORRIS
rope ...... JEFF, LAZO, LASSO, LONGE, REATA, RIATA, LARIAT, MARLINE
rope, cringle
    LEEFANG, LEEFANGE
rope fiber .. DA, COIR, FERU, HEMP, IMBE, JUTE, RHEA, ABACA, SISAL
rope for animals ..... TETHER
rope guide: naut. ...... WAPP
rope loop .... BIGHT

133

a rope, naut. .... **FOX, TYE, STAY, VANG, HAWSER, RATLIN, LANIARD, LANYARD, RATLINE, SNOTTER**
rope to tie boat ..... **PAINTER**
rope, weave .... **REEVE**
rope, yardarm ..... **SNOTTER**
ropes, unite .... **SPLICE**
rosary bead .... **AVE**
rose: Byron .... **GUL**
rose fruit .... **HIP**
rose genus .... **ROSA, ACAENA**
rose-like plant ...... **AVENS**
rose of Sharon
    ALTHEA, ALTHAEA
rose oil derivative .... **ATAR, OTTO, ATTAR, OTTAR**
rose ornament ...... **ROSETTE**
rose, Pers. .... **GUL**
rosewood .... **MOLOMPI**
rosolic acid ... **AURIN, AURINE**
rostellum .... **ROSTEL**
roster .... **LIST, ROTA**
rotate .... **ROLL, GYRATE**
rotating muscle ..... **EVERTOR**
rotating part .... **CAM, ROTOR**
rotation producer .... **TORQUE**
rotten .... **PUTRID**
rouge ...... **RADDLE, RUDDLE**
b rough ...... **RUDE, UNEVEN**
rough, as country ...... **HILLY**
rough copy .... **DRAFT**
rough in voice .... **GRUFF**
rough rock .... **KNAR**
roughness, sea .... **LIPPER**
roulette bet ...... **BAS, NOIR, MILIEU**
round, a .... **ROTA, ROTULA**
round hand .... **RONDE**
round room ...... **ROTUNDA**
Round Table Knight .... **KAY, BORS, BORT, BALAN, BALIN, BOHORT, GARETH, GAWAIN, GALAHAD, PELLEAS**
round-up .... **RODEO**
rounded projection ...... **LOBE**
rounder .... **RAKE, ROUE**
roundworm .... **NEMA, ASCARID, ASCARIS**
rouse . **WAKE, AWAKE, WAKEN**
Rousseau novel, hero ... **EMILE**
route .... **WAY, PATH**
route, plane's fixed ..... **LANE**
routine, fixed .... **ROTE**
row .... **LINE, SPAT, TIER**
rowan tree .... **ASH, SORB**
rowdy: slang .... **B'HOY**
rower .... **OAR**
rower's bench .... **ZYGA, ZYGON, THWART**

c royal authority ...... **SCEPTRE**
royal court, relating to . **AULIC**
royal edict: Fr. .... **ARRET**
royal family, Fr. ..... **VALOIS**
royal rights, having . **PALATINE**
royal rod .. **SCEPTER, SCEPTRE**
royal treasury ...... **FISC, FISK**
royalty, Hawaii .... **ALII**
rub harshly .... **GRATE**
rub off .... **ABRADE**
rub out .... **ERASE**
rub roughly .... **SCRAPE**
rub to polish .... **BUFF, SHINE**
rub to soreness .... **CHAFE**
rubber .... **PARA, LATEX, CAUCHO, ELASTIC**
rubber, black .... **EBONITE**
rubber source ..... **KOKSAGYZ**
rubber, S. Am. . **PARA, CEARA**
rubber tree ...... **ULE, HULE, SERINGA**
rubber, wild .... **CEARA**
rubbery substance
    GUTTA, NOREPOL
rubbish .... **ROT, JUNK, CULCH, RUBBLE**
rubble masonry ..... **MOELLON**
rubella .... **MEASLES**
ruby .... **RED**
ruby red quartz ..... **RUBASSE**
d ruby spinel ... **BALAS, BALASS**
rudder bushing .... **PINTLE**
rudder fish .... **CHOPA**
ruddle .... **KEEL, KIEL**
rudiment .... **GERM**
rudiments .... **ABC**
rue .... **REGRET**
rue herb genus .... **RUTA**
ruff, female ..... **REE, REEVE**
ruffed lemur .... **VARI**
ruffer .... **NAPPER**
ruffle .... **CRIMP**
ruffle, neck ... **JABOT, RUCHE**
RUG .... see also CARPET
rug, long narrow
    KANARA, RUNNER
ruin .... **DOOM**
rule .... **LAW, DOMINEER**
"Rule Britannia" composer
    ARNE
rules, dueling .... **DUELLO**
ruler .... **REGENT**
ruler, Afghanistan ...... **EMIR, AMEER, CALIF, EMEER, CALIPH, SULTAN**
ruler, Arabian .. **EMIR, AMEER, CALIF, EMEER, CALIPH, SULTAN**
RULER, BIBLICAL .... see
    SPECIAL SECTION

a **RULER IN EAST**
　　　　see RULER, ARABIAN
ruler, India .... **NAWAB**
ruler, Morocco
　　　　SHERIF, SHEREEF
ruler, Moslem .. **EMIR, AMEER,
　CALIF, EMEER, CALIPH,
　SULTAN**
ruler of gods .... **ZEUS**
ruler, Oriental .... **CALIF**
ruler, Tunis .... **DEY**
RUMANIA
　　　　see also SPECIAL SECTION
Rumanian composer ... **ENESCO**
Rumanian folk song ... **DOINA**
Rumanian king's title .. **DOMN**
rumen .... **CUD**
ruminant ...... **DEER, GOAT,
　CAMEL, LLAMA, ANTELOPE**
ruminant genus .... **CAPRA**
ruminant, horned **DEER, GOAT**
ruminate ..... **MULL, PONDER**
Rumor personified ...... **FAMA**
rumor, to .... **BRUIT,
　　　　NORATE, REPORT**
b rumple .... **MUSS**
run at top speed ...... **SPRINT**
run before wind .... **SCUD**
run of the mill .... **PAR**
run out .... **PETER**
runner .... **SCARF,
　　　　STOLO, STOLON**
runner, distance ...... **MILER**
runner, plant .. **STOLO, STOLON**
rupees, 100,000 .... **LAC**
rural .... **RUSTIC, PASTORAL**
rural deity ..... **PAN, FAUNUS**
rural poem .... **GEORGIC**
rush .... **HASTE, SPEED**
rush, marsh .... **SPART**
Russell's viper
　　　　DABOIA, DABOYA
RUSSIA ...... see also SOVIET
　　　　and SPECIAL SECTION
Russia, most northern town
　　　　KOLA
Russian .... **RED, RUSS, SLAV,
　　　　KULAK, TATAR**
Russ. basso........... **KIPNIS**
Russ. author .... **BUNIN**

c Russ. beer.**KVAS, QUAS, KVASS**
Russ. community .... **MIR**
Russ. convention ...... **RADA**
Russ. cooperative society.**ARTEL**
Russ. council .... **DUMA**
Russ. dress .... **SARAFAN**
Russ. edict .. **UKASE, DECREE**
Russ. emperor .... **CZAR,
　　　　TSAR, TZAR**
Russ. fiddle .... **GUDOK**
Russ. folk dance .... **KOLO**
Russ. girl's name .... **OLGA**
Russ. hemp .... **RINE**
Russ. labor union ...... **ARTEL**
Russ. lagoon .... **LIMAN**
Russ. Lapland capital ... **KOLA**
Russ. leather .... **YUFT**
Russ. liquid measure ... **STOF,
　　　　STOFF, STOOF**
Russ. log hut .... **ISBA**
Russ. marsh .... **LIMAN**
Russ. mile .... **VERST**
Russ. mountain range
　　　　ALAI, URAL
d Russian mts., pert. to..**ALTAIC**
Russ. name, given . **AKIM, IGOR**
Russ. news agency ...... **TASS**
Russ. official .... **BERIYA**
Russ. opera .... **BORIS**
Russ. peninsula .... **KOLA**
Russ. sea, inland .... **ARAL,
　　　　AZOF, AZOV**
Russ. secret police.**NKVD, OGPU**
Russ. tavern .... **CABACK**
Russ. tax, old .... **OBROK**
Russ. tea urn ...... **SAMOVAR**
Russ. trade guild ...... **ARTEL**
Russ. vehicle .. **ARBA, ARABA**
Russ. village .... **MIR**
Russ. whip .... **PLET**
Russ. writer ... **GORKI, GORKY**
Russ. "yes" .... **DA**
rust .... **EAT, ERODE**
Rustam's father .... **ZAL**
rustic .... **BOOR, RUBE, CARL,
　CARLE, YOKEL, BUCOLIC,
　PEASANT**
Ruth's husband .... **BOAZ**
Ruth's son .... **OBED**
rye, disease of .... **ERGOT**

S

a sable .... SOBOL, MARTEN
sac .... BURSA
saccharine source .... TAR
sack fiber .... JUTE
sack, to .... LOOT
saclike cavity .... BURSA
sacred asp, symbol ... URAEUS
sacred bull, Egypt . APIS, HAPI
sacred chalice .... GRAIL
sacred city, India ... BENARES
sacred enclosure, Gr. .... SEKOS
sacred fig .... PIPAL
sacred Hindu word .... OM
sacred image .... ICON, IKON
sacred lily .... LOTUS
sacred object: Oceania .. ZOGO
sacred picture .... ICON, IKON
sacred place .... SHRINE
sacred place, Gr.
            ABATON, HIERON
sacred tree, Hindu .. BO, PIPAL
sacrifice, place of ..... ALTAR
b sacrificial drink, Zoroaster's
                        SOMA
sacrificial offerings .... HIERA
sad: comb. form ...... TRAGI
sad cry .... ALAS, ALACK
sad: music .... MESTO
saddle horses, fresh . REMUDA
saddle knob .... POMMEL
saddle, rear of .... CANTLE
safe .... SECURE
safe place ...... PORT, HAVEN
safe: thief's slang ...... PETE
safety lamp .... DAVY
safflower .... KUSUM
saga .... EDDA
sage .... WISE
sagacious .... WISE,
            ASTUTE, SAPIENT
sage genus .... SALVIA
sail fastener .... CLEW
sail-line .... EARING
sail nearer wind .... LUFF
sail, square .... LUG
sail, square, edge of ... LEECH
sail, triangular .... JIB
sail yard: Scot. .... RAE
sail's corner .... CLEW
"Sails" of constellation Argo
                        VELA
sailboat .... YAWL, KETCH
sailing race .... REGATTA
SAILING VESSEL .... see
            VESSEL, SAILING
sailmaker's awl ..... STABBER

c sailor.GOB, TAR, SALT, SEADOG
sailor, India .... LASCAR
St. Anthony's cross ...... TAU
saint, British .... ALBAN
saint, Buddhist
        ARAHT, ARHAT, ARAHAT
St. Catherine's home ... SIENA
saint, female: abbr. ...... STE
saint, 14th century ..... ROCH
St. Francis' birthplace .. ASSISI
St. John's-bread ..... CAROB
"St. Louis Blues" composer
                        HANDY
saint, Moslem .... PIR
St. Paul, deserter from . DEMAS
St. Vitus dance ...... CHOREA
sainte: abbr. .... STE
saint's relic box ...... CHASSE
salad green ...... UDO, CRESS,
        KERSE, CRESSE, ENDIVE
salamander .. EFT, EVET, NEWT
salient angle .... CANT
Salientia, the .... ANURA
sally .... START, SORTIE
"Sally in Our Alley" composer
                        CAREY
salmon, female .... HEN
d salmon, male .... COCK
salmon net .... MAUD
salmon, silver .... COHO
salmon, third year ..... MORT
salmon, 2 yr. .. SMOLT, SPROD
salmon, young .. PARR, GRILSE
salt .... SAL, HALITE, SALINE
salt factory .... SALTERN
salt lake, Turkestan ..... SHOR
salt of tartaric acid .. TARTAR
salt pond or spring ... SALINA
salt, resembling ...... HALOID
salt, rock .... HALITE
salt, solution .. BRINE, SALINE
salt tax .... GABELLE
salt tree, Tamarisk ..... ATLE
salted .... ALAT
saltpeter .... NITER, NITRE
saltwort .... KALI
saltworks .... SALINA
salty water .... BRINE
salutation .... AVE
salutation: Ir. ...... ACHARA
Salvation Army leader . BOOTH
salver .... TRAY
salvia .... CHIA
Sambal language .... TINO
sambar deer .... MAHA, RUSA
same .... ILK, DITTO

a same place: abbr. ...... IBID
samlet .... PARR
Samoan maiden ...... TAUPO
Samoan mollusk .... ASI
Samoan political council.FONO
Samuel, king killed by .. AGAG
Samuel, teacher of .... ELI
Samuel's son .... ABIA
samurai, straying ..... RONIN
sanction .... AMEN, FIAT
sanctuary ...... BEMA, FANE,
NAOS, CELLA
sand .... GRIT
sand bar .... REEF, SHOAL
sand expanses .... AREG
sand hill .... DENE, DUNE
sand island .... BAR
sand, sea bottom .... PAAR
sand snake genus .... ERYX
sandal, Egypt .... TATBEB
sandal, Mex.
HUARACHE, HUARACHO
sandalwood tree .... MAIRE
sandarac powder .... POUNCE
sandarac tree .... ARAR
sandbox tree genus ..... HURA
sandpiper .... REE, RUFF, STIB,
REEVE, STINT
sandpiper, Europ. ...... TEREK
b sandpiper, red .... KNOT
sandpiper, small .... KNOT,
PUME, STINT
sandstone .... GRIT
sandstorm .... HABOOB
sandwich .... HERO
Sandwich Island discoverer
COOK
sandy .... ARENOSE
Sankhya philos. term ... GUNA
Sanskrit dialect .... PALI
Sanskrit precept
SUTRA, SUTTA
Sanskrit school .... TOL
Sao —, Brazil .... PAULO
Sao Salvador .... BAHIA
sap spout .... SPILE
sapodilla ... SAPOTA, SAPOTE
sapota tree .... ACANA
Saracen ..... MOOR, MOSLEM
Sarah's slave .... HAGAR
sarcasm .... IRONY
Sardinia gold coin ... CARLINE
sargeant fish .... SNOOK
Sargon's capital ...... ACCAD
Sarmatia cave-dwellers . TAURI
sartor .... TAILOR
sash, C. Amer. .... TOBE
sash, Jap. kimono .... OBI
sassafras tree .... AGUE
Satan .... DEVIL
Satan: Arab .... EBLIS

c satellite .... MOON, PLANET
satellite .... LUNIK, SPUTNIK,
PIONEER, EXPLORER,
VANGUARD, ATLAS-
SCORE, DISCOVERER
satellite, navigation . TRANSIT
satellite, television .... TIROS
satellite's path .... ORBIT
satiate .. CLOY, GLUT, SATE
satirical .... DRY
satisfaction Maori ...... UTU
satisfy ... SATE, SUIT, PLEASE
saturate . SOAK, IMBUE, STEEP
Saturn, satellite of ..... DIONE
Saturn's rings projection.ANSA
Saturn's wife .... OPS
Saturnalia .... ORGY
satyr .... FAUN
sauce .... GRAVY
sauce, Chinese, Oriental .. SOY
sauce, fish .... ALEC
sauce, peppery ..... TABASCO
sauce, tomato ...... CATSUP,
CATCHUP, KETCHUP
saucy .... PERT
Saul's army leader .... ABNER
Saul's chief herdsman .. DOEG
Saul's father .... KISH
Saul's grandfather . NER, ABIEL
Saul's successor .... DAVID
Saul's uncle .... NER
Sault Ste. Marie .... SOO
saurel fish .... SCAD
d sausage, spiced ..... SALAME,
SALAMI
savage .... FERAL
Savage Island language . NIUE
save .... HOARD, STINT,
REDEEM, CONSERVE
saviour .... REDEEMER
savory .... SAPID, TASTY
saw .... ADAGE, AXIOM,
MAXIM, SAYING
saw-leaved centaury
BEHN, BEHEN
saw, notched like .... SERRATE
saw notching .... REDAN
saw, surgical TREPAN,TREPHINE
sawbill duck .... SMEW
sawlike organ, or part .. SERRA
sawlike parts . SERRAS, SERRAE
sawtooth ridge .... SIERRA
saxhorn .... TUBA
Saxon god .... ER, EAR
Saxon king ...... INE, ALFRED
Saxony natives .... SORBS
say .... UTTER
say again .... ITERATE
saying ... MOT, SAW, ADAGE,
AXIOM, MAXIM
sayings .... LOGIA

a
scabbard fish .... HIKU
scabbard, put into .. SHEATHE
scaffolding .... STAGING
scale .... GAMUT
scale, syllable of .. DO, FA, LA,
MI, RE, SO, TI, SOL
scale under blossom
PALEA, PALET
scales, having large . SCUTATE
scallop ..... CRENA, CRENAE
scallops, cut in small .... PINK
scalloped .... CRENATE
scalp disease .... FAVI, FAVUS
scamp ...... ROGUE, RASCAL
SCANDINAVIAN
see also NORSE
SCANDINAVIAN . see also
SWEDEN, NORWAY, in
SPECIAL SECTION
Scandinavian ... DANE, SWEDE
Scand., ancient .... NORSE
Scand. countryman ..... GEAT
Scand. explorer .... ERIC
Scand. fertility god .... NJORD
Scand. legend .... SAGA
Scand. measure .... ALEN
Scand. nation .... GEATAS
Scandinavians in Russia
ROS, RUS

b
scanty .... SPARSE
scar, resembling a .... ULOID
scarce .... RARE
scarcely: Lat. VIX
scare away .... SHOO
scarf .... BOA, TIE,
ASCOT, ORALE
scarf, long .... STOLE
scarf, Sp. Am. .... TAPALO
scarlet flower .... SALVIA
Scarlett O'Hara's home .. TARA
scatter ... SOW, TED, STREW
scatter: dial. .... SCOAD
scatter on .... LITTER
scattered: Her. .... SEME
scenario .... SCRIPT
scene .... VIEW, TABLEAU
scene of action.ARENA, SPHERE
scenic view .... SCAPE
scent .... ODOR, AROMA
scented .... OLENT
schedule .... LIST
scheme .... PLAN, PLOT
schism .... RENT
scholar .... PEDANT
scholars, Moslem .... ULEMA
scholarship .... BURSE
school, boy's .... PREP
school, Fr. ...... ECOLE, LYCEE
school grounds ...... CAMPUS

c
SCHOONER ... see also BOAT,
SHIP, VESSEL
schooner, 3-masted ..... TERN
sciences .... ARTS
scientific farmer . AGRONOMIST
scientific study: abbr. . ANAT.
scientist, Am. . UREY, HOOTON,
PARRAN, COMPTON,
WAKSMAN, MILLIKAN
scientist, Austr. .... MEITNER
scientist, Czech .... CORI
scientist, Dan. .... BOHR
scientist, Eng. .... HOGBEN,
FLEMING, HALDANE
scientist, Ger. .. BAADE, HABER
scientist, Ital. .... FERMI
scissors .... SHEARS
scoff .... GIBE, JEER, JIBE,
RAIL, SNEER
scold .... JAW, NAG, RATE
scold: dialect .... FRAB
scone: Scot. ..... FARL, FARLE
scoop .... DIP
scoot: Scot. ..... SKYT, SKITE
scope .. AREA, AMBIT, RANGE
scorch .... CHAR, SEAR,
SERE, SINGE
score .... TALLY
scoria .... SLAG, DROSS

d
scorpion fish .... LAPON
Scotch cake .... SCONE
scoter .... COOT
Scotland .... SCOTIA
Scott character .... ELLEN
Scott heroine .... ELLEN
Scott, poem by .... MARMION
SCOTTISH
see Pages of SCOTTISH WORDS
Scot. alderman .... BAILIE
Scot. author .... BARRIE
Scot. chemist .... URE, DEWAR
Scot. chief landholder
THANE, THEGN
Scot. cultural congress ... MOD
Scot. explorer .... RAE
Scot. highlander .... GAEL
Scot. king .... BRUCE
Scot. lord ..... THANE, THEGN
Scot. pillory .... JOUG
Scot. playwright .... BARRIE
Scot. poet .... BURNS
Scot. pottage .... BROSE
Scot. proprietor .... LAIRD
Scot. scholar .... NICOLL
Scot. singer .... LAUDER
SCOTTISH WORDS:
accept .... TAE
advise .... REDE
afraid .... RAD, RADE
age .... EILD

a

against	GIN
alder tree	ARN, ELLER
an	AE
animal, lean	RIBE
any	ONY
article	TA
ashes	ASE
ask	AX
at all	AVA
away	AWA
awry	AJEE
babbler	HAVEREL
ball	BA
bank	BRAE
barter	TROKE
beg	SORN
bind	OOP
biscuit	BAKE
blockhead	CUIF, NOWT
bloodhound	LYAM
bone	BANE
bound	STEND
breeches	TREWS
broth	BREE, BROO
brow of hill	SNAB
built	BAG
burden	BIRN
bushel	FOU
calves	CAUR, CAURE

b

came	CAM
catch	KEP
chalk	CAUK
check	WERE
chest	KIST
child	BAIRN
church	KIRK, KURK
comb	KAME
contend	KEMP
court, bring to	SIST
cut	KNAP, SNEG
dairymaid	DEY
damage	TEEN
damaged	LESED
dare	DAUR
devil	DEIL
did not know	KENNA
die	DEE
dig	HOWK
dining room	SPENCE
do	DAE, DIV
do not know	KENNA
dread	DREE
drip	SIE, SYE
dusty	MOTTY
earth	EARD
elder	ELLER
else	ENSE
empty	TOOM
endeavor	ETTLE
endure	DREE

c

extra	ORRA
eye	EE
eyes	EEN, EES
family	ILK
fidget	FIKE
firth	KYLE
fishing expedition	DRAVE
fit of sulks	GEE
flax refuse	PAB, POB
fog	DAG, HAR, HAAR
foretell	SPAE
give	GIE
glimpse	STIME
grandchild	OY, OYE
grant as property	DISPONE
great-grandchild	IEROE
grief	TEEN
have	HAE
hawk	ALLAN
heavy	THARF
hill	BEN, DOD, BRAE, DODD
hillside	BRAE
howl	YOWT
hurt	LESED
injure	TEEN
injured	LESED
intent	ETTLE
keg	KNAG

d

kinsman	SIB
kiss	PREE
knead	ELT
knock	KNOIT
lake	LOCH
leap	LOUP, LOWP, STEND
learning	LEAR
list of candidates	LEET
loaf	SORN
lop	SNATHE
lout	CUIF
love	LOE
loyal	LEAL
marriage portion	DOTE
millrace	LADE
mire	GLAUR
mist	URE
mountain	BEN
mouth, river	BEAL
mouth	BEAL
mud	GLAIR
must	MAUN
name	IAN
near, nearest	NAR
no	NAE
none	NANE
not matched	ORRA
now	NOO
nowhere	NAEGATE
oak	AIK

(Scottish words continued 140)

139

a
oatmeal dish .... BROSE
odd .... ORRA
old age .... EILD
once .... ANES
one .... AIN, ANE, YIN
otherwise .... ELS
out .... OOT
own ...... AIN, ANE, AWN
pantry .... SPENCE
parlor .... BEN
payment .... MENSE
paw ground .... PAUT
peat cutter .... PINER
pig .... GRICE
pike .... GED, GEDD
pillory .... TRONE
pipe .... CUTTY
pluck wool .... ROO
pool .... DIB, CARR,
                LINN, LLYN
present .... GIE
pretty .... GEY
prop .... RANCE
propriety .... MENSE
prune .... SNED
puddle .... DUB
pull .... PU
quagmire .... HAG
quarter of a year ... RAITH
relieve .... LISS

b
revenue, church .... ANNAT
ridge of a hill .... SHIN
river .... DOON
rowboat .... COBLE
sailyard .... RAE
same .... ILK
scone .... FARL, FARLE
scoot .... SKYT, SKITE
scratch .... RIT
seep .... SIPE
seize .... VANG
self .... SEL
serve .... KAE
severe blow .... DEVEL
sheepfold .... REE
sheepstick .... KED
sheep walk .... SLAIT
shelter ...... BIELD, SHEAL
sift .... SIE
since .... SIN, SYNE
slope .... BRAE
slouch .... LOUCH
sly .... SLEE
small .... SMA
snow .... SNA
so .... SAE
son of .... MAC
song .... STROUD
sore .... SAIR
sorrow .... TEEN
sow .... SOO

c
steward .... MORMAOR
stipend .... ANNAT
stone.STANE, STEAN, STEEN
stretch .... STENT
stupid one .... CUIF
suffer .... DREE
summit .... DOD, DODD
sweetheart .... JO
than .... NA
to .... TAE
toe .... TAE
tone .... TEAN
trench .... GAW
truant, play .... TRONE
try .... ETTLE
tune .... PORT
turnip .... NEEP
uncanny .... UNCO
uncle .... EME
urge .... ERT
very .... VERA
vex .... FASH
village .... REW
void, to render ...... CASS
waterfall ... LIN, LYN, LINN
wealthy .... BIEN
weep .... ORP
week .... OUK
well .... AWEEL

d
weighing machine ... TRON,
                     TRONE
wet .... WAT
whirlpool ..... WEEL, WIEL
whiskey drink ..... ATHOL,
                     ATHOLE
widow's third .... TERCE
workhouse .... AVER
year, ¼ of .... RAITH
yell .... GOWL
scoundrel .... ROGUE, VARLET
scout unit . DEN, PACK, TROOP
scow .... BARGE, LIGHTER
scow: Fr. .... ACON
scrap, table .... ORT
scraps of literature ...... ANA
scrape ... RAKE, RASP, GRAZE
scrape bottom .... DREDGE
scratch .... MAR, RAKE
scrawny animal .... SCRAG
screamer bird .... CHAJA
screed .... TIRADE
screen .... SIFT, SHADE
screen, altar ...... REREDOS
screen, wind ...... PARAVENT
script, modern Syriac ... SERTA
script, upright .... RONDE
scripture, early .... ITALA
scripture passage .... TEXT
scriptures, occult interpretation
                       CABALA
scrutinize .... EYE, SCAN

140

a scuffle .... MELEE
sculptor of "Thinker" . RODIN
scum, metal .... DROSS
scup .... BREAM, PORGY
scuppernong ..... MUSCADINE
scuttle .... HOD
scuttle, coal .... HOD
scythe .... SY, SYE
scythe handle . SNATH, SNEAD,
    SNEED, SNATHE
sea anemone .. POLYP, OPELET
sea bird ... ERN, ERNE, GULL,
    SKUA, SCAUP, TERN, FUL-
    MAR, GANNET, PETREL,
    SCOTER
sea bird, north .... PUFFIN
sea cow . DUGONG, MANATEE
sea cucumber ...... TREPANG
sea demon, Teut. ...... WATE
sea duck ...... COOT, EIDER,
    SCAUP, SCOTER
sea eagle .... ERN, ERNE
sea-ear .... ABALONE
sea: Fr. .... MER
sea girdles .... CUVY
sea god .... LER, TRITON,
    NEPTUNE
sea god, Gr. . NEREUS, TRITON,
    POSEIDON
sea god, Rom. ...... NEPTUNE
sea god, Teut. .. HLER, AEGIR
sea goddess, Norse ...... RAN
b sea green .... CELADON
sea gull, Eur. .... MEW
sea, kept bow on . ATRY, ATRIE
sea lettuce ..... ALGA, LAVER
sea lettuce genus ULVA, ULUA
sea marker .... DAN
sea pheasant .... SMEE
sea robber .... PIRATE
sea mile, Austral. ...... NAUT
sea nymph .... NEREID
sea shell .... TRITON
    (see also SHELL)
sea skeleton .... CORAL
sea slug genus . DOTO, ELYSIA
sea snail . WELK, WILK, WHELK
sea snake, Asia ...... KERRIL
sea soldier .... MARINE
sea worm . SAO, LURG, NEREIS
seal .... SIGIL
seal, eared .... OTARY
seal, fur .... URSAL
seal, letter .... CACHET
seal, official .... SIGNET
seal, papal .... BULLA
seal, young .... PUP
seals, group of .... POD
seamark .... BEACON
seamen: Brit. .... RATINGS
seamlike ridge .... RAPHE

c seams of boat, fill ..... CALK
SEAPORT .... see PORT
search .... GROPE
search for .... HUNT, SEEK
search for food ...... FORAGE
season ...... AGE, FALL, SALT,
    TIDE, SPRING
season, church . LENT, ADVENT
season, Fr. .... ETE
seasons, goddesses of .. HORAE
seasonal phenomenon .. EPACT
seasoning .... SAGE, SALT
seasoning herb .... SAGE,
    BASIL, THYME
seat, chancel .... SEDILE
seat, long ...... PEW, SETTEE
seat of oracle of Zeus.DODONA
seat, Rom. .... SELLA
seaweed ... ORE, AGAR, ALGA,
    KELP, ALGAE, LAVER,
    VAREC
seaweed ashes .... KELP
seaweed, brown .... KELP
seaweed, edible .... AGAR
seaweed, edible Hawaiian .LIMU
seaweed, purple .... LAVER
seaweed, purple, Jap. ... NORI
seaweed, red .... DULSE
Seb, consort of .... NUT
d secluded .... REMOTE
second . ABET, TRICE, MOMENT
second brightest star ... BETA
second-growth crop ... ROWEN
Second Punic War's end,
    site of .... ZAMA
second team .... SCRUB
secondary .... BYE, LESS
secret .... RUNE, ARCANE,
    COVERT, MYSTERY,
    ESOTERIC
secret agent .... SPY
secret society, Afr..EGBO, PORO
secret society in Sierra Leone
    PORO
secrets .... ARCANA
secrets, one learning ... EPOPT
secretion, sweet
    LAAP, LERP, LAARP
sect .... CULT
sect, Nepal . ACHAR, ACHARA
section of journey .... LEG
secular ... LAY, LAIC, LAICAL
secure .. FIX, GET, PIN, FAST,
    NAIL, SAFE, FASTEN
secure firmly . MOOR, ANCHOR
secure with rope .... BELAY
security .... BOND
Sec'y of State, 1933-44 .. HULL
sedate .... STAID
sedative .... NEMBUTAL

141

a sediment .... LEES, SILT,
DREGS, SILTAGE
see .... ESPY, LOOK
see: Lat. .... VIDE
seed .... PIP, PIT, GRAIN,
SPORE, PYRENE
seed coat or covering .. ARIL,
HULL, HUSK, TESTA, TEG-
MEN, TESTAE, TEGUMEN,
TEGIMINA
seed, edible ...... PEA, BEAN,
LENTIL, PINOLE
seed, edible, Asia .... SESAME
seed, immature .... OVULE
seed, lens-shaped ..... LENTIL
seed, nutlike .... PINON
seed, opium poppy ..... MAW
seed plant .... ENDOGEN
seeds, remove .... GIN
seedless plant .... FERN
seek to attain .... ASPIRE
seem .... LOOK
seesaw .... TEETER
segment, last .... TELSON
segment of body ..... SOMITE
segment of circle .... ARC
segment, pert. to ...... TORIC
seine .... NET
seize .... NAB, GRAB, GRASP,
USURP, ARREST, COLLAR

b seize: archaic .... REAVE
selections, literary
ANA, ANALECTA
self .... EGO
self-assurance .... APLOMB
self-defense, art of ..... JUDO
self-denying .... ASCETIC
self-education doctrine
BIOSOPHY
self-locking nut ..... PALNUT
self-reproach .... REMORSE
sell .... VEND
seller .... COSTER,
VENDER, VENDOR
semblance .... GUISE
semester .... TERM
semi-precious stone
ONYX, SARD
semicircular room ...... APSE
semidiameter .... RADIUS
semidiameters .... RADII
Seminole chief ..... OSCEOLA
Semitic deity .... BAAL
sen, tenth of .... RIN
senate house ....,..... CURIA
senate houses .... CURIAE
Senator, former ...... BORAH
send back ... REMIT, REMAND
send money .... REMIT

c send out .... EMIT, ISSUE
sending forth .... EMISSIVE
Senegambia gazelle .... KORIN
senility .... DOTAGE
senior .... ELDER
senior: Fr. .... AINE
senna, source of ...... CASSIA
sennet .... SPET
sense .... FEEL
senseless .... INANE
sensitive .... SORE
sentence, analyze ...... PARSE
sentence part .... CLAUSE
"Sentimental Journey" author
STERNE
sentinel, mounted ... VEDETTE
separate . SIFT, APART, SECERN
separated .... APART
separation .... SCHISM
sequence, 3-card ..... TIERCE
sequester .... ISOLATE
Sequoia national park ... MUIR
seraglio .... HAREM, SERAI
serene .... SERENO
serf .... ESNE
serf, Rom. .... COLONA
serf, Spartan, ancient .. HELOT
sergeant fish .... COBIA
series .... SET, GAMUT
series, in a .... SERIATIM

d series of tones .... SCALE
serious ..... GRAVE, EARNEST
sermon .... HOMILY
serow .... JAGLA
SERPENT ..... see also SNAKE
serpent, Egypt. myth .... APEPI
serpent goddess, Egypt. . BUTO
serpent, Gr. .... SEPS
serpent, large .. BOA, PYTHON
serpent monster ...... ELLOPS
serpent, myth. ...... BASILISK
serpent worship ...... OPHISM
serpentine .... OPHITE
servant.......... BOY, MAN,
MAID, MENIAL
servant, India .... HAMAL,
FERASH, HAMMAL
servant, man's .... VALET
servant, P. I. .... BATA
servants, for .... MENIAL
serve soup .... LADLE
server .... TRAY
service, religious .... MASS
service tree .... SORB
servile .... MENIAL
serving boy .... PAGE
sesame .... TIL, TEEL
sesame oil ..... BENI, BENNE
sesame seed .... GINGILI
session, hold .... SIT, MEET

a

set aside .... DEFER
set in type .... PRINT
set limits to .... STINT
set price .... RATE
set system .... ROTE
set thickly .... STUD
setback .... REVERSE
Seth's brother .... CAIN
Seth's mother .... EVE
Seth's son .... ENOS
setting .... SCENE, MILIEU
setting sun, Egyp. god of.TEM,
    TUM, ATMU, ATUM
settled .... ALIT
settler .... BOOMER
seven .... SEPT
Seven Dwarfs ... DOC, DOPEY,
    HAPPY, GRUMPY, SLEEPY,
    SNEEZY, BASHFUL
seven, group of .... HEPTAD,
    PLEIAD, SEPTET, SEPTETTE
"Seventh Heaven" heroine
    DIANE
seventh order, of ...... SEPTIC
seventh, pert. to ..... SEPTAN
sever .... CUT, LOP, REND
severe .... STERN
severely criticize ...... PAN,
    SLATE, ROAST

b

sew hawk's eyelids ...... SEEL
"Seward's —," Alaska . FOLLY
sexes, common to both.EPICENE
shabby .... WORN
shabby woman .... DOWD
shackle .... BOND, GYVE,
    IRON, FETTER
shad .... ALLIS, ALOSA,
    ALOSE, ALLICE
shaddock .. POMELO, PUMELO
shade .... HUE, SCREEN
shade of difference .. NUANCE
shade of meaning ... NUANCE
shaded walk .... MALL
shadow .... TAIL
shadow, eclipse .... UMBRA
shaft .... POLE, SPINDLE
shaft column, feather .. SCAPE
shaft horse .... THILLER
shaft of column .... FUST
shaft, wooden .... ARROW
shafter .... HORSE
shake ..... JAR, JOLT, NIDGE
Shakespeare's elf ...... PUCK
Shakespeare's river .... AVON
Shakespeare's theatre .. GLOBE
Shakespeare's wife .... ANNE
Shakesperian clown .. BOTTOM
Shakesperian forest ... ARDEN
Shakesperian king ...... LEAR

c

Shakesperian shrew ..... KATE
Shakesperian villain ..... IAGO
shallow receptacle ...... TRAY
sham .... FAKE
Shamash, wife of .... AI, AYA
"Shane," star of .... LADD
Shang dynasty .... YIN
shank .... CRUS, SHIN
shanks .... CRURA
shanty .... HUT
shape .... FORM, MOLD
shaped like a club .. CLAVATE
shaped like a needle
    ACUATE, ACERATE
shaping tool ... LATHE, SWAGE
share .... LOT, RATION
share .... PARTAKE
shark .... TOPE
shark, Eur. small .... TOPE
shark, long-nosed ..... MAKO
shark, nurse .... GATA
shark parasite fish ... REMORA
sharp .... ACERB,
    ACUTE, ACUATE
sharp .... CHEAT
sharp ridge .... ARETE
sharpen ... EDGE, HONE, WHET
sharpshooter .. JAGER, SNIPER
shavetail: abbr. .... LT
shawl .... MAUD, PAISLEY

d

shea tree .... KARITE
sheaf of grain: Her. .... GERB
shear .... CLIP
sheath, petiole .... OCREA
Sheba: Lat. .... SABA
shed, as feathers MOLT, MOULT
shed for sheep .... COTE
sheen .... GLOSS
sheep ...... EWE, RAM, MERINO
sheep, Afr. domestic ... ZENU
sheep, Afr. wild
    ARUI, UDAD, AOUDAD
sheep, Asia wild .... ARGALI
sheep, Asia, wild, mountain
    SHA, SNA, RASSE, URIAL,
    BHARAL, NAHOOR, OORIAL
sheep cry .... BAA, MAA
sheep disease .. COE, GID, ROT
sheep dog .... COLLIE
sheep, Eng. black-faced LONK
sheep, female .... EWE
sheep genus .... OVIS
sheep in 2nd year
    TEG, TEGG, BIDENT
sheep, India, wild .. SHA, SNA,
    URIAL, NAHOOR, OORIAL
sheep, large-horned
    AOUDAD, ARGALI
sheep, Leicester ...... DISHLEY
sheep, male .... RAM, TUP

Sheep

sheep, N. Afr. wild .... ARUI, UDAD, AOUDAD
sheep, of .... OVINE
sheep owner, Bibl. ..... NABAL
sheep pasture, old Eng. .. HEAF
sheep, pert. to .... OVINE
sheep, Tibet .... SHA, SNA, URIAL, BHARAL, NAHOOR, OORIAL
sheep tick .... KED, KADE
sheep, unshorn .. HOGG, HEDER
sheep walk: Scot. .... SLAIT
sheep, wild .. SHA, SNA, ARUI, UDAD, RASSE, BHARAL, NAHOOR, AOUDAD, ARGALI, OORIAL
sheep, young .... TAG, TEG
sheepfold .... REE, COTE
sheeplike .... OVINE
sheepskin leather ..... BOCK, ROAN, SKIVER
sheerly .... SOLELY
shekel, ¼, Hebrew ...... REBA
shelf .... LEDGE
shelf above altar ... RETABLE
shell .... BOMB
shell .. TEST, LORICA, TUNICA
shell beads .... PEAG
shell, large .... CONCH
shell, marine .... TRITON
shell money .... ULLO, COWRY, UHLLO, COWRIE
shellfish, edible CRAB, ABALONE, SCALLOP
shelter .... LEE, COTE, SHED, HAVEN, SCREEN
shelter, hillside .... ABRI
shelter: Scot. .. BIELD, SHEAL
shelter, to .... ALEE
sheltered .... ALEE
Shem descendant ..... SEMITE
Shem's brother .... HAM
Shem's son LUD, ARAM, ELAM, ASSHUR
Sheol .... HADES
shepherd prophet ...... AMOS
shepherd's crook PEDA, PEDUM
shepherd's pipe .... OAT, REED
shepherd's song .. MADRIGAL
shepherdess, "Winter's Tale" MOPSA
sheriff substitute ..... ELISOR
sheriff's men .... POSSE
Sherwood .... FOREST
Shetland court president FOUD
Shetland hill pasture ... HOGA
shield .... ECU, EGIS, AEGIS, PAVIS, DEFEND, PROTECT
shield, Athena's .... AEGIS
shield, Austral. .... MULGA
shield-bearing or border. ORLE

shield, medieval .... ECU
shield, Rom. SCUTA, SCUTUM, CLIPEUS
shield-shaped PELTATE, SCUTATE
shield, small .... ECU
shield strap .... ENARME
shield's corner: Her. CANTON
shift .... VEER
shift position. GIBE, GYBE, JIBE
shin .... CNEMIS
shine GLOW, GLISTEN, ERADIATE
shingle, wedge-shaped .. SHIM
shingles .... ZONA
shining .... NITID
Shinto deity .... KAMI
Shinto temple .... SHA
Shinto temple gate .... TORII
ship ..... KEEL, SEND, LINER, TANKER, TENDER, VESSEL, CARAVEL
ship, back part .... STERN
ship boat .... GIG, DORY
ship body or frame ..... HULL
ship bow, curve of ...... LOOF
ship canvas .... SAIL
ship clock .... NEF
ship drainage hole .. SCUPPER
ship employee .... STEWARD
ship, 1st Northwest Passage GJOA
ship, forward part BOW, PROW
ship, fur-hunting ..... SEALER
ship, ironclad ...... MONITOR
ship: Jap. ...... MARO, MARU
ship keel, rear part ..... SKEG
ship, large .... TONNER
ship, lowest part ...... BILGE
ship, Medit. ... SETEE, SETTEE
ship, middle part ...... WAIST
ship mooring place DOCK, BERTH
ship, oar-propelled ... GALLEY
ship, part of RIB, DECK, HULL, KEEL
ship plank .... STRAKE
ship platform .... DECK
ship pole .... MAST, SPAR
ship shaped clock .... NEF
ship side, opp. middle ABEAM
ship timber, bevel ..... SNAPE
ship timber curve .... SNY
ship timber, extra ..... RIDER
ship wheel .... HELM
ship, wrecked .... HULK
ship, 1-masted .... SLOOP
ship, 2-masted ... BRIG, SNOW
ship's kitchen .... GALLEY
shipboard covering .... CAPOT

shipbuilding curve ..... SNY
shipbuilding piece
SPALE, THWART
shipworm .... BORER, TEREDO
shipwreck, causing
NAUFRAGEOUS
shirk .... GOLDBRICK
SHIRT .... see also GARMENT
shirt .... KAMIS, CAMISE
shirt, Oriental .... CAMISE
shoal .... REEF
shoal water deposit .... CULM
shock .... STUN,
APPAL, APPALL, TRAUMA
shock absorber ..... SNUBBER
shod, as monks ..... CALCED
shoe .... GAITER, SANDAL
shoe form .... LAST
shoe front .... VAMP
shoe gripper .... CLEAT
shoe, heavy.BROGAN, BROGUE
shoe latchet .... TAB
shoe, mule .... PLANCH
shoe part
LAST, RAND, WELT, INSOLE
shoe strip ...... RAND, WELT
shoe, wooden ... GETA, SABOT
shoe, wooden-soled ..... CLOG
shoes .... SHOON
shoes, Mercury's winged
TALARIA
shoelace .... LACET
shoemakers' saint ... CRISPIN
shoemaker's tool ...... AWL
shoot .... BAG, POT
shoot at from ambush   SNIPE
shoot at, marble to ...... MIG
shoot, cotton .... RATOON
shoot, plant .... BINE, CION,
GEMMA, SPRIT,
STOLO, STOLON
shoot, small .... SPRIG
shoot, sugar cane ... RATOON
shooter, hidden ...... SNIPER
shooter marble .... TAW,
AGATE, AGGIE
shooting match .... TIR
shooting match: Fr. ...... TIR
shooting star .... LEONID
shop .... STORE
shop, Rom. wine ... TABERNA
shops, Rom. wine .. TABERNAE
shop's name plate ..... FACIA
shore .... COAST, STRAND
SHORE BIRD . see BIRD, SHORE
short .... CURT,
BRIEF, TERSE, STUBBY

short-breathed .... PURSY
short comedy sketch .... SKIT
short-spoken ... CURT, TERSE
short tail .... SCUT
shorten .... CUT, DELE, ELIDE
shortly
ANON, SOON, PRESENTLY
Shoshonean .... UTE
shoulder blade ..... SCAPULA
shoulder, of the
ALAR, SCAPULAR
shoulder ornament
EPAULET, EPAULETTE
shoulder, road .... BERM
shoulder wrap .... SHAWL
shout.CRY, CALL, ROAR, YELL
shove .... PUSH
shovel .... SPADE
show as false .... BELIE
show off .... FLAUNT
show place, Rom. .... CIRCUS
show, street .... RAREE
"Showboat" author .... FERBER
showy .... LOUD
shrew .... ERD, TARTAR
shrewd.SAGE, CANNY, ASTUTE
shrike genus .... LANIUS
shrill .... PIPY
shrill, to .... STRIDULATE
shrimplike crustacean   PRAWN
shrine .... ALTAR
shrink .... CONTRACT
shroud-stopper: naut. ... WAPP
SHRUB .... see also TREE
shrub and tree .... ALDER
shrub, Asia .... CHE
shrub, berry-bearing ... ELDER
shrub, berry, Pacific ... SALAL
shrub, Chin. .... TEA
shrub, Congo medical .. BOCCA
shrub, desert
RETEM, OCOTILLO
shrub, Eng. .... HEATH
shrub, evergreen ... BOX, YEW,
TITI, ERICA, HEATH, SAL-
AL, OLEANDER
shrub, flowering ITEA, AZALEA,
PRIVET, SPIREA, SPIRAEA,
SYRINGA
shrub genus BIXA, INGA, ITEA,
ROSA, ALDER, IXORA,
AZALEA
shrub, Hawaiian ..... OLONA
shrub, low spiny .... GORSE
shrub, Medit. .... CAPER
shrub, poisonous
SUMAC, SUMACH
shrub, prickly .... CAPER

a shrub, Rhus genus
              SUMAC, SUMACH
shrub, strong-scented .. BATIS
shrub with grapelike fruit
              SALAL
shrub, yellow flowers OLEASTER
shun .... AVOID, DODGE
shut up .... IMMURE
shy .... JIB, BALK
SIAM .. see also SPECIAL SEC-
     TION
Siamese .... THAI
Siam. coin .... ATT
Siam. garment ...... PANUNG
Siam. group .... KUI, LAO
Siam. monetary unit .... BAHT
Siamese twin ... ENG, CHANG
SIBERIAN .. see also RUSSIAN
Siberian .... TATAR
Siberian wild cat ..... MANUL
Siberian squirrel ..... MINIVER
sibilant sound .... HISS
Sicilian resort .... ENNA
sickle, curved like ... FALCATE
sickle: variant .... SIVE
side, jewel's .... FACET
side arm .... GUN,
     SWORD, PISTOL, REVOLVER
b side: Lat. .... LATUS
side of head ... LORA, LORUM
side, pert. to
              COSTAL, LATERAL
side-post, door's ...... JAMB
sidetrack .... SHUNT
side street, Chin. ... HUTUNG
side timber: naut. ..... BIBB
side, toward the .... LATERAD
sidereal .... ASTRAL
sidewalk .... PAVEMENT
sidewalk edge ... CURB, KERB
sidewinder .... CROTALUS
sidle .... EDGE
Siegfried's murderer ... HAGEN
siesta .... NAP
sieve .... SIFT, PUREE, BOLTER
sieve for clay .... LAUN
Sif, son of .... ULL, ULLR
sift .... SCREEN
sift: dialect .... REE
sift: old Eng. .... LUE
sift: Scot. .... SIE
sifter .... SIEVE
sigh .... SOUF, SOUGH
sight, come into ...... LOOM
sight, dimness of ..... CALIGO
sight on gun .... BEAD
sight, pert. to .... OCULAR
sign ... MARK, OMEN, TOKEN

c sign, music .... PRESA, SEGNO
sign: old Eng. .... SEIN
sign, pert. to .... SEMIC
sign up ..... ENROL, ENROLL
signal for attention ...... PST
signal for parley ... CHAMADE
signal to act .... CUE
signal to begin .... CUE
signature, affix
              SIGN, ENDORSE
signet .... SIGIL
signify ...... MEAN, DENOTE
"Silas Marner" author .. ELIOT
silence .... GAG, HUSH
silence: music .... TACET
silent ... MUM, MUTE, TACIT
silica .... SAND, SILEX
silica, rich in .... ACIOLIC
silicate .... MICA
silk-cotton tree CEIBA, KAPOK
silk-cotton tree fiber
              KAPOK, KUMBI
silk fabric ..... GROS, MOFF,
              PEKIN, SATIN, TULLE
silk filament .... BRIN
silk, fine .... CRIN, TULLE
silk, heavy .... GROS
silk in cocoon .... BAVE
silk, India ... ROMAL, RUMAL
d silk, old heavy ..... CAMACA
silk, raw .... GREGE
silk substitute ...... NYLON,
              RAYON, ORLON, DACRON
silk thread .... FLOSS
silk, twilled .... ALMA
silk, unravel .... SLEAVE
silken .... SERIC
silkworm, Assam ... ERI, ERIA
silkworm, China ...... TASAR
silkworm disease .... UJI
silly .... INANE
silver: Her. .... ARGENT
silver lactate .... ACTOL
silver ore .... PACO
silver, uncoined, in ingots SYCEE
silverfish .. TARPON, TARPUN
silverize .... PLATE
silvery .... ARGENT
silvery-white metal .. COBALT
simian .... APE
similar .... LIKE, SUCH
Simon .... PETER
simper .... SMIRK
simple .... EASY, MERE
simple sugar .... OSE
simpleton .... ASS, DAW, OAF,
     BOOB, COOT, FOOL, GABY,
     GAWK, GOWK, SIMP,
     GOOSE
simulate
     APE, SHAM, FEIGN, PRETEND

146

sin .... ERR, EVIL
sin, grief for ..... ATTRITION
Sinai .... HOREB
Sinbad's bird .... ROC
since .... AGO
since: Scot. .... SIN, SYNE
Sinclair Lewis character CASS
sine — non .... QUA
sine qua — .... NON
sinew .... TENDON
sinewy .... WIRY
sing .... LILT, CAROL
sing, as a round ...... TROLL
sing softly .... CROON
sing, Swiss style
    JODEL, YODEL, YODLE
singer, synagogue ... CANTOR
singing bird .... OSCINE
singing girl, Egyptian .. ALMA,
    ALME, ALMAH, ALMAI,
    ALMEH
singing, suitable for .... MELIC
single .... ONE, BILL, MONO,
    ONLY, UNAL
single out .... CHOOSE
single: prefix .... MONO
single thing ...... ONE, UNIT
singleton .... ACE
sink, as putt .... HOLE
sink: geol. .... DOLINA
sinuous .. WAVY, SERPENTINE
sinus cavities .... ANTRA
Sioux, Siouan .... OTO, OTOE
sir: India .... MIAN
sir: Malay .... TUAN
siren, Rhine .... LORELEI
Sisera's killer .... JAEL
sister .... NUN, SIB
"Sistine Madonna" painter
    RAPHAEL
sitatunga, Afr. ...... NAKONG
sitting
    POSING, SEANCE, SESSION
sitting on .... ASTRIDE
situation, difficult .... STRAIT
siva snake .... COBRA
Siva, wife of DEVI, KALI, SATI
six, group of
    SENARY, SESTET, SEXTET
six-line verse SESTET, SESTINA
six on a die .. CISE, SICE, SISE
six, series of .... HEXAD
six: Sp. .... SEIS
sixpence: slang .... SICE
sixteen annas .... RUPEE
sixth: music .... SEXT
sixth sense: abbr. ...... ESP
size of shot ...... BB, FF, TT
sizing .... SEALER
skate .... RAY
skate genus .... RAIA

skating area .... RINK
skegger .... PARR
skein of yarn .... RAP, HANK
skeletal .... BONY
skeleton, sea animal
    CORAL, SPONGE
skeptic .... AGNOSTIC
sketch ...... DRAW, OUTLINE
ski, heel spring .... AMSTUTZ
ski race .... SLALOM
ski run ..... SCHUSS, SLALOM
ski wax .... KLISTER
skier, mark of ..... SITZMARK
skiing position .... VORLAGE
skiing, zigzag .... SLALOM
skilled person .... ADEPT
skillful ...
    ABLE, DEFT, ADEPT, HABILE
skillfully .... ABLY
skim over .... SKIP
skin .... FLAY, DERMA
skin, deeper layer ..... CUTIS
skin, design on
    TATOO, TATTOO
skin disease ... ACNE, MANGE,
    PSORA, TETTER
skin disease, horse's .. CALORIS
skin disease, Peru ...... UTA
skin infection .... LEPRA
skin layer .... DERM, CUTIS,
    DERMA, CORIUM, ENDERON
skin of a beast .... FELL
skin, pert. to .. DERIC, DERMIC
skinflint .... MISER
skink, Egypt. .... ADDA
skip .... OMIT
skip a stone .... DAP
skip happily .... CAPER
skipjack .... ELATER
skirmish .... MELEE
skirt, ballet .... TUTU
skirt section .... PANEL
skittle .... PIN
skulk .... LURK
skull, pert. to .. INIAL, INION
skull protuberance .... INION
skullcap, Arab. ...... CHECHIA
skunk .. CHINCHA, CHINCHE
sky .... FIRMAMENT
sky god, Assyrian ...... ANAT
sky: Chin. .... TIEN
sky god, Babyl. .... ABU, ANU
sky god, Norse .... TIU,
    TIW, TYR, ZIO, ZIU
sky, highest part .... ZENITH
sky: Polyn. .... LANGI
sky serpent, Vedic ...... AHI
slab, engraved .... TABLET
slab, flooring, decorative DALLE
slag .... DROSS, SCORIA

a slam .... BANG
slam in cards .... VOLE
slander ...... LIBEL, ASPERSE
slang .... ARGOT
slant .... BEVEL, SLOPE
slanted edge .... BEVEL
slanted: naut. .... ARAKE
slanting .... SKEW, ASKEW
slanting type .... ITALIC
slantingly, drive .... TOE
slap .... CUFF, SPANK
slash .... JAG, SLISH
slater's tool, same as slate-
    trimming tool
slate-trimming tool
            SAX, ZAT, ZAX
Slav .... SERB
Slav, ancient
        VEND, WEND, VENED
Slav, E. Ger. .... WEND
Slav in Saxony .... SORB
slave .... ESNE, SERF, THRALL
slave, fugitive ..... MAROON
slave, Spartan .... HELOT
sled, Swiss .... LUGE
sled to haul logs ...... TODE
sleep .... NAP, NOD, DOZE
sleep, deep .... SOPOR
sleep lightly .... DOZE
b sleeping .... DORMANT
sleeping place BED, COT, BERTH
sleeping sickness fly .. TSETSE
sleeve, large .... DOLMAN
sleigh .... PUNG
sleight-of-hand .... MAGIC
slender .... LANK, LEAN,
        SLIM, THIN, REEDY
slender woman .... SYLPH
slice, bacon .... RASHER
slice of meat .... COLP
slice, thick .... SLAB
slick .... LOY
slide .... SKID, SLUE
sliding door, Jap. ... FUSUMA
sliding piece .... CAM
sliding valve .... PISTON
slight .... MERE, SLIM, FAINT
slight intentionally SLUR, SNUB
slimy .... OOZY
sling around .... SLUE
slip.ERR, BONER, GLIDE, LAPSE
slip by .... ELAPSE
slip out of course ...... SLUE
slip, plant .... CION, CUTTING
slipknot .... NOOSE
slipper ...... MULE, MOYLE
slipper, P. I. .... CHINELA
slope ...... RAMP, GRADIENT
slope: fort. .... GLACIS

c slope of vein or lode ... HADE
slope: Scot .... BRAE
slope of land ...... VERSANT
slope, steep ... SCARP, ESCARP
sloping edge
        BASIL, BEZEL, BEZIL
sloth, three-toed .... AI
sloth, two-toed .... UNAU
slouch: Scot. .... LOUCH
slow .... POKY
slow loris .... KOKAM
slow: music .. TARDO, LARGO
    LENTO, ADAGIO, ANDANTE
slower: music .... RIT
sluggish .... DOPEY
sluice .... CLOW
slump .... RECESSION
slur over .... ELIDE
slushy mass .... POSH
sly look .... LEER, OGLE
sly: old Eng. .... SLEE, SLOAN
sly: Scot. .... SLEE
smack ...... BUSS, KISS, SLAP
small .... WEE, TINY,
        PETIT, PETTY, PETITE
small amount .. DRAM, MINIM
small arachnid .... MITE
small bottle .... VIAL
small bunch .... WISP
d small case .... ETUI
small cluster .... SPRIG
small coin .... MITE
small creature MITE, MINIMUS
small dog .... POM, PUG,
        PUP, PEKE, FEIST
small goby, Atlantic ... MAPO
small: law .... PETIT
small marine animal .... SALP
small monkey .... LEMUR
small pearl .... PEARLET
small poem .... ODELET
small: Scot. .... SMA
small stream RUN, RILL, RILLET
small: suffix .... ING
small weight ... GRAM, MITE
smallest .... LEAST
smallest integer .... ONE
smallpox .... VARIOLA
smaragd .... EMERALD
smart .... STING
smart CHIC, ASTUTE, CLEVER
smartly dressed ... CHIC, TRIG
smear on .... DAUB
smell, disagreeable
        OLID, REEK, FETOR
smelting mixture ..... MATTE
smelting waste .. SLAG, DROSS
smirch .... SULLY
smith, aided Siegfried .. MIME

smock .... CAMISE
smoke .... FUME, REEK
smoke-colored .... FUMOUS
smoke, wisp of .... FLOC
smoked beef ...... PASTRAMI
smokeless powder ..... FILITE
smoking .... AREEK
smoking pipe ... BRIAR, BRIER
smoking pipe, Oriental
HOOKAH, NARGILE
smoky .... FUMID
smooth
EVEN, IRON, LEVEL, PREEN
smooth-breathing ...... LENE
smooth, make ..... LEVIGATE
smooth: phonetics ...... LENE
smooth-spoken .... GLIB
smoothing tool .... PLANE
snail, large.WHELK, ABALONE
snail, marine .... TRITON
snake ..... ASP, BOA, ADDER,
VIPER, PYTHON, REPTILE
snake, Amer. .. ADDER, RACER
snake-bite antidote
GUACO, CEDRON
snake, black .... RACER
snake charmer's clarinet BEEN
snake-haired woman GORGON,
MEDUSA, STHENO, EURYALE
snake, India .... COBRA,
KRAIT, DABOIA, DABOYA
snake-like .... SINUOUS
snake, S. Amer. ...... ABOMA
snake, tree .... LORA
snake, venomous, Ind..BONGAR
snakes, pert. to ..... OPHIOID
snakebird .... DARTER
snakeroot, white ...... STEVIA
snap up bargains ...... SNUP
snapper ...... SESI, PARGO
snapper fish: Maori .. TAMURE
snapper: N. Z. ...... TAMURE
snare .. GIN, NET, WEB, TRAP
snarl .... GNAR, GNARR
snatch .... GRAB, SEIZE
sneer.GIBE, JIBE, FLEER, SCOFF
sniff .... NOSE
snipe, Europ. .... BLEATER
snipe's cry .... SCAPE
snoring .... STERTOR
snow field, Alpine.FIRN, NEVE
snow goose genus ...... CHEN
snow, ground down .... LOLLY
snow house
IGLU, IGLOE, IGLOO, IGLOU
snow leopard .... OUNCE
snow lily .... VIOLET
snow, living in .... NIVAL
snow mouse .... VOLE

snow panther .... OUNCE
snow runner .... SKI, SKEE
snow: Scot. .... SNA
SNOW WHITE
see SEVEN DWARFS
snuff .... RAPPEE
snuffbox bean
CACOON, MACKAYBEAN
snug .... COSY, COZY
snuggery .... NEST
so .... THUS, TRUE, VERY
so be it! .... AMEN
so much: music ...... TANTO
so: Scot. .... SAE
soak .... RET, SOG, SOP, WET
soak flax .... RET
soap, fine .... CASTILE
soap-frame bar .... SESS
soap: pharm. .... SAPO
soap plant .... AMOLE
soap substitute ...... AMOLE
soap vine .... GOGO
soapstone .... TALC
soapy mineral .... TALC
sober .... GRAVE, STAID
social affair .... TEA
social division .... CASTE
social unit or group .... SEPT
society, entrance into .. DEBUT
society swell .... NOB
sock, Jap. .... TABI
sock, Rom. .... UDO
sod .... TURF
sodium alum .... MENDOZITE
sodium carbonate .... TRONA
sodium chloride .... SALT
sodium chloride: pharm. .. SAL
sodium compound ..... SODA
sodium nitrate .. NITER, NITRE
sofa .... DIVAN
soft
LOW, EASY, WAXY, TENDER
soft area on bill .... CERE
soft drink
ADE, POP, COLA, SODA
soft feathers ... DOWN, EIDER
soft ice from floes ..... LOLLY
soft job ..... SNAP, SINECURE
soft mass .... WAD
soft palate .... VELUM
soft palate lobe ...... UVULA
soft palate, pert. to
VELAR, UVULAR
soft palates .... VELA
soft-spoken .... MEALY
soften in temper ..... RELENT
softly: music .... SOAVE
soil: comb. form .... AGRO
soil, organic part .... HUMUS

a
soil, rich .... LOAM
soil, sticky .. GOMBO, GUMBO
soil, type of .... PEDOCAL
solar disc ...... ATEN, ATON
solar over lunar year,
    excess of .... EPACT
soldier: Am. Rev. .. BUCKSKIN
soldier, Austral., N. Z. ANZAC
soldier, Brit. .... ATKINS
soldier, former .... LANCER
soldier, Gr. .... HOPLITE
soldier, Indo-Brit. ..... SEPOY
soldier, native India .. SEPOY
soldier's shelter ..... FOXHOLE
sole .... PELMA
sole of foot .... VOLA
sole of plow .... SLADE
solemn declaration. VOW, OATH
solicit .... BEG, URGE,
    COURT, CANVASS
solicitor's chamber ...... INN
solicitude .... CARE
solid .... CONE, CUBE, PRISM
solid, become GEL, SET, HARDEN
solid: comb. form ..... STEREO
solidify .. GEL, SET, HARDEN
solitary .... LONE, ONLY, SOLE
solo .... ARIA
Solomon's aid giver ... HIRAM

b
Solomon's temple rebuilder
    HIRAM
solution .... KEY
solution, strength of
    TITER, TITRE
solvent .... ACETONE
solvent, treat with .. SOLUTIZE
some .... ANY
somite .... MEROSOME
son: Fr. .... FILS
son-in-law .... GENER
son: Ir. .... MAC
son of .... MAC
son of Agrippina .... NERO
son of Joktan .... OPHIR
son of Reuben .... PALLU
son of: Scot. .... MAC
song ...... LAY, ODE, DITE,
    DITTY, MELOS, TROLL
song, Christmas
    NOEL, CAROL, WASSAIL
song for solo voices ..... GLEE
song: Ger. .... LIED
song, Hawaiian .... MELE
song, Jap. .... UTA
song, morning: poet. .. MATIN
song, of a .... MELIC
song of praise, joy
    PEAN, PAEAN, ANTHEM
"Song of the South" Uncle
    REMUS

c
song, operatic .... ARIA
song, religious
    HYMN, CHANT, ANTHEM
song, sacred
    HYMN, CHANT, ANTHEM
song, sad .... DIRGE
song: Scot. .... STROUD
song, simple .... DITTY
song, Sp. .... CANCION
song thrush ... MAVIE, MAVIS
sonship .... FILIETY
soon .... ANON
sooner .... ERE, ERER
soot .... COOM, SMUT
soot: old Eng. .... SOTE
soothe .... EASE, LULL
soothing ANODYNE, LENITIVE
soothsayer .... SEER
Sophocles, play by ... OEDIPUS
soprano, prima donna .. ALDA,
    BORI, PONS, RISE,
    RAISA, CALLAS, STEBER
sora bird .... RAIL
sorceress .... CIRCE
sorceress, Hindu .... USHA
sorceress, myth. ...... LAMIA
sorceress, "Odyssey," Greek
    CIRCE

d
sorcery, W. Ind.
    OBE, OBI, OBEAH
sore, make .... RANKLE
sore: Scot. .... SAIR
sorghum variety .... MILO
sorrow ..... DOLOR, REMORSE
sorrow, feel
    RUE, LAMENT, REPENT
sorrowful . SAD, BLUE, DOLENT
sort .... KIND,
    CLASS, GROUP, SPECIES
sortie .... SALLY
sortilege .... LOT
sorting machine ..... GRADER
soul .... ANIMA
soul, Egyp. .... BA, KA
soul, Hindu .. ATMA, ATMAN
sound .. TONE, NOISE, VALID
sound, kind of ..... PALATAL
sound loudly .. BLARE, LARUM
sound, monotonous
    HUM, DRONE
sound perception .... EAR
sound, pert. to ...... SONANT
sound reasoning .... LOGIC
sound, resemblance of
    ASSONANT
sound, solid .... KLOP
sound the ocean
    PLUMB, FATHOM

a sound waves, of ...... **AUDIO**	*c* spa, Bohemian .... **BILIN**

sound waves, of ...... **AUDIO**
sound, without ..... **ASONANT**
sounding .... **SONANT**
soundless .... **ASONANT**
soup, heavy .. **PUREE, POTAGE**
soup spoon .... **LADLE**
soup, thick .... **BISK, HOOSH, PUREE, BISQUE**
soup vessel .... **TUREEN**
soupfin shark .... **TOPE**
sour .... **ACID, ACERB, ACIDIC, ACETOSE**
sour curdled milk: Nor. .. **SKYR**
sour-leaved plant ..... **SORREL**
sour milk drink.**LEBAN, LEBEN**
source, mineral .... **ORE**
source, obsidian's ...... **LAVA**
soursop .... **ANNONA**
south: Sp. .... **SUR**
South African .... **BOER**
SOUTH AFRICA ..... see also SPECIAL SECTION
S. Afr. assembly .... **RAAD**
S. Afr. dialect .... **TAAL**
S. Afr. Dutch .... **BOER, TAAL**
S. Afr. garter snake .... **ELAPS**
S. Afr. grass country .... **VELD**
S. Afr. greenhorn ..... **IKONA**
S. Afr. gully .... **DONGA**
S. Afr. "out" .... **UIT**
b S. Afr. town .... **STAD**
S. Afr. village .... **KRAAL**
SOUTH AMERICA .... see also SPECIAL SECTION
South American animal . **TAPIR**
S. Amer. bird ... **GUAN, JACU, SYLPH, TURCO, SERIEMA**
S. Amer. game bird **TINAMOU**
S. Amer. Indian group .... **GES**
S. Amer. lizard .... **TEJU**
S.Amer.tree **VERA,CEBIL,FOTUI**
S. Amer. ungulate .... **TAPIR**
"South Pacific" hero .... **EMILE**
Southern Cross constellation **CRUX**
Southern France .... **MIDI**
Southern river .... **PEEDEE**
Southern state: abbr. .... **ALA**
Southwest river .... **RED**
sovereign (coin) .... **SKIV**
sovereignty .... **EMPERY**
SOVIET .... see also RUSSIAN
Soviet news agency ..... **TASS**
Soviet newspaper .... **PRAVDA**
sow .... **PIG, GILT**
sow .... **SEED, PLANT**
sow: Prov. Eng. .... **YELT**
sow: Scot. .... **SOO**
sower .... **SEEDER**
sown: her. .... **SEME**
soybean .... **SOJA, SOYA**

spa, Eng. .... **BATH**
spa, Ger. .... **EMS, BADEN**
space between bird's eye and bill ..... **LORA, LORE, LORUM**
space between triglyphs **METOPE**
space, small **AREOLA, AREOLE**
spaces on bird's face **LORAE, LORES**
spade .... **LOY, SHOVEL**
spade, narrow .... **LOY, SPUD**
spade-shaped .... **PALACEOUS**
spade, turf .... **SLANE**
Spain, ancient .... **IBERIA**
SPANISH see also SPAIN, SPECIAL SECTION
SP. ARTIST see SP. PAINTER
Sp. belle .... **MAJA**
Sp. cellist .... **CASALS**
Sp. coin, old .... **PISTOLE**
Sp. dance ..... **JOTA, BOLERO**
Sp. epic .... **CID**
Sp. explorer **CORTEZ, BALBOA, CORTES**
d Sp. fabric .... **CREA**
Sp. fortress commander .. **CAID**
Sp. game of ball .... **PELOTA**
Sp. general, duke.**ALBA, ALVA**
Sp. hero .... **CID**
Sp. kettle .... **OLLA**
Sp. lady ..... **DONA, SENORA**
Sp. length unit .... **VARA**
Sp. man .... **DON, SENOR**
Sp. nun .... **AVILA**
Sp. painter **GOYA, MIRO, SERT, PICASSO**
Sp. poet .... **ENCINA**
Sp. pot .... **OLLA**
Sp. title.**DON, SENOR, SENORA**

SPANISH WORDS:
(tilde omitted throughout)
abbey .... **ABADIA**
afternoon .... **TARDE**
annatto seeds ... **ACHIOTE**
another .... **OTRO**
article .... **EL, LA, LAS, LOS, UNO**
ass .... **ASNO**
aunt .... **TIA**
bay .... **BAHIA**
bean .... **HABA**
before .... **ANTES**
being .... **ENTE**
black .... **NEGRA**
blue .... **AZUL**
box canyon .... **CAJON**

a

boy .... NINO
bravo! .... OLE
bull .... TORO
but .... PERO
canal .... CANO
chaperon . DUENA, DUENNA
chest .... CAJETA
chief .... JEFE, ADALID
child .... NINO
church .... IGLESIA
city .... CIUDAD
clay building.ADOBE, TAPIA
cloak .... CAPA
clothes .... ROPA
corral .... ATAJO
cut .... TAJO
day .... DIA
dining hall .... SALA
dove .... PALOMA
drawing room .... SALA
estuary .... RIA
evening .... TARDE
evil .... MALO
first .... PRIMUS
for .... POR
friend .... AMIGO
funds .... CAJA
girl .... NINA
God .... DIOS
gold .... ORO

b

good-bye .... ADIOS
grass fiber rope ...... SOGA
grille .... REJA
gulch .... ARROYO
gypsy .... GITANO
hall .... SALA
hamlet .... ALDA
harbor entrance ..... BOCA
health .... SANO
hello .... HOLLA
hill . ALTO, CERRO, MORRO
hillside .... FALDA
hotel .... POSADA
house .... CASA
Indian .... INDIO
inlet .... RIA, ESTERO
jail keeper .... CAID
judge .... JUEZ
king .... REY
lady .... DAMA
lake .... LAGO
landmark .... SENAL
latter .... ESTE
lawsuit .... ACTO
letter .... CARTA
lime .... LIMA
love .... AMOR
man .... HOMBRE
manservent .... MOZO
mayor .. ALCADE, ALCALDE

c

mouth .... BOCA
movie house .... CINE
meadow .... VEGA
my .... MIO
of .... DE
open space .... COSO
other .... OTRA
parish priest .... CURA
peak .... PICO
people .... GENTE
pine .... PINO
pole .... PALO
pole, wooden .... PALO
porridge .... ATOLE
post office .... CORREO
pot .... OLLA
priest .... CURA, PADRE
queen .... REINA
ragged person .... ROTO
raisin .... PASA
red .... ROJO
river .... RIO
road .... CAMINO
room .... SALA
rum .... RON
saint, feminine .... SANTA
she .... ELLA
silver .... PLATA
six .... SEIS
snake .... CULEBRA

d

song .... CANCION
south .... SUR
street ...... CALLE, CALLI
sweet potato ..... CAMOTE
tall .... ALTA
this .... ESTA, ESTE
three .... TRES
to be .... SER, ESTE
tomorrow .... MANANA
trench .... TAJO
uncle .... TIO
very .... MUY
water .... AGUA
wax .... CERA
wit .... SAL
with .... DE
work .... OBRA
yes .... SI
you .... TE

spar ...... BOX, BOOM, GAFF,
            MAST, YARD, SPRIT
spar for colors .... GAFF
spar, heavy .... BARITE
spar, loading .... STEEVE
spar, small .... SPRIT
spare .... LEAN, EXTRA,
            GAUNT, LENTEN
sparkle .... GLITTER
sparkling, as wine . MOUSSEUX
sparrow, hedge .... DONEY

Sparta queen .... LEDA
Spartan army division .. MORA
Spartan magistrate ... EPHOR
spasm .... FIT, TIC, JERK
spawning place .... REDD
speak
UTTER, ORATE, DECLAIM
speak: comb. form ..... LALO
speak, inability to ... ALALIA
speak theatrically ..... EMOTE
speaker ... ORATOR, LOCUTOR
speaking tube, pilot's.GOSPORT
spear .... DART, LANCE
spear, Afr. ASSAGAI, ASSEGAI
spear, fish .... GIG, GAFF
spear-like weapon PIKE, LANCE
spear-shaped .... HASTATE
spear, 3-prong ..... TRIDENT
spear thrower, Austral.
WOMERA
special: Moslem law
KHAS, KHASS
species .... KIND, SORT
specific date .... DAY
specified time .... DATE
specimen .... SAMPLE
speck .... DOT, MOTE, FLECK
speckle .... DOT, STIPPLE
spectacle .... PAGEANT
specter .... BOGY, BOGEY,
GHOST, SHADE
speech ... LECTURE, ORATION
speech, art of ..... RHETORIC
speech defect
LISP, ALOGIA, STAMMER
speech goddess, Hindu
VAC, DEVI, VACH
speech, local .... PATOIS
speech, long .... SPIEL
speech, loss of ...... APHASIA
speech peculiarity ..... IDIOM
speech, violent ...... TIRADE
speechless ...... DUMB, MUTE
speed ...... HIE, RUN, PACE,
RACE, HASTE, HASTEN,
RAPIDITY
speed, at full .... AMAIN
spelt .... ADOR, EMMER
Spenser heroine .... UNA
Spenser's name for Ireland
IRENA
sphere .... ORB
sphere of action ..... ARENA
spice .... MACE
spice ball .... FAGOT, FAGGOT
spicknel .... MEU, MEW
spicy .... RACY
spider crab genus MAIA, MAJA
spider fluid: Pharm. ARANEIN

spider monkey
QUATA, ATELES, COAITA
spider nest .... NIDUS
spigot .... TAP
spike .... EAR, GAD, BROB
spikenard .... NARD
spin
BIRL, REEL, TWIRL, ROTATE
spinal column ... AXIS, AXON
spinal cord .... MYELON
spinal membrane ...... DURA
spindle .... COP, AXLE
spindle, yarn .... HASP
spine .... AXIS, AXON
spine bones .... SACRA
spine, slender .... SETA
spineless cactus ...... CHAUTE
spiniform .... SPINATE
spinning jenny .... MULE
spiny shrub genus ...... ULEX
spiral formation ..... VOLUTE
spire ornament .... EPI
spirit .... ELAN, SOUL, METAL
spirit: Egyp. myth ..... BA, KA
spirit: Ger. .... GEIST
spirit, Ir. . BANSHEE, BANSHIE
spirit lamp .... ETNA
spirit, Moslem ..... JIN, JINN,
GENIE, GENII, JINNI, JINNEE
spirit of air .... ARIEL
spirit of evil .. DEMON, DEVIL
spirit of man: Egypt ..... AKH
spirit raiser .. ELATER, ELATOR
spirits and water ...... GROG
spirits of the dead .... MANES
spirited .... EAGER, CONMOTO
spirited horse .... STEED
spiritual body: Egypt. ... SAHU
spiritual struggle ..... PENIEL
spiritualist meeting ... SEANCE
splash .... LAP
spleen .... MILT
splendid .... GRAND
splendor .... ECLAT
splendor, goddess of: Hindu
UMA
split .... RIT, RENT, RIVE,
CLEFT, RIVEN, CLEAVE
split pulse .... DAL
spoil .... ROT, BOTCH
spoil, as eggs .... ADDLE
spoils of war .... LOOT
spoken .... ORAL
spoken word .... AGRAPH
spokes, having .... RADIAL
sponge, calcareous ... LEUCON
sponge gourd ... LOOF, LOOFA
sponge on ..... MUMP, LEACH
sponge spicule, bow-shaped
OXEA, TOXA, PINULUS
sponge, young .... ASCON

a
spongewood .... SOLA
sponsor .... PATRON
sponsorship ...... EGIS, AEGIS
spool .... REEL
spore .... SEED
spore cluster .... SORUS
spore fruit of rust fungi
    AECIA, TELIA, AECIUM,
          TELIUM
spore sac, fungus ASCI, ASCUS
sport .... RUX, GAME,
     GOLF, PLAY, POLO
sports arena STADIA, STADIUM
sports center ... RINK, ARENA
sports hall .... GYM
spot in mineral ..... MACLE
spot on card .... PIP
spotted .... PIED, PINTO,
   DAPPLED, MACULOSE
spotted cavy .... PACA
spotted deer KAKAR, CHITAL
spotted moth ...... FORESTER
spotted sting-ray ..... OBISPO
spotted, to make
    DAPPLE, STIPPLE
spouse .... MATE, WIFE
spray .... ATOMIZE
spray, sea .... LIPPER

b
spread .... TED
spread by peening .... RIVET
spread by report
     BRUIT, NORATE
spread out .... FAN
spread rumor .... GOSSIP
spread the word .... TELL
spread to dry, as hay .... TED
sprightly .... PERT, PEART
spring .... SPA
spring back .... RESILE
spring: Bible .... AIN
spring-like .... VERNAL
spring: old Eng. .... KELD
spring, mineral .... SPA
spring rice, India ...... BORO
spring, small .... SEEP
springs, warm ...... THERMAE
springboard .... BATULE
sprinkle DEG, WATER, SPARGE
sprinkling: her. .... SEME
sprint .... RUN, RACE
sprite .. ELF, FAY, PIXY, PIXIE
sprite, tricksy .... ARIEL
sprout ... CION, GROW, SCION
spruce ... TRIG, TRIM, NATTY
spruce, Jap. .... YEDDO
spruce, white ...... EPINETTE
spume .... FOAM
spun wool .... YARN
spur .... GAD, GOAD, CALCAR
spur of mountain ..... ARETE

c
spur part .... ROWEL
spur wheel .... ROWEL
spurs, having .... CALCARATE
spurt .... JET, GUSH
spy, garment-trade slang KEEK
spy, British, Revolution ANDRE
squama .... ALULA
squander .... SPEND
square dance .... REEL
square-meshed net ..... LACIS
squash .... PEPO,
  CRUSH, GOURD, FLATTEN
squash bug .... ANASA
squaw .... MAHALA
squawfish .... CHUB
squid genus .... LOLIGO
squirrel fur, Siberian
    CALABAR, CALABER
squirrel, ground Europ. ... SISEL
squirrel-like animal DORMOUSE
squirrel skin .... VAIR
squirrel's nest ... DRAY, DREY
ST. .... see SAINT
stab .... GORE
stabilize .... STEADY
stable .... FIRM, SOLID
stable compartment ... STALL
stable-keeper, royal .. AVENER
stables, royal .... MEWS
stableman .... OSTLER

d
stack of hay .... RICK
staff .... ROD, MACE
staff-bearer .... MACER
staff, bishop's ...... CROSIER
staff of office .... MACE
staff, royal SCEPTER, SCEPTRE
stag ..... DEER, HART, MALE
stage direction
  MANET, SENET, EXEUNT
stage equipment ...... PROPS
stage extra ..... SUPE, SUPER
stage horn signal .... SENNET
stage setting .... SCENE
stage whisper .... ASIDE
stagger .... REEL
stagger: Prov. Eng. ...... STOT
stagnation .... STASIS
stagnation, blood ..... STASIS
stain, DYE, SOIL, SPOT, TASH
stair part ...... RISER, TREAD
stair post .... NEWEL
staircase spindle .... SPEEL
stake .... ANTE, WAGER
stake, like a .... PALAR
stake, pointed ..... PALISADE
stake, poker .... ANTE
stakes .... POT
stakes, —, Epsom Downs Race
     OAKS
stale .... TRITE
stalk .... STEM

a stalk, flower .. **SCAPE, PEDICEL**
stalk, frond .... **STIPE**
stalk, plant .... **CAULIS**
stalk, short .... **STIPE**
stalk, sugarcane ..... **RATOON**
stall in mud .... **STOG**
stammer .... **HAW, HEM**
stammering sound .... **ER**
stamp .... **MARK, SIGIL**
stamp battery block ..... **VOL**
stamp of approval .... **OK**
stamp-sheet part .... **PANE**
stamping device .... **DIE**
stamping machine ..... **DATER**
stanch .... **STEM**
stand .... **RISE**
stand .. **BEAR, ABIDE, ENDURE**
stand, cuplike .... **ZARF**
stand in awe of .... **FEAR**
stand, small
 TABORET, TAROURET
stand, 3-legged **TRIPOD, TRIVET**
standard . **PAR, FLAG, ENSIGN**
standard. **NORM, TYPE, NORMA**
standard of chemical strength
 TITER
standard, Turk .... **ALEM**
standing .... **STATUS**
stannum .... **TIN**
stanza, last .... **ENVOY**
b stanza, Nor. .... **STEV**
stanza, part of .... **STAVE**
star .... **ASTRO**
star, blue .... **VEGA**
star, brightest .... **COR**
star cluster, distant
 NEBULA, NEBULAE
star, day .... **SUN**
star, evening .... **VENUS,**
 HESPER, VESPER, HESPERUS
star facet .... **PANE**
star, fixed .... **SUN, ALYA**
star: Fr. .... **ETOILE**
star in Aquarius .... **SKAT**
star in Aquilla .... **ALTAIR**
star in Argo .... **NAOS**
star in Big Dipper ..... **PHAD**
star in Bootes .... **IZAR**
star in Cetus .... **MIRA**
star in Cygenus **SADR, DENEB**
star in Draco .... **ADIB, JUZA**
star in Eridanus .. **AZHA, BEID**
star in Leo .. **DUHR, REGULUS**
star in Lyra ... **VEGA, WEGA**
star in Orion .... **RIGEL**
star in Pegasus **ENIF, MATAR**
star in Pleiades .... **MAIA**
star in Perseus .... **ATIK**
star in Scorpio ..... **ANTARES**

c star in Serpens .... **ALYA**
star in Taurus ..**NATH, PLEIAD**
star in Virgo .... **SPICA**
star near Mizar .... **ALCOR**
star, new .... **NOVA**
star-shaped .... **STELLATE**
star-shaped spicule
 ACTER, ACTINE
star, temporary .... **NOVA**
stars, dotted with ...... **SEME**
stars, pert. to .... **ASTRAL**
starch ...... **AMYL, ARUM,**
 SAGO, FARINA, CASSAVA
starchy rootstock .... **TARO**
starfish .... **ASTEROID**
stark mad .... **RAVING**
starnose .... **MOLE**
— Starr, comic strip character
 BRENDA
starred lizard **AGAMA, HARDIM**
start ... **BEGIN, SALLY, ROUSE**
starvation .... **INEDIA**
starwort .... **ASTER**
state .... **AVER**
STATE .. see also **GAZETTEER**
STATE FLOWERS . see page 208
state, New England: abbr. .. **RI**
state of affairs .... **PASS**
state, pert. to .... **CIVIL**
d state of: suffix .... **ERY**
state of being: suffix .... **URE**
state precisely ...... **SPECIFY**
stately home .. **DOME, ESTATE**
statements, confused
 RIGMAROLE
statesman, Brit. .... **PITT**
station .. **POST, DEPOT, PLACE**
stationary .... **FIXED, STATIC**
stationary motor part **STATOR**
statistician .... **STATIST**
statute .... **ACT, LAW**
stave, barrel .... **LAG**
stay .... **WAIT, TARRY**
stay rope .... **GUY**
stays .... **CORSET**
stead .... **LIEU, PLACE**
steal **COP, ROB, GLOM, SNITCH**
steal cattle .... **RUSTLE**
steal: Eng. .... **GLOM**
steal, Eng. dialect ...... **NIM**
steel beam .... **GIRDER**
steel: Ger. .... **STAHL**
steel splint, armor skirt
 TACE, TASSE, TASSET
steep .... **RET, SOP**
steep .... **SHEER**
steep in lime .... **BOWK**
steer wildly .... **YAW**
steer, young: Prov. Eng. .. **STOT**

155

a steering, direct ship's
COND, CONN
steersman .... COX
stellar ...... ASTRAL, STARRY
stem
CION, CORM, SCAPE, STALK
stem, fungus .... STIPE
stem, hollow .... CANE
stem, jointed .... CULM
stem of hop .... BINE
stem, rudimentary .. CAULICLE
stem, ship's .... PROW
stench .... ODOR, FETOR
stentorian .... LOUD
step .... GRADE, PHASE
step ... PACE, STAIR, TREAD
step, dance ..... PAS, CHASSE
step up to mark .... TOE
step, upright part of .. RISER
steps, outdoor .... PERRON
steps over fence ...... STILE
steppes, storm on ..... BURAN
stern GRIM, HARSH, AUSTERE
steward: Scot. ..... MORMAOR
stick .. BAR, BAT, ROD, CANE,
WAND, BATON, MUNDLE
stick .... GLUE,
PASTE, ADHERE, CLEAVE
stick, conductor's ..... BATON
stick together ...... COHERE
stick used in hurling .. CAMAN
b sticks, bundle of ...... FAGOT
stickler for formality .. TAPIST
sticky substance ... GOO, GUM
stiffly nice .... PRIM
stigma .... BRAND
stigmatic point of mango NAK
still .... BUT, YET
stimulant, coffee
CAFFEIN, CAFFEINE
stimulant, tea THEIN, THEINE
stimulate .. FAN, WHET, ELATE
sting .... BITE, SMART
stinging ant .... KELEP
stinging herb .... NETTLE
stingy .... MEAN
stint .... TASK
stipend, church ..... PREBEND
stipend: Scot. .... ANNAT
stipulation .... CLAUSE
stir .. ADO, MIX, TODO, ROUSE
stir up .... RILE, ROIL
stitch .... PUNTO
stitchbird .... IHI
stitched fold .... TUCK
stithy .... ANVIL
stock .... BREED
stock .... STORE
stock exchange, membership in
SEAT
stock exchange, Paris BOURSE

c stock market crash .... PANIC
stockade: Russ. .... ETAPE
stocking run .... LADDER
stockings .... HOSE
stocky .... STUB
stolen goods .... SWAG
stomach .... MAW, CRAW
stomach division, ruminant's
OMASUM
stomach, first .... RUMEN
stomach, ruminant's ... TRIPE
stone .. AGATE, LAPIS, SLATE
Stone Age tool .... CELT,
EOLITH, NEOLITH
stone, aquamarine .... BERYL
stone, breastplate .... JASPER
stone chest .... CIST
stone chip .... SPALL
stone: comb. form ..... LITH
stone-cutter's chisel .... DROVE
stone fruit .... DRUPE
stone, green . BERYL, OLIVINE
stone hammer .... MASH
stone, hard .... ADAMANT
stone heap ..... CARN, KARN,
CAIRN, CARNE, CAIRNE
stone, hollow .... GEODE
stone implement ...... CELT,
EOLITH, NEOLITH
stone, like a .... LITHOID
stone, monument .... MENHIR
d stone paving block ..... SETT
stone pillar .... STELE
stone, red ...... SARD, SPINEL
stone roller fish ...... TOTER
stone, rough .... RUBBLE
stone: Scot. .... STEAN, STEEN
stone set .... PAVER
stone, squared ...... ASHLAR
stone to death .... LAPIDATE
stone, woman turned to NIOBE
stone worker .... MASON
stone, yellow TOPAZ, CITRINE
stonecrop
ORPIN, SEDUM, ORPINE
stonecutter MASON, LAPICIDE
stonecutter's chisel ... DROVE
stoneware: Fr. .... GRES
stool pigeon .... NARK
stop ..... DAM, BALK, HALT,
STEM, WHOA, DESIST
stop, as engine .. CONK, STALL
stop by accident .... STALL
stop: naut. ... AVAST, BELAY
stop short .... BALK
stoppage .... JAM
stopper .... BUNG, PLUG
storage battery plate ... GRID
storage place BIN, BARN, SILO
store, army .... CANTEEN
store fodder .... ENSILE

a storehouse .... ETAPE
storehouse, army ..... DEPOT
storehouse, India .... GOLA
storehouse, public ..... ETAPE
stork .... MARABOU
storm FUME, FURY, RAGE, RAVE
storm, away from ...... ALEE
storm, dust .... SIMOON
storm: Fr. .... ORAGE
storm god, Babyl. ZU, ADAD,
ADDA, ADDU
story, Norse .... SAGA
story, short .... CONTE
stoss, opposite of .... LEE
stout .... BURLY
stout, kind of .... PORTER
stove .... ETNA, RANGE
"Stowe" character
EVA, TOM, TOPSY
straight .... DIRECT
straight-edge .... RULER
strain .... EXERT
strained .... TENSE
strainer .... SIEVE
strainer, wool cloth ... TAMIS
Straits Settlement region
PENANG
strange .... ODD
strap on falcon's leg .... JESS
strap-shaped .... LORATE

b strass .... PASTE
stratagem .... RUSE, WILE
stratagem, sudden ...... COUP
stratum .... LAYER
straw hat ...... BAKU, MILAN
stray .... ERR
stray .... WAIF
stray animal .... CAVY
streak .... ROE, LINE, VEIN,
STRIA, STRAKE, STRIAE
streaky .... LINY, ROWY
stream
FLOW, RILL, BOURN, RIVER
streamlet ...... RILL, RUNNEL
street Arab .... GAMIN
street: It., Sp. .. CALLE, CALLI
street, narrow .... LANE
street roisterer .... MUN
street urchin .... ARAB
street, Venice water .. RIO, RII
strength .... POWER
strengthening .... ROBORANT
stress .... ICTUS
stressed beat, syllable .. ARSIS
stretch: Scot. .... STENT
stretched out .... PROLATE
stretcher .... LITTER
stretching frame .... TENTER,
STENTER
strewn with flowers: Her. SEME

c strife .... WAR
strife, civil .... STASIS
strike .. BAT, HIT, RAP, CONK,
SLOG, SLUG, SOCK, SWAT,
WHAM, SMITE
strikebreaker ..... FINK, SCAB
striking effect .... ECLAT
string of mules .... ATAJO
stringy .... ROPY
strip .. BARE, DIVEST, STRAKE
strip of land ... DOAB, DUAB
strip of wood .... LATH
strip off skin .... FLAY
strip, oxhide, S. Afr. ... RIEM
strip, wood, metal ... SPLINE
stripe .... BAR, BAND, WALE,
WEAL, STREAK
stripe of color: zool. .. PLAGA
stripling .... BOY, LAD
strive .... AIM, VIE
strobile .... CONE
stroke .... FIT, ICTUS
stroke, brilliant .... COUP
stroll .... AMBLE
strong-arm man .... GOON
strong, as cigars .... MADURO
strong desire .... HUNGER
strong man .... SAMSON
strong man, Gr. .... ATLAS
strong point .... FORTE

d strong-scented ... OLID, RANK
strongbox .... SAFE
stronghold .. FORT, SION, ZION
struck with horror ... AGHAST
structure, tall .... TOWER
struggle .... COPE
struggle helplessly. FLOUNDER
struggled .... HOVE
stud .... BOSS
student in charge ... MONITOR
studio, art .... ATELIER
study ...... CON, PORE, READ
study group .... SEMINAR
stuff .... PAD, RAM, CRAM
stuffing .... KAPOK
stum .... MUST
stumble: prov. Eng. ...... STOT
stump of branch .... SKEG
stunted trees .... SCRUB
stupefied .... MAZED
stupefy .... DAZE, MAZE,
STUN, BESOT
stupid .... CRASS, DENSE
stupid person ...... ASS, OAF
CLOD, COOT, DOLT, LOON,
LOUT, LOWN, MOKE
stupor .... COMA, SOPOR
sturgeon, small ..... STERLET
style .... MODE, NAME
style of art .... DADA, GENRE

157

a stylet, surgical ...... TROCAR
stymie .... IMPEDE
Styx ferryman ...... CHARON
subbase .... PLINTH
subdued shade .... PASTEL
subject ...... TOPIC, VASSAL
subject in grammar .... NOUN
subjoin .... ADD
sublime .... NOBLE
submarine PIGBOAT, SNORKEL
submit .... BOW, YIELD
subordinate
　　　　MINOR, DEPENDENT
subside
　EBB, SINK, ABATE, RELAPSE
substance, lustrous .... METAL
substances, class of .... LIPIN
substantiate .... VERIFY
substantive word .... NOUN
substitute
　　　VICE, PROXY, ERSATZ
substitute for: suffix .... ETTE
subtle emanation ...... AURA
subtle variation ..... NUANCE
subtract .... DEDUCT
subway, Eng. .... TUBE
subway entrance ...... KIOSK
subway, Fr. .... METRO
success .... HIT, WOW

b succession .... LINE
successively .... AROW
succinct .... TERSE
succor .... AID
succulent plant .. ALOE, HERB
such .... SO
sucking fish ... PEGA, REMORA
Sudan lake .... CHAD
Sudan native .... FUL
Sudan Negroid .... SERE
Sudan people .... HAUSA
sudden attack: Med. .. ICTUS
suet .... TALLOW
suffer .... LET, BIDE
suffer from hunger
　　　　　CLEM, STARVE
suffer: Scot. .... DREE
sufficient: poet. .... ENOW

SUFFIXES:
　　act of .... TION
　　action .... ANCE
　　adjective .... ENT, IAL, INE,
　　　　　ISH, IST, ITE, OUS
　　agent .... URE
　　alcohol .... OL
　　carbohydrate .... OSE
　　chemical or chemistry . ANE,
　　ENE, IDE, INE, OLE, ONE,
　　ENOL, ITOL, OLIC

c common ending ENT, INE,
　　　　　　ING, ION
common suffix ..... ES, ESE,
　　　ESS, INE, IVE, ETTE,
　　　YNONE
condition .... ATE, ILE, ISE,
　　　ANCE, SION, STER
comparative ...... IER, IOR
compound .... ICAL, ILITY
diminutive .... ET, IE, ULA,
　　　　　ULE, ETTE
feminine ... INA, INE, ELLA
feminine noun .... ESS
follower .... IST, ITE
forming nouns from verbs . ER
full of .... OSE
inflammation .... ITIS
inhabitant of .... ITE
into .... EN
like .... OID
little .... ET
made of .... EN
make .... ISE
medical .... IA, OMA
mineral .... ITE, LITE
native of .... ITE
noun ... IA, OR, ATE, ENT,
　ERY, ESS, IER, ISE, IST,
　ITE, ANCY, ENCE, ENSE,
　STER

d noun ending .... STER
noun forming diminutive . CLE
number .... TEEN
or ordinal number .... ETH
oil .... OL, OLE
one who .... IST, STER
one who does .... IST
order of animals .... INI
ordinal .... ETH
origin, denoting ...... OTE
participle .... ING
person .... ER
plural .... (old EN), ES
quality .... ANCE, ILITY
rocks, of .... ITE, LITE
science of .... ICS
skin .... DERM
small .... ING
state of .... ERY, ANCE
state of being .... URE
substitute for .... ETTE
superlative .... EST
sympathizer .... ITE
town .... TON
tumor .... OMA
verb .... ISE, ESCE
with mineral names ... LITE
zoological .... ATA
Sufi disciple .... MURID
sugar .... OSE, SUCROSE
sugar cane disease ..... ILIAU

sugar cane residue .. **BAGASSE**
sugar, crude .... **GUR**
sugar, fruit .... **KETOSE**
sugar, raw ...... **CASSONADE**
sugar, simple .... **OSE**
sugar source .... **CANE**
suggestion .... **CUE, HINT**
suit of mail .... **ARMOR**
suitable. **APT, FIT, PAT, PROPER**
suitcase ... **BAG, GRIP, VALISE**
suitor .... **SWAIN**
sullen .. **DOUR, GLUM, MOROSE**
sullen, act .... **MOPE**
sullen, be ...... **POUT, SULK**
sully .... **SOIL, DIRTY**
sultan, Turkish .... **SELIM**
sultan's order .... **IRADE**
sultan's residence ...... **SERAI**
sultanate .... **OMAN**
sultry .... **HUMID**
Sulu Moslem .... **MORO**
"sum," infinitive following **ESSE**
sum paid as punishment .. **FINE**
sumac genus .... **RHUS**
sumac, P. I. .... **ANAM, ANAN**
Sumatra squirrel shrew .. **TANA**
Sumatra wildcat ...... **BALU**
Sumatran silk .... **IKAT**
"summa — laude" ...... **CUM**
summary
    DIGEST, PRECIS, EPITOME
summer: Fr. .... **ETE**
summer-house
    ARBOR, PERGOLA
summer, pert. to ..... **ESTIVAL**
summit
    APEX, KNAP, PEAK, SPIRE
summits .... **APICES**
summon .... **CALL, CITE,**
    PAGE, CLEPE, EVOKE
sun .... **SOL, HELIOS**
sun apartments ..... **SOLARIA**
sun bittern .... **CAURALE**
sun: comb. form .... **HELIO**
sun disk .... **ATEN, ATON**
sun-dried brick
    DOBE, DOBY, ADOBE, DOBIE
sun god, Babyl. .. **UTU, UTUG,**
    BABBAR, SHAMASH
sun god, Egypt. ..... **RA, TEM,**
    TUM, AMON, AMEN,
    AMUN, ATMU, ATUM
sun god, Gr., Rom. ...... **SOL,**
    APOLLO, HELIOS
sun god, Inca .... **INTI**
sun, halo around .... **CORONA**
sun, pert. to .... **SOLAR**
sun porches .... **SOLARIA**
sun tree, Jap. .... **HINOKI**

sunbaked building
    DOBE, DOBY, ADOBE, DOBIE
Sunday of Lent, 4th .. **LAETARE**
sunder
    PART, REND, SPLIT, DIVIDE
sundial, style of ..... **GNOMON**
sunfish .... **BREAM**
sunfish genus .... **MOLA**
sunken fence .... **AHA, HAHA**
sunset, occurring at **ACRONICAL**
sunspot center
    UMBRA, UMBRAE
supercilious person ..... **SNOB**
superfluous: Fr. ...... **DE TROP**
superintendent, office
    MANAGER
superior, most .... **BEST, TOPS**
superior quality: Fr. .... **LUXE**
superiority, belief in .. **RACISM**
superlative, absolute .. **ELATIVE**
superlative ending ...... **EST**
supernatural .... **OCCULT**
supernatural being, Melanesia
    ADARO
supernatural power, E. Afr. **NGAI**
supernatural power, Polyn.
    MANA
superscribe .... **DIRECT**
superstition, object of
    FETICH, FETISH
supper .... **TEA**
supplication, make ..... **PRAY**
supply .... **STOCK, ENDUE**
supply, fresh .... **RELAY**
supply of horses ...... **REMUDA**
support ...... **LEG, RIB, ABET,**
    BACK, PROP, BRACE
support, one-legged .. **UNIPOD**
suppose ... **ASSUME, IMAGINE**
suppose: archaic .... **TROW**
suppress ...... **ELIDE, QUASH**
Supreme Being, Hebrew . **IHVH,**
    JHVH, JHWH, YHVH, YHWH
surety agreement ...... **BOND**
surf, roar of .... **ROTE**
surface, attractive ... **VENEER**
surface of gem .... **FACET**
surface of a tool .... **FACE**
surfeit .... **CLCY, GLUT, SATE**
surfeited .... **BLASE**
surge .... **TIDE, BILLOW**
surgeon's instrument .. **TREPAN,**
    TROCAR, ABLATOR, LE-
    VATOR, SCALPEL
surgical thread .... **SETON**
Surinam toad .... **PIPA**
surly .... **GRUFF, SULLEN**
surmise .. **INFER, GUESS, OPINE**
surnamed: Fr. .... **DIT**

a surpass ...... **CAP, TOP, BEST**
surplice, chorister's .... **COTTA**
surplus .... **EXTRA, EXCESS**
surrender
      CEDE, YIELD, DEDITION
surrender: law .... **REMISE**
surround **GIRD, BESET, INARM**
surrounding area ...... **ZONE**
surtout .... **COAT**
survey .... **MAP, POLL**
surveyor's assistant .. **RODMAN**
surveyor's instrument
      ROD, ALIDADE
surveyor's rod, sight on **TARGET**
Susa inhabitant ..... **ELAMITE**
suspend .... **HANG**
suspenders .... **BRACES**
suture .... **SEAM**
svelte .... **SLIM, TRIM**
swab .... **MOP**
swain .... **LOVER**
swallow **BOLT, GULP, MARTIN**
swallow, sea .... **TERN**
swamp ..... **BOG, FEN, MARSH,**
    MORASS, SLEW, SLOO, SLUE
swamp gas .. **MIASM, MIASMA**
swamp, S. Afr. ... **VLEI, VLEY**
swampy belt, India ..... **TERAI**
swan, female .... **PEN**
swan genus .... **OLOR**

b swan, male .... **COB**
swan, whistling .... **OLOR**
swap .... **TRADE**
sward .... **SOD, TURF**
swarm .... **NEST, HORDE**
swarthy .... **DUN, DARK**
swastika .... **FYLFOT**
sway .... **ROCK, ROLL**
swear .... **AVER, CURSE**
sweat ...... **SUDOR, PERSPIRE**
SWEDISH .... see also SPECIAL
   SECTION—SWEDEN
Swedish:
    beer .... **OL**
    tea .... **TE**
    toe .... **TA**
    you .... **ER**
Swedish coin .... **ORE**
Swedish county, district .. **LAN**
Swedish explorer ...... **HEDIN**
Swedish order of merit .. **VASA**
Swedish royal guard **DRABANT**
Swedish sculptor ...... **MILLES**
sweep, scythe's ...... **SWATH**
sweet flag .. **SEDGE, CALAMUS**
sweet gale .... **GAGL**
sweet liquid .... **NECTAR**
sweet potato
   YAM, BATATA, OCARINA
sweet potato: Sp. .... **CAMOTE**

c sweet red wine .... **ALICANTE**
sweet-smelling
    OLENT, REDOLENT
sweet spire .... **ITEA**
sweetfish .... **AYU**
sweetheart: Ir. .... **GRA**
sweetheart: Scot. .... **JO**
sweetmeat: Fr. .... **DRAGEE**
sweetsop .... **ATA,**
   ATES, ATTA, ANNONA
swell .... **DILATE**
swell of water .... **WAVE**
swelling **LUMP, NODE, EDEMA**
swelling on plants ..... **GALL**
swerve .... **SHY, SKEW**
swift .... **FAST, FLEET**
swift, common .... **CRAN**
swift horse .. **ARAB, PACOLET**
swiftly, run .... **DART, SCUD**
swimming .... **NATANT**
swimming bell .. **NECTOPHORE**
swindle **GIP, GYP, DUPE, SWIZ**
swindler .... **COZENER**
swine .. **HOG, PIG, SOW, BOAR**
swine, feeding of ... **PANNAGE**
swine fever .... **ROUGET**
swine genus .... **SUS**
swing music .... **JIVE**
swing musician ...... **HEPCAT**

d swinish .... **PORCINE**
swipe .... **GLOM**
swirl .... **EDDY, GURGE**
SWISS .. see also SPECIAL SEC-
   TION—SWITZERLAND
Swiss capital ... **BERN, BERNE**
Swiss card game .... **JASS**
Swiss critic .... **AMIEL**
Swiss patriot .... **TELL**
Swiss state .... **CANTON**
switch .... **TOGGLE**
swollen .... **TURGID**
swoon .... **FAINT**
swoon: old Eng. .... **SWEB**
sword ... **PATA, EPEE, BLADE,**
   SABER, SABRE, RAPIER
sword, Arthur's
   EXCALIBAR, EXCALIBUR
sword, curved .. **SABER, SABRE**
sword, fencing .... **EPEE**
sword, matador's ... **ESTOQUE**
sword, medieval .... **ESTOC**
sword, Norse myth. ... **GRAM**
sword, put away ... **SHEATHE**
sword, St. George's
   ASCALON, ASKELON
sword-shaped .... **ENSATE**
sword, Siegfried's ..... **GRAM**
sword, slender .... **RAPIER**
swordsman's dummy stake **PEL**
syllable, last .... **ULTIMA**

a syllable, scale .... **DO, FA, LA,**
 MI, RE, SO, TI, SOL
syllable, short .. **MORA, MORAE**
sylvan deity **PAN, FAUN, SATYR**
SYMBOL, CHEMICAL .... see
 SPECIAL SECTION
symbol .... **TOKEN**
symbol of authority ... **MACE**
symbol of Crusaders ... **CROSS**
symbol of protection .... **EGIS**
sympathizer: suffix ...... **ITE**
synagogue .... **SHUL, TEMPLE**
syncopated music ...... **RAG**
syncope ...... **FAINT, SWOON**
synod, Russian .... **SOBOR**
syntax, give the .... **PARSE**

c synthetic fabric or fiber **NYLON,**
 ORLON, RAYON, DACRON
synthetic rubber
 BUNA, ELASTOMER
Syria, ancient .... **ARAM**
Syrian, ancient port ... **SIDON**
Syrian bear .... **DUBB**
Syrian bishop's title .... **ABBA**
Syrian city, old ...... **ALEPPO**
system .... **ISM**
system of rule ...... **REGIME**
system of rules .... **CODE**
system of weights ..... **TROY**
system of worship ...... **CULT**
systematic regulation ... **CODE**

T

b

T-shaped .... **TAU**
tab .... **FLAP, LABEL**
tabard .... **CAPE**
table mountain, Abyssin. **AMBA**
tableland .... **MESA**
tablet .... **PAD, SLATE**
taboo, opposite of .... **NOA**
tabor, Moorish
 ATABAL, ATTABAL
Tacoma's Sound ...... **PUGET**
tack: naut. .... **BUSK**
tact .... **FINESSE**
tackle, anchor .... **CAT**
tael, part of .... **LI**
tag .... **LABEL**
tag, metal .... **AGLET, AIGLET**
Tagalog for river .... **ILOG**
Tahitian national god ... **ORO**
Tai race branch .... **LAO**
tail, of ... **CAUDAL, CAUDATE**
tail of coin .... **VERSO**
tail, rabbit's .... **SCUT**
tail: zool. .... **CAUDA**
tailor .... **SARTOR**
Taino fetish ..... **ZEME, ZEMI**
Taj Mahal site .... **AGRA**
take away by force ... **REAVE**
take away: law .... **ADEEM**
take back .... **RECANT**
take effect again ..... **REVEST**
take off .... **DOFF**
take one's ease .... **REST**
take on cargo ... **LADE, LOAD**
take out **DELE, ELIDE, EXPUNGE**
take part .... **SIDE**
take up again ...... **RESUME**
take up weapons .... **ARM**
tale .... **SAGA, YARN, STORY**
tale, medieval Fr. .... **LAI**

d

tale, Norse .... **SAGA**
"Tale of Two Cities" girl **LUCIE**
"Tales of a Wayside —" .. **INN**
talent .... **FLAIR**
talented .... **SMART**
talisman .... **CHARM**
talisman, Afr. .... **GRIGRI**
talk .... **GAB, GAS, CHAT,**
 PRATE, PALAVER
talk: slang .... **YAK**
talk freely .... **DESCANT**
talk pompously
 ORATE, HARANGUE
talk, rambling ... **RIGMAROLE**
talk wildly ..... **RANT, RAVE**
Tallinn .... **REVAL**
tallow tree .... **CERA**
tally .... **SCORE**
Talmud commentary .. **GEMARA**
talon .... **CLAW, NAIL**
tamarack .... **LARCH**
tamarisk .... **ATLE**
tame, as hawks .... **MAN**
tan .... **BUFF, BEIGE**
tan skins .... **TAW**
tanager ...... **YENI, REDBIRD**
tanager, S. Am. **HABIA, LINDO**
tanbark .... **ROSS**
tangle ...... **SNARL, SLEAVE**
tangled mass ..... **MAT, SHAG**
tanning gum .... **KINO**
tanning, plant for ..... **ALDER**
tanning shrub **SUMAC, SUMACH**
tanning tree, India **AMLA, AMLI**
tantalize .... **TEASE**
Tantalus' daughter .... **NIOBE**
tantra .... **AGAMA**
tantrum .... **RAGE**
tap **PAT, COCK, SPIGOT, FAUCET**

a
tapering dagger ..... **ANLACE**
tapering piece .... **SHIM**
tapestry **ARRAS, TAPIS, DOSSER**
tapestry center .... **ARRAS**
tapeworm .... **TAENIA**
tapeworm larva ..... **MEASLE**
tapioca-like food ..... **SALEP**
tapioca source
    CASAVA, CASSAVA
tapir, S. Amer. ...... **DANTA**
Tapuyan .... **GE**
tarboosh .... **FEZ**
target .... **BUTT**
Tariff Act writer ..... **SMOOT**
Tarkington character .... **SAM**
tarnish .... **SPOT, SULLY**
taro ... **GABE, GABI, DASHEEN**
taro paste .... **POI**
taro root ... **EDO, EDDO, KALO**
tarpaulin .... **PAULIN**
tarpon .... **SABALO**
tarradiddle .... **FIB, LIE**
tarry .... **BIDE, WAIT,**
    STAY, LINGER
tarsus .... **ANKLE**
tarsus, insect .... **MANUS**
tart .... **ACID**
tartar, crude .. **ARGAL, ARGOL**
Tartini's B-flat .... **ZA**

b
task .... **DUTY, CHORE,**
    STENT, STINT
task, punishing ...... **PENSUM**
taste ...... **SIP, SUP, SAPOR,**
    SNACK, PALATE
tasteful .... **ELEGANT**
tasty .... **SAPID**
Tatar .... **HU**
Tatar dynasty, China .... **WEI**
Tatar tribe, W. Siberia .. **SHOR**
tattle .... **BLAB**
tattler, idle .... **GOSSIP**
Tattler publisher ...... **STEELE**
tau cross .... **ANKH**
taunt ..... **JEER, MOCK, TWIT**
taut .... **TENSE**
taut, pull .... **STRETCH**
tavern .... **INN**
tax .. **CESS, GELD, LEVY, SCOT,**
    SESS, STENT, ASSESS, EX-
    CISE, IMPOST
tax, church .... **TITHE**
tea .... **CHA, CHAA**
tea, black
    PECO, BOHEA, PEKOE
tea bowl .... **CHAWAN**
tea box
    CADDY, CALIN, CANISTER
tea, China .... **BOHEA**
tea, Chin. green ...... **HYSON**

c
tea genus .... **THEA**
tea-growing region ... **ASSAM**
tea, kind of
    OOPAK, OOLONG, OOPACK
tea, Labrador .... **LEDUM**
tea, marsh .... **LEDUM**
tea, medicinal **PTISAN, TISANE**
tea, oriental .... **CHA**
tea, Paraguay .. **MATE, YERBA**
tea, rolled .. **CHA, TCHA, TSIA**
tea tree .... **TI**
teacake .... **SCON, SCONE**
teacher .... **DOCENT, MENTOR**
teacher, Hebrew ...... **RABBI**
teacher, Islam religious
    ALIM, MOLLA, MULLA
teacher, Jewish .... **RAB, REB**
teacher, Moslem
    ALIM, MOLLA, MULLA
teacher, Xenophon's .**ISOCRATES**
teacher's association: abbr. **NEA**
team of horses .... **SPAN**
team, 3-horse ...... **RANDEM**
teamster's command **GEE, HAW**
tear .... **RIP, REND, RENT**
tear apart
    REND, TATTER, DIVULSE
tease .... **TWIT, BOTHER**
technical name: biol. ... **ONYM**
technique .... **ART**
tedious writer .... **PROSER**

d
teern .... **RAIN, POUR**
teeth, false ...... **DENTURES**
teeth, incrustation .. **TARTAR**
Telamon's son .... **AJAX**
telegraph inventor .... **MORSE**
telegraph key ...... **TAPPER**
telegraph signal ... **DOT, DASH**
telegraph, underwater .. **CABLE**
telegraphic speed unit .. **BAUD**
telephone exchange **CENTRAL**
telephone inventor ..... **BELL**
telephone wire .... **LINE**
telescope part .... **LENS**
television .... **VIDEO**
television broadcast **TELECAST**
television cable .... **COAXIAL**
television recording **KINESCOPE**
television tube
    MONOSCOPE, ICONSCOPE
tell **IMPART, RELATE, NARRATE**
tell in detail .... **RECOUNT**
Tell, site of legend ...... **URI**
telling blow ...... **COUP, ONER**
temper .... **ANNEAL**
temper, fit of .... **PET**
temperament: Ger. .... **GEMUT**
"Tempest" sprite ..... **ARIEL**
"Tempest" slave ... **CALIBAN**
temple .. **FANE, RATH, RATHA**
temple, Asian .... **PAGODA**

a

temple chamber, Gr. ... **NAOS**
temple, inner part ..... **CELLA**
temple: Siam. .... **VAT, WAT**
temple tower, India .. **SHIKARA**
tempo: music .... **TAKT**
temporary decline ..... **SLUMP**
temporary fashion .... **FAD**
temporary relief ... **REPRIEVE**
tempt .... **LURE, TOLE**
temptation .... **ALLURE**
ten .... **DECAD**
ten ares .... **DECARE**
Ten Commandments
   DECALOG, DECALOGUE
"Ten Days that Shook the
   World" author ..... **REED**
ten million ergs .... **JOULE**
tenant .... **LESSEE**
tenant, early Ir. .... **SAER**
tend .... **SERVE**
tender .... **SOFT, OFFER**
tending toward .... **FOR**
tendril: bot. .... **CAPREOL**
tennis score .... **LOVE, DEUCE**
tennis shoe .... **SNEAKER**
tennis stroke **ACE, LOB, LOBB**
tennis term .... **LET**
Tennyson character .... **ENID,**
    ARDEN

b

Tennyson heroine
   ELAIN, ELAINE
Tennyson sailor ...... **ENOCH**
tenon .... **COG**
tenonlike piece .. **COAG, COAK**
tenor, famous ..... **MELCHIOR**
tense .... **TAUT**
tent dweller
   KEDAR, SCENITE
tent dwelling Arabs ... **KEDAR**
tent flap .... **FLY**
tentmaker, the .... **OMAR**
tents .... **CAMP**
tentacle .... **FEELER**
tenth part .... **DECI, TITHE**
tepid .... **WARM**
Tereus' son .... **ITYS**
term .... **NAME**
term .... **SESSION**
term: algebra .... **NOME**
TERM, GEOMETRY ...... see
   GEOMETRY, GEOMETRIC
term in office .... **TENURE**
term, math. .... **SINE, COSINE**
term of address .... **SIR, SIRE,**
    MADAM
termagant .... **SHREW**
terminable .... **ENDABLE**
termite, P. I. .... **ANAI, ANAY**
tern .... **SKIRR**

c

tern, black .... **DARR**
tern genus .... **STERNA**
tern, Hawaii .... **NOIO**
terpene alcohol .... **NEROL**
terpene compound . **TEREBENE**
terrapin .... **EMYD,**
   POTTER, SLIDER
terrapin, red-bellied
   POTTER, SLIDER
terrestrial .... **GEAL**
terrible .... **DIRE**
terrier, kind of .. **SKYE, CAIRN**
terrier, Scottish breed of . **SKYE**
terrified .... **AFRAID**
territorial division .... **AMT**
territory .... **LAND, SOIL**
territory, additional
   LEBENSRAUM
territory, enclosed .. **ENCLAVE**
terror .... **PANIC**
terrorist .... **GOON**
tessellated .... **MOSAIC**
tessera .... **TILE**
test .... **ASSAY, TEMPT,**
   TRIAL, EXAMINE
test ground .... **BOSE**
testament .... **WILL**
testifier .... **DEPONENT**
testify ...... **DEPONE, DEPOSE**

d

tetrachord, upper tone of .**NETE**
Teutonic, ancient ...... **GOTH**
Teutonic barbarian ..... **GOTH**
Teutonic deity .... **ER**
Teut. Fate ...... **NORN, URTH**
TEUTONIC GODS, GODDESSES,
   DEITY see **NORSE SPECIAL**
   SECTION
Teut. legendary hero ... **OFFA**
Teut. letter of alphabet . **RUNE**
Teut. people .... **GEPIDAE**
Teut. sea goddess ...... **RAN**
Teut. sky god .. **TY, TIU, TIW,**
   TYR, ZIO, ZIU, TYRR
Texas shrine .... **ALAMO**
textile screw pine
   ARA, PANDAN
texture .... **WALE,**
   WOOF, GRAIN
Thailand .... **SIAM**
Thames estuary .... **NORE**
than: Ger. .... **ALS**
than: Scot. .... **NA**
thankless person .... **INGRATE**
that is: abbr. ...... **E.G., I.E.**
that not .... **LEST**
that one: Lat. .... **ILLE**

a

that which follows .... SEQUEL
thatch, grass to .... NETI
thatching palm .... NIPA
the: Ger. .... DAS, DER
"The Ballad of Reading —"
GAOL
"The Jairite" .... IRA
"The Lion of God" .... ALI
"The Red" .... ERIC
the same: Lat. .... IDEM
the squint .... SKEN
theatre ...... ODEA, ODEON,
ODEUM, STAGE
theatre box seat .... LOGE
theatre district ...... RIALTO
theatre floor .... PIT
theatre, Grecian ...... ODEA,
ODEON, ODEUM
theatre group .... ANTA
theatre, part of Greek . SKENE,
SCENA, SCENAE, SKENAI
theatre sign .... SRO
"Theban Bard" ...... PINDAR
Thebes deity ... AMEN, AMON,
AMUN, MENT, AMENT, MENTU
Thebes, king of
CREON, OEDIPUS
theme .... MOTIF
theme: music .... TEMA
then .... ANON

b

then: music .... POI
theoretical .... PLATONIC
there: Fr. .... VOILA
therefore .... ERGO
theseli veil .... TEMPE
Theseus' father ..... AEGEUS
thesis, opp. of .... ARSIS
thespian .... ACTOR
Thessaly, king of .... AEOLUS
Thessaly mountain ...... OSSA
Thessaly valley .... TEMPE
they: Fr. .... ILS
thick-lipped .... LABROSE
thicket .. BOSK, SHAW, COPSE,
COPPICE, SPINNEY
thicket: dialect .... RONE
thicket, game .... COVERT
thickness .... PLY
thief, gypsy .... CHOR
thief: Yiddish .... GANEF,
GANOF, GONOF
thigh bone .... FEMUR
thigh, of the .... FEMORAL
thin ...... LANK, LEAN, RARE,
SHEER, DILUTE, PAPERY,
SPARSE, TENUOUS
thin cake .... WAFER
thin: comb. form .... SERO
thin disk .... WAFER
thin layer .... FILM

c

"Thin Man" dog ...... ASTA
"Thin Man" wife .... NORA
thin-toned .... REEDY
thin out .... ATTENUATE
thing: law (Latin) .... RES
things added ...... ADDENDA
things done .... ACTA
things to be done
AGENDA, AGENDUM
think ... DEEM, TROW, OPINE
think: archaic .... WIS
think (over) .... MULL, MUSE
third: comb. form .... TRIT
third day, every .... TERTIAN
third king of Judah ...... ASA
third: music .... TIERCE
Third Reich special police: abbr.
SS
thirst-tortured king: Gr. myth
TANTALUS
thirsty .... DRY, ADRY
thirty: Fr. .... TRENTE
thirty, series of .... TRENTAL
this: Fr. .... CE
this: Sp. .... ESTA, ESTE
this one: Lat. ...... HIC, HAEC
thither .... THERE
Thomas Hardy heroine ... TESS
thong .... STRAP
thong, braided .... ROMAL
thong-shaped .... LORATE

d

thong, S. Afr. .... RIEM
Thor's stepson ..... ULL, ULLR
Thor's wife .... SIF
thorax, crustacean's . PEREION
thorn ... BRIAR, BRIER, SPINE
thorn apple .... METEL
thorn, bearing a ..... SPINATE
thornback ray .. DORN, ROKER
Thorne Smith character. TOPPER
thorny plant ... BRIAR, BRIER
thorny shrub .... NABK, NUBK
thoroughfare ...... WAY, ROAD,
AVENUE, STREET
thoroughgoing ...... ARRANT
those .... YON, YOND
those in power or office ... INS
thou: Fr. .... TU
thought .... IDEA
thought: comb. form .... IDEO
thoughts, form .... IDEATE
thousand .... MIL
thousand: comb. form . MILLE
Thrace, ancient people of EDONI
thrall .... ESNE, SLAVE
thrash .... LAM, BEAT
thread: comb. form .... NEMA
thread, cotton .... LISLE
thread, guiding ball of .. CLEW
thread-like .... NEMALINE
thread-like process ..... HAIR

a thread-like structure ... **FILUM**
thread, of a .... **FILAR**
threads, cross .... **RETICLE**
threads crossed by woof . **WARP**
threads crossing warp
WEFT, WOOF
threads, lengthwise .... **WARP**
threaded fastener .... **NUT**
threaten ... **IMPEND, MENACE**
three ...... **TER, TRIO, TRIAD**
three: Ger. .... **DREI**
three: Ital. .... **TRE**
three-legged stand
TRIPOD, TRIVET
three-masted ship
XEBEC, FRIGATE
3 parts, divided into: Her.
TIERCE
3.1416 .... **PI**
three: Sp. .... **TRES**
three-spot .... **TREY**
threefold .... **TRINE, TREBLE,
TERNARY, TERNATE**
threefold: comb. form .... **TER**
threshold .... **SILL**
threshold, psychology ... **LIMEN**
thrice: music .... **TER**
thrifty ..... **FRUGAL, SAVING**
thrive ..... **BATTEN, PROSPER**
b throat ...... **GORGE, GULLET**
throat: Lat. .... **GULA**
throat, pert. to .... **GULAR**
throb .. **BEAT, PULSE, PULSATE**
throe .... **PANG**
throng .. **MOB, HORDE, SWARM**
through .... **PER**
through: prefix .... **DIA**
throw .... **CAST, PITCH**
throw aside .... **FLING**
throw back .... **REPEL**
thrush ...... **VEERY, MISSEL**
thrush, Hawaiian ..... **OMAO**
thrush, India .... **SHAMA**
thrush, missel . **MAVIE, MAVIS**
thrust .... **LUNGE**
thrust back .... **REPEL**
thrust down .... **DETRUDE**
thunderfish .... **RAAD**
thurible .... **CENSER**
Thuringian city .... **JENA**
Thursday, source of name.**THOR**
thus .... **SO, SIC**
thus far .... **YET**
thwart .... **FOIL**
Tiber tributary .... **NERA**
Tibetan chief .... **POMBO**
Tibetan ox .... **YAK**
Tibetan priest .... **LAMA**
Tibetan tribe .... **CHAMPA**

c tibia .... **CNEMIS**
Tichborne Claimant ... **ORTON**
tick .... **ACARID**
tick genus .... **ARGAS**
tick, S. Amer. ..... **CARAPATO**
tickets, sell illegally ... **SCALP**
tickle .... **TITILLATE**
Ticonderoga's commander **GATES**
tidal flood ...... **BORE, EAGRE**
tidal wave, flow or bore.**EAGRE**
tidbit .... **CATE**
tide, lowest high .... **NEAP**
tidings .... **NEWS, WORD**
tidings, glad .... **GOSPEL,
EVANGEL, EVANGILE**
tidy ...... **NEAT, REDO, TRIM**
tie ...... **BIND, BOND, LASH,
TRUSS, CRAVAT**
tie, kind of .... **ASCOT**
tie-breaking game ... **RUBBER**
tie off .... **LIGATE**
tie, railroad .... **SLEEPER**
tier .... **ROW**
tiger cat, S. Amer. ..... **CHATI**
tiger, Persian ..... **SHER, SHIR**
tight ... **SNUG, TAUT, TENSE**
tight place .. **FIX, JAM, MESS**
tighten: naut. .... **FRAP**
tightly stretched .... **TENSE**
til .... **SESAME**
d tile, hexagonal .... **FAVI**
tile, roofing .... **PANTILE**
tilelike .... **TEGULAR**
till the earth .... **FARM, PLOW**
tilled land ... **ARADA, ARADO**
tiller .... **HELM**
tilt .... **TIP, CANT, LIST**
tilt .... **JOUST**
tilting: naut. .... **ALIST**
timber bend .... **SNY**
timber, flooring ...... **BATTEN**
timber, nautical .... **KEVEL**
timber, pine: Asia .... **MATSU**
timber rot .... **DOAT, DOTE**
timber truck .... **WYNN**
timber wolf .... **LOBO**
timbrel ..... **TABOR, TABOUR**
time .... **ERA, TEMPI, TEMPO**
time before .... **EVE**
time being .... **NONCE**
time gone by .... **PAST**
time out .... **RECESS**
time, space of .... **WHILE**
time value, equalling in
DIMORIC
times, old .... **ELD, YORE**
timetable .... **SCHEDULE**
timid .... **SHY, PAVID**
timorous .... **TREPID**
timothy .... **HAY**
Timothy's mother: Bib. ... **LOIS**

tin .... CAN, STANNUM
tin, containing .... STANNOUS
tin foil .... TAIN
tin plate .... TAIN
tin roofing .... TERNE
tinamou Her. ..... OR, GULES,
    VERT, AZURE, SABLE,
    ARGENT, PURPURE
tinder .... PUNK, AMADOU
tine .... PRONG
tine of antler .... SNAG
tinge .... TAINT
tinge deeply .... IMBUE
tingle of feeling .... THRILL
tinkle .... TING
tiny bird, W. Ind. ...... TODY
tip .... END, FEE, APEX, KNAP
tip .... CANT, LEAN,
    TILT, CAREEN
tipping .... ALIST, ATILT
tiptoe, on .... ATIP
tire .... FAG, JADE
tire casing .... SHOE
tire, face of .... TREAD
tire support .... RIM
tissue .... TELA
tissue, of a .... TELAR
tissue, pert. to .... TELAR
TITAN . see SPECIAL SECTION,
    GREEK MYTH page 200
Titania's husband .... OBERON
titanic iron-ore sand . ISERENE
titlark .... PIPIT
title ..... EARL, NAME, TERM
title, baronet's .... SIR
title, Benedictine .... DOM
title, church .... PRIMATE
title, East .... COJA, HOJA
title, Ethiopian .... RAS
title Hindu gives Moslem
    MIAN
title, India .... AYA, NAWAB,
    SAHEB, SAHIB
title, Jewish . RAB, REB, RABBI
title, knight's .... SIR
title, king's .... SIRE
title, lady's ... DAME, MADAM
title, Moslem .... AGA, ALI,
    MOLLA, MULLA,
    SHERIF, SHEREFF
title of address .. MME., MRS.,
    SIR, MAAM, MADAM
title of honor, Moslem . SAYID,
    SAIYID, SAYYID
title of kings of Edessa . ABGAR
title of respect ..... SIR, SIRE,
    MADAME
title of respect, Afr. ..... SIDI

title of respect, India .... SRI,
    SHRI, SAHIB, SHREE,
    HUZOOR
title of respect, Malay .. TUAN
title, Oriental .... BABA
title, Persian MIR, AZAM, KHAN
title, Spanish DOM, DON, SENOR
title to property or land . DEED
title, Turkish .. PACHA, PASHA
titleholder .... TITLIST
titmice, genus of ...... PARUS
titmouse .... MAG, PARUS
tittle .... JOT, IOTA, WHIT
Titus Andronicus' daughter
    LAVINIA
Tiwaz .... ER, TIU
to .... FOR, UNTO
to: prefix .... AP
to: Scot. .... TAE
to be: Fr. .... ETRE
to be: Lat. .... ESSE
"to be," part of ...... AM, IS,
    ARE, WAS
to go: Fr. .... ALLER
to love: Fr. .... AIMER
to the point that ...... UNTIL
to use: Lat. .... UTOR
toad genus .... BUFO
toad, huge .... AGUA
toad, order of .... ANURA
toad, tree genus .... HYLA
toadfish .... SAPO
toast, bit of .... SIPPET
toasting word .... SALUD,
    SKOAL, PROSIT
tobacco ash . DOTTEL, DOTTLE
tobacco, chewing .... QUID
tobacco, coarse
    SHAG, CAPORAL
tobacco, Cuban .... CAPA
tobacco, low grade ...... SHAG
tobacco, Peru .... SANA
tobacco, roll .... CIGAR
toddy palm juice ...... SURA
toe .... DIGIT
toe, fifth .... MINIMUS
toe: Scot. .... TAE
togs .... DUDS
toilet case .... ETUI
Tokyo Bay city .... CHIBI
Tokyo, old name ... EDO, YEDO
tolerable .... SOSO
toll .... FEE, KNELL
Tolstoi heroine .... ANNA
tomb, Moslem TABUT, TABOOT
tomboy .... HOIDEN, HOYDEN
tomcat .... GIB
tone down .... SOFTEN
tone, lack of .... ATONY
tone, of .... TONAL
tone quality .... TIMBRE

tone: Scot. .... TEAN
tones, series of ...... OCTAVE
tongue, gypsy .... CHIB
tongue of Agni .... KALI
tongue, pert. to ..... GLOSSAL
tongue, using the ..... APICAL
tongue, wagon .... NEAP
tonic .... ROBORANT
tonic, dried India
      CHIRATA, CHIRETTA
tonic herb ...... ALOE, TANSY
Tonkin native .... THO
too early .... PREMATURE
too much: Fr. .... TROP
tool, boring .... AWL, BIT,
      AUGER, GIMLET
tool, cutting .. AX, ADZ, AXE,
  HOB, SAW, SAX, SYE, ADZE
tool, engraver's
      BURIN, MATTOIR
tool, enlarging ...... REAMER
tool, grass-cutting .... SITHE,
     SCYTHE, SICKLE
tool, machine .... LATHE
tool, molding .... DIE
tool, pointed .... BROACH
tool, post hole digging .... LOY
tool shaper .... SWAGER
tool, splitting .... FROE, FROW
tool, stone, prehistoric
     CELT, EOLITH
tool, threading ...... CHASER
tool's biting edge .... BIT
tooth ..... COG, TINE, MOLAR,
   CANINE, CUSPID, FANG
tooth-billed pigeon ... DODLET
tooth, canine .... CUSPID
tooth: comb. form .... ODONT
tooth, gear .... COG
tooth: Lat. .... DENS
tooth-like ornament .. DENTIL
tooth, long FANG, TUSH, TUSK
tooth pulp .... NERVE
toothed formation ..... SERRA
toothed margin, having
     DENTATE
toothed wheel .... GEAR
toothless .... EDENTATE
toothless mammals . EDENTATA
top .... APEX, CAP, LID
top-notch .... AONE
top ornament ..... EPI, FINIAL
topaz humming bird ..... AVA
topee material .... SOLA
toper .... SOT, SOUSE
topic .... THEME
topmast crossbar support .. FID
topsail .... RAFFE
torment .... BAIT, ANNOY,
    DEVIL, HARRY, TEASE
torn: archaic .... REFT

torn place .... RENT
torrid region or zone .. TROPIC
tortoise .... GALAPAGO
tortoise, fresh water .... EMYD
tortoise, marsh genus ... EMYS
tortoise, order of ... CHELONIA
torturer .... RACKER
"Tosca" villain ...... SCARPIA
toss ...... CAST, FLIP, HURL,
     FLING, PITCH
tosspot ... . SOT
total ...... ADD, SUM, UTTER
total abstinence .. NEPHALISM
totalitarian ruler ... DICTATOR
totem pole .... XAT
toucan .... TOCO
toucan, S. Am. .... ARACARI
touch .... ABUT
touch lightly .... PAT
touch, organ of .... PALP
touch, pert. to HAPTIC, TACTIC,
    TACTILE, TACTUAL
touch sense, pert. to .. HAPTIC
touchwood .... PUNK
tough .... WIRY, HARDY,
    ROWDY, CHEWY
tour: It. .... GIRO
tourmaline, colorless
     ACHROITE
tow .... PULL, DRAW
towai .... KAMAHI
toward: Lat. .... AD
toward stern ..... AFT, ABAFF,
    ABAFT, ASTERN
towel .... WIPER
towel fabric .... HUCK, TERRY
tower, Bibl. .... BABEL
tower, India .... MINAR
tower, little .... TURRET
tower, mosque, slender
     MINARET
towering .... STEEP
towhead .... BLOND, BLONDE
town, Arcadia ancient ... ALEA
town: Cornish prefix ..... TRE
town: Dutch .... STAD
town: Ger. .... STADT
town, India pilgrimage . SORON
town: It. .... CASAL, CASALE
town: Jap. .... MACHI
town: suffix .... TON
township, ancient Attica . DEME
townsman .... CIT
toxic protein .... ABRIN
toy with .... TRIFLE
trace .... TINGE, VESTIGE
track .... TRACE
track, animal ... RUN, SLOT,
    SPUR, SPOOR
track circuit .... LAP

a track of ship .... WAKE
track, deer's .... SLOT
track, otter's .... SPUR, SPOOR
track, put off .... DERAIL
track, put on another
  SHUNT, SWITCH
tracker, India .... PUGGI
tract .... LOT, AREA
tract of farm land ...... FIELD
trade .... SWAP, SWOP
  BARTER, TRAFFIC
trade .... METIER
trade agreement ..... CARTEL
trader ..... DEALER, MONGER
trader selling to soldiers
  SUTLER
trading exchange .... PIT
trading vessel of Ceylon
  DONI, DHONI
traditional story .... SAGA
traduce .... SLUR, DEFAME
traffic .... TRADE
trail .... SLOT, SPOOR, TRACK
train of attendants
  SUITE, RETINUE
train, overhead .... EL
train, slow, many-stops . LOCAL
tramp .... BO, HOBO
trample .... TREAD
tranquil or tranquilize

b   SERENE, SOOTHE
transaction ...... DEAL, SALE
transfer .... CEDE
transfer, property
  DEED, GRANT
transfer, sovereignty .. DEMISE
transferer, property .. ALIENOR
transform .... CONVERT
transgress .... ERR, SIN
transit coach .... BUS
"— transit gloria mundi" . SIC
translator of Freud, Amer.
  BRILL
transmit .... SEND
transom .... TRAVE
transpire .... OCCUR, HAPPEN,
  DEVELOP
transverse pin .... TOGGLE
trap .... SNARE, ENSNARE
trap door .... DROP
trap, mouse: dial. .... TIPE
trap, rabbit: dial. ...... TIPE
trappings .... REGALIA
travel .... TREK
traveler .... PASSENGER
tray .... SALVER, SERVER
tread softly ...... PAD, SNEAK
treasure .... ROON, TROVE
treasurer, college ..... BURSAR
treasury agents .... TMEN
treat .... USE

c   treat with acid ..... ACIDIZE
treat with malice .... SPITE
treatment .... USE
tree   (3 letters) ASH, ELM,
  FIR, LIN, OAK, YEW;
  (4 letters) AKEE, AMLA,
  AMLI, ANAM, ANDA,
  ARAR, ASAK, AULU, AUSU,
  AUZU, BARU, BIJA, BITO,
  BIWA, BOBO, BOGO, DALI,
  DILO, DOON, DOUM, DUKU,
  EBOE, EJOO, GOAI, GUAO,
  HINO, IFIL, IPIL, KINO,
  KIRI, KOPI, KOZO, LIME,
  LINN, MAKO, MYXA,
  NAIO, NEEM, NIOG, NIPA,
  ODUM, OHIA, PALM, PELU,
  PINE, PUKA, RATA, RIMU,
  ROKA, SAUL, SHEA, SUPA,
  TALA, TARA, TAWA, TEAK,
  TEIL, TEYL, TOON, TORO,
  TUNG, TUNO, TUWI, UPAS,
  WHAU, YATE, YAYA, YPIL;
  (5 letters) ASPEN; (6 let-
  ters) LINDEN
tree, African .... AKEE, BAKU,
  COLA, KOLA, ROKA,
  SHEA, AEGLE, ARTAR
d   tree, Afr. & Asia .... SIRIS
tree, Afr. gum .... BUMBO
tree, Afr. tallow .... ROKA
TREE, AMER. TROPICAL...see
  TREE, TROPICAL AMER.
tree, Argentine timber ... TALA
TREE, ASIATIC .. see ASIATIC
  TREE
tree, arrow poison ...... UPAS
TREE, AUSTRAL. .... see
  AUSTRAL. TREE
tree, Bengal quince ...... BEL
tree, black gum ...... TUPELO
tree, body of .... TRUNK
tree, boxwood yielding . SERON
tree, buckwheat .... TITI
tree, butter .... SHEA
tree, caucho-yielding ..... ULE
tree, chicle .... SAPOTA
tree, Chin. ... GINKO, GINKGO
tree clump, prairie .... MOTTE
tree cobra .... MAMBA
tree, coniferous (cone) .. FIR,
  YEW, PINE, LARCH
TREE. E. IND. ... see E. IND.
  TREE and TREE, IND.
TREE, EVERGREEN .... see
  EVERGREEN
tree, flowering ..... CATALPA
tree genus .... MABA
tree genus, Afr. .... OCHNA

a   tree genus, elms
          ULMUS, CELTIS
tree genus, small ... CATALPA
tree, gum .... ICICA
tree, hardwood ASH, OAK, IPIL
tree, India .... DAR, MEE, SAJ,
     SAL, AMLA, AMLI, DHAK,
     MYXA, NEEM, SHOQ, MA-
     HUA, BANYAN
tree knot .... BURL
tree, locust .... ACACIA
tree, maidenhair ..... GINKGO
tree, Malay .... TERAP
tree, Medit. .... CAROB
tree, mimosaceous ...... SIRIS
tree moss .... USNEA
tree, N. Am.
     TAMARAC, TAMARACK
TREE, N. Z.
     see NEW ZEALAND TREE
tree, oak .... ENCINA
tree of olive family ..... ASH
tree, Pacific .... KOU
tree, palm .. GRIGRI, GRUGRU
tree, palm, Asiatic .... ARENG
TREE, P.I. ..... see P. I. TREE
tree, pod .... CAROB
tree, resinous ...... FIR, PINE,
          BALSAM
tree, showy Asia .... ASAK
b   tree-snake .... LORA
tree, sun, Jap. .... HINOKI
tree, swamp .... ALDER
tree, tamarisk salt ...... ATLE
tree, tea .... TI
tree, thorny .... ACACIA
tree tiger .... LEOPARD
tree toad genus .... HYLA
tree, tropical .... EBOE, PALM,
     BALSA, MANGO, COLIMA,
     SAPOTA, LEBBEK
tree, tropical Amer. CEBA, DALI,
     GUAO, CEIBA, COLIMA,
     GUAMA, CEDRON
tree trunk .... BOLE
tree, W. Ind. .... GENIP,
          SAPOTE, LIBIDIBI
trees of a region .... SILVA
treeless plain .... PAMPAS,
          TUNDRA, STEPPES
tremble ...... QUAKE, DIDDER
trembling ..... ASPEN, TREPID
trench .... SAP
trench extension .... SAP
trench, rear wall of .. PARADOS
trend .... TENOR
trespass .. INFRINGE, INTRUDE

c   trespass for game .... POACH
trespass to recover goods
          TROVER
triad .... TRIO
trial .... TEST
triangle .... TRIGON, SCALENE
triangle, side of .... LEG
triangular insert .... GORE
tribal symbol .... TOTEM
TRIBE
     see also SPECIAL SECTION
tribe ...... CLAN, FOLK, RACE
TRIBE, BIBLICAL .... see
          SPECIAL SECTION
tribe: Bib. tent-dwellers.KEDAR
tribe division, Rom.
          CURIA, CURIAE
TRIBE, ISRAELITE .... see
          ISRAELITE TRIBE
TRIBESMAN .. see TRIBES in
     SPECIAL SECTION
tribulation .... TRIAL
tribunal .... BAR, FORUM
tribute .... SCAT, SCATT
tribute: Gaelic .... CAIN
trick FLAM, GAWD, JEST, RUSE,
     WILE, DODGE, FICELLE,
     STRATAGEM
tricks, game for no .... NULLO
tricks, win all .... CAPOT
d   Trieste measure .. ORNA, ORNE
trifle ...... TOY, DOIT, FICO,
     STRAW, NIGGLE, PALTER
trifling ...... SMALL, SLIGHT
trig .... NEAT, TRIM
trigonometry function
          SINE, COSINE
trigonometry line ..... SECANT
trill, bird's .... TIRALEE
trim .... NEAT, TRIG,
          ADORN, DECORATE
trimmed .... SNOD
trimming, dress . GIMP, RUCHE
trimmings, overlapping . FLOTS
Trinidad tree .... CYP
trinket .... GAUD
triple .... TRI, TREBLE
triplet .... TRIN
tripletail, P. R. .... SAMA
tripod, 6-footed .... CAT
Tripoli: measure . see page 188
"Tristram Shandy" author
          STERNE
Tristram's beloved ..... ISOLT,
     YSEUT, ISAUDE, ISAULT,
     ISEULT, ISOLDE, ISOLTA,
     ISOUDE, ISULTE
trite .. BANAL, CORNY, STALE
triton ...... EFT, EVET, NEWT

troche ...... PASTIL, ROTULA,
PASTILE, PASTILLE
TROJAN .... see also TROY
Trojan hero .. PARIS, ENEAS,
AENEAS, AGENOR, DARDAN,
HECTOR, HEKTOR, ACHILLES
trolley .... TRAM
troop-carrying group: abbr.
ATS
troop, division, Gr. .... TAXIS
troops .... MEN
troops, spread .... DEPLOY
trophy .... CUP
tropic .... SOLAR
tropical Am. bird genus
CACICUS
tropical disease . BUBA, BUBAS
tropical fever .... DENGUE
TROPICAL FRUIT .... see
FRUIT, TROPICAL
tropical plant .... TARO
tropical shrub genus INGA, SIDA
trot .... JOG, AMBLE
trouble ... ADO, AIL, WORRY,
EFFORT, MOLEST
troubles .... ILLS
troublesome person
PEST, AGITATOR
trough, inclined ...... CHUTE
trough, mining .... SLUICE
trout, British .. SEWEN, SEWIN
trout, brook .... CHAR
trowel, plasterers' .... DARBY
Troy .... ILION, ILIUM
Troy, founder of .... ILUS
Troy, land of .... TROAS
Troy, last king of ..... PARIS,
PRIAM, PRIAMOS
Troy, of ancient ILIAC, ILIAN
Troy: poetic .... ILIUM
truant, play: Scot. ..... TRONE
truck ...... LORRY, CAMION
trudge .... PACE, PLOD, SLOG
true copy: law .... ESTREAT
true olives .... OLEA
trumpet ..... HORN, CLARION
trumpet call, reveille .... DIAN
trumpet, mouth of .... CODON
trumpet shell .... TRITON
trumpeter perch .... MADO
trumpeter, pigeon-like . AGAMI
trundle, as ore .... RULL
trunk of body .... TORSO
trunkfish .... CHAPIN
truss up .... TIE
trust .... RELY, TROW,
RELIANCE
trustee of a wakf.MUTAWALLI
trusting .... RELIANT
truth: Chin. .... TAO

truth drug ...... PENTOTHAL
Truth personified .... UNA
try .... TEST, ESSAY, ATTEMPT
try to equal ... VIE, EMULATE
tsetse fly .... MAU, KIVU
tsetse fly genus .... GLOSSINA
tub .... VAT, KNAP, KNOP
tub, brewer's .... KEEVE
tub, broad .... KEELER
tub, wooden: dialect ...... SOE
tube .... DUCT
tube, glass ... PIPET, PIPETTE
tube, plane's .... PITOT
tuber delicacy ...... TRUFFLE
tuber, edible OCA, OKA, YAM,
TARO, POTATO
tuber, orchid .... SALEP
tuber, S. Amer. .... OCA, OKA
Tuesday, god who gave name to
TIU, TYR
tuft .... CREST
tuft: bot. .... COMA
tufted plant .... MOSS
tulip tree .... POPLAR
TUMERIC ..... see TURMERIC
tumor .... OMA, WEN
tumor, skin .... WEN
tumult .... RIOT
tune .... AIR, ARIA,
SONG, MELODY
tune, bagpipe .... PORT
tune: Scot. .... PORT
tungstite ..... OCHER, OCHRE
tuning fork ...... DIAPASON
Tunis, ruler of ...... BEY, DEY
tunnel, train, Alps .... CENIS
tunny .... AMIA, TUNA
turban, Oriental .... MANDIL
turbid, make .... ROIL
turf .... SOD
turf, bit of: golf ...... DIVOT
Turkestan town dwellers . SART
turkey buzzard .... AURA
turkey red .... MADDER
turkeys, collection of .. RAFTER
Turkic person TATAR, TARTAR
Turkic person, 8th century
OGOR
Turkish army corps ..... ORDU
Turkish army officer ..... AGA
Turkish caliph .... ALI
Turkish chamber .. ODA, ODAH
Turkish chieftain ...... AMIR,
ZAIM, AMEER
Turkish commander . AGA, ALI
Turkish copper coin .... PARA
Turkish decree .... IRADE
Turkish flag .... ALEM
Turkish general .... AGA
Turkish gold coin ...... LIRA,
ALTUN, MAHBUB

a Turkish government .... **PORTE**
Turkish govt. summer residence
YALI
Turkish governor .. **VALI, WALI**
Turkish hostelry ..... **IMARET**
Turkish judge .... **CADI, KADI**
Turkish leader .... **AGA**
Turkish liquor .... **MASTIC**
Turkish magistrate. **CADI, KADI**
Turkish military district . **ORDO**
Turkish money of account
ASPER
Turkish officer .. **AGA, AGHA**
Turkish oxcart . **ARBA, ARABA**
Turkish palace .... **SERAI**
Turkish pavilion .... **KIOSK**
Turkish president, former
INONU
Turkish regiment .... **ALAI**
Turkish standard . **ALEM, TOUG**
Turkish sultan .... **SELIM**
Turkish title .... **AGA, AGHA,**
BABA, EMIR, EMEER,
PASHA, BASHAW
Turkish tribesman ..... **TATAR**
Turkish tribesman, Persia
GHUZ
Turkoman tribesman **SEID, SHIK**
turmeric .... **REA, ANGO**
b turmoil .... **WELTER**
turn ..... **BEND, GYRE, VEER,**
ROTATE, SWERVE
turn aside. **SKEW, VEER, SHUNT**
turn back to .... **REVERT**
turn direction .... **VERT**
turn inside out .... **EVERT**
turn over: mus. .... **VERTE**
turning point ... **CRISES, CRISIS**
turning: prefix .... **ROTO**
turnover .... **PIE**
turnip ... **BAGA, NEEP, SWEDE**
turnip: Scot. .... **NEEP**
turpentine derivative
ROSIN, PINENE
turpentine distillate .... **ROSIN**
turpentine resin
ALK, GALLIPOT, GALIPOT
turtle, Amazon .... **ARRAU**
turtle, edible
TERAPIN, TERRAPIN
turtle, edible part of . **CALIPEE**
turtle enclosure ...... **CRAWL**
turtle genus .... **EMYS**
turtle, hawkbill .... **CARET**
turtle, order of .... **CHELONIA**
Tuscany art city .... **SIENA**
tusk, elephant .... **IVORY**
tutelary god ..... **LAR, LARES**
tutor .... **TUTE**

c TV advertiser ...... **SPONSOR**
"Twelfth Night" clown .. **FESTE**
"Twelfth Night" heroine
VIOLA
twelve and one-half cents . **BIT**
twenty-fourth part
CARAT, KARAT
twenty quires .... **REAM**
twice .... **BIS**
twice: prefix .... **BI**
twig, willow .. **WITHE, WITHY**
twilight .... **EVE, DUSK,**
GLOAM, EVENTIDE
twilled coth .... **REP**
twilled wool fabric ..... **SERGE**
twin .... **GEMEL**
twin crystal .... **MACLE**
twin gods, Teut. .... **ALCIS**
twine .... **COIL, WIND, TWIST**
twining stem .... **BINE**
twist ..... **PLY, COIL, FEAK,**
KINK, SKEW, GNARL,
WREATHE, CONTORT
twist inwards .... **INTORT**
twist out of shape ..... **WARP**
twisted .... **AWRY, SKEW,**
TORTILE
twisted roll of fibers .... **SLUB**
twisted spirally .... **TORSE**
twitch .... **TIC**
d twitching .... **TIC**
two .... **DUO, DUAD, PAIR**
two ears, affecting the **DIOTIC**
two elements, having . **BINARY**
two feet, verse of ..... **DIPODY**
two-footed ... **BIPED, BIPEDAL**
two-horse chariot .... **BIGA**
two-hulled boat . **CATAMARAN**
two-masted ship . **YAWL, ZULU**
two-month period .. **BIMESTER**
two, music for .... **DUET**
two notes, group of .... **DUOLE**
two-pronged, as sponges
DICELLATE
two-pronged weapon .. **BIDENT**
two-spot .... **DEUCE**
two tenacles, having. **DICEROUS**
two-toed sloth .... **UNAU**
two-wheeled vehicle **GIG, CART**
two-year-old sheep
TEG, TEGG, BIDENT
."Two Years Before the Mast"
author .... **DANA**
twofold .. **DUAL, TWIN, BINAL**
twofold: prefix .... **DI**
tycoon .... **NABOB**
tymp arch of furnace ... **FAULD**
Tyndareus, wife of ..... **LEDA**
type collection .... **FONT**

Type

a type, conforming to . **TYPICAL**
type face .... **RUNIC, CASLON**
type, 5½ point .... **AGATE**
type, jumbled .... **PI, PIE**
type, kind of .... **ELITE**
type measure .... **EM, EN**
type metal piece ...... **QUAD**
type, mixed .... **PI, PIE**
type of script .... **RONDE**
type part .... **KERN**
type set .... **FONT**

c type size ..... **PICA, AGATE,**
BREVIER
type, slanting .... **ITALIC**
type square .... **EM**
type tray .... **GALLEY**
typewriter roller ..... **PLATEN**
Tyr, Norse war god .... **ER**
tyrant .... **DESPOT**
tyrant of Rome .... **NERO**
Tyre, king of .... **HIRAM**
Tyre, princess of .... **DIDO**
tyro .... **NOVICE**

U

Uganda native .... **KOPI**
ukase .... **EDICT**
Ukraine legislature ..... **RADA**
"Ulalume" author .... **POE**
ulexite .... **TIZA**
ultra-conservative ...... **TORY**
ULYSSES ... see also **ODYSSEUS**
Ulysses' swineherd ... **EUMAEUS**
Ulysses' voyages .... **ODYSSEY**
umbrella .... **GAMP**
umbrella finial, Burma .... **TEE**
umbrella, India ...... **CHATTA**
umbrella part .... **RIB**
b umpire .... **REFEREE**
unaccented vowel sound **SCHWA**
unadulterated .... **PURE**
unaffected .. **SIMPLE, ARTLESS**
Unalaskan .... **ALEUT**
unaspirate .... **LENE**
unassuming
MODEST, NATURAL
unbeliever .... **HERETIC**
unbleached ..... **ECRU, BEIGE**
unburnt brick .. **DOBE, ADOBE**
Uncas' beloved .... **CORA**
uncanny ...... **EERY, EERIE,**
WEIRD
unceasing **ETERNAL, PERPETUAL**
uncinate .... **HAMATE**
uncivil .... **RUDE**
uncle, dial. .... **EME**
uncle: Scot. .... **EME**
"Uncle Remus" author
HARRIS
"Uncle Remus" rabbit ... **BRER**
unclean: Jewish law .... **TREF**
unclose .... **OPE, OPEN**
uncommon .... **RARE, SPECIAL**
unconcerned .... **CALM, OPEN,**
SERENE
unconscious state ...... **COMA**
unconstrained .... **EASY**

uncouth person ... **CAD, BOOR,**
YAHOO, GALOOT
unction .... **BALM**
unctuous .... **OILY, SUAVE**
under .... **INFRA, NEATH,**
SOTTO, NETHER
under: Fr. .... **SOUS**
under: naut. .... **ALOW**
under: prefix .... **SUB**
under side, pert. to .. **VENTRAL**
undergo: obs. .... **DREE**
underground bud .... **BULB**
d underground reservoir, natural
water .... **CENOTE**
underground stream, S. Afr.
AAR
underhand, throw ...... **LOB**
undernsong .... **TIERCE**
undershirts .... **SKIVVIES**
undersized animal ...... **RUNT**
understand .... **GRASP**
understanding ... **KEN, SENSE,**
ENTENTE
underwater box ..... **CAISSON**
underworld .... **HADES, SHEOL**
underworld, Egypt.
DUAT, AMENTI
underworld god ... **DIS, PLUTO**
underworld god, Egypt. **OSIRIS,**
SERAPIS
underworld goddess ...... **HEL**
underwrite ... **ENSURE, INSURE**
undeveloped .... **LATENT**
undraped .... **NUDE**
undulant fever .. **BRUCELLOSIS**
undulating .... **WAVY**
undulation .... **WAVE**
unequal .... **UNIQUE**
unequal angled ..... **SCALENE**
unequal conditions ...... **ODDS**
uneven .... **ODD, EROSE**
unevenly shaped .... **EROSE**

a unfadable .... FAST
unfair move .... FOUL
unfair shove in marbles . FULK
unfasten ..... UNTIE, LOOSEN
unfavorable .... BAD, ILL
unfeeling ... HARSH, CALLOUS
unfermented grape juice
　　　　　　　　　　STUM
unfit to eat, make . DENATURE
unfledged bird .... EYAS
unfold .... EVOLVE
unguent, Roman wrestlers'
　　　　　　　　　　CEROMA
ungula .. CLAW, HOOF, NAIL
ungulate, S. Am. ...... TAPIR
unhappy .... SAD, BLUE,
　　　　　MOROSE, RUEFUL
unicorn fish ...... LIJA, UNIE
uniform .... EVEN
uniform in hue .. FLAT, FLOT
uninteresting .... DULL
union .... MERGER
union, labor ... AFL, CIO, ILA,
　　　　　　　ITA, ILGWU
union, political .... BLOC
union, Russ. workers' ... ARTEL
unique person .... ONER
unique thing: slang ..... ONER
unit .... ACE, ONE
b unit of capacity ...... FARAD
unit of conductance ..... MHO
unit of electrical intensity:
　abbr. .... AMP
unit of electrical resistance or
　reluctance .... REL
unit of electricity . OHM, WATT,
　　　　　FARAD, WEBER
unit of electromotive force
　　　　　　　　　　VOLT
unit of energy .... ERG,
　　　　　RAD, ERGON
unit of fluidity .... RHE
unit of force .... DYNE
unit of heat .... CALORIE
unit of illumination ..... PHOT
unit of jet propulsion .... JATO
unit of light .... PYR, LUMEN,
　　　　　　　　　HEFNER
unit of power .... DYNE
unit of power, electric ... OHM,
　　　WATT, FARAD, WEBER
unit of pressure BARAD, BARIE
unit of reluctance .... REL
unit of resistance .... OHM
unit of weight .... WEY
unit of work ..... ERG, ERGON
unit, pert. to ...... MONADIC
unit, power ratio .... BEL

c unite .... WED, ALLY, JOIN,
　　KNIT, WELD, YOKE,
　　MERGE, INTEGRATE
unite edges .... RABBET
UNITED STATES
　　　　　　see AMERICAN
unity .... ONE
univalent element .... MONAD
universal .. WORLD, GENERAL
universal language ... RO, IDO
universe .... WORLD, COSMOS
universe: Hindu .... LOKA
universe, pert. to ... COSMIC
university degree-holder
　　　　　　　LICENTIATE
University in Conn. ..... YALE
unkeeled .... RATITE
unkind ILL
unknown Hindu god ...... KA
unless .... BUT, SAVE
unless: Lat. .... NISI
unlock .... OPE, OPEN
unmarried .... CELIBATE
unmatched .... ODD
unmixed .... PURE, SHEER
unmusical clang ...... TONK
unnecessary .... NEEDLESS
unplowed strip .... HADE
unpredictable .... ERRATIC
d unprincipled person .... CAD,
　　SCAMP, BOUNDER,
　　REPROBATE
unprofitable, as rents .... SECK
unrefined .... EARTHY
unrelenting . IRON, ADAMANT
unruffled ..... CALM, SERENE
unruly outbreak .... RIOT
unruly person .... RANTIPOLE
unsophisticated .... NAIVE
unsorted flour .... ATA, ATTA
unspoken .... TACIT
unstable ... ASTATIC, ERRATIC
unsuitable ..... INAPT, INEPT
untamed .... WILD, FERAL
untidy person .... SLOB
untidiness .... MESS, MUSS
until .... TILL
untrained .... RAW
unusual ...... RARE, EXOTIC
unusual person or thing . ONER
unwavering .... SURE, STEADY
unwholesome ILL
unwieldly thing .... HULK
unwilling ..... LOTH, LOATH,
　　　　　　　　　AVERSE
unwilling, be: archaic ... NILL
unyielding .. FIRM, ADAMANT
unyielding: naut. .... FAST

173

Up

up: comb. form .... ANO
Upanishad .... ISHA
upland plain .... WOLD
upbraid ...... CHIDE, SCOLD, REPROACH
upon ...... EPI, ATOP, ONTO
upon: law .... SUR
Upper Nile Negro ...... MADI
Upper Nile tribesman ... MADI
Upper Silurian .... ONTARIAN
uppermost part .... TOP
upright ...... ERECT, HONEST
upright column .... STELE
upright piece .... JAMB, STUD
uprising .... REVOLT
uproar .... DIN
upward, heave: naut. ... SCEND
uraeus .... ASP
Uranus' satellite .... ARIEL
urban office-holder ... MAYOR
urchin ..... IMP, TAD, GAMIN
Urfa, modern .... EDESSA
urge .... EGG, PLY, YEN, IMPEL, PRESS
urge: Scot. .... ERT

urial .... SHA
urticaria .... HIVES
urus .... TUR
us: Ger. .... UNS
usage .... WONT
use a divining rod ..... DOWSE
use, be of .... AVAIL
use exertions .... STRIVE
use one's efforts .... EXERT
used up ...... ATE, DEPLETED
useful ..... UTILE, PRACTICAL
useless .... IDLE, FUTILE, OTIOSE, INUTILE
usual .... NORMAL
Utah State flower .... SEGO
utmost .... LAST, FINAL, GREATEST
utmost hyperbole .... ELA
utter .... SAY, SHEER, SPEAK, STARK
utter, as greeting .... BID
utter loudly ..... VOCIFERATE
uttered ... ORAL, SAID, SPOKE
utterly .... STARK
Uz, brother of .... ARAN

V

V-shaped piece ...... WEDGE
vacant .... IDLE, EMPTY
vacuum .... VOID
vacuum, opposite of .. PLENUM
vacuum tube .... DIODE
vagabond . VAG, HOBO, TRAMP
vague .... HAZY, LOOSE
vainglory .... PRIDE
valance, short .... PELMET
vale ..... DALE, DELL, VALLEY
Vali, mother of .... RIND
valiant ... BRAVE, STALWART
Valkyrie .... DIS, NORN
valley ..... DALE, DELL, VAIL, VALE, GLADE
valley, deep .... COULEE
valley, Jordan .... GHOR
value .... RATE, PRIZE, WORTH, APPRAISE
value, thing of little ... TRIFLE
valve .... COCK
vampire .... LAMIA
van .... FORE
vandal .... HUN
vanish .... EVANESCE
vanity .... PRIDE
vanity case .... ETUI
vantage, place of ...... COIGN
vapid .... INANE, STALE

vapor .... STEAM
vapor: comb. form ..... ATMO
vapor: dialect.......... ROKE
vapor in air ...... HAZE, MIST
Varangians .... ROS
variable .... PROTEAN
variable, most ...... PROTEAN
variable star .... MIRA, NOVA
variation, small SHADE, NUANCE
variegated .... SHOT
variegated in color PIED, CALICO
variety .... KIND
variety of bean SOY, LIMA, PINTO
various: comb. form VARI, VARIO
varnish ingredient LAC, COPAL, RESIN
varnish, kind of SHELLAC, SHELLACK
varnish material .... ELEMI
vase .... URN
vat ...... BAC, TUB, CISTERN
vat, beer ... GAAL, GAIL, GYLE
vat, brewer's ... KIVE, KEEVE
vat, large .... KEIR, KIER
vault .... SAFE

a vault, church .... **CRYPT**
vaulted alcove .... **APSE**
vaunt .... **BRAG, BOAST**
vector, that which turns a
　　　　　　　　　　　VERSOR
Vedic dialect .... **PALI**
VEDIC GODS
　　see SPECIAL SECTION
veer ..... **SHY, TURN, SHIFT**
veer off .... **SHEER**
vegetable ... **PEA, BEAN, BEET,
KALE, OCRA, OKRA, OKRO,
CHARD, ENDIVE, TOMATO,
WOBBIE, CELTUCE**
vegetable fuel .... **PEAT**
vegetables, pod .... **PEASE**
vehicle .... **CAR, CART,
CYCLE, HANSOM**
vehicle, Am. Ind.
　　TRAVOIS, TRAVOISE
vehicle 4-wheeled .... **LANDAU**
vehicle, light, India ... **TONGA**
vehicle, Near East ..... **ARABA**
vehicle, Russ. .... **TROIKA**
vehicle, war .... **TANK**
veil, chalice .... **AER**
vein: Lat. .... **VENA**
b vein of body .... **CAVA**
vein, ore .... **LODE, SCRIN**
vein, ore: prov. Eng. .... **ROKE**
vein, ore beside .... **RIDER**
vein, throat .... **JUGULAR**
vellum .... **PARCHMENT**
velocity per second ..... **VELO**
velum .... **PALATE**
velvet .... **PANNE**
velvet grass .... **HOLCUS**
vend .... **SELL**
vendetta .... **FEUD**
venerable .... **OLD, HOARY**
"Venerable" monk ...... **BEDE**
venerate ..... **ESTEEM, REVERE**
veneration .... **AWE**
Venetian nobleman ..... **DOGE**
Venetian painter ..... **TITIAN**
Venetian red .... **SIENA**
Venetian resort .... **LIDO**
Venetian rose .... **SIENA**
Venetian traveler ...... **POLO**
Venezuela copper center **AROA**
Venezuela Ind. language **PUME**
vengeance goddess ...... **ARA**
Venice marble bridge ..**RIALTO**
Venice canals .... **RII**
Venice district .... **RIALTO**
ventral .... **HEMAD, HAEMAD**
venture .... **DARE**

c Venus, island of ..... **MELOS**
Venus' son .... **CUPID**
Venus, youth loved by **ADONIS**
veranda, Dutch, S. Afr. **STOEP**
veranda, Hawaii ...... **LANAI**
veranda, India .... **PYAL**
verb form .... **IS, AM, ARE,
WAS, TENSE**
verbal .... **ORAL**
verbal ending .. **ED, ER, ES, ING**
verbal noun .... **GERUND**
verbal rhythm .... **METRE**
verbally .... **ALOUD**
Verdi heroine .... **AIDA**
verily .... **YEA, AMEN**
verity .... **TRUTH**
versatile .... **MOBILE**
verse .... **LINE, STICH**
verse, Fr. .... **RONDEL**
verse, Ir. .... **RANN**
verse, pert. to kind of **IAMBIC**
version, Bible .... **ITALA**
vertebral bones **SACRA, SACRUM**
verticle line, in a ..... **APEAK**
verticle timber: naut. ... **BITT**
vertigo .... **DINUS**
very .... **SO**
very abundant ... **LUXURIANT**
very: Fr. .... **TRES**
very: Scot. .... **VERA**
d very: Span. .... **MUY**
Ve's brother .... **ODIN**
vesicle, skin .... **BLISTER**
VESSEL .. see also BOAT, SHIP,
GALLEY
vessel .... **ARK**
vessel, anat. ...... **VAS, VASA**
vessel, Arab .... **DOW, DHOW**
vessel, chemical .... **ETNA**
vessel, coasting, E. Ind.
　　　　　　　　　　PATAMAR
vessel, cooking .... **PAN, POT**
vessel, drinking ...... **GOURD**
vessel for liquors .. **DECANTER**
vessel, glass .... **BOCAL**
vessel, Gr. **CADUS, AMPHORA**
vessel, heating .... **ETNA**
vessel, large .... **TANK**
vessel, liquor .... **FLAGON**
vessel, Medit. .. **SETEE, MISTIC**
vessel, Rom. .... **PATERA**
vessel, sacred ...... **PIX, PYX**
vessel, sailing .... **SAIC,
SETEE, XEBEC**
vessel, shallow .... **BASIN**
vessel, supply .... **COALER**
vessel, 3-masted
　　　　XEBEC, FRIGATE
vessel, 2-masted **YAWL, ZULU**

a vessel with two handles, Gr. .. **DIOTA**
vessel's curved planking .. **SNY**
vestal .... **CHASTE**
vestige .. **IOTA, RELIC, TRACE**
vestment .. **ALB, COPE, AMICE, EPHOD, STOLE**
vestment, white .. **ALB, AMICE**
vesuvianite, brown ... **EGERAN**
vetch .... **TARE**
vetch, bitter .... **ERS**
vetch, India .... **AKRA**
vetiver, grass .... **BENA**
vex **GALL, RILE, ROIL, HARRY**
vex persistently ...... **NETTLE**
vex: Scot. .... **FASH**
vexed .... **RILY**
via .... **PER**
viands .... **DIET**
viands, dainty .... **CATES**
Viaud's pseudonym ...... **LOTI**
vibrate .... **THRILL**
vibration: music .... **TREMOLO**
vice .... **SIN**
viceroy .... **VALI**
Vichy Premier .... **LAVAL**
vicious man .... **YAHOO**
victim .... **PREY**
victorfish .... **AKU**
victor's crown .... **LAUREL**
victory, Eng. .. **CRECY, CRESSY**
victory trophy .... **SCALP**
b victuals .... **FOOD**
"— victus," woe to the conquered .... **VAE**
"—vide," "which see" .. **QUAE**
vie with .... **EMULATE**
Viennese park .... **PRATER**
view .... **SCENE, VISTA**
vigilant .... **WARY, ALERT**
vigor .... **PEP, VIM, VIS, ZIP, FORCE**
Viking ... **ERIC, OLAF, ROLLO**
Viking explorer .... **ERIC**
vilify .... **REVILE**
village .. **DORP, VILL, HAMLET**
village, Afr. .... **KRAAL**
village, Java .... **DESSA**
village, Russ. .... **MIR**
village, Scot. .... **REW**
village, S. Afr. native ... **STAD**
villain .... **KNAVE**
villein .... **CEORL**
vindicate .... **AVENGE**
vindication .... **REVENGE**
vine .... **IVY, BINE**
vine: comb. form .... **VITI**
vine, N. Z. .... **AKA**
vine, P. I. .... **IYO**

c vine, woody ... **ABUTA, LIANA**
"vin du —," wine of the country .... **CRU**
vinegar of ale .... **ALEGAR**
vinegar, pert. to ...... **ACETIC**
vinegar worm .... **EEL, NEMA**
vinous .... **WINY**
viol, ancient type ...... **REBEC**
viol, bass .... **GAMBA**
viol, Shetlands .... **GUE**
viola .... **ALTO**
violent .... **HOT**
violet-odored ketone .. **IRONE**
violin, bass .... **CELLO**
violin, early .. **REBAB, REBEC**
violin, famous .... **STRAD**
violin, It. .. **AMATI, CREMONA**
violin, small .... **KIT**
violin, tenor ..... **ALTO, VIOLA**
violinist .... **ELMAN, YSAYE**
viper .... **ASP, ADDER**
viper genus .... **ECHIS**
viper, horned .... **CERASTES**
Virgil's hero .. **ENEAS, AENEAS**
Virgin Mary pictured mourning **PIETA**
virus-fighting substance **ANTIVIRAL**
visage .... **FACE**
viscous **LIMY, ROPY, SIZY, SLIMY**
d viscous substance .. **TAR, SLIME**
Vishnu, incarnation, 7th **RAMA**
Vishnu, soul of universe **VASU**
Vishnu's bow .... **SARAN**
Vishnu's serpent ...... **NAGA**
visible juncture .... **SEAM**
Visigoth king **ALARIC, ALARIK**
vision, defective ..... **ANOPIA**
vision, pert. to .... **OPTIC**
visionary ...... **AIRY, IDEAL, DREAMY, UNREAL, IDEALIST**
visit ...... **SEE, CALL, HAUNT**
visit at sea .... **GAM**
visit between whalers ... **GAM**
vison .... **MINK**
vital energy .... **HORME**
vital fluid .... **SAP**
vital principle .... **SOUL**
vitalize .... **ANIMATE**
vitamin ... **CITRIN, ADERMIN, ANEURIN, TORULIN**
vitamin B **NIACIN, THIAMINE**
vitamin B2 .... **FLAVIN**
vitamin H .... **BIOTIN**
vitiate .... **SPOIL, TAINT, POLLUTE, INVALIDATE**
vitriol-infused earth .... **SORY**
vituperate .... **SCOLD**

a vivacious ..... AIRY, BRIGHT
vivacity .... ELAN, LIFE
vocal flourish ...... ROULADE
vocation .... CAREER
"— voce" .... SOTTO
voice .... SAY
voice
    ALTO, BASS, VOCE, TENOR
voice: It. .... VOCE
voice: Lat. .... VOX
voice, loss of ...... APHONIA
voiced .... SONANT
voiced, not .... ASONANT
voiceless .... SPIRATE
voiceless consonant ..... SURD
void .... NUL, NULL,
    ABYSS, SPACE, INVALID
void, to make.ANNUL, CANCEL
void, to render: Scot. ... CASS
voided escutcheon ...... ORLE
volcanic cinder .... SCORIA
volcanic islands, Atlantic
                        FAROE
volcanic rock
    TUFA, TUFF, LATITE
volcanic scoria-matter
                    LAVA, SLAG
volcano .. ETNA, AETNA, PELEE
volcano crater .... MAAR
volcano hole .... CRATER

c volcano, Martinique Is. .. PELEE
volcano mouth ...... CRATER
volcano, P. I. .... APO
volcano pit .... CRATER
volcano, Sicily   ETNA, AETNA
volcano, W. Indies .... PELEE
volition .... WILL
volt-ampere .... WATT
Voltaire .... AROUET
Voltaire play: Fr. ..... ZAIRE
voluble .... GLIB
volume .... MO, TOME
vomiting .... EMESIS
voodoo charm .... MOJO
voodoo snake deity .... ZOMBI
vote .... BALLOT
vote into office .... ELECT
vote, right to .... FRANCHISE
vote, take a .... POLL
votes ...... AYES, NOES, YEAS
vouch for .... SPONSOR
voucher .... CHIT, NOTE
"vous —": Fr., you are .. ETES
vowel, line over ..... MACRON
vowel suppression .... ELISION
voyaging .... ASEA
vulcanite .... EBONITE
Vulcan's wife .... MAIA
vulgar .... COARSE
vulture AURA, URUBU, CONDOR

W

b "W", old English .... WEN
wade across .... FORD
wading bird IBIS, RAIL, CRANE,
    EGRET,   HERON,   STILT,
    AVOCET,   AVOSET,   JAC-
    ANA, FLAMINGO
wag .... WIT
wages .... PAY
Wagner heroine . ELSA, SENTA,
                    ISOLDE
Wagnerian role .... ERDA
wagon .. CART, DRAY, WAIN
wagon pin .... CLEVIS
wagon, Russ. .... TELEGA
wagon shaft .... THILL
wagon tongue .... NEAP, POLE
wagtail .... LARK
wahoo, fish .... PETO
wail .... KEEN, LAMENT
waist ...... CAMISA, TAILLE
waistcoat VEST, GILET, JERKIN
wait .... BIDE
waken ...... ROUSE, AROUSE

d wale .... WELT
Wales emblem .... LEEK
walk ..... PACE, STEP, TREAD
walk affectedly ...... MINCE
walk heavily .... PLOD, SLOG
walk, inability to .... ABASIA
walk lamely .... LIMP
walk stiffly .... STALK
walk, tree-lined .... ALAMEDA
walking stick ... CANE, STILT
wall, arena .... SPINA
wall around fortified place
                    RAMPART
wall, divided by .... SEPTATE
wall: Fr. .... MUR
wall material .... COB
wall, of a .... MURAL
wall paneling .... WAINSCOT
wall piece TEMPLET, TEMPLATE
wall section .... DADO, PANEL
wall, squeeze against .. MURE
walls .... SEPTA
wallaba tree, Brazil ..... APA
walled city, Nigeria ..... KANO

a wallflower .... KEIRI
wallop .... LAM
wallow .... WELTER
walrus .... MORSE
wampum PEAG,SEWAN,SEAWAN
wan .... ASHY, PALE, ASHEN
wand .... BATON
wander .. ERR, HAAK, ROAM,
ROVE, RAMBLE, DIGRESS
wander idly .... GAD
wanderer .... VAG, NOMAD
"Wandering Jew" author .. SUE
wane .... EBB
want .... LACK, NEED, DESIRE
wapiti .... ELK
war-club, medieval ..... MACE
war correspondent
PYLE, BALDWIN
war cry, ancient Gr. ... ALALA
war god .... ARES, MARS
war god, Babyl. ... IRA, IRRA
war god, Norse TY, TYR, TYRR
war god, Teut. .... ER
war goddess, Gr. ...... ENYO
war horse .... CHARGER
war, religious ...... CRUSADE
war, Russ.-Eng. .... CRIMEA
war vessel .... CRUISER
warble .. SING, TRILL, YODEL
b ward off ..... FEND, AVERT,
PARRY, REPEL, STAVE
ward politician ...... HEELER
warden, fire .... RANGER
warehouse .... DEPOT
warehouse room .... LOFT
warm .... CALID, TEPID
warning of danger: biol.
SEMATIC
warning signal .... SIREN
warning system, attack
DEW, BMEWS
warp yarn .... ABB
warrant, from monarch BERAT
warrior, Samoa .... TOA
warship, sailing ..... FRIGATE
wary .... CAGY
was not: dialect .... NAS
wash .... LAVE
wash leather .... LOSH
wash out .... ELUTE
washings: chem. ..... ELUATE
Washington Irving character RIP
wasp .... HORNET
wasps, the .... VESPA
waste .... LOSS
waste allowance .... TRET
waste away GNAW, ATROPHY
waste fiber .... NOIL
waste land .... MOOR
waste matter .... DROSS
waste silk ..... KNUB, FRISON

c waste time .... IDLE
wastes, growing in .. RUDERAL
watch .... SEE, GLOM
watch chain .... FOB
watchdog, Hel's .... GARM
watchful .... ALERT
watchful guardian .... ARGUS
watchful, name meaning IRA
watchman, alert ...... ARGUS
watchman, night ..... SERENO
watchtower .... MIRADOR
water .. SPRINKLE, IRRIGATE
water arum .... CALLA
water chestnut, Chin. ... LING
water cock .... KORA
water, covered by .... AWASH
water: Fr. .... EAU, EAUX
water: Lat. .... AQUA
water lily .... LOTUS
water passage SLUICE, STRAIT
water pipe
HOOKA, HOOKAH, NARGILE
water raising device
TABUT, TABOOT
water reservoir, natural
CENOTE
water scorpion genus ... NEPA
water, seek .... DOUSE
water, sound of ...... PLASH
water: Sp. .... AGUA
d water spirit
ARIEL, SPRITE, UNDINE
water sprite ..... NIX, NIXIE
water sprite: Gaelic .. KELPIE
water surface .... RYME
water vessel, India
LOTA, LOTO, LOTAH
water wheel
NORIA, DANAIDE, TURBINE
water wheel, Persian .. NORIA
water's surface: naut. ... RYME
watercourse ... LADE, BROOK,
CANAL, RIVER, STREAM
watered apearance .... MOIRE
watered silk .... MOIRE
waterfall, Scot. LIN, LYN, LINN
watering place .. SPA, BADEN
waterproof canvas ..... TARP
waterskin .... MATARA
watertight, make CALK, CAULK
waterway .... BAYOU, CANAL
waterway, narrow ..... STRAIT
watery .... SEROUS
watery: comb. form .... SERO
wattle tree .... BOREE
wattled honeyeater
IAO, MANUAO
wave .... FLY, SEA
wave-crest comb. ...... COOM
wave: Fr. .... ONDE
wave, huge .... SEA

a waver .... FALTER, TEETER
wavy: Her.
          UNDE, UNDY, NEBULE
wax .... CERE
wax ointment .... CERATE
wax, pert. to .... CERAL
wax: Sp. .... CERA
wax, yellow or white CERESIN
waxy chemical .... CERIN
waxy substance .... CERIN
way ...... VIA, MODE, ROUTE
way of walking .... GAIT
way out .... EGRESS
wayside — .... INN
wayside stop, India .. PARAO
we: Lat. .... NOS
weak .... PUNY, FRAIL,
     DEBILE, EFFETE, FEEBLE
weak cider .... PERKIN
weaken .... SAP, LABEFY,
     VITIATE, ENERVATE, EN-
     FEEBLE
weakfish, S. Am. .... ACOUPA
weakness .... ATONY
weal .... WALE
wealth, man of .... NABOB
wealthy: Scot. .... BIEN

b weapon .... LANCE,
     SPEAR, SWORD, MUSKET
weapon, ancient .... CELT
weapon, dagger-like .. BALAS
weapon: Fr. .... ARME
weapon, gaucho's BOLA, BOLAS
weapon, Maori .... PATU
weapon, medieval ..... ONCIN
weapon, N. Z. .... PATU
weapon, P. I. .... BOLO
weapon, S. Am. .. BOLA, BOLAS
wear away EAT, ERODE, ABRADE
wear away slowly ... CORRODE
wear by friction .... RUB
wear off .... ABRADE
wearing down .... ATTRITION
weary .... BORE, TIRE
weasel VARE, ERMINE, FERRET
weasel: Eng.
          STOT, STOAT, STOTE
weather indicator BAROMETER
weathercock .... VANE
weaverbird ..... BAYA, MAYA
weaverbird, S. Afr. .... TAHA
weaver's bobbin on shuttle PIRN
weaver's reed .... SLEY
weaving frame .... LOOM
weaving term .... LISSE
weaving tool .... EVENER

c web .... TELA
web-footed bird . DUCK, LOON,
                    GOOSE
web-like membrane ..... TELA
web-spinning
          RETIARY, TELARIAN
wed .... MARRY
wedding anniversaries 1st,
     PAPER; 2nd, COTTON;
     3rd, CANDY OR LEATHER;
     4th, SILK, FRUIT, FLOW-
     ERS, or LEATHER; 5th,
     WOODEN; 6th, IRON OR
     CANDY; 7th, WOOL, COP-
     PER, OR FLORAL; 8th,
     WOOL, BRONZE, OR POT-
     TERY; 9th, WILLOW OR
     POTTERY; 10th, TIN; 11th,
     STEEL; 12th, SILK OR LIN-
     EN; 13th, LACE; 14th,
     IVORY; 15th, CRYSTAL;
     20th, CHINA; 25th, SIL-
     VER; 30th, PEARL; 35th,
     CORAL; 40th, RUBY OR
     EMERALD; 45th, RUBY OR
     SAPPHIRE; 50th, GOLDEN;

d   55th, EMERALD; 75th,
     DIAMOND
wedge, entering . COIN, COIGN,
          QUOIN, COIGNE
wedge-like piece ..... QUOIN
wedge-shaped ...... CUNEATE
wedge-shaped piece GIB, SHIM
wedge, steel .... FROE
Wednesday, source of name
          WODEN
weed .... TARE, DARNEL
weed, coarse .... DOCK
week ..... SENNET, SENNIGHT
week day .... FERIA
weep
     CRY, SOB, BOHO, LAMENT
weep, Scot. .... ORP
weeping statue .... NIOBE
weeping woman, Gr. myth NIOBE
weft .... WOOF
WEIGHT .. see also SPECIAL
     SECTION
weight .... TON, HEFT
weight allowance TARE, TRET
weight, ancient
          MINA, TALENT
weight, ancient: var. ... MNA
weight, Asiatic .... TAEL
weight, balance .... RIDER

179

a weight, Danish .... ORT
weight, India ...... SER, TOLA
weight machine: Scot.
TRON, TRONE
weight, metric unit of .. GRAM
weight of England ..... STONE
weight of silk before
degumming .... PARI
weight, pert. to .... BARIC
weight system .... TROY
weir .... DAM
weird .... EERY, EERIE
welcome .... GREET
well, Bib. .... AIN
well-bred people .... GENTRY
"well done" .. EUGE, BRAVO
well done: Eng. .... EUGE
well: Fr. .... BIEN
well: It. & Lat. .... BENE
well: Scot. .... AWEEL
Welsh dog .... CORGI
Welsh god of sea .... DYLAN
Welshman .... CELT
welt .... WALE
wen .... TALPA
Wend of Saxony .... SORB
wergeld .... CRO
W. Australia capital ... PERTH
W. Afr. timber tree ... ODUM
b W. Afr. tribe IBO, BUBE, BUBI
W. Ind. bayberry AUSU, AUZU
W. Ind. fish
BOGA, CERO, TESTAR
W. Ind. idol. ..... ZEME, ZEMI
W. Ind. isle ... CUBA, HAITI
W. Ind. key .... CAY
W. Ind. scrapper .... CAJI
W. Ind. shrub plant .... ANIL
West Point mascot ..... MULE
West Pointer
PLEB, CADET, PLEBE
West Saxon king .... INE
Western division of Osset DIGOR
Western European CELT, KELT
Western Indian .... UTE
Western shrub .... SAGE
"Western Star" author BENET
Western state .... UTAH
Westphalian city ..... HERNE
wet: Scot. .... WAT
wet .... ASOP, MOIST
whale .... CET, ORC, ORK,
CETE, BELUGA, GRAMPUS
whale carcass KRANG, KRENG
whale hunter .... AHAB
whale oil cask .... RIER
whale-shark .... MHOR
whale tail part .... FLUKE
whale, white .... BELUGA

c whale, white Caspian
HUSE, HUSO
whales .... CETE
whales, herd of ... GAM, POD
whales, pert. to .... CETIC
whales, school of .. GAM, POD
whalebone .... BALEEN
wharf..KEY, PIER, QUAI, QUAY
what is it? obs. .... ANAN
whatnot .... ETAGERE
wheal .... WALE, WEAL
wheat disease .... BUNT
wheat, German EMMER, SPELT
wheat, India ..... SUJI, SUJEE
wheat, kind of EMMER, SPELT
wheat middlings .. SEMOLINA
wheedle .... COG, COAX
wheedling .... BUTTERY
wheel .... ROTA
wheel band .... STRAKE
wheel center HOB, HUB, NAVE
wheel, furniture ..... CASTER
wheel, grooved ..... SHEAVE
wheel horse .... POLER
wheel part .... HUB, RIM,
FELLY, SPOKE
wheel projection .... CAM
wheel shaft .... AXLE
wheel-shaped .... ROTATE
wheel spindle .. AXLE, ARBOR
d wheel tread .... TIRE
wheels, pert. to ...... ROTAL
where: Lat. .... UBI
whetstone, fine . BUHR, HONE
whey of milk .. SERA, SERUM
which see: abbr. .... QV
whiff .... PUFF
while .... AS, WHEN
whimper .... MEWL, PULE
whin .... GORSE
whine .... PULE
whinny .... NEIGH
whip CAT, BEAT, FLOG, LASH
whip, cowboy .... CHICOTE
whip mark ..... WALE, WEAL
whip, Russ. .... KNOUT
whipsocket .... SNEAD
whirl .... REEL, SPIN
whirlpool .... EDDY, GURGE,
VORTEX
whirlpool: Scot. .... WEEL, WIEL
whirlwind in Atlantic ...... OE
whirring sound .... BIRR
whiskers .... BEARD, GOATEE
whiskey: Ir. .... POTEEN
whiskey drink: Scot.
ATHOL, ATHOLE
whist win .... SLAM
whistle .... PIPE, SIREN
whit .... BIT, JOT,
ATOM, DOIT, IOTA

a white acid, pert. to .. TROPIC
white alkaline .... SODA
white ant, P. I. .. ANAI, ANAY
white, bitter compound LININ
white: comb. form ..... ALBO
"White Elephant" land .. SIAM
white ermine LASSET, MINIVER
white-flecked .... ROAN
White Friar ..... CARMELITE
white: Ir. .... BAWN
white man: P. I. ... CACHILA
white matter, brain .... ALBA
white oak .... ROBLE
white poplar .... ABELE
white spruce ...... EPINETTE
white with age .... HOAR
whitefish .... CISCO
whiten .... ETIOLATE
whitish .... HOARY
whitlow grass .... DRABA
Whittier heroine .... MAUD
whiz ..... PIRR, WHIR, ZIZZ
whoa .... HOLLA
whole amount .... GROSS
whole: comb. form ...... TOTO
wholesome .... SALUTARY
wholly .... ALL
wicked .... EVIL
wicker basket .... CESTA,
KIPSY, PANNIER

b wicker basket, Guiana PEGALL
wickerwork .... RATAN
wickerwork hut .... JACAL
wicket, croquet .... HOOP
wide-mouthed vessel
EWER, OLLA
widgeon .... SMEE
widgeon genus .... MARECA
widow .... RELICT
widow in cards .... SKAT
widow monkey .... TITI
widow's bit or coin ..... MITE
widow's third: Scot. .... TERCE
wield .... PLY, USE
wife, Moroccan ruler's SHERIFA
wife ... FEME, FRAU, FEMME
wife's property .... DOS
wig .... PERUKE
wigwam .. TIPI, TEPEE, TEEPEE
wild .... FERAL, SAVAGE
wild animals, collection of
ZOO, MENAGERIE
wild animal's trail
SLOT, SPUR, SPOOR
wild apple .... CRAB, DOUCIN
wild ass, Afr. ...... QUAGGA
wild ass, Asia ...... ONAGER
wild boar genus .... SUS
wild buffalo, India
ARNA, ARNI, ARNEE

c wild buffalo, Malay ... GAUR,
SLADANG, SALADANG,
SELADANG
wild cat, Siberia, Tibet, steppes
MANUL
wild cattle, India GAUR, GOUR
wild cry .... EVOE
wild dog .... DHOLE
wild dog genus .... THOS
wild dog, Japan ..... TANATE
"Wild Duck" author .... IBSEN
wild garlic .... MOLY
wild ginger .... ASARUM
wild hog .... BOAR
wild honeybee, E. Ind. DINGAR
wild horse of Tartary TARPAN
wild lime .... COLIMA
wild olive tree ..... OLEASTER
wild ox .... ANOA
wild ox, Malay. ..... BANTENG
wild plum .... SLOE
wild plum, Calif. ...... ISLAY
wild sheep, Asia
RASSE, ARGALI
wild sheep, horned . MOUFLON
wild sheep, India ... SHA, SNA,
URIAL, NAHOOR, OORIAL
wild sheep, N. Afr.
ARUI, UDAD, AOUDAD
wild sheep, Tibet .... SHA

d SNA, BHARAL, NAHOOR
wild turnip .... NAVEW
wild vanilla .... LIATRIS
wildcat .... BALU, LYNX
wildcat, Afr. & India .. CHAUS
wildcat, S. Am. .... EYRA
wildcat, Sumatra ...... BALU
wildebeest .... GNU
wile .... ART
will addition .... CODICIL
will, one inheriting from
DEVISEE
will, one making .... DEVISOR
will power, loss of .... ABULIA
William: Ir. .... LIAM
William I, half brother of ODO
William the Conqueror's
daughter .... ADELA
willingly .... LIEF
willow .... ITEA, OSIER
willow, Europ. ..... SALLOW
willow genus, Virginia ... ITEA
Wilson's thrush ...... VEERY
wilt .... FADE, DROOP
wily .... FOXY
wimple .... GORGET
win .... GAIN
winch .... WHIN
wind .... GALE
wind, Adriatic .... BORA

a wind, Andes ... **PUNA, PUNO**
wind, Austral. ...... **BUSTER**
wind, away from .... **ALEE**
wind, cold Malta .... **GREGALE**
wind, cold Medit. .... **MISTRAL**
wind, cold Swiss Alps **BISE, BIZE**
wind: comb. form .... **ANEMO**
wind-deposited loam ... **LOESS**
wind, dry, from Sahara .. **LESTE**
wind, east .... **EURUS**
wind god, Babyl.
　　　　　ADAD, ADDA, ADDU
wind god, Hindu ...... **VAYU**
wind god, pert. to
　　　　　EOLIAN, AEOLIAN
wind, hot, dry ...... **KAMSIN,
　　SIMOOM, SIMOON, SIROCCO**
wind, hot, Medit. .... **SOLANO**
wind indicator .. **SOCK, VANE**
wind instrument
　　HORN, OBOE, PIPE, BUGLE
wind, Levant .... **ETESIAN**
wind, Madeira .... **LESTE**
wind, Medit. .... **ETESIAN**
wind, Medit., poet. ..... **SIROC**
wind, Mesop. ....,.... **SHAMAL**
wind, north .... **BOREAS**
wind off Faroe Islands .... **OE**
wind, Peru Andes **PUNA, PUNO**
wind, sand-laden
　　SAMIEL, SIMOOM, SIMOON
b wind, Sahara .... **LESTE**
wind, South .. **NOTUS, AUSTER**
wind, southeast .... **EURUS**
wind, southwest .... **AFER**
wind, Trieste, cold ..... **BORA**
wind, warm dry **FOHN, FOEHN**
wind, west .... **AFER**
winds, south, Peru ..... **SURES**
windborne .... **AEOLIAN**
windflower .... **ANEMONE**
windlass .... **CAPSTAN**
windmill sail .... **AWE**
window lead .... **CAME**
window ledge .... **SILL**
window part .... **SASH**
window, semipolygonal .. **ORIEL**
window setter .... **GLAZIER**
windrow .... **SWATH**
windstorm
　　OE, BURAN, TORNADO
windstorm, Asia **BURA, BURAN**
wine ...... **VIN, HOCK, PORT,
　　SACK, VINO, MEDOC, TO-
　　KAY, CLARET, MALAGA,
　　MUSCAT, SHERRY, MO-
　　SELLE**
wine, Am. .... **CATAWBA**
wine, ancient .... **MASSIC**
wine cask .... **TUN, BUTT**
wine city, It. .... **ASTI**

c wine cup .... **AMA**
wine, delicacy of: Fr. ... **SEVE**
wine disorder .... **CASSE**
wine district, Calif. .... **NAPA**
wine drink .... **NEGUS**
wine, dry .... **SEC, BRUT**
wine, golden .... **BUAL**
wine, heavy .... **TOKAY**
wine, honey and ...... **MULSE**
wine, Madeira .... **BUAL**
wine measure, Trieste
　　　　　ORNA, ORNE
wine merchant .... **VINTNER**
wine, new .... **MUST**
wine pitcher, Gr. .... **OLPE**
wine, red **PORT, TINTA, CLARET**
wine, sweet .... **MUSCAT**
wine, sweet: Fr. ...... **MASDEU**
wine, to make .... **VINT**
wine vessel ...... **AMA, OLPE,
　　　　AMULA, CHALICE**
wine, white .... **HOCK,
　　　SHERRY, SAUTERNE**
wineberry, N. Z. ...... **MAKO**
wing .... **ALA, PENNA,
　　　　PINNA, PINION**
wing, bastard .... **ALULA**
wing, beetle .... **TEGMAN,
　　TEGMINA, TEGUMEN**
wing: Fr. .... **AILE**
d wing-footed animal .. **ALIPED**
winglike .... **ALAR**
wing-like part ..... **ALA, ALAE**
wing movement .... **FLAP**
wing tip, pert. to ... **ALULAR**
wings .... **ALAE**
wings, divested of
　　DEALATA, DEALATED
wings, having .. **ALAR, ALATE**
wings: her. .... **VOL, AILE**
winged figure, Gr.
　　IDOLON, IDOLUM, EIDOLON
winged fruit, indehiscent
　　　　　SAMARA
winged god ..... **EROS, CUPID**
winged seed .... **SAMARA**
winged victory .... **NIKE**
wingless .... **APTERAL**
wingless invertebrates **APTERA**
wink rapidly .... **BAT**
winning at bridge ...... **SLAM**
winnow .... **FAN**
winter, pert. to .... **BRUMAL,
　　HIEMAL, HYEMAL, HIBERNAL**
winter squash .... **CUSHAW**
wipe out .... **ERASE**
wire measure .... **MIL**
wire service .... **AP, UP,
　　　INS, UPI, REUTERS**

wires, cross .... **RETICLE**
Wisconsin college ...... **RIPON**
wisdom ...... **LORE, GNOSIS**
wisdom god of: Babyl.
    NABU, NEBO
wisdom goddess of: Gr.
    ATHENA, PALLAS
wisdom, goddess of: Rom.
    MINERVA
wise .... **SAGE, SENSIBLE**
wise adviser .... **MENTOR**
wise man
  SAGE, SOLON, NESTOR
Wise Men .... **MAGI, GASPAR,**
  MELCHIOR, BALTHASAR
wise men, A-S .... **WITAN**
wisecrack .. **GAG, JOKE, QUIP**
wish for ..... **YEARN, DESIRE**
wish undone .... **RUE**
wisp of hair .... **TATE**
wit .... **WAG, HUMOR**
wit: Sp. .... **SAL**
witless chatter .... **GAB**
witch ... **HAG, HECAT, LAMIA,**
  HECATE, HECCAT, HEKATE
witch city .... **SALEM**
witch doctor .... **GOOFER**
witch in "Faerie Queene"
    DUESSA
witchcraft .... **OBEAH**
with: Fr. .... **AVEC**
with: Ger. .... **MIT**
with joy .... **FAIN**
with: prefix .... **SYN**
withdraw .. **RECEDE, REMOVE,**
  RETIRE, SECEDE, RETRACT
wither .... **FADE**
withered .... **SERE**
within ...... **INTO, INTERIOR**
within: comb. form
  ESO, ENDO, ENSO, ENTO
within: prefix .... **ENDO**
without: comb. form ..... **ECT**
without energy .... **ATONY**
without: Fr. .... **SANS**
without: Ger. .... **OHNE**
without: Lat. .... **SINE**
without: poetic .... **SANS**
without teeth, claws, lion
    MORNE
without veins ...... **AVENOUS**
witness .... **SEE**
witness, law . **TESTE, DEPONENT**
witness, to bear ...... **ATTEST**
witty remark ..... **MOT, QUIP**
witty reply .... **REPARTEE**
wobble .... **TEETER**
Woden .... **ODIN**
woe .... **MISERY**
woe is me .... **ALAS**

wolf, gray .... **LOBO**
wolf, Odin's ...... **GERE, GERI**
wolf, timber .... **LOBO**
wolfhound .... **ALAN**
wolfish .... **LUPINE**
wolframite .... **CAL**
wolverine genus .... **GULO**
woman diplomat, first U.S.
    OWEN
woman: Gr. .... **GYNE**
woman, ill-tempered
  SHREW, VIRAGO
woman personified, Ir.
  EMER, EIMER
woman's name (3 letters) **ADA,**
  AMY, ANN, EVA, EVE, FAY,
  IDA, INA, MAE, MAY, NAN,
  RAE, UNA, ZOE, (4 let-
  ters) **AFRA, ALIX, ALMA,**
  ALYS, ANNA, ANNE, AVIS,
  BONA, CARA, CLOE, CORA,
  DORA, EDNA, ELLA, ELSA,
  EMMA, ENID, ERMA, ETTA,
  INEZ, JANE, JEAN, JOAN,
  JUNE, LEAH, LIDA, LILA,
  LOIS, LORA, LUCY, MARY,
  MAUD, MYRA, NONA,
  NORA, OLGA, RITA, ROSA,
  ROSE, RUTH, SARA, VERA,
  VIDA, (5 letters) ALICE,
  ANITA, CLARE, DELIA,
  DIANA, ELAIN, ELSIE,
  ERICA, FAITH, FLORA,
  GRACE, IRENE, SARAH,
  SELMA, (6 letters) AL-
  THEA, BERTHA, DAPHNE,
  EDWINA, ELAINE, EMILIA,
  PHOEBE, (7 letters) ABI-
  GAIL, CELESTE, LAVINIA
woman's nickname **CAT, DEB,**
  HAT, KIT, LOU, MAB, MAG,
  MEG, SAL, SUE, ABBY,
  ADDY, BESS, BETH, CARO,
  DORA, GAIL, JILL, JOSY,
  JUDY, JULE, KATE, KATY,
  LINA, LISA, LULU, MART,
  MIMI, MINA, MOLL, NELL,
  NINA, ROXY, SUSY, TAVE,
  TAVY, TESS, TINA, XINA,
  SALLY, SALLIE
Wonderland girl ...... **ALICE**
wont .... **HABIT**
wood .... **ALOE**
wood apple, Ind. .... **BEL**
wood, black .... **EBONY**
wood, flexible .... **EDDER**
wood, fragrant . **ALOES, CEDAR**
wood: comb, form ...... **XYLO**
wood: Fr. .... **BOIS**
wood gum .... **XYLAN**

a
wood, light .... **BALSA**
wood, long piece .... **POLE**
wood: obsolete .... **WOLD**
wood, piece of .... **SLAT,**
            SPRAG, BILLET
wood pussy .... **SKUNK**
wood robin, N. Z. ...... **MIRO**
wood sorrel .... **OCA, OKA**
wood, timber: P. I. ... **CAHUY**
woodchuck .... **MARMOT**
woodchuck: dialect **MOONACK**
wooden .... **TREEN**
wooden brick .... **DOOK**
wooden collar, convict's **CANG**
wooden pail .... **SOE**
wooden peg .... **SKEG**
wooden shoe **SABOT, PATTEN**
woodland deity **FAUN, SATYR**
woodland god .... **PAN**
woodpecker genus **JYNX, YUNX**
woodpecker, green **HICKWALL**
woodpecker group ...... **PICI**
woodpecker, red-bellied . **CHAB**
woodpecker, small ... **PICULE**
woodpeckers, of ...... **PICINE**
woodwind
    OBOE, BASSOON, CLARINET
woodworking tool ..... **SAPPER**
woodworm .... **TERMITE**
woody fiber .... **BAST**

b
woody hill .... **HOLT**
woody plant .... **TREE**
woof .... **WEFT**
wool ...... **ANGORA, MERINO**
wool cluster .... **NEP**
wool, coarse .... **GARE**
wool fat . **LANOLIN, LANOLINE**
wool: Lat. .... **LANA**
wool measure .... **HEER**
wool package .... **FADGE**
wool, reclaimed ...... **MUNGO**
woolen cloth .... **ETAMINE**
woolen cloth, coarse, twilled
            KERSEY
woolen fabric .... **FRISCA**
woolen thread .... **YARN**
woolly ...... **LANATE, LANOSE**
woolly pyrol .... **URD**
word by word .... **LITERAL**
word expressing action .. **VERB**
word meanings, pert. to
            SEMANTIC
word of affirmation .... **AMEN**
word of choice .... **OR**
word of God .... **LOGOS**
word of honor, promise
            PAROL, PAROLE
word of mouth, by
            PAROL, PAROLE
word of ratification .... **AMEN**
word, scrambled ... **ANAGRAM**

c
work
    MOIL, TOIL, CHARE, LABOR
WORK .. see also **COMPOSITION**
work aimlessly .... **POTTER**
work at steadily .... **PLY**
work hard
    PEG, MOIL, TOIL, SLAVE
work, in terms of heat **ERGON**
work, musical
    OPUS, OPERA, ORATORIO
work persistently .... **PEG**
work, piece of .... **JOB, STINT**
work: Sp. .... **OBRA**
work unit .... **ERG, ERGON**
workbasket .... **CABA, CABAS**
worker .... **HAND,**
        OPERANT, OPERATOR
worker ant .... **ERGATE**
worker: comb. form .. **ERGATE**
worker's group, worldwide .. **ILO**
worker's union, Soviet .. **ARTEL**
workhorse: Scot ...... **AVER**
working boat, Chesapeake Bay
            FLATTIE
workman, mine .... **CAGER**
workman, S. Afr. .... **VOLK**
workshop .... **ATELIER**
world: Hindu myth ...... **LOKA**
world, holder of .... **ATLAS**
World War I battle site

d
            MONS, MARNE
World War I group . **AEF, AMEX**
World War II area ...... **ETO**
worm .. **ESS, TINEA, ANNELID**
worm, African .... **LOA**
worm, bait .... **LURG**
worm, eye-infesting ...... **LOA**
worm, S-shaped .... **ESS**
worm track, fossil .. **NEREITE**
worn, as rope .... **MAGGED**
worn by friction .... **ATTRITE**
worn out .... **EFFETE**
worn-out horse
            NAG, HACK, PLUG
worry .... **RUX, CARE, CARK,**
            FRET, STEW
worship .... **ADORE**
worship, form of ..... **RITUAL**
worship, house of .... **BETHEL**
worship, object of ...... **IDOL**
worship of saints ...... **DULIA**
worship, place of
        ALTAR, TEMPLE
worthless **BAD, RACA, TRASHY**
worthless bit from table .. **ORT**
worthless rock ...... **GANGUE**
wound: Her. .... **VULN**
wound mark .... **SCAR**
wrangle .... **HAGGLE**
wrap .... **SWATHE, SWADDLE**

a wrapping .... PLIOFILM
wrath .... IRE
wrathful .... IRATE
wreath .... CHAPLET
wreath: Her. .... TORSE
wreathe .... COIL, WIND
wrest .... REND
wrestle .... TUSSLE
wrestling throw ... HIPE, HYPE
wriggling .... EELY
wrinkle .... RUCK, RUGA,
SEAM, RUGAE, RIMPLE
wrinkled ... RUGATE, RUGOSE
wrist .... CARPUS
wrists .... CARPI
wrist bone .... CARPAL
wrist guard .... BRACER
writ of execution ..... ELEGIT
writ, sheriff's .... VENIRE
writ to arrest .... CAPIAS

c write .... PEN, SCRIVE
write comments ...... POSTIL
write music .... NOTATE
writer .... DITER, SCRIBE
writer, Ger. .... MANN
writing instrument ...... PEN
writing on the wall
MENE, TEKEL
writing paper size ...... CAP
writing table .... ESCRITOIRE
writing well, art of .. RHETORIC
wrong ...... OUT, EVIL, AMISS
wrong: Lat. .... MALA, MALUM
wrong, legal .... TORT
wrong: prefix .... MIS
wrongdoing .... EVIL
wrongdoing, serious .... CRIME
wryneck .... LOXIA
Wyoming peak, highest
GANNETT

Y

Y, in Middle Eng. .. YOK, YOGH
Y's .... WIES
yacht .... SAIL
yacht pennant .... BURGEE
Yale .... ELI
b yam, Hawaii .... HOI
yam, white
UBE, UBI, UVE, UVI
Yang, opposite of .... YIN
Yangtze tributary .... HAN
Yap Island stone money ... FEI
yarn ... GARN, TALE, CREWEL
yarn count .... TYPP
yarn for warp .... ABB
yarn measure ..... LEA, HEER
yarn projection KNAP, KNOP
yarn, quantity of ...... SKEIN
Yarura language .... PUME
yataghan .... BALAS
youpon holly ...... CASSENA
yawn .... GAPE
yawn: obs. .... GANE
yearly .... ETESIAN
yearly church payment ANNAT
yearn .... ACHE, LONG
year's crops .... ANNONA
yeast .... BEES
yeast, brewer's .... BARM
yeast, Jap. .... KOJI
yeast, wild .... ANAMITE
yell: Scot. .... GOWL
yellow ...... AMBER, OCHER,
OCHRE, MELINE, CITRINE
yellow-brown .... TOPAZ
yellow bugle .... IVA

yellow dye plant .... AMIL
yellow fish .... ORF, ORFE
yellow ide .... ORF, ORFE
yellow iris .... SEDGE
yellow ocher .... SIL
d yellow pigment .... SIL
yellow wood .... AVODIRE
yellowhammer, Eur. .. AMMER
yellowish .... SALLOW
yelp .... KIYI, YOUP
Yemenite .... ARAB
Yemen's capital .... SANA
yes: Sp. .... SI
yesterday: Fr. .... HIER
yesterday, pert. to HESTERNAL
yet .... E'EN, STILL
yew, pert. to .... TAXINE
yield CEDE, ACCEDE, CONCEDE
Yogi .... SWAMI
yoke bar, S. Afr. .... SKEY
yokel ...... OAF, HICK, RUBE
yolk of egg .... VITELLUS
yolky .... EGGY
yon .... THERE
yorker: cricket .... TICE
Yorkshire city .... LEEDS
Yorkshire river .... URE, OUSE
you: It. .... TU
you: Sp. .... TE
young animal
CUB, PUP, COLT, WHELP
young female hog ... GILT
young girl of Burma ... MIMA
young hog ... SHOAT, SHOTE
young kangaroo .... JOEY

Young

a young man, handsome **ADONIS**
young ox: Eng. .... **STOT**
young plant .... **SET**
young rowdy ...... **HOODLUM**
youngest son .... **CADET**
youngster
    KID, TAD, TOT, SHAVER
youth .... **LAD**
youth .... **GOSSOON**
youth shelter .... **HOSTEL**

c youthful: zool. .... **NEANIC**
Yucatan Indian .... **MAYA**
yucca-like plant .... **SOTOL**
Yugoslav .... **SERB, CROAT**
Yugoslav leader .... **TITO**
Yum-Yum's friend
    KOKO, NANKIPOO
Yutang .... **LIN**

Z

b zeal .... **ELAN, ARDOR**
zealot .... **BIGOT**
zealous .... **AVID**
Zebedee, son of **JOHN, JAMES**
zebra, young .... **COLT**
zebrawood .... **ARAROBA**
zebu-yak hybrid **ZO, ZOH, ZOBO**
zenith .... **TOP, ACME, PEAK**
zenith, opposite of .... **NADIR**
Zeno's follower .... **STOIC**
zeppelin .... **BLIMP**
Zeppelin .... **GRAF**
zero .... **CIPHER**
zest .... **TANG**
zetetic .... **SEEKER**
Zeus, epithet of ..... **AMMON**
Zeus, maiden loved by
    IO, LEDA, EUROPA
Zeus, mother of .... **RHEA**
Zeus, old Doric name for **ZAN**
Zeus' daughter
    ATE, HEBE, IRENE
Zeus' sister .... **HERA**

d Zeus' son ..... **ARES, ARCAS,**
    MINOS, APOLLO
Zeus' wife ..... **HERA, METIS**
Zilpah's son ..... **GAD, ASHER**
zinc in slabs .... **SPELTER**
zinc ingot .... **SPELTER**
Zionist group .... **ITO**
zipper .... **TALON**
zodiac sign ...... **LEO, ARIES,**
  LIBRA, VIRGO, CANCER,
  PISCES, TAURUS, SCORPIO
Zola novel .... **NANA**
zone .... **AREA**
zone: Lat. .... **ZONA**
zoophyte, marine ...... **CORAL**
Zophah, son of ...... **BEERA**
Zoroastrian .. **PARSI, PARSEE**
Zoroastrian bible .... **AVESTA**
zounds .... **OONS**
Zulu headman ..... **INDUNA**
Zulu language .... **BANTU**

SPECIAL SECTION

READY REFERENCE WORD LISTS

In one compact section, here are lists of the most useful and widely-used word categories. Some of these words, having certain customary definitions, are also listed in the definitions' section of this book, but these complete word lists will be of greatest help when you are confronted with GENERALIZED definitions such as "Roman goddess," "South American Indian," "Heraldic term," or "African tribe."

All words in each separate listing are placed according to the number of their letters. This is a tremendous advantage to puzzle solvers, who are more concerned with the length of a word than with its alphabetical placement.

MEASURES

AREA MEASURES

AR, ARE, ACRE, DECARE (10 ARES), CENTIAR, CENTIARE
Annam .... MAU, QUO, SAO
Bengal .... BEGA
Czechoslovakia ... LAN, MIRA
Dutch E. Ind. ....BOUW
England, Old .... HYDE
Japan .... BU, SE, TAN
Norway .... MAL, MAAL
Paraguay .... LINO
Poland .... MORG
Rome, Ancient ...... CLIMA, CLIMATA
Serbia .... RIF, RALO
Shetlands, Orkney .... URE
Siam .... RAI, NGAN
Sweden .... MORGEN

DRY MEASURES

PECK, PINT, STERE
Algeria .... TARRI
Austria .... MUTH
Borneo .... GANTANG
Brazil .... MOIO
Burma .... TENG
Calcutta .... KUNK, RAIK
Channel Is. .... CABOT
China .... HO, HU
Dutch .... KOP, ZAK
Egypt .... KADA, KILAH
Hebrew .... CAB, KAB, KOR, EPHA, OMER, SEAH, EPHAH
Italy .... SALM, SALMA
Japan .... SHO
Morocco .... SAHH
Netherlands .... KOP, ZAK
Portugal .... MEIO, PIPA
Russia .... LOF
Tangier .... MUDD
Tunis ..... SAA, SAAH, UEBA

LENGTH, DISTANCE MEASURES

ELL, ROD, FOOT, HAND, INCH, MILE, YARD, METER, METRE, PERCH, MICRON, FURLONG
Annam .... LY, GON, NGU
Brazil .... PE
Calcutta .... DHAN, JAOB
China .... HU, LI, PU, TU, CH'IH, TCHI, TSUN
Czechoslovakia .. SAH, LATRO
Denmark FOD, MIL, MUL, ALEN
Domin. Repub. .... ONA
Dutch .... DUIM, VOET
D. E. Indies .... DEPA
Egypt .. PIC, PIK, KHET, THEB
Eritrea .... CUBI
Estonia .... LIIN, SULD
France .... AUNE
Greece .. PIC, PIK, BEMA, PIKI POUS, ACAENA
Hebrew .... EZBA
Iceland .... FET, ALIN, LINA
India .. GAZ, GEZ, GUZ, JOW, KOS, JAOB, KOSS
Italy .... CANNA
Japan .. BU, JO, RI (marine), CHO, DJO, KEN, RIN, HIRO

Java .... PAAL
Libya .... DRA, PIK, DRAH
Malabar .... ADY
Malacca .... ASTA
Netherlands .... DUIM, VOET
Norway .... FOT, ALEN
Persia ...... GAZ, GEZ, GUZ, ZAR, ZER
Poland .... MILA, PRET
Prussia .... RUTE
Rangoon . LAN, DAIN, TAUN
Rome, ancient ...... ACTUS, .. GRADUS, STADIA, STADIUM
Russia .... FUT, VERST
Siam .... WA, KUP, NIU, SEN, SOK, WAH, NIOU, SAWK
Spain .... BARA, CODO, DEDO, VARA
Sweden ...... FOT, REF, FAMN
Switzerland .... TOISE
Tripoli .... DRA, DRAA
Turkey .... PIC, PIK, KHAT, ZIRA

(liquid measures on page 189)

WEIGHTS

KIP, TON, GRAM, KILO, CARAT,
    GRAIN, OUNCE, CENTRAL
Abyssinia .... KASM, NATR,
    OKET, ALADA, NETER
Annam .... BINH
Arabia .... KELA
Austria .... UNZE
Bavaria .... GRAN
Brazil .... ONCA
Bulgaria .... OKA, OKE
Burma ...... VIS, KYAT, VISS
Calcutta .. PANK, PAWA, RAIK
China .... LI, FEN, HAO, KIN
    SSU, TAN, YIN, TAEL
Columbia .... SACO
Denmark ES, ORT, VOG, ESER,
    PUND
Dutch .... ONS, LOOD
Dutch E. Ind ...... TJI, HOEN,
    TALI, WANG
Egypt ... KAT, KET, OKA, OKE,
    HEML, KHAR, OHIA, OKIEH
England .... STONE
Estonia .... NAEL, PUUD
Ethiopia .... See Abyssinia
France .... GROS
Germany .... LOT, LOTE,
    LOTH, STEIN
Greece .... MNA, MINA,
    OBOLE, OBOLUS
Guinea .... AKEY, PISO,
    UZAN, SERON

Hebrew .... BEKA, REBA
India .... SER, BHAR, PALA,
    RATI, TOLA, VISS, RATTI
Italian .... SALM, SALMA
Japan ...... KIN, SHI, MORIN
Malay .... CHEE
Malta .... SALM, SALMA
Mexico .... LIBRA, ONZA
Mongolia .... LAN
Morocco .... ARTEL
Moslem .... ROTL
Netherlands ...... ONS, LOOD
Norway .... PUND
ORIENT ...... MANN, ROTL,
    TAEL, ARTAL
Palestine ...... ROTLA, ZUZA
Persia .... SER
Poland .... LUT
Portugal GRAO, ONCA, LIBRA
Rangoon .... RUAY
Rome, Ancient ...... AS, BES,
    LIBRA, SOLIDUS
Russia .... LAN, PUD,
    DOLA, POOD, POUD
Siam .... PAI, KLAM,
    KLOM, TICAL
Shetland Island .. URE (ounce)
Spain .... ONZA
Sweden ASS, ORT, STEN, UNTZ
Turkey ..... OCK, OKA, OKE,
    KILE, OCHA, KERAT

LIQUID MEASURES

TUN, DRAM, GILL, PINT,
MINIM
Abyssinia ...... CUBA, KUBA
Annam .... TAO
Arabia .... SAA
Austria .... FASS
Brazil .... PIPA
Burma .... BYEE, SEIT
China .... KO, QUEI, SHIH
Cyprus .... CASS
Dutch .. (old) AAM, AUM, KAN
Egypt .... HIN
England .... PIN, CRAN
Ethiopia .... see ABYSSINIA
Germany .... AAM, EIMER
Hebrew .... HIN

Hungary .... AKO
Japan .... KOKU, SHO
Malaya .... PAU
Netherlands . AAM, AUM, KAN
Portugal .... BOTA, PIPA
Rangoon .... BYEE, SEIT
Rome, Ancient .... URNA
Russia ... STOF, STOFF, STOOF
Somaliland .... CABA
Spain .... COPA
Sweden .... AM, AMAR, KAPP
Switzerland ..... IMMI, SAUM
Tangier .... KULA
Trieste .... ORNA, ORNE
Yugoslavia .... AKOV

COINS, MONEY

Abyssinia ..... BESA, GIRSH, TALARI
Afghanistan .... AMANIA
Albania .... LEK
Anglo-Saxon .... ORA, SCEAT
Annam .... QUAN
Austria .... DUCAT
Biblical .. BEKA, MITE (small), SHEKEL, TALENT
Brazil .... REI
Bulgaria ... LEV, LEW, DINAR
Chile .... COLON
China .. LI, CASH, TAEL, TIAO, YUAN, PU (early)
Colombia .... REAL
Costa Rica .... COLON
Czechslovakia ...... DUCAT, KRONE (plural, KRONEN)
Denmark ... ORA, ORE, ORAS, KRONE (plural, KRONER)
Dutch OORD, DALER, GULDEN, STIVER
D. E. Indies ..... BONK, DUIT
Egypt .... GIRSH
England ... ORA, RIAL (gold), RYAL, RYEL, GROAT, PENCE, FLORIN, GUINEA
Equador .... SUCRE
Ethiopia ..... see ABYSSINIA
Europe .... (old) GROS, DUCAT
France .. ECU (old), SOL, SOU, AGNEL (old), FRANC, LIARD (old), LOUIS, OBOLE, BESANT or BEZANT (old).
Genoa .... JANE (old)
Germany ..... MARK, KRONE (former), TALER, THALER
Ger. E. Africa .... PESA
Greece .. OBOL or OBOLI (old), STATER (old)
Hungary ...... GARA, PENGO
Iceland .... AURAR, EYRIR, KRONA
India.LAC, PIE, ANNA, DAWM, FELS, HOON, LAKH, PICE (small bronze), TARA, MOHUR (old), RUPEE
Iran .... see PERSIA
Iraq .... DINAR
Ireland .... RAP (old)

Italy .... LIRA, LIRE, SOLDO, TESTER, TESTON, TESTONE, TESTOON
Japan .... BU, RIN, SEN, YEN, OBAN
Latvia .... LAT, LATU
Lithuania .. LIT, LITAI, LITAS
Macao .... AVO
Malaya TRA (tin, pewter), TRAH
Mexico ..... PESO, CENTAVO
Montenegro .... PARA
Morocco .... OKIA, RIAL
Nepal .... MOHAR
Netherlands .... DAALDER
Norway .... ORE, KRONE (KRONER)
Oman .... GAJ, GAZ, GOZ, GHAZI
Persia.PUL, KRAN, POUL, RIAL DARIC, DINAR, MOHUR (old), TOMAN, STATER
Peru .... SOL, DINERO
Poland .... DUCAT
Portugal ..... JOE, REI, PECA, DOBRA (former)
Rome, ancient . SEMIS, DINDER
Roman ...... AS, AES, ASSES, SOLIDUS
Rumania ..... LEU, LEY, BANI
Russia . COPEC, KOPEK, RUBLE
Siam .... AT, ATT, BAHT, TICAL or TIKAL
Sicily .... TARI
Somaliland .... BESA
South Africa ...... DAALDER
Spain ..... COB, DURO, PESO, REAL, DOBLA (old), PESETA, PISTOLE (old)
Sweden ORE, KRONA (KRONOR), KRONE (KRONER)
Switzerland .... BATZ
Thailand .... see SIAM
Timor .... AVO
Turkey ..... LIRA (gold), PARA, ALTUN (gold), ASPER, MAHBUB (gold), PIASTER
United States .. CENT, DIME, EAGLE
Venice .... BETSO (old silver)
Yugoslavia .... DINAR

TRIBES (Including Peoples, Natives)

EUROPE:
Abyssinian .... SHOA
Albania .... GEG, CHAM,
 GHEG, TOSK
Balto-Slav .... LETT
Celtic on Danube .... BOII
Finnish near Volga ..... VEPS,
 VEPSA
Finnish, Ingria .... VOT, VOTE,
 VOTH, WOTE
Lithuania .... BALT
Syryenian .... KOMI
Teuton, ancient .... UBII

MIDDLE EAST:
Arab .... AUS, IBAD
Bedouin .... ABSI, HARB
Turkey .... KURD
East Turkey .... KURD
Persia .... see under ASIA

ASIA:
Afghanistan .... SAFI
Assam ..... AO, AKA; AHOM,
 GARO, NAGA
Borneo .. DYAK, IBAN; DAYAK
Burma .... WA, LAI, KAW,
 MON, WAS; AKHA, CHIN,
 KADU, KUKI, TSIN; KAREN
Caucasus ... IMER, KURI, LASI,
 LAZE, LAZI, SVAN; OSSET,
 SVANE
Celebes, Malayan .... BUGI
China, Miao .... HEH
China, Nord .... USUN, UZUN;
 USSUN
China, Tatar .... TOBA
India .... AWAN, BHIL,
 BHEEL, TURI
Kolarian (India) .... BHAR
Japan, aborigine .. AINO, AINU
Madagascar .... HOVA
Manchu .... DAUR
Mongol .... CHUD
Nepal .... AOUL, KHAS
Persia .... LUR, KURD,
 FARSI, IRANIAN
Tibet .... CHAMPA

AFRICA:
Bantu .... KUA; BANE, BAYA,
 BIHE, BULE, FANG, FUNG,
 GOGO, GOLO, GOMA,
 GUHA, HAKU, HEHE, JAGA,
 LUBA, MAKA, NAMA,

SOGA, SUKU, VIRA, YAKA,
 ZULU (largest); KAFIR;
 KAFFIR
Bedouin .... ABSI
Berber DAZA, RIFF, TEDA, TIBU
Bushman ... SAN, SAAN, QUNG
Congo .... FIOT, SUSU
Central Africa ... ABO; BULO,
 DOMA, KALI, KURI, LURI,
 YAKO; LUREM
Dahomey .... FON, FONG
East Africa ... JUR, LUR, YAO;
 AKKA, ALUR, ASHA, BARI,
 BONI, GOLO, MADI, NUER,
 VITI
Gold Coast .... AKAN, AKIM,
 AKRA
Hamitic ... AFAR, BEJA, BENI,
 BOGO, GALA, HIMA
Kaffir .... XOSA, ZULU
Kenya .... BONI
Lake Albert ..... ALUR, LURI
Liberia .... GI, KRA, KRU,
 TOMA, VAI, VEI, KROO
Libya ..... FUL, FULA, MZAB
Mozambique .... YAO
Nigeria .. ARO, EDO, IBO, IJO;
 BENI, BINI, EBOE, EKOI,
 IDJO, IDYO, IDZO, NUPE;
 BENIN
Nilotic .... SUK, BARI
Pygmy .... AKKA, DOKO
Slave Coast .... EGBA
Sudan ... FUL, FUR, VEI; FULA,
 GOLO, MABA, MEGE,
 NUBA, SUSU, TAMA
West Africa ... GA; AJA, EWE,
 IBO, KRU, KWA; AGNI,
 AKIM, APPA, BAGA, BINI,
 EFIK, EGBA, EKOI, GENG,
 GOLA, HABE, IKWE, JEBU,
 JOAT, JOLA, KETU, NALU,
 ONDO, REMO, SAPE, TCHI,
 TSHI, YACA, WARI

ALASKA:
Aleutians .... ATKA

GREENLAND .... ITA

AUSTRALIA .... KOKO
NEW GUINEA .... KARON

SOUTH AMERICA:
Fr. Guiana .... BONI

191

Alaska .... ALEUT, SITKA

Algonquin or Algonkian
Indians ... FOX, SAC, WEA;
CREE, SAUK; MIAMI; LEN-
APE, OTTAWA, PIEGAN;
SHAWNEE

Amazon .... (lower) MURA,
(upper) ANDOA

Apache .... LIPAN

Araucanian .... AUCA

Arawak ..... ARAUA, CAMPA,
INERI

Arikara .... REE

Arizona .. HANO, HOPI, MOKI,
PIMA, TEWA, YUMA;
MOQUI; APACHE

Athapascan Indians ..... DENE,
HUPA, TAKU; LIPAN,
TINNE; APACHE, NAV-
AHO

Aymara .... COLLA

Bolivia ...... ITE, URO, URU;
ITEN, LECA, MOJO, MOXO,
URAN; CHOLO

Brazil ...... GE; YAO; CAME,
DIAU, MAKU, MURA, PURI,
PURU, TUPI; ACROA,
ANDOA, ARAUA, CARIB,
GUANA, SIUSI; ZAPARO

Caddoan Indians .. REE; ADAI;
IONI, CADDO, BIDAI;
PAWNEE

California ...... HUPA, KOSO,
MONO, NOZI, POMO, SERI,
TATU, YANA; MAIDU,
YANAN; SALINA

Canada .... AHT, CREE, DENE,
TAKU; NISKA, TINNE;
SARCEE

Carib .... YAO, TRIO

Carolina .... CATAWBA

Chaco .... TOBA

Chile .... AUCA

Colorado .... UTE

Colombia .... BORO, DUIT,
MUSO, MUZO, TAMA,
TAPA; CHOCO; COLIMA

Costa Rica ...... BOTO VOTO

Cowichan Indians .. NANAIMO

Dakotas .. REE, SIOUX, TETON;
MANDAN, SANTEE;
ARIKARA

Delaware .... LENAPE

Ecuador: ..... CARA (extinct);
ANDOA, ARDAN

Eskimo .... ATKA; ALEUT

Florida: .... CALUSA

Fuegan .... ONA

Great Lakes .... ERIE; HURON

Guatemala ...... MAM; CHOL,
ITZA, IXIL, IXLI, MAYA,
ULVA, VOTO; KICHE, PIPIL

Honduras .... PAYA

Iowa .... FOX, SAC; SAUK

Indiana .... WEA; MIAMI

Iroquoian Indians,
Iroquois: .... ERIE, HURON,
CAYUGA, MOHAWK,
ONEIDA, SENECA

Jalisco: .... CORA

Keresan Indians: . SIA; ACOMA

Kusan .... COOS

Lesser Antilles .... INERI

Mayan Indians: ... MAM, CHOL

Mexico ... MAM, CHOL, CORA,
MAYA, MIXE, PIMA, PIME,
SERI, TECA, TECO, WABI;
AZTEC, OTOMI, SERIA;
TOLTEC

Miami .... WEA

Mississippi ..... TIOU, BILOXI

Montana ...... CROW, HOHE

Muskohegan Indians: . CREEK,
YAMASI, CHOCTAW,
SEMINOLE

Nebraska .... KIOWA

Nevada .... PAIUTE

New Mexico . SIA, PIRO, TANO,
TAOS, TEWA, ZUNI;
ACOMA, KERES, PECOS

New York .... SENECA

Nicaragua . MIXE, RAMA, ULVA

Oklahoma .. KAW, OTO; LOUP,
OTOE; CADDO, CREEK,
KANSA, KIOWA, OSAGE,
PONCA; PAWNEE

Oregon .... COOS, KUSAN,
MODOC, CHINOOK

Panamint .... KOSO
Panama .... CUNA, CUEVA
Pawnee Indians .... LOUP
Payaguas .... AGAZ
Peru: .... ANDE, ANTI, BORO,
    CANA, INCA, INKA, LAMA,
    PEBA, PIBA, PIRO, YNCA;
    CAMPA, CHIMU, CHOLO,
    COLAN, YUNCA; CHANCA;
    QUICHU
Peru South .... CANA, COLLA,
                    CHANCA
Piman Indians .. CORA, JOVA,
    MAYO, PIMA, XOVA, YAKI,
    YAQUI
Plains Indians ... CREE, CROW;
    KIOWA, OSAGE; PONCA,
    TETON, PAWNEE
Pueblo Indians .. HOPI, MOKI,
    TANO, TAOS, ZUNI;
    KERES, MOQUI
Rio Grande .... TANO
Sacramento Valley ..... YANA
Salishan Indians ..... ATNAH,
                    LUMMI
Shoshonean Indians .... UTE;
    HOPI,   KOSO,   MOKI,
    MONO;   MOQUI,   PIUTE;
    UINTA, PAIUTE
Siouan Indians ... KAW, OTO;
    CROW,   IOWA,   OTOE;

KANSA, OMAHA, OSAGE,
PONCA; BILOXI, DAKOTA,
MANDAN; CATAWBA

Sonora .... JOVA, PIMI, SERI

South America (widely
    distributed) .... GES, ONA,
    YAO; LULE, MOXO, PANO,
    PIRO, TOBA;   CARIB,
    INERI; ARAWAK

South Carolina ..... CATAWBA

Tacanan Indians ..... CAVINA

Tanoan .... TEWA

Tapuyan Indians .... GE, GES,
                GHES, ACROA

Texas .... LIPAN

Tierra del Fuego: .... ONA

Tlingit: .... AUK, SITKA

Tupian .... ANTA

Utah: .... UTE

Washington .... HOH, LUMMI,
                    MAKAH

Yucatan .... MAYA

Yukian .... TATU

Yukon .... TAKU

Yuncan .... CHIMU

ARMOR

Head	COIF, HELM; ARMET, VISOR; BEAVER, CAMAIL; BASINET, HAUBERK
Neck	GORGET
Shoulder	AILETTE, PAULDRON, EPAULIERE, PASSEGARDE
Body	TACE; CULET, TASSE; CORIUM, GORGET, LORICA, TASSET; CUIRASS, HAUBERK, SURCOAT; BRAGUETTE
Arm	BRASSARD, PALLETTE, VAMBRACE; CUBITIERE, REREBRACE
Hand	GAUNTLET
Thigh	CUISH, TASSE, TUILE; CUISSE, TASSET, TUILLE
Leg, foot	JAMB, JAMBE; GREAVE; CHAUSSE, PEDIEUX; SOLLERET
Complete suit	BARD, MAIL; BARDE

HERALDRY—HERALDIC TERMS

Heraldic bearings: BEND, ENTE, FESS, ORLE, FESSE, GIRON, GYRON, LAVER, PHEON; SALTIRE

Heraldic tinctures: gold, OR; fur, PEAN, VAIR, VAIRE; green, VERT; blue, AZURE; red, GULES; black, SABLE; orange, TENNE; silver, ARGENT; blood-red, MURREY; purple, PURPURE

attitude of animal SEJANT, GARDANT, PASSANT, RAMPANT

ball	ROUNDEL
band	FESS, ORLE, FESSE
barnacle	BREY
bend	COTISE
bird	MARTLET
circle	BEZANT, ANNULET
colter	LAVER
creature	LION, PARD; BISSE, WYVER; CANNET, WYVERN; GRIFFON, MARTLET
cross	CRUX, NOWY, PATY; FLORY, FORMY, PATEE, PATTE; CLECHE; SALTIRE
curved in middle	NOWY
curves, made of	NEBULE
division	PALE, PALY
dog, short-eared	ALANT
drops, seme of	GUTTE
duck	CANNET, CANETTE
fillet	ORLE
fish trap	WEEL
flower strewn	SEME
flying in air	FLOTANT
fountain	SYKE
grafted	ENTE
headless	ETETE
horizontal band	see band
leaves, having	POINTE
lines	UNDE, UNDY, URDY, NEBULY
lozenge	FUSIL, MASCLE
manacle	TIRRET
pointed	URDE
powdered	SEME
scattered	SEME
sheaf of grain	GERB, GERBE
shield	PAVIS
shield division	ENTE
shield's corner	CANTON
silver	ARGENT
sitting	ASSIS
snake	BISSE
sown	SEME
spangled	SEME
star-strewn	SEME
strewn	SEME
three parts, divided into	TIERCE
triangle	GIRON, GYRON
two-winged	VOL
voided escutcheon	ORLE
walking	PASSANT
wavy	ONDE, UNDE, UNDY, UNDEE, NEBULE
winged	VOL, AILE
wound	VULN
wreath	ORLE, TORSE

CHEMICAL ELEMENTS

METALLIC ELEMENTS	NON-METALLIC ELEMENTS	GASEOUS ELEMENTS
TIN	ARGON	ARGON
GOLD	BORON (inert)	CHLORINE
IRON	CARBON	FLUORINE
LEAD	HELIUM	HELIUM
ZINC	IODINE	HYDROGEN
CERIUM	NEON (inert)	KRYPTON
CESIUM	RADON-NITON	NEON (inert)
COBALT	SILICON	NITROGEN
COPPER	XENON	OXYGEN
ERBIUM		XENON
NICKEL		
RADIUM		
SILVER		
SODIUM		
YTTRIUM		

CHEMICAL SYMBOLS

Solver: Important Note—it is not necessary to list for you the chemical symbol of every element. The Chemical Symbol of any element not given below is found simply by writing down the first 2 letters of the name of the element. For example: Ruthenium's chemical symbol is simply RU.

Alabamine, **AB**
antimony, **SB;**
arsenic, **AS;**
boron, **B;**
cadmium, **CD;**
cesium, **CS;**
chlorine, **CL;**
chromium, **CR;**
columbium, **CB;**
copper, **CU;**
curium, **CM;**
gadolinium, **GD;**
gold, **AU;**

hafnium, **HF;**
iron, **FE**
lead, **PB;**
magnesium, **MG;**
manganese, **MN;**
mercury, **HG;**
neodymium, **ND;**
palladium, **PD;**
protoactinium, **PA;**
platinum, **PT;**
radon, **RN;**
rhenium, **RE;**
rubidium, **RB;**

samarium, **SM;**
silver, **AG;**
sodium, **NA;**
strontium, **SR;**
terbium, **TB;**
thallium, **TL;**
thulium, **TM;**
tin, **SN;**
ytterbium, **YB;**
zinc, **ZN;**
zirconium, **ZR;**

BIBLICAL REFERENCES

BOOKS OF THE BIBLE

Names and order of books of the:

OLD TESTAMENT

1 GENESIS	11 KINGS 1	21 ECCLESIASTES	30 AMOS
2 EXODUS	12 KINGS 2	22 SONG OF	31 OBADIAH
3 LEVITICUS	13 CHRONICLES 1	SOLOMON	32 JONAH
4 NUMBERS	14 CHRONICLES 2	23 ISAIAH	33 MICAH
5 DEUTERONOMY	15 EZRA	24 JEREMIAH	34 NAHUM
6 JOSHUA	16 NEHEMIAH	25 LAMENTATIONS	35 HABAKKUK
7 JUDGES	17 ESTHER	26 EZEKIEL	36 ZEPHANIAH
8 RUTH	18 JOB	27 DANIEL	37 HAGGAI
9 SAMUEL 1	19 PSALMS	28 HOSEA	38 ZECHARIAH
10 SAMUEL 2	20 PROVERBS	29 JOEL	39 MALACHI

Names and order of books of the:

NEW TESTAMENT

1 MATTHEW	9 GALATIANS	15 TIMOTHY 1	23 JOHN 1
2 MARK	10 EPHESIANS	16 TIMOTHY 2	24 JOHN 2
3 LUKE	11 PHILIPPIANS	17 TITUS	25 JOHN 3
4 JOHN	12 COLOSSIANS	18 PHILEMON	26 JUDE
5 THE ACTS	13 THESSALON-	19 HEBREWS	27 REVELATION
6 ROMANS	IANS 1	20 JAMES	
7 CORINTHIANS 1	14 THESSALON-	21 PETER 1	
8 CORINTHIANS 2	IANS 2	22 PETER 2	

BIBLICAL PROPHETS

AMOS (minor), ESAY, EZRA, JOEL (minor), HOSEA (minor), JONAH (minor), MICAH (minor), MOSES, DANIEL (major), NAHUM (minor), ELISHA, HAGGAI (minor), ISAIAH (major), EZEKIEL (major), JEREMIAH (major)

BIBLICAL PATRIARCHS

REU: ADAM, EBER, ENOS, NOAH, SETH, SHEM; ISAAC, JACOB, JARED, NAHOR, PELEG, SERUG, TERAH; LAMECH

BIBLICAL RULERS

OG; ASA (Judah), GOG, IRA; AGAG, AHAB, AHAZ, AMON, ELAH, JEHU, OMRI, SAUL; CYRUS, DAVID, DEBIR, HEROD, HIRAM, JORAM, NADAB, PEKAH, PIRAM, REZIN, SIHON, ZIMRI; ABIJAH, BAASHA. CAESAR, DARIUS, HEZION, HOSHEA, JAPHIA, JOSHUA, JOSIAH, JOTHAM, UZZIAH

BIBLICAL PEOPLES—TRIBES

DAN, GOG; ANAK, ARAD, CUSH, EMIM, MOAB, PHUD, PHUT (o.t.); ARKITE, HAMITE, HIVITE, KENITE, SEMITE, SHELAH, SINITE; EDOMITE, HITTITE, LEHABIM, MOABITE, REPHAIM

BIBLICAL PLACES

City . DAN, GATH, GAZA, ZOAR; BABEL, EKRON, SODOM; HEBRON

Country .... EDOM, ENON, SEBA; SHEBA

Hill, Jerusalem's .... ZION

Kingdom .... ELAM, MOAB; SAMARIA

Land .... NOD

Land of plenty .... GOSHEN

Mt. HOR, EBAL, NAIN, NEBO, PEOR; HOREB, SEIR, SINA, SINAI, TABOR; ARARAT, GILEAD, HERMON

Place .... ENON, AENON; JORDAN, SHILOH

Pool .... SILOAM

Region .. ARAM, EDAR; BASHAN

Town ...... CANA (1st miracle), NAIN (miracle site); BETHEL

River .... ARNON, JORDAN

BIBLICAL MEN

OG, UZ; ARA, DAN, ELI, GOG, HAM, IRA, LOT, NUN, URI; ABEL, AMOS, BOAZ, CAIN, CUSH, DOEG, EBAL, ENON, ENOS, ESAU, HETH, IRAD, JADA, JEHU, JOAB, KISH, LEVI, MASH, MOAB, OBAL, OBED, OMAR, OREB, OZEM, SETH, SODI, ULAM, UNNI, URIA; AARON (high priest), ABIAH, ABIEL, AHIRA, AMASA, ANNAS, CALEB, CHUZA, ENOCH, HAMAN, HARAN, HIRAM, HOHAM, IBZAN, ISAAC, JACOB, JAMES, JARED, MASSA, MOREH, NABAL, NAHBI, NAHOR, OPHIR, REZON, SACAR, TERAH, URIAH, ZAHAM; SAMSON; ANANIAS, ISHMAEL

BIBLICAL WOMEN

EVE; ADAH, JAEL, LEAH, MARY, RUTH; DINAH, EGLAH, HAGAR, JULIA, JUNIA, LYDIA, MERAB, NAOMI, PHEBE, RAHAB, SARAH, SARAI, SHUAH, TAMAR; ABITAL, BILHAH, DORCAS, ESTHER, HANNAH, HOGLAH, MAACAH, MAHLAH, MICHAL, MILCAH, MIRIAM, PERSIS, RACHEL, RIZPAH, SALOME, VASHTI, ZILLAH, ZILPAH; ABIGAIL, HAMUTAL

BIBLICAL NAMES

ED, ER; IRI, NER, ONO, REI, TOI; ABIA, ADER, ANER, ANIM, ASOM, DARA, ELON, ENOS, IRAD, IVAH, REBA; ABIAM, AHIRA, AMASA, ASEAS

GODS (DEITIES), GODDESSES AND MYTHOLOGY

ASSYRIAN GODS
    ANAT (sky), **ASUR or ASSUR** (war)

BABYLONIAN GODS
    Chief gods: **EA, ABU or ANU, BEL**
    EA (chief), **ZU** (wind), **ABU or ANU** (chief, sky, sun), **BEL** (chief), **HEA** (see EA), **IRA** (war), **SIN** (moon), **UTU** (sun), **ADAD or ADDA or ADDU** (wind, storm), **APSU** (chaos), **ENKI** (see EA), **ENZU** (see SIN), **IRRA** (war), **NABU or NEBO** (wisdom), **UTUG** (sun), **DAGAN** (earth), **ETANA** (eagle rider), **SIRIS** (alcoholic drinks), **BABBAR** (sun), **SHAMASH** (sun)

BABYLONIAN GODDESSES
    AI or AYA (consort of Shamash), **ERUA** (mother), **NINA** (watery deep), **NANAI** (daughter of Anu), **ISTAR or ISHTAR** (chief, love)

BRYTHONIC GODDESS
    DON (ancestress of gods)

CELTIC GODS—GODDESS
    ANA, ANU, DANA, DANU (mother, queen), **LER** (sea), **LUG, LUGH** (light, sun), **DAGDA** (chief)

CYMRIC GODS
    GWYN, LLEU, LLEW (solar)

EGYPTIAN GODS
    RA (sun), **SU** (solar deity), **BES** (evil, pleasure), **GEB** (earth), **KEB** (earth), **MIN** (procreation), **SEB** (earth), **SET** (evil), **SHU** (see SU), **TEM or TUM** (sun), **AANI** (dog-headed ape, sacred to Thoth), **AMEN** (king), **AMON** (sun and king), **AMUN** (king), **ATMU or ATUM** (sun), **BESA** (see BES), **HAPI** (the Nile as a god), **KHEM** (see MIN), **MENT** (falcon-headed), **PTAH** (Memphis god), **SETH** (evil), **SOBK** (crocodile-headed), **AMMON** (see AMEN), **HORUS** (hawk-headed), **MENTU** (see MENT), **SEBEK** (see SOBK), **THOTH** (wisdom, magic), **OSIRIS** (underworld), **SERAPIS** (see OSIRIS)

EGYPTIAN GODDESSES
    MA (same as MAAT), **MUT** (Amen's wife), **NUT** (heavens), **ANTA, APET** (maternity), **BAST** (cat- or lion-headed), **BUTO** (serpent), **ISIS** (cow-headed, Horus' mother), **MAAT** (truth, justice), **SATI** (queen), **ATHOR** (see HATHOR), **HATHOR** (love, mirth, cow-headed)

EGYPTIAN MYTH

BA (soul of man), KA (body of man), NU (chaos), AKH (spirit of man), NUN (see NU), APIS (sacred bull), ATEN (solar disk), DUAT (see AMENTI), HAPI (Nile or Amenti's jinnee), AMENTI (underworld region)

GREEK GODS

DIS (underworld), PAN (field, flocks, forest), ZAN (old name for Zeus), ARES (war, Eris' brother), EROS (love), ZEUS (chief of Olympian gods), COMUS (mirth and revelry), EURUS (southeast wind), HADES (underworld), KOMOS (see COMUS), MOMUS (ridicule), PLUTO (underworld), AEOLUS (wind), APOLLO (sun, youth), AUSTER (south wind), BOREAS (north wind), CRONUS (a Titan, Rhea's spouse; harvest), HELIOS (sun), HERMES (herald), KRONOS (see CRONUS), NEREUS (sea), PLUTUS (wealth), TRITON (sea), BACCHUS (wine), POSEIDON (sea)

GREEK GODDESSES

GE (earth, mother of Titans), ARA (destruction, retribution, vengeance), ATE (discord, mischief, infatuation), EIR (healing), EOS (dawn), ALEA (ATHENA), CORA (see KORE), DICE or DIKE (one of Horae), ENYO (Ares' mother, war), ERIS (discord, sister of Ares), GAEA or GAIA (see GE), HEBE (youth), HERA (queen), HORA (one of Horae), KORE (vegetation), LEDA (Tyndareus' wife), NIKE (victory), RHEA (mother of gods, wife of Kronos), UPIS, ARTEMIS, HORAE (three goddesses of seasons), IRENE (peace), METIS (Zeus' first wife), MOIRA (fate or Fates), ATHENA (wisdom), CLOTHO (a Fate, thread spinner), CYBELE (nature), EIRENE (see IRENE), HECATE (moon, magic), MOERAE (see MOIRA), PALLAS (wisdom), SELENA and SELENE (moon), ARTEMIS (moon, woods, nature), ATROPOS (one of the Fates, thread cutter), DEMETER (grain, agriculture), CHLORIS (flowers), NEMESIS (revenge), LACHESIS (one of the Fates, thread length), APHRODITE (love)

GREEK MYTH

IO (Zeus' beloved changed to a heifer), INO (Cadmus' daughter), PAN (field, flocks, forest), ANAX (one of Dioscuri), AUGE (Arcadian princess), CEYX (Halcyone's husband turned into kingfisher), CLIO (Muse of History), FAUN (see PAN), IDAS (hero, killed Castor), IOLE (Hercules' captive), LETO (Apollo's mother), MAIA (Hermes' mother), OTUS (giant killed by Apollo), ALTIS (sacred grove, Olympic games), ATLAS (held up heavens), CREON (Oedipus' brother-in-law), DIONE (Aphrodite's mother), ENEAS (Troy's defender), ERATO (Clio's sister), HADES (underworld), HELLE (fell into Hellespont with golden fleece), HYDRA (9-headed monster), MINOS (king), NIOBE (weeping stone), SATYR (part-horse demigod), THEIA (Hyperion's sister, wife), ADONIS (beautiful youth), AENEAS (see ENEAS), AGENOR (Trojan warrior), ALECTO (a Fury), DAPHNE (Apollo's nymph turned into tree), EUROPA (carried off by Zeus in form of white bull), HECTOR (Trojan warrior), NEREID (sea nymph to Poseidon), NESTOR (wise king, fought Troy), THETIS (Achilles' mother), TITHON (see TITHONUS), TRITON (sea demigod,

Poseidon's son), URANIA (astronomy), ARIADNE (Theseus' love),
ATHAMAS (Ino's husband), CENTAUR (half man, half horse), CYCLOPS
(1-eyed giant), ERINYES, (avenging spirits), EUTERPE (Muse of Music),
SILENUS (woodland deity, horse-goat-human), ATALANTA (picked up
golden apples—lost the race), TARTARUS (infernal regions), TITHONUS
(immortal king of Troy, Eos' favorite), TISIPHONE (one of Erinyes)
The Gorgons: MEDUSA, STHENO, EURYALE
The Graces: AGLAIA, THALIA
The Titans or Titanesses: primeval deities: GAEA or GE (mother of
Titans). URANUS (father of Titans). Titans: RHEA, COEUS, CREUS,
THEIA, CRONUS or KRONOS, PHOEBE, THEMIS

HINDU GODS
KA (unknown), AGNI (fire), AKAL (Immortal), CIVA (see SIVA), DEVA
or DEWA (divine being), KAMA (love), RAMA (incarnation of Vishnu),
SIVA (supreme), VAYU (wind), YAMA (judge of dead), BHAGA (love),
DYAUS (heaven, sky), VISHNU (supreme), KRISHNA (avatar of Vishnu)

HINDU GODDESSES
SRI (beauty, wealth, luck, Vishnu's wife), UMA (splendor), VAC (speech),
DEVI (any divinity, Siva's consort), KALI (evil), SHRI (see SRI), USAS
(dawn), VACH (see VAC), SHREE (see SRI), MATRIS (mothers), LAKSHMI
(see SRI)

HINDU MYTH
BANA (1,000-arm giant), KALI (tongue of Agni), KETU (Rahu's tail),
NAGA (Vishnu's serpent), RAHU (dragon, swallows sun), USHA (Bana's
daughter)

INCA GOD
INTI (sun)

IRISH—see CELTIC

NORSE GODS
ER (war), TY (see TIU), VE (Odin's brother, slayed Ymir), EAR (see ER),
LOK (see LOKI), TIU (sky, war, Tiwaz), TIW (see TIU), TYR (sky, war),
ULL (bow skill), VAN (sea), ZIO (sky), ZIU (see ZIO), FREY (fertility),
HLER (sea), HOTH (blind god), LOKE or LOKI (discord, mischief), ODIN
chief god, war, wisdom, slayed Ymir), THOR (thunder), TYRR (war),
ULLR (see ULL), VALE (see VALI), VALI (Odin's son), VANS (see
VANIR), VILI (Odin's brother), AEGIR (sea), AESIR (chief), ALCIS (twin
gods), BALDR (see BALDER), BRAGE or BRAGI (poetry), DONAR (see
THOR), HODER or HOTHR (see HOTH), VANIR (early race of gods),
WODAN or WODEN or WOTAN (see ODIN), BALDER or BALDUR (light)
The Aesir or chief gods: TIU, TYR, ULL, FREY, LOKI, ODIN, THOR,
VALI, BRAGI, DONAR, WODEN, BALDER

NORSE GODDESSES

EIR (healing), HEL (Loki's daughter, underworld, dead), RAN (sea, death, wife of Aegir), SIF (Thor's wife), URD (destiny), VOR (betrothal), ERDA (earth), FREA or FRIA (see FRIGG), GERD (Frey's wife), HELA (see HEL), NORN (fate), RIND (Odin's wife, Vali's mother), SAGA (golden beaker), URTH (see URD), FREYA (love, beauty), FRIGG (Odin's wife), NANNA (flowers), NORNA or NORNS (see NORN), FREYJA (see FREYA)

NORSE MYTH

ASK (see ASKR), DIS (female spirit), ASKR (first man), ATLI (king), EGIL (story hero), GARM (Hel's watchdog, slays Tyr), GERI (Odin's wolf), IDUN (Bragi's wife), MARA (nightmare demon), NATT or NOTT (night), WATE (giant), YMIR or YMER ("rime-cold giant"), EGILL (see EGIL), MIMIR (giant), ASGARD (abode of gods)

PHOENICIAN GODDESS
ASTARTE (fertility, love)

ROMAN GODS

DIS (underworld), SOL (sun), AMOR (love), FAUN (field, herds, half goat), JOVE (chief god), MARS (war), MORS (death), COMUS (mirth, joy), CUPID (love), EURUS (southeast wind), KOMOS (see COMUS), MANES (spirits of dead, gods of underworld), ORCUS (dead), APOLLO (sun, music), AUSTER (south wind), BOREAS (north wind), FAUNUS (rural deity), VULCAN (fire), NEPTUNE (sea)

ROMAN GODDESSES

NOX or NYX (night), OPS (harvest, plenty), DIAN (moon, chase, woods), IRIS (rainbow, Zeus' messenger), JUNO (queen), LUNA (moon), MAIA (Vulcan's consort), NONA (Fate), SPES (hope), CERES (earth, grain, agriculture, vegetation), DIANA (see DIAN), EPONA (horses), FIDES (faith), FAUNA (field), FLORA (flowers), MORTA (a Fate), PARCA (a Fate), SALUS (prosperity), TERRA (earth), VENUS (love), VESTA (hearth), ANNONA (crops), AURORA (dawn), DECUMA (a Fate), PARCAE (the Fates), VACUNA (Sabine huntress)
The Fates or Parcae: NONA, MORTA, DECUMA

TEUTONIC GODS—see NORSE GODS

TEUTONIC GODDESSES—see NORSE GODDESSES

VEDIC GODS—see HINDU GODS

VEDIC GODDESSES—see HINDU GODDESSES

WELSH GOD
DYLAN

FIRST AND LAST NAMES

(common to crossword puzzles)

You often find in crossword puzzles definitions like "Writer Aldous ——" or "—— Pavlova." The following list contains the most commonly used names, first names and last names. The part of the name which is usually given in the definition is here in light-face type, arranged alphabetically. The rest of the person's name follows in bold-face type.

Aaron .... **BURR**
Abbott .... **BUD**
Adams .... **MAUDE**
Addams ...... **JANE**
Adelina ...... **PATTI**
Adolph ...... **OCHS**
Adolphe ...... **ADAM**
Adoree ..... **RENEE**
Aherne ..... **BRIAN**
Alan .. **HALE, LADD, PATON, REED**
Albani ...... **EMMA**
Alban .... **BERG**
Albert ..... **ANKER, CAMUS**
Aldo .... **RAY**
Aldous .... **HUXLEY**
Alexis ...... **KIVI**
Alexander
    FLEMING, POPE, SEROV
Alexandre .. **DUMAS**
Alfred ..... **DRAKE, LUNT**
Alfred B. ... **NOBEL**
Alighieri .... **DANTE**
Allegra .... **KENT**
Allen ...... **ETHAN, IDA, MEL**
Allison ...... **FRAN**
Allyson ...... **JUNE**
Alois .... **LANG**
Alonzo ...... **CANO**
Ambler ...... **ERIC**
Ambrose ... **BIERCE, FLEMING**
Amon ..... **CARTER**
Amundsen .. **ROALD**
Anatole ... **FRANCE**
Andersen .... **HANS**
Andre .... **GIDE**
Andrews .... **DANA**
Andy ..... **DEVINE**
Aneurin Bevan . **NYE**
Angelo ... **GIOTTO, MOSSO, PATRI**

Anita .... **LOOS**
Anna .. **CASE, HELD, STEN, NEAGLE**
Anthony ...... **EDEN, SUSAN, TUDOR**
Anton ...... **DOLIN**
Anya .... **SETON**
Arden ... **EVE, TONI**
Arnaz ...... **DESI**
Arnold .... **HAP**
Arsene ..... **LUPIN**
Artemus .... **WARD**
Arthur Conan.**DOYLE**
Ataturk .... **KEMAL**
Attlee ... **CLEMENT**
Auguste .... **RODIN**
Autry .... **GENE**
Axel .... **GADE**
Bagnold ...... **ENID**
Bailey ...... **PEARL**
Bainter ...... **FAY**
Bambi .... **LINN**
Bampton ..... **ROSE**
Barkley ..... **ALBEN**
Bartok .... **BELA**
Barton ...... **CLARA**
Basie ...... **COUNT**
Baxter ...... **ANNE**
Bayes .... **NORA**
Beerbohm .... **MAX**
Beery .... **NOAH**
Begley .... **ED**
Ben ...... **HOGAN**
Bennett ...... **CERF**
Benzell ...... **MIMI**
Berg .... **ALBAN**
Berger ...... **ERNA**
Bernard ..... **SHAW**
Bernhardt .. **SARAH**
Bernie .... **BEN**
Bert .... **LAHR**
Best .... **EDNA**
Bette ...... **DAVIS**
Betty .... **FIELD**
Bevin ..... **ERNEST**
Billings ...... **JOSH**

Billy . **ROSE, SUNDAY**
Blanche ..... **RING, SWEET**
Blandish ... **SERENA**
Blas ...... **GIL, RUY**
Bloch .... **RAY**
Blum .... **LEON**
Blyth .... **ANN**
Bohr .... **NIELS**
Boleyn ..... **ANNE**
Bolger ...... **RAY**
Bolivar ..... **SIMON**
Bonar .... **LAW**
Bonheur ..... **ROSA**
Bowman ..... **LEE**
Boyd .... **ORR**
Bradley ..... **OMAR**
Brendel ...... **EL**
Bret .... **HARTE**
Brigham ... **YOUNG**
Brodie ..... **STEVE**
Brown ... **JOE EVAN**
Broz .... **TITO**
Bruce ..... **CABOT**
Brynner ..... **YUL**
"Buffalo Bill" . **CODY**
Bull .... **OLE**
Burl .... **IVES**
Burns .... **BOB**
Burr .... **AARON**
Burrows ...... **ABE**
Byington ... **SPRING**
Cabeza de ... **VACA**
Calloway ..... **CAB**
Cameron ...... **ROD**
Camillo Benso
    CAVOUR
Canada .... **LEE**
Cantor .... **IDA**
Capek ...... **KAREL**
Carl .... **CORI**
Carl Marie von
    WEBER
Carney .... **ART**
Carnera .... **PRIMO**
Carrel ..... **ALEXIS**

Carrie Chapman ...... CATT
Carrie Jacobs . BOND
Carrillo .... LEO
Carroll . BAKER, LEO
Carter ...... AMON
Case .... ANNA
Cassals ..... PABLO
Castle ...... IRENE, VERNON
Cather ...... WILLA
Catherine .... PARR
Cavalieri ..... LINA
Celeste ..... HOLM
Champion .. GOWER
Chaney .... LON
Channing ... CAROL
Chaplin ..... LETA, OONA
Chapman ..... CEIL
Charisse ...... CYD
Charles .... BEARD, BUSH, DANA, ELIOT, GREY, LAMB, LEVER, READE
Charlie ..... CHASE
Charlotte . BRONTE, CORDAY
Chase .... ILKA
Chekhov ... ANTON
Chic .... SALE
Christie ... AGATHA
Claire .... INA
Clare . BOOTH LUCE
Clarence ..... DAY
Clark .... MARK
Claude .... MONET, RAINS
Clemens .... MARK, TWAIN
Cleveland .. AMORY
Clifton ...... WEBB
Cobb ...... LEE, TY
Cole .. NAT "KING"
Columbo .... RUSS
Conde .... NAST
Connelly .... MARC
Conquest ..... IDA
Conway ..... SHIRL
Cordell ...... HULL
Cornel ..... WILDE
Correll, C. J. . ANDY
Coty .... RENE
Count .... BASIE
Coward ...... NOEL
Cox .... WALLY
Crane .... HART
Cregar ...... LAIRD
Cronyn ..... HUME
Curie .. EVE, MARIE

D.D.E. .... IKE
Dailey .... DAN
Dale .... EVANS
Daniel ...... DEFOE
Davis .... JEFF
Day .... LARAINE
de l'Enclos . NINON
de Leon .... PONCE
de Maupassant . GUY
Deborah ..... KERR
Deems .... TAYLOR
Delmar ...... VINA
Dennis .. DAY, KING
Descartes .... RENE
De Valera .. EAMON
Devine ...... ANDY
Dewey .... TOM
Dionne .. ANNETTE, CECILE, EMELIE, MARIA, OLIVA, YVONNE
Dolin .... ANTON
Donald ...... COOK, CRISP, MEEK, NOVIS
Donlevy .... BRIAN
Donna .... REED
Dorfmann .... ANIA
Doris . DAY, DOLON, DUKE
Dorothy . DIX, GISH, STONE
Dors .... DIANA
Doubleday .. ABNER
Doyle ..... ARTHUR CONAN
Drew .... ELLEN
Duke .... DORIS
Dumas .... AINE
Duncan ..... SARA, TODD
Dunn .... EMMA
Dunne .... IRENE
Durocher . LEO, LIP, LIPPY
Duryea .... DAN
Dvorak .... ANTON
Dwight .... MOODY
Eakers .... IRA
Eames ...... EMMA
Eamon de .. VALERA
Early .... STEVE
Eartha .... KITT
Eckener ..... HUGO
Eddie .... FOY
Edgar .... POE
Edith . ADAMS, DAY, PIAF
Edna . BEST, FERBER, MILLAY
Edouard .... MANET

Eduard ...... BENES
Eduard ...... LALO
Edvard ...... GRIEG
Edward ..... ELGAR, GAY, SILL
Edward Everett . HALE
Edwards ...... GUS
Edwin ..... BOOTH, WEEKS
Eggerth ... MARTA
Egon .... PETRI
Ekberg ...... ANITA
Eleanor .... STEBER
Eleanora ..... DUSE
Elias .... HOWE
Elihu .... ROOT
Ellen .... TERRY
Ellington .... DUKE
Ellsworth .... VINES
Emerson .... FAYE, RALPH WALDO
Emile .... ZOLA
Emily ..... BRONTE, POST
Emma ...... EAMES
En-lai .... CHOU
Enoch ..... ARDEN
Enrico ...... FERMI
Erik .... SATIE
Erikson ..... LIEF
Ernest ...... BEVIN, SETON
Ernie ... FORD, PYLE
Errol ...... LEON
Ethan ..... ALLEN, FROME
Ethel ..... WATERS
Ethelbert .... NEVIN
Eugene . DEBS, FIELD
Eva .... GABOR
Eva Marie ... SAINT
Evans .... DALE
Ewell .... TOM
Eydie ...... GORME
Eyre .... JANE
Ezra ...... POUND, STONE
F.P.A. ...... ADAMS
Fabrizi ..... ALDO
Ferber .... EDNA
Ferdinand .... FOCH
Fernando ... LAMAS
Ferrer .. JOSE, MEL
Filippino .... LIPPI
Fitzgerald .... ELLA
Fitzhugh ...... LEE
Florence ... BATES, REED
Foch .... NINA
Ford .... EDSEL, ERNIE, HENRY

203

Foscolo ...... UGO
Fournier ... ALAIN
Fra Filippo ... LIPPI
Frances ...... ALDA
Francis .... BACON,
     DRAKE
Francis Scott ... KEY
Francesco ... NITTI
Franchot .... TONE
Franck ...... CESAR
Francoise ... SAGAN
Frank ...... BACON,
  BUCK, CAPRA,
  CRAVEN, FAY
Frankie .... CARLE,
     LAINE
Frans .... HALS
Franz ...... LEHAR
Frome ...... ETHAN
Gabor . EVA, MAGDA,
     ZSA ZSA
Gale . STORM, ZONA
Gam .... RITA
Gardner . AVA, ERLE
Gavin .... MUIR
George .... ADE,
  BROWN, CLARK,
  CUSTER, DEWEY,
  ELIOT, GOBEL,
  OHM, PATTON,
  SAND
George Bernard
     SHAW
Geraldine .... PAGE
Gershwin ...... IRA
Gertrude .... BERG,
     STEIN
Gil .... BLAS
Giuseppe .... BELLI
Glasgow ..... ELLEN
Glenn .... FORD
Gluck ...... ALMA
Gorin .... IGOR
Gosden, F. F. .. AMOS
Gould .... JAY
Graham ..... BILLY
Grant ...... WOOD
Gray ... ASA, ZANE
Greco .... JOSE
Gregor .... MENDEL
Griffith ..... ANDY
Gueden .... HILDE
Guido .... RENI
Guiseppe .... VERDI
Guitry ...... SACHA
Gustavus .... SWIFT
Guy .... MOLLET
Gypsy Rose .... LEE
H.S.T. .... TRUMAN
Hagen .... UTA
Hal .... MARCH

Hale .... ALAN
Hallstrom .... IVAR
Hals ...... FRANS
Halsey ...... BULL
Hansson ...... OLA
Harold . TEEN, UREY
Harriet Beecher
     STOWE
Harris .. JOEL, PHIL
Hart ...... CRANE
Harte .... BRET
Havoc .... JUNE
Hayward .... SUSAN
Hayworth .... RITA
Hazel ...... SCOTT
Heifetz .... JASCHA
Heinrich .... HEINE
Held .... ANNA
Henri ...... PETAIN
Henrik ..... IBSEN
Henry .... HUDSON
Herbert ..... ALAN
Herbert George
     WELLS
Hernando de .. SOTO
Hess ...... MYRA
Heywood .. BROUN
Hobson .... LAURA
Hogan .... BEN
Holt .... TIM
Holtz .... LOU
Horace ...... MANN
Horne ...... LENA
Houston ...... SAM
Howard ...... PYLE
Howe ...... ELIAS
Hubbel .... CARL
Hugh ...... LAING
Hunter .. IAN, KIM,
   TAB, EVAN
Hus .... JAN
Hyerdahl .... THOR
Ian .... HUNTER
Ida Bailey ... ALLEN
Igor ...... GORIN
Ilka .... CHASE
Immanuel ... KANT
Ina .... CLAIRE
Inonu ...... ISMET
Irene ..... CASTLE,
   DUNNE, RICH
Iris .... MANN
Irving ..... BERLIN
Irvin S. ..... COBB
Isaac ...... STERN
Ismet ...... INONU
Italo .... TAJO
Ives .... BURL
J. Carrol .... NAISH
Jack ..... LONDON,
   OAKIE, PARR,

Jacob .... WEBB
Jacob .... RIIS
Jagger ..... DEAN
James ..... BARRIE,
  BARTON, BEARD,
  FARLEY, HILL,
  AGEE, WATT
James Montgomery
     FLAGG
Jan .. HUS, PEERCE,
  SMUTS, STEEN
Jane AUSTEN, COWL,
     EYRE
Janet ...... BLAIR,
  GAYNOR, LEIGH
Janis .... PAIGE
Jannings ..... EMIL
Jay .... GOULD
Jean-Paul .. MARAT
Jeanmaire ... RENEE
Jeanne ..... CRAIN,
     EAGELS
Jeffreys .... ANNE
Jenkins .... ALLEN
Jenny .... LIND
Jerome ...... KERN
Jessica ..... TANDY
Jimmy ...... SAVO
Joel Chandler
     HARRIS
Johan .... SARS
Johann Sebastian
     BACH
John . AGAR, ALDEN,
  BROWN, DALY,
  DEWEY, DREW,
  GAY, GOLDEN,
  HAY, KEATS,
  LITEL, LODER,
  LUND, RAITT
John Godfrey . SAXE
John Philip . SOUSA
John Wilkes . BOOTH
Johnnie ...... RAY
Johnny ... MERCER
Johnson . OSA, VAN
Jolson .... AL
Jonas .... SALK
Jonathan .... SWIFT
Jonson .... BEN
Johnston .... ALVA
Jose .... GRECO
Juanita ...... HALL
Jobal ...... EARLY
Juhani .... AHO
Jules ...... VERNE
Julia Ward .. HOWE
Julie ...... ADAMS
June ...... HAVER,
  HAVOC, LANG
Kaltenborn .. HANS

Karel ..... CAPEK
Karl .... MARX
Kay .... STARR
Kaye .... NORA
Kazan .... ELIA
Keith .... IAN
Kelly . GENE, EMMET
Kenton ...... STAN
Khachaturian .ARAM
Khan .. AGA, ALI,
ALY
Kibbee .... GUY
Kiepura ...... JAN
Kim ...... HUNTER
Kitchell .... IVA
Knight .... ERIC
Koussevitzky . SERGE
Kovacs ...... ERNIE
Kurt .... ADLER
Kyser .... KAY
Lafcadio ... HEARN
Lagerkvist .... PAR
Lagerlof .... SELMA
Lahr .... BERT
Laing ...... HUGH
Lanchester ... ELSA
Lange .... HOPE
Lanny .... ROSS
Lardner ..... RING
Lauck, Chester . LUM
Laura Hope . CREWS
Laurel .... STAN
Laurence .. STERNE,
OLIVIER
Laurie ...... PIPER
Law .... BONAR
Lazarus ..... EMMA
Learned ..... HAND
Lee . OMA, CANADA
Le Gallienne ... EVA
Lehmann ... LOTTE
Lehr .... LEW
Lena ...... HORNE
Leslie ...... BANKS
Levant ...... OSCAR
Levene ...... SAM
Levenson .... SAM
Lew .. AYRES, CODY
Lewin, Liliane . LILO
Lewis . ADA, JOHN,
LAWES, STONE,
TED
"Light-horse Harry"
LEE
Lillian . GISH, ROTH
Lillie ... BEA, PEEL
Lily .... PONS
Linkletter .... ART
Linn .... BAMBI
Liszt .... FRANZ
Lollobrigida .. GINA

Lombardo ..... GUY
Long .... HUEY
Loos .... ANITA
Loren ..... SOPHIA
Lorre .... PETER
Louise ...... ANITA
Lowell .... AMY
Lucas .. FOSS, SCOTT
Lucrezia ..... BORI
Ludwig ...... EMIL
Lugosi .... BELA
Luise ...... RAINER
Lupescu ... MAGDA
Lupino ...... IDA
Lynn .... BARI
Lyons .... GENE
Mack .... TED
MacMahon .. ALINE
Madame de .. STAEL
Madge ..... EVANS
Magnani ... ANNA
Major ..... BOWES
Malbin ... ELAINE
Mann IRIS, HORACE
Marco .... POLO
Maria ..... CALLAS
Marie ...... CURIE
Mario ..... LANZA
Mark ...... CLARK
Markey ..... ENID
Marner ..... SILAS
Marquette .... PERE
Marquis ...... DON
Marshall ..... ALAN
Martha HYER, RAYE
Martini ..... NINO
Mary .... ASTOR,
GARDEN, URE
Mary Baker .. EDDY
Marx ...... CHICO,
HARPO, KARL
Masaryk JAN, TOMAS
Mason ..... JAMES,
PAMELA
Massey CURT, ILONA
Mata .... HARI
Maude .... ADAMS
Maurice .... RAVEL
Maxwell .... ELSA
Maynard ..... KEN
McCarey ..... LEO
McCoy .... TIM
Meg ...... MUNDY
Mel .. ALLEN, OTT,
TORME
Menken.ADA, HELEN
Merimee PROSPER
Meriwether .. LEWIS
Merkel .... UNA
Merman ..... ETHEL
Meyerson .... BESS

Milton ...... CROSS
Miranda ...... ISA
Mischa ..... AUER,
ELMAN
Mitzi ...... GREEN
Mollet .... GUY
Montagu .... LOVE
Montez ..... LOLA,
MARIA
Moorhead .. AGNES
Morgana FATA, NINA
Morini ...... ERICA
Mostel ...... ZERO
Mowbray ... ALAN
Mundt ...... KARL
Munson ...... ONA
Murray .. DON, JAN,
KEN, MAE
Musial ...... STAN
Myra .... HESS
Nahum ...... TATE
Nazimova .... ALLA
Ned ...... SPARKS
Neilson ...... ADA
Nelson ...... GENE,
MILES
Nethersole ... OLGA
Nicholas .... AMATI
Nicholas Murray
BUTLER
Nikolaidi ... ELENA
Niels .... BOHR
Noel ..... COWARD
Nora . BAYES, KAYE
Novello ..... IVOR
O. Henry . PORTER
O'Casey ..... SEAN
O'Connor ..... UNA
Ogden . NASH, REID
Oley ...... SPEAKS
Oliver ..... HARDY
Olsen .... OLE
Oma .... LEE
Onegin .... EUGEN
O'Neill ..... OONA
Opie .... READ
Oren .... ROOT
Orlando ... LASSO
Oscar .... LEVANT,
WILDE
Ott .... MEL
Page .... PATTI
Paine .... TOM
Palmer LILLI
Parker ...... FESS
Pastor ..... TONY
Pasternak ... BORIS
Paton ..... ALAN
Paul ..... DRAPER,
MUNI, POTTER
Pauline ...... LORD

Pauling ..... LINUS
Pavlova .... ANNA
Peerce .... JAN
"Peewee" .... REESE
Peggy ...... WOOD
Pendleton .... NAT
Peron . EVA, EVITA,
JUAN
Peter ...... ARNO,
LORRE, MUNCH
Petina .... IRRA
Petri .... EGON
Philip .. HALE, NERI
Picon ...... MOLLY
Pierre ...... CURIE,
LOTI
Pieter ..... HOOCH
Pinky .... LEE
Polo .... MARCO
Ponce de .... LEON
Pons .... LILY
Ponselle ..... ROSA
Porter ...... COLE
Pound ...... EZRA
Preminger .... OTTO
Priscilla ... ALDEN,
MULLEN
Proust .... MARCEL
Pyle .... ERNIE
Rainer ...... LUISE
Raines ...... ELLA
Rains ...... CLAUDE
Ralph Adams . CRAM
Rathbone .... BASIL
Ray .... ALDO,
BLOCH, NOBLE
Read .... OPIE
Rebecca ..... WEST
Red, the ..... ERIC
Reed ALAN, DONNA
Reese .. "PEEWEE"
Regan ...... PHIL
Rehan .... ADA
Reinhardt .... MAX
Rene .... COTY
Rex .... BEACH,
BELL, STOUT
Rhodes ...... CECIL
Richard ...... BYRD,
CONTE, DIX,
HOWE, LONG
Rip .... TORN
Rita .... GAM
Robb .... INEZ
Robert .... ALDA,
BURNS, DONAT,
FULTON, PEEL,
TAFT
Rodzinski .. ARTUR
Roger ..... BACON,
PRYOR, RICO

Romain .. ROLLAND
Romero .... CESAR
Rooney .... PAT
Root . ELIHU, OREN
Rosa .... RAISA
Rubinstein . ANTON
Rudolf ...... BING
Ruth ..... DRAPER
Rutherford .... ANN
S.F.B. ..... MORSE
Saint, — Marie EVA
St. John .... ADELA
St. Vincent Millay
EDNA
Salmon P. .. CHASE
Sam .... HOUSTON,
SNEAD
Samuel .... LOVER,
MORSE
Sand ..... GEORGE
Sande .... EARL
Sandra .... DEE
Sayao .... BIDU
Scheffer ...... ARY
Schipa ...... TITO
Scholem ..... ASCH
Seegar ...... ALAN
Segovia ... ANDRES
Seton ...... ANYA
Sevareid ..... ERIC
Shaw ...... ARTIE
Shawn .... TED
Sheldon ..... HERB
Shelley ..... PERCY
BYSSHE, WINTERS
Short .... ADAM
Shriner ..... HERB
Shubert ...... LEE
Siddons .... SARAH
Sidney .... LANIER
Signe ...... HASSO
Silvers .. PHIL, SID
Sinclair ..... LEWIS
Skinner ...... OTIS
Slagle ...... SUSIE
Slavenska .... MIA
Smith . AL, ALFRED
Snead .... SAM
Sonny ...... TUFTS
Sophia ..... LOREN
Sothern ...... ANN
Sparks .... NED
Speaker ..... TRIS
Speaks ..... OLEY
Spewack ..... BELLA
Spitalny ..... PHIL
Stanford ... WHITE
Steen .... JAN
Stephen .. CRANE,
LONG
Stephen V. .. BENET

Sterling ...... JAN
Steve ...... BRODY
Stevens MARK, RISE
Stoker ...... BRAM
Storm ...... GALE
Stravinsky .... IGOR
Struthers .... BURT
Sullivan .... ED
Sunday .... BILLY
Susan B. . ANTHONY
Syngman ... RHEE
Tab ...... HUNTER
Tajo .... ITALO
Tamiroff .... AKIM
Tanguay ..... EVA
Tarbell .... IDA
Tarkington .. BOOTH
Taylor ..... DEEMS
Teasdale .... SARA
Tegner .... ESAIAS
Templar ... SIMON
Templeton .. ALEC
Tennessee .. ERNIE
Teresa ..... AVILA
Terry ...... ELLEN
Tex .... RITTER
Theda ...... BARA
Thelma .... RITTER
Thomas ARNE, BATA,
DYLAN, GRAY,
HARDY, HICKS,
HOOD, MANN,
NAST, WOLFE
Thornton .. WILDER
Tilden .... BILL
Tillstrom ... BURR
Tim .... HOLT
"Tinker to —"
EVERS, CHANCE
Tiselius ...... ARNE
Tito .... BROZ
Tolstoy ..... LEO
Tom ...... EWELL,
MIX, PAINE
Torme ...... MEL
Torn .... RIP
Truex ...... ERNIE
Truman ... CAPOTE
Trygve .... LIE
Tse-tung .... MAO
Turpin .... BEN
Twain ...... MARK
Uriah .... HEEP
Ulric ..... LENORE
Vallee ..... RUDY
Van .... GUS
Vance ...... ETHEL
Velez ...... LUPE
Venerable, the BEDE
Verdon .... GWEN
Verdugo .... ELENA

Verne ...... JULES	Weber and —	William Randolph
Vernon .... CASTLE	FIELDS	HEARST
Victor BORGE, HUGO	Weill .... KURT	William Rose BENET
Vincent ..... PRICE	Wheeler ..... BERT	William Sidney
Vitus ..... BERING	White .... PEARL,	PORTER
Vivien ..... LEIGH	WILLIAM ALLEN	Williams ... ROGER,
Vivienne .... SEGAL	Whitelaw .... REID	TED
Vladimir ... LENIN	Whitfield .... MAL	Wills CHILL, HELEN
W.C. ...... FIELDS	Whitman .... WALT	Winslow .... HOMER
W. Mackenzie . KING	Whitney ..... ELI	Winterhalter . HUGO
Wallace .. HENRY,	Wilbur ..... CROSS	Wolfert ...... IRA
AGARD, LEW	Wilhelm von . OPEL	Wynn .... ED
Wallach .... ELI	Willa .... CATHER	Xavier ..... CUGAT
Wally .... PIP	William .. BOOTH,	Young ... CY, GIG,
Walter ..... ABEL,	HANDY, HART,	ALAN
BRUNO, REED	HOLDEN, HULL,	Youskevitch .. IGOR
Warburg .... OTTO	INGE, PENN,	ZaSu .... PITTS
Washington	PITT	Zebulon ..... PIKE
BOOKER	William Butler YEATS	Zernial .... GUS
Waugh ...... ALEC	William Cullen	Zetterling .... MAI
Webb .... ALAN	BRYANT	Zola ...... EMILE
		Zorina ...... VERA

PRESIDENTS OF THE UNITED STATES

(In order)

1. GEORGE WASHINGTON	20. JAMES ABRAM GARFIELD
2. JOHN ADAMS	21. CHESTER ALAN ARTHUR
3. THOMAS JEFFERSON	22. GROVER CLEVELAND
4. JAMES MADISON	23. BENJAMIN HARRISON
5. JAMES MONROE	24. GROVER CLEVELAND
6. JOHN QUINCY ADAMS	25. WILLIAM McKINLEY
7. ANDREW JACKSON	26. THEODORE ROOSEVELT
8. MARTIN VAN BUREN	27. WILLIAM HOWARD TAFT
9. WILLIAM HENRY HARRISON	28. WOODROW WILSON
10. JOHN TYLER	29. WARREN GAMALIEL HARDING
11. JAMES KNOX POLK	30. CALVIN COOLIDGE
12. ZACHARY TAYLOR	31. HERBERT CLARK HOOVER
13. MILLARD FILLMORE	32. FRANKLIN DELANO
14. FRANKLIN PIERCE	ROOSEVELT
15. JAMES BUCHANAN	33. HARRY S. TRUMAN
16. ABRAHAM LINCOLN	34. DWIGHT DAVID EISENHOWER
17. ANDREW JOHNSON	35. JOHN FITZGERALD KENNEDY
18. ULYSSES SIMPSON GRANT	36. LYNDON BAINES JOHNSON
19. RUTHERFORD BIRCHARD	37. RICHARD MILHOUS NIXON
HAYES	

U.S. STATE GENERAL INFORMATION TABLE

STATE	Abbreviation	Rank by Area	Rank by Population
ALABAMA	Ala.	29	19
ALASKA	Alas., Alsk.	1	50
ARIZONA	Ariz.	6	35
ARKANSAS	Ark.	27	32
CALIFORNIA	Calif., Cal.	3	2
COLORADO	Colo.	8	33
*CONNECTICUT	Conn.	48	26
*DELAWARE	Del., Dela.	49	46
†DISTRICT OF COLUMBIA	D.C.		
FLORIDA	Fla.	22	12
*GEORGIA	Ga.	21	16
HAWAII	H., Haw.	47	44
IDAHO	Id., Ida.	13	42
ILLINOIS	Ill.	24	4
INDIANA	Ind.	38	10
IOWA	Ia.	25	23
KANSAS	Kan., Kans.	14	29
KENTUCKY	Ky.	37	21
LOUISIANA	La.	31	20
MAINE	Me.	39	36
*MARYLAND	Md.	42	22
*MASSACHUSETTS	Mass.	45	9
MICHIGAN	Mich.	23	7
MINNESOTA	Minn.	12	18
MISSISSIPPI	Miss.	32	28
MISSOURI	Mo.	19	13
MONTANA	Mont.	4	41
NEBRASKA	Nebr.	15	34
NEVADA	Nev.	7	49
*NEW HAMPSHIRE	N.H.	44	45
*NEW JERSEY	N.J.	46	8
NEW MEXICO	N.M.	5	39
*NEW YORK	N.Y.	30	1
*NORTH CAROLINA	N.C.	28	11
NORTH DAKOTA	N.D.	17	43
OHIO	O.	35	6
OKLAHOMA	Okla.	18	27
OREGON	Ore.	10	31
*PENNSYLVANIA	Penna., Pa., Penn.	33	3
*RHODE ISLAND	R.I.	50	37
*SOUTH CAROLINA	S.C.	40	25
SOUTH DAKOTA	S.D.	16	40
TENNESSEE	Tenn.	34	17
TEXAS	Tex.	2	5
UTAH	Ut.	11	38
VERMONT	Vt.	43	47
*VIRGINIA	Va.	36	15
WASHINGTON	Wash.	20	24
WEST VIRGINIA	W. Va.	41	30
WISCONSIN	Wisc., Wis.	26	14
WYOMING	Wyo.	9	48

†District   *One of The Thirteen Original States

State Capital	State Nickname	State Flower
Montgomery	Yellow Hammer, Cotton, Heart of Dixie	Goldenrod
Juneau	The Last Frontier	Forget-Me-Not
Phoenix	Grand Canyon, Sunset Land, Apache	Saguaro Cactus
Little Rock	Wonder, Land of Opportunity, Bear	Apple Blossom
Sacramento	Golden, Grizzly Bear	Golden Poppy
Denver	Centennial, Rover	Columbine
Hartford	Constitution, Nutmeg	Mountain Laurel
Dover	First, Diamond, Blue Hen	Peach Blossom
		American Beauty Rose
Tallahassee	Sunshine, Everglade, Live Oak, Peninsula	Orange Blossom
Atlanta	Empire State of the South, Peach, Cracker	Cherokee Rose
Honolulu	Paradise of the Pacific	Hibiscus
Boise	Gem, Potato	Lewis Mockorange
Springfield	Prairie, Sucker	Violet
Indianapolis	Hoosier	Peony
Des Moines	Hawkeye, Corn	Wild Rose
Topeka	Sunflower, Corn Cracker, Garden, Jayhawk	Sunflower
Frankfort	Blue Grass	Goldenrod
Baton Rouge	Pelican, Creole, Sugar	Magnolia
Augusta	Pine Tree, Lumber, Potato	Pine Cone and Tassel
Annapolis	Old Line, Free, Cockade	Black-Eyed Susan
Boston	Bay, Old Colony	Arbutus
Lansing	Wolverine	Apple Blossom
St. Paul	North Star, Gopher, Land of 10,000 Lakes	Moccasin Flower
Jackson	Magnolia, Bayou	Magnolia
Jefferson City	Show Me, Bullion	Hawthorn
Helena	Treasure, Bonanza	Bitterroot
Lincoln	Beef, Cornhusker, Antelope	Goldenrod
Carson City	Sagebrush, Silver, Battle-Born	Sagebrush
Concord	Granite	Lilac
Trenton	Garden	Violet
Santa Fe	Sunshine	Yucca
Albany	Empire, Excelsior	Rose
Raleigh	Tar Heel, Old North, Turpentine	Dogwood
Bismarck	Sioux, Flickertail	Wild Prairie Rose
Columbus	Buckeye	Scarlet Carnation
Oklahoma City	Sooner	Mistletoe
Salem	Beaver, Webfooter	Oregon Grape
Harrisburg	Keystone, Quaker	Mountain Laurel
Providence	Little Rhody, Gunflint	Violet
Columbia	Palmetto	Yellow Jessamine
Pierre	Coyote, Sunshine	Pasque Flower
Nashville	Volunteer, Big Bend	Iris
Austin	Lone Star	Bluebonnet
Salt Lake City	Beehive, Mormon	Sego Lily
Montpelier	Green Mountain	Red Clover
Richmond	Old Dominion, Cavalier, "Mother of Presidents"	Dogwood
Olympia	Evergreen, Chinook	Rhododendron
Charleston	Mountain, Panhandle	Great Rhododendron
Madison	Badger, Cheese	Violet
Cheyenne	Equality	Indian Paintbrush

GAZETTEER

OR

GEOGRAPHICAL DICTIONARY

Cities, States, Countries, Counties, Provinces, Towns, Rivers, Communes, Ports and Harbors, Regions, Lakes, Mountains, Islands, Volcanoes, Settlements, Kingdoms, Districts, Divisions, Peninsulas, Mountain Ranges, Nomes, etc.; n = North; s = South

A

ABYSSINIA ..... city, **HARAR**, **GONDAR**, **HARRAR**; town, **ADOWA**, (s) **MEGA**, province, **TIGRE**; river, **OMO**, **ABBA**; lake, **TANA**, **TSANA**

ADRIATIC ... port and harbor, **FIUME**; peninsula, **ISTRIA**; resort, **LIDO**

AEGEAN .... river, **STRUMA**; island, **MELOS**, **SAMOS**, **TENOS**; gulf, **SAROS**

AFGHANISTAN .. city, **HERAT**

AFRICA .... (see also SOUTH AFRICA page 216)

AFRICA .. (n) country, **TUNIS**, **UGANDA**, **ALGERIA**, **TUNISIA**, **TUNISIE**; lake, **NYASA**; province, **LAGOS**, **NATAL**; river, **UMO**, **NILE**, **TANA**, **CONGO**, **NIGER**; city (n) **ORAN**, **DAKAR**, **TUNIS**; mountains, **ATLAS**; region, **CONGO**, **NUBIA**, **SUDAN**, **SOUDAN**; port (w) **DAKAR**

ALABAMA ...... city, **SELMA** **ANNISTON**

ALASKA .. city, **NOME**, **SITKA**; island, **ADAK**, **ATKA**, **ATTU**; peninsula, **UNGA**; mountain, **ADA**; inlet, **COOK**; river, **YUKON**; highest peak in North Amer., **McKINLEY**; glacier, **MUIR**

ALBANIA ... capital, **TIRANA**; river, **DRIN**

ALEUTIANS ... islands, **ADAK**, **ATKA**, **ATTU**

ALGERIA .... city, port, **ORAN**

ALPS ...... mountain, **BLANC**, **MATTERHORN**

ANNAM .. .... capital, **HUE**

ANTARCTIC .... sea, **ROSS**

ARABIA .. city, **ADEN**, **BEDA**, **BERA**, **SANA**; state, **ASIR**, **OMAN**, **YEMEN**; port, **ADEN**; district, **TEMA**; kingdom, **NEJD**; gulf, **ADEN**, **OMAN**

ARCTIC .. gulf, **OB**; sea, **KARA**

ARIZONA . city, **MESA**, **YUMA**; river, **GILA**

ARMENIA .... river, **ARAS**

ASIA . mountains, **ALTAI**; lake, **ARAL**; sea, **ARAL**; river, **OB**, **ILI**, **AMUR**, **LENA**, **ONON**, **TIGRIS**; kingdom, **NEPAL**, **SIAM**; country, **ANAM**, **IRAK**, **IRAN**, **BURMA**, **CHINA**, **KOREA**, **SYRIA**, **TIBET**, **SITSANG**; kingdom E. Asia, **KOREA**; desert, **GOBI**

ASIA MINOR .. district, **IONIA**; mountains, **IDA**

ASIATIC .... (see ASIA)

AUSTRIA .. city, **GRAZ, WEIN, VIENNA**; river, **MUR, ENNS, RAAB, RABA**

AUSTRALIA .. peninsula, **EYRE**; river, **SWAN**; city **PERTH**

AZORES ..... port and harbor, **HORTA**; island, **PICO, FAYAL, FLORES**; volcano, **PICO, (ALTO)**

B

BALEARIC ISLANDS .... port, **PALMA**; island, **MAJORCA**

BALTIC island, **OSEL** (opposite **RIGA**); gulf, **RIGA**; capital, **RIGA**; river, **ODER**

BAVARIA .. river, **NAB, ISAR, NAAB**

BELGIAN CONGO .. river, **UELE**

BELGIUM .. city, **HUY, MONS, GHENT, LIEGE, MALINES**; commune (town), **ANS, ATH, SPA, LEDE, MONS, NIEL, ROUX, NAMUR**; river, **LYS, YSER, MEUSE, SENNE**; port and harbor, **OSTEND**; province, **LIEGE**

BOHEMIA .. river, **ELBE, ISER**; mountains, **ORE**

BOMBAY .. city, **POONA**; district, **SURAT**; seaport and harbor, **SURAT**

BOTHNIA .... islands, **ALAND**

BRAZIL .... city, **RIO, BELEM**; port and harbor, **PARA, BELEM, NATAL, SANTOS, PELOTAS**; state, **PARA, BAHIA**; river, **APA, ICA, PARA**; capital, **RIO**

BRITISH WEST INDIES . island, **NEVIS**

BULGARIA ..... capital, **SOFIA**

BURMA (see also INDIA).capital (former) **AVA**, (present) **RANGOON**; district, **PROME**

C

CALIFORNIA .... city, **LODI**,

NAPA, POMONA, ALAMEDA, SALINAS; town, OJAI; county, NAPA, YOLO, MODOC, MADERA; lake, TAHOE; mountain peak, LASSEN, SHASTA; valley, NAPA

CANADA .. mountains, **LOGAN, ROBSON**; peninsula, **GASPE**; province, **ALBERTA (ALTA.), BRITISH COLUMBIA (B.C.), MANITOBA (MAN.) NEW BRUNSWICK (N.B.), NEW-FOUNDLAND (NEWF.), NOVA SCOTIA (N.S.), ONTARIO (ONT.), PRINCE EDWARD ISLAND (P.E.I.), QUEBEC (QUE.), SASKATCHEWAN (SASK.)**; national park, **JASPER**

CANAL ZONE .. city, **ANCON, COLON**; lake, **GATUN**

CARIBBEAN .... island, **CUBA**

CAROLINES .. island, **PALAU (PELEW), PONAPE, TRUK, YAP**

CAPE VERDE.island, **SAL, FOGO**

CASPIAN .. seaport and harbor, **BAKU**

CENTRAL AFRICA ..... region, **SUDAN, SOUDAN**

CENTRAL AMERICA .... river, **LEMPA**

CEYLON .... province, **UVA**

CHANNEL ISLANDS island, **SARK**

CHILE ..... river, **LOA**; port, harbor, town, **ARICA**

CHINA .. city, **AMOY, IPIN, CANTON**; port and harbor, **AMOY**; kingdom old, **WU, SHU, WEI**; river, **SI, HAN, KAN, PEI, AMUR, HWAI, CANTON**; province, **AMOY, AMUR, HONAN**; mountains, **OMEI**; division, **MIAO**

COLORADO .... city, **LAMAR, PUEBLO, DURANGO**; park, **ESTES**; town, **OURAY**; range, **RATON**; mountain, **OSO, EOLUS**; peak, **OSO**; county, **OTERO**; resort, **ASPEN**

COLOMBIA .... river, MAGDALENA; city, CALI

CONGO .... river, UELE

CONNECTICUT town, DARIEN, ANSONIA, MERIDEN

CORSICA ... port and harbor, BASTIA

CRETE .... port and harbor, CANDIA; capital, CANEA; mountain, IDA

CRIMEA .... port and harbor, KERCH; river, ALMA

CUBA .... town, GUINES

CYCLADES .. island, IOS, NIOO, MILO, SYRA, DELOS, MELOS, TENOS, THERA

CZECHOSLAVAKIA ..... city, BRNO; BRUNN; river, EGER, GRAN, HRON, IPEL, ISER, ODER, OHRE, MOLDAU; region, SUDETEN; capital, PRAGUE (PRAHA); mountains, ORE

D

DENMARK .... island off, ALS, AERO; islands, FAROE

DOMINICAN REPUBLIC .. city, MOCA

DUTCH ...... see Netherlands

DUTCH EAST INDIES .. Island, BALI, JAVA NIAS; island group, ARU, ALOR, LETI; gulf, BONI; capital, BATAVIA

E

EAST ASIA .. kingdom, KOREA

EAST EUROPEAN . river, DRAU, TISA, DRAVA, DRAVE, TISZA, THEISS

EAST INDIES . see also (Dutch) East Indies) island, BORNEO

ECUADOR ..... province, ORO

EGYPT .. city, SAIS, CAIRO; ancient city, THEBES; town,

KISH; province, GIZA; river, NILE

ENGLAND .. city, ELY, BATH, YORK, LEEDS, COVENTRY; port and harbor, HULL, DOVER, POOLE; town, ETON; river, ALN, CAM, DEE, EXE, NEN, URE, AVON, NENE, OUSE, TEES, TYNE, TRENT; county, KENT, YORK, BERKS, BUCKS, DERBY, DEVON, ESSEX, HANTS, WILTS, DORSET, SURREY, SUSSEX

ESTONIA ..... island, SAARE; province, SAARE; capital, REVAL

ETHIOPIA ...... see Abyssinia

EUROPE .... river, ISAR, OISE, URAL, DANUBE; lake, BALATON (largest); peninsula, IBERIA; resort, LIDO

F

FIJI .... capital, SUVA

FINLAND .. port and harbor, ABO, KEM, PORI; town, northern, ENARE; lake, ENARE; islands, ALAND

FLORIDA ...... county, DADE; resort, DELAND; city, OCALA; cape, SABLE

FRANCE .... city, AIX, DAX, PAU, AGEN, ALBI, CAEN, LAON, LYON, METZ, NICE, OPPY, VAUX, ARLES, ARRAS, BLOIS, DINAN, LILLE, (n) NESLE, PARIS, SEDAN, TULLE, CANNES, NANTES, SEVRES; colony, ALGERIA; commune, EU, AUX, AUBY, BRON, ISSY, LOOS, MERU, ORLY, SENS, VIMY, VIRE, CENON; port and harbor, CAEN, MEZE, (s) SETE, BREST; resort, PAU, NICE, CANNES; department, VAR, GARD, JURA, NORD, ORNE, MEUSE, VENDEE; river, AIN, LOT, LYS, AIRE, AUDE, CHER, EURE, LOIR, OISE, ORNE, RHIN, SAAR, YSER, AISNE, ISERE, LOIRE (largest) MARNE, MEUSE, SAONE, SARRE, SEINE, SELLE (small), (n) VESLE, MOSELLE; Mount, BLANC; mountains, JURA; region, ANJOU, ALSACE

FRENCH EQUATORIAL AFRICA
river, **SHARI**

FRENCH INDO-CHINA
see Indo China

FRENCH MOROCCO .. capital,
RABAT; city, **RABAT**

FRENCH WEST AFRICA
city, **DAKAR**

FRIENDLY ISLANDS .. **TONGA**

G

GEORGIA ..... city, **MACON**,
SPARTA, **AUGUSTA**

GERMANY ... city, **EMS, ULM,
BONN** (capital W. Germany),
**GERA, JENA, LAHR, LINZ,
EMDEN, ESSEN, NEUSS;** com-
mune town, **AUE, WALD;** spa,
AIX, BADEN; canal, **KIEL;**
river, **EMS, ALLE, EDER, EGER,
ELBE, ISAR, MAIN, ODER, PRUT,
REMS, RUHR, SAAR, LIPPE,
MOSEL, REGEN, RHINE, SAONE,
WESER;** mountain, **ORE, HARZ;**
state, **HESSE;** district, **ALSACE;**
region, **SUDETEN**

GOLD COAST . port and harbor,
KETA

GREAT BARRIER ISLAND **OTEA**

GREECE .... city, **ELIS,
SPARTA, SPARTE;** colony, an-
cient, **IONIA;** island, **COS, IOS,
KOS, NIO, MILO, SCIO, SERO,
CRETE, DELOS, MELOS, PAROS,
SAMOS, IONIAN;** mountain,
OETA, OSSA, HELICON; nome,
ELIS; river, **ARTA;** peninsula,
MOREA; region, **DORIS;** dis-
trict, ancient, **ATTICA**

GREENLAND .... town, settlement, base, **ETAH**

GUAM .. city, capital, **AGANA;**
port and harbor, **APRA**

GUATEMALA .. volcano, **AGUA**

H

HAWAII .. chief city, **HILO;**
island, **MAUI, OAHU;** district,

HANA; islet, **KURE**

HEBRIDES, INNER ..... island,
IONA, SKYE, UIST

HOLLAND .. see NETHELANDS

HONDURAS ...... port. **TELA**

HONSHU .... bay, **ISE;** port
and harbor, **KOBE**

HUNGARY ...... city, **BUDA,
PECS;** commune, town, **ERLAU;**
river, **RAAB**

HYOGO .... capital, **KOBE**

I

IDAHO ...... capital, **BOISE;**
town, **ARCO**

ILLINOIS . city, **PANA, ALEDO,
ELGIN, PEKIN, CANTON, MO-
LINE, PEORIA, SPARTA**

INDIA .. capital, **MADRAS;**
city, **AGRA, DELHI, POONA,
SIMLA, MADRAS, BENARES;**
commune, town, **ARCOT, SOR-
ON;** kingdom (n) **NEPAL;** state,
**DHAR, JATH, JIND, ASSAM,
MYSORE, GWALIOR;** province,
**SIND, SWAT, ASSAM, BERAR,
DELHI, MADRAS;** Portuguese
possession, **GOA;** river, **SIND,
SWAT, GANGA, INDUS, KABUL,
GANGES;** district, **SIMLA, SA-
TARA**

INDIA, NORTH
see NORTH INDIA

INDIANA .... city **GARY,
PERU, MARION**

INDOCHINA . country, **ANAM,
ANNAM;** kingdom, **ANAM,
ANNAM:** city, **HUE, HANOI,
SAIGON;** region, **LAOS;** state,
ANAM, LAOS; port and harbor,
ANNAM

INDONESIA .... island. **AROE,
BALI, JAVA, TERNATE,
CELEBES;** island group, **KAI,
OBI**

IOWA .. city **AMES** (college);
county, **IDA**

IRAQ ..... capital, **BAGDAD, BAGHDAD**; port and harbor, **BASRA**

IRAN .... see **PERSIA**

IRELAND .. old capital, **TARA**; port and harbor, **COBH, TRALEE**; county, **MAYO, CLARE**; island, **ARAN**; river, **LEE, BANN, ERNE, NORE**; lake, **REE, ERNE**; town, **TARA**

ISLE OF WIGHT .... port and harbor, **COWES**

ISRAEL ..... port and harbor, **ACRE, HAIFA**; plain, **SHARON**; desert, **NEGEB**

ITALY .. capital, **ROMA, ROME**; city, **BARI, COMO, PISA, ROMA, ROME, MILAN, PARMA, SIENA, TRENT, NAPLES, SIENNA, VENICE,** (s) **CASERTA**; commune or town, **BRA, ARCO, ASTI, ATRI, DEGO, ESTE, LARI, NOLA, SAVA, TODI, ADRIA, ASOLA, PADUA, TURIN, EMPOLI**; resort, **LIDO**; port and harbor, **OSTIA, TRANI**; province, **ALBA, CONI, POLA, ROMA, ZARA, UDINE**; river, **PO, ADDA, ARNO, NERA, RENO, PIAVE, TIBER**; lake, **COMO, ISEO, NEMI**; strait, **OTRANTO**; gulf, **SALERNO**

J

JALAUN ...... capital, **ORAI**

JAPAN ...... capital, **TOKIO, TOKYO** (old name **EDO**); resort city, **HONSHU**; capital, **NARA**; city, **KOBE, KOFU, CHIBA, OSAKA, OTARU, TOKIO, TOKYO**; harbor or port or seaport, **OSAKA, OTARU**; island, **HONDO** (largest), **SADO**; volcano, **ASO, FUJI**; bay, **ISE**; province, old, **ISE, IYO, YAMATO**; mountain, **FUJI**

K

KANSAS .. city, **ARMA, IOLA, SALINA**; county, **OSAGE**; river, **OSAGE**

KOREA ... city, **KEIJO, SEOUL**

KASHMIR .... river, **INDUS**

KENTUCKY .. county, **ADAIR LA RUE**

KENYA .. (Africa) river, **TANA**

L

LATVIA .. capital, port, **RIGA**; river, **AA**

LEBANON ...... port, **SIDON**

LIBYA ..... port and harbor, **DERNA**; capital, **TRIPOLI**

LITHUANIA .. seaport, **VILNA**

LITTLE AMERICA .. sea, **ROSS**

LUZON ...... province, **ABRA** river, **ABRA, AGNO**

M

MAINE ... bay, **CASCO**; town, **BATH,** (University) **ORONO**; city, **SACO**

MALAYA ...... state, **PERAK, JOHORE**; region, **PENANG**; island, **BALI, JAVA, TIMOR**; port, **PEKAN**

MALAY ARCHIPELAGO island, **CELEBES**

MALTA .... island, **GOZO**

MARTINIQUE . volcano, **PELEE**

MASSACHUSETTS ...... city, **SALEM, NEWTON**; cape, **ANN, COD**; mountain, **TOM**

MEDITERRANEAN . island, **IOS, GOZO, RODI, CAPRI, CRETE, MALTA**; gulf, **TUNIS**; resort, **LIDO, NICE**

MESOPOTAMIA .. river, **TIGRIS**

MEXICO .... town, **TULA**; state, **COLIMA**; lake, **CHAPALA**

MICHIGAN ..... city, **ALMA, CLARE, FLINT, SPARTA**; county, **EATON**

MINDANAO ... volcano, **APO**; gulf, **DAVAO**

MISSISSIPPI .... city, **BILOXI**; river, **YAZOO**

MISSOURI .... city, **SEDALIA**; resort, **AVA**; river, **SAC**

MOLUCCA ...... island, **OBI**, **TERNATE**

MONGOLIA ..... desert, **GOBI**

MONTANA ..... city, **BUTTE**; river, **TETON**

MOROCCO .. region, **RIF, RIFF**; mountains, **ANTI ATLAS**; province, **SUS**; port and harbor, **RABAT**; town, **IFNI**

MOZAMBIQUE ... town, **IBA**; port and harbor, **BEIRA**

N

NEBRASKA .. city, **ORD**; river, **LOUP, PLATTE**; county, **OTOE**; capital, **LINCOLN**

NEPAL .... mountain, **API**

NETHERLANDS ... city, **EDAM, UTRECHT**; commune or town, **EDE, EPE, BEEK, ECHT, ELST, OLST, UDEN, GEMERT**; port and harbor, **EDAM**; river, **EEM, MAAS** (Dutch Meuse), **MAES, RIJN, WAAL**; island, **SUMATRA**

NEVADA ... city, **ELY, ELKO, RENO**; lake, **TAHOE**

NEW GUINEA .. city, port and harbor, **LAE**; island, **PAPUA**

NEW HAMPSHIRE ..... lake, **OSSIPEE**; city, **KEENE, NASHUA, LACONIA**; county, **COOS**

NEW HEBRIDES .... port and harbor, **VILA**; island, **EPI, TANA, EFATE, TANNA**

NEW JERSEY .. city, **TRENTON**; river, **RARITAN**

NEW MEXICO .. town, **TAOS**; river, **GILA**; resort, **TAOS**

NEW YORK ...... city, town, **ROME, TROY, OLEAN, UTICA, ELMIRA, MALONE, OSWEGO**; island, **STATEN**; county, **TIOGA**; village, **ILION**

NEWFOUNDLAND peninsula, **AVALON**

NEW ZEALAND .... lake, **TAUPO**; island, reef, **OTEA**

NIGERIA .. town, **ABA, IWO, LERE**; region, **BENIN**

NICARAGUA ..... city, **LEON**

NORMANDY ..... town, **ST. LO**

NORTH CAROLINA ... river, **HAW, TAR, PEE DEE** (Yadkin); cape, **FEAR**; county, **ASHE**

NORTH DAKOTA . city, **MINOT**

NORTHUMBERLAND river, **TYNE**

NORTH INDIA kingdom, **NEPAL**

NORTH VIETNAM capital, **HANOI**

NORWAY .... capital, **OSLO**; river, **TANA**; city, **HAMAR**

O

OHIO .... county, **ROSS**; city, **ADA** (college town Ohio Northern), **KENT, LIMA, BEREA, ELIDA, NILES, XENIA, CANTON, FOSTORIA**

OKINAWA .. port and harbor, **NAWA, NAHA**

OKLAHOMA ...... city, **ADA, ENID, SHAWNEE**

OREGON .... city, **SALEM, ASTORIA**; peak, **HOOD**

ORKNEYS .... island, **HOY**

P

PACIFIC ISLANDS ... island, **LAU, YAP, FIJI, GUAM, SULU, TRUK, WAKE, LEYTE, SAMOA, TAHITI**; island group, **PELEW**

PAKISTAN .... city, **LAHORE**; river, **INDUS**

PALESTINE .. (see also separate Biblical lists on page 197); mountain, **EBAL, SION, ZION, TABOR, HERMON** (highest); valley, **GHOR**; plain, **ONO**; area, **BEISAN**; port, **ACRE, GAZA**; town, **GAZA**

PANAMA .... port, **COLON**

PARAGUAY ...... city, **ITA**; river, **APA**

PENNSYLVANIA .. city, **ERIE, EASTON, CHESTER, TYRONE**; port, **ERIE**

PERSIA ... city, **NIRIZ, SUSA, RESHT**

PERU ...... department, **ICA**; capital, **LIMA**; city, **ICA**; cold district, **PUNO**; port and harbor, (s) **ILO, CALLAO**; river, **ICA**

PHILIPPINE ISLANDS (see also Luzon and Mindanao); city, **IBA, CEBU, NAGA, ILOILO**; mountain or peak, **IBA, APO**; volcano, **APO**; port and harbor, **ILOILO, BATANGAS**; province, **DAPA**; island, **CEBU, SULU, BATAN SAMAR, PANAY**

POLAND ... city, **LIDA, LODZ, LWOW, POSEN, SRODA**; river, **SAN, STYR, BIALA, VISLA, STRYPA, VISTULA**

PORTUGAL ...... cape, **ROCA**

PUNJAB .... river, **INDUS**

Q

QUEBEC .... peninsula, **GASPE**; district and town, **LEVIS**

R

RAJPUTANA ... district, **ABU**

ROUMANIA ..... city, **ARAD, IASI**; department, **ALBA**; river, **OLT**

RUSSIA .... city, **KIEF, OMSK, OREL**; port and harbor, **OREL,** ODESSA; commune, town, **KOLA**; river, **OB, OM, DON, ILI, OKA, ROS, UFA, DUNA, LENA, NEVA, ONON, SEIM, URAL, TEREK**; lake, **ONEGA**; sea, **ARAL, AZOF, AZOV**; mountains, **ALAI, URAL, ALTAI**; peninsula, **KOLA, KRIM, CRIMEA**; lake in European Russia, **SEG**; state in Dagestan, **AVAR**; region, **OMSK**

S

SAMOA
port, capital and harbor, **APIA**

SAVAGE ISLAND . island, **NIUE**

SAXONY . commune, town, **AUE**

SCOTLAND .. port and harbor, **OBAN**; seaport, **AYR**; county, **AYR, BUTE**; river, **DEE, TAY** (largest), **DOON, SPEY, TYNE, AFTON**; city, **AYR**; mountains, **IME**; lake, **AWE, LOCH**: district, **ATHOLE, ATHOLL**; island off, **ARRAN**

SERBIA ...... department or capital, **NIS, NISH**

SIBERIA .... (see also Russia) river, **OB, ENISEI, YENISEI**

SICILY ...... volcano, **ETNA, AETNA**; commune, town, **RAGUSA**; city, **ENNA**; province, **ENNA**; resort, **ENNA**

SOCIETY ISLANDS
island, **TAHITI**

SOUTH AFRICA district, **RAND**; river, **VAAL**

SOUTHEAST AFRICA
district, **NIASSA, NYASSA**

SOUTHWEST AFRICA
port and harbor, **DAKAR**

SOUTH AMERICA . river, **BENI, PLATA, YAPURA**; district, **CHACO**; mountains, **ANDES**

SOUTH CAROLINA
river, **SANTEE**

SOUTH DAKOTA capital, **PIERRE**

SOUTH PACIFIC .... isle, FIJI, BALI, COOK, SAMOA

SOUTHWEST .... river, PECOS

SPAIN .... city, JACA, JAEN, LEON, AVILA; province, ADRA, JAEN, LEON, LUGO, AVILA, MALAGA; port and harbor, ADRA, NOYA, VIGO, PALOS, MALAGA; river, EBRO, MINHO, TAGUS; kingdom, LEON, CASTILE; commune, town, ORIA

SPANISH MOROCCO (see also Morocco) port and harbor, CEUTA; district, IFNI

SUMATRA .... district, DELI

SWEDEN .. river, UME, LULE; island off ALAND; port and harbor, MALMO, OREBRO; strait, ORESUND

SWITZERLAND .... city, BEX, BALE, BERN, GENF, SION, BASLE, BERNE, LOCARNO; commune, town, AY, BAAR, BIEL, CHUR, RUTI, WALD, AARAU, MORAT; canton, URI ZUG, BERN, VAUD, ZOUG, BASLE, BERNE; river, AAR, AARE; lake, ZUG, JOUY, LUCERNE; mountain, TODI, VISO, MATTERHORN; resort, DAVOS; capital, BERN, BERNE; town, see commune

SYRIA .... city, ALEP, HOMS, ALEPPO; port and harbor, SIDON

T

TAHITI .... capital, PAPEETE

TEXAS .... county, CLAY, CARSON; city, WACO, LAREDO, ABILENE

TIBET . capital, LASSA, LHASA; river, INDUS

TRANS-JORDON .. mountain, HOR; mountain range, SEIR

TUNISIA ..... capital, TUNIS

TURKEY .... city, ADANA, ANGORA; river, ARAS; vilayet, ORDU, URFA; island, TENEDOS
TUSCANY ...... river, ARNO

U

UTAH .... city, HEBER, LOGAN; mountains, UINTA

V

VENEZUELA .... state, LARA; island, ARUBA; river, PAO

VERMONT ...... city, BARRE

VIRGINIA .... river, DAN, RAPIDAN

VIRGIN ISLANDS capital, CHARLOTTE AMALIE

W

WALES .... river, DEE, USK; lake, BALA

WASHINGTON .. city, TACOMA

WEST AUSTRALIA capital. PERTH

WEST INDIES .... isle, island, CUBA, HAITI, NEVIS

WISCONSIN .... city, RIPON, RACINE

WYOMING .... city, CASPER, LARAMIE; highest mountain peak, GANNETT; range, TETON

Y

YEMEN .... capital, SANA

YORKSHIRE .... river, OUSE; city, LEEDS

YUGOSLAVIA ... island, RAB, ARBE, SOLTA; city, NIS; river, SAVA, DRINA, NARENTA; district and province, BANAT

YUKON .... city, DAWSON; river, HESS, PEEL, ROSS

217

THE WORD-FINDER
with cross-references

FOR THE SOLVER

You can complete any unfinished 2-, 3-, or 4-letter word in the crossword you are working by using this WORD-FINDER. Even though you are at first unable to locate it in the Definition section for some reason, if you have just two letters of your wanted word (just one if it's a 2-letter word) you can find it here.

The WORD-FINDER words are listed according to the following Letter-Combination system:

XX - -   (for cases when the first two letters are known)
- XX -   (when the second and third letters are known)
- - XX   (when the last two letters are known)
X - - X   (when the first and last letters are known)

Let us say that you need to complete a word that is four letters long.

STEP ONE: Find the Letter-Combination that is the same as the letters which you have written into the crossword puzzle. Have you, for example, found "ON" as the end of a 4-letter word? Then turn to the "- - ON" Letter-Combination. Of course, since the WORD-FINDER is thorough-going, a number of words, all containing the same letter combination, are listed under this Letter-Combination.

- - ON Acon, agon, Amon, anon,
Avon, axon, azon, bion,
boon, cion, coon, Dion,
doon, ebon, Enon, Eton,
faon, Gaon, hoon, icon,
iron, Leon, lion, loon,
moon, neon, etc.

STEP TWO: You may know, after looking through the words listed under your Letter-Combination, the word which is the only correct possibility. If not, you now begin to eliminate words in the list by working with the words in the crossword puzzle which CROSS your unfinished word. You do this by experimentally inserting words from the Letter-Combination list. When the experimental insert produces such impossible-looking combinations with the crossing word as "bv," "pv" etc. it can be discarded.

STEP THREE: After eliminating the words which make highly unlikely or "impossible" combinations with the crossing words, you still may not be sure how to complete your unfinished puzzle. Here you make use of the invaluable CROSS-REFERENCE listings following the words in the WORD-FINDER. Each number following a word is the number of the page of the Definitions Section on which the word and one of its definitions will be found. The alphabetical letters a, b, c, d indicate in exactly which section of the definition page you will be able to locate the word with its meaning.

Example: adat (90b,95d)

On page 90 of this Dictionary, in section b of the page, you will find the word ADAT in bold face type. The definition is "law, D. E. Ind". On page 95, section d, you will find another cross-reference to ADAT. The definition reads "Malay law."

STEP FOUR: Now re-examine the definition in your puzzle. Eliminate words in the WORD-FINDER by comparing definitions until you arrive at the "logical candidate" word for which you have been looking. Definitions in this dictionary and those in your puzzle will not always agree in exact wording. In that case, let the general meaning of the definitions be your guide. Everyday words are not always cross-referenced in this WORD-FINDER, nor are some words of exceptional terminology. Only some of the words listed in the Special Section are cross-referenced. If your definition calls for a word likely to be found in the Special Section, it is recommended that you look there first.

TWO-LETTER WORDS

A - Aa (47a), aa (90b), Ab (48d,75b,102a), ab (63d), AC (39d), ad (90a,112d,167d), ae (42b,43c,d,122b,139a), Ae (82c,115d), ah (52c), ai (143c,148c), al (8c,80c,102c,104b), am (166c,175c), an (11b, 13b), Ao (13d,88b,c,116c), AP (107a,182d), ap (122d,166c), ar (88b,91c,98a,99b,110c), as (51b,67b,92b,126a,133a,b,180d), at (25c,32c,106a,123a,128a), au (63a,69c), aw (44a), ax (40c,139a, 167a), ay (7c,8b,9b,28d,55a,60a)

- A Aa (47a), aa (90b), BA (42a), Ba (150d,153c), ba (139a), da (9b,37a, 56a,133d,135d), DA (124d), ea (43c), EA (15b,68a), fa (108b,138a, 161a), Ga (69c), ha (52c), ia (43d,158c), ja (66d), ka (45c), Ka (68c, 77b,150d,153c,173c), la (13b,61a,83a,108b,138a,151d,161a), ma, MA (42a), Ma (69a,b,85d), na (140c,163d), NA (36c), oa (43c,d), pa (60b,106d), ra (108b), Ra (159b), SA (36c), ta (112d,139a,160b), VA (83a), va (105a), wa (188), Wa (24c,d,88c), ya, za (162a)

B - BA (42a), ba (139a,150d,153c), bb (147b), be, bi (122d,171c), bo (23d,24c,136a,168a), bu (190), by (18b,32c,106a)

- B ab (63d,) Ab (48d,75b,102a), bb (147b), FB (59c), HB (59c), ob (122b), QB (59c)

C - ce (62d,164c), CE (42a)

- C DC (39d), ec (122c)

D - da (9b,37a,56a,133d,135d), DA (124d), DC (39d), DD (42a). de (63d,89b,122b,122c,124a,152c,d), di (68c,89b,108b,122b,122c, 122d,171d), dm (131c), do (108b,138a,161a)

- D ad, (90a,112d,167d), DD (42a), ed (175c), Ed (18d), id (26d, 40c,51c,57a,b,d), od (8d,59d,79c), td (32a)

E - ea (43c), EA (15b,68a), ec (122c), ed (175c), Ed (18d), ee (139c), EE (42a), ef (91c), eg (59d,163d), eh (52c), el (13b,42a,47a,99b, 151d,168a), El (68a,108a), em (91c,98a,123d,172a,c), en (15b, 29c,50a,91c,98a,119d,123d,158c,d,172a), eo (34a), er (35b,76c, 137d,155a,158c,d,160b,175c), Er (18d,68c,85c,163d,166c,172c, 178a), es (49b,50a,66c,119d,158c,d,175c), et (10b,61a,b,89a,158c), ex (60b,91c,122c)

- E ae (42b,43c,d,122b,139a), Ae (82c,115d), be, CE (42a), Ce (62d), ce (164c), de (63d,89b,122b,c,124a,152c,d), ee (139c), EE (42a), Ge (47d,69a), he (91c), ie (74c,158c,163d), LE (59c), le (13b,61a, 108b), me (108b,124b), Me. (124d), ne (35b,106b), oe (43c,54d, 82d,180d,182a,b), pe (91c), Pe. (124d), re (6b,10b,35d,108b,122b, 129b,138a,161a), RE (59c), se (35b,108b), te (43a,62d,108b,131c, 152d,160b,185d), Ve (63c,109c), we (48c,124b), We (92b), ye (124b)

F - fa (108b,138a,161a), FB (59c), ff (147b), Fi (108b), Fo (23d), fu (42c,84c), Fu (30b)

- F ef (91c), ff (147b), if (35d,125a), LF (16d), of (6b), RF 16d)

G - Ga (69c), Ge (47d,69a), Gi (91d), go (64c,90d)

- G eg (59d,163d), Og (16d,18c)

H - ha (52c), HB (59c), he (91c), hi (52c), ho (39b,79a), Ho (87c), Hu (101c,108a,162b)

- H ah (52c), eh (52c), oh (52c), Rh (20c), sh (17b,43c,79c,126d), th (43c)

I - ia (43d,158c), id (26d,40c,51c,57a,b,d), ie (74c,158c,163d), if (35d, 125a), il (122c), im (122c), in (9d,123a), io (74b,74c,103c,115b), Io (25a,85d,95c,186b), ir (' 9d,122c), Ir (10a,28a,82b), is (51a,166c, 175c), Is (15b,23c,86c), i* (124b)

- I ai (143c,148c), bi (122d,1?1c), d. (68c,89b,108b,122b,c,d,171d), fi (108b), Gi (91d), hi (52c) .i (30a,b,37b,98a,108b,161b), mi (43b, 108b,138a,161a), pi (71b,85d,91c,165a,172a), ri (84c,96d,98a, 108b), RI (106c), si (108b,152d,185d), ti (92b,108b,113a,b,120d, 138a,161a,162c,169b), xi (91c)

J - ja (66d), jo (140c,160c), Jo (8c,94b), ju (121a)

K - ka (45c), Ka (68c,77b,150d,153c,173c), ko (22c,87c,121a)

- K OK (155a)

L - la (13b,61a,83a,108b,138a,151d,161a), le (13b,61a,108b), LE (59c), Lf (16d), li (30a,b,37b,98a,108b,161b), Lt (143c), LT (59c), lu (65a), lo (17d,93d)

- L al (8c,80c,102c,104b), Al (96b), el (13b,42a,47a,99b,151d,168a), El (68a,108a), il (122c), ol (29c,158b,d,160b)

M - ma, Ma (69a,b,85d), MA (42a), me (108b,124b), Me. (124d), mi (43b,108b,138a,161a), mo (21d,81c,101c), Mo (88c,177c), mu (10a, 30a,60c,71a,91c), my (52c,124c)

- M am (166c,175c), em (91c,98a,123d,172a,c), dm (131c), im (122c), om (49a,77a,77b,105c,136a), um (52c,76c)

N - na (140c,163d), NA (36c), ne (35b,106b), no (42b,106b), No (84b), nu (71b,91c), Nu (29a,49a)

- N an (11b,13b), en (15b,29c,50a,91c,98a,119d,123d,158c,d,172a), in (9d,123a), on (8b,9a,60c106a,123a), un (34c,122c)

O - oa (43c,d), ob (122b), od (8d,59d,79c), oe (43c,54d,82d,180d, 182a,b), of (6b), Og (16d,18c), oh (52c), OK (155a), ol (29c, 158b, d,160b), om (49a,77a,b,105c,136a), on (8b,9a,60c,106a,123a), oo (34a,74b), or (9b,36a,37b,69c,158c,166a,184b), os (21d,67b,104a, 131b), ow (52c), ox (10c,22c), oy (139c)

- O Ao (13d,88b,c,116c), bo (23d,24c,136a,168a), do (108b,138a 161a), eo (34a), Fo (23d), go (64c,90d), ho (39b,79a), Ho (87c), io (74b,c,103c,115b), Io (25a,85d,95c,186b), jo (140c,160c), Jo (8c, 94b), ko (22c,87c,121a), lo (17d,93d), mo (21d,81c,101c), Mo (88c, 177c), no (42b,106b), No (84b), oo (34a,74b), Ro (13c,81d,88c,131c, 173c), so (76a,108b,125a,138a,158b,161a,165b,175c), to (10b, 13c), uo (43d), vo (91a), yo, zo (13d,186b)

P - pa (60b,106d), pe (91c), Pe. (124d), pi (71b,85d,91c,165a,172a), pu (30b,140a)

- P ap (122d,166c), AP (107a,182d), up (123a), UP (107a,182d)

Q - QB (59c), q.v. (180d)

R - ra (108b), Ra (159b), re (6b,10b,35d,108b,122b,129b,138a,161a), RE (59c), RF (16d), Rh (20c), ri (84c,96d,98a,108b), RI (106c), Ro (13c,81d,88c,131c,173c), RT (59c)

- R ar (88b,91c,98a,99b,110c), er (35b,76c,137d,155a,158c,d,160b, 175c), Er (18d,68c,85c,163d,166c,172c,178a), ir (99d,122c), Ir (10a, 28a,82b), or (9b,36a,37b,69c158c,166a,184b), Ur (6b,28d,94a, 100d)

S - SA (36c), se (35b,108b), Se, sh (17b,43c,79c,126d), si (108b,152d, 185d), so (76a,108b,125a,138a,158b,161a,165b,175c), SS (16d, 164c), Su (127a), Sw (35b), Sy (141a)

- S as (51b,67b,92b,126a,133a,b,180d), es (49b,50a,66c,119d,158c, d,175c), is (51a,166c,175c), Is (15b,23c,86c), os (21d,67b,104a, 131b), S.S. (16d,164c), us (124b)

T - ta (112d,139a,160b), td (32a), te (43a,62d,108b,131c,152d,160b, 185d), th (43c), ti (92b,108b,113a,b,120d,138a,161a,162c,169b), to (10b,13c), tt (147b), tu (83c,164d,185d), Ty (68c,109c,163d, 178a)

- T at (25c,32c,106a,123a,128a), et (10b,61a,b,89a,158c), It (124b), Lt (143c), LT (59c), RT (59c), tt (147b), ut (72b,108b), Ut (67a)

U - um (52c,76c), un (34c,122c), Uo (43d), up (123a), Ur (6b,28d, 94a,100d), UP (107a,182d), us (124b), ut (72b,108b), Ut (67a), Uz (48c)

- U au (63a,69c), bu (190), fu (42c,84c), Fu (30b), Hu (101c,108a, 162b), ju (121a), lu (65a), mu (10a,30a,60c,71a,91c), nu (71b, 91c), Nu (29a,49a), pu (30b,140a), Su (127a), tu (83c, 164d, 185d), Wu (30b), Zu (68c,157a)

V - va (105a), Va (83a), Ve (63c,109c), vo (91a)

- V q.v. (180d)

W - wa (188), Wa (24c,d,88c), we (48c,124b), We (92b), Wu (30b), wy (91c)

- W aw (44a), ow (52c), sw (35b)

X - xi (91c)

- X ax (40c,139a,167a), ex (60b,91c,122c), ox (10c,22c)

Y - ya, ye (124b), yo

- Y ay (7c,8b,9b,28d,55a,60a), by (18b,32c,106a), my (52c,124c), sy (141a), oy (139c), Ty (68c,109c,163d,178a), wy (91c)

Z - za (162a), zo (13d,186b), Zu (68c,157a)

- Z Uz (48c)

THREE-LETTER WORDS

AA - aal (47c,80c,104b), aam (47a,49d,93a), aar (172d), Aar (131a)

A - A aba (12a,25d,32b,33a,65b), Ada (110a,112c,183c), aea (26a,36d), aga (35a,39a,48b,102d,103a,b,111c,166b,170d,171a), aha (52c,55c, 159c), aka (88b,c,176b), Aka (13d), ala (6d,13a,15c,61a,133d,

222

182c,d), **Ala** (151b), **ama** (26a,28d,31a,35b,39c,95b,108d,111c, 117b,182c), **ana** (10b,33c,60d,93a,98c,122b,d,140d,142b), **Ana** (28a,68d,100c), **apa** (23a,177d), **ara** (33a,114a,116a,118b,163d), **Ara** (9b,18c,36b,c,68d,69b,c,85a,95a,175b), **Asa** (6a,18c,71a,84d, 86d,164c), **ata** (58d,97d,158d,160c,173d), **Ata** (79c,80d,94d, 95d,100a,106b,117a,), **ava** (78d,86a,116a,120d,139a,167b), **Ava** (24c), **awa** (100a,139a), **aya** (77b,166b)

- AA   **baa** (143d), **maa** (97d,143d), **saa** (98a), **taa** (112d)

AB -   **aba** (12a,25d,32b,33a,65b), **abb** (58b,178b,185b), **ABC** (134d), **Abe** (71a,96a,123a), **Abi** (76c), **Abo** (25d), **Abt** (34c), **abu** (17a), **Abu** (15b,42a,55a,68a,c,147d)

A - B   **abb** (58b,178b,185b), **alb** (65b,176a)

- AB   **Bab** (15a), **cab** (75c), **dab** (46a,57b,58b,d,114d,115c), **gab** (29b, 78a,116c,122a,161c,183a), **jab** (120b,125c), **kab** (75c), **lab, Mab** (54b,126b,183d), **nab** (13b,26c,27b,142a), **pab** (139c), **rab** (17c,75c, 85b,102d,162c,166b), **Rab** (45a), **tab** (29b,39c,58b,86a,128d,145a)

AC -   **ace** (7a,26c,52d,57a,77d,110c,114c,120b,147a,163a,173a), **ach** (8b, 48a,52c,66b,80c), **aci** (29c), **act** (41d,55b,119c,155d), **acu** (34c), **acy** (34c)

A - C   **ABC** (134d), **arc** (31b,39d,92a,126a,127c,142a)

- AC   **bac** (31b,55c,174d), **fac** (41c), **lac** (53c,99d,130c,135b,174d), **Mae** (96a,140b,150b), **pac** (73b,94c,100d), **sac** (15d,121d), **Sac** (80c), **tac** (34d,130a), **Vac** (153b), **zac** (27c)

AD -   **Ada** (110a,112c,183c), **add** (10d,11d,14c,158a,167c), **ade** (18c, 149d), **Ade** (9c,53b), **ado** (22b,24d,35b,64c,78d,121d,156b,170a), **ady** (188), **adz** (40c,167a)

A - D   **aid** (14a,15b,64c,75d,158b), **add** (10d,11d,14c,158a,167c), **and** (36a,119d)

- AD   **bad** (55a,173a,184d), **cad** (22b,23b,75c,172c,173d), **dad, fad** (38b, 108c,163a), **gad** (58c,100a,b,127d,132b,153c,154b,178a), **Gad** (84a, 186d), **had, lad** (22c,25b,55b,157c,186a), **mad** (10c,82b), **pad** (39d, 59c,76c,157d,161a,168b), **rad** (50b,138d,173b), **sad** (29c,42c,94c, 98c,104a,150d,173a), **tad** (22c,174a,186a), **wad** (94d,97b,109c, 112b,149d)

AE -   **aea** (26a,36d), **AEF** (184d), **aer** (8b,28d,34a,b,175a), **acs** (23c, 89a,101c,132d,133a,b), **aet** (89a,109d), **Aex** (46d)

A - E   **Abe** (71a,96a,123a), **ace** (7a,26c,52d,57a,77d,110c,114c,120b, 147a,163a,173a), **ade** (18c,149d), **Ade** (9c,53b), **age** (51d,66a,92a, 97c,98c,116b,141c), **ake** (60a,107a), **ale** (17c,18c,50c,55d,92d, 104c), **ame** (37a,62d,131b), **ane** (61c,140a,158b), **ape** (36d,79d, 100a,101d,146d), **are** (51a,88b,98a,99b,110c,166c,175c), **ase** (51a, 139a), **Ase** (79b,115d), **ate** (81a,108c,158c,174c), **Ate** (20c,68b,d, 69a,b,116c,186b), **ave** (54c,71d,73a,122a,134a,136d), **awe** (81d, 100a,130d,175b,182b), **axe** (30c,40c,167a), **aye** (7c,9b,55a,60a)

- AE   **dae** (139b), **eae** (34b), **hae** (139c), **kae** (84a,140b), **Mae** (183c), **nae** (139d), **rae** (136b,138d,140b), **Rae** (183c), **sae** (140b,149c), **tae** (138d,140c,166c,d), **vae** (176b)

AF -   **AFL** (173a), **Afr.** (36c), **aft** (14a,15b,17d,128b,167d)

A - F   **AEF** (184d), **Alf** (96a)

223

- AF gaf (12b), kaf (12b), Kaf (104a), oaf (22a,45b,146d,157d,185d), Qaf (104a)

AG - aga (35a,39a,48b,102d,103a,b,111c,166b,170d,171a), age (51d, 66a,92a,97c,98c,116b,141c), ago (25a,69d,114d,147a)

- AG bag (26c,139a,145b,159a), cag (81d,109d), dag (11b,118c,139c), Dag (108c), fag (55a,166a), gag (146c,183a), hag (140a,183a), jag (124d,148a), lag (93c,155d), mag (73b,95b,166c), Mag (183d), nag (73d,78b,138c,184d), rag (59b,77c,100c,133c,161a), sag (46b), tag (45a,54c,65a,87b,144a), vag (174b,178a), wag (85b,104a,183a), zag (84a)

AH - aha (52c,55c,159c), Ahi (32c,147d), ahu (24c,41d,65d,103d,120d)

A - H ach (8b,48a,52c,66b,80c), akh (153d), ash (24d,33c,49c,73d,134b, 168c,169a), auh (52c)

- AH bah (52c), dah (24c,87a), hah (52c), Jah (84d), Mah (10b,57c, 102b), pah (52c,60b,106d), rah (29b), sah (188), wah (113c), yah (52c)

AI - aid (14a,15b,64c,75d,158b), aik (139d), ail (170a), aim (42d,43d, 67d,109b,125d,157c), ain (18d,91c,110c,124b,140a,154b,180a), air (11c,12c,42b,44c,53a,96b,98c,99d,125b,170c), ait (82d,132a), Aix (46d)

A - I Abi (76c), aci (29c), Ahi (32c,147d), Ali (7b,12a,25c,48b,55a,60c, 92d,101a,103a,164a,166b,170d), ami (61d), ani (19b,d,20b,39b), api (34a,76d), Ari (18d), asi (137a), ati (106d,107a), Ati (45d,106b, 113c,117a)

- AI hai (55c), kai (59c), Kai (14d,84c), lai (98b,161b), Lai (24c,d,88c), mai (62a), rai (188), sai (101d), tai (84b,111c,121b), Tai (80d), Vai (91d)

- AJ gaj (190), raj (129c), saj (48a,169a), taj (75a,97d)

AK - aka (176b), Aka (13d,88b,c), ake (60a,170a), akh (153d), ako (189), aku (57c,176a)

A - K aik (139d), alk (171b), ark (21a,29d,38a,58b,60d,175d), ask (38b, 82a,126c), auk (19b)

- AK dak (95c), hak (46d), lak (38a), nak (156b), oak (73d,168c,169a), sak (37c), Sak (88c), yak (112c,161d,165b), zak (188)

AL - ala (6d,13a,15c,61a,133d,182c,d), Ala. (151b), alb (65b,176a), ale (17c,18c,50c,55d,92d,104c), Alf (96a), Ali (7b,12a,25c,48b,55a,60c, 92d,101a,103a,164a,166b,170d), alk (171b), all (35c,118a,126d, 181a), alp (24b,103d,115c), als (66d,163d), alt (66c,76c,109c), aly (95d)

A - L aal (47c,80c,104b), AFL (173a), ail (170a), all (35c,118a,126d,181a), awl (145b,167a)

- AL aal (47c,80c,104b), bal (9d,37b,61a,61b), cal (183c), Cal (123a), dal (117d,153d), gal, Hal (69d), ial (158b), mal (34a,b,44a,52b,62c, 122b), Mal (94b), pal (35b,38d), sal (29c,48a,136d,149d,152d, 169a,183a), Sal (183d), tal (40c,77a,113b), Zal (135d)

AM - ama (26a,28d,31a,35b,39c,95b,108d,111c,117b,182c), ame (37a, 62d,131b), ami (61d), amo (79a,89c), amp (49b,173b), amt (37d, 40d,108a,163c), amy (63c), Amy (8c,94b,183c)

224

A - M   **aam** (47a,49d,93a), **aim** (42d,43d,67d,109b,125d,157c), **arm** (22d, 60c,81b,92b,124b,161b), **aum** (189)

- AM   **aam** (47a,49d,93a), **bam** (29b), **cam** (48b,65d,95a,98b,134a,139b, 148b,180c), **dam** (30c,49c,55b,156d,180a), **gam** (76b,176d,180c), **ham** (98a,144b), **Ham** (18d,107c), **jam** (123a,156d,165c), **lam** (51b, 58b,93d,164d,178a), **Mam** (192), **pam** (26c,65a,87a,105b), **Ram** (36b), **ram** (17a,45b,50b,79c,112b,121d,143d,157d), **Sam** (96a, 162a), **tam** (74d), **yam** (48c,121d,160b,170c)

AN -   **ana** (10b,33c,60d,93a,98c,122b,d,140d,142b), **Ana** (28a,68d,100c), **and** (36a,119d), **ane** (61c,140a,158b), **ani** (19b,d,20b,39b), **Ann** (183c), **ano** (19d,20b,34d,122d,174a), **Ans** (92a), **ant** (49d,60b,81b, 118c), **Anu** (15b,28a,68a,d,75b,88c,147d), **any** (14b,150b)

A - N   **ain** (18d,91c,110c,124b,140a,154b,180a), **Ann** (183c), **arn** (8c, 139a), **awn** (12c,17b,140a)

- AN   **ban** (81d,97a,124a), **can** (24c,36c,123a,166a), **dan** (24c,97c), **Dan** (18c,39c,77d,83a,84a,141b), **ean** (17d,23b,88a), **fan** (43a,154b), 156b,182d), **Gan** (132d), **Han** (16c,30b,185b), **Ian** (85b,96a,139d), **kan** (93a), **lan** (37b,37d,160b), **man** (29c,60c,64c,65a,142d,161d), **Nan** (183c), **pan** (34a,61a,104a,175d), **Pan** (56a,68a,68b,76b,120c, 135b,161a,184a), **ran** (73d), **Ran** (7c,107d,141a,163d), **san** (91c, **San** (24d), **tan** (23d,33c,46a,72d,90d), **van** (7b,59d,60a,63d,90c), **wan** (113a), **Zan** (186b)

A - O   **Abo** (25d), **ado** (22b,24d,35b,64c,78d,121d,156b,170a), **ago** (25a, 69d,114d,147a), **ako** (189), **amo** (79a,89c), **ano** (19d,20b,34d, 122d,174a), **Apo** (122b,177c), **Aro** (107a,111c), **Aso** (84c), **azo** (107c)

- AO   **dao** (117a), **hao** (189), **iao** (78a,96c,178d), **Lao** (80d,88c,146a, 161b), **mao** (115b), **Mao** (30b), **sao** (141b), **Sao** (113c), **tao** (10d, 131c,170b), **Tao** (117a), **Yao** (30a,c,104b),

AP -   **apa** (23a,177d), **ape** (36d,79d,100a,101d,146d), **api** (34a,76d), **apo** (122b), **Apo** (177c), **apt** (11d,23b,32b,58a,80b,92b,114d,116d, 124b,159a)

A - P   **alp** (24b,103d,115c), **amp** (49b,173b), **asp** (7b,32b,149a,174a, 176c)

- AP   **bap** (93b,132d), **Bap** (124d), **cap** (19d,39a,43a,53a,74d,160a,167b, 185c), **dap** (43b,c,46b,91b,147d), **gap** (11b,23a,29b,76c,110d,128a), **hap** (17d,28d), **Jap**, **lap** (31b,37d,59b,127a,131d,153d,167d), **map** (27a,29b,54a,98d,160a), **nap** (65a,117d,146b,148a), **pap** (59c), **rap** (90d,110a,147c,157c), **sap** (45d,52d,85c,169b,176d,179a), **tap** (55a,114d,153c), **yap** (16c,29b,122a)

AR -   **ara** (33a,114a,116a,118b,163d), **Ara** (8c,9b,36b,c,68d,69b,c, 85a,95a,175b), **arc** (31b,39d,92a,126a,127c,142a), **are** (51a,88b, 98a,99b,110c,166c,175c), **Ari** (18d), **ark** (21a,29d,38a,58b,60d, 175d), **arm** (22d,60c,81b,92b,124b,161b), **arn** (8c,139a), **Aro** (107a, 111c), **ars** (13b,89a), **Ars** (112c), **art** (22d,38b,39c,43b,56c,124a, 162c,181d), **aru** (80c,82b), **Aru** (82d)

A - R   **aar** (172d), **Aar** (131a), **aer** (8b,28d,34a,b,175a), **Afr.** (36c), **air** (11c,12c,42b,44c,53a,96b,98c,99d,125b,170c)

- AR   **aar** (172d), **Aar** (131a), **bar** (37c,39a,46a,52c,76d,78b,91a,124a,

137a,156a,157c,169c), **car** (16a,61d,93b,175a) **dar,** (65c,111b, 169a), **ear** (14c,d,28c,63d,64a,73c,111b,116a,124b,137d,150d, 153c), **far** (44c), **gar** (57b,c,d,106b), **har** (139c), **jar** (31d,70d,143b), **lar** (24c,51d,67a,78d,95d,101d,171b), **mar** (40b,44a,79a,d,81a, 140d), **Mar** (93d), **nar** (139d), **oar** (20b,124c,134b), **par** (15a,51a, 51b,c,69d,107c,135b,155a) **sar** (57d), **tar** (8c,68a,94d,111c,118c, 136a,c,176d), **war** (157c), **yar** (72a), **zar** (188)

AS - **Asa** (6a,18c,71a,84d,86d,164c), **ase** (51a,139a), **Ase** (79b,115d), **ash** (24d,33c,49c,73d,134b,168c,169a), **asi** (137a), **ask** (38b,82a, 126c) **Aso,** (84c), **asp** (7b,32b,149a,174a,176c), **ass** (17b,20c,45b, c,59c,110c,112b,146d,157d)

A - S **aes** (23c,89a,101c,132d,133a,b), **als** (66d,163d), **Ans** (92a), **ars** (13b,89a), **Ars** (112c), **ass** (17b,20c,45b,c,59c,110c,112b,146d, 157d), **aus** (66c), **Aus** (98b)

- AS **bas** (62a,d,129d,134b), **das** (13b,15d,36d,66b,d,164a), **fas** (44d,89d, 129d), **gas** (10b,29b,59a,116d,161c), **has, kas** (32c,47a), **las** (13b, (151d), **mas** (34b,55b,119a) **nas** (74a,89c,178b), **pas** (40d, 156a), **ras** (6c,26b,48b,51d,53d,61c,75a,111c,123c,166b), **vas** (46d, 89d,119c,133b,175d), **was** (166c,175c), **Was** (24d)

AT - **ata** (58d,97d,158d,160c,173d), **Ata** (79c,80d,94d,95d,100a, 106b,117a), **ate** (81a,108c,158c,174c), **Ate** (20c,68b,d,69a,b, 116c,186b), **ati** (106d,107a), **Ati** (45d,106b,113c,117a), **att** (146a)

A - T **Abt** (35c), **act** (41d,55b,119c,155d), **aet** (89a,109d), **aft** (14a,15b, 17d,128b,167d), **ait** (82d,132a), **alt** (66c,76c,109c), **amt** (37d,40d, 108a,163c), **ant** (49d,60b,81b,118c), **apt** (11d,23b,32b,58a,80b,92b, 114d,116d,124b,159a), **art** (22d,38b,39c,43b,56c,124a,162c,181d), **att** (146a), **aut** (34d,89d)

- AT **bat** (39c,107c,156a,157c,182d), **cat** (10a,45b,55b,71d,161b,169d, 180d,183d), **eat** (37b,96b,135d,179b), **fat** (110a,124a), **gat** (28d, 72c,131a), **hat** (74d), **Hat** (183d), **Jat** (80d,125c), **kat** (105d), **lat** (24a,33d,106b,118a), **mat** (46d,50d,94d,117c,161d), **Mat** (96a), **nat** (7a,24c,24d,106a), **oat** (15a,28b,70b,144b), **pat** (11d,116d, 159a,161d,167c), **Pat** (96a), **rat** 16a,42d,73b,132c), **sat** (13d), **tat** (48c,72d,87c), **Tat** (82a), **vat** (31b,36c,163a,170c), **wat** (73d,140d, 163a,180b), **xat** (167c), **zat** (148a)

AU - **auh** (52c), **auk** (19b), **aum** (189), **aus** (66c), **Aus** (98b), **aut** (34d, 89d), **aux** (6d,61a)

A - U **abu** (17a), **Abu** (15b,42a,55a,68a,c,147d), **acu** (34c), **ahu** (24c,41d, 65d,103d,120d), **aku** (57c,176a), **Anu** (15b,28a,68a,d,75b,88c, 147d), **aru** (80c,82b), **Aru** (82d), **ayu** (160c)

- AU **eau** (63a,178c), **gau** (66d,67a), **mau** (170c,188), **pau** (130c), **Pau** (48c,76a), **tau** (71b,91c,136c,161a), **vau** (91c), **Yau** (30c)

AV - **ava** (78d,86a,116a,120d,139a,167b), **Ava** (24c), **ave** (54c,71d,73a, 122a,134a,136d)

- AV **gav** (72d), **lav** (72d), **tav** (91c)

AW - **awa** (100a,139a), **awe** (81d,100a,130d,175b,182b), **awl** (145b,167a), **awn** (12c,17b,140a)

- AW **baw** (52c), **caw** (19b,d), **daw** (39a,70b,84a,146d), **gaw** (140c), **haw** (35a,52c,74d,91a,155a,162c), **jaw** (97d,138c), **law** (26b,33a,40a,

48c,60b,85d,91a,111b,134d,155d), maw (38b,d,72c,111a,121a, 142a,156c), paw (32d,59c,73c), raw (20c,39a,105d,173d), saw (7a, 11b,40c,54c,97d,125a,137d,167a), taw (90d,91c,96c,d,145b,161d), waw (12b,91c), yaw (43a,155d)

AX - axe (30c,40c,167a)

A - X Aex (46d), Aix (46d), aux (6d,61a)

- AX lax (93d,130a), Max (96a), pax (89d,115b), sax (40c,148a,167a), tax (13a,14a,80a,91d), wax (28b,72a,80b,120c), zax (148a)

AY - aya (77b,143c,166b), aye (7c,9b,55a,60a), ayu (160c)

A - Y acy (34c), ady (188), aly (95d), amy (63c), Amy (8c,94b,183c), any (14b,150b)

- AY bay (12d,16c,33c,73d,78b,81b,90a,128d), cay (82d,180b), day (153a), fay (32c,54b,154b), Fay (183c), gay, Gay (17d), hay (52c, 55c,165d), jay (19b,91c), kay (82d), Kay (13b,134b), lay (16a,25c,80a,98b,107d,141d,150b), may (74d), May (183c), nay (42b,106b), pay (35b,128c,130a,d,177b), ray (38a,49a,57b, 58b,147b), Ray (96a), say (131c,174c,177a), way (37d,96b,134b, 164d)

AZ - azo (107c)

A - Z adz (40c,167a)

- AZ gaz (188,190), Laz (27d)

BA - baa (143d), Bab (15a), bac (31b,55c,174d), bad (55a,173a,184d), bag (26c,139a,145b,159a), bah (52c), bal (9d,37b,61a,b), bam (29b), ban (81d,97a,124a), bap (93b,132d), Bap. (124d), bar (37c, 39a,46a,52c,76d,78b,91a,124a,137a,156a,157c,169c), bas (62a,d, 129d,134b), bat (39c,107c,156a,157c,182d), baw (52c), bay (12d, 16c,33c,73d,78b,81b,90a,128d)

B - A baa (143d) boa (36c,55b,106a,125d,138b,142d,149a)

- BA aba (12a,25d,32b,33a,65b), iba (117a)

B - B Bab (15a), bib, bob (57c,115d), Bob (96a), bub (22c)

- BB abb (58b,178b,185b), ebb (6a,15b,41c,43c,104a,128c,158a,178a)

B - C bac (31b,55c,174d), BSC (42a)

- BC ABC (134d)

B - D bad (55a,173a,184d), bed (60c,148b), bid (35a,82a,109d,111b, 174c), bud (22c)

BE - bed (60c, 148b), bee (46b,81b,91c,108c), beg (38b,150a), bel (64a, 93c,168d,173b,183d), Bel (15b,68a,126d), ben (78c,81b,102c,115c), Ben (12d,77c,96a,106c,139d,140a), ber (85c), Bes (68b,119c), bet, bey (70b,170d)

B - E bee (46b,81b,91c), bye (38c,141d)

- BE Abe 71a,96a,123a), obe (31d,87d,150d), ube (185b)

B - G bag (26c,139a,145b,159a), beg (38b,150a), big, bog (97a,160a), bug (24b,66b,81b)

B - H bah (52c), boh (24c)

BI - bib, bid (35a,82a,109d,111b,174c), big, Bim (16c), bin (22c,59a, 78a,128c,156d), bis (50a,90a,102c,130b,171c), bit (46a,86b,114c, 167a,b,171c,180d), biz

- BI Abi (76c), obi (55d,67b,84c,137b,150d), ubi (90a,180d,185b)

B - K Bok (9c)

B - L bal (9d,37b,61a,61b), bel (64a,93c,168d,173b,183d), Bel (15b,68a, 126d), Bul (25d,102a)

B - M bam (29b), Bim (16c), bum (21b)

B - N ban (81d,97a,124a), ben (78c,81b,102c,115c,139d,140a), Ben (12d, 77c,96a,106c), bin (22a,59a,78a,128c,156d), bon (30a,61d,86b,88c), Bon (84b), bun (25b,73b)

BO - boa (36c,55b,106a,125d,138b,142d,149a), bob (57c,115d), Bob (96a), bog (97a,160a), boh (24c), Bok (9c), bon (30a,61d,86b,88c), Bon (84b), boo, Bor (120c), Bos (27c), bot (59a,88d), bow (11c,21b, 39d,60a,107c,109a,125a,144d,158a), box (36a,128c,145d,152d), boy (142d,157c), Boz (43b,115d)

B - O boo

- BO Abo (25d), ebo (28b,110a), Ibo (107a,180a)

B - P Bap. (124d), bap (93b,132d)

B - R bar (37c,39a,46a,52c,76d,78b,91a,124a,137a,156a,157c,169c), ber (85c), Bor (120c), bur (123b)

BS - BSC (42a)

B - S bas (62a,d,129d,134b), Bes (68b,119c), bis (50a,90a,102c,130b, 171c), Bos (27c), bus (125b,168b)

B - T bat (39c,107c,156a,157c,182d), bet, bit (46a,86b,114c,167a,b, 171c,180d), bot (59a,88d), but (36a,52b,156b,173c)

- BT Abt (35c)

BU - bub (22c), bud (22c), bug (24b,66b,81b), Bul (25d,102a), bum (21b), bun (25b,73b), bur (123b), bus (125b,168b), but (36a,52b, 156b,173c), buy

- BU abu (17a), Abu (15b,42a,55a,68a,c,147d)

B - W baw (52c), bow (11c,21b,39d,60a,107c,109a,125a,144d,158a)

B - X box (36a,c,128c,145d,152d)

BY - bye (38c,141d)

B - Y bay (12d,16c,33c,73d,78b,81d,90a,128d), bey (70b,170d), boy (142d,157c), buy

B - Z biz, Boz (43b,115d)

CA - cab (75c), cad (22b,23b,75c,172c,173d), cag (81d,109d), cal (183c), Cal (123a), cam (48b,65d,95a,98b,134a,139b,148b,180c), can (24c, 36c,123a,166a), cap (19d,39a,43a,53a,74d,160a,167b,185c), car (16a,61d,93b,175a), cat (10a,45b,55b,71d,161b,169d,180d), Cat (183d), caw (19b,d) cay (82d, 180b)

C - A cha (162b,c)

- CA ECA (8a), oca (48c,112c,116d,133d,170c,184a), Uca (56a)

C - B cab (75c), cob (28c,78b,95d,160b,177d), cub (92d,185d)

C - D cad (22b,23b,75c,172c,173d), Cid (151c,d), cod (57b,c), cud (126c, 135a)

CE - cea (91c), cep (63a), ces (62b), cet (62d,180b)

C - E cee (91c), che (145d), cie (61b,63b), cle (158d), coe (143d),

228

Coe (33c), **cue** (7a,27b,92c,117d,124b,132c,146c,159a)

- CE ace (7a,26c,52d,57a,77d,110c,114c,120b,147a,163a,173a), **ice** (30a, 36d,42d,63d)

C - G cag (81d,109d), **cig, cog** (33a,65d,163b,167b,180c)

CH - cha (162b,c), **che** (145d), **chi** (91c), **Chi** (69c), **cho** (188)

- CH ach (8b,48a,52c,66b,80c), **ich** (66c), **och** (8b), **tch** (52c)

CI - Cid (151c,d), **cie** (61b,63b), **cig, CIO** (173a), **cis** (34c,122c), **cit** (81a,167d)

C - I chi (91c), **Chi** (69c)

- CI aci (29c), **ici** (61d), **Ici** (9b), **LCI** (21b)

- CK ock (189), **tck** (52c)

CL - cle (158d)

C - L cal (183c), **Cal** (123a), **col** (103d,114c)

C - M cam (48b,65d,95a,98b,134a,139b,148b,180c), **com** (122d), **cum** (159b), **cwm** (31b,37b,103d)

C - N can (24c,36c,123a,166a), **con** (7d,29b,83c,116d,157d)

CO - cob (28c,78b,95d,160b,177d), **cod** (57b,c), **coe** (143d), **Coe** (33c), **cog** (33a,65d,163b,167b,180c), **col** (103d,114c), **com** (122d), **con** (7d,29b,83c,116d,157d), **coo** (19b), **Coo** (82d), **cop** (36a,120c, 126d,153c,155d), **cor** (36c,75b,155b), **cos** (91d,132d), **cot** (129b, 148b), **cow** (22c,45b,81d), **cox** (156a), **coy** (16d), **coz**

C - O cho (188), **CIO** (173a), **coo** (19b), **Coo** (82d), **cro** (104c,115b,180a)

C - P cap (19d,39a,43a,53a,74d,160a,167b,185c), **cep** (63a), **cop** (36a, 120c,126d,153c,155d), **cup** (46b,69d,118b,170a), **cyp** (169d)

CR - cro (104c,115b,180a), **cru** (63a,176c), **cry** (25c,124a,145c,179d)

C - R car (16a,61d,93b,175a), **cor** (36c,75b,155b), **cur** (101d)

C - S ces (62b), **cis** (34c,122c), **cos** (91d,132d)

- CS ics (158d)

C - T cat (10a,45b,55b,71d,161b,169d,180d,183d), **cet** (62d,180b), **cit** (81a,167d), **cot** (148b), **cut** (30c,32b,145c)

- CT act (41d,55b,119c,155d), **ect** (35a,122d,183b), **oct** (34a,122c)

CU - cub (92d,185d), **cud** (126c,135a), **cue** (7a,27b,92c,117d,124b,132c, 146c,159a), **cum** (159b), **cup** (46b,69d,118b,170a), **cur** (101d), **cut** (30c,32b,145c)

C - U cru (63a,176c)

- CU acu (34c), **ecu** (58a,144b,c)

CW - cwm (31b,37b,103d)

C - W caw (19b,d), **cow** (22c,45b,81d)

C - X cox (156a)

CY - cyp (169d)

C - Y cay (82d,180b), **coy** (16d), **cry** (25c,124a,145c,179d)

- CY acy (34c), **icy** (65d)

C - Z coz

DA - dab (46a,57b,58b,d,114d,115c), **dad, dae** (139b), **dag** (11b,118c, 139c), **Dag** (108c), **dah** (24c,87a), **dak** (95c), **dal** (117d,153d), **dam**

(30c,49c,55b,156d,180a), **dan** (24c,97c), **Dan** (18c,39c,77d,83a, 84a,141b), **dao** (117a), **dap** (43b,c,46b,91b,147d), **dar** (65c,111b, 169a), **das** (13b,15d,36d,66b,d,164a), **daw** (39a,70b,84a,146d), **day** (153a)

D - A   **dea** (68d,89b), **dha** (99d), **dia** (122b,d,152a,165b), **dra** (188), **dua** (122d)

- DA   **Ada** (110a,112c,183c), **Ida** (103d,183c), **oda** (74a,170d)

D - B   **dab** (46a,57b,58b,114d,115c), **deb**, **Deb** (183d), **dib** (21b,43b,c, 120d,140a), **dub** (25c,46a,c,87a,105b,121a,140a)

D - C   **dec** (122d), **doc** (143a), **duc** (61c)

DD -   **DDS** (42a)

D - D   **dad**, **did**, **dod** (11a,32a,43b,140c), **dud** (21c,54a)

- DD   **add** (10d,11d,14c,158a,167c), **odd** (46b,53a,109b,157a,172d,173c)

DE -   **dea** (68d,89b), **deb**, **Deb** (183d), **dec** (122d), **dee** (91c), **Dee** (131d, 139b), **deg** (154b), **dei** (68d), **den** (38b,44d,74b,130d,133c,140d), **der** (13b,66b,d,164a), **des** (13b,61a,62b,d), **dev** (42a,b), **dew** (41a), **dey** (8d,84a,114c,135a,139b,170d)

D - E   **dae** (139b), **dee** (91c), **Dee** (131d,139b), **die** (27b,54a,65a,155a, 167a), **doe** (41d,55b,127a), **due** (7b,115b,124c), **dye** (33c,154d)

- DE   **ade** (18c,149d), **Ade** (9c,53b), **Ede** (35b,65d), **ide** (40c,57a,b,d, 158b), **ode** (26b,79c,94d,118a,119d,120a,150b)

D - G   **dag** (11b,118c), **Dag** (108c,139c), **deg** (154b), **dig** (52b), **dog** (10b, 45b,59b), **dug**

DH -   **dha** (99d), **dhu** (40b), **Dhu** (28a,87d)

D - H   **dah** (24c,87a), **doh** (113b)

- DH   **edh** (91c)

DI -   **dia** (122b,d,152a,165b), **dib** (21b,43b,c,120d,140a), **did**, **die** (27b, 54a,65a,155a,167a), **dig** (52b), **dii** (68d), **dim** (47a,48b,54a,74d, 94d,109b), **din** (31c,130b,174a), **dip** (26a,79d,117c,138c), **dis** (122b,d), **Dis** (68b,73a,119d,172d,174b), **dit** (62b,d,120a,159d), **div** (42b,139b), **dix** (118b), **Dix** (60b)

D - I   **dei** (68d) **dii** (68d), **dui** (46d)

- DI   **Udi** (108a)

DJ -   **djo** (188)

D - K   **dak** (95c)

D - L   **dal** (117d,153d)

D - M   **dam** (30c,49c,55b,156d,180a), **dim** (47a,48b,54a,74d,94d,109b), **dom** (121c,166b,c), **Dom** (94b), **dum** (45c,67b,113a)

D - N   **dan** (24c,97c), **Dan** (18c,39c,77d,83a,84a,141b), **den** (38b,44d,74b, 130d,133c,140d), **din** (130b,174a), **don** (151d,166c), **Don** (96a), **dun** (19a,39d,46d,71a,97d,115b,160b)

DO -   **Doc** (143a), **dod** (11a,32a,43b,140c), **doe** (41d,55b,127a), **dog** (10b, 45b,59b), **doh** (113b), **dom** (121c,166b,c), **Dom** (94b), **don** (151d, 166c), **Don** (96a), **dop** (39c,43b), **dor** (17d,24b,32b,46b,47a,81b, 85d), **dos** (45d,61a,97a,181b), **dot** (45d,97a,104d,105a,116b,153a, 162d), **dow** (17d,87a,88d,175d)

D - O   **dao** (117a) **djo** (188), **DSO** (99d), **duo** (46d,113a,171d)

- DO   **ado** (22b,24d,35b,64c,121d,156b,170a), **edo** (162a), **Edo** (107a, 166d), **Ido** (13c,81d,88c,173c), **Odo** (181d), **udo** (28a,30c,48c,84b, c,d,136c,149d)

D - P   **dap** (43b,c,46b,91b,147d), **dip** (26a,79d,117c,138c), **dop** (39c,43b)

DR -   **dra** (188), **dry** (46d,85a,137c,164c)

D - R   **dar** (111b,169a), **der** (13b,66b,d,164a), **dor** (17d,24b,32b,46b,47a, 81b,85d), **dur** (95c)

DS -   **DSO** (99d)

D - S   **das** (13b,15d,36d,66b,d,164a), **DDS** (42a), **des** (13b,61a,62b,d), **dis** (122b,d), **Dis** (68b,73a,119d,172d,174b), **dos** (45d,61a,97a,181b)

- DS   **DDS** (42a), **ods** (109a)

D - T   **dit** (62b,d,120a,159d), **dot** (45d,97a,104d,105a,116b,153a,162d)

DU -   **dua** (122d), **dub** (25c,46a,c,87a,105b,121a,140a), **duc** (61c), **dud** (21c,54a), **due** (7b,115b,124c), **dug, dul** (46d), **dum** (45c,67b,113a), **dun** (19a,39d,46d,71a,97d,115b,160b), **duo** (46d,113a,171d), **dur** (95c), **dux** (31d,64a,90c)

D - U   **dhu** (40b), **Dhu** (28a,87d)

D - V   **dev** (42a,b), **div** (42b,139b)

D - W   **daw** (39a,70b,84a), **dew** (41a), **dow** (17d,87a,88d,175d)

D - X   **dix** (118b), **Dix** (60b), **dux** (31d,64a,90c)

DY -   **dye** (33c,154d)

D - Y   **day** (153a), **dey** (8d,84a,114c,135a,139b,170d), **dry** (46d,85a,137c, 164c)

- DY   **ady** (188)

- DZ   **adz** (40c,167a)

EA -   **eae** (34b), **ean** (17d,23b,88a), **ear** (14c,d,28c,63d,64a,73c,111b, 116a,124b,137d,150d,153c), **eat** (37b,96b,135d,179b), **eau** (63a, 178c)

E - A   **ECA** (8a), **eia** (21c,53c,72b,76c,108b,174c), **Ena** (8c,126b), **era** (8a, 51a,116b,165d), **ESA** (8a), **eta** (71a,84c,91c), **Eva** (157a,183c)

- EA   **aea** (26a,36d), **dea** (68d,89b), **Hea** (15b), **kea** (114a,b), **lea** (56a, 97d,114d,185b), **Lea** (22d), **N.E.A.** (162c), **pea** (32d,91b,142a,175a), **rea** (9c,171a), **sea** (19a,52d,58c,112c,178d), **tea** (13d,18c,79c,81a, 145d,149c,159d), **Wea** (192), **yea** (7c,175c), **zea** (95c)

EB -   **ebb** (6a,15b,41c,43c,104a,128c,158a,178a), **ebo** (28b,110a)

E - B   **ebb** (6a,15b,41c,43c,104a,128c,158a,178a), **elb** (85c)

- EB   **deb, Deb** (183d), **Geb** (47d), **Keb** (47d), **neb** (17b,19a,d,115d), **reb** (35d,75c,85b,162c,166b), **Seb** (47d), **web** (50d,70a,98c,99a,106c, 149b)

EC -   **ECA** (8a), **ect** (35a,122d,183b), **ecu** (58a,144b,c)

E - C   **etc** (10b)

- EC   **dec** (122d), **sec** (46c,182c), **tec** (43a)

ED -   **Ede** (35b,65d), **edh** (91c), **edo** (162a), **Edo** (107a,166d)

E - D   Eed (102d), eld (10b,93c,110b,165d), end (8b,67d,120a,125d,130a, 166a), erd (47d,119d,145c)

- ED   bed (60c,148b), Eed (102d), fed, ged (100a,140a), ked (140b,144a), led, Ned (96a), ped (16d,34b), red (33c,38d,59a,127b,134c,135b), Red (151b), sed (89a), ted (74d,138b,154b), Ted (96b), wed (97a, 173c), zed (91c)

EE -   Eed (102d), eel (36a,49c,57a,b,88a,102c,176c), een (52a,139c, 185d), eer (9b,52a), ees (139c)

E - E   eae (34b), Ede (35b,65d), eke (14c,117c), ele (48c), eme (38d,70a, 140c,172b), ene (35b,158b,c), ere (17d,150c), ese (35b,158c), ete (36c,62d,141c,159b), eve (47a,131a,143a,165d,171c), Eve (183c), ewe (88a,143d), Exe (43a), eye (93d,111b,140d)

- EE   bee (46b,81b,91c,108c), cee (91c), dee (91c), Dee (131d,139b), fee (29a,58a,70d,166a,d), gee (35a,91c,100a,131c,139c,162c), lee (74b, 144b), Lee (9c,31c,96a), mee (169a), nee (19d,22b,25c,60b,95c), pee (91c), ree (12c,50a,80c,134d,137a,140b,144a,146b), Ree (25a), see (20a,43c,44a,51c,53c,93d,109b,113c,116a,176d,178c,183b), tee (39d,52b,69d,91c,112d,115d,118b,172a), vee (58a,91c,106a), wee (52c,100c,148c), zee (81b,91c)

EF -   eft (93b,107a,136c,169d)

E - F   elf (54b,154b)

- EF   AEF (184d), kef (12a,46c,75d,88c), nef (32b,144c,d), ref

EG -   egg (32d,80b,81c,112c,174a), ego (51a,79a,142b)

E - G   egg (32d,80b,81c,112c,174a), eng (48a,146a), erg (50b,173b, 184c)

- EG   beg (38b,150a), deg (154b), Geg (8c), keg (27a,105b), leg (37d, 92b,141d,159d,169c), Meg (8c,183d), peg (38c,46b,54d,98a,118a, 184c), teg (45a,54b,171d)

E - H   edh (91c), eth (91c,158d)

- EH   Heh (191), reh (8d)

EI -   ein (66b,c), Eir (69a,75a), eis (66c)

E - I   Eli (18c,d,76c,96a,137a,185a), epi (56c,61c,d,111c,112d,122d, 133c,153c,167b,174a), eri (13d,21c,146d), Eri (18c)

- EI   dei (68d), fei (16a,185b), hei (65a), lei (65b,74c), rei (89b,121c), Rei (18d), Vei (91d), Wei (30b,162b)

EK -   eke (14c,117c)

E - K   elk (22c,90d,178a)

- EK   lek (65c)

EL -   ela (21c,53c,72b,76c,108b,174c), elb (85c), eld (10b,93c,110b, 165d), ele (48c), elf (54b,154b), Eli (18c,d,76c,96a,137a,185a), elk (22c,90d,178a), ell (10d,24b,32c,98a), elm (168c), els (140a), elt (87a,117c,139d), Ely (27c,50b)

E - L   eel (36a,49c,57a,b,88a,102c,176c), ell (10d,24b,32c,98a)

- EL   bel (64a,93c,168d,173b,183d), Bel (15b,68a,126d), eel (36a,49c, 57a,b,88a,102c,176c), gel (32d,73d,150a), Hel (68d,93c,172d), mel (77d), pel (55c,160d), rel (49b,173b), sel (62c,140b), tel (34a, b,122c), zel (40c)

EM -   eme (38d,70a,140c,172b), Ems (125a,151c), emu (19b,58c,111d)

E - M   **elm** (168c)

- EM   **gem** (104b), **hem** (22a,36a,48b,52c,155a), **mem** (91c), **Sem** (107c), **Tem** (143a,159b)

EN -   **Ena** (8c,126b), **end** (8b,67d,120a,125d,130a,166a), **ene** (35b,158b, c), **eng** (48a,146a) **ens** (17d,18a,51a,52d), **ent** (34d,158b,c)

E - N   **ean** (17d,23b,88a), **een** (52a,139c,185d), **ein** (66b,c), **eon** (8a,37b, 51d,116b), **ern** (19c,d,47b,54b,141a)

- EN   **ben** (78c,81b,102c,115c), **Ben** (12d,77c,96a,106c,139d,140a), **den** (38b,44d,74b,130d,133c,140d), **een** (52a,139c,185d), **fen** (21c,97a, 160a), **gen** (31d,76b), **hen** (19a,60c,114c,136c), **ken** (60b,87c,122b, 172d), **men** (38c,116a,117b,170a), **Men** (94d), **pen** (36a,50a,80d, 118b,126d,160a,185c), **sen** (190), **ten** (19a,26c,41c,42b), **wen** (40c, 72a,110a,170c,177b), **yen** (33b,42d,93c,174a), **Zen** (24a)

EO -   **eon** (8a,37b,51d,116b), **Eos** (14d,41a,68d)

E - O   **ebo** (28b,110a), **edo** (162a), **Edo** (107a,166d), **ego** (51a,79a,142b), **eso** (34d,183b), **ETO** (184d), **exo** (122d)

- EO   **geo** (34a,47d), **Leo** (36b,c,92d,186d), **Meo** (27b,80c), **neo** (34a,b, c,100d,106d,108c,122c,d,128c), **Reo** (26c)

EP -   **epi** (56c,61c,d,111c,112d,122d,133c,153c,167b,174a)

E - P   **e.s.p.** (147b)

- EP   **cep** (63a), **hep** (52c), **kep** (139b), **nep** (27c,32d,56a,87c,184b), **pep** (50b,176b), **rep** (53b,d,131a,171c), **yep**, **Zep**

ER -   **era** (8a,51a,116b,165d), **erd** (47d,119d,145c), **ere** (17d,150c), **erg** (50b,173b,184c), **eri** (13d,21c,146d), **Eri** (18c), **ern** (19c,d,47b,54b, 141a), **err** (21a,43a,67d,100c,d,147a,148b,157b,168b,178a), **ers** (20a,176a), **ert** (140c,174a), **ery** (155d,158c,d)

E - R   **ear** (14c,d,28c,63d,64a,73c,111b,116a,124b,137d,150d,153c), **eer** (9b,52a), **Eir** (69a,75a), **err** (21a,43a,67d,100c,d,147a,148b,157b, 168b,178a), **Eur.** (36c)

- ER   **aer** (8b,28d,34a,b,175a), **ber** (85c), **der** (13b,66b,d,164a), **eer** (9b, 52a), **ger** (8d,36d,75c,124d), **her** (124b,c), **ier** (50a,158c), **Ker** (71b, 95d), **Ler** (23d,28a,b,64b,106c,141a), **mer** (62c,141a), **ner** (137c), **o'er** (6b,112a), **per** (25c,122d,165b,176a), **ser** (80d,83b,d,116c, 152d,180a), **ter** (34d,122d,165a), **xer** (34a), **zer** (188)

ES -   **ESA** (8a), **ese** (35b,158c), **eso** (34d,183b), **esp** (147b), **ess** (39d,78a, 91c,158c,184d), **est** (50a,61c,62a,79b,89c,158d,159c)

E - S   **ees** (139c), **eis** (66c), **els** (140a), **Ems** (125a,151c), **ens** (17d,18a, 51a,52d), **Eos** (14d,41a,68d), **ers** (20a,176a), **ess** (39d,78a,91c,158c, 184d)

- ES   **aes** (23c,89a,101c,132d,133a,b), **Bes** (68b,119c), **ces** (62b), **des** (13b,61a,62b,d), **ees** (139c), **Ges** (151b), **les** (13b,61a), **mes** (62b), **nes** (26b), **oes** (109a), **pes** (59d), **res** (80a,89d,91a,97c,164c), **ses** (61d), **yes** (7c,55a)

ET -   **eta** (71a,84c,91c), **etc** (10b), **ete** (36c,62d,141c,159b), **eth** (91c, 158d), **ETO** (184d)

E - T   **eat** (37b,96b,135d,179b), **ect** (35a,122d,183b), **eft** (93b,107a,136c, 169d), **elt** (87a,117c,139d), **ent** (34d,158b,c), **ert** (140c,174a), **est** (50a,62a,79b,89c,158d,159c)

- **ET**   **aet** (89a,109d), **bet, cet** (62d,180b), **get** (44d,64b,109b,141d), **jet** (20b,35a,154c), **ket** (189), **let** (9a,76d,77c,116b,130a,158b,163a), **met** (28d), **net** (26c,32a,50d,53b,60d,99a,124a,142a,149b), **pet** (26d,37c,55a,59b,162d), **ret** (58b,95a,149c,155d), **set** (7b,11d,13a, 23c,32b,33c,37c,58a,73d,109b,118c,121c,142c,150a,186a), Set (52b, 68a,b,111d), **vet, wet** (40d,46a,101a,124a,127c,149c), **yet** (18b, 24d,64c,77c,80a,108c,156b,165b)

- **EU**   **Eur.** (136c)

- **E - U**   **eau** (63a,178c), **ecu** (58a,144b,c), **emu** (19b,58c,111d)

- **EU**   **feu** (55d,61c,88b), **heu** (8b,30c,52c), **jeu** (61d), **leu** (190), **meu** (153b), **peu** (62a), **Reu** (115d)

- **EV**   **Eva** (157a,183c), **eve** (47a,131a,143a,165d,171c), **Eve** (183c)

- **EV**   **dev** (42a,b), **lev** (33b) **rev**

- **EW**   **ewe** (88a,143d)

- **EW**   **dew** (41a), **few, hew** (40a), **Jew, lew** (190), **Lew** (96a), **mew** (25b, 27b,50a,55b,72c,74d,101b,141b,153b), **new** (11a,63c,88d,111c, 128c), **pew** (30d,52c,57d,120b,141c), **rew** (75c,140c,176b), **sew, yew** (36a,52a,b,145d,168c,d)

- **EX**   **Exe** (43a), **exo** (122d)

- **EX**   **Aex** (46d), **hex** (18c), **lex** (90b), **rex** (86c,96a), **sex, vex** (7c,10d, 44c,82c)

- **EY**   **eye** (93d,111b,140d)

- **E - Y**   **Ely** (27c,50b), **ery** (155d,158c,d)

- **EY**   **bey** (70b,170d), **dey** (8d,84a,114c,135a,139b,170d), **fey** (49c), **gey** (140a), **hey** (25c,52c), **key** (14c,82d,88b,117c,118c,150b,180c), **ley** (190), **Ney** (63b,97b,105d), **rey** (86c,152b), **sey** (120c), **wey** (173b)

- **EZ**   **fez** (75a,162a), **gez** (188), **nez** (62b), **tez** (125c), **yez**

- **FA**   **fac** (41c), **fad** (38b,108c,163a), **fag** (55a,166a), **fan** (43a,154b, 156b,182d), **far** (44c), **fas** (44d,89d,129d), **fat** (110a,124a), **fay** (32c,54b,154b), **Fay** (183c)

- **F - A**   **Fha** (8a), **fra** (23c,63c,101d,123b,129d)

- **FA**   **MFA** (42a)

- **F - B**   **fib** (162a), **fob** (29b,59b,113b,178c), **fub** (29b,119d)

- **F - C**   **fac** (41c)

- **F - D**   **fad** (38b,108c,163a), **fed, fid** (16b,54d,118a,167b), **fod** (188)

- **FE**   **fed, fce** (29a,58a,70d,166a,d), **fei** (16a,185b), **fen** (21c,97a,160a), **feu** (55d,61c,88b), **few, fey** (49c), **fez** (75a,162a)

- **F - E**   **fce** (29a,58a,70d,166a,d), **fie** (52c,59d), **foe** (111a)

- **FE**   **ife** (22c,75d)

- **FF**   **off** (6b,15c,44c,76a)

- **F - G**   **fag** (55a,166a), **fig, fog** (109b), **fug** (129a)

- **FH**   **FHA** (8a)

- **F - H**   **foh** (52c)

- **FI**   **fib** (162a), **fid** (16b,54d,118a,167b), **fie** (52c,59d), **fig, fin** (86a), **fir** (16a,36a,52a,168c,d,169a), **fit** (7a,11d,51b,75a,114a,123a, 124c,126a,153a,157c,159a), **fix** (7b,10a,13a,14c,43a,c,141d,165c)

234

F - I   fel (16a,185b)

FL -   flo, flu, fly (58c,81b,163b,178d)

F - L   Ful (158b)

- FL   AFL (173a)

F - N   fan (43a,154b,156b,182d), **fen** (21c,97a,160a), **fin** (86a), **Fon** (40b), **fun**

FO -   fob (29b,59b,113b,178c), **fod** (188), **foe** (111a), **fog** (109b), **foh** (52c), **Fon** (40b), **foo** (42c), **fop** (38a,40d,46d), **for** (123d,163a, 166c), **fot** (188), **fou** (139a), **fox** (134a)

F - O   Flo, foo (42c), **fro** (15b)

- FO   Ufo (59a)

F - P   fop (38a,40d,46d)

FR -   fra (23c,63c,101d,123b,129d), **fro** (15b), **fry** (57d)

F - R   far (44c), **fir** (16a,36a,52a,168c,d,169a), **for** (123d,163a,166c), **fur**

- FR   Afr. (36c)

F - S   fas (44d,89d,129d)

F - T   fat (110a,124a), **fit** (7a,11d,51b,75a,114a,123a,124c,126a,153a, 157c,159a), **fot** (188), **fut** (188)

- FT   aft (14a,15b,17d,128b,167d), **eft** (93b,107a,136c,169d), **oft** (63c)

FU -   fub (29b,119d), **fug** (129a), **Ful** (158b), **fun, fur, fut** (188)

F - U   feu (55d,61c,88b), **flu, fou** (139a)

F - W   few

F - X   fix (7b,10a,13a,14c,43a,c,141d,165c), **fox** (134a)

F - Y   fay (32c,54b,154b), **Fay** (183c), **fey** (49c), **fly** (58c,81b,163b,178d), **fry** (57d)

F - Z   fez (75a,162a)

GA -   gab (29b,78a,116c,122a,161c,183a), **gad** (58c,100a,127d,132b, 153c,154b,178a), **Gad** (84a,186d), **gaf** (12b), **gag** (146c,183a), **gaj** (190), **gal, gam** (76b,176d,180c), **Gan** (132d), **gap** (11b,23a,29b, 76c,110d,128a), **gar** (57b,c,d,106b), **gas** (10b,29b,59a,116d,161c), **gat** (28d,72c,131a), **gau** (66d,67a), **gav** (72d), **gaw** (140c), **gay, Gay** (17d), **gaz** (188,190)

G - A   goa (65d,104b,126c), **Goa** (121c), **gra** (59b,94b,160c)

- GA   aga (35a,39a,48b,102d,103a,b,111c,166b,170d,171a)

G - B   gab (29b,78a,116c,122a,161c,183a), **Geb** (47d), **gib** (17b,38b,95d, 166d,179d), **gob** (97b,136c)

G - D   gad (58c,100a,b,127d,132b,153c,154b,178a), **Gad** (84a,186d), **ged** (140a), **Ged** (100a), **gid** (143d), **god** (42a), **God** (84d)

GE -   Geb (47d), **Ged** (100a,140a), **gee** (35a,91c,100a,131c,139c,162c), **Geg** (8c), **gel** (32d,73d,150a), **gem** (104b), **gen** (31d,76b), **geo** (34a, 47d), **ger** (8d,36d,75c,124d), **Ges** (151b), **get** (44d,64b,109b,141d), **gey** (140a), **gez** (188)

G - E   gee (35a,91c,100a,131c,139c,162c), **gie** (139c,140a), **gue** (176c)

- GE   age (51d,66a,92a,97c,98c,116b,141c)

G - F   gaf (12b)

G - G   gag (146c,183a), Geg (8c), gig (26d,28d,57c,105b,127a,144c,153a, 171d), gog (95b)

- GG   egg (32d,80b,81c,112c,174a)

GH -   ghi (24d)

- GH   ugh (52c)

GI -   gib (17b,38b,95d,166d,179d), gid (143d), gie (139c,140a), gig (26d,28d,57c,105b,127a,144c,153a,171d), gin (37c,92d,139a,142a, 149b), gip (29b,160c), git (101a)

G - I   ghi (24d), goi (107c), gri (75c,78b)

G - J   gaj (190)

G - L   gal, gel (32d,73d,150a), gul (134a)

G - M   gam (76b,176d,180c), gem (104b), gum (7b,53c,80b,130c,156b), gym (154a)

GN -   gnu (11a,181d)

G - N   gan (132d), gen (31d,76b), gin (37c,92d,139a,142a,149b), gon (188), gun (56d,131a,146a)

GO -   goa (65d,104b,126c), Goa (121c), gob (97b,136c), god (42a), God (84d), gog (95b), goi (107c), gon (188), goo (156b), Gor (81a), got, goy (107c), goz (190)

G - O   geo (34a,47d), goo (156b)

- GO   ago (25a,69d,114d,147a), ego (51a,79a,142b)

G - P   gap (11b,23a,29b,76c,110d,128a), gip (29b,160c), gup (70a), gyp (29b,42a,160c)

GR -   gra (59b,94b,160c), gri (75c,78b), grr (52c), gry (78b)

G - R   gar (57b,c,d,106b), ger (8d,36d,75c,124d), Gor (81a), grr (52c), gur (159a)

G - S   gas (10b,29b,59a,116d,161c), Ges (151b), Gus (96a)

G - T   gat (28d,72c,131a), get (44d,64b,109b,141d), git (101a), got, gut (114d,130a)

GU -   gue (176c), gul (134a), gum (7b,53c,80b,130c,156b), gun (56d, 131a,146a), gup (70a), gur (159a), Gus (96a), gut (114d,130a), guy (55b,131b,155d), Guy (96a), guz (188)

G - U   gau (66d,67a), gnu (11a,181d)

- GU   ngu (188

G - V   gav (72d)

G - W   gaw (140c)

GY -   gym (154a), gyp (29b,42a,160c)

G - Y   gay, Gay (17d), gey (140a), goy (107c), gry (78b), guy (55b,131b, 155d), Guy¹ (96a)

G - Z   gaz (188,190), gez (188), goz (190), guz (188)

HA -   had, hae (139c), hag (140a,183a), hah (52c), hai (55c), hak (46d), Hal (69d), ham (98a,144b), Ham (18d,107c), Han (16c,30b,185b), hao (189) hap (17d,28d), har (139c), has, hat (74d), Hat (183d), haw (35a,52c,74d,91a,155a,162c), hay (52c,55c,165d)

H - A   Hea (15b), hia (114b), hoa (39b)

236

- **HA**   aha (52c,55c,159c), cha (162b,c), dha (99c), **FHA** (8a), **Kha** (88d, 106b), sha (110c,143d,144a,c,174c,181c)

H - B   hob (40c,56d,100c,124b,167a,180c), hub (28b,118b,180c)

H - C   hic (52c,90a,164c)

H - D   had, hid, hod (23b,32d,102d,141a)

HE -   Hea (15b), Heh (191), hei (65a), Hel (68d,93c,172d), hem (22a,36a, 48b,52c,155a), hen (19a,60c,114c,136c), hep (52c), her (124b,c), heu (8b,30c,52c), hew (40a), hex (18c), hey (25c,52c)

H - E   hae (139c), hie (79a,153b), hoe (39c), hue (33c,143b)

- **HE**   che (145d), rhe (59a), she (124b), **She** (73a), the (13b)

H - G   hag (140a,183a), hog (45b,117c,160c), hug (32c,49d)

H - H   hah (52c), Heh (191), Hoh (80d), hsh (79c), huh (52c)

HI -   hia (114b), hic (52c,90a,164c), hid, hie (79a,153b), him (124b), hin (189), hip (52c,54b,85b,133c,134a), hir (76a), his (124c), hit (32d,157c,158a)

H - I   hai (55c), hei (65a), hoi (52c,74b,185b), hui (14a,30b,56d,114c)

- **HI**   Ahi (32c,147d), chi (91c), **Chi** (69c), ghi (24d), ihi (57c,156b), phi (91c)

H - K   hak (46d)

H - L   Hal (69d), Hel (68d,93c,172d)

H - M   ham (98a,144b), **Ham** (18d,107c), hem (22a,36a,48b,52c,155a), him (124b), hum (24d,46b,150d)

- **HM**   ohm (49b,67a,173b)

H - N   Han (16c,30b,185b), hen (19a,60c,114c,136c), hin (189), Hun (16c,21d,174b)

HO -   hoa (39b), hob (40c,56d,100c,124b,167a,180c), hod (23b,32d,102d, 141a), hoe (39c), hog (45b,117c,160c), Hoh (80d), hoi (52c,74b, 185b), hop (40b), **Hor** (103d), hot (10c,176c), how, hoy (16c,52c)

H - O   hao (189)

- **HO**   cho (188), mho (49b,173b), oho (52c), **Rho** (71b,91c), sho (188), tho (52a), **Tho** (167a), who (129c)

H - P   hap (17d,28d), hep (52c), hip (52c,54b,85b,133c,134a), hop (40b), hup (35a), hyp

H - R   har (139c), her (124b,c), hir (76a), **Hor** (103d), **Hur** (91d)

- **HR**   ihr (66d)

HS -   hsh (79c)

H - S   has, his (124c)

H - T   hat (74d), **Hat** (183d), hit (32d,157c,158a), hot (10c,176c), hut (143c)

HU -   hub (28b,118b,180c), hue (33c,143b,) hug (32c,49d), huh (52c), hui (14a,30b,56d,114c), hum (24d,46b,150d), Hun (16c,21d,174b), hup (35a), **Hur** (91d), hut (143c)

H - U   heu (8b,30c,52c)

- **HU**   ahu (24c,41d,65d,103d,120d), dhu (40b), **Dhu** (28a,87d), phu (38c), **Shu** (30b,127a)

H - W haw (35a,52c,74d,91a,155a,162c), hew (40a), how
H - X hex (18c)
HY - hyp
H - Y hay (52c,55c,165d), hey (25c,52c), hoy (16c,52c)
- HY shy (16d,99d,128c,160c,165d,175a), thy, why (52c)

IA - ial (158b), ian (85b,96a,139d), iao (78a,96c,178d)
I - A iba (117a), Ida (103d,183c), Ila (16b), ILA (173a), ina (158c),
Ina (183c), Ira (18c,d,41a,68c,82c,96a,164a,178a,c), Ita (51b,71d,
94d,95d,106b,117a), ITA (173a), iva (76a,97b,127b,185b) iwa
(63c), iya (95b,108d,111c)
- IA dia (122b,d,152a,165b), hia (114b), Lia (82b), mia (83c), pia (13b,
22d,48a,120d), ria (38c,51d,81b,152a,b), Sia (80c), tia (151d), via
(132a,133a,b,179a)
IB - iba (117a), Ibo (107a,180b)
- IB bib, dib (21b,43b,c,120d,140a), fib (162a), gib (17b,38b,95d,166d,
179d), jib (38b,136b,146a), mib (8d,96c), nib (17b,19d,115d),
rib (37c,85b,90c,98a,144d,159d,172a), sib (86b,129c,139d,147b)
IC - ice (30a,36d,42d,63d), ich (66c), ici (61d), Ici (9b), ics (158d),
icy (65d)
- IC hic (52c,90a,164c), pic (188), sic (90a,165b,168b), tic (104d,153a,
171c,d)
ID - Ida (103d,183c), ide (40c,57a,b,d,158b), Ido (13c,81d,88c,173c)
I - D Ind (80c)
- ID aid (14a,15b,64c,75d,158b), bid (35a,82a,109d,111b,174c), Cid
(151c,d), did, fid (16b,54d,118a,167b), gid (143d), hid, kid (67d,
85b,90d,186a), lid (167b), mid (9d,28b,73b), nid (72a,106b,c,116d),
old (158c), rid (32a,44a,60d), Sid (96a)
IE - ier (50a,158c)
I - E ice (30a,36d,42d,63d), ide (40c,57a,b,d,158b), ife (22c,75d), Ike
(123a), ile (62a,63b,158c), ine (29c,158b,c), Ine (10c,137d,180b),
ire (10c,30c,52b,64c,125a,130b,185a), ise (40d,158c,d), Ise (78a,
84c), ite (59b,81a,105d,130c,158b,c,d,161a), ive (158c)
- IE cie (61b,63b), die (27b,54a,65a,155a,167a), fie (52c,59d), gie
(139c,140a), hie (79a,153b), lie (53a,69d,162a), nie (53c), pie
(42d,85d,95b,114d,171b,172a), rie (28c,70d,97d), sie (46c,66d,
139b,140b,146b), tie (10a,14c,38b,45d,51a,88d,109b,127c,138b,
170b), vie (36c,157c,170c)
IF - ife (22c,75d)
- IF Lif (107d), rif (188), Sif (164d), vif (62a), Zif (102a)
I - G ing (114b,d,148d,158c,d,175c), Ing (10c,115b)
- IG big, cig, dig (52b), fig, gig (26d,28d,57c,105b,127a,144c,
153a,171d), jig (40b,d), mig (8d,96c,145b), Mig (118d), nig (33b,
40a,46a), pig (27a,45b,99a,151b,160c), rig (51b,112a), tig (46b),
wig (73b), zig (84a)
IH - ihi (57c,156b), ihr (66d)
I - H ich (66c), ish (158b), Ith (10a,28a,82b,99d)

238

I - I ici (61d), ici (9b), ihi (57c,156b), ini (158d), iri (18a,d,75a)

- II dii (68d), oii (105c), rii (157b,175b)

IJ - ijo (107a)

IK - ike (123a)

I - K ilk (31d,54c,86b,136d,139c,140b), ink (20b,40c), irk (10d)

- IK aik (139d), pik (188)

IL - iia (16b), ILA (173a), ile (62a,63b,158c), ilk (31d,54c,86b,136d, 139c,140b), iii (43d,121a,173a,c,d), ILO (184c), iis (62b,d,164b)

I - L ial (158b), iii (43d,121a,173a,c,d)

- IL ail (170a), kil (82b), lii (72d), mil (80b,110c,164d,182d), Mil (10a), nil (108c), oil (11a,71a), pil (34b), sil (30c,185c,d), til (142d)

IM - imp (42b,127d,174a), imu (15d)

I - M ism (45a,79b,161c)

- IM aim (42d,43d,67d,109b,125d,157c), Bim (16c), dim (47a,48b,54a, 74d,94d,109b), him (124b), Jim (96a), Kim (86d), lim (21a), mim (12b), nim (96d,155d), rim (22a,48b,96d,116b,124b,166a,180c), Sim (96b), Tim (43b), vim (50b,176b)

IN - ina (158c), Ina (183c), ind (80c), ine (29c,158b,c), Ine (10c, 137d,180b), ing (114b,d,158c,d,175c) Ing (10c,115b), ini (158d), ink (20b,40c), inn (72b,73b,78c,132b,150a,161c,162b,179a), Inn (41a), Ino (14b,25b), ins (164d), INS (107a,182d)

I - N ian (85b,96a,139d), inn (72b,73b,78c,132b,150a,161c,162b,179a), Inn (41a), ion (11c,29a,49b,101b,114c,158c)

- IN ain (18d,91c,110c,124b,140a,154b,180a), bin (22c,59a,78a,128c, 156b), din (31c,130b,174a), ein (66b,c), fin (86a), gin (37c,92d, 139a,142a,149b), hin (189), jin (42b,153c), kin (30b,81c,129d) Kin (30b), lin (140c,168c,178d), Lin (115d,186c), Min (29d,68b, 113c), nin (107d), pin (45d,54d,141d,147d), rin (33b,142b), sin (91c,140b,147a,168b,176a), Sin (102b), tin (36c,99a,b,108b,155a, 179c), vin (63a,182b), win (7a,17b,64b,123b), yin (140a), Yin (30b, 143c,185b)

IO - ion (11c,29a,101b,114c,158c), ior (50a,158c), ios (74d), IOU (124b)

I - O iao (78a,96c,178d), Ibo (107a,180b), Ido (13c,81d,88c,173c), Ijo (107a), ILO (184c), Ino (14b,25b), iso (34a,122c,d), Ito (84a,c, 186d), iyo (7d,176b)

- IO CIO (173a), mio (152c), rio (33a,131d,132a,152c,157b), Rio (23a), tio (152d), Zio (147d,163d)

I - P imp (42b,127d,174a)

- IP dip (26a,79d,117c,138c), gip (29b,160c), hip (52c,54b,85b,133c, 134a), kip (17c,72d,76c,189), lip (48b,58b,80a,131c), nip (20c, 29b,45d,46a,b,115c,118a), pip (11d,44a,121d,142a,154a), Pip (43b), rip (87b,130a,162c), Rip (178b), sip (46b,79d,104a,162b), tip (26b,d,50a,70d,77b,78a,120a,165d), yip (16c), zip (24b,50b, 176b)

IR - ira (18c,d,41a,68c,82c,96a,164a,178a,c), ire (10c,30c,52b,64c,

125a,130b,185a), Iri (18a,d,75a), irk (10d)

I - R ier (50a,158c), ihr (66d), ior (50a,158c)

- IR air (11c,12c,42b,44c,53a,96b,98c,99d,125b,170c), Eir (69a,75a), fir (16a,36a,52a,168c,d,169a), hir (76a), mir (29d,135c,d,166c,176b), pir (103a,b,136c), sir (163b,166b), tir (61d,62c,87a,145b), vir (89c)

IS - ise (40d,158c,d), Ise (78a,84c), -ish (158b), ism (45a,79b,161c), iso (34a,122c,d), ist (7b,34b,43a,59b,66c,158c,d)

I - S ics (158d), ils (62b,d,164b), ins (164d), INS (107a,182d), ios (74d), its (124c)

- IS bis (50a,90a,102c,130b,171c), cis (34c,122c), dis (122b,d), Dis (68b,73a,119d,172d,174b), eis (66c), his (124c), lis (54b, 58b,60c,62a,92b), Lis (47a), mis (122b,c,d,185c), nis (23d,67d, 68a,87c), Nis (19d), ris (131d), sis (67b,129c), tis, vis (59d,89b,d, 90b,176b), wis (79d,164c)

IT - Ita (51b,71d,94d,95d,106b,117a), ITA (173a), ite (59b,81a,105d, 130c,158b,c,d,161a), Ite (130c), Ith (10a,28a,82b,99d), Ito (84a, c,186d), its (124c)

I - T ist (7b,34b,43a,59b,66c,158c,d)

- IT ait (82d,132a), bit (46a,86b,114c,167a,b,171c,180d), cit (81a, 167d), dit (62b,d,120a,159d), fit (7a,11d,51b,75a,114a,123a,124c, 126a,153a,157c,159a), git (101a), hit (32d,157c,158a), kit (112a, 176c), Kit (96a,183d), lit, mit (56c,66d,183b), nit (48d), pit (52b, 142a,164a,168a), rit (148c,140b,153d), sit (98c,116a,121c,130c, 142d), tit (19c,130d), uit (47a,111d,151a), wit (78d,85b,177b)

I - U imu (15d), I.O.U. (124b)

- IU piu (102c), Tiu (7c,68c,147d,163d,166c,170c), Ziu (147d,163d)

IV - iva (76a,97b,127b,185b), ive (158c), ivy (32b,38c,176b)

- IV div (42b,139b), Liv (93b)

IW - iwa (63c)

- IW Tiw (68c,147d,163d)

- IX Aix (46b), dix (118b), Dix (60b), fix (7b,10a,13a,14c,43a,c,141d, 165c), mix (156b), nix (23d,108c,178d), pix (31a,51d,175d), six (26c), vix (89d,138b)

IY - iya (95b,108d,111c), iyo (7d,176b)

I - Y icy (65d), ivy (32b,38c,176b)

- IZ biz, viz (105b)

JA - jab (120b,125c) jag (124d,148a) Jah (84d), jam (123a,156d,165c), Jap, jar (31d,70d,143b), Jat (80d,125c), jaw (97d,138c), jay (19b, 91c)

J - B jab (120b,125c), jib (38b,136b,146a), job (30d,184c), Job (96a)

JE - jet (20b,35a,154c), jeu (61d), Jew

J - E Joe (96a)

J - G jag (124d,148a), jig (40b,d), jog (82c,85c,170a), jug (118c,123d)

J - H Jah (84d)

JI - jib (38b,136b,146a), jig (40b,d), Jim (96a), jin (42b,153c)

- JI tji (189), uji (146d)

J - M Jam (123a,156d,165c), Jim (96a), Jum (39c)

J - N Jin (42b,153c)

JO - Job (30d,184c), Job (96a), Joe (96a), Jog (82c,85c,170a), Jot (82a, 114c,166c,180d), Jow (188), Joy

- JO djo (188), Ijo (107a)

J - P Jap

J - R Jar (31d,70d,143b), Jur (107b)

J - S Jus (61d,90b)

J - T Jat (80d,125c), Jet (20b,35a,154c), Jot (82a,114c,166c,180d), Jut 53a,124a)

JU - Jug (118c,123d), Jum (39c), Jur (107b), Jus (61d,90b), Jut (53a, 124a)

J - U Jeu (61d)

J - W Jaw (97d,138c), Jew, Jow (188)

J - Y Jay (19b,91c), Joy

KA - kab (75c), kae (84a,140b), kaf (12b), Kaf (104a), kai (59c), Kai (14d,84c), kan (93a), kas (32c,47a), kat (105d), kay (82d), Kay (13b,134b)

K - A kea (114a,b), Kha (88d,106b), koa (74c), Kra (11b,91d), Kua (95c)

- KA aka (176b), Aka (13d,88b,c), oka (170c,184a,189)

K - B kab (75c), Keb (47d), kob (11a)

K - D ked (140b,144a), kid (67d,85b,90d,186a)

KE - kea (114a,b), Keb (47d), ked (140b,144a), kef (12a,46c,75d,88c), keg (27a,105b), ken (60b,87c,122b,172d), kep (139b), Ker (71b, 95d), ket (189) key (14c,82d,88b,117c,118c,150b,180c)

K - E kae (84a,140b)

- KE ake (60a,107a), eke (14c,117c), Ike (123a), oke (189)

K - F kaf (12b), Kaf (104a), kef (12a,46c,75d,88c)

K - G keg (27a, 105b)

KH - Kha (88d,106b)

- KH akh (153d)

KI - kid (67d,85b,90d,186a), kil (82b), Kim (86d), kin (30b,81c, 129d), Kin (30b), kip (17c,72d,76c,189), kit (112a,176c), Kit (96a, 183c)

K - I kai (59c), Kai (14d,84c), koi (26d), kri (75c,96d), Kri (75c) Kui (86a,88c,146a)

- KI ski (149c)

K - L kil (82b), Kol (18b), kyl (76d,79b)

K - M Kim (86d)

K - N kan (93a), ken (60b,87c,122b), kin (30b,81c), Kin (30b)

KO - koa (74c), kob (11a), koi (26d), Kol (18b), kop (76d), kor (75c), Kos (77c,82d), kou (169a)

- KO ako (189), TKO (22c)

K - P kep (139b), kip (17c,72d,76c,189), kop (76d), kup (188)

241

KR - Kra (11b,91d), kri (75c,96d), Kru (91d)

K - R Ker (71b,95d), kor (75c)

K - S kas (32c,47a), Kos (77c,82d)

K - T kat (105d), ket (189), kit (112a,176c), Kit (96a,183d)

KU - Kua (95c), Kui (86a,88c,146a), kup (188)

K - U kou (169a), Kru (91d)

- KU aku (57c,176a)

KY - kyl (76d,79b)

K - Y kay (82d), Kay (13b,134b), key (14c,82d,88b,117c,118c,150b, 180c)

- KY sky (56d)

LA - lab, lac (53c,99d,130c,135b,174d), lad (22c,25b,55b,157c,186a), lag (93c,155d), Lai (24c,d,88c), lai (98b,161b), lak (38a), lam (51b, 58b,93d,164d,178a), lan (37b,d,160b), Lao (80d,88c,146a,161b), lap (31b,37d,59b,127a,131d,153d,167d), lar (24c,51d,67a,78d,95d, 101d,171b), las (13b,151d) lat (24a,33d,106b,118a), lav (72d), law (26b,33a,40a,48c,60b,85d,91a,111b,134d,155d), lax (93d,130a), lay (16a,25c,80a,98b,107d,141d,150b), Laz (27d)

L - A lea (56a,97d,114d,185b), Lea (22d), Lia (82b), loa (7d,53c,97d,184d)

- LA ala (6d,13a,15c,61a,133d,182c,d), Ala. (151b), ela (21c,53c,72b, 76c,108b,174c), lla (16b), ILA (173a), ola (113b), ula (72c,158c)

L - B lab, LLB (42a), lob (15d,23b,94c,100b,163a,172d)

- LB alb (65b,176a), elb (85c), LLB (42a)

LC - LCI (21b)

L - C lac (53c,99d,130c,135b,174d)

L - D lad (22c,25b,55b,157c,186a), led, lid (167b), LLD (42a), lud (100a), Lud (23c,144b)

- LD eld (10b,93c,110b,165d), LLD (42a), old (8a,71a,77c,123c,175b)

LE - lea (56a,97d,114d,185b), Lea (22d), led, lee (74b,144b), Lee (9c, 31c,96a), leg (37d,92b,141d,159d,169c), lei (65b,74c), lek (65c), Leo (36b,c,92d,186d), Ler (23d,28a,b,64b,106c,141a), les (13b, 61a), let (9a,76d,77c,116b,130a,158b,163a), leu (190), lev (33b), lew (190), Lew (96a), lex (90b), ley (190)

L - E lee (74b,144b), Lee (9c,31c,96a), lie (53a,69d,162a), loe (139d), lue (146b), lye (8d,27d,93b)

- LE ale (17c,18c,50c,55d,92d,104c), cle (158d), ele (48c), ile (62a,63b, 158c), ole (24b,29b,113b,152a,158b,d), ule (23a,27d,134c,158c, 168d)

L - F Lif (107d), lof (188)

- LF Alf (96a), elf (54b,154b)

L - G lag (93c,155d), leg (37d,92b,141d,159d,169c), log (64a,128d), lug (27a,45d,47b,73c,136b), Lug (28b)

LI - Lia (82b), lid (167b),, lie (53a,69d,162a), Lif (107d), lil (72d), lim (21a), lin (92c,140c,168c,178d), Lin (115d,186c), lip (48b,58b,80a, 131c), lis (54b,58b,60c,62a,92b), Lis (47a), lit, Liv (93b)

L - I   lai (98b,161b), Lai (24c,d,88c), LCI (21b), lei (65b,74c), loi (62a)

- LI   Ali (7b,12a,25c,48b,55a,60c,92d,101a,103a,164a,166b,170d), Eli (18c,d,76c,96a,137a,185a)

L - K   lak (38a), lek (65c), Lok (15d,68b)

- LK   alk (171b), elk (22c,90d,178a), ilk (31d,54c,86b,136d,139c,140b)

LL -   LLB (42a), LLD (42a)

L - L   lil (72d)

- LL   all (35c,118a,126d,181a), ell (10d,24b,32c,98a), ill (43d,121a,173a, c,d), Ull (7c,68c,146b,164d)

L - M   lam (51b,58b,93d,164d,178a), lim (21a), lum (30a)

- LM   elm (168c), olm (48c), ulm (49c), Ulm (40d)

L - N   lan (37b,d,160b), lin (140c,168c,178d), Lin (115d,186c), Lon (86c, 96a), lyn (140c,178d)

LO -   loa (7d,53c,97d,184d), lob (15d,23b,94c,100b,163a,172d), loe (139d), lof (188), log (64a,128d), loi (62a), Lok (15d,68b), Lon (86c, 96a), loo (65a), lop (30c,40a,46b,143a), los (13b,151d), lot (24b, 28d,55a,65d,114a,119c,143c,150d,168a), Lot (6b,73d), Lou (96a, 183d), low (16c,149d), loy (121c,148b,151c,167a)

L - O   Lao (80d,88c,146a,161b), Leo (36b,c,92d,186d), loo (65a), Luo (107b), Lwo (107b)

- LO   Flo, ILO (184c), ulo (34b,80d)

L - P   lap (31b,37d,59b,127a,131d,153d,167d), lip (48b,58b,80a,131c), lop (30c,40a,46b,143a)

- LP   alp (24b,103d,115c)

L - R   lar (24c,51d,67a,78d,95d,101d,171b), Ler (23d,28a,28b,64b,106c, 141a), Lur (116c)

LS -   Lst (21a,b,88b)

L - S   las (13b,151d), les (13b,61a), lis (54b,58b,60c,62a,92b), Lis (47a), los (13b,151d), lys (58b,92b)

- LS   als (66d,163d), els (140a), ils (62b,d,164b)

L - T   lat (24a,33d,106b,118a), let (9a,76d,77c,116b,130a,158b,163a), lit, lot (24b,28d,55a,65d,114a,119c,143c,150d,168a), Lot (6b,73d), Lst (21a,b,88b), lut (189)

- LT   alt (66c76c,109c), elt (87a,117c,139d), Olt (41a)

LU -   lud (100a), Lud (23c,144b), lue (146b), lug (27a,45d,47b,73c,136b), Lug (28b), lum (30a), Luo (107b), Lur (116c), lut (189), lux (79d)

L - U   leu (190), Lou (96a,183d)

- LU   flu, ulu (87a)

L - V   lav (72d), lev (33b), Liv (93b)

LW -   Lwo (107b)

L - W   law (26b,33a,40a,48c,60b,85d,91a,111b,134d,155d), lew (190), Lew (96a), low (16c,149d)

L - X   lax (93d, 130a), lex (90b), lux (79d)

LY -   lye (8d,27d,93b), lyn (140c,178d), lys (58b,92b)

L - Y   lay (98b,107d,141d,150b), ley (190), loy (121c,148b,151c,167a)

- LY   aly (95d), **Ely** (27c,50b), **fly** (58c,81b,163b,178d), **ply** (59b,90b, 118d,164b,171c,174a,181b,184c), **sly** (13b,38b,64c,81b,132c)

L - Z   Laz (27d)

MA -   maa (97d,143d), **Mab** (54b,126b,183d), **Mac** (96a,140b,150b), **mad** (10c,82b), **Mae** (183c), **mag** (73b,95b,166c), **Mag** (183d), **Mah** (10b, 57c,102b), **mai** (62a), **mal** (34a,b,44a,52b,62c,122b), **Mal** (94b), **Mam** (192), **man** (29c,60c,64c,65a,142d,161d), **mao** (115b), **Mao** (30b), **map** (27a,29b,54a,98d,160a), **mar** (40b,44a,79a,d,81a,140d), **Mar** (93d), **mas** (34b,55b,119a), **mat** (46d,50d,94d,117c,161d), **Mat** (96a), **mau** (170c,188), **maw** (38b,d,72c,111a,121a,142a,156c), **Max** (96a), **may** (74d), **May** (183c)

M - A   maa (97d,143d), **MFA** (42a), **mia** (83c), **mna** (71d,179d), **moa** (19b), **Mya** (31c)

- MA   ama (26a,28d,31a,35b,39c,95b,108d,111c,117b,182c), **oma** (158c,d, 170c), **sma** (140b,148d), **Uma** (43a,69b,153d)

M - B   Mab (54b,126b,183d), **mib** (8d,96c), **mob** (39a,127a,165b)

M - C   Mac (96a,140b,150b)

M - D   mad (10c,82b), **mid** (9d,28b,73b), **Mod** (138d), **mud** (6c)

ME -   mee (169a), **Meg** (8c,183d), **mel** (77d), **mem** (91c), **men** (38c,116a, 117b,170a), **Men** (94d), **Meo** (27b,80c), **mer** (62c,141a), **mes** (62b), **met** (28d), **meu** (153b), **mew** (25b,27b,50a,55b,72c,74d,101b,141b, 153b)

M - E   Mae (183c), **mee** (169a), **Mme.** (166b), **Moe** (96a)

- ME   ame (37a,62d,131b), **eme** (38d,70a,140c,172b), **Mme.** (166b), **ume** (11d)

MF -   MFA (42a)

M - G   mag (73b,95b,166c), **Mag** (183d), **Meg** (8c,183d), **mig** (8d,96c, 145b), **Mig** (118d), **mug** (46b,54a,65a)

MH -   mho (49b,173b)

M - H   Mah (10b,57c,102b)

MI -   mia (83c), **mib** (8d,96c), **mid** (9d,28b,73b), **mig** (8d,96c,145b), **Mig** (118d), **mil** (80b,110c,164d,182d), **Mil** (10a,82b), **mim** (12b), **Min** (29d,68b,113c), **mio** (152c), **mir** (29d,135c,d,166c,176b), **mis** (122b,c,d,185c), **mit** (56c,66d,183b), **mix** (156b)

M - I   mai (62a), **Moi** (80d)

- MI   ami (61d)

M - L   mal (34a,b,44a,52b,62c,122b), **Mal** (94b), **mel** (77d), **mil** (80b,110c, 164d,182d), **Mil** (10a,82b), **mol** (58b,70c), **mul** (188)

MM -   Mme. (166b)

M - M   Mam (192), **mem** (91c), **mim** (12b), **mom, mum** (30d,95a,146c)

MN -   mna (71d,179d)

M - N   man (29c,60c,64c,65a,142d,161d), **men** (38c,116a,117b,170a), **Men** (94d), **Min** (29d,68b,113c), **mon** (15d,84b) **Mon** (24c), **mun** (157b)

MO -   moa (19b), **mob** (39a,127a,165b), **Mod** (138d), **Moe** (96a), **Moi** (80d), **mol** (58b,70c), **mom, mon** (15d,84b), **Mon** (24c), **moo** (94b), **mop** (160a), **mos** (59b), **mot** (126d,130a,137d,183b), **mow** (32b,40a)

M - O   mao (115b), Mao (30b), Meo (27b,80c), mho (49b,173b), mio (152c), moo (94b), Mro (88c)

- MO   amo (79a,89c), omo (34d)

M - P   map (27a,29b,54a,98d,160a), mop (160a)

- MP   amp (49b,173b), imp (42b,127d,174a)

MR -   Mro (88c), Mrs. (166b), Mru (80d,88c)

M - R   mar (40b,44a,79a,d,81a,140d), Mar (93d), mer (62c,141a), mir (29d, 135c,d,166c,176b), mur (63a,177d)

M - S   mas (34b,55b,119a), mes (62b), mis (122b,c,d,185c), mos (59b), Mrs. (166b), Mus (104a,132c)

- MS   Ems (125a,151c)

M - T   mat (46d,50d,94d,117c,161d), Mat (96a), met (28d), mit (56c,66d, 183b), mot (126d,130a,137d,183b), mut (39c), Mut (9b,127a)

- MT   amt (37d,40d,108a,163c)

MU -   mud (6c), mug (46b,54a,65a), mul (188), mum (30d,95a,146c), mun (157b), mur (63a,177d), Mus (104a,132c), mut (39c), Mut (9b,127a), muy (152d,175d)

M - U   mau (170c,188), meu (153b), Mru (80d,88c)

- MU   emu (19b,58c,111d), imu (15d), SMU (40b), umu (112a)

M - W   maw (38b,d,72c,111a,121a,142a,156c), mew (25b,27b,50a,55b,72c, 74d,101b,141b,153b), mow (32b,40a)

M - X   Max (96a), mix (156b)

MY -   Mya (31c)

M - Y   may (74d), May (183c), muy (152d,175d)

- MY   amy (63c), Amy (8c,94b,183c)

NA -   nab (13b,26c,27b,142a), nae (139d), nag (73d,78b,138c,184d), nak (156b), Nan (183c), nap (65a,117d,146b,148a), nar (139d), nas (74a, 89c,178b), nat (7a,24c,d,106a), nay (42b,106b)

N - A   NEA (162c), noa (35b,124a,161a), NRA (8a,20d)

- NA   ana (10b,33c,60d,93a,98c,122b,d,140d,142b), Ana (28a,68d,100c), Ena (8c,126b), ina (158c), Ina (183c), mna (71d,179d), Ona (26b, 64a), sna (105b,140b,143d,144a,149c,181c,d), Una (54a,153b, 170c,183c)

N - B   nab (13b,26c,27b,142a), neb (17b,19a,d,115d), nib (17b,19d,115d), nob (38c,74d,84a,149d) nub (67b,94d,95c,118c,124d)

N - D   Ned (96a), nid (72a,106c,116d), nod (17c,46c), Nod (18d,25b)

- ND   and (36a), end (8b,67d,120a,125d,130a,166a), Ind (80c), und (66b)

NE -   N.E.A. (162c), neb (17b,19a,d,115d), Ned (96a), nee (19d,22b,25c, 60b,95c), nef (32b,144c,d), neo (34a,b,c,100d,106d,108c,122c,d, 128c), nep (27c,32d,56a,87c,184b), ner (137c), nes (26b), net (26c, 32a,50d,53b,60d,99a,124a,142a,149b), new (11a,63c,88d,111c, 128c, Ney (63b,97b,105d), nez (62b)

N - E   nae (139d), nee (19d,22b,25c,60b,95c), nie (53c,66c), NNE (35b), nye (72a,116d), Nye (9c,18b)

- NE   ane (61c,140a,158b), ene (35b,158b,c), ine (29c,158b,c), Ine (10c, 137d,180b), NNE (35b), one (79a,b,80b,d,124b,147a,148d,173a,c), une (13b,61a,62b,95c)

N - F nef (32b,144c,d)

NG - ngu (188)

N- G nag (73d,78b,138c,184d), nig (33b,40a,46a), nog (20c,46a,48d,54d, 100b,115d,118a)

- NG eng (48a,146a), ing (114b,d,148d,158c,d,175c), Ing (10c,115b)

N - H nth (42a)

NI - nib (17b,19d,115d), nid (72a,106c,116d), nie (53c,66c), nig (33b, 40a,46a), nil (108c), nim (96d,155d), nin (107d), nip (20c,29b,45d,46a,b,115c,118a), nis (23d,67d,68a,87c), Nis (19d), nit (48d), nix (23d,108c,178d)

- NI ani (19b,d,20b,39b), ini (158d), oni (11b), uni·(34c,118d,122c), Uni (51d)

N - K nak (156b)

- NK ink (20b,40c)

N - L nil (108c), nul (108c,177a)

N - M nim (96d,155d), nom (62b,125a), Nym (54c,76a)

NN - NNE (35b), NNW (35b)

N - N Nan (183c), nin (107d), non (34c,62b,89c,106b,122c,147a), nun (24c,91c,117d,147b), Nun (29a,85c)

- NN Ann (183c), inn (72b,73b,78c,150a,161c,162b,179a), Inn (41a)

NO - noa (35b,124a,161a), nob (38c,74d,84a,149d), nod (17c,46c,148a), Nod (18d,25b), nog (20c,46a,48d,54d,100b,115d,118a), nom (62b, 125a), non (34c,62b,89c,106b,122c,147a), noo (108c,139d), nor (10b,36a,37b,92b), nos (62b,90a,179a), not (78b,106b), now (60b, 79d), Nox (69b)

N - O neo (34a,b,c,100d,106d,108c,122c,d,128c), noo (108c,139d)

- NO ano (19d,20b,34d,122d,174a), Ino (14b,25b), ono (34a), Ono (18d,118d), uno (83c,151d)

N - P nap (65a,117d,146b,148a), nep (27c,32d,56a,87c,184b), nip (20c, 29b,45d,46a,b,115c,118a)

NR - NRA (8a,20d)

N - R nar (139d), ner (137c), nor (10b,36a,37b,92b), nur (67d)

N - S nas (74a,89c,178b), nes (26b), nis (23d,67d,87c), Nis (19d), nos (62b,90a,179a)

- NS Ans (92a), ens (17d,18a,51a,52d), ins (164d), INS (107a,182d), ons (38c), uns (66d,174c)

NT - nth (42a)

N - T nat (7a,24c,d,106a), net (26c,32a,50b,53d,60d,99a,124a,142a, 149b), nit (48d), not (78b,106b), nut (24c,32d,38b,54d,64a,65d, 86b,141c,165a), Nut (69a)

- NT ant (49d,60b,81b,118c), ent (34d,158b,c), TNT (53a)

NU - nub (67b,94d,·¨c,118d,124d), nul (108c,177a), nun (24c,91c,117d, 147b), Nun (29,85c,129d), nur (67d), nut (24c,32d,38b,54d,64a, 65d,86b,141c,165 Nut (69a)

N - U ngu (188)

- NU   **Anu** (15b,28a,68a,d,75b,88c,147d), **gnu** (11a,181d), **Unu** (24d)

N - W   **new** (11a,63c,88d,111c,128c), **NNW** (35b), **now** (60b,79d)

- NW   **NNW** (35b), **WNW** (35b)

N - X   **nix** (23d,108c,178d), **Nox** (69b), **Nyx** (69b)

NY -   **nye** (72a,116d), **Nye** (9c,18b), **Nym** (54c,76a), **Nyx** (69b)

N - Y   **nay** (42b,106b), **Ney** (63b,97b,105d)

- NY   **any** (14b,150b), **ony** (139a), **sny** (18a,39d,43d,87a,119a,144d,145a,
165d,176a)

N - Z   **nez** (62b)

OA -   **oaf** (22a,45b,146d,157d,185d), **oak** (73d,168c,169a), **oar** (20b,124c,
134b), **oat** (15a,28b,70b,144b)

O - A   **oca** (48c,112c,116d,133d,170c,184a), **oda** (74a,170d), **oka** (170c,
184a,189), **ola** (113b) **oma** (158c,d,170c), **Ona** (26b,64a), **OPA**
(8a), **ora** (10c,40d,41b,45b,83a,c,101c,104a,122d,123d), **ova** (48d),
oxa (29c)

- OA   **boa** (36c,55b,106a,125d,138b,142d,149a), **goa** (65d,104b,126c),
Goa (121c), **hoa** (39b), **koa** (74c), **loa** (7d,53c,184d), **Loa** (97d), **moa**
(19b), **noa** (35b,124a,161a), **poa** (20d,70d,97d), **roa** (23d,87a), **toa**
(17c,178b), **Zoa** (20b)

OB -   **obe** (31d,87d,150d), **obi** (55d,67b,84c,137b,150d)

O - B   **orb** (50a,53c,67d,153b)

- OB   **bob** (57c,115d), **Bob** (96a), **cob** (28c,78b,95d,160b,177d), **fob** (29b,
59b,113b,178c), **gob** (97b,136c), **hob** (40c,56d,100c,124b,167a,
180c), **job** (30d,184c), **Job** (96a), **kob** (11a), **lob** (15d,23b,94c,100b,
163a,172d), **mob** (39a,127a,165b), **nob** (38c,74d,84a,149d), **pob**
(121b,129b,139c), **rob** (119d,155d), **Rob** (96a), **sob** (39b,179d)

OC -   **oca** (48c,112c,116d,133d,170c,184a), **och** (8b), **ock** (189), **oct** (34a,
122c)

O - C   **orc** (28c,70c,180b)

- OC   **Doc** (143a), **roc** (19c,53b,54a,147a), **soc** (44c,85d)

OD -   **oda** (74a,170d), **odd** (46b,53a,109b,157a,172d,173c), **ode** (26b,79c,
94d,118a,119d,120a,150b), **Odo** (181d), **ods** (109a)

O - D   **odd** (46b,53a,109b,157a,172d,173c), **oid** (158c), **old** (8a,71a,77c,
123c,175b), **Ord** (25b,60b)

- OD   **cod** (57b,c), **dod** (11a,32a,43b,140c), **fod** (188), **god** (42a), **God**
(84d), **hod** (23b,32d,102d,141a), **Mod** (138d), **nod** (17c,46c), **Nod**
(18d,25b), **pod** (76b,78d,91b,141b,180c), **rod** (6a,72d,88b,131a,
154d,156a,160a), **sod** (160b,170d), **tod** (24d,60c,83d), **Vod** (16a)

OE -   **o'er** (6b,112a), **oes** (109a)

O - E   **obe** (31d,87d,150d), **ode** (26b,79c,94d,118a,119d,120a,150b), **oke**
(189), **ole** (24b,29b,113b,152a,158b,d), **one** (79a,b,80d,124b,147a,
148d,173a,c), **ope** (172b,173c), **ore** (39a,99b,108a,115b,141c,151a,
160b), **ose** (102a,146d,158b,c,d,159a), **owe, ote** (158d), **oye** (139c)

- OE   **coe** (143d), **Coe** (33c), **doe** (41d,55b,127a), **foe** (111a), **hoe**
(39c), **Joe** (96a), **loe** (139d), **Moe** (96a), **poe** (114b), **Poe** (9c,d,128a,
172a), **roe** (27d,41d,48d,57b,76d,95b,157b), **soe** (170c,184a), **toe**
(43c,69d,148a,156a), **voe** (17a,81b), **woe** (25b), **Zoe** (36b,183c)

OF - off (6b,15c,44c,76a), oft (63c)

O - F oaf (22a,45b,146d,157d,185d), off (6b,15c,44c,76a), orf (57b,185c), ouf (52c)

- OF lof (188)

- OG bog (97a,160a), cog (33a,65d,163b,167b,180c), dog (10b,45b,59b), fog (109b), gog (95b), hog (45b,117c,160c), jog (82c,85c,170a), log (64a,128d), nog (20c,46a,48d,54d,100b,115d,118a), sog (149c), tog (46a), vog (189)

OH - ohm (49b,67a,173b), oho (52c)

O - H och (8b)

- OH boh (24c), doh (113b), foh (52c), Hoh (80d), poh (52c), soh (52c, 72d,) zoh (13d,186b)

OI - oid (158c), oii (105c), oil (11a,71a)

O - I obi (55d,67b,84c,137b,150d), oii (105c), oni (11b), ori (34a), ovi (34a)

- OI goi (107c), hoi (52c,74b,185b), koi (26d), loi (62a), Moi (80d), poi (44a,59c,74c,117a,162a,164b), roi (55c,62a,133d), toi (62b,d,63a), Toi (18d), yoi (52c,79a)

OK - oka (170c,184a,189), oke (189)

O - K oak (73d,168c,169a), ock (189), ork (180b), ouk (140c)

- OK Bok (9c), Lok (15d,68b), Rok (87c), sok (188), yok (10c,185a)

OL - ola (113b), old (8a,71a,77c,123c,175b), ole (24b,29b,113b,152a, 158b,d), olm (48c), Olt (41a)

O - L oil (11a,71a), owl

- OL col (103d,114c), Kol (18b), mol (58b,70c), sol (108b), Sol (117b, 159b), tol (137b), vol (155a,182d)

OM - oma (158c,d,170c), omo (34d)

O - M ohm (49b,67a,173b), olm (48c)

- OM com (122d), dom (121c,166b,c), Dom (94b), mom, nom (62b,125a), pom (45a,148d), rom (72d), tom (95d), Tom (96b,157a), yom (41a)

ON - Ona (26b,64a), one (79a,b,80b,d,124b,147a,148d,173a,c), oni (11b), ono (34a), Ono (18d,118d), ons (38c) ony (139a)

O - N own (6d)

- ON bon (30a,61d,86b,88c), Bon (84b), con (7d,29b,83c,116d,157d), don (151d,166c), Don (96a), eon (8a,37b,51d,116b), Fon (40b), gon (188), ion (11c,29a,49b,101b,114c,158c), Lon (86c,96a), mon (15d,84b), Mon (24c), non (34c,62b,89c,106b,122c,147a), ron (152c), Ron (86c,88a), son (42d,75d), ton (158d,167d,179d), von (66d,67a), won, yon (44c,112a,164d)

OO - oop (139a), oot (140a)

O - O Odo (181d), oho (52c), omo (34d), ono (34a), Ono (18d,118d), oro (34c,122c,152a), Oro (161b), oto (34a) Oto (147b)

- OO boo, coo (19b), Coo (82d), foo (42c), goo (156b), loo (65a), moo (94b), noo (108c,139d), roo (140a), soo (127d,140b,151b), Soo (137c), too (18b,102c), woo, zoo (181b)

OP - OPA (8a), ope (172b,173c), Ops (28c,69a,b,74a,137c), opt (30c)

O - P oop (139a), orp (140c,179d)

- OP cop (36a,120c,126d,153c,155d), dop (39c,43b), fop (38a,40d,46d), hop (40b), kop (76d), lop (30c,40a,46b,143a), mop (160a), oop (139a), pop (52d,53a,130b,149d), sop (23b,35d,149c,155d), top (38c,52b,118b,123d,160a,174a,186b), wop

OR - ora (10c,40d,41b,45b,83a,c,101c,104a,122d,123d), orb (50a,53c, 67d,153b), orc (28c,70c,180b), Ord (25b,60b), ore (39a,99b,108a, 115b,141c,151a,160b), orf (57b,185c), orl (34a), ork (180b), oro (34c,122c,152a), Oro (161b), orp (140c,179d), orr (77c), ort (59b, 90d,91a,102c,129b,140d,180a,184d), ory (36c)

O - R oar (20b,124c,134b), oer (6b,112a), orr (77c), our (124c)

- OR Bor (120c), cor (36c,75b,155b), dor (17d,24b,32b,46b,47a,81b,85d), for (123d,163a,166c), Gor (81a), Hor (103d), lor (50a,158c), kor (75c), nor (10b,36a,37b,92b), por (152a), tor (38b,76d,85d,115c, 124b,132b,c), Vor (69a)

OS - ose (102a,146d,158b,c,d,159a), ost (15d,86b)

O - S ods (109a), oes (109a), ons (38c), Ops (28c,69a,b,74a,137c), ous (158b)

- OS Bos (27c), cos (91d,132d), dos (45d,61a,97a,181b), Eos (14d,41a, 68d), ios (74d), Kos (77c,82d), los (13b,151d), mos (59b), nos (62b, 90a,179a), ros (37b), Ros (138a,174a), SOS

OT - ote (158d), oto (34a), Oto (147b)

O - T oat (15a,28b,70b,144b), oct (34a,122c), oft (63c), Olt (41a), oot (140a), opt (30c), ort (59b,90d,91a,102c,129b,140d,180a,184d), ost (15d,86b), out (6b,14b,60b,69d,80a,108b,185c)

- OT bot (59a,88d), cot (129b,148b), dot (45d,97a,104d,105a,116b,153a, 162d), fot (188), got, hot (10c,176c), jot (82a,114c,166c,180d), lot (24b,28d,55a,65d,114a,119c,143c,150d,168a), Lot (6b,73d), mot (126d,130a,137d,183b), not (78b,106b), oot (140a), pot (120b, 145b,154d,175d), rot (22b,134c,143d,153d), sot (46c,167b,c), tot (186a), Vot (56d)

OU - ouf (52c), ouk (140c), our (124c), ous (158b), out (6b,14b,60b,69d, 80a,108b,185c)

- OU fou (139a), IOU (124b), kou (169a), Lou (96a,183d), sou (63b), you

OV - ova (48d), ovi (34a)

OW - owe, owl, own (6d)

- OW bow (11c,21b,39d,60a,107c,109a,125a,144d,158a), cow (22c,45b, 81d), dow (17d,87a,88d,175d), how, jow (188), low (16c,149d), mow (32b,40a), now (60b,79d), pow, row (44c,56b,92c,109a,126b, 127d,165c), sow (45b,117c,119a,138b,160c), tow (45d,58b,75d, 125b), vow (119c,150a), wow (52c,158a), yow (52c)

OX - oxa (29c)

- OX box (36a,c,128c,145d,152d), cox (156a), fox (134a), Nox (69b), pox (44a), vox (90a,177a)

OY - oye (139c)

O - Y ony (139a), ory (36c)

- OY boy (142d,157c), coy (16d), goy (107c), hoy (16c,52c), joy, loy (121c,148b,151c,167a), Roy, soy (17b,137c,74d), toy (169d)

- OZ   Boz (43b,115d), coz, goz (190)

PA -   pab (139c), pac (73b,94c,100d), pad (39d,59c,76c,157d,161a,168b), pah (52c,60b,106d), pal (35b,38d), pam (26c,65a,87a,105b), pan (34a,61a,104a,175d), Pan (56a,68a,b,76b,120c,135b,161a,184a), pap (59c), par (15a,51a,b,c,69d,107c,135c,155a), pas (40d,156a), pat (11d,116d,159a,161d,167c), Pat (96a), Pau (48c,76a,130c), paw (32d,59c,73c), pax (89d,115b), pay (35b,128c,130a,d,177b)

P - A   pea (32d,91b,142a,175a), pia (13b,22d,48a,120d), poa (20d, 70d,97d), pta (6a), pua (74c,76a)

- PA   apa (23a,177d), OPA (8a), spa (75b,100b,130c,154b,178d)

P - B   pab (139c), pob (121b,129b,139c)

P - C   pac (73b,94c,100d), pic (188)

P - D   pad (39d,59c,76c,157d,161a,168b), ped (16d,34b), pod (76b,78d, 91b,141b,180c), pud (59d,73c,115a)

PE -   pea (32d,91b,142a,175a), ped (16d,34b), pee (91c), peg (38c,46b, 54d,98a,118a,184c), pel (55c,160d), pen (36a,50a,80d,118b,126d, 160a,185c), pep (50b,176b), per (25c,122d,165b,176a), pes (59d), pet (26d,37c,55a,59b,162d), peu (62a), pew (30d,52c,57d,120b, 141c)

P - E   pee (91c), pie (42d,85d,95b,114d,171b,172a), poe (114b), Poe (9c, d,128a,172a), pre (17d,122b,c), pue (52c), Pye (50d,55a)

- PE   ape (36d,79d,100a,101d,146d), ope (172b,173c)

P - G   peg (38c,46b,54d,98a,118a,184c), pig (27a,45b,99a,151b,160c), pug (45a,101a,108a,148d)

PH -   phi (91c), phu (38c)

P - H   pah (52c,60b,106d), poh (52c)

PI -   pia (13b,22d,48a,120d), pic (188), pie (42d,85d,95b,114d, 171b,172a), pig (27a,45b,99a,151b,160c), pik (188), pil (34b), pin (45d,54d,141d,147d), pip (11d,44a,121d,142a,154a), Pip (43b), pir (103a,b,136c), pit (52b,142a,164a,168a) piu (102c), pix (31a,51d, 175d)

P - I   phi (91c), poi (44a,59c,74c,117a,162a,164b), psi (91c)

- PI   api (34a,76d), epi (56c,61c,d,111c,112d,122d,133c,153c,167b, 174a), UPI (107a,182d)

P - K   pik (188)

PL -   ply (59b,90b,118d,164b,171c,174a,181b,184c)

P - L   pal (35b,38d), pel (55c,160d), pil (34b), pul (190), Pul (14a)

P - M   pam (26b,65a,87a,105b), pom (45a,148d)

P - N   pan (34a,61a,104a,175d), Pan (56a,68a,b,76b,120c,135b,161a, 184a), pen (36a,50a,80d,118b,126d,160a,185c), pin (45d,54d,141d, 147d), pun (119c)

PO -   poa (20d,70d,97d), pob (121b,129b,139c), pod (76b,78d,91b,141b, 180c), poe (114b), Poe (9c,d,128a,172a), poh (52c), poi (44a,59c, 74c,117a,162a,164b), pom (45a,148d), pop (52d,53a,130b,149d), por (152a), pot (120b,145b,154d,175d), pow, pox (44a)

P - O   pro (59d,126d), Pwo (88c)

- **PO**   **apo** (122b), **Apo** (177c)

P - P   **pap** (59c), **pep** (50b,176b), **pip** (11d,44a,121d,154a), **Pip** (43b), **pop** (52d,53a,130b,149d), **pup** (141b,148d,185d)

PR -   **pre** (17d,122b,c), **pro** (59d,126d), **pry** (52b,91d,98b,123d)

P - R   **par** (15a,51a,b,c,69d,107c,135b,155a), **per** (25c,122d,165b,176a), **pir** (103a,b,136c), **por** (152a), **pur, pyr** (92a,b,122c,173b)

PS -   **psi** (91c), **pst** (25c,126d,146c)

P - S   **pas** (40d,156a), **pes** (59d), **pus**

- **PS**   **Ops** (28c,69a,b,74a,137c)

PT -   **Pta** (6a)

P - T   **pat** (11d,116d,159a,161d,167c), **Pat** (96a), **pet** (26d,37c,55a,59b, 162d), **pit** (52b,142a,164a,168a), **pot** (120b,145b,154d,175d), **pst** (25c,126d,146c), **put** (65a,69d,90b)

- **PT**   **apt** (11d,23b,32b,58a,80b,92b,114d,116d,124b,159a), **opt** (30c)

PU -   **pua** (74c,76a), **pud** (59d,73c,115a), **pue** (52c), **pug** (45a,101a,108a, 148d), **pul** (190), **Pul** (14a), **pun** (119c), **pup** (141b,148d,185d), **pur, pus, put** (65a,69d,90b), **puy** (61d)

P - U   **Pau** (48c,76a,130c), **peu** (62a), **phu** (38c), **piu** (102c)

PW -   **Pwo** (88c)

P - W   **paw** (32d,59c,73c), **pew** (30d,52c,57d,120b,141c), **pow**

P - X   **pax** (89d,115b), **pix** (31a,51d,175d), **pox** (44a), **pyx** (31a,51d,175d)

PY -   **Pye** (50d,55a), **pyr** (92a,b,122c,173b), **pyx** (31a,51d,175d)

P - Y   **pay** (35b,128c,130a,d,177b), **ply** (59b,90b,118d,164b,171c,174a, 181b,184c), **pry** (52b,91d,98b,123d), **puy** (61d)

- **PY**   **spy** (44a,51c,52b,141d)

QA -   **Qaf** (104a)

Q - A   **qua** (13c,80a,89c,147a)

Q - E   **que** (62d)

Q - F   **Qaf** (104a)

Q - I   **qui** (62d)

Q - O   **quo** (188)

QU -   **qua** (13c,80a,89c,147a), **que** (62d), **qui** (62d), **quo** (188)

RA -   **rab** (17c,75c,85b,102d,162c,166b), **Rab** (45a), **rad** (50b,138d,173b), **rae** (136b,138d,140b), **Rae** (183c), **rag** (59b,77c,100c,133c,161a), **rah** (29b), **rai** (188), **raj** (129c), **ram** (17a,45b,50b,79c,112b,121d, 143d,157d), **Ram** (36b), **ran** (73d), **Ran** (7c,107d,141a,163d), **rap** (90d,110a,147c,157c), **ras** (6c,26b,48b,51d,53d,61c,75a,111c,123c, 166b), **rat** (16a,42d,73b,132c), **raw** (20c,39a,105d,173d), **ray** (38a, 49a,57b,58b,147b), **Ray** (96a)

R - A   **rea** (9c,171a), **ria** (38c,51d,81b,152a,b), **roa** (23d,87a), **rua** (118c), **Rua** (16b)

- **RA**   **ara** (33a,114a,116a,118b,163d), **Ara** (9b,18c,36b,c,68d,69b,c,85a, 95a,175b), **dra** (188), **era** (8a,51a,116b,165d), **fra** (23c,63c,101d, 123b,129d), **gra** (59b,94b,160c), **Ira** (18c,d,41a,68c,82c,96a,164a, 178a,c), **Kra** (11b,91d), **NRA** (8a,20d), **ora** (10c,40d,41b,45b,83a,c,

251

101c,104a,122d,123d), **tra** (33b)

R - B **rab** (17c,75c,85b,102d,162c,166b), **Rab** (45a), **reb** (35d,75c,85b, 162c,166b), **rib** (37c,85b,90c,98a,144d,159d,172a), **rob** (119d, 155d), **Rob** (96a), **rub** (6b,24d,28c,43c,120c,179b)

- RB **orb** (50a,53c,67d,153b)

R - C **roc** (19c,53b,54a,147a)

- RC **arc** (31b,39d,92a,126a,127c,142a), **orc** (28c,70c,180b)

R - D **rad** (50b,138d,173b), **red** (33c,38d,59a,127b,134c,135b), **Red** (151b), **rid** (32a,44a,60d), **rod** (6a,72d,88b,131a,154d,156a,160a), **rud** (26d,57b)

- RD **erd** (47d,119d,145c), **Ord** (25b,60b), **urd** (17b,184b), **Urd** (68d,107d)

RE - **rea** (9c,171a), **reb** (35d,75c,85b,162c,166b), **red** (33c,38d,59a,127b, 134c,135b), **Red** (151b), **ree** (12c,50a,80c,134d,137a,140b,144a, 146b), **Ree** (25a), **ref, reh** (8d), **rei** (89b,121c), **Rei** (18d), **rel** (49b, 173b), **Reo** (26c), **rep** (53b,d,131a,171c), **res** (80a,89d,91a,97c), **ret** (58b,95a,149c,155d), **Reu** (115d), **rev, rew** (75c,140c,176b), **rex** (86c,96a), **rey** (86c,152b)

R - E **rae** (136b,138d,140b), **Rae** (183c), **ree** (12c,50a,80c,134d,137a, 140b,144a,146b), **Ree** (25a), **rhe** (59a,173b), **rie** (28c,70d,97d), **roe** (27d,41d,48d,57b,76d,95b,157b), **rue** (76a,b,129c,150d,183a), **rye** (28b,70b,72d,92d)

- RE **are** (51a,88b,98a,99b,110c,166c,175c), **ere** (17d,150c), **ire** (10c, 52b,30c,64c,125a,130b,185a), **ore** (39a,99b,108a,115b,141c,151a, 160b), **pre** (17d,122b,c), **tre** (37b,83c,122d,165a,167d), **ure** (40a, 139d,155d,158b,d), **Ure** (138d,185d)

R - F **ref, rif** (188)

- RF **orf** (57b,185c)

R - G **rag** (59b,77c,100c,133c,161a), **rig** (51b,112a), **rug**

- RG **erg** (50b,173b,184c)

RH - **rhe** (59a,173b), **rho** (71b,91c)

R - H **rah** (29b), **reh** (8d)

RI - **ria** (38c, 51d, 81b, 152a, b), **rib** (37c, 85b, 90c, 98a, 144d, 159d,172a), **rid** (32a,44a,60d), **rie** (28c,70d,97d), **rif** (188), **rig** (51b, 112a), **rii** (157b,175b), **rim** (22a,48b,96d),116b,124b,166a,180c), **rin** (33b,142b), **rio** (33a,131d,132a,152c,157b), **Rio** (23a), **rip** (87b, 130a,162c), **Rip** (178b), **ris** (131d), **rit** (140b,148c,153d)

R - I **rai** (188), **rei** (89b,121c), **Rei** (18d), **rii** (157b,175b), **roi** (55c,62a, 133d)

- RI **Ari** (18d), **eri** (13d,21c,146d), **Eri** (18c), **gri** (75c,78b), **Iri** (18a,d, 75a), **kri** (75c,96d), **ori** (34a), **sri** (60c,77b,166c), **Sri** (17c), **tri** (122d,169d), **Uri** (162d)

R - J **raj** (129c)

R - K **Rok** (87c)

- RK **ark** (21a,29d,38a,58b,60d,175d), **irk** (10d), **ork** (180b)

R - L **rel** (49b,173b)

R - M **ram** (17a,45b,50b,79c,112b,121d,143d,157d), **Ram** (36b), **rim** (22a,

48b,96d,116b,124b,166a,180c), **rom** (72d), **rum** (8c,92d)

- RM   **arm** (22d,60c,81b,92b,124b,161b)

R - N   **ran** (73d), **Ran** (7c,107d,141a,163d), **rin** (33b),142b), **ron** (152c), **Ron** (86c,88a), **run** (10d,23c,58d,110d,148d,153b,154b,167d)

- RN   **arn** (8c,139a), **ern** (19c,d,47b,54b,141a), **urn** (36c,174d)

RO -   **roa** (23d,87a), **rob** (119d,155d), **Rob** (96a), **roc** (19c,53b,54a,147a), **rod** (6a,72d,88b,131a,154d,156a,160a), **roe** (27d,41d,48d,57b,76d, 95b,157b), **roi** (55c,62a,133d), **Rok** (87c), **rom** (72d), **ron** (152c), **Ron** (86c,88a), **roo** (140: **ros** (37b), **Ros** (138a,174d), **rot** (22b, 134c,143d,153d), **row** (44·,56b,92c,109a,126b,127d,165c), **Roy**

R - O   **Reo** (26c), **rho** (71b,91c), **rio** (33a,131d,132a,152c,157b), **Rio** (23a), **roo** (140a)

- RO   **Aro** (107a,111c), **cro** (104c,115b,180a), **fro** (15b), **Mro** (88c), **oro** (34c,122c,152a), **Oro** (161b), **pro** (59d,126d), **S.R.O.** (6a,164a), **Uro** (192)

R - P   **rap** (90d,110a,147c,157c), **rep** (53b,d,131a,171c), **rip** (87b, 130a,162c), **Rip** (178b)

- RP   **orp** (140c,179d)

R - R   **rur** (132b)

- RR   **err** (21a,43a,67d,100c,d,147a,148b,157b,168b,178a), **grr** (52c), **orr** (77c)

R - S   **ras** (6c,26b,48b,51d,53d,61c,75a,111c,123c,166b), **res** (80a,89d, 91a,97c,164c), **ris** (131d), **ros** (37b), **Ros** (138a,174d), **rus** (89b), **Rus** (138a)

- RS   **ars** (13b,89a), **Ars** (112c), **ers** (20a,176a), **Mrs.** (166b)

R - T   **rat** (16a,42d,73b,132c), **ret** (58b,95a,149c,155d), **rit** (140b,148c, 153d), **rot** (22b,134c,143d,153d), **rut** (73a)

- RT   **art** (22d,38b,39c,43b,56c,124a,162c,181d), **ert** (140c,174a), **ort** (59b,90d,91a,102c,129b,140d,180a,184d)

RU -   **rua** (118c), **Rua** (16b), **rub** (6b,24d,28c,43c,120c,179b), **rud** (26d, 57b), **rue** (76a,b,129c,150d,183a), **rug**, **rum** (8c,92d), **run** (10d,23c, 58d,110d,148d,153b,154b,167d), **rur** (132b), **rus** (89b), **Rus** (138a), **rut** (73a), **rux** (154a,184d)

R - U   **Reu** (115d)

- RU   **aru** (80c,82b), **Aru** (82d), **cru** (63a,176c), **Kru** (91d), **Mru** (80d,88c), **Uru** (192)

R - V   **rev**

R - W   **raw** (20c,39a,105d,173d), **rew** (75c,140c,176b), **row** (44c,56b,92c, 109a,126b,127d,165c)

R - X   **rex** (86c,96a), **rux** (154a,184d)

RY -   **rye** (28b,70b,72d,92d)

R - Y   **ray** (38a,49a,57b,58b,147b), **Ray** (96a), **rey** (86c,152b), **Roy**

- RY   **cry** (25c,124a,145c,179d), **dry** (46d,85a,137c,164c), **ery** (155d,158c, d), **fry** (57d), **gry** (78b), **ory** (36c), **pry** (52b,91d,98b,123d), **try** (7c, 10d,14c,50a,51c,130a), **wry** (13d)

SA -   **saa** (98a), **sac** (15d,121d), **Sac** (80c), **sad** (29c,42c,94c,98c,104a,

150d,173a), **sae** (140b,149c), **sag** (46b), **sah** (188), **sai** (101d), **saj** (48a,169a), **sak** (37c), **Sak** (88c), **sal** (29c,48a,136d,149d,152d, 169a,183a), **Sal** (183d), **Sam** (96a,162a), **san** (91c), **San** (24d), **sao** (141b), **Sao** (113c), **sap** (45d,52d,85c,169b,176d,179a), **sar** (57d), **sat** (13d), **saw** (7a,11b,40c,54c,97d,125a,137d,167a), **sax** (40c,148a,167a), **say** (131c,174c,177a)

S - A   **saa** (98a), **sea** (19a,52d,58c,112c,178d), **sha** (110c,143d,144a,c, 174c,181c), **sia** (80c), **sma** (140b,148d), **sna** (105b,140b,143d,144a, 149c,181c,d), **spa** (75b,100b,130c,154b,178d), **sta** (13c,91b,104d, 105a), **sua** (89d),

- SA   **Asa** (6a,18c,71a,84d,86d,164c), **ESA** (8a)

S - B   **Seb** (47d), **sib** (86b,129c,139d,147b), **sob** (39b,179d), **sub** (90a, 122d,172c)

S - C   **sac** (15d,121d), **Sac** (80c), **see** (46c,182c), **sic** (90a,165b,168b), **soe** (44c,85d)

- SC   **BSC** (42a)

S - D   **sad** (29c,42c,94c,98c,104a,150d,173a), **sed** (89a), **Sid** (96a), **sod** (160b,170d), **sud** (59a)

SE -   **sea** (19a,52d,58c,112c,178d), **Seb** (47d), **see** (46c,182c), **sed** (89a), **see** (20a,43c,44a,51c,53c,93d,109b,113c,116a,176d,178c,183b), **sel** (62c,140b), **Sem** (107c), **sen** (190) **ser** (80d,83b,d,116c, 152d,180a), **ses** (61d), **set** (7b,11d,13a,23c,32b,33c,37c,58a,73d, 109b,118c,121c,142c,150a,186a), **Set** (52b,68a,b,111d), **sew, sex, sey** (120c)

S - E   **sae** (140b,149c), **see** (20a,43c,44a,51c,53c,109b,113c,116a,176d, 178c,183b), **she** (124b), **She** (73a), **sie** (46c,66d,139b,140b,146b), **soe** (170c,184a), **SSE** (35b), **ste** (62c,136c), **sue** (119c), **Sue** (63a, 178a,183d), **sye** (40c,46c,139b,141a,167a)

- SE   **ase** (51a,139a), **Ase** (79b,115d), **ese** (35b,158d), **ise** (40d,158c,d), **Ise** (78a,84c), **ose** (102a,146d,158b,c,d,159a), **SSE** (35b), **use** (7b, 47a,49d,64c,109b,168b,c,181b)

S - F   **Sif** (164d)

S - G   **sag** (46b), **sog** (149c)

SH -   **sha** (110c,143d,144a,c,174c,181c), **she** (124b), **She** (73a), **sho** (188), **Shu** (30b,127a), **shy** (16d,99d,128c,160c,165d,175a)

S - H   **sah** (188), **soh** (52c,72d)

- SH   **ash** (24d,33c,49c,73d,134b,168c,169a), **hsh** (79c), **ish** (158b), **ush**

SI -   **Sia** (80c), **sib** (86b,129c,139d,147b), **sic** (90a,165b,168b), **Sid** (96a), **sie** (46c,66d,139b,140b,146b), **Sif** (164d), **sil** (30c,185c,d), **Sim** (96b), **sin** (91c,140b,147a,168b,176a), **Sin** (102b), **sip** (46b,79d, 104a,162b), **sir** (87a,163b,166b), **sis** (67b,129c), **sit** (98c,116a,121c, 130c,142d), **six** (26c)

S - I   **sai** (101d), **Sia** (80c), **ski** (149c), **sri** (60c,77b,166c), **Sri** (17c), **sui** (30b)

- SI   **asi** (137a), **psi** (91c)

S - J   **saj** (48a,169a)

SK -   **ski** (149c), **sky** (56d)

S - K   sak (37c), Sak (88c), sok (188), Suk (107b)

- SK   ask (38b,82a,126c)

SL -   sly (13b,38b,64c,81b,132c)

S - L   sal (29c,48a,136d,149d,152d,169a,183a), Sal (183d), sel (62c, 140b), sil (30c,185c,d), sol (108b), Sol (117b,159b)

SM -   sma (140b,148d), SMU (40b)

S - M   Sam (96a,162a), Sem (107c), Sim (96b), sum (8a,123a,167c)

- SM   ism (45a,79b,161c)

SN -   sna (105b,140b,143d,144a,149c,181c), sny (18a,39d,43d,87a,119a, 144d,145a,165d,176a)

S - N   san (91c), San (24d), sen (190), sin (91c,140b,147a,168b,176a), Sin (102b), son (42d,75d), sun (75d,111a,117b,155b), syn (122d,183b)

SO -   sob (39b,179d), soc (44c,85d), sod (160b,170d), soe (170c,184a), sog (149c), soh (52c,72d), sok (188), sol (108b) Sol (117b,159b), son (42d,75d), soo (127d,140b,151b), Soo (137c), sop (23b,35d, 149c,155d), SOS, sot (46c,167b,c), sou (63b), sow (45b,117c,119a, 138b,160c), soy (17b,137c,174d)

S - O   sao (141b), Sao (113c), sho (188), soo (127d,140b,151b), Soo (137c), S.R.O. (6a,164a)

- SO   Aso (84c), DSO (99d), eso (34d,183b), iso (34a,122c,d)

SP -   spa (75b,100b,130c,154b,178d), spy (44a,51c,52b,141d)

S - P   sap (45d,52c,85c,169b,176d,179a), sip (46b,79d,104a,162b), sop (23b,35d,149c,155d), sup (46b,104a,162b)

- SP   asp (7b,32b,149a,174a,176c), e.s.p. (147b)

S - Q   suq (22a,97a)

SR -   sri (60c,77b,166c), Sri (17c), S.R.O. (6a,164a)

S - R   sar (57d), ser (80d,83b,d,116c,152d,180a), sir (87a,163b,166b), sur (34a,62b,d,104b,151a,152d,174a)

SS -   SSE (35b), ssu (189), SSW (35b)

S - S   ses (61d), sis (67b,129c), SOS, sus (117c), Sus (160c,181b)

- SS   ass (17b,20c,45b,c,59c,110c,112b,146d,157d), ess (39d,78a,91c, 158c,184d)

ST -   sta (13c,91b,104d,105a), ste (62c,136c), sty (50a,53c)

S - T   sat (13d), set (7b,11d,13a,23c,32b,33c,37c,58a,73d,109b,118c, 121c,142c,150a,186a), Set (52b,68a,b,111d), sit (98c,116a,121c, 130c,142d), sot (46c,167b,c)

- ST   est (50a,61c,62a,79b,89c,158d,159c), ist (7b,34b,43a,59b,66c,158b, c,d), LST (21a,88b), ost (15d,86b), pst (25c,126d,146c), tst (81d, 126d)

SU -   sua (89d), sub (90a,122d,172c), sud (59a), sue (119c), Sue (63a, 178a,183d), Sui (30b), Suk (107b), sum (8a,123a,167c), sun (75d, 111a,117b,155b), sup (46b,104a,162b), suq (22a,97a), sur (34a,62b, d,104b,151a,152d,174a), sus (117c), Sus (160c,181b)

S - U   Shu (30b,127a), SMU (40b), sou (63b), ssu (189)

- SU   ssu (189)

S - W   saw (7a,11b,40c,54c,97d,125a,137d,167a), sew, sow (45b,117c, 119a,138b,160c), SSW (35b)

- SW   SSW (35b), WSW (35b)

S - X   sax (40c,148a,167a), sex, six (26c)

SY -   sye (40c,46c,139b,141a,167a), syn (122d,183b)

S - Y   say (131c,174c,177a), sey (120c), shy (16d,99d,128c,160c,165d, 175a), sky (56d), sly (13b,38b,64c,81b,132c), sny (18a,39d,43d,87a, 119a,144d,145a,165d,176a), soy (17b,137c,174d), spy (44a,51c, 52b,141d), sty (50a,53c)

TA -   taa (112d), tab (29b,39c,58b,86a,128d,145a), tac (34d,130a), tad (22c,174a,186a), tae (138d,140c,166c,d), tag (45a,54c,65a,87b, 144a), tai (84b,111c,121b), Tai (80d), taj (75a,97d), tal (40c,77a, 113b), tam (74d), tan (23d,33c,46a,72d,90d), tao (10d,131c, 170b), Tao (117a), tap (55a,114d,153c), tar (8c,68a,94d,111c,118c, 136a,c,176d), tat (43b,48c,72d,87c), Tat (82a), tau (71b,91c,136c, 161a), tav (91c), taw (90d,91c,96c,d,145b,161d), tax (13a,14a,80a, 91d)

T - A   taa (112d), tea (13d,18c,79c,81a,145d,149c,159d), tia (151d), toa (17c,178b), tra (33b), tua (117a)

- TA   ata (58d,97d,158d,160c,173d), Ata (79c,80d,94d,95d,100a,106b, 117a), eta (71a,84c,91c), Ita (51b,71d,94d,95d,106b,117a), ITA (173a), Pta (6a), sta (13c,91b,104d,105a), uta (53c,84d,93b,147c, 150b)

T - B   tab (29b,39c,58b,86a,128d,145a), tub (21a,27a,36c,174d)

TC -   tch (52c), tck (52c)

T - C   tac (34d,130a), tec (43a), tic (104d,153a,171c,d)

- TC   etc (10b)

T - D   tad (174a,186a), ted (74d,138b,154b), Ted (96b), tod (24d,60c,83d)

TE -   tea (13d,18c,79c,81a,145d,149c,159d), tec (43a), ted (74d,138b, 154b), Ted (96b), tee (39d,52b,69d,91c,112d,115d,118b,172a), teg (45a,54b,143d,144a,171d), tel (34a,b,122c), Tem (143a,159b), ten (19a,26c,41c,42b), ter (34d,122c,165a), tez (125c)

T - E   tae (138d,140c,166c,d), tee (39d,52b,69d,91c,112d,115d,118b, 172a), the (13b), tie (10a,14c,38b,45d,51a,88d,109b,127c,138b, 170b), toe (43c,69d,148a,156a), tre (37b,83c,122d,165a,167d), tue (114b), tye (28c,134a)

- TE   ate (81a,108c,158c,174c), Ate (20c,68b,d,69a,b,116c,186b), ete (36c,62d,141c,159b), ite (59b,81a,105d,130c,158b,c,d,161a), ote (158d), ste (62c,136c), Ute (145c,180b)

T - G   tag (45a,54c,65a,87b,144a), teg (45a,54b,143d,144a,171d), tig (46b), tog (46a), tug (45d,125b), tyg (46b)

TH -   the (13b), tho (52a), Tho (167a), thy

T - H   tch (52c)

- TH   eth (91c,158d), lth (10a,28a,82b,99d), nth (42a)

TI -   tia (151d), tic (104d,153a,171c,d), tie (10a,14c,38b,45d, 51a,88d,109b,127c,138b,170b), tig (46b), til (142d), Tim (43b), tin (36c,99a,b,108b,155a,179c), tio (152d), tip (26b,d,50a,70d,77b,78a,

120a,165d), **tir** (61d,62c,145b), **tis**, **tit** (19c,130d), **Tiu** (7c,68c, 147d,163d,166c,170c), **Tiw** (68c,147d,163d)

T - I   tai (84b,111c,121b), **Tai** (80d), **tji** (189), **toi** (62b,d,63a), **Toi** (18d), **tri** (122d,169d), **tui** (47c,114b,117a), **Twi** (69c)

- TI   ati (106d,107a), **Ati** (45d,106b,113c,117a)

TJ -   tji (189)

T - J   taj (75a,97d)

TK -   TKO (22c)

T - K   tck (52c)

T - L   tal (40c,77a,113b), **tel** (34a,b,122c), **til** (142d), **tol** (137b)

T - M   tam (74d), **Tem** (143a,159b), **Tim** (43b), **tom** (95d), **Tom** (96b, 157a), **tum** (26d), **Tum** (143a,159b)

TN -   TNT (53a)

T - N   tan (23d,33c,46a,72d,90d), **ten** (19a,26c,41c,42b), **tin** (36c,99a,b, 108b,155a,179c), **ton** (158d,167d,179d), **tun** (23b,27a,182b)

TO -   toa (17c,178b), **tod** (24d,60c,83d), **toe** (43c,69d,148a,156a), **tog** (46a), **toi** (62b,d,63a), **Toi** (18d), **tol** (137b), **tom** (95d), **Tom** (96b, 157a), **ton** (158d,167d,179d), **too** (18b,102c), **top** (38c,52b,118b, 123d,160a,174a,186b), **tor** (38b,76d,85d,115c,124b,132b,c), **tot** (186a), **tow** (45d,58b,75d,125b), **toy** (169d)

T - O   tao (10d,131c,170b), **Tao** (117a), **tho** (52a), **Tho** (167a), **tio** (152d), **TKO** (22c), **too** (18b,102c), **two** (26c,37d,80a,93a)

- TO   ETO (184d), **Ito** (84a,c,186d), **oto** (34a), **Oto** (147b)

T - P   tap (55a,114d,153c), **tip** (26b,d,50a,70d,77b,78a,120a,165d), **top** (38c,52b,118b,123d,160a,174a,186b), **tup** (115a,117d,127d,143d)

TR -   tra (33b), **tre** (37b,83c,122d,165a,167d), **tri** (122d,169d), **try** (7c, 10d,14c,50a,51c,130a)

T - R   tar (8c,68a,94d,111c,118c,136a,c,176d), **ter** (34d,122d,165a), **tir** (61d,62c,145b), **tor** (38b,76d,85d,115c,124b,132b,c), **tur** (14d,27c, 68a,79b,117d,174c), **tyr** (7c,68c,147d,163d,170c,178a)

TS -   tst (81d,126d)

T - S   tis

- TS   its (124c)

T - T   tat (43b,48c,72d,87c), **Tat** (82a), **tit** (19c,130d), **TNT** (53a), **tot** (186a), **tst** (81d,126d), **tut** (52c)

- TT   att (146a)

TU -   tua (117a), **tub** (21a,27a,36c,174d), **tue** (114b), **tug** (45d,125b), **tui** (47c,114b,117a), **tum** (26d), **Tum** (143a,159b), **tun** (23b,27a, 182b), **tup** (115a,117d,127d,143d), **tur** (14d,27c,68a,79b,117d, 174c), **tut** (52c)

T - U   tau (71b,91c,136c,161a), **Tiu** (7c,68c,147d,163d,166c,170c)

- TU   utu (35b,137c), **Utu** (96c,107a,159b)

T - V   tav (91c)

TW -   Twi (69c), **two** (26c,37d,80a,93a)

T - W   taw (90d,91c,96c,d,145b,161d), **Tiw** (68c,147d,163d), **tow** (45d, 58b,75d,125b)

257

T - X   **tax** (13a,14a,80a,91d)

TY -   **tye** (28c,134a), **tyg** (46b), **Tyr** (7c,68c,109c,147d,163d,170c,178a)

T - Y   **thy, toy** (169d), **try** (7c,10d,14c,50a,51c,130a)

- TY   **sty** (50a,53c)

T - Z   **tez** (125c)

U - A   **Uca** (56a), **ula** (72c,158c), **Uma** (43a,69b,153d), **Una** (54a,153b, 170c,183c), **uta** (53c,84d,93b,147c,150b), **uva** (64a,70c)

- UA   **dua** (122d), **Kua** (95c), **pua** (74c,76a), **qua** (13c,80a,89c,147a), **rua** (118c), **Rua** (16b), **sua** (89d), **tua** (117a)

UB -   **ube** (185b), **ubi** (90a,180d,185b)

- UB   **bub** (22c), **cub** (92d,185d), **dub** (25c,46a,c,87a,105b,121a,140a), **fub** (29b,119d), **hub** (28b,118b,180c), **nub** (67b,94d,95c,118c 124d), **rub** (6b,24d,28c,43c,120c,179b), **sub** (90a,122d,172c), **tub** (21a,27a,36c,174d)

UC -   **Uca** (56a)

- UC   **duc** (61c)

UD -   **Udi** (108a), **udo** (28a,30c,48c,84b,c,d,136c,149d)

U - D   **und** (66b), **urd** (17b,184b), **Urd** (68d,107d)

- UD   **bud** (22c), **cud** (126c,135a), **dud** (21c,54a), **lud** (100a), **Lud** (23c, 144b), **mud** (6c), **pud** (59d,73c,115a), **rud** (26d,57b), **sud** (59a)

U - E   **ube** (185b), **ule** (23a,27d,134c,158c,168d), **ume** (11d), **une** (13b, 61a,62b,95c), **ure** (40a,139d,155d,158b,d), **Ure** (138d,185d), **use** (7b,47a,49d,64c,109b,168b,c,181b), **Ute** (145c,180b), **uve** (185b)

- UE   **cue** (7a,27b,92c,117d,124b,132c,146c,159a), **due** (7b,115b,124c), **gue** (176c), **hue** (33c,143b), **lue** (146b), **pue** (52c), **que** (62d), **rue** (76a,b,129c,150d,183a), **sue** (119c), **Sue** (63a,178a,183d), **tue** (114b)

UF -   **ufo** (59a)

- UF   **ouf** (52c)

UG -   **ugh** (52c)

- UG   **bug** (24b,66b,81b), **dug, fug** (129a), **hug** (32c,49d), **jug** (118c, 123d), **lug** (27a,45d,47b,73c,136b), **Lug** (28b), **mug** (46b,54a,65a), **pug** (45a,101a,108a,148d), **rug, tug** (45d,125b), **vug** (28a,66a)

U - H   **ugh** (52c), **ush**

- UH   **auh** (52c), **huh** (52c)

UI -   **uit** (47a,111d,151a)

U - I   **ubi** (90a,180d,185b), **Udi** (108a), **uji** (146d), **uni** (34c,118d,122c), **Uni** (51d), **UPI** (107a,182d), **Uri** (162d), **uvi** (185b)

- UI   **dui** (46d), **hui** (14a,30b,56d,114c), **Kui** (86a,88c,146a), **qui** (62d), **Sui** (30b), **tui** (47c,114b,117a)

UJ -   **uji** (146d)

- UK   **auk** (19b), **ouk** (140c), **Suk** (107b)

UL -   **ula** (72c,158c), **ule** (23a,27d,134c,158c,168d), **Ull** (7c,68c,146b, 164d), **ulm** (49c), **Ulm** (40d), **ulo** (34b,80d), **ulu** (87a)

U - L   **Ull** (7c,68c,146b,164d)

258

- UL   Bul (25d,102a), Ful (158b), gul (134a), mul (188), nul (108c,177a), pul (190), Pul (14a)

UM -   Uma (43a,69b,153d), ume (11d), umu (112a)

U - M   ulm (49c), Ulm (40d)

- UM   àum (189), bum (21b), cum (159b), dum (45c,67b,113a), gum (7b, 53c,80b,130c,156b), hum (24d,46b,150d), Jum (39c), lum (30a), mum (30d,95a,146c), rum (8c,92d), sum (8a,123a,167c), tum (26d), Tum (143a,159b)

UN -   Una (54a,153b,170c,183c), und (66b), une (13b,61a,62b,95c), uni (34c,118d,122c), Uni (51d), uno (83c,151d), uns (66d,174c), Unu (24d)

U - N   urn (36c,174d)

- UN   bun (25b,73b), dun (19a,39d,46d,71a,97d,115b,160b), fun, gun (56d,131a,146a), Hun (16c,21d,174b), mun (157b), nun (24c,91c, 117d,129d,147b), Nun (29a,85c), pun (119c), run (10d,23c,58d, 110d,148d,153b,154b,167d), sun (75d,111a,117b,155b), tun (23b, 27a,182b), wun (24c), Yun (88d)

U - O   udo (28a,30c,48c,84b,c,d,136c,149d), ufo (59a), ulo (34b,80d), uno (83c,151d), Uro (192)

- UO   duo (46d,113a,171d), Luo (107b), quo (188)

UP -   UPI (107a,182d)

- UP   cup (46b,69d,118b,170a), gup (70a), hup (35a), kup (188), pup (141b,148d,185d), sup (46b,104a,162b), tup (115a,117d,127d, 143d)

- UQ   suq (22a,97a)

UR -   urd (17b,184b), Urd (68d,107d), ure (40a,139d,155d,158b,d), Ure (138d,185d), Uri (162d), urn (36c,174d), Uro (192), Uru (192)

- UR   bur (123b), cur (101d), dur (95c), Eur. (36c), fur, gur (159a), Hur (91d), Jur (107b), Lur (116c), mur (63a,177d), nur (67d), our (124c), pur, rur (132b), sur (34a,62b,d,104b,151a,152d,174a), tur (14d,27c,68a,79b,117d,174c)

US -   use (7b,47a,49d,64c,109b,168b,c,181b), ush

U - S   uns (66d,174c)

-US   aus (66c), Aus (98b), bus (125b,168b), Gus (96a), jus (61d,90b), Mus (104a,132c), ous (158b), pus, rus (89b,138a), sus (117c), Sus (160c,181b)

UT -   uta (53a,84d,93b,147c,150b), Ute (145c,180b), utu (35b, 137c), Utu (96c,107a,159b)

U - T   uit (47a,111d,151a)

- UT   aut (34d,89d), but (36a,52b,156b,173c), cut (30c,32b,145c), fut (188), gut (114d,130a), hut (143c), jut (53a,124a), lut (189), mut (39c), Mut (9b,127a), nut (24c,32d,38b,54d,64a,65d,86b,141c, 165a), Nut (69a), out (6b,14b,60b,69d,80a,108b,185c), put (65a, 69d,90b), rut (73a), tut (52c)

U - U   ulu (87a), umu (112a), Unu (24d), Uru (192), utu (35b,137c), Utu (96c,107a,159b)

UV -   uva (64a,70c), uve (185b), uvi (185b)

259

- **UX**   **aux** (6d,61a), **dux** (31d,64a,90c), **lux** (79d), **rux** (154a,184d)
- **UY**   **buy**, **guy** (55b,131b,155d), **Guy** (96a), **muy** (152d,175d), **puy** (61d)
- **UZ**   **guz** (188)

VA - **Vac** (153b), **vae** (176b), **vag** (174b,178a), **Vai** (91d), **van** (7b,59d, 60a,63d,90c), **vas** (46d,89d,119c,133b,175d), **vat** (31b,36c,163a, 170c), **vau** (91c)

V - A **via** (132a,133a,b,179a)

- **VA** **ava** (78d,86a,116a,120d,139a,167b), **Ava** (24c), **Eva** (157a,183c), **iva** (76a,97b,127b,185b), **ova** (48d), **uva** (64a,70c)

V - C **Vac** (153b)

V - D **Vod** (16a)

VE - **vee** (58a,91c,106a), **Vei** (91d), **vet**, **vex** (7c,10d,44c,82c)

V - E **vae** (176b), **vee** (58a,91c,106a), **vie** (36c,157c,170c), **voe** (17a,81b)

- **VE** **ave** (54c,71d,73a,122a,134a,136d), **eve** (47a,131a,143a,165d,171c), **Eve** (183c), **ive** (158c), **uve** (185b)

V - F **vif** (62a)

V - G **vag** (174b,178a), **vog** (189), **vug** (28a,66a)

VI - **via** (132a,133a,b,179a), **vie** (36c,157c,170c), **vif** (62a), **vim** (50b, 176b), **vin** (63a,182b), **vir** (89c), **vis** (59d,89b,d,90b,176b), **vix**, (89d,138b), **viz** (105b)

V - I **Vai** (91d), **Vei** (91d)

- **VI** **ovi** (34a), **uvi** (185b)

V - L **vol** (155a,182d)

V - M **vim** (50b,176b)

V - N **van** (7b,59d,60a,63d,90c), **vin** (63a,182b), **von** (66d,67a)

VO - **Vod** (16a), **voe** (17a,81b), **vog** (189), **vol** (155a,182d), **von** (66d, 67a), **Vor** (68d), **Vot** (56d), **vow** (119c,150a), **vox** (90a,177a)

V - R **vir** (89c), **Vor** (68d)

V - S **vas** (46d,89d,119c,133b,175d), **vis** (59d,89b,d,90b,176b)

V - T **vat** (31b,36c,163a,170c), **vet**, **Vot** (56d)

VU - **vug** (28a,66a)

V - U **Vau** (91c)

V - W **vow** (119c,150a)

V - X **vex** (7c,10d,44c,82c), **vix** (89d,138b), **vox** (90a,177a)

V - Z **viz** (105b)

- **VY** **ivy** (32b,38c,176b)

WA - **wad** (94d,97b,109c,112b,149d), **wag** (85b,104a,183a), **wah** (113c), **wan** (113a), **war** (157c), **was** (166c,175c), **Was** (24d), **wat** (73d, 140d,163a,180b), **waw** (12b,91c), **wax** (28b,72a,80b,120c), **way** (37d,96b,134b,164d)

W - A **Wea** (192)

- **WA** **awa** (100a,139a), **iwa** (63c)

W - B **web** (50d,70a,98c,99a,106c,149b)

W - D **wad** (94d,97b,109c,112b,149d), **wed** (97a,173c)

WE - Wea (192), web (50d,70a,98c,99a,106c,149b), wed (97a,173c), wee (52c,100c,148c), Wei (30b,162b), wen (40c,72a,110a,170c,177b), wet (40d,46a,101a,124a,127c,149c), wey (173b)

W - E wee (52c,100c,148c), woe (25b), wye (91c)

- WE awe (81d,100a,130d,175b,182b), ewe (88a,143d), owe

W - G wag (85b,104a,183a), wig (73b)

WH - who (129c), why (52c)

W - H wah (113c)

WI - wig (73b), win (7a,17b,64b,123b), wis (79d,164c), wit (78d,85b, 177b)

W - I Wei (30b,162b)

- WI Twi (69c)

- WL awl (145b,167a), owl

- WM cwm (31b,37b,103d)

WN - WNW (35b)

W - N wan (113a), wen (40c,72a,110a,170c,177b), win (7a,17b,64b,123b), won, wun (24c) wyn (110a)

- WN awn (12c,17b,140a), own (6d)

WO - woe (25b), won, woo, wop, wow (52c,158a)

W - O who (129c), woo

- WO Lwo (107b), Pwo (88c), two (26c,37d,80a,93a)

W - P wop

WR - wry (13d)

W - R war (157c)

WS - WSW (35b)

W - S was (166c,175c), Was (24d), wis (79d,164c)

W - T wat (73d,140d,163a,180b), wet (40d,46a,101a,124a,127c), wit (78d,85b,177b)

WU - wun (24c)

W - W waw (12b,91c), WNW (35b), wow (52c,158a), WSW (35b)

W - X wax (28b,72a,80b,120c)

WY - wye (91c), wyn (110a)

W - Y way (37d,96b,134b,164d), wey (173b), why (52c), wry (13d)

XA - xat (167c)

- XA oxa (29c)

XE - xer (34a)

- XE axe (30c,40c,167a), Exe (43a)

- XO exo (122d)

X - R xer (34a)

X - T xat (167c)

YA - yah (52c), yak (112c,161d,165b), yam (48c,121d,160b,170c), Yao (30a,c,104b), yap (16c,29b,122a), yar (72a), Yau (30c), yaw (43a, 155d)

Y - A yea (7c,175c)

- YA aya (77b,166b), Aya (143c), Iya (95b,108d,111c), Mya (31c)

YE - yea (7c,175c), yen (33b,42d,93c,174a), yep, yes (7c,55a), yet (18b, 24d,64c,77c,80a,108c,156b,165b), yew (36a,52a,b,145d,168c,d) yez

- YE aye (7c,9b,55a,60a), bye (38c,141d), dye (33c,154d), eye (93d, 111b,140d), lye (8d,27d,93b), nye (72a,116d), Nye (9c,18b), oye (139c), Pye (50d,55a), rye (28b,70b,72d), sye (40c,46c,139b,141a, 167a), tye (28c,134a), wye (91c)

- YG tyg (46b)

Y - H yah (52c)

YI - yin (140a), Yin (30b,143c,185b), yip (16c)

Y - I yoi (52c,79a)

Y - K yak (112c,161d,165b), yok (10c,185a)

- YL kyl (76d,79b)

Y - M yam (48c,121d,160d,170c), yom (41a)

- YM gym (154a), Nym (54c,76a)

Y - N yen (33b,42d,93c,174a), yin (140a), Yin (30b,143c,185b), yon (44c,112a,164d), Yun (88d)

- YN lyn (140c,178d), syn (122d,183b), wyn (110a)

YO - yoi (52c,79a), yok (10c,185a), yom (41a), yon (44c,112a,164d), you, yow (52c)

Y - O Yao (30a,c,104b)

- YO iyo (7d,176b)

Y - P yap (16c,29b,122a), yep, yip (16c)

- YP cyp (169d), gyp (29b,42a,160c), hyp

Y - R yar (72a)

- YR pyr (92a,b,122c,173b), Tyr (7c,68c,109c,147d,163d,170c,178a)

Y - S yes (7c,55a)

- YS lys (58b,92b)

Y - T yet (18b,24d,64c,77c,80a,108c,156b,165b)

YU - Yun (88d)

Y - U Yau (30c), you

- YU ayu (160c)

Y - W yaw (43a,155d), yew (36a,52a,b,145d,168c,d), yow (52c)

- YX Nyx (69b), pyx (31a,51d,75d)

Y - Z yez

ZA - zac (27c), zag (84a), zak (188), Zal (135d), Zan (186b), zar (188), zat (148a), zax (148a)

Z - A zea (95c), Zoa (20b)

Z - C zac (27c)

Z - D zed (91c)

ZE - zea (95c), zed (91c), zee (81b,91c), zel (40c), Zen (24a), Zep, zer (188)

Z - E zee (81b,91c), Zoe (36b,183c)

Z - F	**Zif** (102a)
Z - G	**zag** (84a), **zig** (84a)
Z - H	**zoh** (13d,186b)
ZI -	**Zif** (102a), **zig** (84a), **Zio** (147d,163d), **zip** (24b,50b,176b), **Ziu** (147d,163d)
Z - K	**zak** (188)
Z - L	**Zal** (135d), **zel** (40c)
Z - N	**Zan** (186b), **Zen** (24a)
ZO -	**zoa** (20b), **Zoe** (36b,183c), **zoh** (13d,186b), **zoo** (181b)
Z - O	**Zio** (147d,163d), **zoo** (181b)
- ZO	**azo** (107c)
Z - P	**Zep, zip** (24b,50b,176b)
Z - R	**zar** (188), **zer** (188)
Z - T	**zat** (148a)
Z - U	**Ziu** (147d,163d)
Z - X	**zax** (148a)

FOUR-LETTER WORDS

AA - - Aalu (6b,48d), Aani (45a,48d), Aare, Aaru (6b,48d)

- AA - baal (142b), baas (97c), caam (93d), Faam (111a), gaal (23b,174d), Haab (97d), haaf (57d), haak (57b,178a), haar (139c), kaan (93d, 116c), kaat (105d), laap (51d,91b,141d), maal (188), ma'am (95a, 166b), maar (177a), Maas (132a), Maat (69a,b,85d), Naab, naam (44c), Naam (105b), paal (188), paar (28c,137a), raab (32d), raad (14a,49b,151a,165b), Raad (151a), raas (91b), Saad (12b), saah (188), saal (66c,73b), Saan (24d), Saar (63b,102d,132a), Taal (7d, 88c,151a), taar (12b), Waac, waag (71d,101d)

- - AA blaa, chaa (162b), draa (188)

A - - A Abba (20a,55a,161c), Abfa (76b), Abia (18d,137a), abra (26b), Abra, acca (53b,d), acta (41d,123d,128d,164c), adda (147d), Adda (68c,119d,157a,182a), aera (8a), Aeta (94d,100a,106b,117a), Afra (183c), agha (35a,171a), agla (7a), agra (26d,34d), Agra (161b), agua (152d,166c,178c), Aida (110d,175c), Aira (70d), Akha (86a,c), akia (74c), Akka (125d), akra (176a), Akra (191), akua (120d), alba (98b,181a), Alba (151d), Alca (14c,128b), alda (152b), Alda (110d,150c), Alea (14b,31c,167d), alfa (70d), alga (141b,c), alia (89d), alla (6d), alma (40d,53d,146d,147a), Alma 38d, 183c), alta (89c,152d), Alva (151d), Alya (155b,c), amba (161a), amia (22c,170d), amla (48a,161d,168c,169a), amma (6a), amra (77c), anba (36d), anda (23a,168c), anna (190), Anna (110c,166d, 183c), anoa (28a,60a,112c,181c), ansa (73c,93d,137c), anta (83d, 117c,d,121a), Anta (164a), apia (121b), aqua (90a,178c), arba (135d,171a), arca (9a,22c,29d,115a,130a), Arca (101b), area (37d, 38a,44c,53a,93b,110d,127d,138c,168a,186d), aria (8b,98c,150a,c, 170c), arna (24a,181b), Aroa (175b), arpa (83b), arra (47d,52c,82b),

263

Arta (72b), **Arya** (80d), **asea** (39b,177c), **Asha** (191), **Asia** (48a), **asta** (188), **Asta** (107a,164c), **Atka** (11a), **atma** (150d), **atta** (58d, 90c,97d,160c,173d), **Atta** (94d,95d,100a,106b,117a), **atua** (120d), **Auca** (192), **aula** (66c,73b), **aura** (44c,49c,66a,96b,158a,170d, 177c), **Ausa, Azha** (155b)

AB -- abas (61c), **Abba** (20a,55a,161c), **abbe** (32b,63b,123b), **Abby** (183d), **ABC's** (57a), **abed** (130c), **Abel** (7a,25b), **abet** (8b,15b,50a, 59b,75d,81c,141d,159d), **Abfa** (76b), **Abia** (18d,137a), **Abib** (102 a,b), **Abie** (96b,107a), **abir** (129a), **able** (26b,35b,126a,147c), **ably** (147c), **aboo** (17a), **Abot** (100c), **Abou** (48b,55a), **abox** (22d), **abra** (26b), **Abra, abri** (61c,62c,144b), **Absi** (191), **abut** (22a, 167c)

-AB - baba (108d,120c,166c,171a), **babe, Babi** (116c), **babu** (77a), **baby,** caba (184c), **Faba, gabe** (162a), **gabi** (162a), **gaby** (59c,146d), **haba** (151d), **habe** (191), **Maba** (103a,168d), **mabi** (58d), **nabk** (30d, 164d), **nabo** (117a), **Nabu** (68c,183d), **Raba, rabi** (38d,74a), **Rabi** (14b,117b), **saba** (56a,117a), **Saba** (143d), **sabe, tabi** (84c, 149d), **tabu** (59d,111d), **Wabi** (192)

-- AB Ahab (18c,26c,85b,86d,100d,116a,180b), **Arab** (30a,78b,c,106a, 107c,157b,160c,185d), **blab** (162b), **brab** (113b), **chab** (184a), **crab** (39b,144b,181b), **doab** (157c), **drab** (23d,29c,33d,46d,53b,d), **duab** (157c), **frab** (138c), **grab** (105b,142a,149b), **Haab** (97d), **Joab** (41a), **knab** (107a), **Moab** (18d,85a,86d,94a), **Naab, raab** (32d), **scab** (80b, 107d,157c), **slab** (148b), **snab** (23c,139a), **stab** (14c,87a,117c), **swab** (102b)

A -- B Abib (102a,b), **Adib** (155b), **Agib** (12a,42d), **Ahab** (18c,26c,85b, 86d,100d,116a,180b), **Arab** (30a,78b,c,106a,107c,157b,160c,185d)

AC -- acca (53b,d), **Acer** (96c), **ache** (79a,112d,185b), **acht** (66c), **achy,** acid (151a,162a), **Acis** (64b), **acle** (13d,82c,115d), **acme** (39c,115c, 186b), **acne** (147c), **acon** (62c,140d), **acor** (6d), **acre** (39b,56a,88b), **Acre, acta** (41d,123d,128d,164c), **acth** (13b), **acto** (152b), **Acts,** actu (7a,89a), **acus** (89d,118a), **acyl** (6d)

-A C- Bach (35c), **back** (75d,76d,159d), **Caca** (67a), **caco** (73b), **dace** (57a,b), **each, face** (159d,176c), **fact** (7a,128b), **hack** (40a,77c, 184d), **Jaca** (84a), **jack** (26c,58a,127c), **Jack** (96b), **jacu** (19a,151b), **lace** (58b,179c), **lack** (178a), **lact** (34c), **lacy, mace** (49d,108d,153b, 154d,161a,178a), **mack, nach, paca** (132c,154a), **pace** (64b,98a, 153b,156a,170b,177d), **pack** (24b,140d), **paco** (9b,146d), **pacs** (94c), **pact** (8a), **raca** (19a,59c,130b,184d), **race** (116a,153b,154b, 169c), **rack** (32c,64b), **racy** (153b), **sack** (43d,118a,119d,182b), **saco** (189), **tace** (13a,155d), **tack** (28d,37d,54c), **tact** (43c,d,116a), **Vach** (153b), **Waco, Zach** (96b)

-- AC utac (22d), **Waac**

A -- C aesc (12d,64d), **alec** (10a,57c,d,76c,137c), **amic** (9d), **avec** (63a, 183a)

AD -- adad (52c,56a), **Adad** (68c,157a,182a), **Adah** (25b,51b), **Adam** (26b,96a,111c) adan (102d), **Adar** (85c,102a), **adat** (90b,95d), **adda** (147d), **Adda** (68c,119d,157a,182a), **Addu** (68c,157a,182a), **Addy** (183d), **aden** (34b), **Aden, Ader** (18d), **Ades** (73a), **Adib** (155b), **adit** (51a,100a,114d), **admi** (65d), **ador** (153b), **adry** (164c), **adze** (40c,167a)

264

•AD•   Badb (82b), **bade, cade** (25c,27a,76c,85d,116d), **Cade** (50c), **cadi** (12a,103a,171a), **cady** (69d), **Dada** (13b,63a,157d), **dado** (41c,111c, 115c,177d), **Eads** (23b,24b,50b,82a), **fade** (181d,183b), **fado** (121c), **fady, gade, hade** (66a,148c,173c), **hadj** (98b,118a), **jade** (33c,65d,71d,166a), **jadu** (95a), **jady, kada** (188), **kade** (144a), **kadi** (103a,171a), **Kadu** (191), **lade** (24c,26d,43c,93b,100a,132a,139d, 161b,178d), **Ladd** (143c), **lady, made, Madi** (174a), **mado** (14d,57a, 170b), **padi** (131b), **rada** (135c,172a), **rade** (138d), **sadd** (33a,40b, 58c,107b), **sade** (91d), **sadh** (77a), **sado** (26d,84d), **sadr** (94a), **Sadr** (155b), **vade** (42c,67d,89b), **wadd** (109c), **wade, wadi** (46c,106a, 109a,128a,132a), **wady** (109a,128a,132a)

••AD   adad (52c,56a), **Adad** (68c,157a,182a), **arad** (13a,c,84a), **bead** (17a, 122a,146b), **brad** (54d,67c,105b), **Chad** (158b), **clad** (46a,82a), **dead, diad** (113a), **duad** (113a,171d), **dyad** (113a), **ecad** (73a, 119b), **egad** (100a,109a), **Fuad** (54d), **glad** (85c), **goad** (80b,154b), **grad** (28b), **head** (29d), **Ibad** (191), **Irad** (18d), **Joad** (50c), **lead** (35d,43d,72b,74d,81a), **load** (24c,26d,161b), **mead** (46a,78a,97d, 99b), **Mead** (78a), **orad** (104a), **Phad** (155b), **quad** (33c,172a), **raad** (14a,49b,151a,165b), **read** (116d,157d), **road** (37d,164d), **Saad** (12b), **scad** (31a,57a,78b,88d,137c), **shad** (27d,57a,b,c), **spad** (105b), **Spad** (118d), **stad** (151b,167d,176b), **swad** (94d), **toad** (10a, 17a,63d,126d), **udad** (143d,144a,181c), **woad** (20d,47c)

A••D   abed (130c), **acid** (151a,162a), **adad** (52c,56a), **Adad** (68c,157a, 182a), **aged** (110a), **alod** (51c,55d,88a,124c), **amid** (9d,50a), **apod** (59d), **arad** (13a,c,84a), **arid** (46c,85a), **Arnd** (67a), **Arod** (86c), **avid** (47b,71a,186b)

AE••   aera (8a), **aeri** (34a), **aero** (8b,34a,b,58c,59a), **aery** (47b,51d,106c), **aesc** (12d,64d), **Aeta** (94d,95d,100a,106b,117a)

•AE•   Caen, **daer** (22b), **daez, faex** (46a), **Gaea** (47d,69a), **Gael** (28a,96c, 138d), **haec** (90a,164c), **haem** (122b), **Jael** (147b), **laet** (60d), **nael** (189), **saer** (163a), **tael** (91d,179d), **waeg** (19b,72c,87a), **waer** (40b)

••AE   alae (182d), **blae** (93b), **brae** (76d,139a,c,140b,148c), **Irae** (43c), **koae** (74b), **quae** (176b), **spae** (139c)

A••E   Aare, **abbe** (32b,63b,123b), **Abie** (96b,107a), **able** (26b,35b,126a, 147c), **ache** (79a,112d,185b), **acle** (13d,82c,115d), **acme** (39c,115c, 186b), **acne** (147c), **acre** (39b,56a,88b), **Acre, adze** (40c,167a), **agee** (13d,15c,38d), **ague** (30a,55d,95c,137b), **aide** (7b,14a,75d), **aile** (62b,63a,182c,d), **aine** (49b,62c,142c), **aire** (82c), **Aire, ajee** (15c,139a), **akee** (168c), **alae** (182d), **albe** (133a) aiee (15c,75d,144b,157a,182a), **Alle** (14c), **alme** (40d,147a), **aloe** (7d,20a,76a,b,92b,98b,119b,158b,167a,183d), **amie** (61d), **ance** (158b,c,d), **Ande** (193), **ange** (61a), **Anne** (50c,84a,143b,183c), **ante** (87a,89a,115b,120b,122b,125d,154d), **a-one** (52b,167b), **apse** (9b, 20a,31a,128c,130a,142b,175a), **arme** (63a,179b), **Arne** (35c,50c, 134d), **asse** (25a,60d,74a), **atle** (136d,161d,169b), **Aude, auge** (123c,132b), **aune** (188), **axle** (153c,180c)

AF••   afar (44c), **Afar** (6c), **afer** (48a,182b), **affy** (18b), **Afra** (183c)

•AF•   baff (69d), **baft** (14a,53b), **cafe, daff** (125d), **daft** (59c), **gaff** (57c, d,152d,153a), **haft** (76d), **Kafa** (6c), **raff** (75b), **raft** (27b,33c,58c, 75b), **safe** (141d,157d,174d), **Safi** (191), **Taft** (29d), **Wafd** (49a), **waft** (20d,58c)

- - AF   deaf, goaf (104b), Graf (37c,66b,67a,107c,186b), haaf (57d), heaf (144a), leaf (55c,73c,119b), loaf (79b,94b), neaf (58a,73c), Olaf (108a,176b), Piaf (63c), Wraf

A - - F   alef (91c), alif (12b), arif (127d), atef (39a,48d), Azof (20b,135d)

AG - -   Agag (18c,86c,137a), agal (17c,36d), Agao (6c,73c), agar (7d,28c, 39c,103c,141c), Agau (73c), Agaz (193), aged (110a), agee (13d, 15c,38d), ager (47c,56a,89b,c,131d,133b), agha (35a,171a), Agib (12a,42d), agio (52c,60a,101c,123a), Agis (86d), agla (7a), agni (88a,89c), Agni (56d,68b), agog (47b,52c,86b), agon (12c,36c,41b, 55d,71b), agra (26d,34d), Agra (161b), agri (89b), agro (149d), agua (152d,166c,178c), ague (30a,55d,95c,137b)

- AG -   baga (171b), bago (13d), cage (36a), cagy (178b), dagg (118c), dagh (76d), Dago, gage (28d,98a,119c,d), gagl (160b), hagg, hagi (84b), Iago (54b,111d,143c), Jaga (191), jagg, kago (113a), kagu (106c), lago (83b,152b), mage (95b), magg (95b), Magh (102a), magi (123c), Magi (95b,116c,183a), naga (13d,33a,55b,127c), Naga (24c,77a,88c,176d), Nagy (78d), Paga (117a), page (51b,59b, 142d,159b), raga (56d,105a), rage (10c,30c,157a,161d), ragi (28b), saga (79b,91a,138a,157a,161b,c,168a), Saga, sage (13a,90d,100c, 141c,145c,180b,183a), sago (54c,59b,113b,125b,155c), sagy, vagi (38b), wage (27a,115b), yage (23a)

- - AG   Agag (18c,86c,137a), brag (21a,175a), coag (45d,118a,163b), crag (132c), drag (74a,125b), flag (16b,50d,82b,88c,115a,155a), knag (115d,139c), krag (131c), peag (144a,178a), quag (21c,102c), shag (73b,105b,161d,166d), skag (7d,46d), slag (46c,99a,138c,148d, 177a), snag (11b,27b,35c,87c,124b,166a), stag (65a,98d), swag (22a,156c), waag (71d,101d)

A - - G   Agag (18c,86c,137a), agog (47b,52c,86b), ajog, areg (116a,137a)

AH - -   Ahab (18c,26c,85b,86d,100d,116a,180b), Ahaz (86d), ahem, Ahet (49a,102a), ahey (52c), Ahir (27b), Ahom (88c), ahoy (106a), ahum

- AH -   bahi (60c), baho (122a), baht (146a), haha (55c,159c), kaha (123d), kahu (14d), maha (28c,88c,136d), mahr (103a), Oahu, paha (67b), pahi (21b,26a), paho (122a), Rahu (42b,48b), saha, sahh (188), Saho (6c), sahu (153d), taha (179b), tahr (68a,76d)

- - AH   Adah (25b,51b), Amah (95b,108d,111c), arah (52c), ayah (108d), blah, drah (188), Elah (18c,86d), Etah (51c,71d), eyah (95b,108d, 111c), Ivah (18d), kyah (19a), Leah (19a,84a,87b,183c), Noah (88a, 99b), odah (170d), opah (23b,57a,b,86d), prah (21b,26a,95c,d), Ptah (48d,98c), saah (188), seah (188), shah (116c), Utah (180b), yeah

A - - H   acth (13b), Adah (25b,51b), aich (9a), Alph (132a), amah (95b, 108d,111c), ankh (38d,162b), arah (52c), arch (29d,38b,39d,123d, 132c), ayah (108d)

AI - -   aich (9a), Aida (110d, 175c), aide (7b,14a,75d), aile (62b,63a,182c, d), aine (49b,62c,142c), Aino (84a,c), aint, Ainu (84a,c), aipi (27a), Aira (70d), aire (82c), Aire, airs (123b), airy (177a,176d)

- AI -   bail (43c), bain (61a), bait (15d,51a,94d,167b), caid (35a,151d, 152b), cain (169c), Cain (6a,7a,50d,88a,104c,143a), Dail (49a, 82b, c), dain (188), dais (119b), fail, fain (42d,67c,183b), fair (17a,55d),

266

fait (6d,61b), Gaia (47d,69a), gail (23b,174d), Gail (183d), gain (7a, b,124a,181d), gait (96b,179a), haik (57b,65b,108a), hail (6d,15a, 71d), hair (56b,164d), jail (123d), Jain (77b), kaid (29d,66a), kaif (88c), kaik (96c), kail (18c,22a.25a,79b), Kain, kair, laic (32b,90b, 107d,124a,141d), laid, lain, lair (37c,42b), Lais (17c), lait (62a), Maia (76b,109a,153b,155b,177c), maid (45b.142d), mail (12d,99b, 121c), maim (43d,81a,105c), main (29d,35d,123d), mais (61b), Naia (33a), naid (63c), naif (74b,105d). naik, nail (31d,54d,141d,161d, 173a), naio (107a,168c), Nair (45d), nais (63c,132a), paid (129c), pail, pain (7c), pair (22d,37d,85b,171d), pais (37d), qaid (35a), raia (107d), Raia (147b), raid (59d,80c), raik (188,189), rail (16b,19b,c, 37a,97b,138c,150c,177b), rain (121d,162d), raip (36d), rais (26c, 29d,75a,103b), Rais (106b), saic (86b,91d,175d), said (174c), Said (42d,101a,121b), sail (144c,185a), sain (20c,38d,48a), sair (140b, 150d), sais (48d,71d), tail (11d,27d,59b,143b), tain (166a), tair (68a,76d), tait (14d), vail (94b,124a,174b), vain (81a), vair (64c, 154c), waif (157b), wail (39b,88a), wain (177b), Wain, wait (26d, 42b,92c,155d,162a), zaim (170d), zain (41a)

--AI alai (171a), Alai (135c), anai (163b,181a), chai (72d), goai (106d, 168c), ngai (48a,159c), peai (98b), quai (88b,117c,180c), Thai (146a)

A--I Aani (45a,48d), abri (61c,62c,144b), Absi (191), admi (65d), aeri (34a), agni (88a,89c), Agni (56d,68b), agri (89b), aipi (27a), alai (171a), Alai (135c), Albi (58a), alii (74c,134c), ambi (34a,122c), amli (48a,161d,168c,169a), ammi (98c), amoi (62a), anai (163b, 181a), Andi (27d), anti (7d,111a,122b), Anti (193), apii (74c), arni (24a,181b), arui (11b,143d,144a,181c), asci (154a), assi (77d), Asti 83d,182b), Atli (14c,72b,79a,107d), Atri, auri (34a)

AJ-- ajar (110c), Ajax (71b,162d), ajee (15c,139a), ajog

-AJ- baju (84a), caja (152a), caji (180b), gajo (107c), haje (33a,48d), maja (151c), Maja (153b), majo, Naja (33a), pajo (122a), raja (77a, 123c), Raja, tajo (152a,d), yaje (23a)

AK-- Akal (56d), Akan (191), akee (168c), akey (189), Akha (86a,c), akia (74c), Akim (135d,191), akin (8b,92b,129c), Akka (125d), akov (189), akra (176a), Akra (191), akua (120d)

-AK- baka (52b), bake (139a), baku (26d,157b,168c), cake, caky, fake (123a,143c), faky, hake (57a,b), hakh (46d), hako (115b), haku (86d), jake (40d), Jake (96b), jako (71a), kaka (114b), kaki (84c, 106d), lake (117d), lakh (110c), laky, make (35b,36d,54a,123a) maki (91b), mako (18a,19a,20d,143c,168c,182c), Maku (192), oaks (154d), oaky, rake (41b,44c,134b,140d), Saka (10a), sake (84b,125d), saki (39c,84b,102a), take, takt (105a,163a), Taku (80c), taky, waka (26a), wake (134b,168a), wakf (103a), waky, Yaka (191), Yaki (193)

--AK Anak (67a), asak (13d,168c,169a), beak (19a), coak (45d,118a, 163b), dhak (48a,169a), Dyak (22b), feak (39d,1.71c), flak (11a), haak (57b,178a), Irak (99a,d), kiak (51c), kyak (51c), leak (110c), peak (9a,38c,159b,186b), siak (72d), soak (46c,137c), teak (41a, 48a,168c), weak (55b)

A--K amok (18b,63c), Anak (67a), asak (13d,168c,169a), asok (13d), Atik (155b)

AL·· alae (182d), alai (171a), Alai (135c), alan (45a,79a,183), Alan, alar (15c,145c,182d), alas (52c,136b,183b), alat (136d), alay (96c), alba (98b,181a), Alba (151d), albe (133a), Albi (58a), albo (34d,181a), Alca (14c,128b), alco (45b), alda (152b), Alda (110d, 150c), Alea (14b,31c,167d), alec (10a,57c,d,76c,137c), alee (15c, 75d,144b,157a,182a), alef (91c), alem (98b,155a,170d,171a), alen (40d,138a), alfa (70d), alga (141b,c), Algy (96b), alia (89d), alif (12b), alii (74c,134c), alim (103b,162c), alin (188), alit (44b,143a), Alix (183c), alky, alla (6d), Alle (14c), allo (34c), ally (14a,35c,d, 173c), alma (40d,53d,146d,147a), Alma (38d,183c), alme (40d, 147a), alms (29a), alod (51c,55d,88a,124c), aloe (7d,20a,76a,b,92b, 98b,119b,158b,167a,183d) alop (13d,46b,93d), alow (18a,172c), Alph (132a), Alps (85d), also (10b,18b,80a), alta (89c,152d), alto (152b,176c,177a), alum (14a,45c), Alur (191), Alva (151d), Alya (155b,c), Alys (183c)

·AL· Aalu (6b,48d), Bala (26c,66a), bald (16c), bale (24b,74a), bali, Bali, balk (118c,146a,156d), ball, balm (110a,172c), Balt (93a), balu (104b,159a,181d), cale (72d), calf, calk (78c,109a,141c,178d), call (145c,159b,176d), calm (8d,11d,112b,118d,126c,d,172b,173d), calo (72d), calp (92b), calx (23c,75c,112c), dale (43c,128a,174b), dali (168c,169b), fala (129b), fall (46b,141c), falx (133b), gala (55d), Gala (191), gale (181d), gall (6c), gall (19a,28c,29b,82c,160c, 176a), galt, hala (112b), hale (125b), Hale (9d,131a), half (101a), hall (37b,114d), halm, halo (14d,31b,92a,107b,131d), Hals (47a), halt (13b,28a,38d,156d), lalu (48d), kala (19a), kale (22a,25a, 119b,175a), kali (26d,67c,136d,167a), Kali (147b), kalo (162a), lala (129b), lalo (16b,34d,153a), Lalo (35c), mala (89b,c,90a,94b, 97d,109d,185c), male (154d), Male (45d), mall (27b), mall (95d,124b,143b), malm (32a,92b), malo (23a,74c,152a), malt (17c), Nala (77a), pala (189), Pala (88b), pale (113a,117c,178a), pall (122b), Pali (23d,24a,137b,175a), pall (32d,81b,112a), palm (59b, 168c,169b), palo (152c), palp (11a,55b,58b,167c), paly (194), rale (7c,23a,29d,41b), ralo (188), sala (152a,b,c), Sala (50c), sale (14c,61c,62b,c,168b), salp (109c,148d), salt (35d,105b,123a,136c, 141c,149d), tala (16d,113a,168c,d), talc (28d,63b,99c,100b,122a, 149c), tale (91a,185b), tall (189), talk, tall (118d), vale (54c,128a, 174b), Vale (7c,109c), vali (171a,176a), Vali (7c,109c), wale (70b, 131b,157c,163d,179a,180a,c,d), wali (171a), walk, wall, Walt (96b), Yale (173c), yali (171a)

··AL agal (17c,36d), Akal (56d), Aral (135d), aval (70c), axal (120b), Baal (142b), beal (139d), bual (182c), coal (49c,64a), cral, deal (11d,16c,36c,44c,81a,168b), dhal (12b), dial (25c), dual (45c,171d), eral (51a), etal (89a), foal (78c), gaal (23b,174d), geal (47d,163c), goal (8b,109b,120b,125d), heal, ical (158c), keal (25a), kral, leal (54b,94c,139d), maal (188), meal (72a,130b), Neal, odal (48a,88b, 112c), opal (20a,65d,67b,82b) oral (114a,153d,174c,175c), oval (48d,49c,127a), paal (188), peal (131c,d), pyal (175c), real (7a), rial (190), ryal (110a,190), saal (66c,73b), seal (10c,d,54d,64c,96a, 118b,128a), sial (112a), Taal (7d,88c,151a), teal (19b,20d,46c,d), udal (76b,88b,131c), unal (147a), ural, Ural (135c), uval (70c), veal, vial (148c), weal (124d,157c,180c,d), zeal (12c,55d)

A··L Abel (7a,25b), acyl (6d), agal (17c,36d), Akal (56d), amil (45a,48a,

268

185c), **amyl** (155c), **anil** (47c,80d,180b), **Aoul** (191), **Aral** (135d), **aril** (142a), **aval** (70c), **axal** (120b), **axil** (10c), **azul** (151d)

AM – – **amah** (95b,108d,111c), **amar** (189), **amba** (161a), **ambi** (34a,122c), **ambo** (125b,128b), **amen** (14a,80b,94a,137a,149c,175c,184b), **Amen** (86d,127d,159b,164a), **amer** (61b), **Ames** (9c,82a), **Amex** (184d), **amia** (22c,170d), **amie** (9d), **amid** (9d,50a), **amie** (61d), **amil** (45a,48a,185c), **amin** (9d), **amir** (7c,12a,103a,b,123c,170d), **amit** (94a), **amla** (48a,161d,168c,169a), **amli** (48a,161d,168c,169a), **amma** (6a), **ammi** (98c), **ammo** (9d), **ammu** (9d), **amoi** (62a), **amok** (18b,63c), **Amon** (86d,96d,127d,159b,164a), **amor** (152b), **Amor** (39c,68b), **Amos** (96a,144b), **Amoy** (88c), **amra** (77c), **Amun** (86d,127d,159b,164a), **amyl** (155c)

– AM – **came** (182b), **Came** (192), **camp** (163b), **dama** (65d,152b), **dame** (67b,87c,166b), **damn**, **damp** (101a), **Fama** (135a), **fame** (130a), **famn** (188), **Gama** (121c), **game** (64d,154a), **gamp** (172a), **hami** (78a), **iamb** (59c), **jama** (103b), **jamb** (12d,45c,118a,146b,174a), **jami** (103b), **Kama** (56d), **kame** (67b,139b), **kami** (68a,84b), **Kami** (88c,107c,144c), **lama** (23d,24a,91d,165b), **Lamb** (49c), **lame** (38d, 43d,73b), **lamp** (92a,94c), **mama**, **Mama** (116d), **mamo** (19a,d,74b), **Nama** (78c), **name** (8a,11b,d,25c,46c,107c,130b,157d,163b,166b), **Rama** (77a,80b,176d), **rame** (22d), **rami** (22d), **ramp** (65a,80b, 127b,148b), **sama** (105c,169d), **same** (44d,79b), **samh** (56b), **samp** (70b,77d,121b), **Tama** (192), **tame** (45a,b,66a), **Tame**, **tamp** (46b, 112b,121d,127d), **vamp** (80a,145a), **Yama** (57a,68a), **Zama** (73d, 141d)

– – AM **Adam** (26b,96a,111c), **anam** (159a,168c), **Anam**, **Aram** (18d,50c, 105c,144b,161c), **Azam** (166c), **beam**, **Bram** (96a), **caam** (93d), **cham** (20a,29d), **Cham** (8c), **clam** (20b,101b), **cram** (157d), **dram** (46b,110c,121d,148c), **edam** (29c), **Elam** (18d,37d,82a,116c,144b), **enam** (70c,77a), **Enam** (85c), **exam**, **Faam** (111a), **flam** (169c), **foam** (63d,154b), **gram** (29d,99b,148d,160d,180a), **Gram**, **Guam**, **Imam** (25c,102d,103a), **klam** (189), **Liam** (181d), **loam** (47d,150a), **Iyam** (139a), **ma'am** (95a,166b), **miam** (14d), **naam** (44c,105b), **ogam** (82b,c), **olam** (51a,d,75c,81a), **pram** (15a), **ream** (18c,37d, 50d,113d,171c), **roam** (178a), **seam** (85b,d,160a,176d,185a), **sham** (41c,55b,60d,80a,123a,b,146d), **Siam** (163d,181a), **slam** (180d, 182d), **swam**, **team** (38c,72a,113a), **Tiam**, **tram** (170a), **Ulam** (67b), **wham** (157c)

A – – M **Adam** (26b,96a,111c), **ahem**, **Ahom** (88c), **ahum**, **Akim** (135d,191), **alem** (98b,155a,170d,171a), **alim** (103b,162c), **alum** (14a,45c), **anam** (159a,168c), **Anam**, **Anim** (18d), **Aram** (18d,50c,105c,144b, 161c), **arum** (13a,39b,58d,92b,155c), **Arum** (66a), **asem** (9a,49a, 69c), **Asom** (18d), **atom** (101c,114c,180d), **Atum** (143a,159b), **Azam** (166c)

AN – – **anai** (163b,181a), **Anak** (67a), **anam** (159a,168c), **anan** (49a,159a, 180c), **Anas** (46c,d), **Anat** (138c,147d), **Anax** (43c,120c), **anay** (72b,163b,181a), **anba** (36d), **ance** (158b,c,d), **ancy** (158c), **anda** (23a,168c), **Ande** (193), **Andi** (27d), **Andy** (96b), **Aner** (18d,96b), **anes** (110c,140a), **anet** (43c), **anew** (7c), **ange** (61a), **ango** (171a), **anil** (47c,80d,180b), **Anim** (18d), **anis** (55c), **ankh** (38d,162b), **anna** (190), **Anna** (110c,166d,183c), **Anne** (50c,84a,143b,183c),

anoa (28a,60a,112c,181c), **anon** (7d,14d,79d,80b,123a,145c,150c, 164a), **ansa** (73c,93d,137c), **anse** (61d), **ansu** (11d), **anta** (83d, 117c,d,121a), **Anta** (164a), **ante** (87a,89a,115b,120b,122b,125d, 154d), **anti** (7d,111a,122b), **Anti** (193), **anzu** (11d)

- AN -   **Aani** (45a,48d), **Bana** (67a), **banc** (61a,85c), **band** (72a,157c), **bane** (74a,106b,120b,139a), **bang** (75d,105d,148a), **bani** (190), **bank** (18a,58c), **bans, bant** (43c), **Cana** (57a,64b,100c), **cane** (17b, 128a,156a,159a,177d), **Cane, cang** (184a), **cano** (152a), **cant** (28d, 81b,84d,90c,109b,136c,165d,166a), **Dana** (28a,96a,171d), **Dane** (85d,107d,138a), **dang, dank** (40b,101a), **dans** (62a), **Danu** (28a), **fana, fane** (30d,137a,162d), **fang** (167b), **Fano** (51d,96b,113c,d), **gane** (185b), **gang** (38c), **Gano** (132d), **hand** (60c,114c,115d,184c), **hang** (160a), **hank** (147c), **Hano** (125b), **Hans** (66d,96a), **hant** (67a), **jane** (190), **Jane** (183c), **Jann** (102d), **kana** (84d), **Kane** (74c), **k'ang** (30a), **Kano** (84c,177d), **kant** (28d), **Kant** (67a), **lana** (58a,66a,90a,184b), **land** (44a,163c), **lane** (134b,157b), **lank** (148b,164b), **lanx** (133a,b), **mana** (30a,120d,122a,159c), **mand** (28b), **mane, mani** (115c), **mann** (189), **Mann** (9c,48c,185c), **mano** (71d,73d,74b,83b), **Mans** (30a), **Manu** (10a,76d,77a,b), **Manx** (27b, 28a,82d), **many** (108d), **nana** (118b), **Nana** (15c,105d,116d,186d), **nane** (139d), **Pana, pane** (113c,155a,b), **pang** (165b), **Pani** (120c), **pank** (189), **pant, rana** (77a,123c), **Rana** (63d), **rand** (16d,22a, 131b,145a,b), **Rand** (69c), **rang, rani** (72d,77b,123c,127c), **rank** (31d,55d,70b,92c,94d,157d), **rann** (175c), **rant** (41c,127b,128a, 161d), **sana** (56a,166d), **Sana** (185d), **sand** (71d,146c), **sane** (128a), **sang, sank, sano** (152b), **sans** (63a,183b), **tana** (159a), **Tana** (87d), **Tane** (120d), **tang** (30b,58b,186b), **tanh** (97c), **tank** (175a,d), **Tano** (192), **uang** (131a), **vane** (179b,182a), **vang** (72d,134a,140b), **Vans** (107d), **wand** (120b,132c,156a), **wane** (41c,43c), **wang** (189), **want** (41b,42d,87b,106b,122a), **wany, Yana** (192,193), **yang** (30b,70a), **yank, Yank, zany** (24a,32d,59c)

- - AN   **adan** (102d), **Akan** (191), **alan** (45a,79a,183c), **Alan** (96a), **anan** (49a,159a,180c), **Aran** (18c,48c,64d,82d,174c), **Awan** (191), **azan** (102d), **bean** (91b,142a,175a), **bran** (23c,39a,72a,79c,70b), **Bran** (23c,50c), **chan** (26c,130c), **clan** (169c), **Coan** (37b), **cran** (160c), **cyan, dean** (33c,109d), **dhan** (124c), **dian** (46c,130d,170b), **Dian** (68d,69a,c,102b), **duan** (64b), **elan** (12c,41a,50d,62a,153c,177a, 186b), **Eoan** (41a,85b), **Evan** (96a), **Ewan, flan** (39d,40a,114d), **gean** (29c), **Goan, gran, guan** (151b), **Iban** (47c), **Iran** (6a,48c, 116b), **Ivan** (40c,85b,96a), **jean** (37c), **Jean** (183c), **Joan** (183c), **juan** (113a), **Juan** (96a), **kaan** (93d,116c), **khan** (7c,26c,81b,93d, 116c,123c,130c,166c), **kran** (190), **kuan** (30b,c), **Kuan, kwan** (30b), **lean** (128a,148b,152d,164b,166a), **loan, mean** (15a,42b, 146c,156b), **mian** (97c,147b,166b), **moan, ngan, oban** (190), **Olan** (115c), **Oman** (159a), **Onan** (18c,85c), **Oran, oxan, pean** (65c), **plan** (99b,124a,138b), **quan** (190), **roan** (78b,c,114c,128d,144a, 181a), **Saan** (24d), **Sean** (85b,96a), **Shan** (13c,80d,88c,101d), **scan** (52b,93d,98a,116d,128b,c,140d), **span** (23b,107b,113a,128b,162c), **Svan** (27d), **swan** (19b,33a) **tean** (140c167a), **than** (35b), **tran** (7a), **tuan** (95d,147b,166c), **ulan** (27d,88a), **uran** (101d), **Uran, uzan** (189), **wean** (8d,42d), **yean** (88a), **yuan** (190), **Yuan** (30b,101d)

A - - N acon (62c,140d), adan (102d), aden (34b), Aden, agon (12c,36c, 41b,55d,71b), Akan. (191), akin (8b,92b,129c), alan (45a,79a, 183c), Alan (96a), alen (40d,138a), alin (188), amen (14a, 80b,94a,137a,149c,175c,184b), Amen (86d,127d,159b,164a), amin (9d), Amon (86d,96b,127d,159b,164a), Amun (86d,127d, 159b,164a), anan (49a,159a,180c), anon (7d,14d,79d,80b,123a, 145c,150c,164a), Aran (18c,48c,64d,82d,174c), Asin (102a), aten (150a,159b), aton (150a,159b), Avon (143b), Awan (191) axon (106c,153c), ayin (91c), azan (102d), azon (127b)

AO - - aone (52b,167b), Aoul (191)

- AO - faon (33c,55a), gaol (123d), Gaol (164a), Gaon (85b), Jaob, Laos (80d,129c), naos (28a,71c,137a,163a), Naos (155b), paon (115b), Taos (192), Yaou (30c)

- - AO Agao (6c,73c), dhao (24c), grao (189), guao (168c,169b), Miao (30a,b), omao (165b), prao (21b,26a,95c,d), tiao

A - - O aboo (17c), acto (152b), aero (8b,34a,b,58c,59a), Agao (6c,73c), agio (52c,60a,101c,123a), agro (149d), Aino (84a,c), albo (34d, 181a), alco (45b), allo (34c), also (10b,18b,80a), alto (152b,176c, 177a), ambo (125b,128b), ammo (9d), ango (171a), apio (125b), areo (34c), Argo (12c,36b,c), Arno (27a), aroo (80c,82b), arro (52c), arto (34a), asno (151d), Ateo (120d), atmo (34d,174d), auto (34d)

AP - - Apap (102a), apar (12d), aper (32d), Apet (97c), apex (39c,76c, 115c,118b,159b,166a,167b), apia (121b), apii (74c), apio (125b), Apis (17c,24b,49a,125a,136a), apod (59d), apse (9b,20a,31a,128c, 130a,142b,175a), Apsu (29a), Apus (36b,c)

- AP - capa (152a,166d), cape (75a,96c,124b,161a), caph (91c), capp (27a), gape (185b), gapo (60a), gapy, Hapi (66a,107b,136a), hapu (106d), jape (85a,b), kapa (74b), kaph (91d), kapp, Lapp (108a), mapo (68a,148d), napa (25c,67d,90d), Napa (182c), nape (15b, 108c,d), napu (29d,80d), papa, pape (19b,113a), rapt (6c,27a,50d), sapa (70c), sapo (149c,166d), tapa (16c,32c,53b,56a,74b,104b,112b, 113d,120d), tape (16a,19a,128d), tapu, wapp (54b,133d,145d), yapa (113b), Yapp (22a)

- - AP Apap (102a), atap (113b), chap (55b), clap (58b), drap (61b,c, 62a), flap (17b,59a,104a,118d,161a,182d), frap (45d,165c), heap (117d), knap (76d,107a,139b,159b,166a,170c,185b), laap (51d,91b, 141d), leap (26c), neap (165c,167a,177b), plap (54b), reap (7a,40a, 74a), shap, slap (24a,128c,148c), snap (23a,36d,38b,48b,54d,56c, 58c,149d), soap, swap (168a), trap (27b,67b,132b,149b), wrap (32b,51a)

A - - P alop (13d,46b,93d), Apap (102a), asop (180b), atap (113b), atip (14b,166a), atop (112a,174a)

AQ - - aqua (90a,178c)

- AQ - waqf (103a)

- - AQ Iraq (99a,d)

AR - - Arab (30a,78b,c,106a,107c,157b,160c,185d), arad (13a,c,84a), arah (52c), Aral (135d), Aram (18d,50c,105c,144b,161c), Aran (18c, 48c,64d,82d,174c), arar (137a,168c), Aras, arba (135d,171a), arca

271

(9a,22c,29d,115a,130a), **Arca** (101b), **arch** (29d,38b,39d,123d, 132c), **area** (37d,38a,44c,53a,93b,110d,127d,138c,168a,186d), **areg** (116a,137a), **areo** (34c), **Ares** (49b,51b,68c,76a,97a,105c,110b, 178a,186d), **aret** (128c), **Argo** (12c,36b,c), **aria** (8b,98c,150a,c, 170c), **arid** (46c,85a), **arif** (127d), **aril** (142a), **aris** (101b), **arme** (63a,179b), **arms, army** (78c), **arna** (24a,181b), **Arnd** (67a), **Arne** (35c,50c,134d), **arni** (24a,181b), **Arno** (27a), **arn't**, **Aroa** (175b), **Arod** (86c), **aroo** (80c,82b), **arow** (92c,158b), **arpa** (83b), **arra** (47d,52c,82b), **arro** (52c), **Arta** (72b), **arto** (34a), **arts** (138c), **arty, arui** (11b,143d,144a,181c), **arum** (13a,39b,58d,92b,155c), **Arum** (66a), **Arya** (80d)

- **AR** - **Aare, Aaru** (6b,48d), **bara** (188), **barb** (20b,57d,78b,117d,120a,b, 124b), **bard** (12d,120a), **bare** (43d,157c), **bari** (79c), **Bari** (37c,83d), **bark** (115c), **barm** (185b), **barn** (156d), **baro** (71a,122c), **barr** (49b), **Bart** (96b), **baru** (168c), **cara** (83a), **Cara** (48b,183c), **card** (33d, 114d), **care** (11b,14c,35d,150a,184d), **cark** (26d,184d), **carl** (115c, 135d), **Carl** (96a), **carn** (156c), **caro** (83a,183d), **carp** (27d,38d, 40c,55a,56c,57a), **carr** (120d,140a), **cart** (171d,175a,177b), **Dara** (18d), **Dard, dare** (28d,41b,42a,74d,175b), **Dare** (57a), **dari** (38a, 70b), **dark** (47a,67d,109b,160b), **darn** (130b), **darr** (163c), **dart** (13b,88a,100c,120b,153a,160c), **Dart** (100c), **earl** (107c), **earn** (42d,64b,99a), **fard** (112d), **fare** (43c,59b,67d,123b), **farl** (138c, 140b), **farm** (165d), **faro** (65a), **gara** (190), **garb** (32c,46a), **gare** (61b,c,62c,127c,184b), **Garm** (178c), **garn** (67d,185b), **Garo** (88c), **Harb** (191), **hard** (109b), **hare** (91b,132c), **hark** (92d), **harl** (16b,56b, 59a), **harm** (40b,81a), **harp** (105a,129a), **hart** (41d,154d), **jarl** (40d, 107d), **kara** (132a), **Kari** (14d), **Karl** (96a), **karn** (156c), **karo** (106d), **Lara** (25c), **lard** (54d,61a,71a,110a), **lari** (78a,101c), **Lari** (72c), **lark** (19a,63d,177b), **larp** (51d), **Lars** (51d,121b), **mara** (114d), **Mara** (24a,d,105b,107b), **marc** (70c), **Marc** (96a), **mare** (78b,108b), **mari** (16a,61d), **mark, Mark** (52a,96a,146b,155a), **marl** (32a,42c, 55d), **maro** (144d), **Mars** (68c,118d,119a,178a), **mart** (49d,97a), **Mart** (96b,183d), **maru** (84c,144d), **Mary** (50c,126b,183c), **nard** (13a, 97c,102b,110a,153c), **Nare** (93c), **nark** (81a,156d), **nary** (108b), **oary, para** (134c,170d), **Para** (18a,51d), **parc** (62b,112c), **pard** (27b, 91b), **pare** (115c,129a), **pari** (34a,180a), **park, parr** (136d,147c), **pars** (89d), **part** (44d,60d,121c,159c), **paru** (57a), **rara** (119a), **rare** (138b,164b,172b,173d), **Sara** (24d,183c), **sard** (26d,28d,65d,111a, 142b,156d), **Sarg** (96d,125c), **sari** (48b,65b,77b), **Sark** (28d), **Sart** (82b, 103b, 170d), **tara** (22a, 55c, 113a, 168c), **Tara** (82b,c,138b), **tare** (9a,18d,41a,176a,179d), **tari** (47d,69a), **tarn** (87d,103d,120d), **taro** (13c,48c,49b,64b,112b,120a,133d,155c,170a, c), **tarp** (26b,178d), **tart** (114d), **vara** (151d), **vare** (179b), **vari** (34d,91b,134d,174d), **vary** (28d,43c), **ward** (31c,55c,86b), **ware** (27d,35a), **warf, warm** (7c,75b,163b), **warn** (7b), **warp** (36c,165a, 171c), **wart** (124d), **wary** (27d,176b), **yard** (152d), **yare** (96b,124b, 128b), **yark** (22c), **yarl** (40d,107d), **yarn** (154b,161b,184b), **yarr** (72a), **Yaru** (48d), **zarf** (39c,155a), **zarp** (120c)

- - **AR** **Adar** (85c,102a), **afar** (44c), **Afar** (6c), **agar** (7d,28c,39c,103c,141c), **ajar** (110c), **alar** (15c,145c,182d), **amar** (189), **apar** (12d), **arar** (137a,168c), **asar** (67b), **atar** (58d,116b,134a), **Avar** (27d,108a), **bear** (27a,50b,113c,155a), **Bhar** (191), **boar** (77c,117c,160c,181c), char (24d,138c,170b), czar (42d,49d,60b,135c), dear, Dhar, duar, Edar (18d), fear (113c,155a), gear (32c,112a,167b), gnar (72a), guar (46c,59d), haar (139c), hear (75b,c,92d), hoar (63d,71a, 181a), inar (65b), Isar (41a,104c,132a), Iyar (102b), izar (65b, 103b,155b), joar (100a), juar (100a), khar (189), knar (87c,134b), kuar (102a), kyar (33a), lear (139d), Lear (37a,143b), liar (98d), maar (177a), near (11d,32c,107b), omar (103b), Omar (48c,51b, 163b), osar (51b,67b,131b), paar (28c), pear (64a), rear (15b,23a, b,24a,51b,76d,127c), roar (145c) Saar (63b,102d,132a), scar (31a, 184d), sear (23d,27d,72d,138c), soar (59a), spar (22c,24c,64b, 97b,100b,144d), star (14a,21c,94c,100c), taar (12b), tear (67c, 87b,130a), thar (68a,76d), tiar (39a,75a,121a), tsar (42d,49d, 60b,135c), tzar (42d,49d,60b,135c), usar (8d,16c), wear (50b), year, Zoar

A - - R   Abir (129a), Acer (96c), acor (6d), Adar (85c,102a), Ader (18d), ador (153b), afar (44c), Afar (6c), afer (48a,182b), agar (7d,28c, 39c,103c,141c), ager (47c,56a,89b,c,131d,133b), Ahir (27b), ajar (110c), alar (15c,145c,182d), Alur (191), amar (189), amer (61b), amir (7c,12a,103a,b,123c,170d), amor (152b), Amor (39c,68b), Aner (18d,96b), apar (12d), aper (32d), arar (137a,168c), asar (67b), Aser (84a), Askr (107d), asor (75c,105a), Asur (68c), atar (58d,116b,134a), Ater (18c), Auer (79a), Avar (27d,108a), aver (7c,14a,15c,41c,95c,140d,155c,160b,184c)

AS - -   asak (13d,168c,169a), asar (67b), asci (154a), asea (39b,177c), asem (9a,49a,69c), Aser (84a), Asha (191), ashy (113a,178a), Asia (48a), Asin (102a), Askr (107d), asno (151d), asok (13d), Asom (18d), asop (180b), asor (75c,105a), asse (25a,60d,74a), assi (77d), asta (188), Asta (107a,164c), Asti (83d,182b), Asur (68c)

- AS -   base (6a,43b,44b,51c,60c,79b,94b,122b), bash, bask (94d), bass (57b,c,177a), bast (16c,56a,117b,184a), Bast (27b), casa (152b), case (22c,36c,81c,91a,108c), cash (101c), cask, Caso (82d), cass (140c,177a), Cass (147a), cast (165b,167c), dash (125c,162d), dasi (77a), ease (7c,8d,35a,100d,129d,130b,c,150c), East (111b), easy (54a,146d,149d,172b), fash (140c,176a), fass (189), fast (56d, 126c,141d,160c,173a,d), gash (40a), gasp (113c), hase (74d), hash, hasp (31d,54d,153c), hast, jass (160d), kasa (48a), kasi (116b), kasm (189), lash (58c,87b,165c,180d), Lasi (191), lass (95b, last (36c,50b,145a,174c), masa (37a), mash (39b,156c), mask (44a,45c), mass (8a,24b,35b,142d), mast (17c,108d,120b,144d,152d), masu (57a,84c), nase (26b,75a,124b), Nash (9c), nasi (34c,108a,115a), Nast (9c,27a), oast (15d,86b,112a), pasa (46a,127c,152c), pasi (94b), pass (110b,155c), past (25c,69d,165d), rasa (51c), rase (42b, d,91d), rash (75a), rasp (56b,70d,140d), sasa (55c), sash (18a,45c, 67b,182b), sass, tash (154d), task (156b), Tass (107a,135d,151b), vasa (46d,114a,160b,175d), Vasa, vase, vast (78d,79d), vasu (106c), Vasu (176d), wash, wasp, wast

- - AS   abas (61c), alas (52c,136b,183b), Anas (46c,d), Aras, baas (97c), bias (43b,123a), blas (6c,49c), Blas (67b), bras (61a), Dyas (66a), ELAS (71c), eyas (106c,173a), gras (78b), Idas (27b,71c), Iras (11b,32a), khas (153a), kras (76d), kvas (135c), Lias (66a), Lyas (66a), Maas (132a), mias (111a), Nias (82d), oras (40d), quas

273

(135c), upas (84d,120b,168c,d), **Usas** (68d), utas (49a,109c), **Xmas,** yeas (177c), **Zoas** (20b)

A - - S abas (61c), **ABC's** (57a), **Acis** (64b), **Acts, acus** (89d, 118a), **Ades** (73a), **Agis** (86d), **Aias, Airs** (123b), alas (52c,136b,183h), alms (29a), **Alps** (85d), **Alys** (183c), **Ames** (9c,82a), **Amos** (96a,144b), **Anas** (46c,d), **Anes** (110c,140a), anis (55c), **Apis** (17c,24b,49a, 125a,136a), **Apus** (36b,c), **Aras, Ares** (49b,51b,68c,76a,97a,105c, 110b,178a,186d), aris (101b), arms, arts (138c), ates (160c), atis (76d,102a), **Aves** (19d), **Avis** (89a,183c), **avus** (89b), axis (28b, 41d,77c,153c), ayes (177c)

AT - - atap (113b), atar (58d,116b,134a), atef (39a,48d), aten (150a, 159b), **Ateo** (120d), **Ater** (18c), ates (160c), **Atik** (155b), atip (14b,166a), atis (76d,102a), **Atka** (11a), atle (136d,161d,169b), **Atli** (14c,72b,79a,107d), atma (150d), atmo (34d,174d), **Atmu** (143a,159b), atom (101c,114c,180d), aton (150a,159b), atop (112a, 174a), **Atri, atry** (141b), atta (58d,90c,97d,160c,173d), **Atta** (94d, 95d,100a,106b,117a), **Attu, atua** (120d), **Atum** (143a,159b)

- AT - bata (30a,142d), **bate** (43c,91b,100d), bath, **Bath** (50d,151c), batt (37c), batz (190), cata (122c), cate (165c), **Cato** (132d,133b), data (54a), date (64a,153a), dato (95c,102c,117a), datu (95c,102c, 117a), eats, fate (42d,52a,87a,94a), gata (143c), gate (51a,121b), **Gath** (117a), hate (6a,43a), hath, **Hati** (48d), jati (27b), jato (173b), **Kate** (143c,183d), kath (14a), **Katy** (183d), lata (85d,95d), late (128c), lath (157c), latu (190), mate (18c,35b,41d,113a,154a,162c), math (77a), **Matt, maty** (80c), **Nata** (15c,47c), **Nate** (22b), **Nath** (155c), **Nato** (6a,8d), natr (189), **Natt** (107b), oath (119c,150a), pata (32c,160d), pate (39a,74d), path (132a,134b), pato (46d), patu (179b), rata (29d,56b,89d,96c,106d,120c,168c), rate (11d,14a,31d, 36b,51d,52a,70b,85c,112b,123b,127d,128a,138c,143a,174b), rath (29a,76d,162d), rati (189), rats, sate (32d,52c,67d,70d,137c,159d), sati, **Sati** (49a,126b,147b), tate (183a), tatt (87c), tatu (12d), **Tatu, Wate** (141a), watt, **Watt** (82a,173b,177c), yate (51d,16Sc), yati (76d), zati (21d)

- - AT adat (90b,95d), alat (136d), **Anat** (138c,147d), beat (58c,87b,131a, 164d,165b,180d), bhat (80c), blat (25b), boat (27b,106a), brat, chat (9b,19c,161c), coat (160a), doat (17a,94b,112a,165d), drat (100a), **Duat** (172d), erat (89c), etat (62d), feat (7a,52d), fiat (35a, 41d,48c,111b,137a), **Fiat** (83c), flat (41b,124b,173a), frat, geat (77d,101a), **Geat** (138a), ghat (32d,88b,103d,132a), gnat (59a, 81b,99c), goat (135a), heat, ikat (53b,159a), kaat (105d), khat (105d), kyat (189), **Maat** (69a,b,85d), meat (59b), moat (44d), neat (165c,169d), peat (64a,175a), piat (11a), plat (22d,96c,114a,119c, 133d), pyat (95b), scat (26b,67a,d,126c,169c), seat (9Sc,156b), shat (87d), skat (181b), **Skat** (155b), slat (58b,89a,117c,184a), spat (112c,126b,134b), stat (72d), swat (15d,20d,32d,157c), **Swat** (103a), that (42b,124b,129c), what (129c)

A - - T abet (8b,15b,50a,59b,75d,81c,141d,159d), **Abot** (100c), abut (22a, 167c), acht (66c), adat (90b,95d), adit (51a,100a,114d), **Ahet** (49a,102a), aint, alat (136d), alit (44b,143a), amit (94a), **Anat** (138c,147d), anet (43c), **Apet** (97c), aret (128c), arn't, aunt (129c)

AU - - **Auca** (192), **Aude, Auer** (79a), auge (123c,132b), aula (66c,73b), aulu (74c,168c), aune (188), aunt (129c), aura (44c,49c,66a,96b, 158a,170d,177c), auri (34a), **Ausa, ausu** (168c,180b), auto (34d) **auza** (168c,180b)

-AU- baud (162d), baul (18b), Baum (9c,112c), cauk (139b), caul (16d, 74d), caur (139a), daub (148d), dauk (95c), Daur (139b), dauw (24c), eaux (178c), faun (56a,68b,137c,161a,184a), gaub (116c), gaud (169d), gaue (67a), Gaul (10a,60d,63c), gaup, gaur (112c, 181c), gaus (67d), gaut (88b,103d,132a), haul (27b,45d), jaun (113a), kaun (93d), laud (122a), laun (146b), maud (53d,136d, 143c), Maud (181a,183c), Maui (120d), maul (73c), maun (139d), naut (141b), Paul (96a), paun (18b), paut (140a), Sauk (192), saul (48a,168c), Saul (18c,86d,115a), saum (189), taun (188), taut (163b,165c), Vaux (63b), yaup

--AU Agau (73c), beau, Diau (192), Drau, Esau (82c,84a,128c), frau (181b), miau (27b,99b), prau (21b,26a,95c,d), sgau (88c), unau (148c,171d), whau (107a,168c)

A--U Aalu (6b,48d), Aaru (6b,48d), Abou (48b,55a), actu (7a,89a), Addu (68c,157a,182a), Agau (73c), Ainu (84a,84c), ammu (9d), ansu (11d), anzu (11d), Apsu (29a), Atmu (143a,159b), **Attu, aulu** (74c,168c), ausu (168c,180b), auzu (168c,180b)

AV-- aval (70c), Avar (27d,108a), avec (63a,183a), aver (7c,14a,15c,41c, 95c,140d,155c,160b,184c), Aves (19d), avid (47b,71a,186b), avis (89a), Avis (183c), Avon (143b), avow (6d,36a,41c,112c), avus (89b)

-AV- bave (61d,146c), cava (116a,175b), cave (27d), cavy (72b,120d, 132c,157b), Dave (96b), Davy (96b,136b), eave (133c), favi (138a, 165d), gave, have, Java (33a), Jave (84d), kava (18c,116a), Kavi (84d), lava (101c,132b,151a,177a), lave (16d,178b), nave (30d,31a, 78d,114b,180c), navy (33c,58b), pave (85a), pavo (115b), Pavo (36b,c), pavy (115b), rave (41c,157a,161d), ravi, Ravi (16b), save (52b,110c,123a,173c), Tave (183d), Tavy (183d), wave (19a, 59a,111c,131d,160c,172d), wavy (147b,172d), yava

--AV Muav (66a), Slav (13c,40c,48b,52a,120b,135b)

A--V akov (189), Azov (20b,135d)

AW-- Awan (191), away (6b,69d,76a,109d,111d), awry (13d,38d,171c)

-AW- bawl, bawn (181a), cawk (133c), dawk (95c), dawm (190), dawn (14d,41b), fawn (33c), gawd (169c), gawk (146d), gawp, hawk (19c, 115c), jawy, kawa (18c,116a), Kawi (84d), kawn (93d), lawn (20a, 37c,53b,92c), pawa (189), pawl (43a,95a), pawn (29c,119c), sawk (188), sawn, tawa (106d,168c), yawl (136b,171d,175d), yawn, yawp

--AW chaw (97c), claw (29c,105b,161d,173a), craw (38d,72c,156c), dhaw (125a), draw (42c,53a,92b,117c,121c,167d), flaw, gnaw (20a,107a, 178b), miaw (27b,99b), shaw (164b), Shaw (50c,53b), slaw, thaw

A--W alow (18a,172c), anew (7c), arow (92c,158b), avow (6d,36a,41c, 112c)

AX-- axal (120b), axil (10c), axis (28b,41d,77c,153c), axle (153c,180c), axon (106c,153c)

-AX- saxe (20d,33c), taxi (13a,125b), taxo (13a), waxy (119c,149d)

-- AX Ajax (71b,162d), Anax (43c,120c), coax (180c), Crax (19b,39d), flax, hoax (41c,122a), Odax (132c), Olax (52b)

A -- X abox (22d), Ajax (71b,162d), Alix (183c), Amex (184d), Anax (43d,120c), apex (39c,76c,115c,118b,159b,166a,167b),

AY -- ayah (108d), ayes (177c), ayin (91c)

- AY - baya (179b), Baya (191), cayo, Daye (123d), days, hayz, kayo (87c), maya (179b), Maya (23d,186c), Mayo (193), raya (19b,23c,76d, 107d), saya (117a), Vayu (68c,182a), ways, yaya (113c,168c)

-- AY alay (96c), anay (72b), away (6b,69d,76a,109d,111d), blay (57d), bray, chay (48a,128d), Clay (9d), dray (27a,154c,177b), esay, flay (147c,157c), fray (56b,60d), gray (33c,77c), Gray (50c), okay (8d), olay (113b), piay (98b), play (63d,154a), pray (18b,51a,159d), quay (88b,117c,180c), ruay (189), shay (110c), slay, stay (72d, 124c,130a,134a,162a), sway (104a)

A -- Y Abby (183d), ably (147c), achy, Addy (183d), adry, (164c), aery (47b,51d,106c), affy (18b), ahey (52c), ahoy (106a), airy (176d, 177a), akey (189), alay (96c), Algy (96b), alky, ally (14a,35c,d, 173c), Amoy (88c), anay (72b,163b,181a), ancy (158c), Andy (96b), army, arty, ashy (113a,178a), atry (141b), away (6b,69d,76a,109d, 111d), awry (13d,38d,171c)

AZ -- Azam (166c), azan (102d), Azha (155b), Azof (20b,135d), azon (127b), Azov (20b,135d), azul (151d)

- AZ - caza, cazi (103a), cazy (103a), Daza (191), daze (157d), dazy, faze (43d), Gaza (117a), gaze, gazi, gazy, haze (100c,174d), hazy (174b), jazz, Kazi (103a), kazy (103a), laze (79b), Laze (191), Lazi (191), lazo (88d,128b,133d), lazy, maze (87b,157d), naze (26b, 124b), Nazi, raze (42b,d,91d), razz (131b), vaza (114a)

-- AZ Agaz (193), Ahaz (86d), Boaz (135d)

A -- Z Agaz (193), Ahaz (86d)

BA -- Baal (142b), baas (97c), baba (108d,120c,166c,171a), babe, Babi (116c), babu (77a), baby, Bach (35c), back (75d,76d,159d), Badb (82b), bade, baff (69d), baft (14a,53b), baga (171b), bago (13d), bahi (60c), baho (122a), baht (146a), bail (43c), bain (61a), bait (15d,51a,94d,167b), baju (84a), baka (52b), bake (139a), baku (26d,157b,168c), Bala (26c,66a), bald (16c), bale (24b,74a), balk (118c,146a,156d), ball, balm (110a,172c), Balt (93a), balu (104b, 159a,181d), Bana (67a), banc (61a,85c), band (72a,157c), bane (74a,106b,120b,139a), bang (75d,105d,148a), bani (190), bank (18a,58c), bans, bant (43c), bara (188), barb (20b,57d,78b,117d, 120a,b,124b), bard (12d,120a), bare (43d,157c), bari (37c,79c), Bari (83d), bark (115c), barm (185b), barn (156d), baro (71a,122c), barr (49b), Bart (96b), baru (168c), base (6a,43b,44b,51c,60c,79b,94b, 122b), bash, bask (94d), bass (57b,c,177a), bast (16c,56a,117b, 184a), Bast (27b), bata (30a,142d), bate (43c,91b,100d), bath, Bath (50d,151c), batt (37c), batz (190), baud (162d), baul (18b), Baum (9c,112c), bave (61d,146c), bawl, bawn (181a), baya (179b), Baya (191)

- BA - abas (61c), Ibad (191), Iban (47c), oban (190)

-- BA Abba (20a,55a,161c), alba (98a,181a), Alba (151d), amba (161a), anba (36d), arba (135d,171a), baba (108d,120c,166c,171a), boba (29d), buba (170a), caba (184c), ceba (169b), cuba (189), Cuba (180b), Egba (191), Elba (105d), ezba (188), Faba, haba (151d), isba (135c), juba (106b), koba (11a), kuba (26d,189), Luba (191), Maba (103a,168d), Nuba (108c), peba (12d), Peba (193), Raba, reba (144a), Reba (18d,86c), saba (56a,117a), Saba (143d), Seba (18c,39d), Toba (80c), tuba (105a,137d), ueba (188)

B - - A   baba (108d,120c,166c,171a), baga (171b), baka (52b), Bala (26c, 66a), Bana (67a), bara (188), bata (30a,142d), baya (179b), Baya (191), Beda (101d), bega (188), Beja (6c,191), beka (189), bela (12a), Bela (18b,48c), bema (28d,31a,114b,119b,125b,137a), bena, (176a), Bera (86d), Besa (68b,119c), beta (71a,91c,141d), biga (171d), bija (168c), bina (77a), bisa (11a), biwa (93d,168c), Bixa (145d), blaa, boba (29d), boca (152b,c), boga (57d,180b), bola (16a, 179b), boma (7d), bona (89d,183c), Bona, bora (181d,182b), bosa (12a), bota (189), boza (12a), brea (100b), buba (170a), buda (83d), buna (161c), bura (182b)

- BB -   Abba (20a,55a,161c), abbe (32b,63b,123b), Abby (183d)

- - BB   bibb (97c,146b), Cobb (9c), dubb (161c), hobb (124b), hubb (118b), jibb, lobb (23b,94c,163a)

B - - B   Badb (82b), barb (20b,57d,78b,117d,120a,b,124b), bibb (97c, 146b), blab (162b), bleb (20c,23d,67c), blob, blub, Bodb (82b), bomb (144a), boob (146d), brab (113b), brob (153c), bulb (37a, 172c)

- BC -   ABC's (57a)

B - - C   banc (61a,85c), bloc (173a), Bosc (115c)

B - - D   bald (16c), band (72a,157c), bard (12d,120a), baud (162d), bead (17a,122a,146b), Beld (155b), bend (39d,171b), bind (33b,165c), biod (59d,79c), bird, bled, bold (41a), bond (92a,101c,141d,143b, 159d,165c), bord (100b), brad (54d,67c,105b), bred (23c,48c,127c), bund (49c,66c,90c), Byrd (9c,120b)

BE - -   bead (17a,122a,146b), beak (19a), beal (139d), beam, bean (91b, 142a,175a), bear (27a,50b,113c,155a), beat (58c,87b,131a,164d, 165b,180d), beau, beck (107c), Beda (101d), Bede (48c,50c,101d, 175b), beef, been (149a), beer (18c), bees (185b), beet (175a), bega (188), behn (137d), Beid (155b), Beja (6c,191), beka (189), bela (12a), Bela (18b,48c,78d), Beli (23c), bell (24c,39d), Bell (162d), belt (16a,31a), bema (28d,31a,114b,119b,125b,137a), bena (176a), bend (39d,171b), bene (18a,83c,90a,106d,122a,180a), beng (43a), beni (116a,142d), Beni (191), beno (113b,117a), bent (80b), benu (49a), Bera (86d), berg (79b), berm (25d,90c,145c), Bern (160d), Bert (96b), Besa (68b,119c), Bess (76c,183d), best (41d, 159c,160a), beta (71a,91c,141d), bete (61a,107c), beth (91c), Beth (8c,183d), bevy (38a,58c)

- BE -   abed (130c), Abel (7a,25b), abet (8b,15b,50a,59b,75d,81c,141d, 159d), Eben (96a), Eber (51a,75c,99d), ibex (67d,68a), obex (22d), obey (35c,75c), Obed (135d), uber (66b)

- - BE   abbe (32b,63b,123b), albe (133a), babe, Bube (180b), cube (66b, 150a), dobe (159b,c,172b), Elbe (108a), gabe (162a), gibe (8a,42c, 84d,100d,138c,144c,149b), gybe (144c), Habe (191), Hebe (39c,

277

69c,186b), **imbe** (37a,56a,133d), **jibe** (8a,33b,35d,37b,42c,100d, 138c,144c,149b), **jube** (28d), **kibe, Kobe** (78a), **lobe** (90c,134b), **lube** (110a), **ribe** (139a), **robe** (65b), **rube** (37d,135d,185d), **Rube** (96b), **sabe, tobe** (7d,137b), **tube** (118b,158a)

B - - E   **babe, bade, bake** (139a), **bale** (24b,74a), **bane** (74a,106b,120b, 139a), **bare** (43d,157c), **base** (6a,43b,44b,51c,60c,79b,94b,122b), **bate** (43c,91b,100d), **bave** (61d,146c), **Bede** (48c,50c,101d,175b), **bene** (18a,83c,90a,106d,122a,180a), **bete** (61a,107c), **bice** (20d, 117d), **Bice** (27b), **bide** (47c,50b,130a,158b), **bike, bile** (30c), **bine** (145b,156a,171c,176b), **bise** (182a), **bite** (29d,156b), **bize** (182a), **blae** (93b), **blue** (33c,98c,102c,150d,173a), **boce** (23b,52a,57b), **bode** (14c,60a,110b,121b), **bole** (31d,32a,169b), **bone, bore** (14c, 25b,46a,116a,165c,179b), **bose** (163c), **brae** (76d,139a,c,140b, 148c), **bree** (139a), **Brie** (29c), **Bube** (180b), **bure** (61b), **byee** (189), **byre** (38a)

- BF -   **Abfa** (76b)

B - - F   **baff** (69d), **beef, biff, buff** (134c,161d)

B - - G   **bang** (75d,105d,148a), **beng** (43a), **berg** (79b), **bing, bong, borg** (40d), **brag** (21a,175a), **brig** (72b,106a,144d), **bung** (119d,156d), **burg** (22b,73c)

BH - -   **Bhar** (191), **bhat** (80c), **bhel** (126d), **Bhil** (191), **b'hoy** (134b), **bhut** (67a)

- - BH   **Cobh** (37a)

B - - H   **Bach** (35c), **bash, bath, Bath** (50d,151c), **beth** (91c), **Beth** (8c, 183d), **bikh** (120b), **binh** (189), **bish** (120b), **blah, booh** (52c), **bosh, both, bruh** (95a), **bukh** (122a), **bush**

BI - -   **bias** (43b,123a), **bibb** (97c,146b), **bibi** (87d), **bice** (20d,117d), **Bice** (27b), **bide** (47c,50b,130a,158b,162a,177b), **bien** (63a,140c,179a, 180a), **bier** (33b,66b), **biff, biga** (171d), **bija** (168c), **bike, bikh** (120b), **bile** (30c), **bilk** (29b,41c,42a), **bill** (17b,147a), **Bill** (96b), **bilo** (131b), **bina** (77a), **bind** (33b,165c), **bine** (145b,156a,171c, 176b), **bing, binh** (189), **Bini** (191), **binn** (22c), **bino** (113b,117a), **biod** (59d,79c), **bion** (117b), **bios** (92a), **bird, birl** (93c,131a,153c), **birn** (31d,139a), **birr** (180d), **bisa** (11a), **bise** (182a), **bish** (120b), **bisk** (120b,151a), **bite** (29d,156b), **biti** (20b), **bito** (7d,57d,168c), **bitt** (54d,175c), **biur** (35a), **biwa** (93d,168c), **Bixa** (145d), **bize** (182a), **bizz**

- BI -   **Abia** (18d,137a), **Abib** (102a,b), **Abie** (96b,107a), **abir** (129a), **ibid** (80a,117a,137a), **ibis** (48d,49a,177b), **ibit** (117a), **obia** (55d), **obit** (41b,64d), **Ubii** (191)

- - BI   **Albi** (58a), **ambi** (34a,122c), **Babi** (116c), **bibi** (87d), **Bubi** (180b), **cubi** (188), **gabi** (162a), **gobi, Gobi** (42d), **kobi** (84b), **mabi** (58d), **rabi** (38d,74a), **Rabi** (14b,117b), **sebi** (34b), **tabi** (84c,149d), **Tybi** (102a), **Wabi** (192), **Yobi**

B - - I   **Babi** (116c), **bahi** (60c), **Bali, bani** (190), **bari** (79c), **Bari** (37c, 83d), **Beli** (23c), **beni** (116a,142d), **Beni** (191), **bibi** (87d), **Bini** (191), **biti** (20b), **Boii** (191), **Boni** (63b), **Bori** (110d,150c), **Bubi** (180b), **Bugi** (191), **buri** (56b)

- - BK   **nabk** (30d,164d), **nubk** (30d,164d), **Sobk** (38d)

B - - K back (75d,76d,159d), balk (118c,146a,156d), bank (18a,58c), bark (115c), bask (94d), beak (19a), beck (107c), bilk (29b,41c,42a), bisk (120b,151a), bock (17c,90d,144a), bonk (190), book, bosk (164b), bowk (155d), buck, bukk (122a), bulk (97b), bunk, busk (17b,37b,55d,161b)

BL - - blaa, blab (162b), blae (93b), blah, blas (6c,49c), Blas (67b), blat (25b), blay (57d), bleb (20c,23d,67c), bled, blet (64a), bleu (61b), blew, blob, bloc (173a), blot, blow, blub, blue (33c,98c,102c,150d, 173a), blup, blur, blut (66b)

- BL - able (26b,35b,126a,147c), ably (147c)

B - - L baal (142b), bail (43c), ball, baul (18b), bawl, beal (139d), bell (24c,39d), Bell (162d), bhel (126d), Bhil (191), bill (17b,147a), Bill (96b), birl (93c,131a,153c), boil, boll (119b,d), bool (39d), bowl, bual (182c), buhl (81a), bull (113c), burl (87c,169a)

B - - M balm (110a,172c), barm (185b), Baum (9c,112c), beam, berm (25d, 90d,145c), boom (152d), Bram (96a), brim

B - - N bain (61a), barn (156d), bawn (181a), bean (91b,142a,175a), been (149a), behn (137d), Bern (160d), bien (63a,140c,179a,180a), binn (22c), bion (117b), birn (31d,139a), Bonn (17d), boon (18b,20c, 55a), born, bran (23c,39a,70b,72a,79c), Bran (23c,50c), bren (72d, 95a), brin (32c,54c,146c), bunn (25b), burn

BO - - boar (77c,117c,160c,181c), boat (27b,106a), Boaz (135d), boba (29d,) bobo (112c,168c), boca (152b,c), boce (23b,52a,57b), bock (17c,90d,144a), Bodb (82b), bode (14c,60a,110b,121b), Bodo (88c), body (72a), Boer (151a), boga (57d,180b), bogo (117a,168c), Boge (191), bogy (153a), boho (117a,179d), Bohr (14b,40d,138c), Boii (191), boil, bois (62b,63a,183d), bojo (117a), boko (52b), bola (16a, 179b), bold (41a), bole (31d,32a,169b), boll (119b,d), bolo (87a, 179b), bolt (13b,54d,58b,132d,160a), boma (7d), bomb (144a), bona (89d), Bona (183c), bond (92a,101c,141d,143b,159d,165c), bone, bong, Boni (63b), bonk (190), Bonn (17d), bony (147c), Bony (96b), boob (146d), booh (52c), book, bool (39d), boom (152d), boon (18b,20c,55a), boor (47a,135d,172c), boot (128d), bora (181d, 182b), bord (100b), bore (14c,25b,46a,116a,165c,179b), borg (40d), Bori (110d,150c), born, boro (154b), Boro (193), Bors (70b,134b), bort (43b), Bort (134b), bosa (12a), Bosc (115c), bose (163c), bosh, bosk (164b), boss (49d,157d), bota (189), both, Boto (192), bott (32a,88d), bout (36c), bouw (188), bowk (155d), bowl, boxy, boza (12a), bozo (55b)

- BO - aboo (17a), Abot (100c), Abou (48b,55a), abox (22d), eboe (28b, 110a,168c,169b), Eboe, ebon (20b), oboe (74b,104d,105a,182a, 184a), obol (29b,110a)

- - BO albo (34d,181a), ambo (125b,128b), bobo (112c,168c), bubo (112c), Egbo (141d), Gobo (84d), hobo (168a,174b), jobo (77c), lobo (165d,183c), nabo (117a), Nebo (68c,102d,103d,183a), umbo (22b), zobo (186b)

B - - O bago (13d), baho (122a), baro (71a,122c), beno (113b,117a), bilo (131b), bino (113b,117a), bito (7d,52d,168c), bobo (112c,168c), Bodo (88c), bogo (117a,168c), Bogo (191), boho (117a,179d), bojo (117a), boko (52b), bolo (87a,179b), boro (154b), Boro (193), Boto

(192), **bozo** (55b), **broo** (139a), **bubo** (112c), **Bufo** (166c), **Buto** (142d), **buyo** (18b), **bygo** (114c)

B - - P blup, bump

BR - - brab (113b), brad (54d,67c,105b), brae (76d,139a,c,140b,148c), brag (21a,175a), Bram (96a), bran (23c,39a,70b,72a,79c), Bran (23c,50c), bras (61a), brat, bray, brea (100b), bred (23c,48c,127c), bree (139a), bren (72d,95a), Brer (172b), Bres, brew (35d), brey (194), Brie (29c), brig (72b,106a,144d), brim, brin (32c,54c,146c), brit (76c), brob (153c), broo (139a), brow, bruh (95a), brut (182c), Brut (23c)

- BR - abra (26b), Abra, abri (61c,62c,144b), Ebro (132a), obra (152d, 184c)

B - - R barr (49b), bear (27a,50b,113c,155a), beer (18c), Bhar (191), bier (33b,66b), birr (180d), biur (35a), blur, boar (77c,117c,160c,181c), Boer (151a), Bohr (14b,40d,138c), boor (47a,135d,172c), Brer (172b), buhr (180d), burr (123b)

- BS - Absi (191)

- - BS dibs (70c), Lubs (94c), nibs (116c), nobs (38c,87a)

B - - S baas (97c), bans, bass (57b,c,177a), bees (185b), Bess (76c,183d), bias (43b,123a), bios (92a), blas (6c,49c), Blas (67b), bois (62b, 63a,183d), Bors (70b,134b), boss (49d,157d), bras (61a), Bres, buss (87a,148c)

- - BT debt (91d,109b)

B - - T baft (14a,53b), baht (146a), bait (15d,51a,94d,167b), Bait (93a), bant (43c), Bart (96b), bast (16c,56a,117b,184a), Bast (27b), batt (37c), beat (58c,87b,131a,164d,165b,180d), beet (175a), belt (16a, 31a), bent (80b), Bert (96b), best (41d,159c,160a), bhat (80c), bhut (67a), bitt (54d,175c), blat (25b), blet (64a), blot, blut (66b), boat (27b,106a), bolt (13b,54d,58b,132d,160a), boot (128d), bort (43b), Bort (134b), bott (32a,88d), bout (36c), brat, brit (76c), brut (182c), Brut (23c), bult (76d), bunt (15d,180c), bust, butt (27a,77b,127d,162a,182b)

BU - - bual (182c), buba (170a), Bube (180b), Bubi (180b), bubo (112c), buck, buda (83d), buff (134c,161d), Bufo (166c), Bugi (191), buhl (81a), buhr (180d), bukh (122a), bukk (122a), bulb (37a,172c), bulk (97b), bull (113c), bult (76d), bump, buna (161c), bund (49c,66c,90c), bung (119d,156d), bunk, bunn (25b), bunt (15d, 180c), buoy (28d,58c), bura (182b), bure (61b), burg (22b,73c), buri (56b), burl (87c,169a), burn, burr (123b), bury (81d), bush, busk (17b,37b,55d,161b), buss (87a,148c), bust, busy, Buto (142d), butt (27a,77b,127d,162a,182b), buxy (115b), buyo (18b) buzz

- BU - abut (22a,167c), ebur (89c)

- - BU babu (77a), kobu (84b), Nabu (68c,183a), tabu (59d,111d), Tibu (191), zebu (22d,80d,112c)

B - - U babu (77a), baju (84a), baku (26d,157b,168c), balu (104b,159a, 181d), baru (168c), beau, benu (49a), bleu (61b)

B - - W blew, blow, bouw (188), brew (35d), brow

280

BY - -   byee, (189), bygo (114c), Byrd (9c,120b), byre (38a)

- - BY   Abby (183d), baby, doby (159b,c), gaby (59c,146d), goby (57d), kiby (29a), ruby (20a,65d,179c), toby (8c,85c,104b), Toby (96b, 125c)

B - - Y   baby, bevy (38a,58c), b'hoy (134b), blay (57d), body (72a), bogy (153a), bony (147c), Bony (96b), boxy, bray, brey (194), buoy (28d,58c), bury (81d), busy, buxy (115b)

B - - Z   batz (190), bizz, Boaz (135d), buzz

CA - -   caam (93d), caba (184c), Caca (67a), caco (73b), cade (25c,27a,76c, 85d,116d), Cade (50c), cadi (12a,103a,171a), cady (69d), Caen, cafe, cage (36a), cagy (178b), caid (35a,151d,152b), cain (169c), Cain (6a,7a,50d,88a,104c,143a), caja (152a), caji (180b), cake, caky, cale (72d), calf, calk (78c,109a,141c,178d), call (145c,159b, 176d), calm (8d,11d,112b,118d,126c,d,172b,173d), calo (72d), calp (92b), calx (23c,75c,112c), came (182b), Came (192), camp (163b), Cana (57a,64b,100c), cane (17b,128a,156a,159a,177d), Cane, cang (184a), cano (152a), cant (28d,81b,84d,90c,109b,136c,165d,166a), capa (152a,166d), cape (75a,96c,124b,161a), caph (91c), Capp (27a), cara (83a), Cara (48b,183c), card (33d,114d), care (11b, 14c,35d,150a,184d), cark (26d,184d), carl (115c,135d), Carl (96a), carn (156c), caro (83a), Caro (183d), carp (27d,38d,40c,55a,56c, 57a), carr (120d,140a), cart (171d,175a,177b), casa (152b), case (22c,36c,81c,91a,108c), cash (101c), cask, Caso (82d) cass (140c, 177a), Cass (147a), cast (165b,167c), cata (122c), cate (165c), Cato (132d,133b), Catt (9d), cauk (139b), caul (16d,74d), caup, caur (139a), cava (116a,175b), cave (27d), cavy (72b,120d,132c, 157b), cawk (133c), cayo, caza, cazi (103a), cazy (103a)

- CA -   ecad (73a,119b), ical (158c), scab (80b,107d,157c), scad (31a,57a, 78b,88d,137c), scan (52b,93d,98a,116d,128b,c,140d), scar (31a, 184d), scat (26b,67a,d,126c,169c)

- - CA   acca (53b,d), Alca (14c,128b), arca (9a,22c,29d,115a,130a), Arca (101b), Auca (192), boca (152b,c), Caca (67a), coca (29d,33a,105d, 113a), cuca (33a,105d), deca (34d,122d), Ecca (66a), esca (11c, 44a,70c), Inca (14b,30a), jaca (84a), juca (27a), mica (82c,100b, 146c), onca (189), orca (86b), paca (132c,154a), peca (190), pica (66b,95b,172c), puca (68a), raca (19a,59c,130b,184d), Teca (192), unca (49a), Ynca (193), yuca (27a)

C - - A   caba (184c), Caca (67a), caja (152a), Cana (57a,64b,100c), capa (152a,166d), cara (83a), Cara (48b,183c), casa (152b), cata (122c), cava (116a,175b), caza, ceba (169b), cela (62d), cena (88d,133a), cepa (110c), cera (152d,161d,179a), chaa (162b), chia (136d), cima (83b,c), Civa (56d), coca (29d,33a,105d,113a), coda (32c,35d,55d, 56c), coja (103b,166b), cola (25b,108d,149d,168c), coma (91c, 157d,170c,172b), copa (88b,113c), cora (65d), Cora (42b,69c,80c, 116b,124d,172b,183c), cota (117a), coxa (77b), crea (92c,151d), cuba (189), Cuba (180b), cuca (33a,105d), Cuna (193), cura (152c), cuya (39b), cyma (101a,b)

C - - B   chab (184a), chib (167a), chob (23c), chub (40c,154c), club (39c), Cobb (9c), comb (38c), crab (39b,144b,181b), crib (96b,120d), curb (130c,146b)

- CC -   acca (53b,d), Ecca (66a), ecce (17d,89a,c)

C - - C   chic (148d), circ (31a), cric (131c), croc (13a,74a)

C - - D   caid (35a,151d,152b), card (33d,114d), Chad (158b), chid, Chud (191), clad (46a,82a), clod (22a,45b,157d), coed, cold (65d), cond (156a), cord (39b,131a), curd (99d)

CE - -   ceba (169b), cede (67b,70c,129d,160a,168b,185d), ceil (92c,112a), cela (62d), cell (39b), celt (30c,123a,156c,167b,179b), Celt (10a, 180a,b), cena (88d,133a), cene (34c), cens (115b), cent (36d), cepa (110c), cepe (48c), cera (152d,161d,179a), cere (19a,114b,149d, 179a), cern (41c), cero (57b,c,d,180b), cess (91d,94c,162b), cest (18a,67b), cete (180b,c), ceto (34a), Ceyx (73b)

- CE -   Acer (96c), icer

- - CE   ance (158b,c,d), bice (20d,117d), Bice (27b), boce (23b,52a,57b), dace (57a,b), dice (65a), duce (29d), ecce (17d,89a,c), ence (158c), esce (158d), face (159d,176c), lace (58b,179c), luce (58c,117d), Luce (7b,35a), mace (49d,108d,153b,154d,161a,178a), mice, nice (54d,119c,130c), Nice (98c), once (60b,79b), pace (64b,98a,153b, 156a,170b,177d), pice (190), puce (33c,d,52a), race (116a,153b, 154b), Rice (46a), sice (71d,147b), syce (71d), tace (13a,155d), tice (9a,38c,51a,185d), vice (31d,158a), voce (83c,177a)

C - - E   cade (25c,27a,76c,85d,116d), Cade (50c), cafe, cage (36a), cake, cale (72d), came (182b), Came (192), cane (17b,128a,156a,159a, 177d), Cane, cape (75a,96c,124b,161a), care (11b,14c,35d,150a, 184d), case (22c,36c,81c,91a,108c), cate (165c), cave (27d), cede (67b,70c,129d,160a,168b,185d), cene (34c), cepe (48c), cere (19a, 114b,149d,179a), cete (180b,c), chee (189), cine (104b,152c), cise (147b), cite (15a,98d,126d,159b), cive (110c), clee (19a,129a), Cloe (183c), clue, code (21c,31a,40c,161c), coke (32d,64a), cole (25a), Cole, come, cone (66b,150a,157c), cope (12b,26b,36c,65b, 157d,176a), core (28b,51c,75b,81b), cose (29b), cote (19b,143d, 144a,b), cove (17a,73d,107d), coze (29b), Cree (192), cube (66b, 150a), cuke (39b), cure (123b,d), cute (39c), cyke (40c), cyme (58d, 69c)

C - - F   calf, chef, clef (104d,105a), coif (73a), cuff (148a), cuif (139a,d, 140c)

C - - G   cang (184a), chug (53a), clog (30c,145b), coag (45d,118a,163b), crag (132c), crig (20d)

CH - -   chaa (162b), chab (184a), Chad (158b), chai (72d), cham (20a,29d), Cham (8c) chan (26c,130c), chap (55b), char (24d,138c,170b), chat (9b,19c,161c), chaw (97c), chay (48a,128d), chee (189), chef, chek (59c), Chen (149b), cher (61b), chew (97c), chez (14b,61a), chiã (136d), chib (167a), chic (148d), chid, ch'ih (188), chil, chin, Chin (30b), chip (69d), chir (29b,116d), chit (67b,98c,108b,116c, 177c), chiv (87a), chob (23c), chol (118d), Chol (192), chop (98a), chor (164b), chou (61b), Chou (30b), chow (45a), choy (48a,128d), chub (40c,154c), Chud (191), chug (53a), chum (38d), Chun (30c), chut!

- CH -   ache (79a,112d,185b), acht (66c), achy, echo (130b,d), Echo (105d), icho (67b), ichu (10b,70d), ocha (189), tcha (162c), tche (13d,30b, 105a), tchi, Tchi, tchu

- - CH   alch (9a), arch (29d,38b,39d,123d,132c), bach, Bach (35c), each, etch, Foch (63b), hoch (52c,66c), Hoch, inch, itch, Koch (66d), lech (102b), loch (88a,139d), much, nach, ouch, rich, Roch (136c), sech (97c), such (146d), Tech, Vach (153b), Zach (96b)

C - - H   caph (91c), Caph, cash (101c), ch'ih (188), Cobh (37a), cosh (35a, 97c), cush (101c), Cush (51d,73c)

Cl - -   cima (83b,c), cine (104b,152c), cinq (61d), cion (42d,70b,145b, 148b,154b,156a), cipo (91d), circ (31a), cirl (24c), cise (147b), cist (22c,29d,156c), cite (15a,98d,126d,159b), cito (89d,126c), cits, city, Civa (56d), cive (110c)

- Cl -   acid (151a,162a), Acis (64b), Scio

- - Cl   asci (154a), deci (163b), foci (28b), fuci (132c), loci (66b,118c), Pici (19c,184a), unci (31d)

C - - I   cadi (12a,103a,171a), Cadi, caji (180b), cazi (103a), chai (72d), coll, Coni, Cori (138c), cubi (188)

- - CK   back (75d,76d,159d), beck (107c), bock (17c,90d,144a), buck, cock (19a,29a,55a,133d,136d,161d,174b), deck (13b,41c, 144d), dick (43a,55b), Dick (96b), dock (40a,117c,144d,179d), duck (26b,53b,179c), hack (40a,77c,184d), heck (100a), hick (185d), hock (91a,115b,182b,c), huck (167d), jack (26c,58a,127c), Jack (96b), jock (96b), Jock, juck (114c), kick, lack (178a), lick lock (54d), luck (28d), mack, mick (82c), mock (131b,162b), muck, neck (83a), nick (30c,108b), nock (13b,108b), pack (24b,140d), peck (24d), pick, puck (44b,68a,77c,100c), Puck (99d,143b), rack (32c,64b), reck (26d,75c), rick (74d,117d), rock (160b), ruck (39a, 185a), sack (43d,118a,119d,182b), seck (173d), sick, sock (157c, 182a), suck, tack (28d,37d,54d), teck (128b), tick (12b,20d,97c), tock (7d,19b), tuck (156b), wick

C - - K   calk (78c,109a,141c,178d), cark (26d,184d), cask, cauk (139b), cawk (133c), chek (59c), coak (45d,118a,163b), cock (19a,29a, 55a,133d,136d), conk (41c,108a,156d,157c), cook (137b), cork (119d), cusk (57b)

CL - -   clad (46a,82a), clam (20b,101b), clan (169c), clap (58b), claw (29c, 105b,161d,173a), clay, Clay (9d), clee (19a,129a), clef (104d,105a), clem (56b,158b), Cleo (126b), clew (16a,33a,77b,136b,164d), Clim (12b), Clio (104d), clip (54d,143d), clod (22a,45b,157d), Cloe (183c), clog (30c,145b), clop, clot (32d,94d), clou (62b), clow (58c,148c), cloy (61b,137c,159d), club (39c), clue, Clym (12b)

- CL -   acle (13d,82c,115d)

C - - L   call (145c,159b,176d), earl (115c,135d), Carl (96a), caul (16d,74d), ceil (92c,112a), cell (39b), chil, chol (118d), Chol (192), cirl (24c), coal (49c,64a), coel (39b), coll (39d,171c,185a), cool (25c,107d), cowl (101c), cral, cull (117c), curl (38d,73b,93b,131d)

- CM -   acme (39c,115c,186b)

C - - M   caam (93d), calm (8d,11d,112b,118d,126c,d,172b), cham (20a,29d), Cham (8c), chum (38d), clam (20b,101b), clem (56b,158b), Clim (12b), Clym (12b), coom (32d,150c,178d), corm (24b,38d,156a), cram (157d), Crom, culm (11a,32d,70d,145a,156a)

CN - -   Cnut (40d,50c)

-CN-   acne (147c)

C--N   Caen, cain (169c), Cain (6a,7a,50d,88a,104c,143a), carn (156c), cern (41c), chan (26c,130c), Chen (149b), chin, Chin (30b), Chun (30c), cion (42d,70b,145b,148b,154b,156a), clan (169c), Coan (37b), coin (19b,37a,100c,101c,179d), conn (43d,156a), coon (121c), corn (39d,95c,123a), coyn (37a), cran (160c), crin (146c), cyan

CO--   coag (45d,118a,163b), coak (45d,118a,163b), coal (49c,64a), Coan (37b), coat (160a), coax (180c), Cobb (9c), Cobh (37a), coca (29d, 33a,105d,113a), cock (19a,29a,55a,133d,136d,161d,174b), coco, (113a), coda (32c,35d,56c), code (21c,31a,40c,161c), codo (188), coed, coel (39b), coho (136d), coif (73a), coil (39d,171c,185a), coin (19b,37a,100c,101c,179d), coir (33a,37a,56a,133d), Coix (70d,85b), coja (103b,166b), coke (32d,64a), coky, cola (25b,108d,149d,168c), cold (65d), cole (25a), Cole, coli, colp (28a,148b), colt (78c,131a, 185d,186b), Colt, coly (104a), coma (91c,157d,170c,172b), comb (38c), come, Como, cond (156a), cone (66b,150a,157c), Coni, conk (41c,108a,156d,157c), conn (43d,156a), cony (127a), cook (137b), cool (25c,107d), coom (32d,150c,178d), coon (121c), coop, Coos, (192), coot (19b,46d,72b,138d,141a,146d,157d), copa (88b,113c), cope (12b,26b,36c,65b,157d,176a), copt (48d), copy, cora (65d), Cora (42b,69c,80c,116b,124d,172b,183c), cord (39b,139a), core (28b,51c,75b,81b), Cori (138c), cork (119d), corm (24b,38d,156a), corn (39d,95c,123a), cose (29b), cosh (35a,97c), coso (152c), coss (98a), cost (29a), cosy (149c), cota (117a), cote (19b,143d,144a,b), coto (16c,90b), Coty (63c), coup (20d,97c,157b,c,162d), cous (38a), cove (17a,73d,107d), cowl (101d), coxa (77b) coyn (37a), coyo (15a,30c), coze (29b), cozy (149c)

-CO-   acon (62c,140d), acor (6d), icon (79d,92b,136a), scob (42a), scon (162c), scop (120a), scot (14a,162b), Scot (64b,132c), scow (21a, 58b)

--CO   alco (45b), caco (73b), coco (113a), Duco, fico (169d), loco (38b, 119b,120b), mico (97a), paco (9b,146d), peco (162b), pico (65a, 152c), poco (83b,93a), saco (189), soco (22d), Teco (192), toco (19b,167c), unco (140c), Waco

C--O   caco (73b), calo (72d), cano (152a), caro (83a), Caro (183d), Caso (82d), Cato (132d,133b), cayo, cero (57b,c,d,180b), ceto (34a), cipo (91d), cito (89d,126c), Cleo (126b), Clio (104d), coco, (113a), codo (188), coho (136d), Como, coso (152d), coto (16c,90b), coyo (15a,30c)

C--P   calp (92b), camp (163b), Capp (27a), carp (27d,38d,40c,55a,56c, 57a), caup, chap (55b), chip (69d), chop (98a), clap (58b), clip (54d,143d), clop, colp (28a,148b), coop, coup (20d,97c,157b,c, 162d), crop (38b), cusp (38c,78b,119a,120a,b)

C--Q   cinq (61d)

CR--   crab (39b,144b,181b), crag (132c), cral, cram (157d), cran (160c), craw (38d,72c,156c), Crax (19b,39d), crea (92c,151d), Cree (192), crew (72a,106a), Crex (37a), crib (96b,120d), cric (131c), crig (20d), crin (146c), cris (40b,95d), croc (13a,74a), Crom, crop (38b), crow (19a), crus (91a,143c), crux (39a,151b)

- CR - acre (39b,56a,88b), **Acre,** ecru (17d,23d,172b), ocra (72c,175a)

C - - R carr (120d,140a), caur (139a), char (24d,138c,170b), cher (61b), chir (29b,116d), chor (164b), coir (33a,37a,56a,133d), cuir (45c,62a), curr (104c), **Czar** (42d,49d,60b,135c)

- - CS ABC's (57a), pacs (94c)

C - - S cass (140c,177a), **Cass** (147a), cens (115b), cess (91d,94c,162b), cits, **Coos** (192), coss (98a), cous (38a), cris (40b,95d), crus (91a, 143c), cuss

- CT - acta (41d,123d,128d,164c), acth (13b), acto (152b), **Acts, actu** (7a, 89a), ecto (34c,122d), octa (122c), octo (34a,89b,122c)

- - CT duct (170c), fact (7a,128b), lact (34c), pact (8a), **Pict** (23c,47d), rect (117b), sect (42b,54a,114c), tact (43c,d,116a)

C - - T cant (28d,81b,84d,90c,109b,136c,165d,166a), cart (171d,175a, 177b), cast (165b,167c), **Catt** (9d), celt (30c,82c,123a,156c,167b, 179b), **Celt** (10a,180a,b), cent (36d), cest (18a,67b), chat (9b,19c, 161c), chit (67b,98c,108b,116c,177c), chut!, cist (22c,29d,156c), clot (32d,94d), coat (160a), colt (78c,131a,185d,186b), **Colt** (131a), coot (19b,46d,72c,138d,141a,146d,157d), **Copt** (48d), cost (29a), cult (141d,161c), curt (145b,c), cyst

CU - - cuba (189), **Cuba** (180b), cube (66b,150a), cubi (188), cuca (33a, 105d), cuff (148a), cuif (139a,d,140c), cuir (45c,62a), cuke (39b), cull (117c), culm (11a,32d,70d,145a,156a), cult (141d,161c), **Cuna** (193), cura (152c), curb (130c,146b), curd (99d), cure (123b), curl (38d,73b,93b,131d), curr (104c), curt (145b,c), cush (101c), **Cush** (51d,73c), cusk (57b), cusp (38c,78b,119a,120a,b), cuss, cute (39c), cuvy (141a), cuya (39b)

- CU - acus (89d,118a), scud (32c,126c,135b,160c), scum (129b), scup (57a,121b), scur (78b), scut (145c,161b)

- - CU jacu (19a,151b), jocu (45b,57a)

C - - U chou (61b), **Chou** (30b), clou (62b)

C - - V chiv (87a)

C - - W chaw (97c), chew (97c), chow (45a), claw (29c,105b,161d,173a), clew (16a,33a,77b,136b,164d), clow (58c,148c), craw (38d,72c, 156c), crew (72a,106a), crow (19a)

C - - X calx (23c,75c,112c), **Ceyx** (73b), coax (180c), **Coix** (70d,85b), **Crax** (19b,39d), **Crex** (37a), crux (39a,151b)

CY - - cyan, cyke (40c), cyma (101a,b), cyme (58d,69c), cyst

- CY - acyl (6d)

- - CY ancy (158c), lacy, **Lucy** (183c), racy (153b)

C - - Y cady (69d), cagy (178b), caky, cavy (72b,120d,132c,157b), cazy (103a), chay (48a,128d), choy (48a,128d), city, clay, **Clay** (9d), cloy (61b,137c,159d), coky, coly (104a), cony (127a), copy, cosy (149c), **Coty** (63c), cozy (149c), cuvy (141a)

CZ - - czar (42d,49d,60b,135c)

C - - Z chez (14b,61a)

DA - - dace (57a,b), **Dada** (13b,63a,157d), dado (41c,111c,115c, 177d), daer (22b), daez, daff (125d), daft (59c), dagg (118c), dagh

(76d), **Dago, Dail** (49a,82b,c), **dain** (188), **dais** (119b), **dale** (43c, 128a,174b), **dali** (168c,169b), **dama** (65d,152b), **dame** (67b,87c, 166b), **damn, damp** (101a), **Dana** (28a,96a,171d), **Dane** (85d,107d, 138a), **dang, dank** (40b,101a), **dans** (62a), **Danu** (28a), **Dara** (18d), **Dard, dare** (28d,41b,42a,74d,175b), **Dare** (57a), **dari** (38a,70b), **dark** (47a,67d,109b,160b), **darn** (130b), **darr** (163c), **dart** (13b,88a, 100c,120b,153a,160c), **dash** (125c,162d), **dasi** (77a), **data** (54a), **date** (64a,153a), **dato** (95c,102c,117a), **datu** (95c,102c,117a), **daub** (148d), **dauk** (95c), **Daur** (139b), **dauw** (24c), **Dave** (96b), **Davy** (96b,136b), **dawk** (95c), **dawm** (190), **dawn** (14d,41b), **Daye** (123d), **days, Daza** (191), **daze** (157d), **dazy**

-DA- adad (52c,56a), **Adad** (68c,157a,182a), **Adah** (25b,51b), **Adam** (26b,96a,111c), **adan** (102d), **Adar** (85c,102a), **adat** (90b,95d), **Edam** (29c), **Edar** (18d), **Idas** (27b,71c), **odah** (170d), **odai** (48a,88b,112c), **Odax** (132c), **udad** (143d,144a,181c), **udal** (76b, 88b,131c)

--DA adda (147d), **Adda** (68c,119d), **Aida** (110d,175c), **alda** (152b), **Alda** (110d,150c), **anda** (23a,168c), **Beda** (101d), **Buda** (83d), **coda** (32c,35d,56c), **Dada** (13b,63a,157d), **Edda** (76b,79b,107d), **Erda** (23d,41a,47d,68d,69a,131d,177b), **Juda, kada** (188), **Leda** (27b, 75d,120c,153a,171d,186b), **Lida** (183c), **meda** (110a), **nuda** (39b), **peda** (114d,144b), **rada** (135c,172a), **Roda** (107b), **sida** (37a, 126c,170a), **soda** (19a,149d,181a), **Teda** (191), **Toda** (45d,76d), **Veda** (77a,b), **Vida** (183c)

D--A Dada (13b,63a,157d), **dama** (65d,152b), **Dana** (28a,96a,171d), **Dara** (18d), **data** (54a), **Daza** (191), **deca** (34d,122d), **depa** (188), **dera** (34c), **deva** (23d,42a,b,56d,77a), **dewa, dika** (23a), **Disa** (111a), **dita** (117a), **diva** (110d,123c), **dola** (189), **dona** (83d,121c,151d), **dopa** (117d), **dora** (70b), **Dora** (36d,41a,43b), **dosa** (74b), **doxa** (48b), **draa** (188), **Duma** (135c), **dura** (153c), **dyna** (34c)

--DB Badb (82b), **Bodb** (82b), **Medb**

D--B daub (148d), **dieb** (84a), **doab** (157c), **doob** (18b), **doub** (18b), **drab** (23d,29c,33d,46d,53b,d), **drib** (46b), **drub** (17b,39c), **duab** (157c), **dubb** (161c), **dumb** (153b)

D--C disc (31b), **douc** (101d)

DD-- DDSC (42a)

-DD- adda (147a), **Adda** (68c,119d,157a,182a), **Addu** (68c,157a,182a), **Addy** (183d), **Edda** (76b,79b), **eddo** (162a), **eddy** (37d, 39d,160d, 180d), **odds** (28d,172d)

--DD dodd (139c,140c), **gedd** (140a), **Ladd** (143c), **ludd** (23c), **mudd** (188), **Nudd** (23c), **Redd** (153a), **Ridd** (94a), **rodd** (38d), **rudd** (26d, 57a,b), **sadd** (33a,40b,58c,107b), **sudd** (40b,58c,107b), **wadd** (109c)

D--D dard, dead, deed (7a,52d,91a,166c,168b), **diad** (113a), **dord** (42c), **dowd** (143b), **duad** (113a,171d), **dyad** (113a)

DE-- dead, deaf, deal (11d,16c,36c,44c,81a,168b), **dean** (33c,109d), **dear, debt** (91d,109b), **deca** (34d,122d), **deci** (163b), **deck** (13b, 41c,144d), **dedo** (188), **deed** (7a,52d,91a,166c,168b), **deem** (36b, 85c,164c), **deep** (124a), **deer** (28c,135a,154d) **defi** (61b), **deft** (147c), **defy** (28d), **degu** (132c), **deil** (139b), **dein** (66d), **dele** (26a, 49c,51b,53a,110b,123d,124c,130a,145c,161b), **dell** (43c,174b),

deme (71b,c,167d), **demi** (34b,122c), **demo** (122d), **demy** (113d), **dene** (137a), **Dene** (192), **dens** (90a,167b), **dent** (42c,77d), **deny** (36d,43d,129b), **depa** (188), **dera** (34c), **dere** (74a,79c), **derm** (147c,158d), **desi** (85d), **desk, deul** (77b), **deus** (68a,89b), **Deva** (23d,42a,b,56d,77a), **Devi** (147b,153b), **dewa, dewy** (101a)

- DE - aden (34b), Aden, Ader (18d), Ades (73a), edel (66c), Eden (6b,50d, 107c,113d,123c), Eder, EDES (71c), idea (54c,108c,124a,164d), idee (61d), idem (89d,164a), Iden (76a), ideo (34b,d), ides (41a, b,133a), odea (105a,164a), odel (48a,112c), Oder (132a)

- - DE aide (7b,14a,75d), Ande (193), Aude, bade, Bede (48c,50c,101d, 175b), bide (47c,50b,130a,158b,162a), bode (14c,60a,110b,121b), cade (25c,27a,76c,85d,116d), Cade (50c), cede (67b,70c,129d, 160a,168b,185d), code (21c,31a,40c,161c), Dode (96b), dude (40d), eide (119c), fade (181d,183b), fide, gade, Gide (63a), hade (66a, 148c,173c), hide (53a), hyde (188), Hyde (45a), inde, jade (33c, 65d,71d,166a), Jude (11c,96a), kade (144a), lade (24c,26d,43c,93b, 100a,132a,139d,161b,178d), lode (42c,99a,111b,175b), made, Mede (10a,b,13c), mide (110a), mode (54d,96b,157d,179a), nide (23c,72a,106c,116d), node (35c,85b,87c,94d,120a,124d,160c), nude (16c), onde (63a,178d), rede (37c,81d,138d), ride (46b,85c), rode (46c), rude (134b,172b), sade (91d), side (13d,22a,b,54a,58a,89a, 161b), tide (39d,75d,109c,141c,159d), Tide, tode (80a,148a), unde (179a), urde (86b), vade (42c,67d,89b), vide (89d,126a,142a), wade, wide (133d)

D - - E dace (57a,b), dale (43c,128a,174b), dame (67b,87c,166b), Dane (85d,107d,138a), dare (28d,41b,42a,74d,175d), Dare (57a), date (64a,153a), Dave (96b), Daye (123d), daze (157d), dele (26a,49c, 51b,53a,110b,123d,124c,130a,145c,161b), deme (71b,c,167d), dene (137a), Dene (192), dere (74a,79c), dice (65a), dike (49c, 91d), Dike (78a), dime, dine, dire (45d,55a,104a,163c), dite (150b), dive (42b,74b,119d), dobe (159b,c,172b), Dode (96b), doge (95b), dole (44c,118c,121c,129d), Dole (74c), dome (39c,133c,155d), done, dope (46c,105d), dore (61d,67b,69d,117d), Dore (50d,63a,b), dose (123a), dote (17a,90b,94b,97a,112a,139d,165d), dove (19a, 117d), doze (148a), dree (139b,140c,158b,172c), duce (29d), dude (40d), duff (125b), duke (107c), dune (137a), dupe (27c,41c, 72c,160c), duse (83c), dyke (49c,91d), dyne (59d)

D - - F daff (125d), deaf, doff (130a,161b), duff (125b)

- DG - edge (22a,96d,131c,143c,146b), edgy (106c)

D - - G dagg (118c), dang, ding (130b), Doeg (137c), dong, drag (74a, 125b), dreg, drug (105d)

DH - - dhak (48a,169a), dhal (12b), dhan (124c), dhao (24c), Dhar, dhaw (125a), dhow (88d,111c,175d)

- - DH sadh (77a), Sadh, yodh (91d)

D - - H dagh (76d), Dagh, dash (125c,162d), dish, doth, drah (188)

DI - - diad (113a), dial (25c), dian (46c,130d,170b), Dian (68d,69a,c, 102b), Diau (192), dibs (70c), dice (65a), dick (43a,55b), Dick (96b), dido (11b,26c,65a,122a), Dido (27a,172c), dieb (84a), diem (89b,116a), dier, dies (41b,89b), diet (14a,54c,84c,91b,176a), Dieu (61d), dika (23a), dike (49c,91d), Dike (78a), dill (13a,117c), dilo

(120d,168c), **dime, dine, ding** (130b), **dino** (34b), **dint** (48c,59d, 122a), **Dion** (96a,152a), **dipt, dire** (45d,55a,104a,163c), **dirk** (40b), **dirt, Disa** (111a), **disc** (31b), **dish, disk** (31b), **diss** (98b), **dita** (117a), **dite** (150b), **diva** (110d,123c), **dive** (42b,74b,119d), **divi, dixi**

-DI- **Adib** (155b, **adit** (51a,100a,114d), **edit** (20d,49d,123a,129a,131a), **idic** (79b), **idio** (34b,c), **odic** (79c,120a), **Odin** (7c,29d,63c,68c,175d, 183b), **odio** (83b), **udic** (108a)

--DI **Andi** (27d), **cadi** (12a,103a), **kadi** (103a,171a), **Lodi** (105d), **ludi** (133b), **Madi** (174a), **medi** (34c), **Midi** (151b), **nidi** (106c), **nodi** (35c,87c), **padi** (131b), **pedi** (34b), **rodi** (98c), **sidi** (103b), **wadi** (46c,106a,109a,128a,132a)

D--I **dali** (168c,169b), **dari** (38a,70b), **dasi** (77a), **deci** (163b), **defi** (61b), **demi** (34b,122c), **desi** (85d), **Devi** (147b,153b), **divi, dixi, doni** (21a,28c,168a), **drei** (66d,165a)

-DJ- **Idjo** (191)

--DJ **hadj** (98b,118a)

D--K **dank** (40b,101a), **dark** (47a,67d,109b,160b), **dauk** (95c), **dawk** (95c), **deck** (13b,41c,144d), **desk, dhak** (48a,169a), **dick** (43a,55b), **Dick** (96b), **dirk** (40b), **disk** (31b), **dock** (40a,117c,144d,179d), **dook** (184a), **duck** (26b,53b,179c), **dunk** (43c,79d), **dusk** (171c), **Dyak** (22b)

-DL- **idle** (174b,c,178c), **idly**

D--L **Dail** (49a,82b,c), **deal** (11d,16c,36c,44c,81a,168b), **dell** (139b), **dell** (43c,174b), **deul** (77b), **dhal** (12b), **dial** (25c), **dill** (13a,117c), **doll** (125c), **dowl, dual** (45c,171d), **duel, dull** (21a,32c,173a), **Dull** (94b)

-DM- **admi** (65d)

D--M **dawm** (190), **deem** (36b,85c,164c), **derm** (147c,158d), **diem** (89b, 116a), **doom** (42d,55a,134d), **dorm, doum** (168c), **dram** (46b,110c, 121d,148c), **drum** (105a), **duim** (188)

-DN- **Edna** (183c)

D--N **dain** (188), **darn, damn, dawn** (14d,41b), **dean** (33c,109d), **dein** (66d), **dhan** (124c), **dian** (46c,130d,170b), **Dian** (68d,69a,c,102h), **Dion** (96a,152a), **Domn** (135a), **doon** (140b,168c), **dorn** (164d), **down** (149d), **duan** (64b)

DO-- **doab** (157c), **doat** (17a,94b,112a,165d), **dobe** (159b,c,172b), **doby** (159b,c), **dock** (40a,117c,144d,179d), **dodd** (139c,140c), **Dode** (96b), **dodo** (19b), **Doeg** (137c), **doer** (8a,116b), **does, doff** (130a,161b), **doge** (95b,175b), **dogy** (46d,103c), **doit** (47a,169d,180d), **Doko** (191), **dola** (189), **dole** (44c,118c,121c,129d), **Dole** (74c), **doll, doll** (125c), **dolt** (20c,59c,157d), **dome** (39c,133c,155d), **Domn** (135a), **domy, dona** (83d,121c,151d), **done, dong, doni** (21a,28c, 168a), **don't, doob** (18b), **dook** (184a), **doom** (42d,55a,134d), **doon** (140b,168c), **door** (51a,121b), **dopa** (117d), **dope** (46c,105d), **dopp** (43c), **dora** (70b), **Dora** (36d,41a,43b,183c,d), **dord** (42c), **dore** (61d,67b,69d,117d), **Dore** (50d,63a,b), **dorm, dorn** (164d), **dorp** (73c,176b), **dorr** (32b), **dory** (21b,58b,144c), **dosa** (74b), **dose** (123a), **doss** (17c), **dost, dote** (17a,90b,94b,97a,112a,139d,165d),

doth, Doto (141b), **doty** (43d), **doub** (18b), **douc** (101d), **doum** (168c), **dour** (67d,159a), **dove** (19a,117d), **dowd** (143b), **dowl, down** (149d), **doxa** (48b), **doxy** (129d), **doze** (148a), **dozy**

-DO- ador (153b), **Edom** (18c,51b,79b,82c,84a), **idol** (48c,54c,55a,75b, 79d,112d,130b,184d), **odor** (138b,156a)

--DO **Bodo** (88c), **codo** (188), **dado** (41c,111c,115c,177d), **dedo** (188), **dido** (11b,26c,65a,122a), **Dido** (27a,172c), **dodo** (19b), **eddo** (162a), **endo** (34d,122d,183b), **fado** (121c), **Jodo** (113d), **judo** (84b,85c, 142b), **Lido** (83d,175b), **ludo** (65a,112b), **mado** (14d,57a,170b), **ordo** (22a,30d,122a,171a), **pedo** (34b), **redo** (165c), **sado** (26d, 84d), **todo** (22b,24d,35b,64c,156b), **undo** (11a,93d), **Yedo** (166d)

D--O dado (41c,111c,115c,177d), **Dago, dato** (95c,102c,117a), **dedo** (188), **demo** (122d), **dhao** (24c), **dido** (11b,26c,65a,122a), **Dido** (27a,172c), **dilo** (120d,168c), **dino** (34b), **dodo** (19b), **Doko** (191), **Doto** (141b), **Duco, duro** (190)

D--P damp (101a), **deep** (124a), **dopp** (43c), **dorp** (73c,176b), **drap** (61b, c,62a), **drip, drop** (43d,54b,100b,114c,168b), **dump**

DR-- draa (188), **drab** (23d,29c,33d,46d,53b,d), **drag** (74a,125b), **drah** (188), **dram** (46b,110c,121d,148c), **drap** (61b,c,62a), **drat** (100a), **Drau, draw** (42c,53a,92b,117c,121c,167d), **dray** (27a,154c,177b), **dree** (139b,140c,158b,172c), **dreg, drei** (66d,165a), **drew, drey** (154c), **drib** (46b), **Drin, drip, drop** (43d,54b,100b,114c,168b), **drub** (17b,39c), **drug** (105d), **drum** (105a), **drun** (132b)

-DR- adry (164c)

--DR sadr (94a), **Sadr** (155b)

D--R daer (22b), **darr** (163c), **Daur** (139b), **dear, deer** (28c,135a,154d), **Dhar, dier, doer** (8a,116b), **door** (51a,121b), **dorr** (32b), **dour** (67d, 159a), **duar, Duhr** (155b), **durr** (70b), **dyer**

-DS- DDSC (42a)

--DS duds (32c,166d), **Eads** (23b,24b,50b,82a), **odds** (28d,172d), **suds** (59a)

D--S dais (119b), **dans** (62a), **days, dens** (90a,167b), **deus** (68a,89b), **dibs** (70c), **dies** (41b,89b), **diss** (98b), **does, doss** (17c), **duds** (32c,166d), **Duns, Dyas** (66a)

D--T daft (59c), **dart** (13b,88a,100c,120b,153a,160c), **debt** (91d,109b), **deft** (147c), **dent** (42c,77d), **diet** (14a,54c,84c,91b,176a), **dint** (48c,59d,122a), **dipt, dirt, doat** (17a,94b,112a,165d), **doit** (47a, 169d,180d), **dolt** (20c,59c,157d), **don't, dost, drat** (100a), **Duat** (172d), **duct** (170c), **duet** (104d,171d), **duit** (190), **Duit** (192), **dunt, dust**

DU-- duab (157c), **duad** (113a,171d), **dual** (45c,171d), **duan** (64b), **duar, Duat** (172d), **dubb** (161c), **duce** (29d), **duck** (26b,53b,179c), **Duco, duct** (170c), **dude** (40d), **duds** (32c,166d), **duel, duet** (104d,171d), **duff** (125b), **Dufy** (63a), **Duhr** (155b), **duim** (188), **duit** (190), **Duit** (192), **duke** (107c), **duku** (95d,168c), **dull** (21a,32c,173a), **Dull** (94b), **Duma** (135c), **dumb** (153b), **dump, dune** (137a), **dunk** (43c, 79d), **Duns, dunt, dupe** (27c,41c,72c,160c), **dura** (153c), **duro** (190), **durr** (70b), **duse** (83c), **dusk** (171c), **dust, duty** (109b,162b)

-DU- idun (107d), **odum** (168c,180a)

- - DU Addu (68c,157a,182a), Jadu (95a), Kadu (191), kudu (11a), ordu (170d), pudu (41d), Urdu (77b), widu (102d), wudu (102d)

D - - U Danu (28a), datu (95c,102c,117a), degu (132c), Diau (192), Dieu (61d), Drau, duku (95d,168c)

D - - W dauw (24c), dhaw (125a), dhow (88d,111c,175d), draw (42c,53a, 92b,117c,121c,167d), drew

DY - - dyad (113a), Dyak (22b), Dyas (66a), dyer, dyke (49c,91d), dyna (34c), dyne (59d,173b)

- DY - idyl (114d), Idyo (191), odyl (59d,79c)

- - DY Addy (183d), Andy (96b), body (72a), cady (69d), eddy (37d,39d, 160d,180d), fady, jady, Judy (125c,183d), lady, sidy (123b), tidy (106a,111b), tody (19b,d,59a,166a), undy (179a), urdy (86b), wady (109a,128a,132a)

D - - Y Davy (96b,136b), dazy, defy (28d), demy (113d), deny (36d,43d, 129b), dewy (101a), doby (159b,c), dogy (46d,103c), domy, dory (21b,58b,144c), doty (43d), doxy (129d), dozy, dray (27a,154c, 177b), drey (154c), Dufy (63a), duty (109b,162b)

- DZ - adze (40c,167a), Idzo (191)

- - DZ Lodz

D - - Z Daez

EA - - each, Eads (23b,24b,50b,82a), eard (139b), earl (107c,166b), earn (42d,64b,99a), ease (7c,8d,35a,100d,129d,130b,c,150c), east, East (111b), easy (54a,146d,149d,172b) eats, eaux (178c), eave (133c),

- EA - bead (17a,122a,146b), beak (19a), beal (139d), beam, bean (91b, 142a,175a), bear (27a,50b,113c,155a), beat (58c,87b,131a,164d, 165b,180d), beau, dead, deaf, deal (11d,16c,36c,44c,81a,168b), dean (33c,109d), dear, feak (39d,171c), fear (113c,155a), feat (7a, 52d), geal (47d,163c), gean (29c), gear (32c,112a,167b), geat (77d, 101a), Geat (138a), head (29d), heaf (144a), heal, heap (117d), hear (75b,c,92d), heat, jean (37c), Jean (183c), keal (25a), lead (35d,43d,72b,74d,81a), leaf (55c,73c,119b), Leah (19a,84a,87b, 183c), leak (110c), leal (54b,94c,139d), lean (128a,148b,152d, 164b,166a), leap (26c), lear (139d), Lear (37a,143b), mead (46a, 78a,97d,99b), Mead (78a), meal (72a,130b), mean (15a,42b,146c, 156b), meat (59b), neaf (58a,73c), Neal, neap (165c,167a,177b), near (11d,32c,107b), neat (165c,169d), peag (144a,178a), peal (98b), peak (9a,38c,159b,186b), peal (131c,d), pean (64c,150b), pear (64a), peat (64a,175a), read (116d,157d), real (7a), ream (18c,37d,50d,113d,171c), reap (7a,40a,74a), rear (15b,23a,b,24a, 51b,76d,127c), seah (188), seal (10c,d,54d,64c,96a,118b,128a), seam (85b,d,160a,176d,185a), Sean (85b,96a), sear (23d,27d,72d, 138c), seat (98c,156b), teak (41a,48a,168c), teal (19b,20d,46c,d), team (38c,72a,113a), tean (140c,167a), tear (67c,87b,130a), veal, weak (55b), weal (124d,157c,180c,d), wean (8d,42a), wear (50b), yeah, Yean (88a), year, yeas (177c), zeal (12c,55d)

- - EA Alea (14b,31c,167d), area (37d,38a,44c,53a,93b,110d,127d, 138c,168a,186d), asea (39b,177c), brea (100b), crea (92c,151d), evea (82a), Evea (95a), flea (81b), Frea, Gaea (47d,69a), idea (54c, 108c,124d,164d), Itea (145d,160c,181d), odea (105a,164a), olea

(170b), **Olea** (110b), **Otea** (71a,82d), **oxea** (153d), **plea** (51a,52d, 122a,130b), **rhea** (37a,56a,111d,133d), **Rhea** (19b,68d,87c,103c, 186b), **shea** (25a,168c,d), **Thea** (162c), **uvea** (53c,82b)

E - - A   **Ecca** (66a), **Edda** (76b,79b,107d,136b), **Edna** (183c), **Egba** (191), **Ekka** (26d), **Elba** (105d), **Elia** (88a,115d), **ella** (152c, 158c), **Ella** (183c), **Elsa** (70a,93c,110d,177b,183c), **Emma** (183c), **Enna** (146a), **epha** (75c), **Erda** (23d,41a,47d,68d,69a,131d,177b), **eria** (13d,146d), **Erma** (183c), **Erua** (103c), **esca** (11c,44a,70c), **esta** (152d,164c), **etna** (75b,153c,157a,175d,177a,c), **Etta** (183c), **evea** (82a,95a), **eyra** (181d), **ezba** (188), **Ezra** (96a)

EB - -   **Eben** (96a), **Eber** (51a,75c,99d), **Ebro** (132a), **eboe** (28b,110a,168c, 169b), **Eboe, ebon** (20b), **ebur** (89c)

- EB -   **ceba** (169b), **debt** (91d,109b), **Hebe** (39c,69c,186b), **Nebo** (68c, 102d,103d,183a), **peba** (12d), **Peba** (193), **Reba** (18d,86c,144a), **Seba** (18c,39d), **sebi** (34b), **ueba** (188), **zebu** (22d,80d,112c)

- - EB   **bleb** (20c,23d,67c), **dieb** (84a), **pleb** (10d,35b,180b), **Sleb** (12a), **sweb** (160d), **theb** (188)

EC - -   **ecad** (73a,119b), **Ecca** (66a), **ecce** (17d,89a,c), **echo** (130b,d), **Echo** (105d), **ecru** (17d,23d,172b), **ecto** (34c,122d)

- EC -   **beck** (107c), **deca** (34d,122d), **deci** (163b), **deck** (13b,41c,144d), **heck** (100a), **lech** (102b), **neck** (83a), **peca** (190), **peck** (24d), **peco** (162b), **reck** (26d,75c), **rect** (117b), **sech** (97c), **seck** (173d), **sect** (42b,54a,114c), **teca, Teca** (192), **Tech, teck** (128b), **Teco** (192)

- - EC   **alec** (10a,57c,d,76c), **Alec** (137a), **avec** (63a,183a), **haec** (90a, 164c), **spec**

E - - C   **epic** (76b,120a), **eric** (115b), **Eric** (71d,96a,107d,138a,164a,176b), **eruc** (37a,56a)

ED - -   **Edam** (29c), **Edar** (18d), **Edda·** (76b,79b,107d,136b), **eddo** (162a), **eddy** (37d,39d,160d,180d), **edel** (66c), **Eden** (6b,50d,107c,113d, 123c), **Eder, Edes** (71c), **edge** (22a,96d,131c,143c,146b), **edgy** (106c), **edit** (20d,49d,123a,129a,131a), **Edna** (183c), **Edom** (18c, 51b,79b,82c,84a)

- ED -   **Beda** (101d), **Bede** (48c,50c,101d,175b), **cede** (67b,70c,129d,160a, 168b,185d), **dedo** (188), **gedd** (140a), **Leda** (27b,75d,120c,153a, 171d,186b), **meda** (110a), **Medb, Mede** (10a,b,13c), **medi** (34c), **peda** (114d,144b), **pedi** (34b), **pedo** (34b), **redd** (153a), **rede** (37c, 81d,138d), **redo** (165c), **Teda** (191), **Veda** (77a,b), **Yedo** (166d)

- - ED   **abed** (130c), **aged** (110a), **bled, bred** (23c,48c,127c), **coed, deed** (7a,52d,91a,166c,168b), **feed** (108c), **fled, Fred** (96b), **gled** (19a, 52a,87a), **heed** (14c,75b,109b), **hued, lied** (66d,150b), **meed** (128c, 131a), **Moed** (100c), **need** (42b,52d,87b,122a,178a), **Obed** (135d), **pied** (96c,103c,114b,117c,154a,174d), **reed** (16a,70d,97b,105a, 111b,118b,144b), **Reed** (163a), **roed, seed** (70b,111c,112c,119a, 151b,154a), **shed** (27a,90c,101b,144b), **sled** (40a), **sned** (93d,125a, 140a), **sped, syed** (103b), **tied, toed, used** (6d,73a), **weed**

E - - D   **eard** (139b), **ecad** (73a,119b), **egad** (100a,109a), **eild** (138d,140a), **elod** (49b,59d,79c), **emyd** (163c,167c), **Enid** (13b,25d,66b,163a, 183c)

EE - -   **eely** (185a), **eery** (172b,180a)

- EE - beef, been (149a), beer (18c), bees (185b), beet (175a), deed (7a, 52d,166c,168b), deem (36b,85c,164c), deep (124a), deer (28c, 135a,154d), feed (108c), feel (72a,142c), fees (128c), Geez (6c, 51d), heed (14c,75b,109b), heel, Heep (41a,43b), heer (47a,184b, 185b), jeel, jeep, jeer (138c,162b), keef (75d), keek (154c), keel (128d,134d,144c,d), keen (15a,88a,177b), keep (123a,130d),·keet (72b), leek (58b,76a,110c,177d), leer (9d,58a,67c,93d,112a,148c), lees (46a,142a), leet (26a,38a,139d), meed (128c,131a), meek (93d,99d), meer, meet (11d,13d,36a,50a,81d,142d), need (42b, 52d,87b,122a,178a), neem (96d,168c,169a), neep (140c,171b), neer (14b,86b,108b), peek (93d), peel (53a,114a), peen (73c), peep (93d,115c), peer (51a,107c), peet (64a), reed (16a,70d,97b,105a, 111b,118b,144b), Reed (163a), reef (129a,137a,145a), reek (49d, 53c,64a,148d,149a), reel (21b,40b,d,153c,154a,c,d,180d), reem (18d), seed (70b,111c,112c,119a,151b,154a), seek (141c), seel (20c,32c,143b), seem (11c), seen, seep (110c,116a,154b), seer (60a,124c,150c), teel (142d), teem (6b,121d), teen (139b,c,140b, 158d), teer (25b,69d), Tees (108a), veer (28d,144c,171b), weed week, weel (16d,57a,140d,180d), weep (39b,88a,104a), weet (19d)

■ - EE agee (13d,15c,38d), ajee (15c,139a), akee (168c), alee (15c,75d, 144b,157a,182a), bree (139a), byee (189), chee (189), clee (19a, 129a), Cree (192), dree (139b,140c,158b,172c), epee (55c,160d), flee, free (44a,70d,131b), ghee (24d), glee (99a,150b), idee (61d), inee (120b), Klee (113a), knee (85b), ogee (40c,101a,b,120b), pree (139d), Rhee (87c), shee (82b), skee (149c), slee (140b,148c), smee (19b,46c,d,118b,119d,141b,181b), Smee (116d), snee (40a, b,43d,87a), Spee (66d,70b), thee (124b), tree (11d,37a,66a,184b), twee, tyee (29d), usee, whee

E - - E ease (7c,8d,35a,100d,129d,130b,c,150c), eave (133c), eboe (28b, 110a,168c,169b), Eboe, ecce (17d,89a,c), edge (22a,96d,131c, 143c,146b), elde (119c), eine (66c), Eire (82b), Elbe (108a), elle (62b,c), else (18b,79b,111d), ence (158c), enne (34c), ense (139b, 158c), ente (70b,151d), epee (55c,160d), Erie (82c,87d), erne (19c, d,47b,54b,141a) Erse (28a,64b,82b), esce (158d), esne (10c,45b, 142c,148a,164d), esse (7a,18a,52d,89a,90a,159a,166c), este (152b, d,164c), Este (55c,83c,112d), etre (61a,c,62d,166c), ette (158a,c,d), euge (180a), evoe (15b,130d,181c), eyre (23c,31b,85c), Eyre

EF - - Efik (191)

- EF - defi (61b), deft (147c), defy (28d), heft (179d), Heft, jefe (152a), jeff (133d), left (42c), reft (32a,42c,44d,167b), teff (6c), weft (39a,165a,184b)

■ - EF alef (91c), atef (39a,48d), beef, chef, clef (104d,105a), elef (91c), fief (55d), keef (75d), kief (75d), lief (181d), reef (129a,137a, 145a), tref (172b)

E - - F elef (91c), Enif (155b)

EG - - egad (100a,109a), Egba (191), Egbo (141d), Eger (49a), eggs (112a), eggy (185d), Egil (107d), egis (14b,d,115a,124d,144b,154a,161a), egol (11b)

- EG - bega (188), degu (132c), hegh, mega (34b,c), pega (57a,130a, 158b), Pegu (24c,102a,127d), sego (24b,25a,92b,174c), tegg (143d,

292

171d), **vega** (110d,152c), **Vega** (155b), **Wega** (155b), **Wegg** (111d), **yegg** (24c)

--EG   **areg** (116a,137a), **Areg, Doeg** (137c), **dreg, Gheg** (8c), **skeg** (7d, 86a,144d,157d,184a), **sneg** (139b), **waeg** (19b,72c,87a)

EH--   **eheu** (52c)

-EH-   **behn** (137d), **Hehe** (191), **jehu** (46b), **Jehu** (18c), **lehr** (67c,112a), **peho** (19b,102c,106d), **sehr** (66d), **tehr** (27c,68a)

--EH   **okeh** (8d,37b)

E--H   **each, Elah** (18c,86d), **Esth** (16a,51d), **Etah** (51c,71d), **etch, eyah** (95b,108d,111c)

EI--   **eide** (119c), **eild** (138d,140a), **eine** (66c) **Eire** (82b)

-EI-   **Beid** (155b), **ceil** (92c,112a), **deil** (139b), **dein** (66d), **feis** (82b), **gein** (67d), **heii** (74b), **hein** (52c,61c), **heir, keif** (75d), **keir** (20c, 174d), **Leif** (107d), **Leir, mein** (30b), **nein** (66c), **meio** (188), **Neil** (96a), **reim** (112c), **rein** (29b,130c), **reis** (26c,29d,75a,103b), **seid** (103b), **Seid** (42d,101a,171a), **Seik** (77b), **Seim** (120c), **sein** (146c), **seip** (110c), **Seir** (51b,94a,103d), **seis** (147b,152c), **seit** (189), **Teig** (96a), **teil** (92b,c,168c), **veil** (74d,76c), **vein** (20d,157b), **weir** (40b,57d), **zein**

--EI   **drei** (66d,165a), **kuei** (44a), **kwei** (44a), **Omei** (24a), **quei** (189), **vlei** (38c,160a)

E--I   **Ekoi** (191), **Enki** (15b), **equi** (122d), **etui** (27a,29b,62c,106b,148d, 166d,174b)

EJ--   **ejoo** (55b,168c)

-EJ-   **Beja** (6c,191), **Nejd, reja** (152b), **Sejm** (120c), **teju** (151b)

EK--   **Ekka** (26d), **Ekoi** (191)

-EK-   **beka** (189), **feke, Peke** (45a,148d), **Reki** (16a), **weka** (58c,106d, 107a,127b), **weki** (55c), **Zeke** (96b)

--EK   **chek** (59c), **esek** (18d), **hoek** (39d), **keek** (154c), **leek** (58b,76a, 110c,177d), **meek** (93d,99d), **peek** (93d,115c), **reek** (49d,53c, 64a,148d,149a), **seek** (141c), **trek** (85c,93c,99d,168b)

E--K   **Efik** (191), **esek** (18d)

EL--   **Elah** (18c,86d), **Elam** (18d,37d,82a,116c,144b), **elan** (12c,41a,50d, 62a,153c,177a,186b), **ELAS** (71c), **Elba** (105d), **Elbe** (108a), **elef** (91c), **Elia** (88a,115d), **Elis** (22c,37d,71b,107c), **ella** (152c,158c, **Ella** (183c), **elle** (62b,c), **elmy, elod** (49b,59d,79c), **Elon** (18c,51b, 108a), **Elsa** (70a,93c,110d,177b,183c), **else** (18b,79b,111d), **Elul** (102b)

-EL-   **bela** (12a), **Bela** (18b,48c,78d), **Beli** (23c), **bell** (24c,39d), **Bell** (162d), **belt** (16a,31a), **cela** (62d), **cell** (39b), **celt** (30c,82c,123a, 156c,167b,179b), **Celt** (10a,180a,b), **dele** (26a,49c,51b,53a,110b, 123d,124c,130a,145c,161b), **dell** (43c,174b), **eely** (185a), **fell** (40a, 58b,76c,115d,147d), **fels** (190), **felt, geld** (162b), **gelt** (101c), **Hela** (93c), **held, helm** (144d,165d), **help** (14a), **kela** (189), **keld** (154b), **kelp** (82a,141c), **Kelt** (180b), **Lely** (47a), **mele** (74b,150b), **melt, Nell** (110a,183d), **pela** (30c), **Pele** (69c,74c), **pelf** (131b), **pelo** (83b), **pelt** (53a), **pelu** (30a,106d,168c), **rely** (16b,170b), **self** (48d,80d), **sell** (97a,115c,175b), **tela** (22d,98c,121b,166a,179c), **tele** (34b,

293

122c), tell (94b), tell (105d,129c,154b), Tell (160d), vela (98c
136b,149d), Vela (36b,c), veld (151a), velo (175b), weld (47c,85b,
173c), Welf (67a), welk (65c,96d,141b), well, welt (36d,131b,
145a,b,177b,d), yell (145c), yelp, yelt (151b)

- - EL   Abel (7a,25b), bhel (126d), coel (39b), duel, edel (66c), esel (66b),
ezel (47a,85d), feel (72a,142c), fuel (65c), Gael (28a,96c,138d),
goel (15a,75c), heel, Jael (147b), jeel, Joel (96a), keel (128d,134d,
144c,d), kiel (128d,134d), Kiel (25d), koel (19a,b,39b), nael (189),
noel (26d,150b), Noel (30d,96a), odel (48a,112c), Orel, peel (53a,
114a), reel (21b,40b,d,153c,154a,c,d,180d), Riel (129a), ryel (190),
seel (20c,32c,143b), tael (91d,179d), teel (142d), tuel, weel (16d,
57d,140d,180d), wiel (140d,180d)

E - - L   earl (107c), edel (66c), Egil (107d), egol (11b), Elul (102b), Emil
(96a), enol (29c,158b), eral (51a), esel (66b), etal (89a), evil (79c,
95d,147a,181a,185c), ezel (47a,85d)

EM - -   Emer (39b,183c), emeu (111d), Emil (96a), Emim (67a,100d), emir
(12a,103a,b,123c,134d,135a,171a), emit (43d,49a,53c,58d,83a,
142c), Emma (183c), emyd (163c,167c), Emys (167c,171b)

- EM -   bema (28d,31a,114b,119b,125b,137a), deme (71b,c,167d), demi
(34b,122c), demo (122d), demy (113d), feme (181b), hemi (122c),
hemo (34a,122b), hemp (26a,37a,56a,133d), kemp (139b), memo
(108b), Nema (34d,48c,134b,164d,176c), nemo (34b), Nemo (56a,
85c), Remi (10b), Rems, seme (45c,138b,151b,154b,155c,157b),
semi (34b,80b,122c,d), tema (12a,164a), Tema, xema (72c), Xema
(12c), zeme (55d,161b,180b), zemi (55d,161b,180b)

- - EM   ahem, alem (98b,155a,170d,171a), asem (9a,49a,69c), clem (56b,
158b), deem (36b,85c,164c), diem (89b,116a), haem (122b), idem
(89d,164a), item (6d,13b,42d,51a,90d,92d,107a,113d,114c), Khem
(113c), neem (96d,168c,169a), poem (51a), reem (18d), riem (76c,
112c,157c,164d), seem (11c), Shem (107c), stem (29b,125a,154d,
155a,156d), teem (6b,121d), them (124b)

E - - M   edam (29c), Edom (18c,51b,79b,82c,84a), Elam (18d,37d,82a,116c,
144b), Emim (67a,100d), enam (70c,77a), Enam (85c), etym
(133d), exam

EN - -   enam (70c,77a,85c), ençe (158c), endo (34d,122d,183b), Enid
(13b,25d,66b,163a,183c), Enif (155b), enin (20d), Enki (15b), Enna
(146a), enne (34c), enol (29c,158b), Enon (18c,d), Enos (7a,18d,52a,
70c,96a,143a), enow (50d,123a,158b), ense (139b,158c), enso
(34d,183b), ente (70b,151d), ento (34b,d,183b), envy (41b), Enyo
(12c,69c,178a), Enzu (102b)

- EN -   bena (176a), bend (39d,171b), bene (18a,83c,90a,106d,122a,
180a), beng (43a), beni (116a,142d), Beni (191), beno (113b,117a),
bent (80b), benu (49a), cena (88d,133a), cene (34c), cens (115b),
cent (36d), dene (137a), Dene (192), dens (90a,167b), dent (42c,
77d), deny (36d,43d,129b), fend (114b,178b), gena (29b), gene
(54a,76b), Gene (96b), gens (42d,132d), gent, genu (6b,18a,87a,
89c), hens (121d), Jena (105d,165b), keno, Kent (90d), lena
(56d), Lena (36b), lend (6d,79d), lene (36b,149a,172b), leno (37c,
53b), lens (67c,95b,111a,129b,162d), lent (54d), Lent (115d,141c),
mend (130b), mene (19a,73d,108d,185c), Ment (54b,164a), menu

(19a,27a), **Menu, nene** (19b,74c), **pend, pene, pent** (36a), **rena** (25b,132c), **rend** (32a,159c,162c,185a), **Reni** (83d), **Reno, rent** (58a,91b,138b,153d,162c,167c), **send** (42c,44b,95c,121c,130a, 144c,168b), **senn** (76b), **Sens** (63b), **sent, tend** (26d,80b,93d,100a), **tene** (34d,131b), **teng** (188), **tent** (26b,115a), **vena** (90a,175a), **vend** (97a,115c,142b), **Vend** (10b,148a), **vent** (8b,11b,110d,112a), **wend** (67d,123d), **Wend** (10b,148a), **went** (42c), **xeno** (34d), **yeni** (19b,161d), **Zend, Zeno** (71b), **zenu** (143d)

• • EN   **aden** (34b), **Aden, alen** (40d,138a), **amen** (14a,80b,94a,137a,149c, 175c,184b), **Amen** (86d,127d,164a), **aten** (150a,159b), **been** (149a), **bien** (63a,140c,179a,180a), **bren** (72d,95a), **Caen, Chen** (149b), **Eben** (96a), **Eden** (6b,50d,107c,113d,123c), **even** (51a,58b,79d,91d, 149a,173a), **glen** (43c), **hien** (30b), **hoen** (189), **Iden** (76a), **Iren** (127c), **Iten** (192), **keen** (15a,88a,177b), **lien** (65c,91a,124c), **mien** (11c,17b,26d,44c,96b), **omen** (14c,59d,60a,121c,123a,146b), **open** (26a,60d,81a,109b,112c,125b,172b,173c), **oven** (15d,78c,86b), **Owen** (96a,183c), **oxen** (10c), **peen** (73c), **pien** (13b), **rien** (62b), **seen, Shen** (68a), **sken** (164a), **sten** (72c,95a), **teen** (139b,c,140b, 158d), **then, tien** (147d), **T-men** (168b), **when** (180d), **wren** (19b,c), **Wren** (50b)

E • • N   **earn** (42d,64b,99a), **Eben** (96a), **ebon** (20b), **Eden** (6b,50d,107c, 113d,123c), **elan** (12c,41a,50d,62a,153c,177a,186b), **Elon** (18c, 51b), **enin** (20d), **Enon** (18c,d), **Eoàn** (41a,85b), **Eoin** (85b), **Erin** (82b), **Eton** (33b,50c,84a), **Evan** (96a), **even** (51a,58b,79d,91d, 149a,173a), **Ewan**

EO • •   **Eoan** (41a,85b), **Eoin** (85b)

• EO •   **feod** (55d), **Leon** (96a), **meou, meow, neon** (65c), **peon** (28c,59c, 99c), **Teos** (82a)

• • EO   **areo** (34c), **Ateo** (120d), **Cleo** (126b), **ideo** (34b,d,164d), **oleo** (34c), **skeo** (57d)

E • • O   **Ebro** (132a), **echo** (130b,d), **Echo** (105d), **ecto** (34c,122d), **eddo** (162a), **Egbo** (141d), **ejoo** (55b,168c), **endo** (34d,122d,183b), **enso** (34d,183b), **ento** (34b,d,183b), **Enyo** (12c,69c,178a), **ergo** (164b)

EP • •   **epee** (55c,160d), **epha** (75c), **epic** (76b,120a), **epos** (51a,76b,120a)

• EP •   **cepa** (110c), **cepe** (48c), **depa** (188), **kepi** (99d), **kept, Nepa** (106b, 178c), **pepo** (39b,64a,70a,98c,125c,154c), **repp** (53b,131a), **seps** (93b,142d), **sept** (31d,82b,143a,149c), **Sept** (45b), **Veps** (191), **wept**

• • EP   **deep** (124a), **Heep** (41a,43b), **jeep, keep** (123a,130d), **neep** (140c, 171b), **peep** (93d,115c), **prep** (138b), **seep** (110c,116a,154b), **skep** (16d,17c,77c), **step** (70b,112b,177b,d), **weep** (39b,88a,104a)

EQ • •   **equi** (122d)

ER • •   **eral** (51a), **erat** (89c), **Erda** (23d,41a,47d,68d,69a,131d,177b), **erer** (17d,150c), **ergo** (164b), **eria** (13d,146d), **eric** (115b), **Eric** (71d, 96a,107d,138a,164a,176b), **Erie** (82c,87d), **Erin** (82b), **Eris** (12c, 68d,109c), **Erma** (183c), **erne** (19c,d,47b,54b,141a), **Eros** (11c, 39c,68b,97c,182d), **Erse** (28a,64b,82b), **erst** (60b), **Erua** (103c), **eruc** (37a,56a), **eryx** (137a)

• ER •   **aera** (8a), **aeri** (34a), **aero** (8b,34a,b,58c,59a), **aery** (47b,51d,106c), **Bera** (86d), **berg** (79b), **berm** (25d,90d,145c), **Bern** (160d), **Bert**

295

(96b), **cera** (152d,161d,179a), **cere** (19a,114b,149d,179a), **cern** (41c), **cero** (57b,c,d, 180b), **dera** (34c), **dere** (74a,79c), **derm** 147c,158d), **eery** (172b,180a), **fern** (142a), **feru** (37a,56a,133d), **gerb** (56d,143d), **Gerd** (63c), **Gere** (183c), **Geri** (183c), **germ** (17d, 99c,134d), **Hera** (69c,85d,110b,126b,186b,d), **herb** (58b,158b), **herd** (39a,46c,72a), **here**, **herl** (16b,59a), **hero** (42b,124d,137b), **Hero** (90c), **Herr** (66c), **hers** (124c), **jerk** (153a), **kerb** (146b), **kere** (75c,128b), **kerf** (40a,108b), **keri** (75c,128b), **kern** (59c,172a), **Kern** (132b), **Kerr**, **Lero** (82d), **lerp** (51d,141d), **mere** (16c,22b, 62a,78b,87d,96c,110c,120d,146d,148b), **merl** (20b), **mero** (72a), **Meru** (77a,103d), **Nera** (165b), **Neri**, **Nero** (8a,126d,133a,172c), **Pera** (60a), **pere** (61c,63b), **peri** (54b,116b,c,122b), **perk** (84d, 93a), **perm** (49b,97d), **pern** (78a), **pero** (152a), **pert** (80a,93a,137c, 154b), **Peru**, **qere** (75c), **qeri** (75c), **sera** (11b,20d,59a,83a,180d), **Serb** (15d,148a,186c), **sere** (24d,46a,46c,138c,183b), **Sere** (158b), **serf** (21d,148a), **seri** (18b), **Seri** (192), **sero** (34d,88d,164b,178d), **Sert** (151d), **tera** (23d,84c), **term** (92b,105b,142b,166b), **tern** (19b, 32d,72c,94a,138c,141a,160a), **terp** (12b,123a), **vera** (140c,151b, 175c), **Vera** (183c), **verb** (7a,114b,184b), **verd** (71d), **veri** (28b), **vert** (71d,166a,171b), **very** (149c), **were** (139b), **werf** (54d), **werl** (15c,27c), **wert**, **zero** (31a,84c,108c), **Zero** (118d)

--ER **Acer** (96c) **Ader** (18d), **afer** (48a,182b), **ager** (47c,56a,89b,c,131d, 133b), **amer** (61b), **aner** (18d,96b), **aper** (32d), **Aser** (84a), **Ater** (18c), **Auer** (79a), **aver** (7c,14a,15c,41c,95c,140d,155c,160b, 184c), **beer** (18c), **bier** (33b,66b), **Boer** (151a), **Brer** (172b), **cher** (61b), **daer** (22b), **deer** (28c,135a,154d), **dier**, **doer** (8a,116b), **dyer**, **Eber** (51a,75c,99d), **Eder**, **Eger** (49a), **Emer** (39b,183c), **erer** (17d, 150c), **eser**, **euer** (66d), **ever** (9b,14b,80b), **ewer** (84c,85c,118c, 181b), **eyer**, **gier** (47b), **goer**, **heer** (47a, 184b, 185b), **hier** (63a, 185d), **Hler** (141a), **hoer**, **icer**, **Imer**, **Iser** (49a), **iter** (22d,76c,85c, 89c,114d,132a,b,133a,b), **jeer** (138c,162b), **kier** (20c,174d), **leer** (9d,58a,67c,93d,112a,148c), **meer**, **neer** (14b,86b,108b), **Oder** (132a), **omer** (51a,75c), **oner** (20d,53a,75c,162d,173a,d), **oser** (61b), **over** (6b,38c,80a,114d,130a), **oxer** (55c), **oyer** (38a,75b,119c), **peer** (51a,93d,107c), **pier** (23a,88b,180c), **rier** (180b) **roer** (72d) **ruer**, **saer** (163a), **seer** (60a,124c,150c), **sher** (65d,165c), **sier** (57a,118b), **ster** (158c,d), **suer** (124d), **teer** (25b 69d), **tier** (118a,134b), **tyer**, **uber** (66b), **user** (49d), **veer** (28d,144c,171b), **vier** (66c), **waer** (40b), **Ymer** (67a,131c), **Yser**

E--R **Eber** (51a,75c,99d), **ebur** (89c), **Edar** (18d), **Eder**, **Eger** (49a), **Emer** (39b,183c,), **emir** (12a,103a,b,123c,171a), **erer** (17d,150c), **eser**, **euer** (66d), **ever** (9b,14b,80b), **ewer** (84d,85c,118c,181b), **eyer**

ES-- **Esau** (82c,84a,128c), **Esay**, **esca** (11c,44a,70c), **esce** (158d), **esek** (18d), **esel** (66b), **eser**, **esne** (10c,45b,142c,148a,164d), **Esop** (53b, 54a), **esox** (57b), **espy** (44a,142a), **esse** (7a,18a,52d,89a,90a,159a, 166c), **esta** (152d,164c), **este** (152b,d,164c), **Este** (55c,83c,d,112d), **Esth** (16a,51d), **Esus**

-ES- **aesc** (12d,64d), **Besa** (68b,119c), **Bess** (76c,183d), **best** (41d,159c, 160a), **cess** (91d,94c,162b), **cest** (18a,67b), **desi** (85d), **desk**, **euer** (66d), **fess** (23c,51b), **fest**, **gest** (7c,41d,52d,133c), **hest** (35a), **jess** (157a), **jest** (169c), **Jesu**, **less** (100c,108b,141d), **lest** (59d,163d),

mesa (49b,76d,119b,161a), **mese** (71c), **mesh** (50d,106c), **mess** (22b,44b,77c,85d,104b,165c,173d), **ness** (26b,75a,124b), **nest** (38b, 74b,130d,149c,160b), **oese** (15d,119c), **pesa** (190), **peso** (99c), **pest** (108c,116b,118d,170a), **rese** (127b), **resh** (91d), **rest** (15d,91b, 104d,105a,115a,b,130a,b,161b), **sesi** (20b,57a,149b), **sess** (149c, 162b), **Tesa** (80c), **Tess** (73d,164c,183d), **test** (26a,51c,144a,169c, 170c), **vest** (32c,177b), **West** (9c,50b,109b), **Yeso** (72d), **zest** (55d, 72d)

● ● ES **Ades** (73a), **Ames** (9c,82a), **anes** (110c,140a), **Ares** (49b,51b,68c, 76a,97a,105c,110b,178a,186d), **ates** (160c), **Aves** (19d), **bees** (185b), **Bres, dies** (41b,89b), **does, EDES** (71c), **fees** (128c), **Ghes** (193), **gres** (156d), **ides** (41a,b,133a), **Ives** (9c,90b), **lees** (46a, 142a), **ones** (116a), **oyes** (38a,39b,75b), **pres** (62b), **spes, Spes** (69a,78a), **Tees** (108a), **tres** (19a,52b,63a,152d,165a,175c), **uses** (18a), **wies** (185a)

E ● ● S **Eads** (23b,24b,50b,82a), **eats, EDES** (71c), **eggs** (112a), **egis** (14b, d,115a,124d,144b,154a,161a), **ELAS** (71c), **Elis** (22c,37d,71b, 107c), **Emys** (167c,171b), **Enns, Enos** (7a,18d,52a,70c,96a,143a), **epos** (51a,76b,120a), **Eris** (12c,68d,109c), **Eros** (11c,39c,68b,97c, 182d), **Esus, etes** (177c), **eyas** (106c,173a)

ET ● ● **Etah** (51c,71d), **etal** (89a), **etat** (62d), **etch, etes** (177c), **etna** (75b, 153c,157a,175d,177a,c), **Eton** (33b,50c,84a), **etre** (61a,c,62d,166c), **Etta** (183c), **ette** (158a,c,d), **etui** (27a,29b,62c,106b,148d,166d, 174b), **etym** (133d)

● ET ● **Aeta** (94d,95d,100a,106b,117a), **beta** (71a,91c,141d), **bete** (61a,107c), **beth** (91c), **Beth** (8c,183d), **cete** (180b,c), **ceto** (34a), **fete** (55d,129b), **geta** (84b,145a), **gett** (44d), **Heth** (77c), **jete** (16a), **Jeth** (102a), **keta** (45a), **Keta, Ketu** (48b), **lete, Leti** (82d), **Leto** (11c), **Lett** (16a,90a,93a), **meta** (132d,133a), **Meta, mete** (9a, 11d,22b,44c,45b,98a,121c), **nete** (71c,108b,163d), **neti** (164a), **nett, pete** (136b), **Pete** (96b), **peto** (57a,177b), **Peto** (76a), **rete** (106c,119c), **seta** (23b,27c,73a,b,123b,153c), **seth** (98d), **Seth** (7a, 52b,68a,b,96a,98d), **seti** (34a), **Seti** (116d), **sett** (115a,156d), **tete** (61d,73b,74d), **teth** (91d), **veta** (104a), **veto** (94a,124a), **Veto, weta** (93c), **yeta** (84c), **zeta** (71b,91c)

● ● ET **abet** (8b,15b,50a,59b,75d,81c,141d,159d), **Ahet** (49a,102a), **anet** (43c), **Apet** (97c), **aret** (128c), **beet** (175a), **blet** (64a), **diet** (14a, 54c,84c,91b,176a), **duet** (104d,171d), **evet** (48d,107a,136c,169d), **fret** (28c,35b,111c,184d), **keet** (72b), **khet** (188), **laet** (60d), **leet** (26a,38a), **meet** (11d,13d,36a,50a,81d,142d), **oket** (189), **peet** (64a), **piet** (29b,95b), **plet** (135d), **poet** (49b), **pret** (188), **pyet** (95b), **spet** (16c,57a,142c), **stet** (91b,123d,124c), **suet** (54d), **tret** (9a,178b,179d), **voet** (188), **weet** (19d), **whet** (143c,156b)

E ● ● T **east, East** (111b), **edit** (20d,49d,123a,129a,131a), **emit** (43d,49a, 53c,58d,83a,142c), **erat** (89c), **erst** (60b), **etat** (62d), **evet** (48d, 107a,136c,169d), **exit** (114d), **eyot** (82d)

EU ● ● **euer** (66d), **euge** (180a)

● EU ● **deul** (77b), **deus** (68a,89b), **feud** (55d,126b,175b), **Geum** (76b), **jeux** (61d), **meum** (27a,89c), **Meum, neue** (66c), **peur** (61c), **Zeus** (135a)

297

--EU bleu (61b), Dieu (61d), eheu (52c), emeu (111d), lieu (118c,155d)

E--U ecru (17d,23d,172b), eheu (52c), emeu (111d), Enzu (102b), Esau (82c,84a,128c)

EV-- Evan (96a), even (51a,58b,79d,91d,149a,173a), evea (82a,95a), ever (9b,14b,80b), evet (48d,107a,136c,169d), evil (79c,95d,147a, 181a,185c), evoe (15b,130d,181c)

-EV- bevy (38a,58c), Deva (23d,42a,b,56d,77a), Devi (147b,153b), hevi (111d), Leve (62a), Levi (84a,90c), levo (91a), levy (14a, 162b), Neva (91b,132a), neve (56d,67c,70c,149b), peva (12d), pevy (91d,94c), reve (61c,104d), revs (131a), seve (63a,182c)

--EV Kiev, Stev (155b)

EW-- Ewan, ewer (84d,85c,118c,181b), ewry (133c)

-EW- dewa, dewy (101a), hewn, mewl (180d), mews (154c), news (165c), newt (48d,136c,169d), sewn, Tewa (193)

--EW anew (7c), blew, brew (35d), chew (97c), clew (16a,33a,77b,136b, 164d), crew (72a,106a), drew, flew, grew, knew, Llew (40c), phew (52c), plew (17c), shew (44c), skew (148a,160c,171c), slew (160a), smew (19b,46d,99a,137d), spew (35a,49a), stew (21c,44b,184d), thew (104c), view (93d,138b), whew

E--W enow (50d,123a,158b)

EX-- exam, exit (114d)

-EX- next (106a), sext (26b,111b,147b), text (21c,140d)

--EX Amex (184d), apex (39c,76c,115c,118b,159b,166a,167b), Crex (37a), faex (46a), flex (18a), ibex (67d,68a), ilex (77d), obex (22d), plex (60b), spex, Ulex (153c)

E--X eaux (178c), eryx (137a), esox (57b)

EY-- eyah (95b,108d,111c), eyas (106c,173a), eyer, eyey (74b), eyot (82d), eyra (181d), eyre (23c,31b,85c), Eyre, eyry (47b,106c)

-EY- Ceyx (73b), teyl (92b,c,168c)

--EY ahey (52c), akey (189), brey (194), drey (154c), eyey (74b), fley (63d), Frey (7c,68b,124d), grey (33c), hoey (114c), joey (86a,185d), Joey (96b,109c), obey (35c,75c), prey (119d,176a), roey (103d), skey (185d), sley (179b), Spey, they (124b), trey (26c,165a), Urey (14b,107c,138c), whey (100a)

E--Y easy (54a), eddy (37d,39d,160d,180d), edgy (106c), eely (185a), eery (172b,180a), eggy (185d), elmy, envy (41b), esay, espy (44a, 142a), ewry (133c), eyey (74b), eyry (47b,106c)

EZ-- ezba (188), ezel (47a,85d), Ezra (96a)

--EZ chez (14b,61a), daez, Geez (6c,51d), Inez (45c,183c), juez (152b), knez (123c), oyez (38a,39b,75b)

FA-- Faam (111a), Faba, face (159d,176c), fact (7a,128b), fade (181d, 183b), fado (121c), fady, faex (46a), fail, fain (42d,67c,183b), fair (17a,55d), fait (6d,61b), fake (123a,143c), faky, fala (129b), fall (46b,141c), falx (133b), Fama (135a), fame (130a), famn (188), fana, fane (30d,137a,162d), fang (167b), fano (51d,96b,113c,d), faon (33c,55a), fard (112d) fare (43c,59b,67d,123b), farl (138c, 140b), farm (165d), faro (65a), fash (140c,176a), fass (189), fast (56d,126c,141d,160c,173a,d), fate (42d,52a,87a,94a), faun (56a,

298

68b,137c,161a,184a), **favi** (138a,165d), **fawn** (33c), **faze** (43d)

-FA- afar (44c), Afar (6c)

--FA Abfa (76b), alfa (70d), gufa (21b,99a), Kafa (6c), kufa (21b,99a), Offa (163d), sofa (44d), tufa (121b,177a), Urfa (99a)

F--A Faba, fala (129b), Fama (135a), fana, flea (81b), fora (133a), Frea, Fria, fuga

F--B flub (22b), frab (138c), frib (43d)

F--C fisc (52c,134c), floc (149a)

--FD Wafd (49a)

F--D fard (112d), feed (108c), fend (114b,178b), feod (55d), feud (55d, 126b,175b), find (44a), fled, fold, fond (7c,94b), food (109a,176b), ford (177b), foud (54d,144b), Fred (96b), Fuad (54d), fund (6d, 101c,130c), fyrd (110a)

FE-- feak (39d,171c), fear (113c,155a), feat (7a,52d), feed (108c), feel (72a,142c), fees (128c), feis (82b), feke, fell (40a,58b,76c,115d, 147d), fels (190), felt, feme (181b), fend (114b,178b), feod (55d), fern (142a), feru (37a,56a,133d), fess (23c,51b), fest, fete (55d, 129b), feud (55d,126b,175b)

-FE- afer (48a,182b)

--FE cafe, fife (59a,105a), jefe (152a), life (19a,177a), nife (37a), orfe (57a,b,185c), rife (6b,c,39d,123b), safe (141d,157d,174d), wife (154a)

F--E face (159d,176c), fade (181d,183b), fake (123a,143c), fame (130a), fane (30d,137a,162d), fare (43c,59b,67d,123b), fate (42d,52a,87a, 94a), faze (43d), feke, feme (181b), fete (55d,129b), fide, fife (59a,105a), fike (139c), file (13a,127d), fine (49b,50a,104b,115d, 159a), fire (13a,43d,44b), five flee, floe (79b), flue (8b,30a), fore (63d,174b), free (44a,70d,131b), froe (32a,167a,179d), fume (129a, 149a,157d), fuse (98c), fute (51c), fuze (98c), fyke (15d)

-FF- affy (18b), offa, Offa (163d), offs (38c)

--FF baff (69d), biff, buff (134c,161d), cuff (148a), daff (125d), doff (130a,161b), duff (125b), gaff (57c,d,152d,153a), goff (32d), guff, huff (58a), jeff (133d), Jeff, jiff (101c), kiff (88c), koff (47a), luff (136b), miff (44c), moff (53b,146c), muff, piff (24b), puff (180d), raff (75b), riff (131d), Riff (18b,102c), ruff (19b,33b,63d, 137a), teff (6c), tiff (126b), toff (40d), tuff (121b,177a)

F--F fief (55d)

F--G fang (167b), flag (16b,50d,82b,88c,115a,155a), flog (180d), Fong (40b), frog (10a,17a,126b), Fung (191)

F--H fash (140c,176a), fish, Foch (63b)

FI-- fiat (35a,41d,48c,111b,137a), Fiat (83c), fico (169d), fide, fief (55d), fife (59a,105a), fike (139c), file (13a,127d), fili, fill (109b), film (164b), filo, fils (62d,150b), find (44a), fine (49b,50a,104b, 115d,159a), fink (19a,56c,157c), Finn (107d), Fiot (191), fire (13a,43d,44b), firm (154c,173d), firn (67c,70c,106c,149b), fisc (52c,134c), fish, fisk (24d,52c,134c), fist (80c), five

-FI- Efik (191), ifil (117a,168c)

--FI defi (61b), Safi (191), sufi (103a,116c)

F - - I   favi (138a,165d), fill, foci (28b), fuci (132c), fuji (84b), Fuji (84d)

F - - J   Funj

F - - K   feak (39d,171c), fink (19a,56c,157c), fisk (24d,52c,134c), flak (11a), folk (116a,169c), fork, fulk (173a), funk (63d,113c)

FL - -   flag (16b,50d,82b,88c,115a,155a), flak (11a), flam (169c), flan (39d,40a,114d), flap (17b,59a,104a,118d,161a,182d), flat (41b, 124b,173a), flaw, flax, flay (147c,157c), flea (81b), fled, flee, flew, flex (18a), fley (63d), flip (167c), flit (41a), flix, floc (149a), floe (79b), flog (180d), flop (54a), flot (173a), flow (157b), flub (22b), flue (8b,30a), flux (28d,58d)

F - - L   fail, fall (46b,141c), farl (138c,140b), feel (72a,142c), fell (40a, 58b,76c,115d,147d), fill (109b), foal (78c), foil (15d,55c,165b), fool (24a,41c,47a,146d), foul (173a), fowl, fuel (65c), full (7b, 130b), furl (132d)

F - - M   Faam (111a), farm (165d), film (164b), firm (154c,173d), flam (169c), foam (63d,154b), form (54d,143c), frim (58d), from

F - - N   fain (42d,67c,183b), famn (188), faon (33c,55a), faun (56a,68b, 137c,161a,184a), fawn (33c), fern (142a), Finn (107d), firn (67c, 70c,106c,149b), flan (39d,40a,114d), fohn (182b)

FO - -   foal (78c), foam (63d,154b), Foch (63b), foci (28b), fogy, fohn (182b), foil (15d,55c,165b), fold, folk (116a,169c), fond (7c,94b), Fong (40b), fono (137a), fons (60c), font (16b,171d,172a), food (109a,176b), fool (24a,41c,47a,146d), foot (115a), fora (133a), ford (177b), fore (63d,174b), fork, form (54d,143c), fort (63d, 157d), foss (44d,100d), foud (54d,144b), foul (173a), four (26c), fowl, foxy (38b,39c,181d)

- - FO   Bufo (166c)

F - - O   fado (121c), fano (51d,96b,113c,d), faro (65a), fico (169d), filo, fono (137a)

F - - P   flap (17b,59a,104a,118d,161a,182d), flip (167c), flop (54a), frap (45d,165c)

FR - -   frab (138c), frap (45d,165c), frat, frau (181b), fray (56b,60d), Frea, Fred (96b), free (44a,70d,131b), fret (28c,35b,111c,184d), Frey (7c,68b,124d), Fria, frib (43d), frim (58d), frit (64c,67c), friz (39d), froe (32a,167a,179d), frog (10a,17a,126d), from, frot (28c), frow (47a,167a)

- FR -   Afra (183c)

F - - R   fair (17a,55d), fear (113c,155a), four (26c)

- - FS   offs (38c)

F - - S   fass (189), fees (128c), feis (82b), fels (190), fess (23c,51b), fils (62d,150b), fons (60c), foss (44d,100d), fuss (22b,35b)

- - FT   baft (14a,53b), daft (59c), deft (147c), gift (123a), haft (76d), heft (179d), Heft, left (42c), lift (49b), loft (14c,69d,104b,178b), raft (27b,33c,58c,75b), reft (32a,42c,44d,167b), rift (30c,32a,58a, 110d), sift (140d,142c,146b), soft (48b,95d,99d,163a), Taft (29d), tuft (24b,32d,38c), waft (20d,58c), weft (39a,165a,184b), yuft (135c)

F--T fact (7a,128b), fait (6d,61b), fast (56d,126c,141d,160c,173a,d), feat (7a,52d), felt, fest, Fiat (83c), fiat (35a,41d,48c,111b,137a), Fiot (191), fist (80c), flat (41b,124b,173a), flit (41a), flot (173a), font (16b,171d,172a), foot (115a), fort (63d,157d), frat, fret (28c, 35b,111c,184d), frit (64c,67c), frot (28c), fust (105c,143b)

FU-- Fuad (54d), fuci (132c), fuel (65c), fuga, fugu (84b), fuji (84b), Fuji (84d), fulk (173a), full (7b,130b), fume (129a,149a,157a), fumy, fund (6d,101c,130c), Fung (191), funk (63d,113c), furl (132d), fury (157a), fuse (98c), fuss (22b,35b), fust (105c,143b), fute (51c), fuze (98c), fuzz (45d)

F--U feru (37a,56a,133d), frau (181b), fugu (84b)

F--W flaw, flew, flow (157b), frow (47a,167a)

F--X faex (46a), falx (133b), flax, flex (18a), flix, flux (28d,58d)

FY-- fyke (15d), fyrd (110a)

--FY affy (18b), defy (28d), Dufy (63a)

F--Y fady, faky, flay (147c,157c), fley (63d), fogy, foxy (38b,39c,181d), fray (56b,60d), Frey (7c,68b,124d), fumy, fury (157a)

F--Z friz (39d), fuzz (45d)

GA-- gaal (23b,174d), gabe (162a), gabi (162a), gaby (59c,146d), gade Gaea (47d,69a), Gael (28a,96c,138d), gaff (57c,d,152d,153a), gage (28d,98a,119c,d), gagl (160b), Gaia (47d,69a), gail (23b, 174d), Gail (183d), gain (7a,b,124a,181d), gait (96b,179a), gajo (107c), gala (55d), Gala (191), gale (181d), gali (6c), gall (19a, 28c,29b,82c,160c,176a), galt, Gama (121c), game (64d,154a), gamp (172a), gane (185b), gang (38c), Gano (132d), gaol (123d), Gaol (164a), Gaon (85b), gape (185b), gapo (60a), gapy, gara (190), garb (32c,46a), gare (61b,c,62c,127c,184b), Garm (178c), garn (67d,185b), Garo (88c), Gary, gash (40a), gasp (113c), gata (143c), gate (51a,121b), Gath (117a), gaub (116c), gaud (169d), gaue (67a), Gaul (10a,60d,63c), gaup, gaur (112c,181c), gaus (67a), gaut (88b,103d,132a), gave, gawd (169c), gawk (146d), gawp, Gaza (117a), gaze, gazi, gazy

-GA- Agag (18c,86c,137a), agal (17c,36d), Agao (6c,73c), agar (7d,28c, 39c,103c,141c), Agau (73c), Agaz (193), egad (100a,109a), ngai (48a,159c), ngan, ogam (82b,c), Sgau (88c)

--GA alga (141b,c), baga (171b), bega (188), biga (171d), boga (57d, 180b), fuga, giga (56a,105a), goga (24a), hoga (144b), inga (145d, 170a), Jaga (191), juga (27a), mega (34b,c), muga, naga (13d, 33a,55b,127c), Naga (24c,77a,88c,176d), Olga (135c,183c), paga (117a), pega (57a,130a,158b), raga (56d,105a), riga (118b), ruga (59b,185a), saga (79b,91a,138a,157a,161b,c,168a), Saga, soga (70d,152b), Soga (191), toga (132d,133a,b), vega (152c), Vega (155b), Wega (155b), yoga (10b,13c,77a), Yuga (76d), zyga (134b)

G--A Gaea (47d,69a), Gaia (47d,69a), gala (55d), Gala (191), Gama (121c), gara (190), gata (143c), Gaza (117a), gena (29b), geta (84b, 145a), giga (56a, 105a), gila (93b), Gita, Gjoa (144d), glia (106c), goga (24a), gola (27b,40c,70c,157a), Goma (191), Gona (106d), gora (81c), Goya (151d), gufa (21b,99a),

Guha (191), guia (90a,101a,165b), guna (106a,137b)

-GB- Egba (191), Egbo (141d)

G--B garb (32c,46a), gaub (116c), gerb (56d,143d), glib (58d,149a,177c), glub, grab (105b,142a,149b), grub (88d), guib (11a)

G--D gaud (169d), gawd (169c), gedd (140a), geld (162b), Gerd (63c), gild (14a,49c,69c,98b), gird (32c,50a,123a,160a), glad (85c), gled (19a,52a,87a), goad (80b,154b), gold, Gond, good, grad (28b), grid (17a,70d,119b,156d)

GE-- geal (47d,163c), gean (29c), gear (32c,112a,167b), geat (77d,101a), Geat (138a), gedd (140a), Geez (6c,51d), gein (67d), geld (162b), gelt (101c), gena (29b), gene (54a,76b), Gene (96b), gens (42d, 132d), gent, genu (6b,18a,87a,89c), gerb (56d,143d), Gerd (63c), Gere (183c), Geri (183c), germ (17d,99c,134d), gest (7c,41d,52d, 133c), geta (84b,145a), gett (44d), Geum (76b)

-GE- aged (110a), agee (13d,15c,38d), ager (47c,56a,89b,c,131d,133b), Eger (49a), ogee (101a,b,120b)

--GE ange (61a), auge (123c,132b), cage (36a), doge (95b,175b), edge (22a,96d,131c,143c,146b), euge (180a), gage (28d,98a,119c,d), huge, Inge (24d,67d,117c,119c), kuge (84c), loge (164a), luge (148a), mage (95b), page (51b,59b,142d,159b), rage (10c,30c,157a, 161d), sage (13a,90d,100c,141c,145c,180b,183a), tige (118a), urge (42d,46b,79d,80a,b,81c,124a,150a), wage (27a,115b), yage (23a)

G--E gabe (162a), gade, gage (28d,98a,119c,d), gale (181d), game (64d, 154a), gane (185b), gape (185b), gare (61b,c,62c,127c, 184b), gate (51a,121b), gaue (67a), gave, gaze, gene (54a,76b), Gene (96b), ghee (24d), gibe (8a,42c,84d,100d,138c,144c,149b), Gide (63a), gime (77d), gite (62a,118d), give (79d,123a), glee (99a, 150b), glue (7b,156a), gone (6b,15c,42c,44c,114d), gore (115d, 117c,154c,169c), guze (128d), gybe (144c), gyle (23b,174d), gyne (34b,55b,183c), gyre (31b,171b), gyve (55d,143b)

G--F gaff (57c,d,152d,153a), goaf (104b), goff (32d), golf (154a), goof, Graf (37c,66b,67a,107c,186b), guff, gulf (6c)

-GG- eggs (112a), eggy (185d)

--GG dagg (118c), hagg, hogg (144a), jagg, magg (95b), migg (96c), nogg (48d), tegg (143d,171d), vugg (28a,66a,132b), Wegg (111d), wigg, yegg (24c)

G--G gang (38c), Gheg (8c), glug, gong, grig (38c,70d,93a), grog (92d, 153d)

GH-- ghat (32d,88b,103d,132a), ghee (24d), Gheg (8c), Ghes (193), ghor (174b), ghos (30b), Ghuz (171a)

-GH- agha (35a,171a)

--GH dagh (76d), hegh, high, Hugh (96a), Lugh (28b), Magh (102a), nigh (106a), ough, pugh, sigh, vugh (28a,66a,136b), yogh (10c, 185a)

G--H gash (40a), Gath (117a), gish (102c), gosh, Goth (16c), gush (35a, 154c)

GI-- gibe (8a,42c,84d,100d,138c,144c,149b), Gide (63a), gier (47b),

gift (123a), **giga** (56a,105a), **gila** (93b), **gild** (14a,49c,69c,98b), **gill** (22d), **gilo** (48a), **gilt** (69c,77c,151b,185d), **gime** (77d), **gimp** (169d), **gink** (48b), **gird** (32c,50a,123a,160a), **girl**, **gire** (38c,83c, 167c), **girt** (50a), **gish** (102c), **gist** (95c,118c), **Gita**, **gite** (62a, 118d), **give** (79d,123a)

-GI -   **Agib** (12a,42d), **agio** (52c,60a,101c,123a), **Agis** (86d), **Egil** (107d), **egis** (14b,d,115a,124d,144b,154a,161a)

- - GI   **Bugi** (191), **hagi** (84b), **jogi** (76d), **magi** (123c), **Magi** (95b,116c, 183a), **ragi** (28b), **sugi** (84b), **vagi** (38b), **yogi** (76d)

G - - I   **gabi** (162a), **gali** (6c), **gazi**, **Geri** (183c), **goai** (106d,168c), **gobi**, **Gobi** (42d), **goli** (105c), **Guti**, **gyri** (22d,131b)

GJ - -   **Gjoa** (144d)

G - - J   **gunj** (70c)

G - - K   **gawk** (146d), **gink** (48b), **gowk** (146d)

GL - -   **glad** (85c), **gled** (19a,52a,87a), **glee** (99a,150b), **glen** (43c), **glia** (106c), **glib** (58d,149a,177c), **glim**, **glis** (45c), **glom** (155d,160d, 178c), **glow** (144c), **glub**, **glue** (7b,156a), **glug**, **glum** (102c,159a), **glut** (52c,70a,137c,159d)

-GL -   **agla** (7a), **iglu** (51c,149b), **ogle** (9d,53c,91a,93d,148c)

- - GL   **gagl** (160b)

G - - L   **gaal** (23b,174d), **Gael** (28a,96c,138d), **gagl** (160b), **gail** (23b,174d), **Gail** (183d), **gall** (19a,28c,29b,82c,160c,176a), **gaol** (123d), **Gaol** (164a), **Gaul** (10a,60d,63c), **geal** (47d,163c), **gill** (22d), **girl**, **goal** (8b,109b,120b,125d), **goel** (15a,75c), **Goll**, **goul** (102a), **gowl** (102a, 140d,185b), **gull** (32d,41c,42a,72c,99b,141a)

G - - M   **Garm** (178c), **germ** (99c,134d), **Geum** (76b), **glim**, **glom** (155d, 160d,178c), **glum** (102c,159a), **gram** (29d,99b,148d,160d,180a), **Gram**, **grim** (156a), **grum** (102c), **Guam**

GN - -   **gnar** (72a), **gnat** (59a,81b,99c), **gnaw** (20a,107a,178b)

-GN -   **agni** (88a,89c), **Agni** (56d,68b)

- - GN   **sign** (121c,146c)

G - - N   **gain** (7a,b,124a,181d), **Gaon** (85b), **garn** (67d,185b), **gean** (29c), **gein** (67d), **glen** (43c), **Goan**, **goon** (157c,163c), **gown**, **gran**, **grin**, **guan** (151b), **Gwyn** (40c,50b)

GO - -   **goad** (80b,154b), **goaf** (104b), **goai** (106d,168c), **goal** (8b,109b, 120b,125d), **Goan**, **goat** (135a), **gobi**, **Gobi** (42d), **gobo** (84d), **goby** (57d), **goel** (15a,75c), **goer**, **goff** (32d), **goga** (24a), **gogo** (16b,24a, 149c), **Gogo** (191), **gola** (27b,40c,70c,157a), **gold**, **golf** (154a) **goli** (105c), **Goll**, **Golo** (191), **Goma** (191), **Gona** (106d), **Gond**, **gone** (6b,15c,42c,44c,114d), **gong**, **good**, **goof**, **goon** (157c,163c), **Goop** (107d), **goor**, **gora** (81c), **gore** (115d,117c,154c,169c), **gory**, **gosh**, **Goth** (16c,163d), **goul** (102a), **gour** (112c,181c), **gout**, **gowk** (146d), **gowl** (102a,140d,185b), **gown**, **Goya** (151d)

-GO -   **agog** (47b,52c,86b), **agon** (12c,36c,41b,55d),71b), **egol** (11b), **Igor** (135d), **Ogor** (170d)

- - GO   **ango** (171a), **Argo** (12c,36b,c), **bago** (13d), **bogo** (117a, 168c), **Bogo** (191), **bygo** (114c), **Dago**, **ergo** (164b), **gogo** (16b,24a,

303

149c), **Gogo** (191), **Hugo** (63a,96a), **Iago** (54b,111d,143c), **kago** (113a), **lago** (83b,152b), **mogo** (74b), **Pogo** (121c), **sago** (54c, 59b,113b,125b,155c), **sego** (24b,25a,92b,174c), **upgo** (13c), **zogo** (136a)

G--O   **gajo** (107c), **Gajo, Gano** (132d), **gapo** (60a), **Garo** (88c), **gilo** (48a), **giro** (38c,83c,167c), **gobo** (84d), **gogo** (16b,24a,149c), **Gogo** (191), **Golo** (191), **grao** (189), **guao** (168c,169b), **Gulo** (183c), **gyro** (34d)

-GP-   **Ogpu** (135d)

G--P   **gamp** (172a), **gasp** (113c), **gaup, gawp, gimp** (169d), **Goop** (107d), **gulp** (46a,79d,160a), **Gump** (43b), **grip** (159a)

GR--   **grab** (105b,142a,149b), **grad** (28b), **Graf** (37c,66b,67a,107c,186b), **gram** (29d,99b,148d,160d,180a), **grao** (189), **gras** (78b), **gray** (33c, 77c), **Gray** (50c), **gres** (156d), **grew, grey** (33c), **grid** (17a,70d, 119b,156d), **grig** (38c,70d,93a), **grim** (156a), **grin, grip** (159a), **gris** (61d), **grit** (137a,b), **grog** (92d,153d), **gros** (47a,53d,146c), **Gros** (63a), **grot** (27d), **grow** (154b), **grub** (43c,88d), **grum** (102c), **Grus** (36b,c,38b)

-GR-   **agra** (26d,34d), **Agra** (161b), **agri** (89b), **agro** (149d), **ogre** (67a, 102a)

G--R   **gaur** (112c,181c), **gear** (32c,167b), **Ghor** (174b), **gier** (47b), **gnar** (72a), **goer, goor, gour** (112c,181c) **guar** (46c,59d), **guhr** (47d)

--GS   **eggs** (112a), **togs** (32c)

G--S   **gaus** (67a), **gens** (42d,132d), **Gens, Ghes** (193), **ghos** (30b), **glis** (45c), **Glis, gras** (78b), **gres** (156d), **gris** (61d), **gros** (47a,53d,146c), **Gros** (63a), **Grus** (36b,c,38b), **gyps, Gyps** (71d)

--GT   **togt** (77c), **Vogt**

G--T   **gait** (96b,179a), **galt, gaut** (88b,103d,132a), **geat** (77d,101a), **Geat** (138a), **gelt** (101c), **gent, gest** (7c,41d,52d,133c), **gett** (44d), **ghat** (32d,88b,103d,132a), **gift** (123a), **gilt** (69c,77c,151b), **girt** (50a), **gist** (95c,118c), **glut** (52c,70a,137c,159d), **gnat** (59a,81b,99c), **goat** (135a), **grit** (137a,b), **grot** (27d), **gust**

GU--   **Guam, guan** (151b), **guao** (168c,169b), **guar** (46c,59d), **gufa** (21b, 99a), **guff, gugu, Guha** (191), **guhr** (47d), **guib** (11a), **gula** (90a, 101a,165b), **gulf** (6c), **gull** (32d,41c,42a,72c,99b,141a), **Gulo** (183c), **gulp** (46a,79d,160a), **Gump** (43b), **guna** (106a,137b), **gunj** (70c), **guru** (77b), **gush** (35a,154c), **gust, Guti, guze** (128d)

-GU-   **agua** (152d,166c,178c), **ague** (30a,55d,95c), **ogum** (82b)

--GU   **degu** (132c), **fugu** (84b), **gugu, kagu** (106c), **Pegu** (24c,102a,127d)

G--U   **genu** (6b,18a,87a,89c), **gugu, guru** (77b)

GW--   **Gwyn** (40c,50b)

G--W   **glow** (144c), **gnaw** (20a,107a,178b), **grew, grow** (154b)

GY--   **gybe** (144c), **gyle** (23b,174d), **gyne** (34b,55b,183c), **gyps, Gyps** (71d), **gyre** (31b,171b), **gyri** (22d,131b), **gyro** (34d), **gyve** (55d, 143b)

--GY   **algy, Algy** (96b), **bogy** (153a), **cagy** (178b), **dogy** (46d,103c), **edgy** (106c), **eggy** (185d), **fogy, logy** (46d), **Nagy** (78d), **orgy** (26d,130d, 137c), **pogy** (57a,88a,98d,103c), **sagy**

304

G - - Y   gaby (59c,146d), Gaby, gapy, Gary, gazy, goby (57d), gory, gray (33c,77c), Gray (50c), grey (33c)

G - - Z   Geez (6c,51d), Ghuz (171a)

HA - -   Haab (97d), haaf (57d), haak (57b,178a), haar (139c), haba (151d), Habe (191), hack (40a,77c,184d) hade (66a,148c,173c), hadj (98b,118a), haec (90a,164c), haem (122b), haft (76d), hagg, hagi (84b), haha (55c,159c), haik (57b,65b,108a), hail (6d,15a,71d), hair (56b,164d), haje (33a,48d), hake (57a,b), hakh (46d), °hako (115b), haku (86d), hala (112b), hale (125b), Hale (9d,131a), half (101a), hall (37b,114d), halm, halo (14d,31b,92a,107b,131d), Hals (47a), halt (13b,28a,38d,156d), hami (78a), hand (60c,114c,115d,184c), hang (160a), hank (147c), Hano (125b), Hans (66d,96a), hant (67a), Hapi (66a,107b,136a), hapu (106d), Harb (191), hard (109b), hare (91b,132c), hark (92d), harl (16b,56b,59a), harm (40b,81a), harp (105a,129a), hart (41d,154d), hase (74d) hash, hasp (31d, 54d,153c), hast, hate (6a,43a), hath, Hati (48d), haul (27b,45d), have, hawk (19c,115c), hayz, haze (100c,174d), hazy (174b)

◾HA -   Ahab (18c,26c,85b,86d,100d,116a,180b), Ahaz (86d), Bhar (191), bhat (80c), chaa (162b), chab (184a), Chad (158b), chai (72d), cham (20a,29d), Cham (8c), chan (26c,130c), chap (55b), char (24d,26c, 170b), chat (9b,19c,161c), chaw (97c), chay (48a,128d), dhak (48a, 169a), dhal (12b), dhan (124c), dhao (24c), Dhar, dhaw (125a), ghat (32d,88b,103d,132a), khan (7c,26c,81b,93d,116c,123c,130c, 166c), khar (189), khas (153a), khat (105d), Phad (155b), shad (27d,57a,b,c), shag (73b,105b,161d,166d), shah (116c), sham (41c, 55b,60d,80a,123a,b,146d), Shan (13c,80d,88c,101d), shap, shat (87d), shaw (164b), Shaw (50c,53b), shay (110c), Thai (146a), than (35b), thar (68a,76d), that (42b,124b,129c), thaw, wham (157c), what (129c), whau (107a,168c)

◾- HA   agha (35a,171a), Akha (86a,c), Asha (191), Azha (155b), epha (75c), Guha (191), haha (55c,159c), Isha (174a), kaha (123d), maha (28c,88c,136d), moha (42b,83d), ocha (189), paha (67b), poha (74c), saha, taha (179b), tcha (162c), Usha (16a,150c),

H - - A   haba (151d), Haba, haha (55c,159c), hala (112b), Hela (93c), Hera (69c,85d,110b,126b,186b,d), hila (53c), Hima (191), hoga (144b), hoja (166b), hola (74c,152b), hora (22a,40b), Hova (95a), Hoya (14d), Hsia (30b,47c), huia (19a,106d), hula (74b), Hupa (192), hura (20a,137a), Hura, Hyla (10a,166d,169b)

H - - B   Haab (97d), Harb (191), herb (58b,158b), hobb (124b), hubb (118b)

H - - C   haec (90a,164c)

H - - D   hand (60c,114c,115d,184c), hard (109b), head (29d), heed (14c, 75b,109b), held, herd (39a,46c,72a), Hild, hind (15b,41d,45a), hold (95c,124c,130d), hood (38a,74d), hued

HE - -   head (29d), heaf (144a), heal, heap (117d), hear (75b,c,92d), heat, Hebe (39c,69c,186b), heck (100a), heed (14c,75b,109b), heel, Heep (41a,43b), heer (47a,184b,185b), heft (179d), Heft, hegh, Hehe (191), heil (74b), hein (52c,61c) heir, Hela (93c), held, helm (144d,165d), help (14a), hemi (122c) hemo (34a,122b), hemp (26a, 37a,56a,133d), hens (121d), Hera (69c,85d,110b),126b,186b,d), herb (58b,158b), herd (39a,46c,72a), here, herl (16b,59a), hero

305

(42b,124d,137b), Hero (90c), Herr (66c), hers (124c), hest (35a), Heth (77c), hevi (111d), hewn

- HE - ahem, Ahet (49a,102a), ahey (52c), bhel (126d), chee (189), chef, chek (59c), Chen (149b), cher (61b), chew (97c), chez (14b,61a), eheu (52c), ghee (24d), Gheg (8c), Ghes (193), Hehe (191), Khem (113c), khet (188), phew (52c), rhea (37a,56a,111d), Rhea (19b,68d, 87c,103c,186b), Rhee (87c), shea (25a,168c,d), shed (27a,90c,101b, 144b), shee (82b), Shem (107c), Shen (68a), sher (65d,165c), shew (44c), Thea (162c), theb (188), thee (124b), them (124b), then, thew (104c), they (124b), whee, when (180d), whet (143c,156b), whew, whey (100a)

-- HE ache (79a,112d,185b), Hehe (191), Hohe (192), tche (13d,30b,105a)

H -- E Habe (191), hade (66a,148c,173c), haje (33a,48d), hake (57a,b), hale (125b), Hale (9d,131a), hare (91b,132c), hase (74d), hate (6a, 43a), have, haze (100c,174d), Hebe (39c,69c,186b), Hehe (191), here, hide (53a), hike, hipe (185a), hire (49d,50b,91b,130a), hive (17c), Hohe (192), hole (6c,11b,110d,118c,147a), home, hone (110a,143c,180d), hope (13d,52d), hose (156c), hove (92a,157d), howe (77d), Howe (17a,82a), huge, hule (23a,134c), Hume (50c), huse (180c), hyde (188), Hyde (45a), hyke, hyle (97c), hype (185a)

H -- F haaf (57d), half (101a), heaf (144a), hoof (173a), huff (58a)

H -- G hagg, hang (160a), hing (13c), hogg (144a), hong (30b), hung

-- HH sahh (188)

H -- H hakh (46d), hash, hath, hegh, Heth (77c), high, hish, hoch, (52c, 66c), Hoch, hoth, Hoth (20c), Hugh (96a), hunh?, hush (17b,146c)

HI -- hick (185d), hide (53a), hien (30b), hier (63a,185d), high, hike, hiku (57a,106d,138a), hila (53c), Hild, hill, hilo (74c), hilt (73c), Hima (191), hind (15b,41d,45a), hing (13c), hino (106d,168c), hint (9a,39c,159a), hipe (185a), hire (49d,50b,91b,130a), hiro, hish, hiss (146a), hist (25c,93d), hive (17c)

- HI - Ahir (27b), Bhil (191), chia (136d), chib (167a), chic (148d), chid, ch'ih (188), chil, chin, Chin (30b), chip (69d), chir (29b,116d), chit (67b,98c,108b,116c,177c), chiv (87a), jhil, ohia (74c,168c), Ohio, Phil (96b), phit (24b), phiz (54a), Rhin, shih (189), Shik (171a), shim (91d,144c,162a,179d), shin (91a,d,140b,143c), ship, shir (36d, 65d,165c), thin (43b,c,148b), this (42b,124b), Whig, whim (26c, 54c,108c), whin (64c,70a,132b,181d), whip (58c,88d), whir (25c, 181a), whit (166c), whiz (25c)

-- HI bahi (60c), Bahi, pahi (21b,26a), tchi, Tchi, tshi, Tshi (69c)

H -- I hagi (84b), hami (78a), Hapi (66a,107b,136a), Hati (48d), heii (74b), hemi (122c), hevi (111d), Holi (77a), hopi (33c), Hopi (12c, 102c,125b), hoti

H -- J hadj (98b,118a)

H -- K haak (57b,178a), hack (40a,77c,184d), haik (57b,65b,108a), hank (147c), hark (92d), hawk (19c,115c), heck (100a), hick (185d), hock (91a,115b,182b,c), hoek (39d), honk (70a), hook (27b,39d), howk (139b), huck (167d), hulk (144d,173d), hunk, husk (53a,78d, 142a)

HL -- Hler (141a)

- - HL buhl (81a), kohl (53c), kuhl (53c)

H - - L hail (6d,15a,71d), hall (37b,114d), harl (16b 56b,59a), haul (27b, 45d), heal, heel, herl (16b,59a), hill, howl (39b), hull (141d,142a, 144c,d), hurl (167c)

H - - M haem (122b), halm, harm (40b,81a), helm (144d,165d), holm (77d, 82d,109a)

- HN - ohne (66d,183b)

- - HN behn (137d), fohn (182b), John (11c,96a,121a,186b)

H - - N hein (52c,61c), hewn, hien (30b), hoen (189), hoon (190), horn (11a, 105a,170b,182a), hymn (150c)

HO - - hoar (63d,71a,181a), hoax (41c,122a), hobb (124b), hobo (168a, 174b), hoch (52c,66c), hock (91a,115b,182b,c), hoek (39d), hoen (189), hoer, hoey (114c), hoga (144b), hogg (144a), Hohe (192), hoja (166b), hoju (84b), hola (74c,152b), hold (95c,124c,130d), hole (6c,11b,110d,118c,147a), Holi (77a), holm (77d,82d,109a), holt (36d,119b,184b), holy, home, homo (122d), homy (38b), hone (110a,143c,180d), hong (30b), honk (70a), hood (38a,74d), hoof (173a), hook (27b,39d), hoon (190), hoop (181b), hoot (112c), hope (13d,52d), hopi (33c), Hopi (12c,102c,125b), hops (17c), hora (22a, 40b), horn (11a,105a,170b,182a), hors (62b), hose (156c), host (13a,51d,104c), Hoth (20c), hoti, hour, Hova (95a), hove (92a, 157d), howe (77d), Howe (17a,82a), howk (139b), howl (39b), Hoya (14d)

- HO - Ahom (88c), ahoy (106a), b'hoy (134b), chob (23c), chol (118d), Chol (192), chop (98a), chor (164b), chou (61b), Chou (30b), chow (45a), choy (48a,128d), dhow (88d,111c,175d), Ghor (174b), ghos (30b), khot, mhor (180b), ohoy (106a), phon (94a), phoo, phos, phot (173b), rhob (64a,85c), Shoa (6c), shod, shoe (166a), shoo (46b,67a,138b), shop, shoq (169a), shor (136d), Shor (162b), shot (9d,43d,90c,174d), shou (41d), show (42b,44c,96b), thob (128a), Thor (7c,68c,99c,100c,109c,165b), Thos (84a,181c), thou (124b), whoa (156d), whom (42b), whoo

- - HO baho (122a), boho (117a,179d), coho (136d), echo (130b,d), Echo (105d), icho (67b), kiho (82a), moho (19a,78a), otho (133a), paho (122a), peho (19b,102c,106d), Saho (6c), soho!, Soho (93c), toho (79a)

H - - O hako (115b), halo (14d,31b,92a,107b,131d), Hano (125b), hemo (34a,122b), hero (42b,124d,137b), Hero (90c), hilo (74c), hino (106d,168c), hiro, hobo (168a,174b), homo (168a,174b), Hugo (63a,96a), huso (180c), hypo (117b)

H - - P harp (105a,129a), hasp (31d,54d,153c), heap (117d), Heep (41a, 43b), help (14a), hemp (26a,37a,56a,133d), hoop (181b), hump (124d)

- HR - Shri (17c,166c)

- - HR Bohr (14b,40d,138c), buhr (180d), Duhr (155b), guhr (47d), lehr (67c,112a), mahr (103a), mohr (65d), rohr (72d), Ruhr, sehr (66d), tahr (68a,76d), tehr (27c,68a)

H - - R haar (139c), hair (56b,164d), hear (75b,c,92d), heer (47a,184b, 185b), heir, Herr (66c), hier (63a,185d), Hier (141a), hoar (63d,

71a,181a), **hoer, hour**

HS - - Hsia (30b,47c)

H - - S Hals (47a), Hans (66d,96a), hens (121d), hers (124c), hiss (146a), hops (17c), hors (62b), hyps

- - HT acht (66c), baht (146a)

H - - T haft (76d), halt (13b,28a,38d,156d), hant (67a), hart (41d,154d), hast, heat, heft (179d), Heft, hest (35a), hilt (73c), hint (9a,39c, 159a), hist (25c,93d), holt (36d,119b,184b), hoot (112c), host (13a, 51d,104c), hunt (141c), hurt

HU - - hubb (118b), huck (167d), hued, huff (58a), huge, Hugh (96a), Hugo (63a,96a), huia (19a,106d), hula (74b), hule (23a,134c), hulk (144d,173d), hull (141d,142a,144c,d), hulu (55b), Hume (50c), hump (124d), hung, hunh?, hunk, hunt (141c), Hupa (192), hura (20a,137a), Hura, hurl (167c), hurt, huse (180c), hush (17b,146c), husk (53a,78d,142a), huso (180c), huzz

- HU - ahum, bhut (67a), chub (40c,154c), Chud (191), chug (53a), chum, (38d), Chun (30c), chut!, Ghuz (171a), jhum, Phud (110b), phut (24b), Phut (110b), rhum (8c), Rhus (159a), shul (161a), shun (15a, 51b,52a), shut, thud, thug (65a), thus (149c), whun (64c,70a)

- - HU ichu (10b,70d), jehu (46b), Jehu (18c), kahu (14d), Oahu, Rahu (42b,48b), sahu (153d), tchu

H - - U haku (86d), hapu (106d), hiku (57a,106d,138a), hoju (84b), hulu (55b)

- HV - IHVH (159d), JHVH (159d), YHVH (159d)

- HW - JHWH (159d), YHWH (159d)

H - - X hoax (41c,122c)

HY - - hyde (188), Hyde (45a), hyke, Hyla (10a,166d,169b), hyle (97c), hymn (150c), hype (185a), hypo (117b), hyps

- HY - whyo (59d,65a)

- - HY achy, ashy (113a,178a)

H - - Y hazy (174b), hoey (114c), holy, homy (38b)

H - - Z Hayz, huzz

IA - - Iago (54b,111d,143c), Ialu (48d), Iamb (59c)

- IA - bias (43b,123a), diad (113a), dial (25c), dian (46c,130d,170b), Dian (68d,69a,c,102b), Diau (192), fiat (35a,41d,48c,111b,137a), Fiat (83c), kiak (51c), Liam (181d), liar (98d), Lias (66a), miam (14d), mian (97c,147b,166b), Miao (30a,b), mias (111a), Mias, miau (27b,99b), miaw (27b,99b), Nias (82d), Piaf (63c), piat (11a), piay (98b), rial (190), siak (72d), sial (112a), Siam (163d,181a), Tiam, tiao, tiar (39a,75a,121a), vial (148c)

- - IA Abia (18d,137a), akia (74c), amia (22c,170d), apia (121b), aria (8b,98c,150a,c), Asia (48a), chia (136d), Elia (88a,115d), eria (13d, 146d), Fria, Gaia (47d,69a), glia (106c), Hsia (30b,47c), huia (19a, 106d), ilia (21d,77b,115d), inia (9b,109b), Inia (28c,45b), ixia (37a), Maia (76b,109a,153b,155b,177c), Naia (33a), obia (55d), ohia (74c, 168c), okia (190), raia (107d), Raia (147b), Soia, tsia (162c), Uria (14c,16d)

308

I - - A   idea (54c,108c,124a,164d), ijma (103b), ikra (27d), ilia (21d,77b, 115d), Inca (14b,30a), inga (145d), inia (9b,109b), Inia (28c,45b), Inka (193), Iola, Iona (28a,82d), iota (71a,85c,91c,114c,166c,176a, 180d), Iowa (193), Irra (68c,178a), isba (135c), Isha (174a), Itea (145d,160c,181d), Itza (192), ixia (37a)

IB - -   Ibad (191), Iban (47c), ibex (67d,68a), ibid (80a,117a,137a), ibis (48d,49a,177b), ibit (117a)

- IB -   bibb (97c,146b), bibi (87d), dibs (70c), gibe (8a,42c,84d,100d,138c, 144c,149b), jibb, jibe (8a,33b,35d,37b,42c,100d,138c,144c,149b), kibe, kiby (29a), nibs (116c), ribe (139a), Tibu (191)

- - IB   Abib (102a,b), Adib (155b), Agib (12a,42d), chib (167a), crib (96b, 120d), drib (46b), frib (43d), glib (58d,149a,177c), guib (11a), snib (54d,93c), stib (19b,47a,137a)

I - - B   iamb (59c)

IC - -   ical (158c), icer, icho (67b), ichu (10b,70d), icon (79d,92b,136a)

- IC -   aich (9a), bice (20d,117d), Bice (27b), dice (65a), dick (43a,55b), Dick (96b), fico (169d), hick (185d), kick, lick, mica (82c,100b, 146c), mice, mick (82c), mico (97a), nice (54d,119c,130c), Nice (98c), nick (30c,108b), pica (66b,95b,172c), pice (190), Pici (19c, 184a), pick, pico (65a,152c), Pict (23c,47d), rice, Rice (46a), rich, rick (74d,117d,154d), sice (71d,147b), sick, tice (9a,38c,51a,185d), tick (12b,20d,97c), vice (31d,158a), wick

- - IC   amic (9d), chic (148d) cric (131c), epic (76b,120a), eric (115b), Eric (71d,96a,107d,138a,164a,176b), idic (79b), laic (32b,90b,107d, 124a,141d), odic (79c,120a), olic (158b), otic (14c,d,47b), saic (86b, 91d,175d), Udic (108a), Uvic (70c)

I - - C   idic (79b)

ID - -   Idas (27b,71c), idea (54c,108c,124a,164d), idee (61d), idem (89d, 164a), Iden (76a), ideo (34b,d,164d), ides (41a,b,133a), idic (79b), idio (34b,c), Idjo (191), idle (174b,c,178c), idly, idol (48c,54c,55a 75b,79d,112d,130b,184d), Idun (107d), idyl (114d), Idyo (191), Idzo (191)

- ID -   Aida (110d,175c), aide (7b,14a,75d), bide (47c,50b,130a,158b, 162a,177b), dido (11b,26c,65a,122a), Dido (27a,172c), eide (119c), fide, Gide (63a) hide (53a), Lida (183c), Lido (83d,175b), mide (110a), Midi (151b), nide (23c,72a,106c,116d), nidi (106c), Ridd (94a), ride (46b,85c), sida (37a,126c,170a), side (13d,22a,b,54a, 58a,89a,161b), sidi (103b,166b), sidy (123b), tide (39d,75d,109c, 141c,159d), tidy (106a,111b), Vida (183c), vide (89d,126a,142a), wide (133d), widu (102d)

- - ID   acid (151a,162a), amid (9d,50a), arid (46c,85a), avid (47b,71a, 186b), Beid (155b), caid (35a,151d,152b), chid, Enid (13b,25d,66b, 163a,183c), grid (17a,70d,119b,156d), ibid (80a,117a,137a), imid (29c), irid (38d,67c), kaid (29d,66a), laid, maid (45b,142d), naid (63c), olid (55d,60c,148d,157d), ooid (48d), Ovid (132d,133b), oxid (112c), paid (129c), qaid (35a), quid (39b,166d), raid (59d,80c), said (174c), Said (42d,101a,121b), seid (103b), Seid (42d,101a, 171a), skid (148b), slid, uvid (101a), void (11a,49d,108d), zoid

I - - D   Ibad (191), ibid (80a,117a,137a), imid (29c), Irad (18d), irid (38d, 67c)

- IE - bien (63a,140c,179a,180a), bier (33b,66b), dieb (84a), diem (89b, 116a), dier, dies (41b,89b), diet (14a,54c,84c,91b,176a), Dieu (61d), fief (55d), gier (47b), hien (30b), hier (63a,185d), kief (75d), kiel (128d,134d), Kiel (25d), kier (20c,174d), Kiev, lied (66d,150b), lief (181d), lien (65c,91a,124c), lieu (118c,155b), mien (11c,17b, 26d,44c,96b), pied (96c,103c,114b,117c,154a,174d), pien (13b), pier (23a,88b,180c), piet (29b,95b), Riel (129a), riem (76c,112c, 157c,164d), rien (62b), rier (180b), sier (57a,118b), tied, tien (147d), tier (118a,134b), vier (66c), view (93d,138b), wiel (140d, 180d), wies (185a)

- - IE Abie (96b,107a), Amie (61d), Brie (29c), Erie (82c,87d), Okie (99d), Opie (50c), plie (32c,59b), soie (62c), unie (173a)

I - - E idee (61d), idle (174b,c,178c), ille (89b,d,163d), imbe (37a,56a, 133d), inde, inee (120b), Inge (24d,67d,117c,119c), inre (35d,80a), Iole (52a,76b,123c), Ione (24b,88d,94d), ipse (44d,89c), Irae (43c), isle (8b,53c,81d,82d,86b,88a), ixle (56a)

IF - - ifil (117a,168c)

- IF - biff, fife (59a,105a), gift (123a), jiff (101c), kiff (88c), life (19a,177a), lift (49b), miff (44c), nife (37a), piff (24b), rife (6b,c, 39d,123b), riff (131d), Riff (18b,102c), rift (30c,32a,58a,110d), sift (140d,142c,146b), tiff (126b), wife (154a)

- - IF alif (12b), arif (127d), coif (73a), cuif (139a,d,140c), Enif (155b), kaif (88c), keif (75d), Leif (107d), luif, naif (74b,105d), waif (157b)

IG - - iglu (51c,149b), Igor (135d)

- IG - biga (171d), giga (56a,105a), high, migg (96c), nigh (106a), riga (118b), Riga, sigh, sign (121c,146c), tige (118a), wigg

- - IG brig (72b,106a,144d), crig (20d), grig (38c,70d,93a), prig (112a, 116c), snig (45d), swig (46a,72c), Teig (96a), trig (106a,148d,154b, 169d), twig, Whig

I - - G ilog (132a,161b)

IH - - IHVH (159d)

- IH - kiho (82a)

- - IH ch'ih (188), shih (189)

I - - H IHVH (159d), inch, itch, Ivah (18d)

II - - Iiwi (19a,74b)

- II - Ilin (188), Riis (9d)

- - II alii (74c,134c), apii (74c), Boii (191), heii (74b), Ubii (191)

I - - I Iiwi (19a,74b), immi (189), impi (86a), Inti (159b), Ioni (192)

IJ - - ijma (103b)

- IJ - bija (168c), Ilja (57a,90d,173a)

IK - - ikat (53b,159a), ikmo (18b), ikon (79d,136a), ikra (27d)

- IK - bike, bikh (120b), dika (23a), dike (49c,91d), Dike (78a), fike (139c), hike, hiku (57a,106d,138a), kiki (27b), kiku (30d), like (13c,37d,146d), mike, Mike (96b), Nike (69c,100c,182d), pika (93a,128a,132c), pike (57a,b,76c,120b,153a), piki (95c), piky,

310

rikk (49a), sika (41d,84b), Sikh (77b), tike (29d), Tiki (120c)

··IK Atik (155b), Efik (191), haik (57b,65b,108a), kaik (96c), naik, raik (188,189), Seik (77b), Shik (171a)

I··K Irak (99a,d), irok (55b)

IL·· ilex (77d), illa (21d,77b,115d), ille (89b,d,163d), ills (170a), ilog (132a,161b), ilot (82d), ilus (88d,170b)

·IL· aile (62b,63a,182c,d), bile (30c), bilk (29b,41c,42a), bill (17b,147a), Bill, bilo (131b), dill (13a,117c), dilo (120d,168c), eild (138d,140a), file (13a,127d), fili, fill (109b), film (164b), filo, fils (62d,150b), glla (93b), gild (14a,49c,69c,98b), gill (22d), gilo (48a), gilt (69c,77c,151b,185d), hila (53c), Hild, hill, hilo (74c), hilt (73c), Jill (183d), jilt, kile (189), kill (38c), kiln (15d,112a), kilo (99b, 122d), kilt, Lila (183c), lill (15d,118a), lilt (93a,131a,147a), lily, mila (188), mild (32a,66a), mile (64c), milk, mill (126c), milo (70b, 87c,150d), Milo, milt (153d), nile (33c,71d), Nile (106b), nill (173d), oily (110b,172c), pile (45d,75b,117c), pili (34b,108d), pill, pily, rile (10c,d,82c,125a,156b,176a), rill (23c,102b,132a,148d,157b), rily (176a), silk (53b,179c), sill (45c,76c,165a,182b), silo (59a, 156d), silt (104b), tile (31d,56d,72b,95b,133c,163c), till (39c,101c, 173d), tilt (26b,d,166a), vila (54b), vile (16c,56c), vili (54b), Vili (109c), vill (176b), vily (54b), wild (38b,173d), wile (13b,41c,157b, 169c), wilk (65c,96d,141b), will (18b,43a,163c,177c), wilt (46b), wily (13b,38b,39c)

··IL amil (45a,48a,185c), anil (47c,80d,180b), aril (142a), axil (10c), bail (43c), Bhil (191), boil, ceil (92c,112a), chil, coil (39d,171c, 185a), Dail (49a,82b,c), deil (139b), Egil (107d), Emil (96a), evil (79c,95d,147a,181a,185c), fail, foil (15d,55c,165b), gail (23b, 174d), Gail (183d), hail (6d,15a,71d), ifil (117a,168c), ipil (117a, 168c,169a), Ixil (192), jail (123d), jhil, kail (8c,22a,25a,79b), mail (12d,99b,121c), moil (46c,184c), nail (31d,54d,141d,161d,173a), Neil (96a), noil (87c,178b), pail Phil (96b), rail (16b,19b,c,37a,97b, 138c,150c,177b), roil (44c,104b,156b,170d,176a), sail (144c,185a), skil (57a), soil (154d,159a,163c), tail (11d,27d,59b,143b), teil (92b, c,168c), toil (46c,184c), vail (94b,124a,174b), veil (74d,76c), wail (39b,88a), ypil (117a,168c)

I··L ical (158c), idol (48c,54c,55a,75b,79d,112d,130b,184d), idyl (114d), ifil (117a,168c), ipil (117a,168c,169a), itol (158b), Ixil (192)

IM·· imam (25c,102d,103a), imbe (37a,56a,133d), Imer, imid (29c), immi (189), impi (86a)

·IM· cima (83b,c), dime, gime (77d), gimp (169d), Hima (191), lima (17b,152b,174d), Lima (31b), limb (12d,22d), lime (25b,27d,31b, 33c,102d,168c), limn (45d,121c), limp (58a,81a,177d), limu (141c), limy (176d), mima (185d), mime (24a,71b,85a,100a), Mime (131d, 148d), mimi (14d), Mimi (87b,110d,125b,183d), nimb (31b, 73b,92a,107b,131d), oime (8b), pima (37c), Pima (192), rima (23a,30c,32a,58a,110d), rime (30c,36a,58a,63d,77c), rimu (79d,106d,129a,168c), rimy (63d), sima (132b) sime (101d), Simi (82d), simp (59c,146d), time (47a,131a), Yima (84a,116b,c), Zimb (6c)

311

--IM Anim (18d), Akim (135d,191), alim (103b,162c), brim, Clim (12b), duim (188), Emim (67a,100d), frim (58d), glim, grim (156a), maim (43d,81a,105c), prim (156b), Seim (120c), shim (91d,144c,162a, 179d), skim (67c), slim (148b,160a), swim (58c), trim (40a,106a, 154b,160a,165c,169d), urim (18d,23a,110a), whim (26c,54c,108c), zaim (170d)

I--M idem (89d,164a), imam (25c,102d,103a), item (6d,13b,42d,51a, 90d,92d,107a,113d,114c)

IN-- inar (65b), Inca (14b,30a), inch, inde, inee (120b), Inez (45c,183c), inga (145d,170a), Inge (24d,67d,117c,119c), inia (9b,109b), Inia (28c,45b), Inka (193), inky (20b), inly, inre (35d,80a), inro (84b,c, 106c), Inti (159b), into (123a,183b)

-IN- aine (49b,62c), Aine (142c), Aino (84a,c), aint, Ainu (84a,c), bina (77a), bind (33b,165c), bine (145b,156a,171c,176b), bing, binh (189), Bini (191), binn (22c), bino (113b,117a), cine (104b, 152c), cinq (61d), dine, ding (130b), dino (34b), dint (48c,59d, 122a), fine (49b,50a,104b,115d,159a), fink (19a,56c,157c), Finn (107d), gink (48b), hind (15b,41d,45a), hing (13c), hino (106d, 168c), hint (9a,39c,159a), jink, jinn (42b,103b,153c), jinx (78a), kina (126d), kind (150d,153a,174d), kine (38a,112c), king (26c, 29c), kink (38b,171c), kino (27c,34c,47c,72c,98b,161d,168c), lina (188), Lina (183d), line (12b,22b,36d,38a,126c,134b,157b,158b, 162d,175c), ling (24c,57a,b,75b,178c), link (36a,81d,85b), Linn (120d,140a,c,168c,178d), lino, lint (46a,58d), liny (157b), Linz (40d), mina (10b,70b,71d), Mina (23a,183d), mind (75c,81d,93d, 109b), mine (69c,79d,111b,124c), Ming (30b,c), mink (176d), mino (84c), mint (13a,33b,58b,76a), minx (116c), miny, nina (152a), Nina (26c,33d,68d,183d), nine (26c,104d), nino (152a), pina (35d,118b), pine (36a,52a,88c,93c,168c,d,169a), ping, pink (26d,33c,60c,138a), pino (152c), pint (67b), piny, rind (53a, 115c), Rind (109c,174b), rine (44d,75d,135c), ring (50a), rink (147c,154a), sina (46c), Sina (102d,103d), Sind, sine (64c,66b,90a, 97c,126a,163b,169d,183b), sing (26d,178a), sinh (97c), sink (41c, 43c,46b,158a), sino (34a), Tina (183d), tind (86b), tine (11b,124b, 167b), ting (166a), Ting (30c), Tino (136d), tint (33c,d,114d), tiny (100c,148c), vina (77a,105a), vine (32b), vino (92d,182b), vint (26c,182c), viny, wind (33b,39d,171c,185a), wine, wing (10d,58c, 59a,118b,d), wink (107a), winy (176c), Xina (183d), zinc (21a), zing

--IN akin (8b,92b,129c), alin (188), amin (9d), Asin (102a), ayin (91c), bain (61a), brin (32c,54c,146c), cain (169c), Cain (6a,7a,50d,88a, 104c,143c), chin, Chin (30b), coin (19b,37a,100c,101c,179d), crin (146c), dain (188), dein (66d), Drin, enin (20d), Eoin (85b), Erin (82b), fain (42d,67c,183b), gain (7a,b,124a), gein (67d), grin, hein (52c,61c), Jain (77b), join (36a,173c), Kain, lain, liin (188), loin (98a), main (29d,35d,123d), mein (30b), nein (66c), Odin (7c, 29d,63c,68c,175d,183b), pain (7c), rain (121d,162d), rein (130c), Rhin, ruin (42d), sain (20c,38d,48a), sein (146c), shin (91a,d,140b, 143c), skin (53a,76c,115c,d), spin (131a,180d), tain (166a), thin (43b,c,148b), trin (169d), Tsin (30b), twin (45c,171d), vain (81a), vein (20d,157c), wain (177b), Wain, whin (64c,70a,132b,181d),

312

zain (41a), zein

I - - N Iban (47c), icon (79d,92b,136a), Iden (76a), Idun (107d), Ikon (79d,136a), Iran (6a,48c,116b), Iren (127c), iron (55c,d,69d,81a, 97b,143b,149a,173d,179c), Iten (192), Ivan (40c,85b,96a)

IO - - Iola, Iole (52a,76b,123c), Iona (28a,82d), Ione (24b,88d,94d), Ioni (192), iota (71a,85c,91c,114c,166c,176a,180d), Iowa (193)

- IO - biod (79c,59d), bion (117b), bios (92a), cion (42d,70b,145b,148b, 154b,156a), Dion (96a,152a), Fiot (191), lion (55b,86c), niog (33a,168c), niou (188), pion (43c,52b), piot (95b), riot (44c, 111d,170c,173d), siol (82c), sion (125c,158c), Sion (75b,c,83a,157d), tion (158b), Tiou (192), viol (105a), Zion (75b,c,83a,157d)

- - IO agio (52c,60a,101c,123a), apio (125b), Clio (104d), idio (34b,c), meio (188), moio (188), naio (107a,168c), noio (107c,163c), odio (83b), Ohio, olio (44b,77c,98c,100d,121d), Scio, skio (57d), trio (104d,165a,169c), Unio (105c)

I - - O Iago (54b,111d,143c), icho (67b), ideo (34b,d,164d), idio (34b,c), Idjo (191), Idyo (191), Idzo (191) ikmo (18b) inro (84b,c,106c), into (123a), ipso (89c), itmo (18b)

IP - - ipil (117a,168c,169a), ipse (44d,89c), ipso (89c)

- IP - aipi (27a), cipo (91d), dipt, hipe (185a), kipp, lipa (54d), nipa (14b, 46b,48a,164a,168c), pipa (159d) pipe (105a,180d,182a), pipi (106d, 119d), pipy (145d), ripa (16b,131d), ripe (58a,97c,98c), Sipe (101a, 110c,140b), tipe (168b), tipi (181b), wipe, Xipe (15c), Zipa (29d), zipp, Zips (40c)

- - IP atip (14b,166a), chip (69d), clip (54d,143d), drip, flip (167c), grip (159a), knip (115c), quip (183a,b), raip (36d), seip (110c), ship, skip (110b,114c,147c), slip (67c,119a), snip (32b,40a), trip (85c), whip (58c,88d)

I - - Q Iraq (99a,d)

IR - - Irad (18d), Irae (43c), Irak (99a,d), Iran (6a,48c,116b), Iraq (99a,d), Iras (11b,32a), Iren (127c), irid (38d,67c), iris (53c 58a,111c), Iris (127c), Irma (96d), irok (55b), iron (55c,d,69d,81a,97b,143b,149a, 173d,179c), Irra (68c,178a), irus (109d)

- IR - Aira (70d), aire (82c), Aire, airs (123b), airy (176d,177a), bird, birl (93c,131a,153c), birn (31d,139a), birr (180d), cirl (24c), circ (31a), dire (45d,55a,104a,163c), dirk (40b), dirt, Eire (82b), fire (13a,43d,44b), firm (154c,173d), firn (67c,70c,106c,149b), gird (32c,50a,123a,160a), girl, giro (38c,83c,167c), girt (50a), hire (49d,50b,91b,130a), hiro, kiri (86a,87c,115a,168c), kirk (31a,139b), lira (28b,79a,170d), lire (62c), Mira (155b,174d) mire (21c,104b), mirk (41a,67d), miro (19a,106d,184a), Miro (113a, 151d), miry, pirn (21b,129a,179b), Piro (192), pirr (181a), rire (62a), sire (17d 55a,59d,124a,163b,166b), siri (18b), tire (15a,21a, 52d,55a,179b,180d), tiro (9b,17d,108c), Vira (191), vire (11a,13b), wire, wiry (147a,167c), zira (188)

- - IR Abir (129a), Ahir (27b), amir (7c,12a,103a,b,123c,170d), chir (29b,116d), coir (33a,37a,56a,133d) cuir (45c,62a), emir (12a, 103a,b,123c,134d,135a,171a), fair (17a,55d), hair (56b,164d), heir, kair, keir (20c,174d), koir (33a), lair (37c,42b), Leir, loir (45c),

313

Loir, Muir (8b,142c), **Nair** (45d), **noir** (61b,134b), **pair** (22d,37d, 85b,171d), **sair** (140b,150d), **Seir** (51b,94a,103d), **shir** (36d,65d, 165c), **skir, soir** (61c), **spir** (97c), **stir** (8a,13a,35b,78d,100d), **tair** (68a,76d), **vair** (64c,154c), **weir** (40b,57d), **whir** (25c,181a), **Ymir** (67a,131c)

I - - R **icer, Igor** (135d), **Imer, inar** (65b), **Isar** (41a,104c,132a), **Iser** (49a), **iter** (22d,76c,85c,89c,114d,132a,b,133a,b), **Iyar** (102b), **izar** (65b,103b), **Izar** (155b)

IS - - **Isar** (41a,104c,132a), **isba** (135c), **Iser** (49a), **Isha** (174a), **Isis** (68d, 78c,111d), **isle** (8b,53c,81d,82d,86b,88a), **ismy** (45a)

- IS - **bisa** (11a), **bise** (182a), **bish** (120b), **bisk** (120b,151a), **cise** (147b), **cist** (22c,29d,156c), **Disa** (111a), **disc** (31b), **dish, disk** (31b), **diss** (98b), **fisc** (52c,134c), **fish, fisk** (24d,52c,134c), **fist** (80c), **gish** (102c), **gist** (95c,118c), **hish, hiss** (146a), **hist** (25c,93d), **kish** (16d,70c), **Kish** (137c), **kiss** (148c), **kist** (29d,58a,139b), **Lisa** (183d), **lisp** (153b), **liss** (54b,58b,60c,129d,140a), **list** (26d,27b, 75b,83d,134a,138b,165d), **mise** (8a,10a,70c), **miss, mist** (46b,59b, 59b,174d), **Nish** (19d), **nisi** (90a,173c), **Oise, Pisa** (90c), **pise** (127d), **pish** (36c,107d), **pisk** (9c,19b), **piso** (189), **pist** (25c), **rise** (49d,80b,155a), **Rise** (110d,150c), **risk** (74d), **risp** (99a), **Riss** (66a), **sise** (62c,147b), **sish** (79c), **sisi** (121b), **sist** (139b), **visa** (114d), **vise** (31d,77d,114d), **viss** (189), **wise** (136b), **wish** (42d), **wisp** (148c), **wist** (87c)

- - IS **acis** (64b), **Agis** (86d), **anis** (55c), **Apis** (17c,24b,49a,125a,136a), **aris** (101b), **atis** (76d,102a), **avis** (89a), **Avis** (183c), **axis** (28b, 41d,77c,153c), **bois** (62b,63a,183d), **Bois, cris** (40b,95d), **dais** (119b), **egis** (14b,d,115a,124d,144b,154a,161a), **Elis** (22c,37d, 71b,107c), **Eris** (12c,68d,109c), **feis** (82b), **glis** (45c), **gris** (61d), **ibis** (48d,49a,177b), **iris** (53c,58a,111c), **Iris** (127c), **kris** (40b,95d), **Isis** (68d,78c,111d), **itis** (158c), **Lais** (17c), **Lois** (165d,183c), **mais** (61b), **nais** (63c,132a), **Otis** (9c,d,24d,82a,111a), **Ovis** (143d), **pais** (37d), **rais** (26c,29d,75a,103b), **Rais** (106b), **reis** (26c,29d,75a, 103b), **Riis** (9d), **sais** (48d,71d), **seis** (147b,152c), **this** (42b,124b), **tris** (122d), **unis** (91b), **Upis** (13b)

I - - S **ibis** (48d,49a,177b), **Ibis, Idas** (27b,71c), **ides** (41a,b,133a), **ills** (170a), **Ilus** (88d,170b), **Iras** (11b,32a), **iris** (53c,58a,111c), **Iris** (127c), **Irus** (109d), **Isis** (68d,78c,111d), **Itys** (163b), **Ives** (9c,90b)

IT - - **itch, Itea** (145d,160c,181d), **item** (6d,13b,42d,51a,90d,92d,107a, 113d,114c), **Iten** (192), **iter** (22d,76c,85c,89c,114d,132a,b,133a,b), **itis** (158c), **itmo** (18b), **itol** (158b), **Itys** (163b), **Itza** (192)

- IT - **bite** (29d,156b), **biti** (20b), **bito** (7d,57d,168c), **bitt** (54d,175c), **cite** (15a,98d,126d,159b), **cito** (89d,126c), **cits, city, dita** (117a), **dite** (150b), **Gita, gite** (62a,118d), **jiti, kite** (19c,49a,74c,d), **kith** (63c), **lite** (158c,d), **lith** (34d,156c), **liti** (60d) **litz** (127b), **mite** (12b,81b,82a,114a,c,148c,d,181b), **mitt** (56c), **mitu** (39d), **mity** (55c), **pita** (9c,28b,56a,83a), **pith** (37a,51c,67b,95c,97a, 119b,126d), **pitt** (50d), **Pitt** (155d), **pito** (9c,28b,83a), **pity** (35b), **rita, Rita** (37b,78d,183c), **rite** (93a,131d), **Sita** (127d), **site** (93b), **sito** (34b), **titi** (20d,102a,145d,168d,181b), **Tito** (186c), **vita** (89c, 92a), **vite** (62b), **viti** (17ob), **with** (10b)

314

- - IT adit (51a,100a,114d), alit (44b,143a), amit (94a), bait (15d,51a, 94d,167b), brit (76c), chit (67b,98c,108b,116c,177c), doit (47a, 169d,180d), duit (190), Duit (192), edit (20d,49d,123a,129a,131a), emit (43d,49a,53c,58d,83a,142c), exit (114d), fait (6d,61b), flit (41a), frit (64c,67c), gait (96b,179a), grit (137a,b), ibit (117a), knit (173c,179b), lait (62a), nuit (62b), obit (41b,64c), omit (49c, 52c,106b,114c,147d), phit (24b), quit (90d,130c), seit (189), skit (145c), slit (40a), spit (120a,132b,c), suit (38a,58a,91a,112a,119c, 137c), tait (14d), trit (34d,164c), twit (162b,c), unit (101c,110c, 147a), wait (26d,42b,92c,155d,162a), whit (166c), writ (91a), Yuit (51c)

I - - T ibit (117a), ikat (53b,159a), ilot (82d)

- IU - biur (35a), Niue (137d), Pius (121a)

I - - U lalu (48d), ichu (10b,70d), iglu (51c,149b)

IV - - Ivah (18d), Ivan (40c,85b,96a), Ives (9c,90b)

- IV - Civa (56d), cive (110c), diva (110d,123c), dive (42b,74b,119d), divi, five, give (79d,123a), hive (17c), jiva (77a), jive (160c), kiva (28c,125b), kive (174d), kivu (170c), live (47c), Livy (132d,133a), rive (32a,153d), siva (67a,120d), Siva (56d,77a), sive (146a), viva (93d), vive (93d), vivo (93a), wive (97a)

- - IV chiv (87a), skiv (151b)

- IW - Biwa (93d,168c), iiwi (19a,74b), kiwi (11d,19a,58c)

IX - - ixia (37a), Ixil (192), ixle (56a)

- IX - Bixa (145d), dixi, Mixe (192), mixy, pixy (154b)

- - IX Alix (183c), Coix (70d,85b), flix, noix (67c)

IY - - Iyar (102b)

- IY - kiyi (185d)

I - - Y idly, inky (20b), Inly, ismy (45a)

IZ - - izar (65b,103b), Izar (155b)

- IZ - bize (182a), bizz, size, sizy (176d), sizz, tiza (172a), zizz (181a)

- - IZ friz (39d), phiz (54a), swiz (160c), whiz (25c)

I - - Z Inez (45c,183c)

JA - - jaca (84a), jack (26c,58a,127c), Jack (96b), jacu (19a,151b), jade (33c,65d,71d,166a), jadu (95a), jady, Jael (147b), Jaga (191), jagg, jail (123d), Jain (77b), jake (40d), Jake (96b), jako (71a), jama (103b), jamb (12d,45c,118a,146b,174a), jami (103b), jane (190), Jane (183c), jann (102d), jaob, jape (85a,b), jarl (40d,107d), jass (160d), jati (27b), jato (173b), jaun (113a), Java (33a), Jave (84d), Jawy, jazz

- JA - ajar (110c), Ajax (71b,162d)

- - JA Beja (6c,191), bija (168c), caja (152a), coja (103b,166b), hoja (166b), lija (57a,90d,173a), maja (151c), Maja (153b), Naja (33a), puja (77a), raja (77a,123c), reja (152b), sɔja (151b)

J - - A Jaca (84a), Jaca, Jaga (191), jama (103b), Java (33a), Jena (105d, 165b), jiva (77a), jota (151c), Jova (193), juba (106b), juca (27a), Juda, juga (27a), jula, jura, Juza (155b)

J - - B jamb (12d,45c,118a,146b,174a), jaob, jibb, Joab (41a)

--JD   Nejd

J--D   Joad (50c)

JE--   jean (37c), Jean (183c), jeel, jeep, jeer (138c,162b), jefe (152a), jeff (133d), Jeff, jehu (46b), Jehu (18c), Jena (105d,165b), jerk (153a), jess (157a), jest (169c), Jesu, jete (16a), Jeth (102a), jeux (61d)

►JE-   ajee (15c,139a)

--JE   haje (33a,48d), yaje (23a)

J--E   jade (33c,65d,71d,166a), Jake (40d), Jake (96b), Jane (190), Jane (183c), jape (85a,b), Jave (84d), jefe (152a), jete (16a), jibe (8a, 33b,35d,37b,42c,100d,138c,144c,149b), jive (160c), joke (183a), jole (29b), Jose (96a), Jove (85d), jube (28d), Jude (11c,96a), juke (114c), Jule (183d), June (183c), jupe (62b,84a), jure (90b), jute (37a,48a,56a,133d,136a), Jute

J--F   jeff (133d), Jeff, jiff (101c)

J--G   jagg, joug (138d), Jung (125a)

JH--   Jhil, jhum, JHVH (159d), JHWH (159d)

J--H   Jeth (102a), josh (85b), JHVH (159d), JHWH (159d)

JI--   jibb, jibe (8a,33b,35d,37b,42c,100d,138c,144c,149b), jiff (101c), Jill (183d), jilt, jink, jinn (42b,103b,153c), jinx (78a), jiti, jiva (77a), jive (160c)

--JI   caji (180b), Caji, fuji (84b), Fuji (84d), koji (185b), suji (180c)

J--I   jarri (103b), jati (27b), Jati, jiti, jogi (76d), joli (62b), joti

J--K   jack (26c,58a,127c), Jack (96b), jerk (153a), jink, jock, Jock (96b), jonk, juck (114c), junk (30a,134c)

J--L   Jael (147b), jail (123d), jarl (40d,107d), jeel, jhil, Jill (183d), Joel (96a), jowl (29b)

-JM-   ijma (103b)

--JM   Sejm (120c)

J--M   jhum, joom (39c)

J--N   Jain (77b), jann, Jann (102d), jaun (113a), jean (37c), Jean (183c), jinn (42b,103b,153c), Joan (183c), John (11c,96a,121a,186b), join (36a,173c), juan (113a), Juan (96a)

JO--   Joab (41a), Joad (50c), Joan (183c), joar (100a), jobo (77c), jock, Jock (96b), jocu (45b,57a), Jodo (113d), Joel (96a), joey (86a, 185d), Joey (96b,109c), jogi (76d), John (11c,96a,121a,186b), join (36a,173c), joke (183a), joky, jole (29b), joli (62b), jolt (143b), jonk, joom (39c), Jose (96a), josh (85b), joss (30b), Josy (183d), jota (151c), joti, joug (138d), Jova (193), Jove (85d), jowl 29b), Jozy

-JO-   ajog, ejoo (55b,168c), Gjoa (144d)

--JO   bojo (117a), gajo (107c), Idjo (191), majo (177c), mojo (177c), pajo (122a, rojo (129a,152c), tajo (152a,d)

J--O   jako (71a), Jako, jato (173b), jobo (77c), Jodo (113d), judo (84b, 85c,142b), Juno (69c,85d,100c,126b)

J--P   jeep, jump

J - - R jeer (162b), joar (100a), juar (100a)

J - - S jass (160d), jess (157a), joss (30b)

J - - T jest (169c), jilt, jolt (143b), just (51b,54b)

JU - - juan (113a), Juan (96a), juar (100a), juba (106b), jube (28d), juca (27a), juck (114c), Juda, Jude (11c,96a), judo (84b,85c,142b), Judy (125c,183d), juez (152b), juga (27a), juju (29b,55d), juke (114c), jula, Jule (183d), jump, June (183c), Jung (125a), junk (30a,134c), Juno (69c,85d,100c,126b), jupe (62b,84a), jura, Jura, jure (90b), jury (38a), just (51b,54b), jute (37a,48a,56a,133d, 136a), Jute, Juza (155b)

- - JU baju (84a), hoju (84b), juju (29b,55d), teju (151b)

J - - U jacu (19a,151b), jadu (95), jehu (46b), Jehu (18c), Jesu, jocu (45b,57a), juju (29b,55d)

J - - X jeux (61d), jinx (78a), jynx (78a), Jynx (184a)

JY - - jynx (78a), Jynx (184a)

J - - Y jady, jawy, joey (86a,185d), Joey (96b,109c), joky, Josy (183d), Jozy, Judy (125c,183d), July, jury (38a)

J - - Z jazz, juez (152b)

KA - - kaan (93d,116c), kaat (105d), kada (188), kade (144a), kadi (103a, 171a), Kadu (191), Kafa (6c), kago (113a), kagu (106c), kaha (123d), kahu (14d), kaid (29d,66a), kaif (88c) kaik (96c), kail (18c, 22a,25a,79b), Kain, kair, kaka (114b), kaki (84c,106d), kala (19a), kale (22a,25a,119b,175a), kali (26d,67c,136d,167a), Kali (147b), kalo (162a), Kama (56d), kame (67b,139b), Kami (68a,84b,88c, 107c,144c), kana (84d), Kane (74c), k'ang (30a), Kano (84c,177d), kant (28d), Kant (67a), kapa (74b), kaph (91d), Kapp, Kara (132a), Kari (14d), Karl (96a), karn (156c), karo (106d), kasa (48a), kasi 116b), kasm (189), Kate (143c,183d), kath (14a), Katy (183d), kaun (93d), kava (18c,116a), Kavi (84d), kawa (18c,116a), Kawi (84d), kawn (93d), kayo (87c), kazi (103a), kazy (103a)

- KA - Akal (56d), Akan (191), ikat (53b,159a), okay (8d), skag (7d, 46d), skat (181b), Skat (155b)

- - KA Akka (125d), Atka (11a), baka (52b), beka (189), dika (23a), Ekka (26d), Inka (193), kaka (114b), loka (173c,184c), pika (93a, 128a,132c), puka (107a,168c), roka (95a,168c,d), Saka (10a), sika (41d,84b), soka (20c), waka (26a), weka (58c,106d,107a,127b), Yaka (191)

K - - A kada (188), Kafa (6c), kaha (123d), kaka (114b), kala (19a), Kama (56d), kana (84d), kapa (74b), kara (132a), kasa (48a), kava (18c 116a), kawa (18c,116a), kela (189), keta (45a), kina (126d), kiva (28c,125b), koba (11a), kola (25b,84a,108d), Kola (135b,c,d), kona (74c), kora (19a,178c), kota (117a), Kota (45d), kuba (26d,189), kufa (21b,99a), kula (189), kusa

K - - B kerb (146b), knab (107a), knob (73c,107c,124d), knub (178b)

K - - D kaid (29d,66a), keld (154b), kind (150d,153a,174d), Kurd (48b, 82a)

KE - - keal (25a), keef (75d), keek (154c), keel (128d,134d,144c,d), keen (15a,88a,177b), keep (123a,130d), keet (72b), keif (75d), keir

317

(20c,174d), kela (189), keld (154b), kelp (82a,141c), Kelt (180b), kemp (139b), keno, Kent (90d), kepi (99d), kept, kerb (146b), kere (75c,128b), kerf (40a,108b), keri (75c,128b), kern (59c,172a), Kern (132b), Kerr, keta (45a), Ketu (48b)

-KE- akee (168c), akey (189), okeh (8d,37b), oket (189), skee (149c), skeg (7d,86a,144d,157d,184a), sken (164a), skeo (57d), skep (16d,17c,77c), skew (148a,160c,171b,c), skey (185d)

--KE bake (139a), bike, cake, coke (32d,64a), cuke (39b), cyke (40c), dike (49c,91d), Dike (78a), duke (107c), dyke (49c,91d), fake (123a,143c), feke, fike (139c), fyke (15d), hake (57a,b), hike, hyke!, jake (40d), Jake (96b), joke (183a), juke (114c), lake (117d), like (13c,37d,146d), Loke (15d,68b), luke, Luke (52a, 96a), make (35b,36d,54a,123a), mike, Mike (96b), moke (45c, 157d), Nike (69c,100c,182d), Peke (45a,148d), pike (57a,b,76c, 120b,153a), poke (108c), rake (41b,44c,134b,140d), roke (174d, 175b), sake (84b,125d), soke (44c,85d), syke (194), take, tike (29d), tuke (26b,53b), tyke (29d), wake (134b,168a), woke, yoke (85b,92d,173c), Zeke (96b)

K--E kade (144a), kale (22a,25a,119b,175a), kame (67b,139b), Kane (74c), Kate (143c,183d), kere (75c,128b), kibe kile (189), kine (38a,112c), kite (19c,49a,74c,d), kive (174d), Klee (113a), knee (85b), koae (74b), Kobe (78a), Kome (71d), kore (107b) Kore (29a, 42b,116b,124d), kuge (84c), Kure (84c), kyle (57a,139c)

--KF wakf (103a), wukf (103a)

K--F kaif (88c), keef (75d), keif (75d), kerf (40a,108b), kief (75d), kiff (88c), koff (47a)

K--G k'ang (30a), king (26c,29c), knag (115d,139c), krag (131c), kung (125b)

KH-- khan (7c,26c,81b,93d,116c,123c,130c,166c), khar (189), khas (153a), khat (105d), Khem (113c), khet (188), khot

-KH- Akha (86a,c)

--KH ankh (38d,162b), bikh (120b), bukh (122a), hakh (46d), lakh (110c), rukh (53b,54a), Sikh (77b)

K--H kaph (91d), kath (14a), kish (16d,70c), Kish (137c), kith (63c), Koch (66d), koph (91d), Kush, kyah (19a)

KI-- kiak (51c), kibe, kiby (29a), kick, kief (75d), kiel (128d,134d), Kiel (25d), kier (20c,174d), Kiev, kiff (88c), kiho (82a), kiki (27b), kiku (30d), kile (189), kill (38c), kiln (15d,112a), kilo (99b,122d), kilt, kina (126d), kind (150d,153a,174d), kine (38a,112c), king (26c,29c), kink (38b,171c), kino (27c,34c,47c,72c,98b,161d,168c), kipp, kiri (86a,87c,115a,168c), kirk (31a,139b), kish (16d,70c), Kish (137c), kiss (148c), kist (29d,58a,139b), kite (19c,49a,74c,d), kith (63c), kiva (28c,125b), kive (174d), kivu (170c), kiwi (11d, 19a,58c), kiyi (185d)

-KI- akia (74c), Akim (135d,191), akin (8b,92b,129c), okia (190), Okie (99d), skid (148b), skil (57a), skim (67c), skin (53a,76c,115c, d), skio (57d), skip (110b,114c,147c), skir, skit (145c), skiv (151b)

--KI Enki (15b), kaki (84c,106d), kiki (27b), Kuki (191), Loki (7c,15d, 68b), maki (91b), moki (127b), piki (95c), Reki (16a), saki (39c,

84b,102a), **Tiki** (120c), **weki** (55c), **yaki** (193)

K - - I kadi (103a,171a), kaki (84c,106d), kali (26d,67c,136d,167a), **Kali** (147b), **Kami** (68a,84b,88c,107c,144c), **Kari** (14d), kasi (116b), **Kavi** (84d), **Kawi** (84d), kazi (103a), kepi (99d), keri (75c,128b), kiki (27b), kiri (86a,87c,115a,168c), kiwi (11d,19a,58c), kiyi (185d), kobi (84b), koji (185b), **Koli** (27b), **Komi** (191), kopi (107a, 168c), **Kopi** (172a), kori (7d,77a), kuei (44a), **Kuki** (191), **Kuli** (27b), **Kuri** (191), kwei (44a)

- KK - **Akka** (125d), **Ekka** (26d)

- - KK bukk (122a), rikk (49a)

K - - K kaik (96c), kiak (51c), keek (154c), kick, kink (38b,171c), kirk (31a,139b), konk (41c), kunk (188), kurk (31a,139b), kyak (51c)

KL - - klam (189), **Klee** (113a), klom (189), klop (150d)

K - - L kail (18c,22a,25a,79b), **Karl** (96a), keal (25a), keel (128d,134d, 144c,d), kiel (128d,134d), **Kiel** (25d), kill (38c), koel (19a,b,39b), kohl (53c), kral, kuhl (53c)

- KM - ikmo (18b)

K - - M kasm (189), **Khem** (113c), klam (189), klom (189)

KN - - **Knab** (107a), knag (115d,139c), knap (76d,107a,139b,159b,166a, 170c,185b), knar (87c,134b), knee (85b), knew, knez (123c), knip (115c), knit (173c,179b), knob (73c,107c,124d), knop (124b,170c, 185b), knor (87c), knot (43c,99d,107c,124d,137b), knub (178b), knur (67d,87c,107c), knut, **Knut** (40d,50c,96a)

K - - N kaan (93d,116c), **Kain**, karn (156c), kaun (93d), kawn (93d), keen (15a,88a,177b), kern (172a), **Kern** (132b), khan (7c,26c,81b,93d, 116c,123c,130c,166c), kiln (15d,112a), kran (190), kuan (30b), **Kuan** (30c), kwan (30b)

KO - - koae (74b), koba (11a), **Kobe** (78a), kobi (84b), kobu (84b), **Koch** (66d), koel (19a,b,39b), koff (47a), kohl (53c), koir (33a), koji (185b), koko (106d,114b), **Koko** (93d,186c), koku (189), kola (25b,84a,108d,168c), **Kola** (135b,c,d), **Koli** (27b), kolo (59b,135c), **Kome** (71d), **Komi** (191), kona (74c), konk (41c), koop (16c), koph (91d), kopi (107a,168c), **Kopi** (172a), kora (19a,178c), **Kora, kore** (107b), **Kore** (29a,42b,116b,124d), kori (7d,77a), koso (6c,80d), **Koso** (192,193), koss (188), kota (117a), **Kota** (45d), koto (84b), kozo (113d,168c)

- KO - akov (189), **Ekoi** (191), ikon (79d,136a)

- - KO boko (52b), **Doko** (191), hako (115b), jako (71a), koko (106d,114b), **Koko** (93d,186c), mako (18a,19a,20d,143c,168c,182c), moko (96c), toko (30c)

K - - O kago (113a), kalo (162a), **Kano** (84c,177d), karo (106d), kayo (87c), keno, kiho (82a), kilo (99b,122d), kino (27c,34c,47c,72c, 98b,161d,168c), koko (106d,114b), **Koko** (93d,186c), kolo (59b, 135c), koso (6c,80d), **Koso** (192,193), koto (84b), kozo (113d,168c), **Kroo** (191)

K - - P **Kapp**, keep (123a,130d), kelp (82a,141c), kemp (139b), kipp, klop (150d), knap (76d,107a,139b,159b,166a,170c,185b), knip (115c), knop (124b,170c,185b), koop (16c)

319

KR • •   krag (131c), kraf, kran (190), kras (76d), kris (40b,95d), Kroo (191)

• KR •   akra (176a), Akra (191), ikra (27d), okra (72c,175a), okro (72c, 175a)

• • KR   Askr (107d)

K • • R   kair, keir (20c,174d), Kerr, khar (189), kier (20c,174d), knar (87c,134b), knor (87c), knur (67d,87c,107c), koir (33a), Kuar (102a), kyar (33a)

• • KS   oaks (154d)

K • • S   khas (153a), kiss (148c), koss (188), kras (76d), kris (40b,95d), kvas (135c)

• • KT   takt (105a,163a)

K • • T   kaat (105d), kant (28d), Kant (67a), keet (72b), Kelt (180b), Kent (90d), kept, khat (105d), khet (188), khot, kilt, kist (29d,58a, 139b), knit (173c,179b), knot (43c,99d,107c,124d,137b), knut, Knut (40d,50c,96a), kyat (189)

KU • •   Kuan (30c), kuan (30b), Kuar (102a), kuba (26d,189), kudu (11a), kuei (44a), kufa (21b,99a), kuge (84c), kuhl (53c), Kuki (191), kuku (19a,106d), kula (189), Kuli (27b), kung (125b), kunk (188), Kurd (48b,82a), Kure (84c), Kuri (191), kurk (31a,139b), kusa, Kush

• KU •   akua (120d), skua (19b,72c,84a,141a)

• • KU   baku (26d,157b,168c), duku (95d,168c), haku (86d), hiku (57a, 106d,138a), kiku (30d), koku (189), kuku (19a,106d), Maku (192), poku (11a), puku (11a), Suku (191), Taku (80c)

K • • U   Kadu (191), kagu (106c), kahu (14d), Ketu (48b), kiku (30d), kivu (1 'Oc), kobu (84b), koku (189), kudu (11a), kuku (19a,106d)

KV • •   k.as (135c)

• KV •   NKVD (135d)

K • • V   Kiev

KW • •   kwan (30b), kwei (44a)

K • • W   knew, know

KY • •   kyah (19a), kyak (51c), kyar (33a), kyat (189), kyle (57a,139c)

• KY •   Skye (163c), skyr (21d,151a), skyt (138c,140b)

• • KY   alky, caky, coky, faky, Inky (20b), joky, laky, oaky, piky, poky (148c), taky, waky

K • • Y   Katy (183d), kazy (103a), kiby (29a)

K • • Z   knez (123c)

LA • •   laap (51d,91b,141d), lace (58b,179c), lack (178a), lact (34c), lacy, Ladd (143c), lade (24c,26d,43c,93b,100a,132a,139d,161b,178d), lady, laet (60d), lago (83b,152b), laic (32b,90b,107d,124a,141d), laid, lain, lair (37c,42b), Lais (17c), lait (62a), lake (117d), lakh (110c), laky, lala (129b), lalo (16b,34d,153a), Lalo (35c), lama (23d,24a,91d,165b), lamb, Lamb (49c), lame (38d,43d,73b), lamp (92a,94c), lana (58a,66a,90a,184b), land (44a,163c), lane (134b, 157b), lank (148b,164b), lant, lanx (133a,b), Laos (80d,129c), Lapp (108a), Lara (25c), lard (54d,61a,71a,110a), lari (78a,101c),

Lari (72c), **lark** (19a,63d,177b), **larp** (51d), **Lars** (51d,121b), **lash** (58c,87b,165c,180d), **Lasi** (191), **lass** (95b), **last** (36c,50b,145a, 174c), **lata** (85d,95d), **late** (128c), **lath** (157c), **latu** (190), **laud** (122a), **laun** (146b), **lava** (101c,132b,151a,177a), **lave** (16d,178b), **lawn** (20a,37c,53b,92c), **laze** (79b), **Laze** (191), **Lazi** (191), **lazo** (88d,128b,133d), **lazy**

-LA- alae (182d), alai (171a), Alai (135c), alan (45a,79a,183c), Alan, alar (15c,145c,182d), alas (52c,136b,183b), alat (136d), alay 5c), blaa, blab (162b), blae (93b), blah, blas (6c,49c), Blas (t 7b), blat (25b), blay (57d), clad (46a,82a), clam (20b,101b), clan (169c), clap (58b), claw (29c,105b,161d,173a), Clay (9d), Elah (18c,86d), elan (12c,41a,50d,62a,153c,177a,186b), Elam (18d,37d, 82a,116c,144b), ELAS (71c), flag (16b,50d,82b,88c,115a,155a), flak (11a), flam (169c), flan (39d,40a,114d), flap (17b,59a,104a, 118d,161a,182d), flat (41b,124b,173a), flaw, flax, flay (147c,157c), glad (85c), klam (189), Olaf (108a,176b), olam (51a,d,75c,81a), Olan (115c), Olax (52b), olay (113b), plan (99b,124a,138b), plap (54b), plat (22b,96c,114a,119c,133d), play (63d,154a), slab (148b), slag (46c,99a,13Sc,148d,177a), slam (180d,182d), slap (24a,128c, 148c), slat (58b,89a,117c,184a), Slav (13c,40c,48b,52a,120b,135b), slaw, slay, Ulam (67b), ulan (27d,8Sa)

--LA agla (7a), alla (6d), amla (48a,161d,168c,169a), aula (66c,73b), Bala (26c,66a), bela (12a), Bela (18b,48c,78d), bola (16a,179b), cela (62d), cola (25b,108d,149d,168c), dola (189), ella (152c, 15Sc), Ella (183c), fala (129b), gala (55d), Gala (191), gila (93b), gola (27b,40c,70c,157a), gula (90a,101a,165b), hala (112b), Hela (93c), hila (53c), hola (74c,152b), hula (74b), Hyla (10a,166d, 169b), Iola, jula, kala (19a), kela (189), kola (25b,84a,108d,168c), Kola (135b,c,d), kula (189), lala (129b), Lila (183c), Lola (27d,97b), mala (S9c,90a,94b,97d,109d,185c), mela (34a,129d), mila (188), Mola (159c), Nala (77a), Nola, olla (36d,44b,84d,113b,121d, 151d,152c,181b), pala (189), Pala (8Sb), pela (30c), Pola, pyla (22d), sala (50c,152a,b,c), Sala (50c), sola (9a,48a,74b,118c, 154a,167b), Sula (65a), tala (16d,113a,168c,d), tela (22d,98c, 121b,166a,179c), tola (48a,80d,180a), Tola (85b), tula (9a), Tula, upla, vela (9Sc,136b,149d), Vela (36b,c), vila (54b), vola (89d), Zola (63a)

L--A lala (129b), lama (23d,24a,91d,165b), lana (5Sa,66a,90a,184b), Lara (25c), lata (85d,95d), lava (101c,132b,151a,177a), Leda (27b, 75d,120c,153a,171d,186b), lena (56d), Lena (36b), Lida (183c), lija (57a,90d,173a), Lila (183c), lima (17b,152b,174d), Lima (31b), lina (18S), Lina (183d), lipa (54d), lira (28b,79a,170d), Lisa (183d), loka (173c,184c), Lola (27d,97b), loma (5Sb,63d), lora (146b,149b, 151c,169b), Lora (183c), lota (24c,121d,178d), Lota, Iowa (19a), Luba (191), luna (103c), Luna (102b), lura (22d,82a), lyra, Lyra (36b,74a)

-LB- alba (9Sb,181a), Alba (151d), albe (133a), Albi (5Sa), albo (34d, 1S1a), Elba (105d), Elbe (10Sa)

--LB bulb (37a,172c)

L--B lamb, Lamb (49c), limb (12d,22d), lobb (23b,94c,163a)

-LC- Alca (14c,12Sb), alco (45b)

321

--LC   **talc** (28d,63b,99c,100b,122a,149c)

L--C   **laic** (32b,90b,107d,124a,141d)

-LD-   **Alda** (110d,150c), **alda** (152b)

--LD   **bald** (16c), **bold** (41a), **cold** (65d), **eild** (138d,140a), **fold, geld** (162b), **gild** (14a,49c,69c,98b), **gold, held, Hild, hold** (95c,124c, 130d), **Keld** (154b), **meld** (26a,41c,99a,118b), **mild** (32a,66a), **mold** (54d,143c), **sold, suld** (188), **told** (129c), **veld** (151a), **weld** (47c, 85b,173c), **wild** (38b,173d), **wold** (47c,60a,118d,174a,184a)

L--D   **Ladd** (143c), **laid, land** (44a,163c), **lard** (54d,61a,71a,110a), **laud** (122a), **lead** (35d,43d,72b,74d,81a), **lend** (6d,79d), **lied** (66d,150b), **load** (24c,26d,161b), **lood** (189) **lord** (107c), **loud** (156a), **Ludd** (23c)

LE--   **lead** (35d,43d,72b,74d,81a), **leaf** (55c,73c,119b), **Leah** (19a,84a, 87b,183c), **leak** (110c), **leal** (54b,94c,139d), **lean** (128a,148b,152d, 164b,166a), **leap** (26c), **lear** (139d), **Lear** (37a,143b), **lech** 102b), **Leda** (27b,75d,120c,153a,171d,186b), **leek** (58b,76a,110c,177d), **leer** (9d,58a,67c,93d,112a,148c), **lees** (46a,142a), **leet** (26a, 38a,139d), **left** (42c), **lehr** (67c,112a) **Leif** (107d), **Leir, Lely** (47a), **lena** (56d), **Lena** (36b), **lend** (6d,79d), **lene** (36b,149a, 172b), **leno** (37c,53b), **lens** (67c,95b,111a,129b,162d), **lent** (54d), **Lent** (115d,141c), **Leon** (96a), **Lero** (82d), **lerp** (51d,141d), **less** (100c,108b,141d), **lest** (59d,163d), **lete, Leti** (82d), **Leto** (11c), **Lett** (16a,90a,93a), **leve** (62a), **Levi** (84a,90c), **levo** (91a), **levy** (14a, 162b)

-LE-   **Alea** (14b,31c,167d), **alec** (10a,57c,d,76c,137c), **alee** (15c,75d, 144b,157a,182a), **alef** (91c), **alem** (98b,155a,170d,171a), **alen** (40d, 138a), **bleb** (20c,23d,67c), **bled, blet** (64a), **bleu** (61b), **blew, clee** (19a,129a), **clef** (104d,105a), **clem** (56b,158b), **clew** (16a,33a,77b, 136b,164d), **elef** (91c), **flea** (81b), **fled, flee, flew, flex** (18a), **fley** (63d), **gled** (19a,52a,87a), **glee** (99a,150b), **glen** (43c), **Hler** (141a), **ilex** (77d), **Klee** (113a), **Lieu** (40c), **Llew** (40c), **olea** (170b), **Olea** (110b), **oleo** (34c), **plea** (51a,52d,122a,130b), **pleb** (10d,35b,180b), **plet** (135d), **plew** (17c), **plex** (60b), **Sleb** (12a), **sled** (40a), **slee** (140b,148c), **slew** (160a), **sley** (179b), **Ulex** (153c), **vlei** (38c, 160a), **vley** (160a)

--LE   **able** (26b,35b,126a,147c), **acle** (13d,82c,115d), **aile** (62b,63a,182c, d), **Alle** (14c), **atle** (136d,161d,169b), **axle** (153c,180c), **bale** (24b, 74a), **bile** (30c), **bole** (31d,32a,169b), **cale** (72d), **cole** (25a), **Cole, dale** (43c,128a,174b), **dele** (26a,49c,51b,53a,110b,123d,124c,130a, 145c,161b), **dole** (44c,118c,121c,129d), **Dole** (74c), **elle** (62b,c), **file** (13a,127d), **gale** (181d), **gyle** (23b,174d), **hale** (125b), **Hale** (9d,131a), **hole** (6c,11b,110d,118c,147a), **hule** (23a,134c), **hyle** (97c), **idle** (174b,c,178c), **ille** (89b,d,163d), **iole** (52a,76b,123c), **isle** (8b,53c,81d,82d,86b,88a), **ixle** (56a), **jole** (29b), **Jule** (183d), **kale** (22a,25a,119b,175a), **kile** (189), **kyle** (57a,139c), **male** (154d), **Male** (45d), **mele** (74b,150b), **mile** (64c), **mole** (19d,23a,24d,85a, 117c,155c), **Mole** (88c), **mule** (45b,148b,153c,180b), **nile** (33c, 71d), **Nile** (106b), **ogle** (9d,53c,91a,93d,148c), **orle** (17b,56b,76a, 144b,177a), **pale** (113a,117c,178a), **Pele** (69c,74c), **pile** (45d,75b, 117c), **pole** (132c,143b,177b,184a), **Pole** (52a), **pule** (180d), **pyle** (34b), **Pyle** (9c,178a), **rale** (7c,23a,29d,41b), **rile** (10c,d,82c,125a,

156b,176a), **role** (114b), **rule** (11b,26b,90b), **sale** (14c,61c,62b,c, 168b), **sole** (52c,57a,b,58b,d,110c,115d,150a), **tale** (91a,185b), **tele** (34b,122c), **tile** (31d,56d,72b,95b,133c,163c), **tole** (9a,51a,99b, 163a), **tule** (24b,27c), **vale** (54c,128a,174b), **Vale** (7c,109c), **vile** (16c,56c), **vole** (97d,104a), **wale** (70b,131b,157c,163d,179a,180a, c,d), **wile** (13b,41c,157b,169c), **Yale** (173c), **Yule** (30d)

L - - E   lace (58b,179c), lade (24c,26d,43c,93b,100a,132a,139d,161b), 178d), lake (117d), lame (38d,43d,73b), lane (134b,157b), late (128c), lave (16d,178b), laze (79b), Laze (191), lene(36b,149a, 172b), lete, leve (62a), life (19a,177a), like (13c,37d,146d), lime (25b,27d,31b,33c,102d,168c), line (12b,22b,36d,38a,126c,134b, 157b,158b,162d,175c), lire (62c), lite (158c,d), live (47c), lobe (90c,134b), lode (42c,99a,111b,175b), loge (164a), Loke (15d,68b), Lome, lone (150a), lope (48b,64b,d), lore (77c,87c,90d,151c,183a), lose (60a,100c), lote (24c,94a), love (163a), lube (110a), luce (58c,117d), Luce (7b,35a), luge (148a), luke, Luke (52a,96a), lune (38c,73b,74d), lupe (19a,64a), lure (41c,51a,54b,163a), lute (11c, 28b,84d,105a,131d), luxe (61c,62d,159c), lyre (11c,81c,105a,111c), lyse

- LF -   alfa (70d)

- - LF   calf, golf (154a), gulf (6c), half (101a), pelf (22a,56c,131b), self (48d,80d), Welf (67a), wolf

L - - F   leaf (55c,73c,119b), Leif (107d), lief (181d), loaf (49b,94b), loof (144c,153d), luff (136b), luif

- LG -   alga (141b,c), Algy (96b), Olga (135c,183c)

L - - G   ling (24c,57a,b,75b,178c), long (38b,185b), lung, lurg (96d,141b, 184d)

L - - H   lakh (110c), lash (58c,87b,165c,180d), lath (157c), Leah (19a,84a, 87b,183c), lech (102b), lith (34d,156c), loch (88a,139d), losh (178b), loth (15a,173d), Lugh (28b), lush (94d)

LI - -   Liam (181d), liar (98d), Lias (66a), lick, Lida (183c), Lido (83d, 175b), lied (66d,150b), lief (181d), lien (65c,91a,124c), lieu (118c, 155d), life (19a,177a), lift (49b), liin (188), lija (57a,90d,173a), like (13c,37d,146d), Lila (183c), lill (15d,118a), lilt (93a,131a, 147a), lily, lima (17b,152b,174d), Lima (31b), limb (12d,22d), lime (25b,27d,31b,33c,102d,168c), limn (45d,121c), limp (58a,81a,177d), limu (141c), limy (176d), lina (188), Lina (183d), line (12b,22b,36d,38a,126c,134b,157b,158b,162d,175c), ling (24c,57a,b,75b,178c), link (36a,81d,85b), linn (120d,140a,c, 168c,178d), lino, lint (46a,58d), liny (157b), Linz (40d), lion (55b, 86c), lipa (54d), lira (28b,79a,170d), lire (62c), Lisa (183d), lisp 153b), liss (54b,58b,60c,129d,140a), list (26d,27b,75b,83d,134a, 138b,165d), lite (158c,d), lith (34d,156c), liti (60d), litz (127b), live (47c), Livy (132d,133a)

- LI -   alia (89d), alif (12b), alii (74c,134c), alim (103b,162c) alin (188), alit (44b,143a), Alix (183c), Clim (12b), Clio (104d), clip (54d, 143d), Elia (88a,115d), Elis (22c,37d,71b,107c), flip (167c), flit (41a), flix, glia (106c), glib (58d,149a,177c), glim, glis (45c), ilia (21d,77b,115d), ille (89b,d), olic (158b), olid (55d,60c,148d,157d), olio (44b,77c,98c,100d,121d), plie (32c,59b), slid, slim (148b,

160a), slip (67c,119a), slit (40a)

- - Ll amli (48a,161d,168c,169a), Atli (14c,72b,79a,107d), Bali, Bell (23c), coli, dali (168c,169b), doli, fili, gali (6c), goli (105c), Holi (77a), joli (62b), kali (26d,67c,136d,167a), Kali (147b), Koli (27b, Kuli (27b), mali (27b), pali (122b), Pali (23d,24a,137b,175a), pili (34b,108d), puli (45a,78d), soli (12c,110c), tali (189), teli (94b), vali (171a,176a), Vali (7c,109c), vili (54b), Vili (109c), wali (171a), yali (171a)

L - - l Lari (72c), lari (78a,101c), Lasi (191), Lazi (191), Leti (82d), Levi (84a,90c), liti (60d), loci (66b,118c), Lodi (105d), Loki (7c,15d, 68b), lori (91b), Loti (63a,176a), ludi (133b), Luri (191)

- LK - alky

- - LK balk (118c,146a,156d), bilk (29b,41c,42a), bulk (97b), calk (78c, 109a,141c,178d), folk (116a,169c), fulk (173a), hulk (144d,173d), milk, mulk (60d), polk (37c), pulk (37c,88d), silk (53b,179c), sulk (159a), talk, volk (66c,105d,116a), Volk, walk, welk (65c,96d, 141b), yolk

L - - K lack (178a), lank (148b,164b), lark (19a,63d,177b), leak (110c), leek (58b,76a,110c,177d), lick, link (36a,81d,85b), lock (54d), lonk (143d), look (11c,53c,142a), luck (28d), lurk (92a, 147d)

LL - - llyn (120d,140a), Lleu (40c), Llew (40c)

- LL - alla (6d), Alle (14c), allo (34c), ally (14a,35c,d,173c), ella (152c, 158c), Ella (183c), elle (62b,c), ille (89b,d,163d), ills (170a), olla (36d,44b,84d,113b,121d,151d,152c,181b), ullo (6a,144a), Ullr (146b,164d)

- - LL ball, bell (24c,39d), Bell (162d), bill (17b,147a), Bill (96b), boll (119b,d), bull (113c), call (145c,159b,176d), cell (39b), cull (117c), dell (43c,174b), dill (13a,117c), doll (125c), dull (21a,32c,173a), Dull (94b), fall (46b,141c), fell (40a,58b,76c,115d,147d), fill (109b), full (7b,130b), gall (19a,28c,29b,82c,160c,176a), gill (22d), Goll, gull (32d,41c,42a,72c,99b,141a), hall (37b,114d), hill, hull (141d,142a,144c,d), Jill (183d), kill (38c), lill (15d,118a), loll (94b,128c), lull (126d,150c), mall (95d,124b,143b), mill (126c), moll, Moll (183d), mull (53b,135a,164c), Nell (110a,183d), nill (173d), Noll (96b,110b), null (108c,177a), pall (32d,81b,112a), pill, poll (74d,160a,177c), pull (45d,167d), rill (23c,102b,132a,148d, 157b), roll (134a,160b), rull (170b), sell (97a,115c,175b), sill (45c, 76c,165a,182b), tall (118d), tell (105d,129c,154b), Tell (160d), till (39c,101c,173d), toll (131c), vill (176b), wall, well, will (18b,43a, 163c,177c), yell (145c)

L - - L leal (54b,94c,139d), lill (15d,118a), loll (94b,128c), lull (25c,126d,150c)

- LM - alma (40d,53d,146d,147a), Alma (38d,183c), alme (40d,147a), alms (29a), elmy, ulme (49c)

- - LM balm (110a,172c), calm (8d,11d,112b,118d,126c,d,172b,173d), culm (11a,32d,70d,145a,156a), film (164b), halm, helm (144d, 165d), holm (77d,82d,109a), malm (32a,92b), palm (59b,163a,169b)

L - - M Liam (181d), loam (47d), loom (11c,146b,179b), lyam (139a)

324

-LN - ulna (21d,39b)

- - LN kiln (15d,112a), vuln (184d)

L - - N Lain, laun (146b), lawn (20a,37c,53b,92c), lean (128a,148b,152d, 164b,166a), Leon (96a), lien (65c,91a,124c), liin (188), limn (45d, 121c), linn (120d,140a,c,168c,178d), lion (55b,86c), llyn (120d, 140a), loan, loin (40a,98a), loon (19a,b,c,157d,179c), lorn (42d, 60b), loun (19a,b), lown (157d)

LO - - load (24c,26d,161b), loaf (79b,94b), loam (47d,150a), loan, lobb (23b,94c,163a), lobe (90c,134b), lobo (165d,183c), loch (88a,139d), loci (66b,118c), lock (54d), loco (38b,119b,120b), lode (42c,99a, 111b,175b), Lodi (105d), Lodz, loft (14c,69d,104b,178b), loge (164a), logy (46d), loin (40a,98a), loir (45c), Loir, Lois (165d,183c), loka (173c,184c), Loke (7c,15d,68b), Loki (7c,15d,68b), Lola (27d, 97b), loll (94b,128c), Lolo (27d,30a), loma (58b,63d), Lome, lone (150a), long (38b,185b), Lonk (143d), lood (189), loof (144c,153d) look (11c,53c,142a), loom (11c,146b,179b), loon (19a,b,c,157d, 179c), loop (31b,107d), Loos, loot (22a,118a,119d,136a,153d), lope (48b,64b,d), lora (146b,149b,151c,169b), Lora (183c), lord (107c), lore (77c,87c,90d,151c,183a), lori (91b), lorn (42d,60b), loro (19a,114b), lory (19a,114a), lose (60a,100c), losh (178b), loss (42c,123d,178b), lost, lota (24c,121d,178d), lote (24c,94a), loth (15a,173d), Loti (63a,176a), loto (65a,121d,178d), lots, loud (156a), loun (19a,b), loup (61d,62a,90c,139d), Loup (193), lour (13d,63d), lout (15c,22a,24b,45b,109a,157d), love (163a), lowa (19a), lown (157d), lowp (90c,139d)

-LO - alod (51c,55d,88a,124c), aloe (7d,20a,76a,b,92b,98b,119b,155b, 167a,183d), alop (13d,46b,93d), alow (18a,172c), blob, bloc (173a), blot, blow, clod (22a,45b,157d), Cloe (183c), clog (30c,145b), clop, clot (32d,94d), clou (62b), clow (58c,148c), cloy (61b,137c, 159d), elod (49b,59d,79c), Elon (18c,51b,108a), floc (149a), floe (79b), flog (180d), flop (54a), flot (173a), flow (157b), glom (155d, 160d,178c), glow (144c), ilog (132a,161b), ilot (82d), klom (189), klop (150d), Olor (160a,b), plod (170b), plop (54b), plot (25a,36b, 118d,138b), plow (39c,165d), ploy (43c), slob (173d), sloe (14a,20b, 64a,119d,181c), slog (157c,170b,177d), sloo (160a), slop, slot (10d, 11b,41d,110d,167d,168a,181b), slow (43c)

- - LO allo (34c), bilo (131b), bolo (87a), calo (72d), dilo (120d,168c), filo, gilo (48a), Golo (191), Gulo (183c), halo (14d,31b,92a), hilo (74c), kalo (162a), kilo (99b,122d), kolo (59b,135c), lalo (16b,34d), Lalo (35c), Lolo (27d,30a), malo (23a,74c,152a), milo (70b,87c), Milo, nolo (42a), orlo (56b,119c), Oslo, palo (152c), pelo (83b), polo (154a), Polo (175b), ralo (188), silo (59a), solo (12c,89a,110c), ullo (6a,144a), velo (175b)

L - - O lago (83b,152b), lalo (16b,34d), Lalo (35c), lazo (88d,128b,133d), leno (37c,53b), Lero (82d), Leto (11c), levo (91a), Lido (83d,175b), lino, lobo (165d,183c), loco (38b,119b,120b), Lolo (27d,30a), loro (19a,114b), loto (65a,121d), ludo (65a,112b)

- LP - Alph (132a), Alps (85d), olpe (90d,182c)

- - LP calp (92b), colp (28a,148b), gulp (46a,79d,160a), help (14a), kelp (82a,141c), palp (11a,55b,58b,167c), pulp, salp (14Sd), yelp

325

L - - P laap (51d,91b,141d), lamp (92a,94c), Lapp (108a), larp (51d), leap (26c), lerp (51d,141d), limp (58a,81a,177d), lisp (153b), loop (31b,107d), loup (61d,62a,90c,139d), Loup (193), lowp (90c,139d), lump (45a,160c)

- - LR Ullr (146b,164d)

L - - R lair (37c,42b), lear (139d), Lear (37a,143b), leer (9d,58a,67c,93d, 112a,148c), lehr (67c,112a), Leir, liar (98d), loir (45c), Loir, lour (13d,63d)

- LS - also (10b,18b,80a), Elsa (70a,93c,110d,177b,183c), else (18b,79b, 111d)

- - LS fels (190), fils (62d,150b), Hals (47a), ills (170a)

L - - S Lais (17c), Laos (80d,129c), Lars (51d,121b), lass (95b), lees (46a, 142a), lens (95b,111a,129b,162d), less (100c,108b,141d), Lias (66a), liss (54b,58b,60c,129d,140a) Lois (165d,183c), Loos, loss (42c,123d,178b), lots, Lubs (94c), Lyas (66a)

- LT - alta (89c,152d), alto (152b,176c,177a)

- - LT Balt (93a), belt (16a,31a), bolt (13b,54d,58b,132d,160a), bult (76d), celt (30c,82c,123a,156c,167b,179b), Celt (10a,180a,b), colt (78c,131a,185d,186b), Colt, cult (141d,161c), dolt (20c,59c,157d), felt, galt, gelt (101c), gilt (69c,77c,151d,185d), halt (13b,28a,38d, 156d), hilt (73c), holt (36d,119b,184b), jilt, jolt (143b), Kelt (180b), kilt, lilt (93a,131a,147a), malt (17c), melt, milt (153d), molt (27a, 143d) pelt (53a), salt (35d,105b,123a,136c,141c,149d), silt (104b, 142a), tilt (26b,d,166a), tolt, volt (49b,78c), Walt (96b), welt (36d,131b,145a,b,177b,d), wilt (46b), yelt (151b)

L - - T lact (34c), laet (60d), lait (62a), lant, last (36c,50b,145a,174c), leet (26a,38a,139d), left (42c), lent (54d), Lent (115d,141c), lest (59d, 163d), Lett (16a,90a,93a), lift (49b), lilt (93a,131a,147a), lint (46a, 58d), list (26d,27b,75b,83d,134a,138b,165d), loft (14c,69d,104b, 178b), loot (22a,118a,119d,136a,153d), lost, lout (15c,22a,24b,45b, 109a,157d), lust (41b)

LU - - Luba (191), lube (110a), Lubs (94c), luce (58c,117d), Luce (7b,35a), luck (28d), lucy, Lucy (183c), Ludd (23c), ludi (133b), ludo (65a, 112b), luff (136b), luge (148a), Lugh (28b), luif, luke, Luke (52a, 96a), lull (25c,126d,150c), lulu (19a,57b,112c), Lulu (183d), lump (45a,160c), luna (103c), Luna (102b), lune (38c,73b,74d), lung, luny (38b), lupe (19a,64a), lura (22d,82a), lure (41c,51a,54b,163a), lurg (96d,141b,184d), Luri (191), lurk (92a,147d), lush (94d), lust (41b), lute (11c,28b,84d,105a,131d), luxe (61c,62d,159c)

- LU - alum (14a,45c), Alur (191), blub, blue (33c,98c,102c,150d,173a), blup, blur, blut (65b), club (39c), clue, Elul (102b), flub (22b), flue (8b,30a), flux (28d,58d), glub, glue (7b,156a), glug, glum (102c, 159a), glut (52c,70a,137c,159d), llus (88d,170b), plug (156d,184d), plum, plup, plus (10b,102c) slub (171c), slue (97b,148b,160a), slug (46b,99b,157c), slum, slur (44b,124c,148b,168a), ulua (57a,74c), Ulua (141b)

- - LU Aalu (6b,48d), aulu (74c,168c), balu (104b,159a,181d), hulu (55b), lalu (48d), iglu (51c,149b), lulu (19a,57b,112c), Lulu (183d), pelu (30a,106d,168c), pulu (74c), Sulu (102c), tolu (16a), Tulu (45d), zulu (171d,175d), Zulu (86a)

L - - U latu (190), lieu (118c,155d), limu (141c), Lieu (40c), lulu (19a,57b, 112c), Lulu (183d)

- LV - Alva (151d), Ulva (141b)

LW - - Lwow

L - - W Llew (40c), Lwow

- - LX calx (23c,75c,112c), falx (133b)

L - - X lanx (133a,b), lynx (26c,181d), Lynx (36b)

LY - - lyam (139a), Lyas (66a), lynx (26c,181d), Lynx (36b), Lyra (36b, 74a), lyre (11c,81c,105a,111c), lyse

- LY - Alya (155b,c), Alys (183c), Clym (12b), Ilyn (120d,140a)

- - LY ably (147c), ally (14a,35c,d,173c), coly (104a), eely (185a), holy, idly, inly, July, Lely (47a), lily, moly (76a,181c), oily (110b, 172c), only (24d,52c,98d,147a,150a), Orly (8b), paly (194), pily, poly (34c,76b), puly, rely (16b,170b), rily (176a), ugly, vily (54b), wily (13b,38b,39c)

L - - Y Lacy, lady, laky, lazy, Lely (47a), levy (14a,162b), lily, limy (176d), liny (157b), livy (132d,133a), logy (46d), lory (19a,114a), lucy, Lucy (183c), luny (38b)

L - - Z Linz (40d), litz (127b), Lodz

MA - - maal (188), ma'am (95a,166b), maar (177a), Maas (132a), Maat (69a,b,85d), Maba (103a,168d), mabi (58d), mace (49d,108d,153b, 154d,161a,178a), mack, made, Madi (174a), mado (14d,57a,170b), mage (95b), magg (95b), Magh (102a), magi (123c), Magi (95b, 116c,183a), maha (28c,88c,136d), mahr (103a), Maia (76b,109a, 153b,155b,177c), maid (45b,142d), mail (12d,99b,121c), maim (43d,81a,105c), main (29d,35d,123d), mais (61b), maja (151c), Maja (153b), majo, make (35b,36d,54a,123a), maki (91b), mako (18a,19a,20d,143c,168c,182c), Maku (192), mala (89b,c,90a,94b, 97d,109d,185c), male (154d), Male (45d), mali (27b), mall (95d, 124b,143b), malm (32a,92b), malo (23a,74c,152a), malt (17c), mama, Mama (116d), mamo (19a,74b), mana (30a,120d,122a, 159c), mand (28b), mane, mani (115c), mann (189), Mann (9c, 48c,185c), mano (71d,73d,74b,83b), Mans (30a), Manu (10a,76d, 77a,b), Manx (27b,28a,82d), many (108d), mapo (68a,148d), mara (114d), Mara (24a,d,105b,107b), marc (70c), Marc (96a) mare (78b), Mare (108b), mari (61d), Mari (16a), mark (146b,155a), Mark (52a, 96a), marl (32a,42c,55d), maro (144d), Mars (68c,118d,119a,129a, 178a), mart (49d,97a), Mart (96b,183d), maru (84c,144d), Mary (50c,126b,183c), masa (37a), mash (39b,156c), mask (44a,45c), mass (8a,24b,35b,142d), mast (17c,108d,120b,144d,152d), masu (57a,84c), mate (18c,35b,41d,113a,154a,162c), math (77a), Matt, maty (80c), maud (53d,71a,136d,143c), Maud (181a,183c), Maui (120d), maul (73c,96b), maun (139d), maya (77a,179b), Maya (23d, 186c), Mayo (193), maze (87b,157d)

- MA - amah (95b,108d,111c), amar (189), imam (25c,102d,103a), Oman (159a), omao (165b), omar (103b), Omar (48c,51b,116c,163b), Xmas

- - MA alma (40d,53d,146d,147a), Alma (38d,183c), amma (6a), atma (150d), bema (28d,31a,114b,119b,125b,137a), boma (7d),

cima (83b,c), **coma** (91c,157d,170c,172b), **cyma** (101a,b), **dama** (65d,152b), **Duma** (135c), **Emma** (183c), **Erma** (183c), **Fama** (1·35a), **Gama** (121c), **Goma** (191), **Hima** (191), **iJma** (103b), **Irma** (96d), **jama** (103b), **Kama** (56d), **lama** (23d,24a,91d,165b), **lima** (17b,152b,174d), **Lima** (31b), **loma** (58b,63d), **mama, Mama** (116d), **mima** (185d), **Nama** (78c), **Nema** (34d,48c,134b,164d,176c), **Numa** (133a), **pima** (37c), **Pima** (192), **puma** (27b,37c,55b,103d), **Rama** (77a,80b,176d), **rima** (23a,30c,32a,58a,110d), **Roma** (83c,d), **sama** (105c,169d), **sima** (132b), **soma** (10c,21c,34a,48a,81d,136b), **Tama** (192), **tema** (12a,164a), **Toma** (191), **xema** (72c), **Xema** (12c), **Yama** (57a,68a), **Yima** (84a,116b,c), **Yuma, Zama** (73d, 141d)

M - - A **Maba** (103a,168d), **maha** (28c,88c,136d), **Maia** (76b,109a,153b, 155b,177c), **maja** (151c), **Maja** (153b), **mala** (89b,c,90a,94b,97d, 109d,185c), **mama, Mama** (116d), **mana** (30a,120d,122a,159c), **mara** (114d), **Mara** (24a,d,105b,107b), **masa** (37a), **maya** (77a, 179b), **Maya** (23d,186c), **meda** (110a), **mega** (34b,c), **mela** (34a, 129d), **mesa** (49b,76d,119b,161a), **meta** (132d,133a), **Meta, mica** (82c,100b,146c), **mila** (188), **mima** (185d), **mina** (10b,70b,71d, 179d), **Mina** (23a,183d), **mira** (174d), **Mira** (155b), **moha** (42b, 83d), **Mola** (159c), **mona** (72b,101d), **mora** (42b,65a,72b,83d,99b, 153a,161a), **mota** (103a), **moxa** (27d,30c), **muga, mura** (84d), **Mura** (192), **Musa** (16a), **muta** (28d,103a), **myna** (19a,c,70b), **Myra** (10a, 31b,183c), **myxa** (168c,169a)

- MB - **amba** (161a), **ambi** (34a,122c), **ambo** (125b,128b), **imbe** (37a,56a, 133d), **umbo** (22b)

- - MB **bomb** (144a), **comb** (38c), **dumb** (153b), **iamb** (59c), **jamb** (12d, 45c,118a,146b,174a), **lamb, Lamb** (49c), **limb** (12d,22d), **nimb** (31b,73b,92a,107b,131d), **numb, rumb** (120b), **tomb, Zimb** (6c)

M - - B **medb, Moab** (18d,85a,86d,94a)

M - - C **marc** (70c), **Marc** (96a)

M - - D **maid** (45b,142d), **mand** (28b), **maud** (53d,71a,136d,143c), **Maud** (181a,183c), **mead** (46a,78a,97d,99b), **Mead** (78a), **meed** (128c, 131a), **meld** (26a,41c,99a,118b), **mend** (130b), **mild** (32a,66a), **mind** (75c,81d,93d,109b), **Moed** (100c), **mold** (54d,143c), **mood** (44c), **mudd** (188), **mund** (124d)

ME - - **mead** (46a,78a,97d,99b), **Mead** (78a), **meal** (72a,130b), **mean** (15a, 42b,146c,156b), **meat** (59b), **meda** (110a), **Medb, Mede** (10a,b,13c), **medi** (34c), **meed** (128c,131a), **meek** (93d,99d), **meer, meet** (11d, 13d,36a,50a,81d,142d), **mega** (34b,c), **mein** (30b), **meio** (188), **mela** (34a,129d), **meld** (26a,41c,99a,118b), **mele** (74b,150b), **melt, memo** (108b), **mend** (130b), **mene** (19a,73d,108d,185c), **Ment** (54b,164a), **menu** (19a,27a), **Menu, meou, meow, mere** (16c,22b, 62a,78b,87d,96c,110c,120d,146d,148b), **meri** (20b), **mero** (72a), **Meru** (77a,103d), **mesa** (49b,76d,119b,161a), **mese** (71c), **mesh** (50d,106c), **mess** (22b,44b,77c,85d,104b,165c,173d), **meta** (132d, 133a), **Meta, mete** (9a,11d,22b,44c,45b,98a,121c), **meum** (27a, 89c), **Meum, mewl** (180d), **mews** (1·54c)

- ME - **amen** (14a,80b,94a,137a,149c,175c,184b), **Amen** (86d,127d,159b, 164a), **amer** (61b), **Ames** (9c,82a), **Amex** (184d), **Emer** (39b,183c),

328

emeu (111d), **Imer, Omei** (24a), **omen** (14c,59d,60a,121c,123a, 146b), **omer** (51a,75c), **smee** (19b,46c,d,118b,119d,141b,181b), **Smee** (116d), **smew** (19b,46d,99a,137d), **T-men** (168b), **Ymer** (67a, 131c)

- - ME **acme** (39c,115c,186b), **alme** (40d), **arme** (63a,179b), **came** (182b), **Came** (192), **come, cyme** (58d,69c), **dame** (67b,87c,166b), **deme** (71b,c,167d), **dime, dome** (39c,133c,155d), **fame** (130a) **feme** (181b), **fume** (129a,149a,157a), **game** (64d,154a), **gime** (77d), **home, Hume** (50c), **kame** (67b,139b), **Kome** (71d), **lame** (38d,43d, 73b), **lime** (25b,27d,31b,102d,168c), **Lome, mime** (24a,71b,85a, 100a), **Mime** (131d,148d), **name** (8a,11b,d,25c,46c,107c,130b,157d, 163b,166b), **nome** (71c,163b), **Nome, oime** (8b), **pome** (11d), **Pume** (137b,175b,185b), **rame** (22d), **rime** (30c,36a,58a,63d,77c), **Rome** (31c,51d), **ryme** (178d), **same** (44d,79b), **seme** (45c,138b,151b, 154b,155c,157b), **sime** (101d), **some** (114b,121c,126a), **tame** (45a, 66a), **Tame, time** (47a,131a), **tome** (21d,177c), **ulme** (49c), **zeme** (55d,161b,180b), **zyme** (55c)

M - - E **mace** (49d,108d,153b,154d,161a,178a), **made, mage** (95b), **make** (35b,36d,54a,123a), **male** (154d), **Male** (45d), **mane, mare** (78b), **Mare** (108b), **mate** (18c,35b,41d,113a,154a,162c), **maze** (87b, 157d), **Mede** (10a,b,13c), **mele** (74b,150b), **mene** (19a,73d,108d, 185c), **mere** (16c,22b,62a,78b,87d,96c,110c,120d,146d,148b), **mese** (71c), **mete** (9a,11d,22b,44c,45b,98a,121c), **mice, mide** (110a), **mike, Mike** (96b), **mile** (64c), **mime** (24a,71b,85a,100a), **Mime** (131d,148d), **mine** (69c,79d,111b,124c), **mire** (21c,104b), **mise** (8a, 10a,70c), **mite** (12b,81b,82a,114a,c,148c,d,181b), **Mixe** (192), **mode** (54d,96b,157d,179a), **moke** (45c,157d), **mole** (19d,23a,24d,85a, 117c,155c), **Mole** (88c), **mope** (92d,159a), **more** (71a), **More** (50b), **Mose** (96b), **mote** (114c,153a), **moue** (61d,62b), **move, mule** (45b, 148b,153c,180b), **mure** (177d), **muse** (65b,93d,120d,164c), **Muse** (68d), **mute** (146c,153b)

M - - F **miff** (44c), **moff** (53b,146c), **muff**

M - - G **magg** (95b), **migg** (96c), **Ming** (30b,c), **morg** (188), **mung** (70d)

MH - - **mhor** (180b)

- - MH **samh** (56b)

M - - H **Magh** (102a), **mash** (39b,156c), **math** (77a), **mesh** (50d,106c), **moth, Moth** (112d), **much, mush** (97d), **muth** (188), **myth** (8b,91a)

MI - - **miam** (14d), **mian** (97c,147b,166b), **Miao** (30a,b), **mias** (111a), **miau** (27b,99b), **miaw** (27b,99b), **mica** (82c,100b,146c), **mice, mick** (82c), **mico** (97a), **mide** (110a), **Midi** (151b), **mien** (11c, 17b,26d,44c,96b), **miff** (44c), **migg** (96c), **mike, Mike** (96b), **mila** (188), **mild** (32a,66a), **mile** (64c), **milk, mill** (126c), **milo** (70b,87c, 150d), **Milo, milt** (153d), **mima** (185d), **mime** (24a,71b,85a,100a), **Mime** (131d,148d), **mimi** (14d), **Mimi** (87b,110d,125b,183d), **mina** (10b,70b,71d,179d), **Mina** (23a,183d), **mind** (75c,81d,93d,109b), **mine** (69c,79d,111b,124c), **ming** (30b,c), **mink** (176d), **mino** (84c), **mint** (13a,33b,58b,76a), **minx** (116c), **miny, Mira** (155b,174d), **mire** (21c,104b), **mirk** (41a,67d), **miro** (19a,106d,184a), **Miro** (113a, 151d), **miry, mise** (8a,10a,70c), **miss, mist** (46b,59b,174d), **mite** (12b,81b,82a,114a,c,148c,d,181b), **mitt** (56c), **mitu** (39d), **mity, Mixe** (192), **mixy**

329

- MI - amia (22c,170d), amic (9d), amid (9d,50a), amie (61d), amil (45a, 48a,185c), amin (9d), amir (7c,12a,103a,b,123c,170d), amit (94a), Emil (96a), Emim (67a,100d), emir (12a,103a,b,123c,134d,135a, 171a), emit (43d,49a,53c,58d,83a,142c), imid (29c), omit (49c, 52c,106b,114c,147d)

- - MI admi (65d), ammi (98c), demi (34b,122c), hami (78a), hemi (122c), immi (189), jami (103b), kami (68a,84b), Kami (88c,107c,144c), Komi (191), mimi (14d), Mimi (87b,110d,125b,183d), rami (22d), Remi (10b), romi (72d), semi (34b,80b,122c,d), Simi (82d), zemi (55d,161b,180b)

M - - I Mabi (58d), Madi (174a), magi (123c), Magi (95b,116c,183a), maki (91b), mali (27b), mani (115c), mari (61d), Mari (16a), Maui (120d), medi (34c), Midi (151b), mimi (14d), Mimi (87b,110d,125b,183d), moki (127b), Moki

M - - J munj (70d)

M - - K Mack, mark (146b,155a), Mark (52a,96a), mask (44a,45c), meek (93d,99d), mick (82c), milk, mink (176d), mirk (41a,67d), mock (131b,162b), monk (28b,63c,129d), mosk (97b,103b), muck, mulk (60d), murk (41a,67d), musk (116b)

- ML - amla (48a,161d,168c,169a), amli (48a,161d,168c,169a)

M - - L maal (188), mail (12d,99b,121c), mall (95d,124b,143b), marl (32a, 42c,55d), maul (73c,96b), meal (72a,130b), merl (20b), mewl (180d), mill (126c), moil (46c,184c), moll, Moll (183d), mull (53b, 135a,164c)

- MM - amma (6a), ammi (98c), ammo (9d), ammu (9d), Emma (183c), immi (189)

M - - M ma'am (95a,166b), maim (43d,81a,105c), malm (32a,92b), meum (27a,89c), Meum, miam (14d)

- MN - omni (34a)

- - MN damn, Domn (135a), famn (188), hymn (150c), limn (45d,121c)

M - - N main (29d,35d,123d), mann (189), Mann (9c,48c,185c), maun (139d), mean (15a,42b,146c,156b), mein (30b), mian (97c,147b, 166b), mien (11c,17b,26d,44c,96b), moan, moon (40b,132c,137c), morn, mown

MO - - Moab (18d,85a,86d,94a), moan, moat (44d), mock (131b,162b), mode (54d,96b,157d,179a), Moed (100c), moff (53b,146c), mogo (74b), moha (42b,83d), moho (19a,78a), mohr (65d), moil (46c, 184c), moio (188), mojo (177c), moke (45c,157d), moki (127b), moko (96c), Mola (159c), mold (54d,143c), mole (19d,23a,24d,85a, 117c,155c), Mole (88c), moll, Moll (183d), molt (27a,143d), moly (76a,181c), mona (72b,101d), monk (28b,63c,129d), mono (34c, 78d,122d,147a), Mono (193), mons (89c), Mons (184d), mont (62b), mood (44c), moon (40b,132c,137c), moor (10a,75b,137b,141d, 178b), Moor (102c,d,111d), moot (41b,44c), mope (92d,159a), mora (42b,65a,72b,83d,99b,153a,161a), more (71a), More (50b), morg (188), morn, moro (19a,56c), Moro (100a,103a,117a,159a), Mors (41b), mort (41b,47a,78b,136d), Mose (96b), mosk (97b,103b), moss (91d,104c,114a,170c), most, mosy (67d), mota (103a), mote (114c,153a), moth, Moth (112d), moto (104b), moue (61d,62b), move, mown, moxa (27d,30c), Moxo (192), mozo (152b)

-MO - amoi (62a), amok (18b,63c), Amon (86d,96b,127d,159b,164a), amor (152b), Amor (39c,68b), Amos (96a,144b), Amoy (88c)

--MO ammo (9d), atmo (34d,174d), Como, demo (122d), hemo (34a, 122b), homo (122d), ikmo (18b), itmo (18b), mamo (19a,b,74b), memo (108b), nemo (34b), Nemo (56a,85c), Pomo (192), Sumo

M--O mado (14d,57a,170b), majo, mako (18a,19a,20d,143c,168c,182c), malo (23a,74c,152a), mamo (19a,74b), mano (71d,73d,74b,83b), mapo (68a,148d), maro (144d), Mayo (193), meio (188), memo (108b), mero (72a), Miao (30a,b), mico (97a), milo (70b,87c, 150d), Milo, mino (84c), miro (19a,106d,184a), Miro (113a,151d), mogo, (74b), moho (19a,78a), moio (188), mojo (177c), moko (96c), mono (34c,78d,122d,147a), Mono (193), moro (19a,56c), Moro (100a,103a,117a,159a), moto (104b), Moxo (192), mozo (152b), Muso (192), Muzo (192), myxo

-MP - impi (86a), umph

--MP bump, camp (163b), damp (101a), dump, gamp (172a), gimp (169d), Gump (43b), hemp (26a,37a,56a,133d), hump (124d), jump, kemp (139b), lamp (92a,94c), limp (58a,81a,177d), lump (45a, 160c), mump (29b,153d), pomp (111d,112d), pump, ramp (65a, 80b,127b,148b), romp (63d), rump, samp (70b,77d,121b), simp (59c,146d), sump (28c,45d,100b), tamp (46b,112b,121d), tump (60a,76d,103d), tymp (20c), vamp (80a,145a)

M--P mump (29b,153d)

-MR - amra (77c), Omri (18c,86d)

M--R maar (177a), mahr (103a), meer, mhor (180b), mohr (65d), moor (10a,75b,137b,141d,178b), Moor (102c,d,111d), Muir (8b, 142c), murr (72b,128b)

-MS - Omsk

--MS alms (29a), arms, Rems

M--S Maas (132a), Mais (61b), Mans (30a), Mars (68c,118d,119a,129a, 178a), mass (8a,24b,35b,142d), mess (22b,44b,77c,85d,104b,165c, 173d), mews (154c), mias (111a), miss, mons (89c), Mons (184d), Mors (41b), moss (91d,104c,114a,170c), muss (135b,173d)

M--T Maat (69a,b,85d), malt (17c), mart (49d,97a), Mart (96b,183d), mast (17c,108d,120b,144d,152d), Matt, meat (59b), meet (11d,13d,36a,50a,81d,142d), melt, Ment (54b,164a), milt (153d), mint (13a,33b,58b,76a), mist (46b,59b,174d), mitt (56c), moat (44d), molt (27a,143d), mont (62b), moot (41b,44c), mort (41b,47a, 78b,136d), most, must (70c,101a,106d,157d,182c), mutt (39c, 101d), myst (71c,123b)

MU -- Muav (66a), much, muck, mudd (188), muff, muga, Muir (8b, 142c), mule (45b,148b,153c,180b), mulk (60d), mull (53b,135a, 164c), mump (29b,153d), mund (124d), mung (70d), munj (70d), mura (84d), Mura (192), mure (177d), murk (41a,67d), murr (72b, 128b), Musa (16a), muse (65b,93d,120d,164c), Muse (68d), mush (97d), musk (116b), Muso (192), muss (135b,173d), must (70c,101a, 106d,157d,182c), muta (28d,103a), mute (146c,153b), muth (188), mutt (39c,101d), Muzo (192)

•MU• Amun (86d,127d,159b,164a), smug, smur (32c,46b,100c), smut (32d,44a,119a,150c)

•-MU ammu (9d), Atmu (143a,159b), limu (141c), rimu (79d, 106d,129a, 168c)

M•-U Maku (192), Manu (10a,76d,77a,b), maru (84c,144d), masu (57a, 84c), menu (19a,27a), Menu, meou, Meru (77a,103d), miau (99b), mitu (39d), Mitu

M•-V Muav (66a)

M•-W meow, miaw (27b,99b)

M•-X Manx (27b,28a,82d), minx (116c)

MY•- myna (19a,c,70b), Myra (10a,31b,183c), myst (71c,123b), myth (8b,91a), myxa (168c,169a), myxo

•MY• amyl (155c), emyd (163c,167c), Emys (167c,171b)

•-MY army (78c), demy (113d), domy, elmy, fumy, homy (38b), ismy (45a), limy (176d), rimy (63d)

M•-Y many (108d), Mary (50c,126b,183c), maty (80c), miny, miry, mity, mixy, moly (76a,181c), mosy (67d)

NA•- Naab, naam (44c,150b), nabk (30d,164d), nabo (117a), Nabu (68c, 183a), nach, nael (189), naga (13d,33a,55b,127c), Naga (24c,77a, 88c,176d), Nagy (78d), Naia (33a), naid (63c), naif (74b,105d), naik, nail (31d,54d,141d,161d,173a), naio (107a,168c), Nair (45d), nais (63c,132a), Naja (33a), Nala (77a), Nama (78c), name (8a, 11b,25c,46c,107c,130b,157d,163b,166b), nana (118b), Nana (15c, 105d,116d,186d), nane (139d), naos (28a,71c,137a,163a), Naos (155b), napa (25c,67d,90d), Napa (182c), nape (15b,108c,d), napu (29d,80d), nard (13a,97c,102b,110a,153c), Nare (93c), nark (81a, 156d), nary (108b), nase (26b,75a,124b), Nash (9c), nasi (34c,108a, 115a), Nast (9c,27a), nata (47c), Nata (15c), Nate (22b), Nath (155c), Nato (6a,8d), natr (189), Natt (107b), naut (141b), nave (30d,31a,78d,114b,180c), navy (33c,58b), naze (26b,124b), Nazi

•NA• anai (163b,181a), Anak (67a), anam (159a,168c), Anam, anan (49a,159a,180c), Anas (46c,d), Anat (138c,147d), Anax (43c, 120c) anay (72b,163b,181a), enam (70c,77a), Enam (85c), gnar (72a), gnat (59a,81b,99c), gnaw (20a,107a,178b), inar (65b), knab (107a), knag (139c), knap (76d,107a,139b,159b,166a,170c,185b), knar (87c,134b), Onan (18c,85c), snab (23c,139a), snag (11b, 27b,35c,87c,124b,166a), snap (23a,36d,38b,48b,54d,56c,58c,149d), unal (147a), unau (148c,171d)

•-NA anna (190), Anna (110c,166d), arna (24a,181b), Bana (67a), bena (176a), bina (77a), bona (89d), Bona (183c), buna (161c), Cana (57a,64b,100c), cena (88d,133a), Cuna (193), Dana (28a,96a, 171d), dona (83d,121c,151d), dyna (34c), Edna (183c), Enna (146a), etna (75b,153c,157a,175d,177a,c), fana, gena (29b), Gona (106d), guna (106a,137b), Iona (28a,82d), Jena (105d,165b), kana (84d), kina (126d), kona (74c), lana (58a,66a,90a,184b), lena (56d), Lena (36b), lina (188), Lina (183d), luna (103c), Luna (102b), mana (30a,120d,122a,159c), mina (10b,70b,71d,179d), Mina (23a, 183d), mona (72b,101d), myna (19a,c,70b), nana (118b), Nana (15c,105d,116d,186d), nina (152a), Nina (26c,33d,68d,183d),

332

nona (89b,107b), **Nona** (69a,114a,183c), orna (169d,182c), **Pana,** pina (35d,118b), puna (10b,33b,104a,119b,182a), rana (77a,123c), **Rana** (63d), rena (132c), sana (56a,166d), **Sana** (185d), sina (46c), **Sina** (102d,103d), tana (159a), **Tana** (87d), **Tina** (183d), tuna (57a, b,123b,170d), ulna (21d,39b), urna (133a), vena (90a,175a), **vina** (77a,105a), **Xina** (183d), **Yana** (192,193), zona (144c,186d)

N - - A   naga (13d,33a,55b,127c), **Naga** (24c,77a,88c,176d), **Naia** (33a), **Naja** (33a), **Nala** (77a), **Nama** (78c), nana (118b), **Nana** (15c,105d, 116d,186d), napa (25c,67d,90d), **Napa** (182c), nata (47c), **Nata** (15c), nema (34d,48c,134b,164d,176c), **Nepa** (106b,178c), **Nera** (165b), **Neva** (91b,132a), **Nina** (26c,33d,68d,183d), nipa (14b, 46b,48a,164a,168c), **Nola, nona** (89b,107b), **Nona** (69a,114a,183c), **Nora** (79b,107a,164c,183c), nota (15c,89c), nova (20c,106d,155c, 174d), noxa, **Nuba** (108c), **Nuda** (39b), **Numa** (133a)

- NB -   anba (36d)

N - - B   **Naab,** nimb (31b,73b,92a,107b,131d), **numb**

- NC -   ance (158b,c,d), ancy (158c), ence (158c), **Inca** (14b,30a), **inch,** onca (189), once (60b,79b), unca (49a), unci (31d), unco (140c), **Ynca** (193)

- - NC   banc (61a,85c), zinc (21a)

- ND -   anda (23a,168c), **Ande** (193), **Andi** (27d), **Andy** (96b), endo (34d, 122d,183b), inde, onde (63a,178d), unde (179a), undo (11a,93d), undy (179a)

- - ND   **Arnd** (67a), band (72a,157c), bend (39d,171b), bind (33b,165c), bond (92a,101c,141d,143b,159d,165c), bund (49c,66c,90c), cond (156a), fend (114b,178b), find (44a), fond (7c,94b), fund (6d,101c, 130c), **Gond,** hand (60c,114c,115d,184c), hind (15b,41d,45a), kind (150d,153a,174d), land (44a,163c), lend (6d,79d), mand (28b), mend (130b), mind (75c,81d,93d,109b), mund (124d), pend, pond, pund (189), rand (16d,22a,131b,145a,b), **Rand** (69c), rend (32a, 159c,162c,185a), rind (53a,115c), **Rind** (109c,174b), rynd (100a), sand (71d,146c), send (42c,44b,95c,121c,130a,144c,168b), **Sind,** tend (26d,80b,93a,100a), tind (86b), tund (121d), vend (97a,115c, 142b), **Vend** (10b,148a), wand (120b,132c,156a), wend (67d,123d), **Wend** (10b,148a), wind (33b,39d,171c,185a), yond (164d), **Zend**

N - - D   naid (63c), nard (13a,97c,102b,110a,153c), need (42b,52d,87b, 122a,178a), **Nejd, NKVD** (135d), **Nudd** (23c)

NE - -   neaf (58a,73c), **Neal,** neap (165c,167a,177b), near (11d,32c,107b), neat (165c,169d), **Nebo** (68c,102d,103d,183a), neck (83a), need (42b,52d,87b,122a,178a), neem (96d,168c,169a), neep (140c, 171b), neer (14b,86b,108b), **Neil** (96a), nein (66c), **Nejd, Nell** (110a, 183d), nema (34d,48c,134b,164d,176c), nemo (34b), **Nemo** (56a,85c), nene (19b,74c), neon (65c), **Nepa** (106b,178c), **Nera** (165b), **Neri, Nero** (8a,126d,133a,150b,172c), ness (26b,75a,124b), nest (38b,74b,130d,149c,160b), nete (71c,108b,163d), neti (164a), nett, neue (66c), **Neva** (91b,132a), neve (56d,67c,70c,149b), **news** (165c), newt (48d),136c,169d), next (106a)

- NE -   **Aner** (18d,96b), anes (110c,140a), anet (43c), anew (7c), inee (120b), **Inez** (45c,183c), knee (85b), knew, knez (123c), oner (20d, 53a,75c,162d,173a,d), ones (116a), sned (93d,125a,140a), snee

(40a,43d,87a), **sneg** (139b)

• • NE acne (147c), aine (49b,62c,142c), Anne (50c,84a,143b,183c), a-one (52b,167b), Arne (35c,50c,134d), aune (188), bane (74a,106b,120b, 139a), bene (18a,83c,90a,106d,122a,180a), bine (145b,156a,171c, 176b), bone, cane (17b,128a,156a,159a,177d), Cane, cene (34c), cine (104b,152c), cone (66b,150a,157c), Dane (85d,107d,138a), dene (137a), Dene (192), dine, done, dune (137a), dyne (59d,173b), eine (66c), enne (34c), erne (19c,d,47b,54b,141a), esne (10c, 45b,142c,148a,164d), fane (30d,137a,162d), fine (49b,50a,104b, 115d,159a), gane (185b), gene (54a), Gene (96b), gone (6b,15c,42c, 44c,114d), gyne (34b,55b,183c), hone (110a,143c,180d), Ione (24b,88d,94d), jane (190), Jane (183c), June (183c), kane (74c), kine (38a,112c), lane (134b,157b), lene (36b,149a,172b), line (12b, 22b,36d,38a,126c,134b,157b,158b,162d,175c), lone (150a), lune (38c,73b,74d), mane, mine (69c,79d,111b,124c), mene (19a,73d, 108d,185c), nene (19b,74c), nine (26c,104d), none (108b), ohne (66d,183b), orne (169d,182c), Orne (25b), pane (113c,155a,b), pene, pine (36a,52a,88c,93c,168c,d,169a), pone (37a,85b), rine (44d,75d, 135c), rone (127c,164b), rune (9b,67a,94a,95a,105c,107d,120a, 141d,163d), sane (128a), sine (64c,66b,90a,97c,126a,163b,169d, 183b), syne (140b,147a), Tane (120d), tene (34d,131b), tine (11b, 124b,167b), tone (6c,118c,150d), tune (8b,12c,98c), tyne, Tyne (108a), vane (179b,182a), vine (32b), wane (41c,43c), wine, zone (44c,50a,160a)

N • • E name (8a,11b,d,25c,46c,107c,130b,157d,163b), nane (139d), nape (15b,108c,d), Nare (93c), nase (26b,75a,124b), Nate (22b), nave (30d,31a,78d,114b,180c), naze (26b,124b), nene (19b,74c), nete (71c,108b,163d), neue (66c), neve (56d,67c,70c,149b), nice (54d, 119c,130c), Nice (98c), nide (23c,72a,106c,116d), nife (37a), Nike (69c,100c,182d), nile (33c,71d), Nile (106b), nine (26c,104d), Niue (137d), node (35c,85b,87c,94d,120a,124d,160c), nome (71c,163b), Nome, none (108b), Nore (163d), nose (118d,125a,149b), note (98c,109b,124b,128d,130a,177c), nove (83b), noze (75a), nude (16c,172d), Nupe (191)

N • • F naif (74b,105d), neaf (58a,73c)

NG • • ngai (48a,159c), ngan

• NG • ange (61a), ango (171a), inga (145d,170a), Inge (24d,67d,117c 119c)

• • NG bang (75d,105d,148a), beng (43a), bing, bong, bung (119d,156d), cang (184a), dang, ding (130b), dong, fang (167b), Fong (40b), Fung (191), gang (38c), gong, hang (160a), hing (13c), hong (30b), hung, Jung (125a), k'ang (30a), king (26c,29c), kung (125b), ling (24c,57a,b,75b,178c), long (38b), lung, Ming (30b,c), mung (70d), pang (165b), ping, pong, pung (22c,148b), Qung (191), rang, ring (50a), Rong (88c), rung (28c,39a), sang, sing (26d,178a), song (12c,170c), sung, Sung (30b), tang (30b,58b,186b), teng (188), ting (166a), Ting (30c), tong (30a,c), tung (110a,168c), uang (131a), vang (72d,134a,140b), wang (189), wing (10d,58c,59a, 118b,d), wong (56a), yang (30b,70a), zing

N • • G niog (33a,168c), nogg (48d)

334

-- NH binh (189), hunh?, sinh (97c), tanh (97c)

N -- H Nach, Nash (9c), Nath (155c), nigh (106a), Nish (19d), Noah (88a, 99b)

NI -- Nias (82d), nibs (116c), nice (54d,119c,130c), Nice (98c), nick (30c,108b), nide (23c,72a,106c,116d), nidi (106c), nife (37a), nigh (106a), Nike (69c,100c,182d), nile (33c,71d), Nile (106b), nill (173d), nimb (31b,73b,92a,107b,131d), nina (152a), Nina (26c, 33d,68d,183d), nine (26c,104d), nino (152a), niog (33a,168c), niou (188), nipa (14b,46b,48a,164a,168c), Nish (19d), nisi (90a, 173c), nito (55c), Niue (137d)

- NI - anil (47c,80d,180b), Anim (18d), anis (55c), Enid (13b,25d,66b, 163a,183c), Enif (155b), enin (20d), inia (9b,109b), Inia (28c,45b), knip (115c), knit (173c,179b), snib (54d,93c), snig (45d), snip (32b,40a), unie (173a), Unio (105c), unis (91b), unit (101c,110c, 147a)

-- NI Aani (45a,48d), agni (88a,89c), Agni (56d,68b), arni (24a,181b), bani (190), beni (116a,142d), Beni (191), Bini (191), Boni (63b), Coni, doni (21a,28c,168a), Ioni (192), mani (115c), omni (34a), Pani (120c), rani (72d,77b,123c,127c), Reni (83d), yeni (19b,161d), Zuni (125b)

N -- I nasi (34c,108a,115a), Nazi, Neri, neti (164a), ngai (48a,159c), nidi (106c), nisi (90a,173c), nodi (35c,87c), nori (8c,141c)

-- NJ Funj, gunj (70c), munj (70d)

NK -- NKVD (135d)

- NK - ankh (38d,162b), Enki (15b), Inka (193), inky (20b)

-- NK bank (18a,58c), bonk (190), bunk, conk (41c,108a,156d,157c), dank (40b,101a), dunk (43c,79d), fink (19a,56c,157c), funk (63d, 113c), gink (48b), hank (147c), honk (70a), hunk, jink, jonk, junk (30a,134c), kink (38b,171c), konk (41c), kunk (188), lank (148b, 164b), link (36a,81d,85b), lonk (143d), mink (176d), monk (28b, 63c,129d), pank (189), pink (26d,33c,60c,138a), punk (9b,166a, 167c), rank (31d,55d,70b,92c,94d,157d), rink (147c,154a), sank, sink (41c,43c,46b,158a), sunk, tank (175a,d), tonk (173c), wink (107a), yank, Yank

N -- K nabk (30d,164d), naik, nark (81a,156d), neck (83a), nick (30c, 108b), nock (13b,108b), nook (37a,130d), nubk (30d,164d)

- NL - inly, only (24d,52c,98d,147a,150a)

N -- L nael (189), nail (31d,54d,141d,161d,173a), Neal, Neil (96a), Nell (110a,183d), nill (173d), noel (26d,150b) Noel (30d,96a), noil (87c, 178b), Noll (96b,110b), noyl (87c), null (108c,177a), nurl (33b,87c)

N -- M naam (44c,105b), Naam, neem (96d,168c,169a), norm (15a,115a, 128a,155a)

- NN - Anna (110c,166d,183c), anna (190), Anne (50c,84a,143b,183c), Enna (146a), enne (34c), Enns

-- NN binn (22c), Bonn (17d), bunn (25b), conn (43d,156a), Finn (107d), Jann (102d), jinn (42b,103b,153c), linn (120d,140a,c,168c,178d), mann (189), Mann (9c,48c,185c), rann (175c), senn (76b), sunn (56a), wynn (165d)

N - - N nein (66c), neon (65c), ngan, noon, Norn (69a,163d,174b), noun (114b,158a)

NO - - Noah (88a,99b), nobs (38c,87a), nock (13b,108b), node (35c,85b, 87c,94d,120a,124d,160c), nodi (35c,87c), noel (26d,150b), Noel (30d,96a), noes (177c), nogg (48d), noil (87c,178b), noio (107c, 163c), noir (61b,134b), noix (67c), Nola, Noll (96b,110b), nolo (42a), nome (71c,163b), Nome, nona (89b,107b), Nona (69a,114a, 183c), none (108b), nono (83b), nook (37a,130d), noon, Nora (79b, 107a,164c,183c), Nore (163d), nori (8c,141c), norm (15a,115a, 128a,155a), Norn (69a,163d,174b), nose (118d,125a,149b), Nosu (27d), nosy, nota (15c,89c), note (98c,109b,124b,128d,130a,177c), Nott (107b), noun (114b,158a), noup (124b), nous (81d,100a, 128b), nova (20c,106d,155c,174d), nove (83b), nowt (106a,139a), nowy (194), noxa, noyl (87c), noze (75a)

- NO - anoa (28a,60a,112c,181c), anon (7d,14d,79d,80b,123a,145c,150c, 164a), enol (29c,158b), Enon (18c,d), Enos (7a,18d,52a,70c,96a, 143a), enow (50d,123a,158b), knob (73c), knop (124b,170c,185b), knor (87c), knot (43c,99d,107c,124d,137b), know, snob (159c), snod (169d), snow

- - NO Aino (84a,c), Arno (27a), asno (151d), beno (113b,117a), cano (152a), dino (34b), fano (51d,96b,113c,d), fono (137a), Gano (132d), Hano (125b), hino (106d,168c), Juno (69c,85d,100c,126b), Kano (84c,177d), keno (161d,168c), kino (27c,34c,47c,72c,98b), leno (37c,53b), lino, mano (71d,73d,74b,83b), mino (84c), mono 34c,78d,122d,147a), Mono (193), nino (152a), nono (83b), pino (152c), puno (182a), Reno, sano (152b), sino (34a), Tano (192), Tino (136d), tuno (28b,168c), vino (92d,182b), xeno (34d), Zeno (71b)

N - - O nabo (117a), naio (107a,168c), Nato (6a,8d), Nebo (68c,102d,103d, 183a), nemo (34b), Nemo (56a,85c), Nero (8a,126d,133a,150b, 172c), nino (152a), nito (55c), noio (107c,163c), nolo (42a), nono (83b)

N - - P neap (165c,167a,177b), neep (140c,171b), noup (124b)

- - NQ cinq (61d)

- NR - inre (35d,80a), inro (84b,c,106c)

N - - R Nair (45d), natr (189), near (11d,32c,107b), neer (14b,86b,108b), noir (61b,134b), nurr (67d)

- NS - ansa (73c,93d,137c), anse (61d), ansu (11d), ense (139b,158c), enso 34d,183b)

- - NS bans, cens (115b), dans (62a), dens (90a,167b), Duns, Enns, fons (60c), gens (42d,132d), Hans (66d,96a), hens (121d), lens (67c, 95b,111a,129b,162d), Mans (30a), mons (89c), Mons (184d), oons (100a,186d), Pons (13d,63c,110d,150c), sans (63a,183b), Sens (63b), sons (98d,109d), Vans (107d)

N - - S nais (63c,132a), naos (28a,71c,137a,163a), Naos (155b), ness (26b, 75a,124b), news (165c), Nias (82d), nibs (116c), nobs (38c,87a), noes (177c), nous (81d,100a,128b)

- NT - anta (83d,117c,d,121a), Anta (164a), ante (87a,89a,115b,120b, 122b,125d,154d), anti (7d,111a,122b), Anti (193), ente (70b,151d),

ento (34b,d,183b), **Inti** (159b), **into** (123a,183b), **onto** (76a,174a), **unto** (166c), **untz** (189)

- - NT aint, arn't, aunt (129c), bant (43c), bent (80b), bunt (15d,180c), cant (28d,81b,84d,90c,109b,136c,165d,166a), **cent** (36d), **dent** (42c,77d), dint (48c,59d,122a), dont, dunt, font (16b,171d,172a), gent, hant (67a), hint (9a,39c,159a), hunt (141c), kant (28d), Kant (67a), **Kent** (90d), lant, lent (54d), **Lent** (115d,141c), lint (46a,58d), **Ment** (54b,164a), mint (13a,33b,58b,76a), mont (62b), oont (25d), pant, pent (36a), pint (67b), pont (55d,61b), punt (21a,58b), rant (41c,127b,128a,161a), **rent** (58a,77c,91b,138b, 153d,162c,167c), runt (47a,172d), sent, tent (26b,115a), tint (33c, d,114d), vent (8b,11b,110d,112a), vint (26c,182c), want (41b, (38b,74b,106b,122a), went (42c), wont (6d,40a,73a,174c)

N - - T Nast (9c,27a), Natt (107b), naut (141b), neat (165c,169d), **nest** (38b,74b,130d,149c,160b), nett, newt (48d,136c,169d), next (106a), **Nott** (107b), nowt (106a,139a), nuit (62b)

NU - - Nuba (108c), nubk (30d,164d), nuda (39b), Nudd (23c), nude (16c, 172d), nuit (62b), null (108c,177a), Numa (133a), numb, **Nupe** (191), nurl (33b,87c), nurr (67d)

- NU - Cnut (40d,50c), knub (178b), knur (67d,87c,107c), knut, Knut (40d,50c,96a), onus (24c,93b,109b), snub (128c,148b), snug (35a, 38b,165c), **Snug** (99d), snup (149b)

- - NU Ainu (84a,c), benu (49a), **Danu** (28a), genu (6b,18a,87a,89c), **Manu** (10a,76d,77a,b), menu (19a,27a), **Menu**, tunu (28b), zenu (143d)

N - - U Nabu (68c,183a), napu (29d,80d), niou (188), **Nosu** (27d)

- NV - envy (41b)

- - NX jinx (78a), jynx (78a), **Jynx** (184a), lanx (133a,b), lynx (26c,181d), **Lynx** (36b), **Manx** (27b,28a,82d), minx (116c), **Yunx** (184a)

N - - X noix (67c)

- NY - **Enyo** (12c,69c,178a), onym (162c), onyx (25d,28d,65d,142b), **Pnyx** (71c)

- - NY bony (147c), **Bony** (96b), cony (127a), deny (36d,43d,129b), liny (157b), luny (38b), many (108d), miny, piny, pony, puny (55b, 179a), tiny (100c,148c), tony, **Tony** (96b), tuny, viny, wany, winy (176c), zany (24a,32d,59c)

N - - Y **Nagy** (78d), nary (108b), navy (33c,58b), nosy, nowy (194)

- NZ - anzu (11d), **Enzu** (102b), onza (189), unze (189)

- - NZ **Linz** (40d)

OA - - **Oahu**, oaks (154d), oaky, oary, oast (15d,86b,112a), oath (119c, 150a)

- OA - boar (77c,117c,160c,181c), **boat** (27b,106a), **Boaz** (135d), coag (45d,118a,163b), coak (45d,118a,163b), coal (49c,64a), **Coan** (37b), coat (160a), coax (180c), doab (157c), doat (17a,94b,112a,165d), **Eoan** (41a,85b), foal (78c), foam (63d,15^b), goad (80b,154b), goaf (104b), goai (106d,168c), goal (8b,109b,120b,125d), **Goan**, goat (135a), hoar (63d,71a,181a), hoax (41c,122a), **Joab** (41a), **Joad** (50c), **Joan** (183c), joar (100a), koae (74b), load (24c,26d,161b), loaf (79b,94b), loam (47d,150a), loan, **Moab** (18d,85a,86d,94a),

337

moan, moat (44d), Noah (88a,99b), road (37d,164d), roam (178a), roan (78b,c,114c,128d,144a,181a), roar (145c), soak (46c,137c), soap, soar (59a), toad (10a,17a,63d,126d), woad (20d,47c), Zoar, Zoas (20b)

--OA anoa (28a,60a,112c,181c), Aroa (175b), Gjoa (144d), pooa (76a, 125b), proa (21b,26a,95c,d), Shoa (6c) stoa (33c,121a,c), tooa (17c), whoa (156d)

O--A obia (55d), obra (152d,184c), ocha (189), ocra (72c,175a), octa (122c), odea (105d,164a), Offa (163d), ohia (74c,168c), okia (190), okra (72c,175a), olea (170b), Olea (110b), Olga (135c,183c), olla (36d,44b,84d,113b,121d,151d,152c,181b), onca (189), onza (189), orca (86b), orna (169d,182c), orra (139c,d,140a), ossa (21d), Ossa (103d,110b,164b), Otea (71a,82d), otra (152c), oxea (153d)

OB-- oban (190), Obed (135d), obex (22d), obey (35c,75c), obia (55d), obit (41b,64c), oboe (74b,104d,105a,182a,184a), obol (29b,110a), obra (152d,184c)

-OB- boba (29d), bobo (112c,168c), Cobb (9c), Cobh (37a), dobe (159b, c,172b), doby (159b,c), gobi, Gobi (42d), gobo (84d), goby (57d), hobb (124b), hobo (168a,174b), jobo (77c), Koba (11a), Kobe (78a), kobi (84b), kobu (84b), lobb (23b,94c,163a), lobe (90c, 134b), lobo (165d,183c), nobs (38c,87a), robe (65b), Sobk (38d), Toba (80c), tobe (7d,137b), toby (8c,85c,104b), Toby (96b,125c), Yobi, zobo (186b)

--OB blob, boob (146d), brob (153c), chob (23c), doob (18b), jaob, knob (73c,107c,124d), rhob (64a,85c), scob (42a), slob (173d), snob (159c), swob (102b), thob (128a)

OC-- ocha (189), ocra (72c,175a), octa (122c), octo (34a,89b,122c)

-OC- boca (152b,c), boce (23b,52a,57b), bock (17c,90d,144a), coca (29d, 33a,105d,113a), cock (19a,29a,55a,133d,136d,161d,174b), coco, dock (40a,117c,144d,179d), Foch (63b), foci (28b), hoch (52c, 66c), hock (91a,115b,182b,c), jock, Jock (96b), jocu (45b,57a), Koch (66d), loch (88a,139d), loci (66b,118c), lock (54d), loco (38b, 119b,120b), mock (131b,162b), nock (13b,108b), poco (83b,93a), Roch (136c), rock (160b), sock (157c,182a), soco (22d), tock (7d, 19b), toco (19b,167c), voce (83c,177a)

--OC bloc (173a), croc (13a,74a), floc (149a)

O--C odic (79c,120a), olic (158b), otic (14c,d,47b)

OD-- odah (170d), odal (48a,88b,112c), Odax (132c), odds (28d,172d), Odea (105a,164a), odel (48a,112c), Oder (132a), odic (79c,120a), Odin (7c,29d,63c,68c,175d,183b), odio (83b), odor (138b,156a), odum (168c,180a), odyl (59d,79c)

-OD- Bodb (82b), bode (14c,60a,110b,121b), Bodo (88c), body (72a), coda (32c,35d,56c), code (21c,31a,40c,161c), codo (188), dodd (139c,140c), Dode (96b), dodo (19b), Jodo (113d), lode (42c,99a,111b,175b), Lodi (105d), Lodz, mode (54d,96b,157d, 179a), node (35c,85b,87c,94d,120a,124d,160c), nodi (35c,87c), Roda (107b), rodd (38d), rode (46c), rodi (98c), soda (19a,149d, 181a), Toda (45d,76d), tode (80a,148a), todo (22b,24d,35b,64c, 156b), tody (19b,d,59a,166a), yodh (91d)

--OD alod (51c,55d,88a,124c), apod (59d), Arod (86c), biod (59d,79c),

338

clod (22a,45b,157d), **elod** (49b,59d,79c), **feod** (55d), **food** (109a, 176b), **good, hood** (38a,74d), **lood** (189), **mood** (44c), **plod** (170b, 177d), **pood** (189), **prod** (67d,80b,106b,120b), **quod** (123d), **rood** (38d,39a,88b), **shod, snod** (169d), **stod** (40d,67d), **trod, wood**

O - - D   **obed** (135d), **olid** (55d,60c,148d,157d), **ooid** (48d), **oord** (190), **orad** (104a), **Ovid** (132d,133b), **oxid** (112c)

OE - -   **oese** (15d,119c)

- OE -   **Boer** (151a), **coed, coel** (39b), **Doëg** (137c), **doer** (8a,116b), **does, goel** (15a,75c), **goer, hoek** (39d), **hoen** (189), **hoer, hoey** (114c), **Joel** (96a), **joey** (86a,185d), **Joey** (96b,109c), **koel** (19a,b,39b), **Moed** (100c), **noel** (26d,150b), **Noel** (30d,96a), **noes** (177c), **poem** (51a), **poet** (49b), **roed, roer** (72d), **roey** (103d), **toed, voet** (188)

- - OE   **aloe** (7d,20a,76a,b,92b,98b,119b,158b,167a,183d), **Cloe** (183c), **eboe** (28b,110a,168c,169b), **evoe** (15b,130d,181c), **floe** (79b), **froe** (32a,167a,179d), **oboe** (74b,104d,105a,182a,184a), **Otoe** (147b), **shoe** (166a), **sloe** (14a,20b,64d,119d,181c)

O - - E   **oboe** (74b,104d,105a,182a,184a), **oese** (15d,119c), **ogee** (40c,101a, b,120b), **ogle** (9d,53c,91a,93d,148c), **ogre** (67a,102a), **ohne** (66d, 183b), **Oime** (8b), **Oise, Okie** (99d), **olpe** (90d,182c), **once** (60b, 79b), **onde** (63a,178d), **ooze** (53c,104b,116a), **orfe** (57a,b,185c), **orle** (17b,56b,76a,144b,177a), **orne** (169d,182c), **Orne** (25b), **oste** (21d,83b), **Otoe** (147b), **Ouse** (132a,185d), **owse**

OF - -   **Offa** (163d), **offs** (38c)

- OF -   **doff** (130a,161b), **goff** (32d), **koff** (47a), **loft** (14c,69d,104b, 178b), **moff** (53b,146c), **sofa** (44d), **soft** (48b,95d,99d,163a), **toff** (40d)

- - OF   **Azof** (20b,135d), **goof, hoof** (173a), **loof** (144c,153d), **poof, roof** (78d), **stof** (135c), **woof** (39a,163d,165a,179d)

O - - F   **Olaf** (108a,176b)

OG - -   **ogam** (82b,c), **ogee** (40c,101a,b,120b), **ogle** (9d,53c,91a,93d,148c), **Ogor** (170d), **Ogpu** (135d), **ogre** (67a,102a), **ogum** (82b)

- OG -   **boga** (57d,180b), **bogo** (117a,168c), **Bogo** (191), **bogy** (153a), **doge** (95b,175b), **dogy** (46d,103c), **fogy, goga** (24a), **gogo** (16b,24a, 149c), **Gogo** (191), **hoga** (144b), **hogg** (144a), **jogi** (76d), **loge** (164a), **logy** (46d), **mogo** (74b), **nogg** (48d), **Pogo** (121c), **pogy** (57a,88a,98d,103c), **soga** (70d,152b), **Soga** (191), **toga** (132d,133a, b), **togs** (32c), **togt** (77c), **Vogt, yoga** (10b,13c,77a), **yogh** (10c, 185a), **yogi** (76d), **zogo** (136a)

- - OG   **agog** (47b,52c,86b), **ajog, clog** (30c,145b), **flog** (180d), **frog** (10a, 17a,126d), **grog** (92d,153d), **ilog** (132a, 161b), **niog** (33a,168c), **slog** (157c,170b,177d), **stog** (155a), **voog** (28a,66a,132b)

OH - -   **ohia** (74c,168c), **Ohio, ohne** (66d,183b), **ohoy** (106a)

- OH -   **boho** (117a,179d), **Bohr** (14b,40d,138c), **coho** (136d), **fohn** (182b), **Hohe** (192), **John** (11c,96a,121a,186b), **kohl** (53c), **moha** (42b,83d), **moho** (19a,78a), **mohr** (65d), **poha** (74c), **rohr** (72d), **soho!, Soho** (93c), **toho** (79a)

- - OH   **booh** (52c), **pooh** (22b,107d)

O - - H   **oath** (119c,150a), **odah** (170d), **okeh** (8d,37b), **opah** (23b,57a,b, 86d), **ouch!, ough**

OI - - oily (110b,172c), oime (8b), Oise

- OI - Boii (191), boil, bois (62b,63a,183d), coif (73a), coil (39d,171c, 185a), coin (19b,37a,100c,101c,179d), coir (33a,37a,56a,133d), Coix (70d,85b), doit (47a,169d,180d), Eoin (85b), foil (15d,55c, 165b), join (36a,173c), koir (33a), loin (40a,98a), loir (45c), Loir, Lois (165d,183c), moil (46c,184c), moio (188), noil (87c,178b), noio (107c,163c), noir (61b,134b), noix (67c), ooid (48d), roil (44c, 104b,156b,170d,176a), Soia, soie (62c), soil (154d,159a,163c), soir (61c), toil (46c,184c), void (11a,49d,108d,174b), zoid

- - OI amoi (62a), Ekoi (191)

O - - I Omei (24a), omni (34a), Omri (18c,86d)

- OJ - bojo (117a), coja (103b,166b), hoja (166b), hoju (84b), koji (185b), mojo (177c), rojo (129a,152c), soja (151b)

OK - - okay (8d), okeh (8d,37b), oket (189), okia (190), Okie (99d), okra (72c,175a), okro (72c,175a)

- OK - boko (52b), coke (32d,64a), coky, Doko (191), joke (183a), joky, koko (106d,114b), Koko (93d,186c), koku (189), loka (173c,184c), Loke (15d,68b), Loki (7c,15d,68b), moke (45c,157d), moki (127b), Moki, moko (96c), poke (108c), poku (11a), poky (148c), roka (95a,168c,d), roke (174d,175b), soka (20c), soke (44c,85d), toko (30c), woke, yoke (85b,92d,173c)

- - OK amok (18b,63c), asok (13d), book, cook (137b), dook (184a), hook (27b,39d), irok (55b), look (11c,53c,142a), nook (37a,130d), pook (68a), rook (19b,29c,39a), sook (22a,25c,97a), took

O - - K Omsk

OL - - Olaf (108a,176b), olam (51a,d,75c,81a), Olan (115c), Olax (52b), olay (113b), Olea (110b,170b), oleo (34c), Olga (135c,183c), olic (158b), olid (55d,60c,148d,157d), olio (44b,77c,98c,100d,121d), olla (36d,44b,84d,113b,121d,151d,152c,181b), Olor (160a,b), olpe (90d,182c)

- OL - bola (16a), bold (41a), bole (31d,32a,169b), boll (119b,d), bolo (87a,179b), bolt (13b,54d,58b,132d,160a), cola (25b,108d,149d, 168c), cold (65d), cole (25a), Cole, coli, colp (28a,148b), colt (78c, 131a,185d,186b), Colt, coly (104a), dola (189), dole (44c,118c, 121c,129d), Dole (74c), doli, doll (125c), dolt (20c,59c,157d), fold folk (116a,169c), gola (27b,40c,70c,157a), gold, golf (154a), goll (105c), Goll, Golo (191), hola (74c,152b), hold (95c,124c,130d), hole (6c,11b,110d,118c,147a), Holi (77a), holm (77d,82d,109a), holt (36d,119b,184b), holy, Iola, Iole (52a,76b,123c), jole (29b), joll (62b), jolt (143b), kola (25b,84a,108d,168c), Kola (135b,c,d), Koli (27b), kolo (59b,135c), Lola (27d,97b), loll (94b,128c), Lolo (27d,30a), Mola (159c), mold (54d,143c), mole (19d,23a,24d,85a, 117c,155c), Mole (88c), moll, Moll (183d), molt (27a,143d), moly (76a,181c), Nola, Noll (96b,110b), nolo (42a), Pola, pole (132c,143b,177b,184a), Pole (52a), polk (37c), poll (74d,160a, 177c), polo (154a), Polo (175b), poly (34c,76b), role (114b), roll (134a,160b), sola (9a,48a,74b,118c,154a,167b), sold, sole (52c, 57a,b,58b,d,110c,115d,150a), soli (12c,110c), solo (12c,89a,110c), tola (48a,80d), Tola (85b,180a), told (129c), tole (9a,51a,99b,163a), toll (131c), tolt, tolu (16a), vola (89d,150a), vole (97d,104a,148a,

149b), **volk** (66c,105d,116a,184c), **Volk, volt** (49b,78c,173b), **wold** (47c,60a,118d,174a,184a), **wolf, yolk, Zola** (63a)

--OL **bool** (39d), **chol** (118d), **Chol** (192), **cool** (25c,107d), **egol** (11b), **enol** (29c,158b), **fool** (24a,41c,47a,146d), **gaol** (123d), **Gaol** (164a), **idol** (48c,54c,55a,75b,79d,112d,130b,184d), **itol** (158b), **obol** (29b, 110a), **pool** (65a,119d,120d), **siol** (82c), **tool** (27c), **viol** (105a), **wool** (58b,179c)

O--L **obol** (29b,110a), **odal** (48a,88b,112c), **odel** (48a,112c), **odyl** (59d, 79c), **opal** (20a,65d,67b,82b), **oral** (114a,153d,174c,175c), **Orel, oval** (48d,49c), **oxyl** (112c)

OM-- **Oman** (159a), **omao** (165b), **omar** (103b), **Omar** (48c,51b,116c, 163b), **Omei** (24a), **omen** (14c,59d,60a,121c,123a,146b), **omer** (51a,75c), **omit** (49c,52c,106b,114c,147d), **omni** (34a), **Omri** (18c, 86d), **Omsk**

-OM- **boma** (7d), **bomb** (144a), **coma** (91c,157d,170c,172b), **comb** (38c), **come, Como, dome** (39c,133c,155d), **Domn** (135a), **domy, Goma** (191), **home, homo** (122d), **homy** (38b), **Kome** (71d), **Komi** (191), **loma** (58b,63d), **Lome, nome** (71c,163b), **Nome, pome** (11d), **Pomo** (192), **pomp** (111d,112d), **Roma** (83c,d), **Rome** (31c,51d), **romi** (72d), **romp** (63d), **soma** (10c,21c,34a,48a,81d,136b), **some** (114b, 121c,126a), **Toma** (191), **tomb, tome** (21d,177c)

--OM **Ahom** (88c), **asom** (18d), **atom** (101c,114c,180d), **boom** (152d), **coom** (32d,150c,178d), **Crom, doom** (42d,55a,134d), **Edom** (18c, 51b,79b,82c,84a), **from, glom** (155d,160d,178c), **joom** (39c), **klom** (189), **loom** (11c,146b,179b), **room** (28d), **stom** (34c), **toom** (139b), **whom** (42b), **zoom**

O--M **odum** (168c,180a), **ogam** (82b,c), **ogum** (82b), **olam** (51a,d,75c, 81a), **onym** (162c), **ovum** (48d)

ON-- **Onan** (18c,85c), **onca** (189), **once** (60b,79b), **onde** (63a,178d), **oner** (20d,53a,75c,162d,173a,d), **ones** (116a), **only** (24d,52c,98d, 147a,150a), **onto** (76a,174a), **onus** (24c,93b,109b), **onym** (162c), **onyx** (25d,28d,65d,142b), **onza** (189)

-ON- **a-one** (52b,167b), **bona** (89d), **Bona** (183c), **bond** (92a,101c,141d, 143b,159d,165c), **bone, bong, Boni** (63b), **bonk** (190), **Bonn** (17d), **bony** (147c), **Bony** (96b), **cond** (156a), **cone** (66b,150a,157c), **Coni, conk** (41c,108a,156d,157c), **conn** (43d,156a), **cony** (127a), **dona** (83d,121c,151d), **done, dong, doni** (21a,28c,168a), **don't, fond** (7c,94b), **Fong** (40b), **fono** (137a), **fons** (60c), **font** (16b,171d,172a), **Gona** (106d), **Gond, gone** (6b,15c,42c,44c,114d), **gong, hone** (110a, 143c,180d), **hong** (30b), **honk** (70a), **Iona** (28a,82d), **Ione** (24b, 88d,94d), **Ioni** (192), **jonk, kona** (74c), **konk** (41c), **lone** (150a), **long** (38b,185b), **lonk** (143d), **mona** (72b,101d), **monk** (28b,63c, 129d), **mono** (34c,78d,122d,147a), **Mono** (193), **mons** (89c), **Mons** (184d), **mont** (62b), **nona** (89b,107b), **Nona** (69a,183c), **none** (108b), **nono** (83b), **oons** (100a,186d), **oont** (25d), **pond, pone** (37a,85b), **pong, Pons** (13d,63c,110d,150c), **pont** (55d,61b), **pony, rone** (127c,164b), **Rong** (88c), **song** (12c,170c), **sons** (98d,109d), **tone** (6c,118c), **tong** (30a,c), **tonk** (173c), **tony, Tony** (96b), **wong** (56a), **wont** (6d,40a,73a), **yond** (164d), **zona** (144c,186d), **zone** (44c,50a,160a)

341

‑‑ON acon (62c,140d), agon (12c,36c,41b,55d,71b), Amon (86d,96b, 127d,159b,164a), anon (7d,14d,79d,80b,123a,145c,150c,164a), aton (150a,159b), Avon (143b), axon (106c,153c), azon (127b), bion (117b), boon (18b,20c,55a), cion (42d,70b,145b,148b,154b, 156a), coon (121c), Dion (96a,152a), doon (140b,168c), ebon (20b), Elon (18c,51b,108a), Enon (18c,d), Eton (33b,50c,84a), faon (33c, 55a), Gaon (85b), goon (157c,163c), hoon (190), icon (79d,92b, 136a), ikon (79d,136a), iron (55c,d,69d,81a,97b,143b,149a,173d, 179c), Leon (96a), lion (55b,86c), loon (19a,b,c,157d,179c), moon (40b,132c,137c), neon (65c), paon (115b), peon (28c,59c,99c), phon (94a), pion (43c,52b), poon (97c), roon (41a,168b), scon (162c), sion (125c,158c), Sion (75b,c,83a,157d), soon (123a), tion (158b), toon (80c,95b,168c), tron (180a), upon (6b), woon (24c), Zion (75b,c,83a,157d) zoon (43a)

O‑‑N oban (190), Odin (7c,29d,63c,68c,175d,183b), Olan (115c), Oman (159a), omen (14c,59d,60a,121c,123a,146b), onan (18c), Onan (85c), open (26a,60d,81a,109b,112c,125b,172b,173c), Oran, oven (15d,78c,86b), Owen (96a,183c), oxan (65c), oxen (10c)

OO‑‑ ooid (48d), oons (100a,186d), oont (25d), oord (190), ooze (53c, 104b,116a), oozy (148b)

‑OO‑ boob (146d), booh (52c), book, bool (39d), boom (152d), boon (18b,20c,55a), boor (47a,135d,172c), boot (128d), cook (137b), cool (25c,107d), coom (32d,150c,178d), coon (121c), coop, Coos (192), coot (19b,46d,72b,138d,141a,146d,157d), doob (18b), dook (184a), doom (42d,55a,134d), doon (140b,168c), door (51a,121b), food (109a,176b), fool (24a,41c,47a,146d), foot (115a), good, goof, goon (157c,163c), Goop (107d), goor, hood (38a,74d), hoof (173a), hook (27b,39d), hoon (190), hoop (181b), hoot (112c), joom (39c), koop (16c), lood (189), loof (144c,153d), look (11c,53c,142a), loom (11c,146b,179b), loon (19a,b,c,157d,179c), loop (31b,107d), Loos, loot (22a,118a,119d,153d), mood (44c), moon (40b,132c, 137c), moor (10a,75b,137b,141d,178b), Moor (102c,d,111d), moot (41b,44c), nook (37a,130d), noon, pooa (76a,125b), pood (189), poof, pooh (22b,107d), pook (68a), pool (65a,119d,120d), poon (97c), poop (41c), poor (33a), poot!, rood (38d,39a,88b), roof (78d), rook (19b,29c,39a), room (28d), roon (41a,168b), root (53a), Roos (67a), sook (22a,25c,97a), soon (123a,145c), soot (20b, 26c,88a), tooa (17c), took, tool (27c), toom (139b), toon (80c, 95b,168c), toot, voog (28a,66a,132b), wood, woof (39a,163d, 165a,179d), wool (58b,179c), woon (24c), yoop, zoon (43a)

‑‑OO aboo (17a), aroo (80c,82b), broo (139a), ejoo (55b,168c), Kroo (191), phoo, shoo (46b,67a,138b), sloo (160a), whoo

O‑‑O octo (34a,89b,122c), odio (83b), Ohio, okro (72c,175a), oleo (34c), olio (44b,77c,98c,100d,121d), omao (165b), onto (76a,174a), ordo (22a,30d,122a,171a), orlo (56b,119c), Oslo, otho (133a), otro (151d), otto (58d,116b,134a), Otto (14c,66d,67a,96a)

OP‑‑ opah (23b,57a,b,86d), opal (20a,65d,67b,82b), open (26a,60d, 81a,109b,112c,125b,172b,173c), Opie (50c), opus (35c,105a,184c)

‑OP‑ copa (88b,113c), cope (12b,26b,36c,65b,157d,176a), Copt (48d),

342

copy, dopa (117d), dope (46c,105d), dopp (43c), hope (13d,52d), hopi (33c), Hopi (12c,102c,125b), hops (17c), koph (91d), kopi (107a,168c), Kopi (172a), lope (48b,64b,d), mope (92d,159a), pope (20a,30d,31c,120d), qoph (91d), rope (36d,88d,128b), ropy (157c, 176d), soph, Sopt (45b), tope (24a,46b,57a,143c,151a), toph (75c), topi (37a,75a,118c), tops (159c)

●●OP alop (13d,46b,93d), asop (180b), atop (112a,174a), chop (98a), clop, coop, crop (38b), drop (43d,54b,100b,114c,168b), Esop (53b,54a), flop (54a), Goop (107d), hoop (181b), klop (150d), knop (124b,170c,185b), koop (16c), loop (31b,107d), plop (54b), poop (41c), prop (159d), scop (120a), shop, slop, stop (73b,111b), swop (168a), trop (62d,167a), yoop

●●OQ shoq (169a)

OR●● orad (104a), oral (114a,153d,174c,175c), Oran, oras (40d), orca (86b), ordo (22a,30d,122a,171a), ordu (170d), Orel, orfe (57a,b, 185c), orgy (26d,130d,137c), orle (17b,56b,76a,144b,177a), orlo (56b,119c), Orly (8b), orna (169d,182c), orne (169d,182c), Orne (25b), orra (139c,d,140a), orts (60d), oryx (11a)

●OR● bora (181d,182b), bord (100b), bore (14c,25b,46a,116a,165c, 179b), borg (40d), Bori (110d,150c), born, boro (154b), Boro (193), Bors (70b,134b), bort (43b), Bort (134b), cora (65d), Cora (42b, 69c,80c,116b,124d,172b,183c), cord (39b,131a), core (28b,51c, 75b,81b), cork (119d), Cori (138c), corm (24b,38d,156a), corn (39d,95c,123a), dora (70b), Dora (36d,41a,43b,183c,d), dord (42c), dore (61d,67b,69d,117d), Dore (50d,63a,b), dorm, dorn (164d), dorp (73c,176b), dorr (32b), dory (21b,58b,144c), fora (133a), ford (177b), fore (63d,174b), fork, form (54d,143c), fort (63d,157d), gora (81c), gore (115d,117c,154c,169c), gory, hora (22a,40b), horn (11a,105a,170b,182a), hors (62b), kora (178c), Kora, kore (107b), Kore (29a,42b,116b,124d), kori (7d,77a), lora (146b,149b,151c,169b), Lora (183c), lord (107c), lore (77c,87c, 90d,151c,183a), lori (91b), lorn (42d,60b), loro (19a,114b), lory (19a,114a), mora (42b,65a,72b,83d,99b,153a,161a), more (71a), More (50b), morg (188), morn, moro (19a,56c), Moro (100a,103a, 117a,159a), Mors (41b), mort (41b,47a,78b,136d), Nora (79b, 107a,164c,183c), Nore (163d), nori (8c,141c), norm (15a,115a, 128a,155a), Norn (69a,163d,174b), oord (190), pore (59d,110d, 111c,120d,157d), pork, Poro (141d), port (73d,136b,140c,170c,d, 182b,c), Rori (16b), sora (19b,c,127b), sorb (11d,103d,134b,142d), Sorb (148a,180a), sore (23d,142c), sori (55c,64a), sorn (139a,d), sors (44d,89b), sort (31d,39c,70b,86b,153a), sory (176d), tora (11a,44d,74a,75c,85c,90b,102d,115d), tore, tori (101b), torn (130a), toro (38a,107a,152a,168c), torp (54c), tort (31c,91a,185c), Tory (23c,36b,94c,172a), word (124b,165c), wore, work (64c,76b), worm, worn (143b), wort (76a,95d,121d), yore (10b,69d,93c,110b, 165d), york (38c), York (50b,c)

●●OR acor (6d), ador (153b), amor (152b), Amor (39c,68b), asor (75c, 105a), boor (47a,135d,172c), chor (164b), door (51a,121b), Ghor (174b), goor, Igor (135d), knor (87c), mhor (180b), moor (10a, 75b,137b,141d,178b), Moor (102c,d,111d), odor (138b,156a), Ogor (170b), Olor (160a,b), poor (33a), shor (136d), Shor (162b), Thor

(7c,68c,99c,100c,109c,165b), **utor** (90a,166c)

O - - R **Oder** (132a), **odor** (138b,156a), **Ogor** (170d), **Oior** (160a,b), **omar** (103b), **Omar** (48c,51b,116c), **omer** (51a,75c), **oner** (20d,53a,75c, 162d,173a,d), **osar** (51b,67b,131b), **oser** (61b), **over** (6b,38c,80a, 114d), **oxer** (55c), **oyer** (38a,75b,119c)

OS - - **osar** (51b,67b,131b), **oser** (61b), **Oslo, ossa** (21d) **Ossa** (103d,110b, 164b), **oste** (21d,83b)

- OS - **bosa** (12a), **Bosa, Bosc** (115c), **bose** (163c), **bosh, bosk** (164b), **boss** (49d,157d), **cosh** (35a,97c), **cose** (29b), **coso** (152c), **coss** (98a), **cost** (29a), **cosy** (149c), **dosa** (74b), **dose** (123a), **doss** (17c), **dost, foss** (44d,100d), **gosh, hose** (156c), **host** (13a,51d,104c), **Jose** (96a), **josh** (85b), **joss** (30b), **Josy** (183d), **koso** (6c,80d), **Koso** (192,193), **koss** (188), **lose** (60a,100c), **losh** (178b), **loss** (42c,123d, 178b), **lost, Mose** (96b), **mosk** (97b,103b), **moss** (91d,104c,114a, 170c), **most, mosy** (67d), **nose** (118d,125a,149b), **Nosu** (27d), **nosy, pose** (14c,15d), **posh** (49b,148c), **post** (89a,95c,155d), **Rosa** (58d, 134a,145d,183c), **rose** (33c), **Rose** (6a,50c,183c), **ross** (16c,161d), **Ross** (50c), **rosy** (21a,111a), **sosh** (81d), **soso** (99c,114c,166c), **tosh** (106a), **Tosk** (8c), **toss** (24a,132d, **Xosa** (86a)

- - OS **Amos** (96a,144b), **bios** (92a), **Coos** (192), **Enos** (7a,18d,52a,70c, 96a,143a), **epos** (51a,76b,120a), **Eros** (11c,39c,68b,97c,182d), **ghos** (30b), **gros** (47a,53d,146c), **Gros** (63a), **Laos** (80d,129c), **Loos, naos** (28a,71c,137a,163a), **Naos** (155b), **phos, Taos** (192), **Teos** (82a), **Thos** (84a,181c)

O - - S **oaks** (154d), **odds** (28d,172d), **offs** (38c), **ones** (116a), **onus** (24c, 93b,109b), **oons** (100a,186d), **opus** (35c,105a,184c), **oras** (40d), **orts** (60d), **Otis** (9c,d,24d,82a,111a), **Otus** (67a), **ours** (124c), **Ovis** (143d), **oyes** (38a,39b,75b)

OT - - **Otea** (71a,82d), **Otho** (133a), **otic** (14c,d,47b), **Otis** (9c,d,24d,82a, 111a), **Otoe** (147b), **otra** (152c), **otro** (151d), **otto** (58d,116b,134a), **Otto** (14c,66d,67a,96a), **Otus** (67a)

- OT - **bota** (189), **both, Boto** (192), **bott** (32a,88d), **cota** (117a), **cote** (19b,143d,144a,b), **coto** (16c,90b), **Coty** (63c), **dote** (17a,90b,94b, 97a,112a,139d,165d), **doth, Doto** (141b), **doty** (43d), **Goth** (16c, 163d), **Hoth** (20c), **hoti, iota** (71a,85c,91c,114c,166c,176a,180d), **jota** (151c), **joti, kota** (117a), **Kota** (45d), **koto** (84b), **Iota** (24c, 121d,178d), **loth** (15a,173d), **lote** (24c,94a), **Loti** (63a,176a), **loto** (65a,121d,178d), **lots, mota** (103a), **mote** (114c,153a), **moth, Moth** (112d), **moto** (104b), **nota** (15c,89c), **note** (98c,109b,124b, 128d,130a,177c), **Nott** (107b), **pott** (113d), **rota** (27c,30d,38a,79a, 92d,133a,134a,b,180c), **rote** (130b,134b,143a,159d), **roti** (62c), **roti** (103b,111c), **roto** (30a,122d,127b,152c,171b), **sote** (150c), **tota** (71d), **tote** (27a,73c), **toto** (8d,15a,34d,89a,181a), **toty** (87b), **vota** (133b), **vote** (60b), **Vote** (56d), **Voth** (191), **Voto** (192), **Wote** (191)

- - OT **Abot** (100c), **blot, boot** (128d), **clot** (32d,94d), **coot** (19b,46d,72b, 138d,141a,146d,157d), **eyot** (82d), **Fiot** (191), **flot** (173a), **foot** (115a), **frot** (28c), **grot** (27d), **hoot** (112c), **ilot** (82d), **khot, knot** (43c,99d,107c,124d,137b), **loot** (22a,118a,119d,136a,153d), **moot** (41b,44c), **phot** (173b), **piot** (95b), **plot** (25a,36b,118d,138b), **poot!, riot** (44c,111d,170c,173d), **root** (53a), **ryot** (115c), **scot** (14a,

344

162b), **Scot** (64b,132c), **shot** (9d,43d,90c,174d), **slot** (10d,11b,41d, 110d,167d,168a,181b), **soot** (20b,26c,88a), **spot** (93b,118c,154d, 162a), **stot** (154d,155d,157d,179b,186a), **swot, toot, trot** (85b, 93d,112d)

O--T   **oast** (15d,86b,112a), **obit** (41b,64c), **oket** (189), **omit** (49c,52c, 106b,114c,147d), **oont** (25d), **oust** (44c,49a,52b,125d)

OU--   **ouch!, ough!, ours** (124c), **Ouse** (132a,185d), **oust** (44c,49a,52b, 125d)

-OU-   **Aoul** (191), **bout** (36c), **bouw** (188), **coup** (20d,97c,157b,c,162d), **cous** (38a), **doub** (18b), **douc** (101d), **doum** (168c), **dour** (67d, 159a), **foud** (54d,144b), **foul** (173a), **four** (26c), **goul** (102a), **gour** (112c,181c), **gout, hour, joug** (138d), **loud** (156a), **loun** (19a,b), **loup** (61d,62a,90c,139d), **Loup** (193), **lour** (13d,63d), **lout** (15c, 22a,24b,45b,109a,157d), **moue** (61d,62b), **noun** (114b,158a), **noup** (124b), **nous** (81d,100a,128b), **pouf, poul** (190), **pour** (162d), **pous** (188), **pout** (159a), **roud** (57a,b), **roue** (41b,44c,127c,134b), **roup** (44a,121d), **rout** (41d,44b,46b), **souf** (146b), **souk** (22a,97a), **soul** (10d,125a,153c,176d), **soup, sour, sous** (62d,172c), **toug** (171a), **toup** (95d), **tour** (31b,85c), **tout** (61a,127a), **youp** (185d), **your** (124c)

--OU   **Abou** (48b,55a), **chou** (61b), **Chou** (30b), **clou** (62b), **meou, niou** (188), **shou** (41d), **thou** (124b), **Tiou** (192), **Yaou** (30c)

O--U   **Oahu, Ogpu** (135d), **ordu** (170d)

OV--   **oval** (48d,49c,127a), **oven** (15d,78c,86b), **over** (6b,38c,80a,114d, 130a), **Ovid** (132d,133b), **Ovis** (143d), **ovum** (48d)

-OV-   **cove** (17a,73d,107d), **dove** (19a,117d), **Hova** (95a), **hove** (92a, 157d), **Jova** (193), **Jove** (85d), **love** (163a), **move, nova** (20c,106d, 155c,174d), **nove** (83b), **rove** (127d,132b,178a), **wove, Xova** (193)

--OV   **akov** (189), **Azov** (20b)

OW--   **Owen** (96a,183c), **owse**

-OW-   **bowk** (155d), **bowl, cowl** (101d), **dowd** (143b), **dowl, down** (149d), **fowl, gowk** (146d), **gowl** (102a,140d,185b), **gown, howe** (77d), **Howe** (17a,82a), **howl** (39b), **howk** (139b), **Iowa** (193), **jowl** (29b), **lowa** (19a), **lown** (157d), **lowp** (90c,139d), **mown, nowt** (106a,139a), **nowy** (194), **powe, rowy** (157b), **town** (73c), **towy** (58b), **yowl, yowt** (139c)

--OW   **alow** (18a,172c), **arow** (92c,158b), **avow** (6d,36a,41c,112c), **blow, brow, chow** (45a), **clow** (58c,148c), **crow** (19a), **dhow** (8Sd,111c, 175d), **enow** (50d,123a,158b), **flow** (157b), **frow** (47a,167a), **glow** (144c), **grow** (154b), **know, Lwow, meow, plow** (39c,165d), **prow** (21b,22c,144d,156a), **scow** (21a,58b), **show** (42b,44c,96b), **slow** (43c), **snow, stow** (112b), **swow** (100a), **trow** (18a,21a,159d,164c, 170b)

OX--   **oxan** (65c), **oxea** (153d), **oxen** (10c), **oxer** (55c), **oxid** (112c), **oxyl** (112c)

-OX-   **boxy, coxa** (77b), **doxa** (48b), **doxy** (129d), **foxy** (38b,39c,181d), **moxa** (27d,30c), **Moxo** (192), **noxa, Roxy** (183d), **toxa** (153d)

--OX   **abox** (22d), **esox** (57b)

O--X   **obex** (22d), **Odax** (132c), **Olax** (52b), **onyx** (25d,28d,65d,142b), oryx (11a)

OY - -   oyer (38a,75b,119c), oyes (38a,39b,75b), oyez (38a,39b,75b)

- OY -   coyn (37a), coyo (15a,30c), Goya (151d), Hoya (14d), noyl (87c), soya (151b)

- - OY   ahoy (106a), Amoy (88c), b'hoy (134b), buoy (28d,58c), choy (48a,128d), cloy (61b,137c,159d), ohoy (106a), ploy (43c), troy (161c,180a), Troy

O - - Y   oaky, oary, obey (35c,75c), ohoy (106a), oily (110b,172c), okay (8d), olay (113b), only (24d,52c,98d,147a,150a), oozy (148b), orgy (26d,130d,137c), Orly (8b)

- OZ -   boza (12a), bozo (55b), coze (29b), cozy (149c), doze (148a), dozy, Jozy, kozo (113d,168c), mozo (152b), noze (75a), ooze (53c, 104b,116a), oozy (148b)

O - - Z   oyez (38a,39b,75b)

PA - -   paal (188), paar (28c), paca (132c,154a), pace (64b,98a,153b,156a, 170b,177d), pack (24b,140d), paco (9b,146d), pacs (94c), pact (8a), padi (131b), paga (117a), page (51b,59b,142d,159b), paha (67b), pahi (21b,26a), paho (122a), paid (129c), pail, pain (7c), pair (22d,37d,85b,171d), pais (37d), pajo (122a), pala (189), Pala (88b), pale (113a,117c,178a), pali (122b), Pali (23d,24a,137b,175a), pall (32d,81b,112a), palm (59b,168c,169b), palo (152c), palp (11a,55b, 58b,167c), paly (194), Pana, pane (113c,155a,b), pang (165b), Pani (120c), pank (189), pant, paon (115b), papa, pape (19b,113a), para (134c,170d), Para (18a,51d), parc (62b,112c), pard (27b, 91b), pare (115c,129a), pari (34a,180a), park, parr (136d,137a, 147c), pars (59d), part (44d,60d,121c,159c), paru (57a), pasa (46a,127c,152c), pasi (94b), pass (110b,155c), past (25c,69d,165d), pata (32c,160d), pate (39a,74d), path (132a,134b), pato (46d), patu (179b), paul, Paul (96a), paun (18b), paut (140a), pave (85a), pavo (115b), Pavo (36b,c), pavy (115b), pawa (189), pawl (43a, 95a), pawn (29c,119c)

- PA -   Apap (102a), apar (12d), opah (23b,57a,b,86d), opal (20a,65d,67b, 82b), spad (105b), Spad (118d), spae (139c), span (23b,107b,113a, 128b,162c), spar (22c,24c,64b,97b,100b,144d), spat (112c,126b, 134b), upas (84d,120b,168c,d)

- - PA   arpa (83b), capa (152a,166d), cepa (110c), copa (88b,113c), depa (188), dopa (117d), Hupa (192), kapa (74b), lipa (54d), napa (25c, 67d,90d), Napa (182c), Nepa, 106b,178c), nipa (14b,46b,48a,164a, 168c), papa, pipa (159d), pupa (30d,81b,c), ripa (16b,131d), ropa (152a), rupa (60b), sapa (70c), supa (168c), tapa (16c,32c,53b, 56a,74b,104b,112b,113d,120d), yapa (113b), Zipa (29d)

P - - A   paca (132c,154a), paga (117a), paha (67b), pala (189), Pala (88b), Pana, papa, para (134c,170d), Para (18a,51d), pasa (46a, 127c,152c), pata (32c,160d), pawa (189), peba (12d), Peba (193), peca (190), peda (114d,144b), pega (57a,130a), pela (30c), Pera (60a), pesa (190), peva (12d), pica (66b,95b,172c), pika (93a,128a, 132c), pima (37c), Pima (192), pina (35d,118b), pipa (159d), Pisa (90c), pita (9c,28b,56a,83a), plea (51a,52d,122a,130b), poha (74c), pola, pooa (76a,125b), proa (21b,26a,95c,d), puca (68a), puja (77a), **puka** (107a,168c), **puma** (27b,37c,55b,103d), **puna** (10b,33b,104a,119b,182a), **pupa** (30d,81b,c), **Puya** (118b), **pyla** (22d)

P - - B pleb (10d,35b,180b)

P - - C parc (62b,112c)

P - - D paid (129c), **pard** (27b,91b), **pend, Phad** (155b), **Phud** (110b), **pied** (96c,103c,114b,117c,154a,174d), **plod** (170b,177d), **pond, pood** (189), **prod** (67d,80b,106b,120b), **pund** (189), **puud** (189)

PE - - peag (144a,178a), **peai** (98b), **peak** (9a,38c,159b,186b), **peal** (131c,d), **pean** (64c,150b), **pear** (64a), **peat** (64a,175a), **peba** (12d), **Peba** (193), **peca** (190), **peck** (24d), **peco** (162b), **peda** (114d,144b), **pedi** (34b), **pedo** (34b), **peek** (93d,115c), **peel** (53a,114a), **peen** (73c), **peep** (93d,115c), **peer** (51a,93d,107c), **peet** (64a), **pega** (57a,130a,158b), **Pegu** (24c,102a,127d), **peho** (19b,102c,106d), **Peke** (45a,148d), **pela** (30c), **Pele** (69c,74c), **pelf** (22a,56c,131b), **pelo** (83b), **pelt** (53a), **pelu** (30a,106d,168c), **pend, pene, pent** (36a), **peon** (28c,59c,99c), **pepo** (39b,64a,70a,98c,125c,154c), **Pera** (60a), **pere** (61c,63b), **peri** (54b,116b,c,122b), **perk** (84d,93a), **perm** (49b,97d), **pern** (78a), **pero** (152a), **pert** (80a,93a,137c,154b), **Peru, pesa** (190), **peso** (99c), **pest** (108c,116b,118d,170a), **pete** (136b), **Pete** (96b), **peto** (57a,177b), **Peto** (76a), **peur** (61c), **peva** (12d), **pevy** (91d,94c)

- PZ - aper (32d), **Apet** (97c), **apex** (39c,76c,115c,118b,159b,166a,167b), **epee** (55c,160d), **open** (26a,60d,81a,109b,112c,125b,172b,173c), **spec, sped, Spee** (66d,70b), **spes, Spes** (69a,78a), **spet** (16c,57a, 142c), **spew** (35a,49a), **spex, Spey**

- - PE cape (75a,96c,124b,161a), **cepe** (48c), **cope** (12b,26b,36c,65b,157d, 176a), **dope** (46c,105d), **dupe** (27c,41c,72c,160c), **gape** (185b), **hipe** (185a), **hope** (13d), **hype** (185a), **jape** (85a,b), **jupe** (62b, 84a), **lope** (48b,64b,d), **lupe** (19a,64a), **mope** (92d), **nape** (15b,108c,d), **Nupe** (191), **olpe** (90d), **pape** (19b,113a), **pipe** (105a,180d,182a), **pope** (20a,30d,31c,120d), **ripe** (58a,97c,98c), **rope** (36d,88d,128b), **rype** (19b,125a), **sipe** (101a,110c,140b), **supe** (53a,154d), **sype** (110c), **tape** (16a,19a,128d), **tipe** (168b), **tope** (24a,46b,57a,143c, 151a), **type** (31d,115a,155a), **wipe, Xipe** (15c)

P - - E pace (64b,98a,153b,156a,170b,177d), **page** (51b,59b,142d,159b), **pale** (113a,117c,178a), **pane** (113c,155a,b), **pape** (19b,113a), **pare** (115c,129a), **pate** (39a,74d), **pave** (85a), **Peke** (45a,148d), **Pele** (69c,74c), **pene, pere** (61c,63b), **pete** (136b), **Pete** (96b), **pice** (190), **pike** (57a,b,76c,120b,153a), **pile** (45d,75b,117c), **pine** (36a, 52a,88c,93c,168c,d,169a), **pipe** (105a,180d,182a), **pise** (127d), **plie** (32c,59b), **poke** (108c), **pole** (132c,143b,177b,184a), **Pole** (52a), **pome** (11d), **pone** (37a,85b), **pope** (20a,30d,31c, 120d), **pore** (59d,110d,111c,120d,157d), **pose** (14c,15d), **powe, pree** (139d), **puce** (33c,d,52a), **pule** (180d), **pume** (137b), **Pume** (175b,185b), **pure** (29b,172b,173c), **pyle** (34b), **Pyle** (9c,178a), **pyre** (64c)

P - - F pelf (22a,56c,131b), **Piaf** (63c), **piff** (24b), **poor, pouf, puff** (180d)

- PG - upgo (13c)

P - - G pang (165b), **peag** (144a,178a), **ping, plug** (156d,184d), **pong,**

prig (112a,116c), **pung** (22c,148b)

PH - - **Phad** (155b), **phew** (52c), **Phil** (96b), **phit** (24b), **phiz** (54a), **phon** (94a), **phoo, phos, phot** (173b), **Phud** (110b), **phut** (24b), **Phut** (110b)

- PH - **epha** (75c)

- - PH **Alph** (132a), **caph** (91c), **kaph** (91d), **koph** (91d), **qoph** (91d), **soph, toph** (75c), **umph**

P - - H **path** (132a,134b), **pish** (36c,107d), **pith** (37a,51c,67b,95c,97a, 119b,126d), **pooh** (22b,107d), **posh** (49b,148c), **prah** (21b, 26a,95c,d), **Ptah** (48d,98c), **pugh!, push** (145c)

PI - - **Piaf** (63c), **piat** (11a), **piay** (98b), **pica** (66b,95b,172c), **pice** (190), **Pici** (19c,184a), **pick, pico** (65a,152c), **Pict** (23c,47d), **pied** (96c, 103c,114b,117c,154a,174d), **pien** (13b), **pier** (23a,88b,180c), **piet** (29b,95b), **piff** (24b), **pika** (93a,128a,132c), **pike** (57a,b,76c,120b, 153a), **piki** (95c), **piky, pile** (45d,75b,117c), **pili** (34b,108d), **pill, pily, pima** (37c), **Pima** (192), **pina** (35d,118b), **pine** (36a,52a,88c, 93c,168c,d,169a), **ping, pink** (26d,33c,60c,138a), **pino** (152c), **pint** (67b), **piny, pion** (43c,52b), **piot** (95b), **pipa** (159d), **pipe** (105a, 180d,182a), **pipi** (106d,119d), **pipy** (145d), **pirn** (21b,129a,179b), **Piro** (192), **pirr** (181a), **Pisa** (90c), **pise** (127d), **pish** (36c,107d), **pisk** (9c, 19b), **piso** (189), **pist** (25c), **pita** (9c,28b,56a,83a), **pith** (37a, 51c,67b,95c,97a,119b,126d), **pito** (9c,28b,83a), **Pitt** (50d,155d), **pity** (35b), **Pius** (121a), **pixy** (154b)

- PI - **apia** (121b), **apii** (74c), **apio** (125b), **Apis** (17c,24b,49a,125a,136a), **epic** (76b,120a), **ipil** (117a,168c,169a), **Opie** (50c), **spin** (131a, 180d), **spir** (97c), **spit** (120a,132b,c), **Upis** (13b), **ypil** (117a,168c)

- - PI **aipi** (27a), **Hapi** (66a,107b,136a), **Hopi** (12c,102c,125b), **hopi** (33c), **impi** (86a), **kepi** (99d), **kopi** (107a,168c), **Kopi** (172a), **pipi** (106d,119d), **tipi** (181b), **topi** (37a,75a,118c), **Tupi** (192)

P - - I **padi** (131b), **pahi** (21b,26a), **pali** (122b), **Pali,** (23d,24a,137b,175a), **Pani** (120c), **pari** (34a,180a), **pasi** (94b), **peal** (98b), **pedi** (34b), **peri** (54b,116b,c,122b), **Pici** (19c,184a), **piki** (95c), **pili** (34b, 108d), **pipi** (106d,119d), **puli** (45a,78d), **puri** (80d)

P - - K **pack** (24b,140d), **pank** (189), **park, peak** (9a,38c,159b,186b), **peck** (24d), **peek** (93d,115c), **perk** (84d,93a), **pick, pink** (26d,33c,60c, 138a), **pisk** (9c,19b), **polk** (37c), **pook** (68a), **pork, puck** (44b,68a, 77c,100c), **Puck** (99d,143b), **pulk** (37c,88d), **punk** (9b,166a,167c)

PL - - **plan** (99b,124a,138b), **plap** (54b), **plat** (22d,96c,114a,119c,133d), **play** (63d,154a), **plea** (51a,52d,122a,130b), **pleb** (10d,35b,180b), **plet** (135d), **plew** (17c), **plex** (60b), **plie** (32c,59b), **plod** (170b, 177d), **plop** (54b), **plot** (25a,36b,118d,138b), **plow** (39c,165d), **ploy** (43c), **plug** (156d,184d), **plum, plup, plus** (10b,102c)

- PL - **upla**

P - - L **paal** (188), **pail, pall** (32d,81b,112a), **paul, Paul** (96a), **pawl** (43a, 95a), **peal** (131c,d), **peel** (53a,114a), **Phil** (96b), **pill, poll** (74d, 160a,177c), **pool** (65a,119d,120d), **poul** (190), **pull** (45d,167d), **purl** (87c,104c), **pyal** (175c)

P - - M **palm** (59b,168c,169b), **perm** (49b,97d), **plum, poem** (51a), **pram** (15a), **prim** (156b)

PN - -   **Pnyx** (71c)

P - - N   **pain** (7c), **paon** (115b), **paun** (18b), **pawn** (29c,119c), **pean** (64c, 150b), **peen** (73c), **peon** (28c,59c.99c), **pern** (78a), **phon** (94a), **pien** (13b), **pion** (43c,52b), **pirn** (21b,129a,179b), **plan** (99b,124a, 138b), **poon** (97c)

PO - -   **poco** (83b,93a), **poem** (51a), **poet** (49b), **Pogo** (121c), **pogy** (57a, 88a,98d,103c), **poha** (74c), **poke** (108c), **poku** (11a), **poky** (148c), **pola, pole** (132c,143b,177b,184a), **Pole** (52a), **polk** (37c), **poll** (74d,160a,177c), **polo** (154a), **Polo** (175b), **poly** (34c,76b), **pome** (11d), **Pomo** (192), **pomp** (111d,112d), **pond, pone** (37a,85b), **pong, Pons** (13d,63c,110d,150c), **pont** (55d,61b), **pony, pooa** (76a,125b), **pood** (189), **poof, pooh** (22b,107d), **pook** (68a), **pool** (65a,119d, 120d), **poon** (97c), **poop** (41c), **poor** (33a), **poot!, pope** (20a,30d, 31c,120d), **pore** (59d,110d,111c,120d,157d), **pork, Poro** (141d), **port** (73d,136b,140c,170c,d,182b,c), **pose** (14c,15d), **posh** (49b, 148c), **post** (89a,95c,155d), **pott** (113d), **pouf, poul** (190), **pour** (162d), **pous** (188), **pout** (159a), **powe**

- PO -   **apod** (59d), **epos** (51a,76b,120a), **spot** (93b,118c,154d,162a), **upon** (6b)

- - PO   **cipo** (91d), **gapo** (60a), **hypo** (117b), **mapo** (68a,148d), **pepo** (39b, 64a,70a,98c,125c,154c), **sapo** (149c,166d), **typo** (35c,51b)

P - - O   **paco** (9b,146d), **paho** (122a), **pajo** (122a), **palo** (152c), **pato** (46d), **pavo** (115b), **Pavo** (36b,c), **peco** (162b), **pedo** (34b), **peho** (19b, 102c,106d), **pelo** (83b), **pepo** (39b,64a,70a,98c,125c,154c), **pero** (152a), **peso** (99c), **peto** (57a,177b), **Peto** (76a), **phoo, pico** (65a, 152c), **pino** (152c), **Piro** (192), **piso** (189), **pito** (9c,28b,83a), **poco** (83b,93a), **Pogo** (121c), **polo** (154a), **Polo** (175b), **Pomo** (192), **Poro** (141d), **prao** (21b,26a,95c,d), **puno** (182a), **pyro**

- - PP   **Capp** (27a), **dopp** (43c), **kapp, kipp, Lapp** (108a), **repp** (53b,131a), **typp** (185b), **wapp** (54b,133d,145d), **Yapp** (22a), **zipp**

P - - P   **palp** (11a,55b,58b), **peep** (93d,115c), **plap** (54b), **p'op** (54b), **plup, pomp** (111d,112d), **poop** (41c), **prep** (138b), **prop** (159d), **pulp, pump**

PR - -   **prah** (21b,26a,95c,d), **pram** (15a), **prao** (21b,26a,95c,d), **prau** (21b, 26a,95c,d), **pray** (18b,51a,159d), **pree** (139d), **prep** (138b), **pres** (62b), **pret** (188), **prey** (119d,176a), **prig** (112a,116c), **prim** (156b), **proa** (21b,26a,95c,d), **prod** (67d,80b,106b,120b), **prop** (159d), **prow** (21b,22c,144d,156a), **prut!, Prut** (41a)

- PR -   **spry** (7a,107b)

P - - R   **paar** (28c), **pair** (22d,37d,85b,171d), **parr** (136d,137a,147c), **pear** (64a), **peer** (51a,93d,107c), **peur** (61c), **pier** (23a,88b,180c), **pirr** (181a), **poor** (33a), **pour** (162d), **purr** (104c)

- PS -   **apse** (9b,20a,31a,128c,130a,142b,175a), **Apsu** (29a), **ipse** (44d, 89c), **ipso** (89c)

- - PS   **Alps** (85d), **gyps, Gyps** (71d), **hops** (17c), **hyps, seps** (93b,142d), **tops** (159c), **Veps** (191), **Zips** (40c)

P - - S   **pacs** (94c), **pais** (37d), **pars** (89d), **pass** (110b,155c), **phos, Pius** (121a), **plus** (10b,102c), **Pons** (13d,63c,110d,150c), **pous** (183), **pres** (62b), **puss**

PT - - Ptah (48d,98c)

- - PT Copt (48d), dipt, kept, rapt (6c,27a,50d), sept (31d,82b,143a,149c), Sept (45b), Sopt (45b), wept

P - - T pact (8a), pant, part (44d,60d,121c,159c), past (25c,69d,165d), paut (140a), peat (64a,175a), peet (64a), pelt (53a), pent (36a), pert (80a,93a,137c,154b), pest (108c,116b,118d,170a), phit (24b), phot (173b), phut (24b), Phut (110b), piat (11a), Pict (23c, 47d), piet (29b,95b), pint (67b), piot (95b), pist (25c), Pitt (50d, 155d), plat (22d,96c,114a,119c,133d), plet (135d), plot (25a,36b, 118d,138b), poet (49b), pont (55d,61b), poot!, port (73d,136b, 140c,170c,d,182b,c), post (89a,95c,155d), pott (113d), pout (159a), pret (188), prut!, Prut (41a), punt (21a,58b), putt (69d), pyat (95b), pyet (95b)

PU - - puca (68a), puce (33c,d,52a), puck (44b,68a,77c,100c), Puck (99d,143b), pudu (41d), puff (180d), pugh!, puja (77a), puka (107a,168c), puku (11a), pule (180d), puli (45a,78d), pulk (37c, 88d), pull (45d,167d), pulp, pulu (74c), puly, puma (27b,37c,55b, 103d), pume (137b), Pume (175b,185b), pump, puna (10b,33b, 104a,119b,182a), pund (189), pung (22c,148b), punk (9b,166a, 167c), puno (182a), punt (21a,58b), puny (55b,179a), pupa (30d, 81b,c), pure (29b,172b,173c), puri (80d), purl (87c,104c), purr (104c), Puru (192), push (145c), puss, putt (69d), puud (189), puxy, Puya (118b)

- PU - Apus (36b,c), opus (35c,105a,184c), spud (121d,151c), spun, spur (10d,67d,167d,168a,181b), sput (21c)

- - PU hapu (106d), napu (29d,80d), Ogpu (135d), tapu

P - - U paru (57a), patu (179b), Pegu (24c,102a,127d), pelu (30a,106d, 168c), Peru, poku (11a), prau (21b,26a,95c,d), pudu (41d), puku (11a), pulu (74c), Puru (192)

P - - W phew (52c), plew (17c), plow (39c,165d), prow (21b,22c,144d, 156a)

P - - X plex (60b), Pnyx (71c)

PY - - pyal (175c), pyat (95b), pyet (95b), pyla (22d), pyle (34b), Pyle (9c,178a), pyre (64c), pyro

- - PY copy, espy (44a,142a), gapy, pipy (145d), ropy (157c,176d), typy

P - - Y paly (194), pavy (115b), pevy (91d,94c), piay (98b), piky, pily, piny, pipy (145d), pity (35b), pixy (154b), play (63d,154a), ploy (43c), pogy (57a,88a,98d,103c), poky (148c), poly (34c,76b), pony, pray (18b,51a,159d), prey (119d,176a), puly, puny (55b,179a), puxy

P - - Z phiz (54a)

QA - - Qaid (35a)

Q - - D Qaid (35a), quad (33c,172a), quid (39b,166d), quod (123d)

QE - - qere (75c), qeri (75c)

Q - - E qere (75c), quae (176b)

- - QF waqf (103a)

Q - - G quag (21c,102c), Qung (191)

Q - - H qoph (91d)

350

Q - - I   qeri (75c), quai (88b,117c,180c), quei (189)

Q - - N   quan (190)

QO - -   qoph (91d)

Q - - P   quip (183a,b)

Q - - S   quas (135c)

Q - - T   quit (90d,130c)

QU - -   quad (33c,172a), quae (176b), quag (21c,102c), quai (88b,117c, 180c), quan (190), quas (135c), quay (88b,117c,180c), quei (189), quid (39b,166d), quip (183a,b), quit (90d,130c), quiz, Qung (191), quod (123d)

- QU -   aqua (90a,178c), equi (122d)

Q - - Y   quay (88b,117c,180c)

Q - - Z   quiz

RA - -   raab (32d), raad (14a,49b,151a,165b), raas (91b), Raba, rabi (38d, 74a), Rabi (14b,117b), raca (19a,59c,130b,184d), race (116a,153b, 154b,169c), rack (32c,64b), racy (153b), rada (135c,172a), rade (138d), raff (75b), raft (27b,33c,58c,75b), raga (56d,105a), rage (10c,30c,157a,161d), ragi (28b), Rahu (42b,48b), Raia (107d,147b), raid (59d,80c), raik (188,189), rail (16b,19b,c,37a,97b,138c,150c, 177b), rain (121d,162d), raip (36d), rais (26c,29d,75a,103b), Rais (106b), raja (77a,123c), rake (41b,44c,134b,140d), rale (7c,23a, 29d,41b), ralo (188), Rama (77a,80b,176d), rame (22d), rami (22d), ramp (65a,80b,127b,148b), rana (77a,123c), Rana (63d), rand (16d,22a,131b,145a,b), Rand (69c), rang, rani (72d,77b,123c,127c), rank (31d,55d,70b,92c,94d,157d), rann (175c), rant (41c,127b, 128a,161d), rapt (6c,27a,50d), rara (119a), rare (138b,164b,172b, 173d), rasa (51c), rase (42b,91d), rash (75a), rasp (56b,70d,140d), rata (29d,56b,89d,96c,106d,120c,168c), rate (11d,14a,31d,36b,51d, 52a,70b,85c,112b,123b,127d,128a,138c,143a,174b), rath (29a, 76d,162d), rati (189), rats, rave,(41c,157a,161d), ravi (61b), Ravi (16b), raya (19b,23c,76d,107d), raze (42b,91d) razz (131b)

- RA -   Arab (30a,78b,c,106a,107c,157b,160c,185d), arad (13a,c,84a), arah (52c), Aral (135d), Aram (18d,50c,105c,144b,161c), Aran (18c,48c,64d,82d,174c), arar (137a,168c), Aras, brab (113b), brad (54d,67c,105b), brae (76d,139a,c,140b,148c), brag (21a,175a), Bram (96a), bran (23c,39a,70b,72a,79c), Bran (23c,50c), bras (61a), brat, bray, crab (39b,144b,181b), crag (132c), cral, cram (157d), cran (160c), craw (38d,72c,156c), Crax (19b,39d), draa, drab (23d,29c,33d,46d,53d), drag (74a,125b), drah (188), dram (46b,110c,121d,148c), drap (61b,c,62a), drat (100a), Drau, draw (42c,53a,92b,117c,121c,167d), dray (27a,154c), eral (51a), erat (89c), frab (138c), frap (45d,165c), frat, frau (181b), fray (56b,60d), grab (105b,142a,149b), grad (28b), Graf (37c,66b,67a, 107c,186b), gram (29d,99b,148d,160d,180a), grao (189), gras (78b), gray (33c,77c), Gray (50c), Irad (18d), Irae (43c), Irak (99a,d), Iran (6a,48c,116b), Iraq (99a,d), Iras (11b,32a), krag (131c), kral, kran (190), kras (76d), orad (104a), oral (114a,153d, 174c,175c), Oran, oras (40d), prah (21b,26a,95c,d), pram (15a), prao (21b,26a,95c,d), prau (21b,26a,95c,d), pray (18b,51a,159d), tram (170a), tran (7a), trap (27b,67b,132b,149b), tray (128c,136d,

351

142d,143c), ural, Ural (135c), uran (101d), Wraf, wrap (32b,51a)

- - RA abra (26b), Abra, aera (8a), Afra (183c), agra (26d,34d), Agra (161b), Aira (70d), akra (176a), Akra (191), amra (77c), arra (47d, 52c,82b), aura (44c,49c,66a,96b,158a,170d,177c), bara (188), Bera (86d), bora (181d,182b), bura (182b), cara (83a), Cara (48b, 183c), cora (65d), Cora (42b,69c,80c,116b,124d,172b,183c), cura (152c), Dara (18d), dera (34c), dora (70b), Dora (36d,41a,43b, 183c,d), dura (153c), eyra (181d), Ezra (96a), fora (133a), gara (190), gora (81c), Hera (69c,85d,110b,126b,186b,d), hora (22a,40b), hura (20a,137a), Hura, ikra (27d), Irra (68c, 178a), jura, Jura, Kara (132a), kora (19a,178c), Kora, Lara (25c), lira (28b,79a,170d), lora (146b,149b,151c,169b), Lora (183c), lura (22d,82a), Lyra (36b,74a), mara (114d), Mara (24a,d,105b,107b), mira (174d), Mira (155b), mora (42b,65a,72b,83d,99b,153a,161a), mura (84d), Mura (192), Myra (10a,31b,183c), Nera (165b), Nora (79b,107a,164c,183c), ocra (72c,175a), okra (72c,175a), orra (139c,d,140a), otra (152c), para (134c,170d), Para (18a,51d), Pera (60a), Sara (24d,183c), sera (11b,20d,59a,83a,180d), sora (19b,c, 127b), sura (87c,113b,166d), Syra, tara (22a,55c,113a,168c), Tara (82b,c,138b), tera (23d,84c), tora (11a,44d,74a,75c,85c,90b,102d, 115d), vara (151d), vera (140c,151b,175c), Vera (183c) Vira (191), zira (188)

R - - A Raba, raca (19a,59c,130b,184d), rada (135c,172a), raga (56d,105a), Raia (107d,147b), raja (77a,123c), Rama (77a,176d), rana (77a,123c), Rana (63d), rara (119a), rasa (51c), rata (29d,56b,89d), 96c,106d,120c,168c), raya (19b,23c,76d,107d), reba (144a), Reba (18d,86c), rede (37c,81d), reja (152b), rena (25b,132c), rhea (37a, 56a,111d,133d), Rhea (19b,68d,87c,103c,186b), riga (118b), Riga, rima (23a,30c,32a,58a,110d), ripa (16b,131d), rita, Rita (37b, 78d,183c,), Roda (107b), roka (95a,168c,d), Roma (83c,d), ropa (152a), Rosa (58d,134a,145d,183c), rota (27c,30d,38a,79a,92d, 133a,134a,b,180c), ruga (59b,185a), rupa (60b), rusa, Rusa (41d, 136d), Ruta (76b,134d)

- RB - arba (135d,171a)

- - RB barb (20b,57d,78b,117d,120a,b,124b), curb (130c,146b), garb (32c,46a), gerb (56d,143d), Harb (191), herb (58b,158b), kerb (146b), Serb (15d,148a,186c), sorb (11d,103d,134b,142d), Sorb (148a,180a), verb (7a,114b,184b)

R - - B raab (32d), rhob (64a,85c), rumb (120b)

- RC - arca (9a,22c,29d,115a,130a), Arca (101b), arch (29d,38b,39d,123d, 132c), orca (86b)

- - RC circ (31a), marc (70c), Marc (96a), parc (62b,112c)

- RD - Erda (23d,41a,47d,68d,69a,131d,177b), ordo (22a,30d,122a,171a), ordu (170d), urde (86b), Urdu (77b), urdy (86b)

- - RD bard (12d,120a), bird, bord (100b), Byrd (9c,120b), card (33d,114d), cord (39b,131a), curd (99d), Dard, dord (42c), eard (139b), fard (112d), ford (177b), fyrd (110a), Gerd (63c), gird (32c,50a,123a,160a), hard (109b), herd (39a,46c,72a), Kurd (48b, 82a), lard (54d,61a,71a,110a), lord (107c), nard (13a,97c,102b, 110a,153c), oord (190), pard (27b,91b), sard (26d,28d,65d,111a),

352

142b,156d), **Sard, surd** (82c,177a), **verd** (71d), **ward** (31c,55c,86b), **word** (124b,165c), **Wurd, Wyrd** (107d), **yard** (152d)

R - - D **raad** (14a,49b,151a,165b), **Raad** (151a), **raid** (59d,80c), **rand** (16d, 22a,131b,145a,b), **Rand** (69c), **read** (116d,157d), **redd** (153a), **reed** (16a,70d,97b,105a,111b,118b,144b), **Reed** (163a), **rend** (32a,159c, 162c,185a), **Ridd** (94a), **rind** (53a,115c), **Rind** (109c,174b), **road** (37d,164d), **rodd** (38d), **roed, rood** (38d,39a,88b), **roud** (57a,b), **rudd** (26d,57a,b), **rynd** (100a)

RE - - **read** (116d,157d), **real** (7a), **ream** (18c,37d,50d,113d,171c), **reap** (7a,40a,74a), **rear** (15b,23a,b,24a,51b,76d,127c), **reba** (144a), **Reba** (18d,86c), **reck** (26d,75c), **rect** (117b), **redd** (153a), **rede** (37c, 81d,138d), **redo** (165c), **reed** (16a,70d,97b,105a,111b,118b,144b), **Reed** (163a), **reef** (129a,137a,145a), **reek** (49d,53c,64a,148d,149a), **reel** (21b,40b,d,153c,154a,c,d,180d), **reem** (18d), **reft** (32a,42c, 44d,167b), **reim** (112c), **rein** (29b,130c), **reis** (26c,29d,75a,103b), **reja** (152b), **Reki** (16a), **rely** (16b,170b), **Remi** (10b), **Rems, rena** (25b,132c), **rend** (32a,159c,162c,185a), **Reni** (83d), **Reno, rent** (58a,77c,91b,138b,153d,162c,167c), **repp** (53b,131a), **rese** (127b), **resh** (91d), **rest** (15d,91b,104d,105a,115a,b,130a,b,161b), **rete** (106c,119c), **reve** (61c,104d), **revs** (131a)

- RE - **area** (37d,38a,44c,53a,93b,110d,127d,138c,168a,186d), **areg** (116a, 137a), **areo** (34c), **Ares** (49b,51b,68c,76a,97a,105c,110b), **aret** (128c), **brea** (100b), **bred** (23c,48c,127c), **bree** (139a), **bren** (72d, 95a), **Brer** (172b), **Bres, brew** (35d), **brey** (194), **crea** (92c), **Cree** (192), **crew** (72a,106a), **Crex** (37a), **dree** (139b,140c,158b,172c), **drei** (66d,165a), **dreg, drew, drey** (154c), **erer,** (17d,150c), **Frea, Fred** (96b), **free** (44a,70d,131b), **fret** (28c,35b,111c,184d), **Frey** (7c, 68b,124d), **gres** (156d), **grew, grey** (33c), **Iren** (127c), **Orel, pree** (139d), **prep** (138b), **pres** (62b), **pret** (188), **prey** (119d), **tree** (11d, 37a,56a,184b), **tref** (172b), **trek** (85c,93c,99d,168b), **tres** (19a,52b, 63a,152d,165a,175c), **tret** (9a,178b,179d), **trey** (26c,165a), **Urey** (107c,138c), **wren** (19b,c), **Wren** (50b)

- - RE **Aare, acre** (39b,56a,88b), **Acre, aire** (82c), **Aire, bare** (43d,157c), **bore** (14c,25b,46a,116a,165c,179b), **bure** (61b), **byre** (38a), **care** (11b,14c,35d,150a,184d), **cere** (19a,149d,179a), **core** (28b,51c, 75b,81b), **cure** (123b), **dare** (28d,41b,42a,74d,175b), **Dare** (57a), **dere** (74a,79c), **dire** (45d,55a,104a,163c), **dore** (61d,67b,69d, 117d), **Dore** (50d,63a,b), **Eire** (82b), **etre** (61a,c,62d,166c), **eyre** (23c,31b,85c), **Eyre, fare** (43c,59b,67d,123b), **fire** (13a,43d, 44b), **fore** (63d,174b), **gare** (61b,c,62c,127c), **Gere** (183c), **gore** (115d,117c,154c,169c), **gyre** (31b,171b), **hare** (91b,132c), **here, hire** (49d,50b,91b,130a), **inre** (35d,80a), **jure** (90b), **kere** (75c, 128b), **kore** (107b), **Kore** (29a,42b,116b,124d), **Kure** (84c), **lire** (62c), **lore** (77c,87c,90d,151c,183a), **lure** (41c,51a,54b,163a), **lyre** (11c,81c,105a,111c), **mare** (78b), **Mare** (108b), **mere** (16c,22b,62a, 78b,87d,96c,110c,120d,146d,148b), **mire** (21c,104b), **more** (71a), **More** (50b), **mure** (177d), **Nare** (93c), **Nore** (163d), **ogre** (67a,102a), **pare** (115c,129a), **pere** (61c,63b), **pore** (59d,110d,111c,120d,157d), **pure** (29b,172b,173c), **pyre** (64c), **qere** (75c), **rare** (138b,164b, 172b,173d), **rire** (62a), **sere** (24d,46a,c,138c,183b), **Sere** (158b), **sire** (17d,55a,59d,124a,163b,166b), **sore** (23d,142d), **sure** (173d), **tare** (9a,18d,41a,176a,179d), **tire** (15a,22a,52d,55a,179b,180d), tore, tyre (15a), Tyre (31b,90d,117b), vare (179b), vire (11a,13b), ware (27d,35a), were (139b), wire, wore, yare (96b,124b,128b), yore (10b,69d,93c,110b,165d)

R - - E race (116a,153b,154b,169c), rade (138d), rage (10c,30c,157a, 161d), rake (41b,44c,134b,140d), rale (7c,23a,29d,41b), rame (22d), rare (138b,164b,172b,173d), rase (42b,d,91d), rate 11d,14a,31d,36b,51d,52a,70b,85c,112b,123b,127d,128a,138c,143a, 174b), rave (41c,157a,161d), raze (42b,d,91d), rede (37c,81d,138d), rese (127b), rete (106c,119c), reve (61c,104d), ribe (139a), Rice (46a), ride (46b,85c), rife (6b,c,39d,123b), rile (10c,d,82c,125a, 156b,176a), rime (30c,36a,58a,63d,77c), rine (44d,75d,135c), ripe (58a,97c,98c), rire (62a), rise (49d,80b,155a), Rise (110d,150c), rite (93a,131d), rive (32a,153d), robe (65b), rode (46c), role (114b), Rome (31c,51d), rone (127c,164b), rope (36d,88d,128b), rose (33c), Rose (6a,50c,183c), rote (130b,134b,143a,159d), roue (41b,44c,127c,134b), rove (127d,132b,178a), rube (37d,135d, 185d), Rube (96b), rude (134b,172b), rule (11b,26b,90b), rune (9b,67a,94a,95a,105c,107d,120a,141d,163d), ruse (13b,77c,157b, 169c), rute (188), ryme (178d), rype (19b,125a)

- RF - orfe (57a,b,185c), Urfa (99a)

- - RF kerf (40a,108b), serf (21d,148a), surf (23a), turf (115c,149d, 160b), warf, werf (54d), zarf (39c,155a)

R - - F raff (75b), reef (129a,137a,145a), riff (131d), Riff (18b,102c), roof (78d), ruff (19b,33b,63d,137a)

- RG - Argo (12c,36b,c), ergo (164b), orgy (26d,130d,137c), urge (42d, 46b,79d,80a,b,81c,124a,150a)

- - RG berg (79b), borg (40d), burg (22b,73c), lurg (96d,141b,184d), morg (188), Sarg (96d,125c)

R - - G rang, ring (50a), Rong (88c), rung (28c,39a)

RH - - rhea (37a,56a,111d,133d), Rhea (19b,68d,87c,103c,186b), Rhee (87c), Rhin, rhob (64a,85c), rhum (8c), Rhus (159a)

R - - H rash (75a), rath (29a,76d,162d), resh (91d), rich, Roch (136c), rukh (53b,54a), rush, ruth (35b,118c), Ruth (105b,183c)

RI - - rial (190), ribe (139a), rice, Rice (46a), rich, rick (74d,117d,154d), Ridd (94a), ride (46b,85c), Riel (129a), riem (76c,112c,157c,164d), rien (62b), rier (180b), rife (6b,c,39d,123b), riff (131d), Riff (18b, 102c), rift (30c,32a,58a,110d), riga (118b), Riga, Riis (9d), rikk (49a), rile (10c,d,82c,125a,156b,176a), rill (23c102b,132a,148d, 157b), rily (176a), rima (23a,30c,32a,58a,110d), rime (30c,36a,58a, 63d,77c), rimu (79d,106d,129a,168c), rimy (63d), rind (53a,115c), Rind (109c,174b), rine (44d,75d,135c), ring (50a), rink (147c, 154a), riot (44c,111d,170c,173d), ripa (16b,131d), ripe (58a,97c, 98c), rire (62a), rise (49d,80b,155a), Rise (110d,150c), risk (74d), risp (99a), Riss (66a), rita, Rita (37b,78d,183c), rite (93a,131d), rive (32a,153d)

- RI - aria (8b,98c,150a,c,170c), arid (46c,85a), arif (127d), aril (142a), aris (101b), Brie (29c), brig (72b,106a,144d), brim, brin (32c,54c,146c), brit (76c), crib (96b,120d), cric (131c), crig (20d), crin (146c), cris (40b,95d), drib (46b), Drin, drip, eria (13d,146d), eric (115b), Eric (71d,96a,107d,138a,164a,176b), Erie (82c,87d),

Erin (82b), **Eris** (12c,68d,109c), **Fria, frib** (43d), **frim** (58d), **frit** (64c,67c), **friz** (39d), **grid** (17a,70d,119b,156d), **grig** (38c,70d, 93a), **grim** (156a), **grin, grip** (159a), **gris** (61d), **grit** (137a,b), **irid** (38d,67c), **iris** (53c,58a,111c) **Iris** (127c), **kris** (40b,95d), **prig** (112a, 116c), **prim** (156b), **trig** (106a,148d,154b,169d), **trim** (40a,106a, 154b,160a,165c,169d), **trin** (169d), **trio** (104d,165a,169c), **trip** (85c), **tris** (122d), **trit** (34d,164c), **Uria** (14c,16d), **urim** (18d,23a, 110a), **writ** (91a)

--RI **abri** (61c,62c,144b), **aeri** (34a), **agri** (89b), **Atri,** **auri** (34a), **bari** (37c,79c), **Bari** (83d), **Bori** (110d,150c), **buri** (56b), **Cori** (138c), **dari** (38a,70b), **Geri** (183c), **gyri** (22d,131b), **kari** (14d), **keri** (75c,128b), **kiri** (86a,87c,115a,168c), **kori** (7d,77a), **Kuri** (191), **lari** (78a,101c), **Lari** (72c), **lori** (91b), **Luri** (191), **mari** (61d), **Mari** (16a), **Neri, nori** (8c,141c), **Omri** (18c,86d), **pari** (34a, 180a), **peri** (54b,116b,c,122b), **puri** (80d), **qeri** (75c), **Rori** (16b), **sari** (48b,65b,77b), **seri** (18b), **Seri** (192), **Shri** (17c,166c), **siri** (18b), **sori** (55c,64a), **Tari** (47d,69a), **tori** (101b), **Turi** (191), **vari** (34d,91b,134d,174d), **veri** (28b), **weri** (15c,27c)

R--I **rabi** (38d,74a), **Rabi** (14b,117b), **ragi** (28b), **rami** (22d), **rani** (72d, 77b,123c,127c), **rati** (189), **ravi** (61b), **Ravi** (16b), **Reki** (16a), **Remi** (10b), **Reni** (83d), **rodi** (98c), **romi** (72d), **Rori** (16b), **roti** (62c)

--RK **bark** (115c), **cark** (26d,184d), **cork** (119d), **dark** (47a,67d,109b, 160b), **dirk** (40b), **fork, hark** (92d), **jerk** (153a), **kirk** (31a,139b), **kurk** (31a,139b), **lark** (19a,63d), **lurk** (92a,147d), **mark** (146b, 155a), **Mark** (52a,96a), **mirk** (41a,67d), **murk** (41a,67d), **nark** (81a, 156d), **park, perk** (84d,93a), **pork, Sark** (28d), **Turk** (101d,102d, 106a,111d), **work** (64c,76b), **yark** (22c), **york** (38c), **York** (50b,c)

R--K **rack** (32c,64b), **raik** (188,189), **rank** (31d,55d,70b,92c,94d,157d), **reck** (26d,75c), **reek** (49d,53c,64a,148d,149a), **rick** (74d,117d, 154d), **rikk** (49a), **rink** (147c,154a), **risk** (74d), **rock** (160b), **rook** (19b,29c,39a), **ruck** (39a,185a), **rusk** (23a)

-RL- **orle** (17b,56b,76a,144b,177a), **orlo** (56b,119c), **Orly** (8b)

--RL **birl** (93c,131a,153c), **burl** (87c,169a), **carl** (115c,135d), **Carl** (96a), **cirl** (24c), **curl** (38d,73b,93b,131d), **earl** (107c), **farl** (138c,140b), **furl** (132d), **girl, harl** (16b,56b,59a), **herl** (16b,59a), **hurl** (167c), **jarl** (40d,107d), **Karl** (96a), **marl** (32a,42c,55d), **merl** (20b), **nurl** (33b,87c), **purl** (87c,104c), **yarl** (40d,107d)

R--L **rail** (16b,19b,c,37a,97b,138c,150c,177b), **real** (7a), **reel** (21b,40b,d, 153c,154a,c,d,180d), **rial** (190), **Riel** (129a), **riil** (23c,102b,132a, 148d,157b), **roil** (44c,104b,156b,170d,176a), **roll** (134a,160b), **rotl** (103b,111c), **rull** (170b), **ryal** (110a,190), **ryel** (190)

-RM- **arme** (63a,179b), **arms, army** (78c), **Erma** (183c), **Irma** (96d)

--RM **barm** (185b), **berm** (25d,90d,145c), **corm** (24b,38d,156a), **derm** (147c,158d), **dorm, farm** (165d), **firm** (154c,173d), **form** (54d, 143c), **Garm** (178c), **germ** (17d,99c,134d), **harm** (40b,81a), **norm** (15a,115a,128a,155a), **perm** (49b,97d), **term** (92b,105b,142b,166b), **turm** (132d), **warm** (7c,75b,163b), **worm, wurm** (67c)

R--M **ream** (18c,37d,50d,113d,171c), **reem** (18d), **reim** (112c), **rhum** (8c), **riem** (76c,112c,157c,164d), **roam** (178a), **room** (28d)

-RN- **arna** (24a,181b), **Arnd** (67a), **Arne** (35c,50c,134d), **arni** (24a,181b),

Arno (27a), **arn't**, **erne** (19c,d,47b,54b,141a), **orna** (169d,182c), **orne** (169d,182c), **Orne** (25b), **urna** (133a)

--RN **barn** (156d), **Bern**, 160d), **birn** (31d), **born**, **burn**, **carn** (156c), **cern** (41c), **corn** (39d,95c,123a), **darn** (130b), **dorn** (164d), **earn** (42d, 64b,99a), **fern** (142a), **firn** (67c,70c,106c,149b), **garn** (67d,185b), **horn** (11a,105a,170b,182a), **karn** (156c), **kern** (59c,172a), **Kern** (132b), **lorn** (42d,60b), **morn**, **Norn** (69a,163d,174b), **pern** (78a), **pirn** (21b,129a,179b), **sorn** (139a,d), **tarn** (87d,103d,120d), **tern** (19b,32d,72c,94a,138c,141b,160a), **torn** (130a), **turn** (28d,131a, 175a), **warn** (7b), **worn** (143b), **yarn** (154b,161b,184b)

R--N **rain** (121d,162d), **rann** (175c), **rein** (29b,130c), **Rhin**, **rien** (62b), **roan** (78b,c,114c,128d,144a,181a), **roon** (41a,168b), **ruin** (42d)

RO-- **road** (37d,164d), **roam** (178a), **roan** (78b,c,114c,128d,144a, 181a), **roar** (145c), **robe** (65b), **Roch** (136c), **rock** (160b), **Roda** (107b), **rodd** (38d), **rode** (46c), **rodi** (98c), **roed**, **roer** (72d), **roey** (103d), **rohr** (72d), **roil** (44c,104b,156b,170d,176a), **rojo** (129a, 152c), **roka** (95a,168c,d), **roke** (174d,175b), **role** (114b), **roll** (134a, 160b), **Roma** (83c), **Rome** (31c,51d), **romi** (72d), **romp** (63d), **rone** (127c, 164b), **Rong** (88c), **rood** (38d,39a,88b), **roof** (78d), **rook** (19b,29c,39a), **room** (28d), **roon** (41a,168b), **Roos** (67a), **root** (53a), **ropa** (152a), **rope** (36d,88d,128b), **ropy** (157c,176d), **Rori** (16b), **Rosa** (58d,134a,145d,183c), **rose** (33c), **Rose** (6a,50c,183c), **ross** (16c,161d), **Ross** (50c), **rosy** (21a,111a), **rota** (27c,30d,38a,79a,92d, 133a,134a,b,180c), **rote** (130b,134b,143a,159d), **roti** (62c), **rotl** (103b,111c), **roto** (30a,122d,127b,152c,171b), **roud** (57a,b), **roue** (41b,44c,127c,134b), **roup** (44a,121d), **rout** (41d,44b,46b), **rove** (127d,132b,178a), **rowy** (157b), **Roxy** (183d)

-RO- **Aroa** (175b), **Arod** (86c), **aroo** (80c,82b), **arow** (92c,158b), **brob** (153c), **broo** (139a), **brow**, **croc** (13a,74a), **Crom**, **crop** (38b), **crow** (19a), **drop** (43d,54b,100b,114c,168b), **Eros** (11c,39c,68b,97c,182d), **froe** (32a,167a,179d), **frog** (10a,17a,126d), **from**, **frot** (28c), **frow** (47a,167a), **grog** (92d,153d), **gros** (47a,53d), **Gros** (63a), **grot** (27d), **grow** (154b), **irok** (55b), **iron** (55c,d,69d,81a,97b,143b, 149a,173d,179c), **Kroo** (191), **proa** (21b,26a,95c,d), **prod** (67d,80b, 106b,120b), **prop** (159d), **prow** (21b,22c,144d,156a), **trod**, **tron** (140d,180a), **trop** (62d,167a), **trot** (85b,93d,112d), **trow** (18a,21a, 159d,164c,170b), **trey** (161c,180a)

--RO **aero** (8b,34a,b,58c,59a), **agro** (149d), **arro** (52c), **baro** (71a,122c), **boro** (154b), **Boro** (193), **caro** (83a), **Caro** (183d), **cero** (57b,c,d, 180b), **duro** (190), **Ebro** (132a), **faro** (65a), **Garo** (88c), **giro** (38c, 167c), **gyro** (34d), **hero** (42b,124d,137b), **Hero** (90c), **hiro**, **inro** (84b,c,106c), **karo** (106d), **Lero** (82d), **loro** (19a,114b), **maro** (144d), **mero** (72a), **miro** (19a,106d,184a), **Miro** (113a,151d), **moro** (19a,56c), **Moro** (100a,103a,117a,159a), **Nero** (8a,126d,133a,150b, 172c), **okro** (72c,175a), **otro** (151d), **pero** (152a), **Piro** (192), **Poro** (141d), **pyro**, **sero** (34d,88d,164b,178d), **taro** (13c,48c,49b,64b, 112b,120a,133d,155c,170a,c), **tiro** (9b,17d,108c), **toro** (38a,107a, 152a,168c), **tyro** (9b,17d,108c), **xero** (31a,84c,108c), **Zero** (118d)

R--O **ralo** (188), **redo** (165c), **Reno**, **rojo** (129a), **roto** (30a,122d,127b)

-RP- **arpa** (83b)

--RP **carp** (27d,38d,40c,55a,56c,57a), **dorp** (73c,176b), **harp** (105a,129a),

356

larp (51d), **lerp** (51d,141d), **tarp** (26b,178d), **terp** (12b,123a), **torp** (54c), **turp, warp** (36c,165a,171c), **zarp** (120c)

R--P **raip** (36d), **ramp** (65a,80b,127b,148b), **rasp** (56b,70d,140d), **reap** (7a,40a,74a), **repp** (53b,131a), **risp** (99a), **romp** (63d), **roup** (44a, 121d), **rump**

-RR- **arra** (47d,52c,82b), **arro** (52c), **Irra** (178a), **orra** (139c,d,140a)

--RR **barr** (49b), **birr** (180d), **burr** (123b), **carr** (120d,140a), **curr** (104c), **darr** (163c), **dorr** (32b), **durr** (70b), **Herr** (66c), **Kerr, murr** (72b,128b), **nurr** (67d), **parr** (136d,137a,147c), **pirr** (181a), **purr** (104c), **turr** (24d,105a), **Tyrr** (68c,109c,163d,178a), **yarr** (72a)

R--R **rear** (15b,23a,b,24a,51b,76d,127c), **rier** (180b), **roar** (145c), **roer** (72d), **rohr** (72d), **ruer, Ruhr**

-RS- **Erse** (28a,64b,82b), **erst** (60b), **Ursa** (17b,36b,43d)

--RS **airs** (123b), **Bors** (70b,134b), **hers** (124c), **hors** (62b), **Lars** (51d, 121b), **Mars** (68c,118d,119a,129a,178a), **Mors** (41b), **ours** (124c), **pars** (89d), **sors** (44d,89b)

R--S **raas** (91b), **rais** (26c,29d,75a,103b), **Rais** (106b), **rats, reis** (26c, 29d,75a,103b), **Rems, revs** (131a), **Rhus** (159a), **Riis** (9d), **Riss** (66a), **Roos** (67a), **ross** (16c,161d), **Ross** (50c), **Russ** (135b)

-RT- **Arta** (72b), **arto** (34a), **arts** (138c), **arty, orts** (60d), **Urth** (68d, 107d,163d)

--RT **Bart** (96b), **Bert** (96b), **bort** (43b), **Bort** (134b), **cart** (171d,175a, 177b), **curt** (145b,c), **dart** (19b,88a,100c,120b,153a,160c), **dirt, fort** (63d,157d), **girt** (50a), **hart** (41d,154d), **hurt, mart** (49d,97a), **Mart** (96b,183d), **mort** (41b,47a,78b,136d), **part** (44d,60d,121c, 159c), **pert** (80a,93a,137c,154b), **port** (73d,136b,140c,170c,d,182b, c), **Sart** (82b,103b,170d), **Sert** (151d), **sort** (31d,39c,70b,86d,153a), **tart** (114d), **tort** (31c,91a,185c), **vert** (71d,166a,171b), **wart** (124d), **wert, wort** (76a,95d,121d), **yurt** (101d)

R--T **raft** (27b,33c,58c,75b), **rant** (41c,127b,128a,161d), **rapt** (6c,27a, 50d), **rect** (117b), **reft** (32a,42c,44d,167b), **rent** (58a,77c,91b,138b, 153d,162c,167c), **rest** (15d,91b,104d,105a,115a,b,130a,b,161b), **rift** (30c,32a,58a,110d), **riot** (44c,111d,170c,173d), **root** (53a), **rout** (41d,44b,46b), **runt** (47a,172d), **rust** (37b,112c,119a), **ryot** (115c)

RU-- **ruay** (189), **rube** (37d,135d,185d), **Rube** (96b), **ruby** (20a,65d, 179c), **ruck** (39a,185a), **rudd** (26d,57a,b), **rude** (134b,172b), **ruer ruff** (19b,33b,63d,137a), **ruga** (59b,185a), **Ruhr, ruin** (42d), **rukh** (53b,54a), **rule** (11b,26b,90b), **rull** (170b), **rumb** (120b), **rump, rune** (9b,67a,94a,95a,105c,107d,120a,141d,163d), **rung** (28c,39a), **runt** (47a,172d), **rupa** (60b), **ruru** (19b,102c,106d), **rusa, Rusa** (41d, 136d), **ruse** (13b,77c,157b,169c), **rush, rusk** (23a), **Russ** (135b), **rust** (37b,112c,119a), **Ruta** (76b,134d), **rute** (188), **ruth** (35b,118c), **Ruth** (105b,183c)

-RU- **arui** (11b,143d,144a,181c), **arum** (13a,39b,58d,92b,155c), **Arum** (66a), **bruh** (95a), **brut** (182c), **Brut** (23c), **crus** (91a,143c), **crux** (39a,151b), **drub** (17b,39c) **drug** (105d), **drum** (105a), **drun** (132b), **erua** (103c), **eruc** (37a,56a), **grub** (43c,88d), **grum** (102c), **Grus** (36b,c,38b), **irus** (109d), **prut!, Prut** (41a), **true** (7a,8d,37b,54b, 94c,149c), **urus** (14d,53a,112c)

357

·· RU Aaru (6b,48d), baru (168c), ecru (17d,23d,172b), feru (37a,56a, 133d), guru (77b), maru (84c,144d), Meru (77a,103d), paru (57a), Peru, Puru (192), ruru (19b,102c,106d), Yaru (48d)

R ·· U Rahu (42b,48b), rimu (79d,106d,129a,168c), ruru (19b,102c,106d)

· RV · urva (38b)

RY ·· ryal (110a,190), ryel (190), ryme (178d), rynd (100a), ryot (115c), rype (19b,125a)

· RY · Arya (80d), eryx (137a), oryx (11a), tryp (114a)

·· RY adry (164c), aery (47b,51d,106c), airy (177a,176d), atry (141b), awry (13d,38d,171c), bury (81d), dory (21b,58b,144c), eery (172b, 180a), ewry (133c), eyry (47b,106c), fury (157a), Gary, gory, jury (38a), lory (19a,114a), Mary (50c,126b,183c), miry, nary (108b), oary, sory (176d), spry (7a,107b), Tory (23c,36b,94c,172a), vary (28d,43c), very (149c), wary (27d,176b), wiry (147a,167c)

R ·· Y racy (153b), rely (16b,170b), rily (176a), rimy (63d), roey (103d), ropy (157c,176d), rosy (21a,111a), rowy (157b), Roxy (183d), ruay (189), ruby (20a,65d,179c)

R ·· Z razz (131b)

SA ·· Saad (12b), saah (188), saal (66c,73b), Saan (24d), Saar (63b,102d, 132a), saba (56a,117a), Saba (143d), sabe, sack (43d,118a,119d, 182b), saco (189), sadd (33a,40b,58c,107b), sade (91d), sadh (77a), sado (26d,84d), sadr (94a), Sadr (155b), saer (163a), safe (141d,157d,174d), Safi (191), saga (79b,91a,138a,157a,161b,c, 168a), Saga, sage (13a,90d,100c,141c,145c,180b,183a), sago (54c, 59b,113b,125b,155c), sagy, saha, sáhh (188), Saho (6c), sahu (153d), saic (86b,91d,175d), said (174c), Said (42d,101a,121b), sail (144c,185a), sain (20c,38d,48a), sair (140b,150d), sais (48d, 71d), Saka (10a), sake (84b,125d), saki (39c,84b,102a), sala (152a, b,c), Sala (50c), sale (14c,61c,62b,c,168b), salp (109c,148d), salt (35d,105b,123a,136c,141c,149d), sama (105c,169d), same (44d, 79b), samh (56b), samp (70b,77d,121b), sana (56a,166d), Sana (185d), sand (71d,146c), sane (128a), sang, sank, sano (152b), sans (63a,183b), sapa (70c), sapo (149c,166d), Sara (24d,183c), sard (26d,28d,65d,111a,142b,156d), Sard, Sarg (96d,125c), sari (48b,65b,77b), Sark (28d), Sart (82b,103b,170d), sasa (55c), sash (18a,45c,67b,182b), sass, sate (32d,52c,67d,70d,137c,159d), sati, Sati (49a,126b,147b), Sauk (192), saul (48a,168c), Saul (18c,86d, 115a), saum (189), save (52b,110c,123a,173c), sawk (188), sawn saxe (20d,33c), saya (117a)

· SA · asak (13d,168c,169a), asar (67b), Esau (82c,84a,128c), Esay, Isar (41a,104c,132a), osar (51b,67b,131b), tsar (42d,49d,60b,135c), usar (8d,16c), Usas (68d)

·· SA ansa (73c,93d,137c), Ausa, Besa (68b,119c), bisa (11a), bosa (12a), casa (152b), Disa (111a), dosa (74b), Elsa (70a,93c,110d, 177b,183c), kasa (48a), kusa, Lisa (183d), masa (37a), mesa (49b, 76d,119b,161a), Musa (16a), ossa (21d), Ossa (103d,110b,164b), pasa (46a,127c,152c), pesa (190), Pisa (90c), rasa (51c), Rosa (58d,134a,145d,183c), rusa, Rusa (41d,136d), sasa (55c), Susa (49a), Tesa (80c), Ursa (17b,36b,43d), vasa (46d,114a,160b,175d), Vasa, visa (114d), Xosa (86a)

S - - A   saba (56a,117a), Saba (143d), saga (79b,91a,138a,157a,161b,c, 168a), saha, Saka (10a), sala (152a,b,c), Sala (50c), sama (105c, 169d), sana (56a,166d), Sana (185d), sapa (70c), Sara (24d,183c), sasa (55c), saya (117a), Seba (18c,39d), sera (11b,20d,59a,83a, 180d), seta (23b,27c,73a,b,123b,153c), shea (25a,168c,d), · Shoa (6c), sida (37a,126c,170a), sika (41d,84b), sima (132b), sina (46c), Sina (102d,103d), Sita (127d), siva (67a,120d), Siva (56d,77a), skua (19b,72c,84a,141a), soda (19a,149d,181a), sofa (44d), soga (70d,152b), Soga (191), Soia, soja (151b), soka (20c), sola (9a,48a, 74b,118c,154a,167b), soma (10c,21c,34a,48a,81d,136b), sora (19b, c,127b), soya (151b), stoa (33c,121a,c), Sula (65a), supa (168c), sura (87c,113b,166d), Susa (49a), Syra

- SB -   isba (135c)

S - - B   scab (80b,107d,157c), scob (42a), Serb (15d,148a,186c), slab (148b), Sleb (12a), slob (173d), slub (171c), snab (23c,139a), snib (54d,93c), snob (159c), snub (128c,148b), sorb (11d,103d,134b, 142d), Sorb (148a,180a), stab (14c,87a,117c), stib (19b,47a,137a), stub (156c), swab (102b), sweb (160d), swob (102b)

SC - -   scab (80b,107d,157c), scad (31a,57a,78b,88d,137c), scan (52b,93d, 98a,116d,128b,c,140d), scar (31a,184d), scat (26b,67a,d,126c, 169c), Scio, scob (42a), scon (162c), scop (120a), scot (14a,162b), Scot (64b,132c), scow (21a,58b), scud (32c,126c,135b,160c), scum (129b), scup (57a,121b), scur (78b), scut (145c,161b)

- SC -   asci (154a), esca (11c,44a,70c), esce (158d)

- - SC   aesc (12d,64d), Bosc (115c), DDSC (42a), disc (31b), fisc (52c,134c)

S - - C   saic (86b,91d,175d), spec

S - - D   Saad (12b), sadd (33a,40b,58c,107b), said (174c), Said (42d,101a, 121b), sand (71d,146c), sard (26d,28d,65d,111a,142d,156d), Sard, scad (31a,57a,78b,137c), scud (32c,126c,135b,160c), seed (70b, 111c,112c,119a,151b,154a), seid (103b), Seid 42d,101a, 171a), send (42c,44b,95c,121c,130a,144c,168b), shad (27d,57a, b,c), shed (27a,90c,101b,144b), shod, Sind, skid (148b), sled (40a), slid, sned (93d,125a), snod (169d), sold, spad (105b), Spad (118d), sped, spud (121d,151c), stad (151b,167d,176b), stod (40d,67d), stud (22b,25a,42d,54d,111c,143a,174a), sudd (40b,58c,107b), suld (188), surd (82c,177a), swad (94d), syed (103b), syud (103b)

SE - -   seah (188), seal (10c,d,54d,64c,96a,118b,128a), seam (85b,d,160a, 176d,185a), Sean (85b,96a), sear (23d,27d,72c,138c), seat (98c, 156b), Seba (18c,39d), sebi (34b), sech (97c), seck (173d), sect (42b,54a,114c), seed (70b,111c,112c,119a,151b,154a), seek (141c), seel (20c,32c,143b), seem (11c), seen, seep (110c,116a, 154b), seer (60a,124c,150c), sego (24b,25a,92b,174c), sehr (66d), seid (103b), Seid (42d,101a,171a), Seik (77b), Seim (120c), sein (146c), seip (110c), Seir (51b,94a,103d), seis (147b,152c), seit (189), Sejm (120c), self (48d,80d), sell (97a,115c,175b), seme (45c, 138b,151b,154b,155c,157b), semi (34b,80b,122c,d), send (42c, 44b,95c,121c,130a,144c,168b), senn (76b), Sens (63b), sent, seps, (93b,142d), sept (31d,82b,143a,149c), Sept (45b), sera (11b,20d, 59a,83a,180d), Serb (15d,148a,186c), sere (24d,46a,c,138c,183b), Sere (158b), serf (21d,148a), seri (18b), Seri (192), sero (34d,88d,

164b,178d), **Sert** (151d), **sesi** (20b,57a,149b), **sess** (149c,162b), **seta** (23b,27c,73a,b,123b,153c), **seth** (98d), **Seth** (7a,52b,68a,b,96a, 98d), **seti** (34a), **Seti** (116d), **sett** (115a,156d), **seve** (63a,182c), **sewn, sext** (26b,111b,147b)

-SE- asea (39b,177c), asem (9a,49a,69c), Aser (84a), esek (18d), esel (66b), eser, Iser (49a), oser (61b), used (6d,73a), usee, user (49d), uses (18a), yser

--SE anse (61d), apse (9b,20a,31a,128c,130a,142b,175a), asse (25a, 60d,74a), base (6a,43b,44b,51c,60c,79b,94b,122b), bise (182a), bose (163c), case (22c,36c,81c,91a,108c), cise (147b), cose (29b), dose (123a), duse (83c), ease (7c,8d,35a,100d,129d,130b,c,150c), else (18b,79b,111d), ense (139b,158c), Erse (28a,64b,82b), esse (7a,18a,52d,89a,90a,159a,166c), fuse (98c), hase (74d), hose (156c), huse (180c), ipse (44d,89c), Jose (96a), lose (60a,100c), lyse, mese (71c), mise (8a,10a,70c), Mose (96b), muse (65b,93d, 120d,164c), Muse (68d), nase (26b,75a,124b), nose (118d,125a, 149b), oese (15d,119c), Oise, Ouse (132a,185d), owse, pise (127d), pose (14c,15d), rase (42b,d,91d), rese (127b), rise (49d,80b,155a), Rise (110d,150c), rose (33c), Rose (6a,50c,183c), ruse (13b,77c, 157b,169c), sise (62c,147b), vase, vise (31d,77d,114d), wise (136b)

S--E sabe, sade (91d), safe (141d,157d,174d), sage (13a,90d,100c,141c, 145c,180b,183a), sake (84b,125d), sale (14c,61c,62b,c,168b), same (44d,79b), sane (128a), sate (32d,52c,67d,70d,137c,159d), save (52b,110c,123a,173c), saxe (20d,33c), seme (45c,138b,151b,154b, 155c,157b), sere (24d,46a,c,138c,183b), Sere (158b), seve (63a, 182c), shee (82b), shoe (166a), sice (71d,147b), side (13d,22a,b, 54a,58a,89a,161b), sime (101d), sine (64c,66b,90a,97c,126a,163b, 169d,183b), sipe (101a,110c,140b), sire (17d,55a,59d,124a,163b, 166b), sise (62c,147b), site (93b), sive (146a), size, skee (149c), Skye (163c), slee (140b,148c), sloe (14a,20b,64a,119d,181c), slue (97b,148b,160a), smee (19b,46c,d,118b,119d,141b,181b), Smee (116d), snee (40a,b,43d,87a), soie (62c), soke (44c,85d), sole (52c, 57a,b,58b,d,110c,115d,150a), some (114b,121c,126a), sore (23d, 142c), sote (150c), spae (139c), Spee (66d,70b), supe (53a,154d), sure (173d), syce (71d), syke (194), syne (140b,147a), sype (110c)

S--F self (48d,80d), serf (21d,148a), souf (146b), stof (135c), surf (23a)

SG-- Sgau (88c)

S--G sang, Sarg (96d,125c), shag (73b,105b,161d,166d), sing (26d,178a), skag (7d,46d), skeg (7d,86a,144d,157d,184a), slag (46c,99a,138c, 148d,177a), slog (157c,170b,177d), slug (46b,99b,157c), smug, snag (11b,27b,35c,87c,124b,166a), sneg (139b), snig (45d), snug (35a,38b,165c), Snug (99d), song (12c,170c), stag (65a,98d), stog (155a), sung, Sung (30b), swag (22a,156c), swig (46a,72c)

SH-- shad (27d,57a,b,c), shag (73b,105b,161d,166d), shah (116c), sham (41c,55b,60d,80a,123a,b,146d), Shan (13c,80d,88c,101d), shap, shat (87d), shaw (164b), Shaw (50c,53b), shay (110c), shea (25a, 168c,d), shed (27a,90c,101b,144b), shee (82b), Shem (107c), Shen (68a), sher (65d,165c), shet, shew (44c), shih (189), Shik (171a), shim (91d,144c,162a,179d), shin (91a,d,140b,143c), ship, shir (36d, 65d,165c), Shoa (6c), shod, shoe (166a), shoo (46b,67a,138b), shop, shoq (169a), shor (136d), Shor (162b), shot (9d,43d,90c,174d), shou

(41d), **show** (42b,44c,96b), **Shri** (17c,166c), **shul** (161a), **shun** (15a, 51b,52a), **shut**

● **SH** ● **Asha** (191), **ashy** (113a,178a), **Isha** (174a), **Tshi** (69c), **Usha** (16a, 150c)

● ● **SH** **bash, bish** (120b), **bosh, bush, cash** (101c), **cosh** (35a,97c), **cush** (101c), **Cush** (51d,73c), **dash** (125c,162d), **dish, fash** (140c,176a), **fish, gash** (40a), **gish** (102c), **gosh, gush** (35a,154c), **hash, hish, hush** (17b,146c), **josh** (85b), **kish** (16d,70c), **Kish** (137c), **Kush lash** (58c,87b,165c,180d), **losh** (178b), **lush** (94d), **mash** (39b, 156c), **mesh** (50d,106c), **mush** (97d), **Nash** (9c), **Nish** (19d), **pish** (36c,107d), **posh** (49b,148c), **push** (145c), **rash** (75a), **resh** (91d), **rush, sash** (18a,45c,67b,182b), **sish** (79b), **sosh** (81d), **tash** (154d), **tosh** (106a), **tush** (167b), **wash, wish** (42d)

S ● ● **H** **saah** (188), **sadh** (77a), **sahh** (188), **samh** (56b), **sash** (18a,45c,67b, 182b), **seah** (188), **sech** (97c), **seth** (98d), **Seth** (7a,52b,68a,b,96a, 98d), **shah** (116c), **shih** (189), **sigh, Sikh** (77b), **sinh** (97c), **sish** (79b), **soph, sosh** (81d), **such** (146d)

SI ● ● **siak** (72d), **sial** (112a), **Siam** (163d,181a), **sice** (71d,147b), **sick, sida** (37a,126c,170a), **side** (13d,22a,b,54a,58a,89a,161b), **sidi** (103b, 166b), **sidy** (123b), **sier** (57a,118b), **sift** (140d,142c,146b), **sigh, sign** (121c,146c), **sika** (41d,84b), **Sikh** (77b), **silk** (53b,179c), **sill** (45c,76c,165a,182b), **silo** (59a,156d), **silt** (104b,142a), **sima** (132b), **sime** (101d), **Simi** (82d), **simp** (59c,146d), **sina** (46c), **Sina** (102d, 103d), **Sind, sine** (64c,66b,90a,97a,126a,163b,169d,183b), **sing** (26d,178a), **sinh** (97c), **sink** (41c,43c,46b,158a) **sino** (34a), **siol** (82c), **sion** (125c,158c), **Sion** (75b,c,83a,157d), **sipe** (101a,110c, 140b), **sire** (17d,55a,59d,124a,163b,166b), **siri** (18b), **sise** (62c, 147b), **sish** (79b), **sisi** (121b), **siss, sist** (139b), **Sita** (127d), **site** (93b), **sito** (34b), **siva** (67a,120d), **Siva** (56d,77a), **Sive** (146a), **size, sizy** (176d), **sizz**

● **SI** ● **Asia** (48a), **Asin** (102a), **Hsia** (30b,47c), **Isis** (68d,78c,111d), **tsia** (162c), **Tsin** (30b)

● ● **SI** **Absi** (191), **assi** (77d), **dasi** (77a), **desi** (85d), **kasi** (116b), **Lasi** (191), **nasi** (34c,108a,115a), **nisi** (90a,173c), **pasi** (94b), **sesi** (20b,57a), **sisi** (121b), **susi** (53b,d)

S ● ● **I** **Safi** (191), **saki** (39c,84b,102a), **sari** (48b,65b,77b), **sati, Sati** (49a, 126b,147b), **sebi** (34b), **semi** (34b,80b,122c,d), **seri** (18b), **Seri** (192), **sesi** (20b,57a,149b), **seti** (34a), **Seti** (116d), **Shri** (17c,166c), **sidi** (103b,166b), **Simi** (82d), **siri** (18b), **sisi** (121b), **soli** (12c,110c), **sori** (55c,64a), **sufi** (103a,116c), **sugi** (84b), **suji** (180c), **susi** (53b,d)

SK ● ● **skag** (7d,46d), **skat** (181b), **Skat** (155b), **skee** (149c), **skeg** (7d,86a, 144d,157d,184a), **sken** (164a), **skeo** (57d), **skep** (16d,17c,77c), **skew** (148a,160c,171b,c), **skey** (185d), **skid** (148b), **skil** (57a), **skim** (67c), **skin** (53a,76c,115c,d), **skio** (57d), **skip** (110b,114c,147c), **skir, skit** (145c), **skiv** (151b), **skua** (19b,72c,84a,141a), **Skye** (163c), **skyr** (21d,151a), **skyt** (138c,140b)

● **SK** ● **Askr** (107d)

● ● **SK** **bask** (94d), **bisk** (120b,151a), **bosk** (164b), **busk** (17b,37b,55d, 161b), **cask, cusk** (57b), **desk, disk** (31b), **dusk** (171c), **fisk** (24d,52c,134c), **husk** (53a,78d,142a), **mask** (44a,45c), **mosk** (97b,

361

103b), **musk** (116b), **Omsk, pisk** (9c,19b), **risk** (74d), **rusk** (23a), **task** (156b), **Tosk** (8c), **tusk** (167b)

S--K **sack** (43d,118a,119d,182b), **sank, Sark** (28d), **Sauk** (192), **sawk** (188), **seck** (173d), **seek** (141c), **Seik** (77b), **Shik** (171a), **siak** (72d), **sick, silk** (53b,179c), **sink** (41c,43c,46b,158a), **soak** (46c,137c), **Sobk** (38d), **sock** (157c,182a), **sook** (22a,25c,97a), **souk** (22a,97a), **suck, sulk** (159a), **sunk**

SL-- **slab** (148b), **slag** (46c,99a,138c,148d,177a), **slam** (180d,182d), **slap** (24a,128c,148c), **slat** (58b,89a,117c,184a), **Slav** (13c,40c,48b,52a, 120b,135b), **slaw, slay, Sleb** (12a), **sled** (40a), **slee** (140b,148c), **slew** (160a), **sley** (179b), **slid, slim** (148b,160a), **slip** (67c,119a), **slit** (40a), **slob** (173d), **sloe** (14a,20b,64a,119d,181c), **slog** (157c,170b, 177d), **sloo** (160a), **slop, slot** (10d,11b,41d,110d,167d,168a,181b), **slow** (43c), **slub** (171c), **slue** (97b,148b,160a), **slug** (46b,99b,157c), **slum, slur** (44b,124c,148b,168a)

-SL- **isle** (8b,53c,81d,82d,86b,88a), **Oslo**

S--L **saal** (66c,73b), **sail** (144c,185a), **saul** (48a,168c), **Saul** (18c,86d, 115a), **seal** (10c,d,54d,64c,96a,118b,128a), **seel** (20c,32c,143b), **sell** (97a,115c,175b), **shul** (161a), **sial** (112a), **sill** (45c,76c,165a, 182b) **siol** (82c), **skil** (57a), **soil** (154d,159a,163c), **soul** (10d,125a, 153c,176d)

SM-- **smee** (19b,46c,d,118b,119d,141b,181b), **Smee** (116d), **smew** (19b, 46d,99a,137d), **smug, smur** (32c,46b,100c), **smut** (32d,44a,119a, 150c)

-SM- **ismy** (45a)

--SM **kasm** (189)

S--M **saum** (189), **scum** (129b), **seam** (85b,d,160a,176d,185a), **seem** (11c), **Seim** (120c), **Sejm** (120c), **sham** (41c,55b,60d,80a,123a,b, 146d), **Shem** (107c), **shim** (91d,144c,162a,179d), **Siam** (163d,181a), **skim** (67c), **slam** (180d,182d), **slim** (148b,160a), **slum, stem** (29b, 125a,154d,155a,156d), **stom** (34c), **stum** (70c,105c,131a,173a), **swam, swim** (58c), **swum**

SN-- **snab** (23c,139a), **snag** (11b,27b,35c,87c,124b,166a), **snap** (23a, 36d,38b,48b,54d,56c,58c,149d), **sned** (93d,125a,140a), **snee** (40a, b,43d,87a), **sneg** (139b), **snib** (54d,93c), **snig** (45d), **snip** (32b, 40a), **snob** (159c), **snod** (169d), **snow, snub** (128c,148b), **snug** (35a,38b,165c), **Snug** (99d), **snup** (149b)

-SN- **asno** (151d), **esne** (10c,45b,142c,148a,164d)

S--N **Saan** (24d), **sain** (20c,38d,48a), **sawn, scan** (52b,93d,98a,116d, 128b,c,140d), **scon** (162c), **Sean** (85b,96a), **seen, sein** (146c), **senn** (76b), **sewn, Shan** (13c,80d,88c,101d), **Shen** (68a), **shin** (91a,d,140b, 143c), **shun** (15a,51b,52a), **sign** (121c,146c), **sion** (125c,158c), **Sion** (75b,c,83a,157d), **sken** (164a), **skin** (53a,76c,115c,d), **soon** (123a, 145c), **sorn** (139a,d), **span** (23b,107b,113a,128b,162c), **spin** (131a, 180d), **spun, sten** (72c,95a), **stun** (145a,157d), **sunn** (56a), **Svan** (27d), **swan** (19b,33a)

SO-- **soak** (46c,137c), **soap, soar** (59a), **Sobk** (38d), **sock** (157c,182a), **soco** (22d), **soda** (19a,149d,181a), **sofa** (44d), **soft** (48b,95d,99d, 163a), **soga** (70d,152b), **Soga** (191), **soho!, Soho** (93c), **Soia, soie**

362

(62c), **soll** (154d,159a,163c), **solr** (61c), **soja** (151b), **soka** (20c), **soke** (44c,85d), **sola** (9a,48a,74b,118c,154a,167b), **sold, sole** (52c,57a,b, 58b,d,110c,115d,150a), **soli** (12c,110c), **solo** (12c,89a,110c), **soma** (10c,21c,34a,48a,81d,136b), **some** (114b,121c,126a), **song** (12c, 170c), **sons** (98d,109d), **sook** (22a,25c,97a), **soon** (123a,145c), **soot** (20b,26c,88a), **soph, Sopt** (45b), **sora** (19b,c,127b), **sorb** (11d,103d, 134b,142d), **Sorb** (148a,180a), **sore** (23d,142c), **sori** (55c,64a), **sorn** (139a,d), **sors** (44d,89b), **sort** (31d,39c,70b,86b,153a), **sory** (176d), **sosh** (81d), **soso** (99c,114c,166d), **sote** (150c), **souf** (146b), **souk** (22a,97a), **soul** (10d,125a,153c,176d), **soup, sour, sous** (62d,172c), **soya** (151b)

– SO – **asok** (13d), **asom** (18d), **asop** (180b), **asor** (75c,105a), **Esop** (53b, 54a), **esox** (57b)

– – SO **also** (10b,18b,80a), **Caso** (82d), **coso** (152c), **enso** (34d,183b), **huso** (180c), **ipso** (89c), **koso** (6c,80d), **Koso** (192,193), **Muso** (192), **peso** (99c), **piso** (189), **soso** (99c,114c,166d), **yeso** (72d)

S – – O **saco** (189), **sado** (26d,84d), **sago** (54c,59b,113b,125b,155c), **Saho** (6c), **sano** (152b), **sapo** (149c,166d), **Scio, sego** (24b,25a,92b,174c), **sero** (34d,88d,164b,178d), **shoo** (46b,67a,138b), **silo** (59a,156d), **sino** (34a), **sito** (34b), **skeo** (57d), **skio** (57d), **sloo** (160a), **soco** (22d), **soho!, Soho** (93c), **solo** (12c,89a,110c), **soso** (99c,114c,166d), **Sumo**

SP – – **spad** (105b), **Spad** (118d), **spae** (139c), **span** (23b,107b,113a,128b, 162c), **spar** (22c,24c,64b,97b,100b,144d), **spat** (112c,126b,134b), **spec, sped, Spee** (66d,70b), **spes, Spes** (69a,78a), **spet** (16c,57a, 142c), **spew** (35a,49a), **spex, spey, spin** (131a,180d), **spir** (97c), **spit** (120a,132b,c), **spot** (93b,118c,154d,162a), **spry** (7a,107b), **spud** (121d,151c), **spun, spur** (10d,67d,167d,168a,181b), **sput** (21c)

– SP – **espy** (44a,142a)

– – SP **cusp** (38c,78b,119a,120a,b), **gasp** (113c), **hasp** (31d,54d,153c), **lisp** (153b), **rasp** (56b,70d,140d), **risp** (99a), **wasp, wisp** (24b,148c)

S – – P **salp** (109c,148d), **samp** (70b,77d,121b), **scop** (120a), **scup** (57a, 121b), **seep** (110c,116a,154b), **seip** (110c), **shap, ship, shop, simp** (59c,146d), **skep** (16d,17c,77c), **skip** (110b,114c,147c), **slap** (24a, 128c,148c), **slip** (67c,119a), **slop, snap** (23a,36d,38b,48b,54d,56c, 58c,149d), **snip** (32b,40a), **snup** (149b), **soap, soup, step** (70b,112b, 177b,d), **stop** (73b,111b), **sump** (28c,45d,100b), **swap** (168a), **swop** (168a)

S – – Q **shoq** (169a)

S – – R **Saar** (63b,102d,132a), **sadr** (94a), **Sadr** (155b), **saer** (163a), **sair** (140b,150d), **scar** (31a,184d), **scur** (78b), **sear** (23d,27d,72d,138c), **seer** (60a,124c,150c), **sehr** (66d), **Seir** (51b,94a,103d), **sher** (65d, 165c), **shir** (36d,65d,165c), **shor** (136d), **Shor** (162b), **sier** (57a, 118b), **skir, skyr** (21d,151a), **slur** (44b,124c,148b,168a), **smur** (32c,46b,100c), **soar** (59a), **soir** (61c), **sour, spar** (22c,24c,64b,97b, 100b,144d), **spir** (97c), **spur** (10d,67d,167d,168a,181b), **star** (14a, 21c,94c,100c), **ster** (158c,d), **stir** (8a,13a,35b,78d,100d,104a), **suer** (124d)

– SS – **asse** (25a,60d,74a), **assi** (77d), **esse** (7a,18a,52d,89a,90a,159a, 166c), **ossa** (21d), **Ossa** (103d,110b,164b)

• • SS bass (57b,c,177a), Bess (76c,183d), boss (49d,157d), buss (87a, 148c), cass (140c,177a), Cass (147a), cess (91d,94c,162b), coss (98a), cuss, diss (98b), doss (17c), fass (189), fess (23c,51b), foss (44d,100d), fuss (22b,35b), hiss (146a), jass (160d), jess (157a), joss (30b), kiss (148c), koss (188), lass (95b), less (100c,108b,141d), liss (54b,58b,60c,129d,140a), loss (42c,123d,178b), mass (8a,24b, 35b,142d), mess (22b,44b,77c,85d,104b,165c,173d), miss, moss (91d,104c,114a,170c), muss (135b,173d), ness (26b,75a,124b), pass (110b,155c), puss, Riss (66a), ross (16c,161d), Ross (50c), Russ (135b), sass, sess (149c,162b), siss, Tass (107a,135d,151b), Tess (73d,164c,183d), toss (24a,132d), viss (189)

S • • S sais (48d,71d), sans (63a,183b), sass, seis (147b,152c), sens (63b), seps (93b,142d), sess (149c,162b), siss, sons (98d,109d), sors (44d, 89b), sous (62d,172c), spes, Spes (69a,78a), suds (59a)

ST • • stab (14c,87a,117c), stad (151b,167d,176b), stag (65a,98d), star (14a,21c,94c,100c), stat (72d), stay (72d,124c,130a,134a,162a), stem (29b,125a,154d,155a,156d), sten (72c,95a), step (70b,112b, 177b,d), ster (158c,d), stet (91b,123d,124c), stev (155b), stew (21c,44b,184d), stib (19b,47a,137a), stir (8a,13a,35b,78d,100d, 104a), stoa (33c,121a,c), stod (40d,67d), stof (135c), stog (155a), stom (34c), stop (73b,111b), stot (154d,155d,157d,179b,186a), stow (112b), stub (156c), stud (22b,25a,42d,54d,111c,143a,174a), stum (70c,105c,131a,173a), stun (145a,157d), Styx (29b,73a,105c)

• ST • asta (188), Asta (107a,164c), Asti (83d,182b), esta (152d,164c), este (152b,d,164c), Este (55c,83c,d,112d), Esth (16a,51d), oste (21d,83b)

• • ST bast (16c,56a,117b,184a), Bast (27b), best (41d,159c,160a), bust (165b,167c), cast (18a,67b), dost, dust, east, East (111b), erst (60b), fast (56d,126c,141d,160c,173a,d), fest, fist (80c), fust (105c,143b), gest (7c,41d,52d,133c), gist (95c,118c), gust, hast, hest (35a), hist (25c,93d), host (13a,51d,104c), jest (169c), just (51b,54b), kist (29d,58a,139b), last (36c,50b,145a,174c), lest (59d, 163d), list (26d,27b,75b,83d,134a,138b,165d), lost, lust (41b), mast (17c,108d,120b,144d,152d), mist (46b,59b,174d), most, must (70c,101a,106d,157d,182c), myst (71c,123b), Nast (9c,27a), nest (38b,74b,130d,149c,160b), oast (15d,86b,112a), oust (44c, 49a,52b,125d), past (25c,69d,165d), pest (108c,116b,118d,170a), pist (25c), post (89a,95c,155d), rest (15d,91b,104d,105a,115a,b, 130a,b,161b), rust (37b,112c,119a), sist (139b), test (26a,51c,144a, 169c,170c), vast (78d,79a), vest (32c,177b), wast, west, West (9c, 50b,109b), wist (87c), zest (55d,72d)

S • • T salt (35d,105b,123a,136c,141c,149d), Sart (82b,103b,170d), scat (26b,67a,d,126c,169c), scot (14a,162b), Scot (64b,132c), scut (145c,161b), seat (98c,156b), sect (42b,54a,114c), seit (189), sent, sept (31d,82b,143a,149c), Sept (45b), Sert (151d), sett (115a,156d), sext (26b,111b,147b), shat (87d), shot (9d,43d,90c, 174d), shut, sift (140d,142c,146b), silt (104b,142a), skat (181b), Skat (155b), skit (145c), skyt (138c,140b), slat (58b,89a,117c, 184a), slit (40a), slot (10d,11b,41d,110d,167d,168a,181b), smut (32d,44a,119a,150c), soft (48b,95d,99d,163a), soot (20b,26c,88a), Sopt (45b), sort (31d,39c,70b,86b,153a), spat (112c,126b,134b),

364

spet (16c,57a,142c), spit (120a,132b,c), spot (93b,118c,154d,162a), sput (21c), stat (72d), stet (91b,123d,124c), stot (154d,155d,157d, 179b,186a), suet (54d), suit (38a,58a,91a,112a,119c,137c), swat (15d,20d,32d,157c), Swat (103a), swot

SU -- such (146d), suck, sudd (40b,58c,107b), suds (59a), suer (124d), suet (54d), sufi (103a,116c), sugi (84b), suit (38a,58a,91a,112a, 119c,137c), suji (180c), Suku (191), Sula (65a), suld (188), sulk (159a), Sulu (102c), Sumo, sump (28c,45d,100b), sung, Sung (30b), sunk, sunn (56a), supa (168c), supe (53a,154d), sura (87c,113b, 166d), surd (82c,177a), sure (173d), surf (23a), Susa (49a), susi (53b,d), susu (20c), Susu (191), Susy (183d)

-SU - Asur (68c), Esus, tsun (30b), Usun (191)

--SU ansu (11d), Apsu (29a), ausu (168c,180b), Jesu, masu (57a,84c), Nosu (27d), susu (20c), Susu (191), vasu (106c), Vasu (176d)

S--U sahu (153d), Sgau (88c), shou (41d), Suku (191), Sulu (102c), susu 20c), Susu (191)

SV-- Svan (27d)

S--V skiv (151b), Slav (13c,40c,48b,52a,120b,135b), stev (155b)

SW-- swab (102b), swad (94d), swag (22a,156c), swam, swan (19b,33a), swap (168a), swat (15d,20d,32d,157c), Swat (103a), sway (104a), sweb (160d), swig (46a,72c), swim (58c), swiz (160c), swob (102b), swop (168a), swot, swow (100a), swum

S--W scow (21a,58b), shaw (164b), Shaw (50c,53b), shew (44c), show (42b,44c,96b), skew (148a,160c,171b,c), slaw, slew (160a), slow (43c), smew (19b,46d,99a,137d), snow, spew (35a,49a), stew (21c, 44b,184d), stow (112b), swow (100a)

S--X spex, Styx (29b,73a,105c)

SY-- syce (71d), syed (103b), syke (194), syne (140b,147a), sype (110c), Syra, syud (103b)

--SY busy, cosy (149c), easy (54a,146d,149d,172b), Josy (183d), mosy (67d), nosy, rosy (21a,111a), Susy (183d)

S--Y sagy, shay (110c), sidy (123b), sizy (176d), skey (185d), slay, sley (179b), sory (176d), Spey, spry (7a,107b), stay (72d,124c,130a, 134a), Susy (183d), sway (104a)

S--Z sizz, swiz (160c)

TA-- Taal (7d,88c,151a), taar (12b), tabi (84c,149d), tabu (59d,111d), tace (13a,155d), tack (28d,37d,54d), tact (43c,d,116a), tael (91d, 179d), Taft (29d), taha (179b), tahr (68a,76d), tail (11d,27d,59b, 143b), tain (166a), tair (68a,76d), tait (14d), tajo (152a,d), take, takt (105a,163a), Taku (80c), taky, tala (16d,113a,168c,d), talc (28d,63b,99c,100b,122a,149c), tale (91a,185b), tali (189), talk, tall (118d), Tama (192), tame (45a,b,66a), Tame, tamp (46b,112b, 121d,127d), tana (159a), Tana (87d), Tane (120d), tang (30b,58b, 186b), tanh (97c), tank (175a,d), Tano (192), Taos (192), tapa (16c, 32c,53b,56a,74b,104b,112b,113d,120d), tape (16a,19a,128d), tapu, tara (22a,55c,113a,168c), Tara (82b,c,138b), tare (9a,18d,41a, 176a,179d), Tari (47d,69a), tarn (87d,103d,120d), taro (13c,48c, 49b,64b,112b,120a,133d,155c,170a,c), tarp (26b,178d), tart (114d), tash (154d), task (156b), Tass (107a,135d,151b), tate (183a), tatt

(87c), **tatu** (12d), **Tatu, taun** (188), **taut** (163b,165c), **Tave** (183d),
Tavy (183d), **tawa** (106d,168c), **taxi** (13a,125b), **taxo** (13a)

-TA- atap (113b), atar (58d,116b,134a), Etah (71d,51c), etal (89a), etat
(62d), Ptah (48d,98c), stab (14c,87a,117c), stad (151b,167d,176b),
stag (65a,98d), star (14a,21c,94c,100c), stat (72d), stay (72d,124c,
130a,134a,162a), utac (22d), Utah (180b), utas (49a,109c)

--TA acta (41d,123d,128d,164c), Aeta (94d,95d,100a,106b,117a),
alta (89c,152d), anta (83d,117c,d,121a), Anta (164a), Arta
(72b), asta (188), Asta (107a,164c), atta (58d,90c,97d,160c,173d),
Atta (94d,95d,100a,106b,117a), bata (30a,142d), beta (71a,
91c,141d), bota (189), cata (122c), cota (117a), data (54a),
dita (117a), esta (152d,164c), Etta (183c), gata (143c), geta
(84b,145a), Gita, iota (71a,85c,91c,114c,166c,176a,180d),
jota (151c), keta (45a), kota (117a), Kota (45d), lata (85d,
95d), lota (24c,121d,178d), Lota meta (132d,133a), Meta,
mota (103a), muta (28d,103a), nata (47c), Nata (15c), nota (15c,
89c), octa (122c), pata (32c,160d), pita (9c,28b,56a,83a), rata
(29d,56b,89d,96c,106d,120c,168c), rita, Rita (37b,78d,183c), rota
(27c,30d,38a,79a,92d,133a,134a,b,180c), Ruta (76b,134d), seta
(23b,27c,73a,b,123b,153c), Sita (127d), tota (71d), veta (104a), vita
(89c,92a), vota (133b), weta (93c), yeta (84c), zeta (71b,91c)

T--A taha (179b), tala (16d,113a,168c,d), Tama (192), tana (159a), Tana
(87d), tapa (16c,32c,53b,56a,74b,104b,112b,113d,120d), tara (22a,
55c,113a,168c), Tara (82b,c,138b), tawa (106d,168c), tcha (162c),
teca, Teca (192), Teda (191), tela (22d,98c,121b,166a,179c), tema
(12a,164a), Tema, tera (23d,84c), tesa (80c), Tewa (193), Thea
(162c), Tina (183d), tiza (172a), Toba (80c), Toda (45d,76d), toga
(132d,133a,b), tola (48a,80d,180a), Tola (85b), Toma (191), tooa
(17c), tora (11a,44d,74a,75c,85c,90b,102d,115d), tota (71d), toxa
(153d), tsia (162c), tuba (105a,137d), tufa (121b,177a), tula (9a),
Tula, tuna (57a,b,123b), tuza (119d)

T--B theb (188), thob (128a), tomb

TC-- tcha (162c), tche (13d,30b,105a), tchi, Tchi, tchu

-TC'- etch, itch

T--C talc (28d,63b,99c,100b,122a,149c)

T--D tend (26d,80b,93d,100a), thud, tied, tind (86b), toad (10a,17a,
63d,126d), toed, told (129c), trod, tund (121d)

TE-- teak (41a,48a,168c), teal (19b,20d,46c,d), team (38c,72a,113a),
tean (140c,167a), tear (67c,87b,130a), teca, Teca (192), Tech,
teck (128b), Teco (192), Teda (191), teel (142d), teem (6b,121d),
teen (139b,c,140b,158d), teer (25b,69d), Tees (108a), teff (6c),
tegg (143d,171d), tehr (27c,68a), Teig (96a), teil (92b,c,168c), teju
(151b), tela (22d,98c,121b,166a,179c), tele (34b,122c), teli (94b),
tell (105d,129c,154b), Tell (160d), tema (12a,164a), Tema, tend
(26d,80b,93d,100a) tene (34d,131b), teng (188), tent (26b),
115a), Teos (82a), tera (23d,84c), term (92b,105b,142b,166b),
tern (19b,32d,72c,94a,138c,141a,160a), terp (12b,123a), tesa
(80c), Tess (73d,164c,183d), test (26a,51c,144a,169c,170c), tete
(61d,73b,74d), teth (91d), Tewa (193), text (21c,140d), teyl (92b,
c,168c)

366

-TE- atef (39a,48d), aten (150a,159b), **Ateo** (120d), **Ater** (18c), **ates** (160c), **Itea** (145d,160c,181d), item (6d,13b,42d,51a,90d,92d,107a, 113d,114c), **Iten** (192), iter (22d,76c,85c,89c,114d,132a,b,133a,b), **Otea** (71a,82d), stem (29b,125a,154d,155a,156d), sten (72c,95a), step (70b,112b,177b,d), ster (158c,d), stet (91b,123d,124c), stev (155b), stew (21c,44b,184d)

--TE ante (87a,89a,115b,120b,122b,125d,154d), bate (43c,91b,100d), bete (61a,107c), bite (29d,156b), cate (165c), cete (180b,c), cite (15a,98d,126d,159b), cote (19b,143d,144a,b), cute (39c), date (64a,153a), dite (150b), dote (17a,90b,94b,97a,112a,139d,165d), ente (70b,151d), este (152b,d,164c), **Este** (55c,83c,d,112d), ette (158a,c,d), fate (42d,52a,87a,94a), fete (55d,129b), fute (51c), gate (51a,121b), gite (62a,118d), hate (6a,43a), jete (16a), jute (37a,48a,56a,133d,136a), **Jute, Kate** (143c,183d), kite (19c,49a, 74c,d), late (128c), **lete, lite** (158c,d), lote (24c,94a), lute (11c,28b, 84d,105a,131d), mate (18c,35b,41d,113a,154a,162c), mete (9a, 11d,22b,44c,45b,98a,121c), mite (12b,81b,82a,114a,c,148c,d,181b), mote (114c,153a), mute (146c,153b), **Nate** (22b), nete (71c,108b, 163d), note (98c,109b,124b,128d,130a,177c), oste (21d,83b), pate (39a,74d), pete (136b), **Pete,** rate (11d,14a,31d,36b,51d,52a,70b, 85c,112b,123b,127d,128a,138c,143a,174b), rete (106c,119c), rite (93a,131d), rote (130b,134b,143a,159d), rute (188), sate (32d,52c, 67d,70d,137c,159d), site (93b), sote (150c), tate (183a), tete (61d, 73b,74d), tote (27a,73c), tute (171b), vite (62b), vote (60b), **Vote** (56d), **Wate** (141a), **Wote** (191), yate (51d,168c)

T--E tace (13a,155d), **take,** tale (91a,185b), tame (45a,b,66a), **Tame, Tane** (120d), tape (16a,19a,128d), tare (9a,18d,41a,176a,179d), tate (183a), **Tave** (183d), tche (13d,30b,105a), tele (34b,122c), tene (34d,131b), tete (61d,73b,74d), thee (124b), tice (9a,38c,51a, 185d), tide (39d,75d,109c,141c,159d), tige (118a), tike (29d), tile (31d,56d,72b,95b,133c,163c), time (47a,131a), tine (11b,124b, 167b), tipe (168b), tire (15a,22a,52d,55a,179b,180d), tobe (7d, 137b), tode (80a,148a), tole (9a,51a,99b,163a), tome (21d,177c), tone (6c,118c,150d), tope (24a,46b,57a,143c,151a), tore, tote (27a, 73c), **tree** (11d,37a,66a,184b), **true** (7a,8d,37b,54b,94c,149c), tube (118b,158a), tuke (26b,53b), tule (24b,27c), tune (8b,12c, 98c), tute (171b), **twee, tyee** (29d), tyke (29d), **tyne, Tyne** (108a), type (31d,115a,155a), tyre (15a), **Tyre** (31b,90d,117b)

T--F teff (6c), tiff (126b), toff (40d), tref (172b), tuff (121b,177a), turf (115c,149d,160b)

T--G tang (30b,58b,186b), tegg (143d,171d), **Teig** (96a), teng (188), thug (65a), ting (166a), **Ting** (30c), tong (30a,c,), toug (171a), trig (106a,148d,154b,169d), tung (110a,168c), **twig**

TH-- **Thai** (146a), than (35b), thar (68a,76d), that (42b,124b,129c), **thaw, Thea** (162c), theb (188), thee (124b), them (124b), **then, thew** (104c), they (124b), thin (43b,c,148b), this (42b,124b), thob (128a), **Thor** (7c,68c,99c,100c,109c,165b), **Thos** (84a,181c), thou (124b), **thud, thug** (65a), thus (149c)

-TH- Otho (133a)

--TH acth (13b), **bath, Bath** (50d,151c), beth (91c), **Beth** (8c,183d), **both, doth, Esth** (16a,51d), **Gath** (117a), **Goth** (16c,163d), **hath,**

367

Heth (77c), **Hoth** (20c), **Jeth** (102a), **kath** (14a), **kith** (63c), **lath** (157c), **lith** (34d,156c), **loth** (15a,173d), **math** (77a), **moth, Moth** (112d), **muth** (188), **myth** (8b,91a), **Nath** (155c), **oath** (119c,150a), **path** (132a,134b), **pith** (37a,51c,67b,95c,97a,119b,126d), **rath** (76d,162d), **ruth** (35b,118c), **Ruth** (105b,183c), **seth** (98d), **Seth** (7a,52b,68a,b,96a,98d), **teth** (91d), **Urth** (68d,107d,163d), **Voth** (191), **with** (10b)

T--H **tanh** (97c), **tash** (154d), **Tech, teth** (91d), **toph** (75c), **tosh** (106a), **tush** (167b)

TI-- **Tiam, tiao, tiar** (39a,75a,121a), **Tibu** (191), **tice** (9a,38c,51a,185d), **tick** (12b,20d,97c), **tide** (39d,75d,109c,141c,159d), **tidy** (106a, 111b), **tied, tien** (147d), **tier** (118a,134b), **tiff** (126b), **tige** (118a), **tike** (29d), **Tiki** (120c), **tile** (31d,56d,72b,95b,133c,163c), **till** (39c, 101c,173d), **tilt** (26b,d,166a), **time** (47a,131a), **Tina** (183d), **tind** (86b), **tine** (11b,124b,167b), **ting** (166a), **Ting** (30c), **Tino** (136d), **tint** (33c,d,114d), **tiny** (100c,148c), **tion** (158b), **Tiou** (192), **tipe** (168b), **tipi** (181b), **tire** (15a,22a,52d,55a,179b,180d), **tiro** (9b,17d, 108c), **titi** (20d,102a,145d,168d,181b), **Tito** (186c), **tiza** (172a)

-TI- **Atik** (155b), **atip** (14b,166a), **atis** (76d,102a), **itis** (158c), **otic** (14c, d,47b), **Otis** (9c,d,24d,82a,111a), **stib** (19b,47a,137a), **stir** (8a, 13a,35b,78d,100d,104a)

--TI **anti** (7d,111a,122b), **Anti** (193), **Asti** (83d,182b), **biti** (20b), **Guti, Hati** (48d), **hoti, Inti** (159b), **jati** (27b), **jiti, joti, Leti** (82d), **liti** (60d), **Loti** (63a,176a), **neti** (164a), **rati** (189), **roti** (62c), **sati, Sati** (49a,126b,147b), **seti** (34a), **Seti** (116d), **titi** (20d,102a,145d,168d, 181b), **viti** (176b), **yati** (76d), **zati** (21d)

T--I **tabi** (84c,149d) **tali** (189), **Tari** (47d,69a), **taxi** (13a,125b), **tchi, Tchi, teli** (94b), **Thai** (146a), **Tiki** (120c), **tipi** (181b), **titi** (20d,102a, 145d,168d,181b), **topi** (37a,75a,118c), **tori** (101b), **tshi, Tshi** (69c), **Tupi** (192), **Turi** (191), **tuwi** (117a,168c), **Tybi** (102a)

-TK- **Atka** (11a)

T--K **tack** (28d,37d,54d), **talk, tank** (175a,d), **task** (156b), **teak** (41a, 48a,168c), **teck** (128b), **tick** (12b,20d,97c), **tock** (7d,19b),**tonk** (173c), **took, Tosk** (8c), **trek** (85c,93c,99d,168b), **tuck** (156b), **Turk** (101d,102d,106a,111d), **tusk** (167b)

-TL- **atle** (136d,161d,169b), **Atli** (14c,72b,79a,107d)

--TL **rotl** (103b,111c)

T--L **Taal** (7d,88c,151a), **tael** (91d,179d), **tail** (11d,27d,59b,143b), **tall** (118d), **teal** (19b,20d,46c,d), **teel** (142d), **teil** (92b,c,168c), **tell** (105d,129c,154b), **Tell** (160d), **teyl** (92b,c,168c), **till** (39c,101c, 173d), **toil** (46c,184c), **toll** (131c), **tool** (27c), **tuel**

TM-- **T-men** (168b)

-TM- **atma** (150d), **atmo** (34d,174d), **Atmu** (143a,159b), **itmo** (18b)

T--M **team** (38c,72a,113a), **teem** (6b), **term** (92b,105b,142b,166b), **them** (124b), **tiam, toom** (139b), **tram** (170a), **trim** (40a,106a,154b, 160a,165c,169d), **turm** (132d)

-TN- **etna** (75b,153c,157a,175d,177a,c)

T--N **tain** (166a), **tarn** (87d,103d,120d), **taun** (188), **tean** (140c,167a), **teen** (139b,c,140b,158d), **tern** (19b,32d,72c,94a,138c,141a,160a), than (35b), then, thin (43b,c,148b), tien (147d), tion (158b), T-men (168b), toon (80c,95b,168c), torn (130a), town (73c), tran (7a), trin (169d), tron (140d,180a), Tsin (30b), tsun (30b), tuan (95d,147b,166c), turn (28d,131a,175a), twin (45c,171d)

TO - -   toad (10a,17a,63d,126d), Toba (80c), tobe (7d,137b), toby (8c, 85c,104b), Toby (96b,125c), tock (7d,19b), toco (19b,167c), Toda (45d,76d), tode (80a,148a), todo (22b,24d,35b,64c,156b), tody (19b,d,59a,166a), toed, toff (40d), toga (132d,133a,b), togs (32c), togt (77c), toho (79a), toil (46c,184c), toko (30c), tola (48a,80d,180a), Tola (85b), told (129c), tole (9a,51a,99b,163a), toll (131c), tolt, tolu (16a), Toma (191), tomb, tome (21d,177c), tone (6c,118c,150d), tong (30a,c), tonk (173c), tony, Tony (96b), tooa (17c), took, tool (27c), toom (139b), toon (80c,95b,168c), toot, tope (24a,46b,57a,143c,151a), toph (75c), topi (37a,75a, 118c), tops (159c), tora (11a,44d,74a,75c,85c,90b,102d,115d), tore, tori (101b), torn (130a), toro (38a,107a,152a,168c), torp (54c), tort (31c,91a,185c), Tory (23c,36b,94c,172a), tosh (106a), Tosk (8c), toss (24a,132d), tota (71d), tote (27a,73c), toto (8d,15a,34d, 89a,181a), toty (87b), toug (171a), toup (95d), tour (31b,85c), tout (61a,127a), town (73c), towy (58b), toxa (153d)

- TO -   atom (101c,114c,180d), aton (150a,159b), atop (112a,174a), Eton (33b,50c,84a), itol (158b), Otoe (147b), stoa (33c,121a,c), stod (40d,67d), stof (135c), stog (155a), stom (34c), stop (73b,111b), stot (154d,155d,157d,179b,186a), stow (112b), utor (90a,166c)

- - TO   acto (152b), alto (152b,176c), auto (34d), bito (7d,57d,168c), Boto (192), Buto (142d), Cato (132d,133b), ceto (34a), cito (89d,126c), coto (16c,90b), dato (95c,102c,117a), Doto (141b), ecto (34c,122d), ento (34b,d), into (123a,183b) jato (173b), koto (84b), Leto (11c), loto (65a,121d,178d), moto (104b), Nato (6a,8d), nito (55c), octo (34a,89b,122c), onto (76a,174a), otto (58d,116b,134a), Otto (14c,66d,67a,96a), pato (46d), peto (57a,177b), Peto (76a), pito (9c,28b,83a), roto (30a,122d,127b,152c,171b), sito (34b), Tito (186c), toto (8d,15a,34d,89a,181a), Tyto (16c), unto (166c), veto (94a,124a), Veto, Voto (192)

T - - O   tajo (152a,d), Tano (192), taro (13c,48c,49b,64b,112b,120a,133d, 155c,170a,c), taxo (13a), Teco (192), tiao, Tino (136d), tiro (9b, 17d,108c), Tito (186c), toco (19b,167c), todo (22b,24d,35b,64c, 156b), toho (79a), toko (30c), toro (38a,107a,152a,168c), toto (8d,15a,34d,89a,181a), trio (104d,165a,169c), tuno (28b,168c), typo (35c,51b,123d), tyro (9b,17d,108c), Tyto (16c)

T - - P   tamp (46b,112b,121d,127d), tarp (26b,178d), terp (12b,123a), torp (54c), toup (95d), trap (27b,67b,132b,149b), trip (85c), trop (62d,167a), tryp (114a), tump (60a,76d,103d), turp, tymp (20c), typp (185b)

TR - -   tram (170a), tran (7a), trap (27b,67b,132b149b), tray (128c, 136d,142d,143c), tree (11d,37a,66a,184b), tref (172b), trek (85c, 93c,99d,168b), tres (19a,52b,63a,152d,165a,175c), tret (9a,178b, 179d), trey (26c,165a), trig (106a,148d,154b,169d), trim (40a,106a,154b,160a,165c,169d), trin (169d), trio (104d,165a, 169c), trip (85c), tris (122d), trit (34d,164c), trod, tron (140d, 180a), trop (62d,167a), trot (85b,93d,112d), trow (18a,21a,159d,

369

164c,170b), **troy** (161c,180a), **Troy, true** (7a,8d,37b,54b,94c,149c), **tryp** (114a)

●TR - Atri, atry (141b), etre (61a,c,62d,166c)

● ● TR natr (189)

T ● ● R **taar** (12b), **tahr** (68a,76d), **tair** (68a,76d), **tear** (67c,87b,130a), **teer** (25b,69d), **tehr** (27c,68a), **thar** (68a,76d), **Thor** (7c,68c,99c, 100c,109c,165b), **tiar** (39a,75a,121a), **tier** (118a,134b), **tour** (31b, 85c), **tsar** (42d,49d,60b,135c), **turr** (24d,105a), **tyer, Tyrr** (68c, 109c,163d,178a), **tzar** (42d,49d,60b,135c)

TS ● ● **tsar** (42d,49d,60b,135c), **tshi, Tshi** (69c), **tsia** (162c), **Tsin** (30b), **tsun** (30b)

● ● TS Acts, arts (138c), cits, eats, lots, orts (60d), rats

T ● ● S **Taos** (192), **Tass** (107a,135d,151b), **Tees** (108a), **Teos** (82a), **Tess** (73d,164c,183d), **this** (42b,124b), **Thos** (84a,181c), **thus** (149c), **tngs** (32c), **tops** (159c), **toss** (24a,132d), **tres** (19a,52b,63a,152d,165a, 175c), **tris** (122d)

●TT- **atta** (58d,90c,97d,160c,173d), **Atta** (94d,95d,100a,106b,117a), **Attu, Etta** (183c), **ette** (158a,c,d), **otto** (58d,116b,134a), **Otto** (14c,66d,67a,96a)

● ● TT **batt** (37c), **bitt** (54d,175c), **bott** (32a,88d), **butt** (27a,77b,127d, 162a,182b), **Catt** (9d), **gett** (44d), **Lett** (16a,90a,93a), **Matt, mitt** (56c), **mutt** (39c,101d), **Natt** (107b), **nett, Nott** (107b), **Pitt** (50d,155d), **pott** (113d), **putt** (69d), **sett** (115a,156d), **tatt** (87c), **watt** (173b,177c), **Watt** (82a)

T ● ● T **tact** (43c,d,116a), **Taft** (29d), **tait** (14d), **takt** (105a,163a), **tart** (114d), **tatt** (87c), **taut** (163b,165c), **tent** (26b,115a), **test** (26a, 51c,144a,169c,170c), **text** (21c,140d), **that** (42b,124b,129c), **tilt** (26b,d,166a), **tint** (33c,d,114d), **todt** (66b), **tolt, toot, tort** (31c,91a,185c), **tout** (61a,127a), **tret** (9a,178b,179d), **trit** (34d,164c), **trot** (85b,93d,112d), **tuft** (24b,32d,38c), **twit** (162b,c)

TU ● ● **tuan** (95d,147b,166c), **tuba** (105a,137d), **tube** (118b,158a), **tuck** (156b), **tuel, tufa** (121b,177a), **tuff** (121b,177a), **tuft** (24b,32d, 38c), **tuke** (26b,53b), **tula** (9a), **Tula, tule** (24b,27c), **Tulu** (45d), **tump** (60a,76d,103d), **tuna** (57a,b,123b,170d), **tund** (121d), **tune** (8b,12c,98c), **tung** (110a,168c), **tuno** (28b,168c), **tunu** (28b), **tuny, Tupi** (192), **turf** (115c,149d,160b), **Turi** (191), **Turk** (101d,102d, 106a,111d), **turm** (132d), **turn** (28d,131a,175a), **turp, turr** (24d, 105a), **tush** (167b), **tusk** (167b), **tute** (171b), **tutu** (16a,106d,147d), **tuwi** (117a,168c), **tuza** (119d)

●TU - **atua** (120d), **Atum** (143a,159b), **etui** (27a,29b,62c,106b,148d, 166d,174b), **Otus** (67a), **stub** (156c), **stud** (22b,25a,42d,54d,111c, 143a,174a), **stum** (70c,105c,131a,173a), **stun** (145a,157d), **Utug** (159b), **utum** (19b,112c)

● ● TU **actu** (7a,89a), **Attu, datu** (95c,102c,117a), **Ketu** (48b), **latu** (190), **mitu** (39d), **patu** (179b), **tatu** (12d), **Tatu, tutu** (16a,106d,147d), **yutu** (19b,166a)

T ● ● U **tabu** (59d,111d), **Taku** (80c), **tapu, tatu** (12d), **Tatu, tchu, teju** (151b), **thou** (124b), **Tibu** (191), **Tiou** (192), **tolu** (16a), **Tulu** (45d), **tunu** (28b), **tutu** (16a,106d,147d)

370

TW - - twee, twig, twin (45c,171d), twit (162b,c)

T - - W thaw, thew (104c), trow (18a,21a,159d,164c,170b)

TY - - Tybi (102a), tyee (29d), tyer, tyke (29d), tymp (20c), tyne, Tyne (108a), type (31d,115a,155a), typo (35c,51b,123d), typp (185b), typy, tyre (15a), Tyre (31b,90d,117b), tyro (9b,17d,108c), Tyrr (68c,109c,163d,178a), Tyto (16c)

- TY - etym (133d), Itys (163b), Styx (29b,73a,105c)

- - TY arty, city, Coty (63c), doty (43d), duty (109b,162b), Katy (183d), maty (80c), mity, pity (35b), toty (87b)

T - - Y taky, Tavy (183d), they (124b), tidy (106a,111b), tiny (100c,148c), toby (8c,85c,104b), Toby (96b,125c), tody (19b,d,59a,166a), tony, Tony (96b), tory, Tory (23c,36b,94c,172a), toty (87b), towy (58b), tray (128c,136d,142d,143c), trey (26c,165a), troy (161c,180a), Troy, tuny, typy

TZ - - tzar (42d,49d,60b,135c)

- TZ - Itza (192)

- - TZ batz (190), litz (127b), untz (189)

UA - - uang (131a)

- UA - bual (182c), duab (157c), duad (171d), dual (45c,171d), duan (64b), duar, Duat (172d), Fuad (54d), Guam, guan (151b), guao (168c,169b), guar (46c,59d), juan (113a), Juan (96a), juar (100a), kuan (30b), Kuan (30c), Kuar (102a), Muav (66a), quad (33c,172a), quae (176b), quag (21c,102c), quai (88b,117c,180c), quan (190), quas (135c), quay (88b,117c,180c), ruay (189), tuan (95d,147b, 166c), yuan (190), Yuan (30b,101d)

- - UA agua (152d,166c,178c), akua (120d), aqua (90a,178c), atua (120d), Erua (103c), skua (19b,72c,84a,141a), ulua (57a,74c), Ulua (141b)

U - - A ueba (188), ulna (21d,39b), ulua (57a,74c), Ulua (141b), Ulva (141b), unca (49a), upla, Urfa (99a), Uria (14c,16d), urna (133a), Ursa (17b,36b,43d), urva (38b), Usha (16a,150c), uvea (53c,82b)

UB - - uber (66b), Ubii (191)

- UB - buba (170a), Bube (180b), Bubi (180b), Bubo (112c), cuba (189), Cuba (180b), cube (66b,150a), cubi (188), dubb (161c), hubb (118b), juba (106b), jube (28d), kuba (26d,189), Luba (191), lube (110a), Lubs (94c), Nuba (108c), nubk (30d,164d), rube (37d, 135d,185d), Rube (96b), ruby (20a,65d,179c), tuba (105a,137d), tube (118b,158a)

- - UB blub, chub (40c,154c), club (39c), daub (148d), doub (189), drub (17b,39c), flub (22b), gaub (116c), glub, grub (43c,88d), knub (178b), slub (171c), snub (128c,148b), stub (156c)

- UC - Auca (192), buck, cuca (33a,105d), duce (29d), duck (26b,53b, 179c), Duco, duct (170c), fuci (132c), huck (167d), juca (27a), juck (114c), luce (58c,117d), Luce (7b,35a), luck (28d), lucy, Lucy (183c), much, muck, ouch!, puca (68a), puce (33c,d,52a), puck (44b,68a,77c,100c), Puck (99d,143b), ruck (39a,185a), such (146d), suck, tuck (156b), yuca (27a)

- - UC douc (101d), eruc (37a,56a)

U - - C Udic (108a), Utac (22d)

UD ·· udad (143d,144a,181c), udal (76b,88b,131c), Udic (108a)

· UD · Aude, buda (83d), Buda, dude (40d), duds (32c,166d), Juda, Jude (11c,96a), judo (84b,85c,142b), Judy (125c,183d), kudu (11a), Ludd (23c), ludi (133b), ludo (65a,112b), mudd (188), nuda (39b), Nudd (23c), nude (16c,172d), pudu (41d), rudd (26d,57a,b), rude (134b,172b), sudd (40b,58c,107b), suds (59a), wudu (102d)

·· UD baud (162d), Chud (191), feud (55d,126b,175b), foud (54d,144b), gaud (169d), laud (122a), loud (156a), maud (53d,71a,136d,143c), Maud (181a,183c), Phud (110b), puud (189), roud (57a,b), scud (32c,126c,135b,160c), spud (121d,151c), stud (22b,25a,42d,54d, 111c,143a,174a), syud (103b), thud

U ·· D udad (143d,144a,181c), used (6d,73a), uvid (101a)

UE ·· ueba (188)

· UE · Auer (79a), duel, duet (104d,171d), euer (66d), fuel (65c), hued, juez (152b), kuei (44a), quei (189), ruer, suer (124d), suet (54d), tuel

·· UE ague (30a,55d,95c), blue (33c,98c,102c,150d,173a), clue, flue (8b,30a), gaue (67a), glue (7b,156a), moue (61d,62b), neue (66c), Niue (137d), roue (41b,44c,127c,134b), slue (97b,148b,160a), true (7a,8d,37b,54b,94c,149c)

U ·· E ulme (49c), unde (179a), unie (173a), unze (189), urde (86b), urge (42d,46b,79d,80a,b,81c,150a), usee

· UF · buff (134c,161d), Bufo (166c), cuff (148a), duff (125b), Dufy (63a), gufa (21b,99a), guff, huff (58a), kufa (21b,99a), luff (136b), muff, puff, (180d), ruff (19b,33b,63d,137a), sufi (103a, 116c), tufa (121b,177a), tuff (121b,177a), tuft (24b,32d,38c), yuft (135c)

·· UF pouf, souf (146b)

UG ·· ugly

· UG · auge (123c,132b), Bugi (191), euge (180a), fuga, fugu (84b), gugu, huge, Hugh (96a), Hugo (63a,96a), juga (27a), kuge (84c), luge (148a), Lugh (28b), muga, ough, pugh, ruga (59b,185a), sugi (84b), vugg (28a,66a,132b), vugh (28a,66a,132b), Yuga (76d)

·· UG chug (53a), drug (105d), glug, joug (138d), plug (156d,184d), slug (46b,99b,157c), smug, snug (35a,38b,165c), Snug (99d), thug (65a), toug (171a), Utug (159b)

U ·· G uang (131a), Utug (159b)

· UH · buhl (81a), buhr (180d), Duhr (155b), Guha (191), guhr (47d), kuhl (53c), Ruhr

·· UH bruh (95a)

U ·· H umph, Urth (68d,107d,163d), Utah (180b)

· UI · cuif (139a,d,140c), cuir (45c,62a), duim (188), duit (190), Duit (192), guib (11a), huia (19a,106d), luif, Muir (8b,142c), nuit (62b), quid (39b,166d), quip (183a,b), quit (90d,130c), quiz, ruin (42d), suit (38a,58a,91a,112a,119c,137c), Yuit (51c)

·· UI arui (11b,143d,144a,181c), equi (122d), etui (27a,29b,62c,106b, 148d,166d,174b), Maui (120d)

U--I Ubii (191), unci (31d)

-UJ- fuji (84b), Fuji (84d), juju (29b,55d), puja (77a), suji (180c)

-UK- bukh (122a), bukk (122a), cuke (39b), duke (107c), duku (95d, 168c), juke (114c), Kuki (191), kuku (19a,106d), luke, Luke (52a,96a), puka (107a,168c), puku (11a), rukh (53b,54a), Suku (191), tuke (26b,53b), wukf (103a)

--UK cauk (139b), dauk (95d), Sauk (192), souk (22a,97a)

UL-- Ulam (67b), ulan (27d,88a), Ulex (153c), ullo (6a,144a), Ullr (146b,164d), ulme (49c), ulna (21d,39b), ulua (57a,74c), Uiua (141b), Ulva (141b)

-UL- aula (66c,73b), aulu (74c,168c), bulb 37a,172c), bulk (97b), bull (113c), bult (76d), cull (117c), culm (11a,32d,70d,145a,156a), cult (141d,161c), dull (21a,32c,173a), Dull (94b), fulk (173a), full (7b, 130b), gula (90a,101a,165b), gulf (6c), gull (32d,41c,42a,72c,99b, 141a), Gulo (183c), gulp (46a,79d,160a), hula (74b) hule, (23a, 134c), hulk (144d,173d), hull (141d,142a,144c,d), hulu (55b), jula, Jule (183d), July, kula (189), Kuli (27b), lull (25c,126d,150c), lulu (19a,57b,112c), Lulu (183d), mule (45b,148b,153c,180b), mulk (60d), mull (53b,135a,164c), null (108c,177a), pule (180d), pulk (37c,88d), puli (45a,78d), pull (45d,167d), pulp, pulu (74c), puly, rule (11b,26b,90b), rull (170b), Sula (65a), suld (188), sulk (159a), Sulu (102c), tula (9a), Tula, tule (24b,27c), Tulu (45d), vuln (184d), Yule (30d), zulu (171d,175d), Zulu (86a)

--UL Aoul (191), azul (151d), baul (18b), caul (16d,74d), deul (77b), Elul (102b), foul (173a), Gaul (10a,60d,63c), goul (102a), haul (27b,45d), maul (73c,96b), paul, Paul (96a), poul (190), saul (48a, 168c), Saul (18c,86d,115a), shul (161a), soul (10d,125a,153c, 176d)

U--L udal (76b,88b,131c), unal (147a), Ural (135c), uval (70c)

UM-- umbo (22b), umph

-UM- bump, Duma (135c), dumb (153b), dump, fume (129a,149a,157a), fumy, Gump (43b), Hume (50c), hump (124d), jump, lump (45a, 160c), mump (29b,153d), Numa (133a), numb, puma (27b,37c,55b, 103d), Pume (137b,175b,185b), pump, rumb (120b), rump, Sumo, sump (28c,45d), tump (60a,76d,103d), Yuma

--UM ahum, alum (14a,45c), arum (13a,39b,58d,92b,155c), Arum (66a), Atum (143a,159b), Baum (9c,112c), chum (38d), doum (168c), drum (105a), Geum (76b), glum (102c,159a), grum (102c), jhum, meum (27a,89c), Meum, odum (168c,180a), ogum (82b), ovum (48d), plum, rhum (8c), saum (189), scum (129b), slum, stum (70c,105c,131a,173a), swum, Ulam (67b), utum (19b,112c)

U--M urim (18d,23a,110a), utum (19b,112c)

UN-- unal (147a), unau (148c,171d), unca (49a), unci (31d), unco (140c), unde (179a), undo (11a,93d), undy (179a), unie (173a), Unio (105c), unis (91b), unit (101c,110c,147a), unto (166c), untz (189), unze (189)

-UN- aune (188), aunt (129c), buna (161c), bund (49c,66c,90c), bung (119d,156d), bunk, bunn (25b), bunt (15d,180c), Cuna (193), dune (137a), dunk (43c,79d), Duns, dunt, fund (6d,101c,130c), Fung

373

(191), Funj, funk (63d,113c), guna (106a,137b), gunj (70c), hung, hunh?, hunk, hunt (141c), June (183c), Jung (125a), junk (30a, 134c), Juno (69c,85d,100c,126b), kung (125b), kunk (188), luna 103c), Luna (102b), lune (38c,73b,74d), lung, luny (38b), mund (124d), mung (70d), munj (70d), paun (18b), puna (10b,33b,104a, 119b,182a), pund (189), pung (22c,148b), punk (9b,166a,167c), puno (182a), punt (21a,58b), puny (55b,179a), Qung (191), rune (9b,67a,94a,105c,107d,120a,141d,163d), rung (28c,39a), runt (47a172d), sung, Sung (30b), sunk, sunn (56a), tuna (57a,b,123b, 170d), tund (121d), tune (8b,12c,98c), tung (110a,168c), tuno (28b,168c), tunu (28b), tuny, Yunx (184a), Zuni (125b)

-- UN Amun (86d,127d,159b,164a), Chun (30c), drun (132b), faun (56a, 68b,137c,161a,184a), Idun (107d), jaun (113a), kaun (93d), laun (146b), loun (19a,b), maun (139d), noun (114b,158a), paun (18b), shun (15a,51b,52a), spun, stun (145a,157d), taun (188), tsun (30b), Usun (191), whun (64c,70a)

U -- N ulan (27d,88a), upon (6b), uran (101d), Usun (191), uzan (189)

- UO - buoy (28d,58c), quod (123d)

U -- O ullo (6a,144a), umbo (22b), unco (140c), undo (11a,93d), Unio (105c), unto (166c), upgo (13c)

UP -- upas (84d,120b,168c,d), upgo (13c), Upis (13b), upla, upon (6b)

- UP - dupe (27c,41c,72c,160c), Hupa (192), jupe (62b,84a), lupe (19a, 64a), Nupe (191), pupa (30d,81b,c), rupa (60b), supa (168c), supe (53a,154d), Tupi (192)

-- UP blup, caup, coup (20d,97c,157b,c,162d), gaup, loup (61d,62a,90c, 139d), Loup (193), noup (124b), plup, roup (44a,121d), scup (57a, 121b), snup (149b), soup, toup (95d), yaup, youp (185d)

UR -- Ural (135c), uran (101d), urde (86b), Urdu (77b), urdy (86b), Urey (17b,36b,43d), Urth (68d,107d,163d), urus (14d,53a,112c), urva 150a), Uria (14c,16d), urim (18d,23a,110a), urna (133a), Ursa (17b,36b,43d), Urth (68d,107d,163d), urus (14d,53a,112c), urva (38b)

- UR - aura (44c,49c,66a,96b,158a,170d,177c), auri (34a), bura (182b), bure (61b), burg (22b,73c), buri (56b), burl (87c,169a), burn, burr (123b), bury (81d), cura (152c), curb (130c,146b), curd (99d), cure (123b), curl (38d,73b,131d), curr (104c), curt (145b,c), dura (153c), duro (190), durr (70b), furl (132d), fury (157a), guru (77b), hura (20a,137a), Hura, hurl (167c), hurt, jura, Jura, jure (90b), jury (38a), Kurd (48b,82a), Kure (84c), Kuri (191), kurk (31a,139b), lura (22d,82a), lure (41c,51a,54b,163a), lurg (96d,141b,184d), Luri (191), lurk (92a,147b), mura (84d), Mura (192), mure (177d), murk (41a,67d), murr (72b,128b), nurl (33b,87c), nurr (67d), ours (124c), pure (29b,172b,173c), puri (80d), purl (87c,104c), purr (104c), Puru (192), ruru (19b,102c,106d), sura (87c,113b,166d), surd (82c,177a), sure (173d), surf (23a), turf (115c,149d,160b), Turi (191), Turk (101d,102d,106a,111d), turm (132d), turn (28d, 131a,175a), turp, turr (24d,105a), Wurd, wurm (67c), yurt (101d)

-- UR Alur (191), Asur (68c), biur (35a), blur, caur (139a), Daur (139b), dour (67d,159a), ebur (89c), four (26c), gaur (112c,181c), gour (112c,181c), hour, knur (67d,87c,107d), lour (13d,63d), peur (61c),

374

pour (162d), **scur** (78b), **slur** (44b,124c,148b,168a), **smur** (32c,46b, 100c), **sour, spur** (10d,67d,167d,168a,181b), **tour** (31b,85c), **your** (124c)

U - - R   **uber** (66b), **Ullr** (146b,164d), **usar** (8d,16c), **user** (49d), **utor** (90a, 166c)

US - -   **usar** (8d,16c), **Usas** (68d), **used** (6d,73a), **usee, user** (49d), **uses** (18a), **Usha** (16a,150c), **Usun** (191)

- US -   **Ausa, ausu** (168c,180b), **bush, busk** (17b,37b,55d,161b), **buss** (87a,148c), **bust, busy, cush** (101c), **Cush** (51d,73c), **cusk** (57b), **cusp** (38c,78b,119a,120a,b), **cuss, duse** (83c), **dusk** (171c), **dust, fuse** (98c), **fuss** (22b,35b), **fust** (105c,143b), **gush** (35a,154c), **gust, huse** (180c), **hush** (17b,146c), **husk** (53a,78d,142a), **huso** (180c), **just** (51b,54b), **kusa, Kush, lush** (94d), **lust** (41b), **Musa** (16a), **muse** (65b,93d,120d,164c), **Muse** (68d), **mush** (97d), **musk** (116b), **Muso** (192), **muss** (135b,173d), **must** (70c,101a,106d,157d,182c), **Ouse** (132a,185d), **oust** (44c,49a,52b,125d), **push,** (145c) **puss, rusa, Rusa** (41d,136d), **ruse** (13b,77c,157b,169c), **rush, rusk** (23a), **Russ** (135b), **rust** (37b,112c,119a), **Susa** (49a), **susi** (53b,d), **susu** (20c), **Susu** (191), **Susy** (183d), **tush** (167b), **tusk** (167b),

- - US   **acus** (89d,118a), **Apus** (36b,c), **avus** (89b), **cous** (38a), **crus** (91a, 143c), **deus** (68a,89b), **Esus, gaus** (67a), **Grus** (36b,c,38b), **Ilus** (88d,170b), **irus** (109d), **nous** (81d,100a,128b), **onus** (24c,93b,109b), **opus** (35c,105a,184c), **Otus** (67a), **Pius** (121a), **plus** (10b, 102c), **pous** (188), **Rhus** (159a), **sous** (62d,172c), **thus** (149c), **urus** (14d,53a,112c), **Zeus** (135a)

U - - S   **unis** (91b), **upas** (84d,120b,168c,d), **Upis** (13b), **urus** (14d,53a, 112c), **uses** (18a), **Usas** (68d), **utas** (49a,109c)

UT - -   **utac** (22d), **Utah** (180b), **utas** (49a,109c), **utor** (90a,166c), **Utug** (159b), **utum** (19b,112c)

- UT -   **auto** (34d), **Buto** (142d), **butt** (27a,77b,127d,162a,182b), **cute** (39c), **duty** (109b,162b), **fute** (51c), **Guti, jute** (37a,48a,56a,133d, 136a), **Jute, lute** (11c,28b,84d,105a,131d), **muta** (28d,103a), **mute** (146c,153b), **muth** (188), **mutt** (39c,101d), **putt** (69d), **Ruta** (76b, 134d), **rute** (188), **ruth** (35b,118c), **Ruth** (105b,183c), **tute** (171b), **tutu** (16a,106d,147d), **yutu** (19b,166a)

- - UT   **abut** (22a,167c), **bhut** (67a), **blut** (66b), **bout** (36c), **brut** (182c), **Brut** (23c), **chut!, Cnut** (40d,50c), **gaut** (88b,103d,132a), **glut** (52c,70a,137c,159d), **gout, knut, Knut** (40d,50c,96a), **lout** (15c, 22a,24b,45b,109a,157d), **naut** (141b), **paut** (140a), **phut** (24b), **Phut** (110b), **pout** (159a), **prut!, Prut** (41a), **rout** (41d,44b,46b), **scut** (145c,161b), **shut, smut** (32d,44a,119a,150c), **sput** (21c), **taut** (163b,165c), **tout** (61a,127a)

U - - T   **unit** (101c,110c,147a)

- UU -   **puud** (189)

U - - U   **unau** (148c,171d), **Urdu** (77b)

UV - -   **uval** (70c), **uvea** (53c,82b), **uvic** (70c), **uvid** (101a)

- UV -   **cuvy** (141a)

- UW -   **tuwi** (117a,168c)

- - UW   **bouw** (188), **dauw** (24c)

- **UX** -   buxy (115b), **luxe** (61c,62d,159c), **puxy**
- - **UX**   crux (39a,151b), **eaux** (178c), **flux** (28d,58d), **jeux** (61d), **Vaux** (63b)
U - - X   Ulex (153c)
- **UY** -   buyo (18b), **cuya** (39b), **Puya** (118b)
U - - Y   ugly, **undy** (179a), **urdy** (86b), **Urey** (14b,107c,138c)
UZ - -   uzan (189)
- **UZ** -   auzu (168c,180b), **buzz**, **fuze** (98c), **fuzz** (45d), **guze** (128d), **huzz**, **Juza** (155b), **Muzo** (192), **tuza** (119d), **wuzu** (102d), **zuza** (189)
- - **UZ**   Ghuz (171a)
U - - Z   untz (189)
VA - -   Vach (153b), **vade** (42c,67d,89b), **vagi** (38b), **vail** (94b,124a,174b), **vain** (81a), **vair** (64c,154c), **vale** (54c,128a,174b), **Vale** (7c,109c), **vali** (171a,176a), **Vali** (7c,109c), **vamp** (80a,145a), **vane** (179b, 182a), **vang** (72d,134a,140b), **Vans** (107d), **vara** (151d), **vare** 179b), **vari** (34d,91b,134d,174d), **vary** (28d,43c), **vasa** (46d,114a, 160b,175d), **Vasa, vase, vast** (78d,79d), **vasu** (106c), **Vasu** (176d), **Vaux** (63b), **Vayu** (68c,182a), **vaza** (114a)
- **VA** -   aval (70c), **Avar** (27d,108a), **Evan** (96a), **Ivah** (18d), **Ivan** (40c, 85b,96a), **kvas** (135c), **oval** (48d,49c,127a), **Svan** (27d), **uval** (70c)
- - **VA**   Alva (151d), **cava** (116a,175b), **Civa** (56d), **deva** (23d,42a,42b, 56d,77a), **diva** (100d,123c), **Hova** (95a), **Java** (33a), **jiva** (77a), **Jova** (193), **kava** (18c,116a), **kiva** (28c,125b), **lava** (101c,151a, 177a), **Neva** (91b,132a), **nova** (20c,106d,155c,174d), **peva** (12d), **siva** (67a), **Siva** (56d,77a), **Ulva** (141b), **urva** (38b), **viva** (93d), **Xova** (193), **yava**
V - - A   vara (151d), **vasa** (46d,114a,160b,175d), **Vasa, vaza** (114a), **Veda** (77a,b), **vega** (110d,152c), **Vega** (155b), **vela** (98c,136b,149d), **Vela** (36b,c), **vena** (90a,175a), **vera** (140c,151b,175c), **Vera** (183c), **veta** (104a), **Vida** (183c), **vila** (54b), **vina** (77a,105a), **Vira** (191), **visa** (114d), **vita** (89c,92a), **viva** (93d), **vola** (89d,150a), **vota** (133b)
V - - B   verb (7a,114b,184b)
- - **VD**   NKVD (135d)
V - - D   veld (151a), **vend** (97a,115c,142b), **Vend** (10b,148a), **verd** (71d), **void** (11a,49d,108d,174b)
VE - -   veal, **Veda** (77a,b), **veer** (28d,144c,171b), **vega** (110d,152c), **Vega** (155b), **veil** (74d,76c), **vein** (20d,157b), **vela** (98c,136b,149d), **Vela** (36b,c), **veld** (151a), **velo** (175b), **vena** (90a,175a), **vend** (97a, 115c,142b), **Vend** (10b,148a), **vent** (8b,11b,110d,112a), **Veps** (191), **vera** (140c,151b,175c), **Vera** (183c), **verb** (7a,114b,184b), **verd** (71d), **veri** (28b), **vert** (71d,166a,171b), **very** (149c), **vest** (32c, 177b), **veta** (104a), **veto** (94a,124a), **Veto**
- **VE** -   avec (63a,183a), **aver** (7c,14a,15c,41c,95c,140d,155c,160b,184c), **Aves** (19d), **evea** (82a,95a), **even** (51a,58b,79d,91d,149a,173a), **ever** (9b,14b,80b), **evet** (48d,107a,136c,169d), **Ives** (9c,90b), **oven** (15d,78c,86b), **over** (6b,38c,80a,114d,130a), **uvea** (53c,82b)
- - **VE**   bave (61d,146c), **cave** (27d), **cive** (110c), **cove** (17a,73d,107d),

376

Dave (96b), **dive** (42b,74b,119d), **dove** (19a,117d), **eave** (133c), **five, gave, give** (79d,123a), **gyve** (55d,143b), **have** (92a), **hive** (17c), **hove** (92a), **Jave** (84d), **jive** (160c), **Jove** (85d), **kive** (174d), **lave** (16d,178b), **leve** (62a), **live** (47c), **love** (163a), **move, nave** (30d,31a,78d,114b,180c), **neve** (56d,67c,70c,149b), **nove** (83b), **pave** (85a), **rave** (41c,157a,161d), **reve** (61c,104d), **rive** (32a,153d), **rove** (127d,132b,178a), **save** (52b,110c,123a,173c), **seve** (63a, 182c), **sive** (146a), **Tave** (183d), **vive** (93d), **wave** (19a,59a,111c, 131d,160c,172d), **wive** (97a), **wove**

V--E   **vade** (42c,67d,89b), **vale** (54c,128a,174b), **Vale** (7c,109c), **vane** (179b,182a), **vare** (179b), **vase, vice** (31d,158a), **vide** (89d,126a, 142a), **vile** (16c,56c), **vine** (32b), **vire** (11a,13b), **vise** (31d,77d, 114d), **vite** (62b), **vive** (93d), **voce** (83c,177a), **vole** (97d,104a, 148a,149b), **vote** (60b), **Vote** (56d)

V--G   **vang** (72d,134a,140b), **voog** (28a,66a,132b), **vugg** (28a,66a,132b)

--VH   **IHVH** (159d), **JHVH** (159d), **YHVH** (159d)

V--H   **Vach** (153b), **Voth** (191), **vugh** (28a,66a,132b)

VI--   **vial** (148c), **vice** (31d,158a), **Vida** (183c), **vide** (89d,126a,142a), **vier** (66c), **view** (93d,138b), **vila** (54b), **vile** (16c,56c), **vili** (54b), **Vili** (109c), **vill** (176b), **vily** (54b), **vina** (77a,105a), **vine** (32b), **vino** (92d,182b), **vint** (26c,182c), **viny, viol** (105a), **Vira** (191), **vire** (11a,13b), **visa** (114d), **vise** (31d,77d,114d), **viss** (189), **vita** (89c, 92a), **vite** (62b), **viti** (176b), **viva** (93d), **vive** (93d), **vivo** (93a)

-VI-   **avid** (47b,71a,186b), **avis** (89a), **Avis** (183c), **evil** (79c,95d,147a, 181a,185c), **Ovid** (132d,133b), **Ovis** (143d), **uvic** (70c), **uvid** (101a)

--VI   **Devi** (147b,153b), **divi, favi** (138a,165d), **hevi** (111d), **Kavi** (84d), **Levi** (84a,90c), **ravi** (61b), **Ravi** (16b)

V--I   **vagi** (38b), **vali** (171a,176a), **Vali** (7c,109c), **vari** (34d,91b,134d, 174d), **veri** (28b), **vili** (54b), **Vili** (109c), **viti** (176b), **vlei** (38c,160a)

V--K   **volk** (66c,105d,116a,184c)

VL--   **vlei** (38c,160a), **vley** (160a)

V--L   **vail** (94b,124a,174b), **veal, veil,** (74d,76c), **vial** (148c), **vill** (176b), **viol** (105a)

V--N   **vain** (81a), **vein** (20d,157b), **vuln** (184d)

VO--   **voce** (83c,177a), **voet** (188), **Vogt, void** (11a,49d,108d,174b), **vola** (89d,150a), **vole** (97d,104a,148b,149b), **volk** (66c,105d,116a,184c), **volt** (49b,78c,173b), **voog** (28a,66a,132b), **vota** (133b), **vote** (60b), **Vote** (56d), **Voth** (191), **Voto** (192)

-VO-   **Avon** (143b), **Avow** (6d,36a,41c,112c), **evoe** (15b,130d,181c)

--VO   **levo** (91a), **pavo** (115b), **Pavo** (36b,c), **vivo** (93a)

V--O   **velo** (175b), **veto** (94a,124a), **Veto, vino** (92d,182b), **vivo** (93a), **Voto** (192)

V--P   **vamp** (80a,145a)

V--R   **vair** (64c,154c), **veer** (28d,144c,171b), **vier** (66c)

--VS   **revs** (131a)

V--S   **Vans** (107d), **Veps** (191), **viss** (189)

V--T   **vast** (78d,79d), **vent** (8b,11b,110d,112a), **vert** (71d,166a,171b),

vest (32c,177b), **vint** (26c,182c), **voet** (188), **Vogt, volt** (49b,78c, 173b)

VU - -   **vugg** (28a,66a,132b), **vugh** (28a,66a,132b), **vuln** (184d)

- VU -   **avus** (89b), **ovum** (48d)

- - VU   **kivu** (170c)

V - - U   **vasu** (106c), **Vasu** (176d), **Vayu** (68c,182a)

V - - W   **view** (93d,138b)

V - - X   **Vaux** (63b)

- - VY   **bevy** (38a,58c), **cavy** (72b,120d,132c,157b), **cuvy** (141a), **Davy** (96b,136b), **envy** (41b), **levy** (14a,162b), **Livy** (132d,133a), **navy** (33c,58b), **pavy** (115b), **pevy** (91d,94c), **Tavy** (183d), **wavy** (147b, 172d)

V - - Y   **vary** (28d,43c), **very** (149c), **vily** (54b), **viny, vley** (160a)

WA - -   **Waac, waag** (71d,101d), **Wabi** (192), **Waco, wadd** (109c), **wade, wadi** (46c,106a,109a,128a,132a), **wady** (109a,128a,132a), **waeg** (19b,72c,87a), **waer** (40b), **Wafd** (49a), **waft** (20d,58c), **wage** (27a, 115b), **waif** (157b), **wail** (39b,88a), **wain** (177b), **Wain, wait** (26d, 42b,92c,155d,162a), **waka** (26a), **wake** (134b,168a), **wakf** (103a), **waky, wale** (70b,131b,157c,163d,179a,180a,c,d), **wali** (171a), **walk, wall, Walt** (96b), **wand** (120b,132c,156a), **wane** (41c,43c), **wang** (189), **want** (41b,42d,87b,106b,122a), **wany, wapp** (54b,133d, 145d), **waqf** (103a), **ward** (31c,55c,86b), **ware** (27d,35a), **warf, warm** (7c,75b,163b), **warn** (7b), **warp** (36c,165a,171c), **wart** (124d), **wary** (27d,176b), **wash, wasp, wast, Wate** (141a), **watt** (173b, 177c), **Watt** (82a), **wave** (19a,59a,111c,131d,160c,172d), **wavy** (147b,172d), **waxy** (119c,149d), **ways**

- WA -   **Awan** (191), **away** (6b,69d,76a,109d,111d), **Ewan, kwan** (30b), **swab** (102b), **swad** (94d), **swag** (22a,156c), **swam, swan** (19b,33a), **swap** (168a), **swat** (15d,20d,32d,157c), **Swat** (103a), **sway** (104a)

- - WA   **biwa** (93d,168c), **dewa, Iowa** (193), **kawa** (18c,116a), **Iowa** (19a), **pawa** (189), **tawa** (160d,168c), **Tewa** (193)

W - - A   **waka** (26a), **Wega** (155b), **weka** (58c,106d,107a,127b), **weta** (93c), **whoa** (156d)

W - - C   **Waac**

- - WD   **dowd** (143b), **gawd** (169c)

W - - D   **wadd** (109c), **Wafd** (49a), **wand** (120b,132c,156a), **ward** (31c,55c, 86b), **week, weld** (47c,85b,173c), **wend** (67d,123d), **Wend** (10b, 148a), **wild** (38b,173d), **wind** (33b,39d,171c,185a), **woad** (20d,47c), **wold** (47c,60a,118d,174a,184a), **wood, word** (124b,165c), **Wurd, Wyrd** (107d)

WE - -   **weak** (55b), **weal** (124d,157c,180c,d), **wean** (8d,42d), **wear** (50b), **weed, week, weel** (16d,57d,140d,180d), **weep** (39b,88a,104a), **weet** (19d), **weft** (39a,165a,184b), **Wega** (155b), **Wegg** (111d), **weir** '40b,57d), **weka** (58c,106d,107a,127b), **weki** (55c), **weld** (47c,85b, 173c), **Welf** (67a), **welk** (65c,96d,141b), **well welt** (36d,131b,145a, b,177b,d), **wend** (67d,123d), **Wend** (10b,148a), **went** (42c), **wept, were** (139b), **werf** (54d), **weri** (15c,27c), **wert, west, West** (9c,50b, 109b), **weta** (93c)

- WE - ewer (84d,85c,118c,181b), kwei (44a), **Owen** (96a,183c), **sweb** (160d), twee

-- WE howe (77d), **Howe** (17a,82a), powe

W -- E wade, wage (27a,115b), wake (134b,168a), wale (70b,131b,157c, 163d,179a,180a,c,d), wane (41c,43c), ware (27d,35a), **Wate** (141a), wave (19a,59a,111c,131d,160c,172d), were (139b), whee, wide (133d), wife (154a), wile (13b,41c,157b,169c), wine, wipe, wire, wise (136b), wive (97a), woke, wore, **Wote** (191), wove

W -- F waif (157b), wakf (103a), waqf (103a), warf, **Welf** (67a), werf (54d), wolf, woof (39a,163d,165a,179d), **Wraf**, wukf (103a)

W -- G waag (71d,101d), waeg (19b,72c,87a), wang (189), **Wegg** (111d), Whig wigg, wing (10d,58c,59a,118b,d), wong (56a)

WH -- wham (157c), what (129c), whau (107a,168c), whee!, when (180d), whet (143c,156b), whew, whey (100a), Whig, whim (26c, 54c,108c), whin (64c,70a,132b,181d), whip (58c,88d), whir (25c, 181a), whit (166c), whiz (25c), whoa (156d), whom (42b), whoo!, whun (64c,70a), whyo (59d,65a)

-- WH **JHWH** (159d), **YHWH** (159c)

W -- H wash, wish (42d), with (10b)

WI -- wick, wide (133d), widu (102d), wiel (140d,180d), wies (185a), wife (154a), wigg, wild (38b,173d), wile (13b,41c,157b,169c), wilk (65c,96d,141b), will (18b,43a,163c,177c), wilt (46b), wily (13b,38b,39c), wind (33b,39d,171c,185a), wine, wing (10d,58c, 59a,118b,d), wink (107a), winy (176c), wipe, wire, wiry (147a, 167c), wise (136b), wish (42d), wisp (24b,148c), wist (87c), with (10b), wive (97a)

- WI - swig (46a,72c), swim (58c), swiz (160c), twig, twin (45c,171d), twit (162b,c)

-- WI liwi (19a,74b), **Kawi** (84d), kiwi (11d,19a,58c), tuwi (117a,168c)

W -- I **Wabi** (192), wadi (46c,106a,109a,128a,132a), wali (171a), wekl (55c), weri (15c,27c)

-- WK bowk (155d), cawk (133c), dawk (95c), gawk (146d), gowk (146d), hawk (19c,115c), sawk (188)

W -- K walk, weak (55b), week, welk (65c,96d,141b), wick, wilk (65c, 96d,141b), wink (107a), work (64c,76b)

-- WL bawl, bowl, cowl (101d), dowl, fowl, gowl (102a,140d,185b), howl (39b), jowl (29b), mewl (180d), pawl (43a,95a), yawl (136b,171d, 175d), yowl

W -- L wail (39b,88a), wall, weal (124d,157c,180c,d), weel (16d,57d,140d, 180d), well, wiel (140d,180d), will (18b,43a,163c,177c), wool (58b, 179c)

-- WM dawm (190)

W -- M warm (7c,75b,163b), wham (157c), whim (26c,54c,108c), whom (42b), worm, wurm (67c),

-- WN bawn (181a), dawn (14d,41b), down (149d), fawn (33c), gown, hewn, kawn (93d), lawn (20a,37c,53b,92c), lown (157d), mown, pawn (29c,119c), sawn, sewn, town (73c), yawn

W -- N wain (177b), **Wain**, warn (7b), wean (8d,42d), when (180d), whin

(64c,70a,132b,181d), **whun** (64c,70a), **woon** (24c), **worn** (143b), **wren** (19b,c), **Wren** (50b), **wynn** (165d)

WO · ·   **woad** (20d,47c), **woke, wold** (47c,60a,118d,174a,184a), **wolf, wong** (56a), **wont** (6d,40a,73a,174c), **wood woof** (39a,163d,165a, 179d), **wool** (58b,179c), **woon** (24c), **word** (124b,165c), **wore, work** (64c,76b), **worm, worn** (143b), **wort** (76a,95d,121d), **Wote** (191), **wove**

· WO ·   Lwow, **swob** (102b), **swop** (168a), **swot, swow** (100a)

W · · O   Waco, **whoo, whyo** (59d,65a)

· · WP   gawp, lowp (90c,139d), yawp

W · · P   **wapp** (54b,133d,145d), **warp** (36c,165a,171c), **wasp, weep** (39b, 88a,104a), **whip** (58c,88d), **wisp** (24b,148c), **wrap** (32b,51a)

WR · ·   **Wraf, wrap** (32b,51a), **wren** (19b,c), **Wren** (50b), **writ** (91a)

· WR ·   **awry** (13d,38d,171c), **ewry** (133c)

W · · R   **waer** (40b), **wear** (50b), **weir** (40b,57d), **whir** (25c,181a)

· WS ·   owse

· · WS   **mews** (154c), **news** (165c)

W · · S   **ways, wies** (185a)

· · WT   **newt** (48d,136c,169d), **nowt** (106a,139a), **yowt** (139c)

W · · T   **waft** (20d,58c), **wait** (26d,42b,92c,155d,162a), **Walt** (96b), **want** (41b,42d,87b,106b,122a), **wart** (124d), **wast, watt** (173b,177c), **Watt** (82a), **weet** (19d), **weft** (39a,165a,184b), **welt** (36d,131b, 145a,b,177b,d), **went** (42c), **wept, wert, west, West** (9c,50b,109b), **what** (129c), **whet** (143c,156b), **whit** (166c), **wilt** (46b), **wist** (87c), **wont** (6d,40a,73a,174c), **wort** (76a,95d,121d), **writ** (91a)

WU · ·   **wudu** (102d), **wukf** (103a), **Wurd, wurm** (67c), **wuzu** (102d)

· WU ·   swum

W · · U   **whau** (107a,168c), **widu** (102d), **wudu** (102d), **wuzu** (102d)

W · · W   whew!

WY · ·   **wynn** (165d), **Wyrd** (107d)

· WY ·   **Gwyn** (40c,50b)

· · WY   **dewy** (101a), **jawy, nowy** (194), **rowy** (157b), **towy** (58b)

W · · Y   **wady** (109a,128a,132a), **waky, wany, wary** (27d,176b), **wavy** (147b,172d), **waxy** (119c,149d), **whey** (100a), **wily** (13b,38b,39c), **winy** (176c), **wiry** (147a,167c)

W · · Z   whiz (25c)

· XA ·   **axal** (120b), **exam, oxan** (65c)

· · XA   **Bixa** (145d), **coxa** (77b), **doxa** (48b), **moxa** (27d,30c), **myxa** (168c, 169a), **noxa, toxa** (153d)

X · · A   **xema** (72c), **Xema** (12c), **Xina** (183d), **Xosa** (86a), **Xova** (193)

XE · ·   **xema** (72c), **Xema** (12c), **xeno** (34d)

· XE ·   **oxea** (153d), **oxen** (10c), **oxer** (55c)

· · XE   **luxe** (61c,62d,159c), **Mixe** (192), **saxe** (20d,33c)

X · · E   **Xipe** (15c)

XI · ·   **Xina** (183d), **Xipe** (15c)

- XI - axil (10c), axis (28b,41d,77c,153c), exit (114d), ixia (37a), Ixil (192), oxid (112c)

- - XI dixi, taxi (13a,125b)

- XL - axle (153c,180c), ixle (56a)

XM - - Xmas

XO - - Xosa (86a), Xova (193)

- XO - axon (106c,153c)

- - XO Moxo (192), myxo, taxo (13a)

X - - O xeno (34d), xylo (35a,183d)

X - - S Xmas

- - XT next (106a), sext (26b,111b,147b), text (21c,140d)

XY - - xylo (35a,183d)

- XY - oxyl (112c)

- - XY boxy, buxy (115b), doxy (129d), foxy (38b,39c,181d), mixy, pixy (154b), puxy, Roxy (183d), waxy (119c,149d)

YA - - yage (23a), yaje (23a), Yaka (191), Yaki (193), Yale (173c), yali (171a), Yama (57a,68a), Yana (192,193), yang (30b,70a), yank, Yank, Yaou (30c), yapa (113b), Yapp (22a), yard (152d), yare (96b,124b,128b), yark (22c), yarl (40d,107d), yarn (154b,161b, 184b), yarr (72a), Yaru (48d), yate (51d,168c), yati (76d), yaup, yava, yawl (136b,171d,175d), yawn, yawp, yaya (113c,168c)

- YA - ayah (108d), cyan, dyad (113a), Dyak (22b), Dyas (66a), eyah (95b, 108d,111c), eyas (106c,173a), Iyar (102b), kyah (19a), kyak (51c), kyar (33a), kyat (189), Lyam (139a), Lyas (66a), pyal (175c), pyat (95b), ryal (110a,190)

- - YA Alya (155b,c), Arya (80d), baya (179b), Baya (191), cuya (39b), Goya (151d), Hoya (14d), maya (77a,179b), Maya (23d,186c), Puya (118b), raya (19b,23c,76d,107d), saya (117a), soya (151b), yaya (113c,168c)

Y - - A Yaka (191), Yama (57a,68a), Yana (192,193), yapa (113b), yava, yaya (113c,168c), yeta (84c), Yima (84a,116b,c), Ynca (193), yoga (10b,13c,77a), yuca (27a), Yuga (76d), Yuma

- YB - gybe (144c), Tybi (102a)

- YC - syce (71d)

- YD - hyde (188), Hyde (45a)

- - YD emyd (163c,167c)

Y - - D yard (152d), yond (164d)

YE - - yeah, yean (88a), year, yeas (177c), Yedo (166d), yegg (24c), yell (145c), yelp, yelt (151b), yeni (19b,161d), yeso (72d), yeta (84c)

- YE - ayes (177c), byee (189), dyer, eyer, eyey (74b), oyer (38a,75b, 119c), oyes (38a,39b,75b), oyez (38a,39b,75b), pyet (95b), ryel (190), syed (103b), tyee (29d), tyer

- - YE Daye (123d), Skye (163c)

Y - - E yage (23a), yaje (23a), Yale (173c), yare (96b,124b,128b), yate (51d,168c), yoke (85b,92d,173c), yore (10b,69d,93c,110b,165d), Yule (30d)

- **YG** - bygo (114c), zyga (134b)
- **Y - - G** yang (30b,70a), yegg (24c)
- **YH - -** YHVH (159d), YHWH (159d)
- **Y - - H** yeah, YHVH (159d), YHWH (159d), yodh (91d), yogh (10c,185a)
- **YI - -** Yima (84a,116b,c)
- **- YI -** ayin (91c)
- **- - YI** kiyi (185d)
- **Y - - I** Yaki (193), yall (171a), yati (76d), yeni (19b,161d), Yobi, yogi (76d)
- **- YK -** cyke (40c), dyke (49c,91d), fyke (15d), hyke!, syke (194), tyke (29d)
- **Y - - K** yank, Yank, yark (22c), yolk, york (38c), York (50b,c)
- **- YL -** gyle (23b,174d), Hyla (10a,166d,169b), hyle (97c), kyle (57a, 139c), pyla (22d), pyle (34b), Pyle (9c,178a), Xylo (35a,183d)
- **- - YL** acyl (6d), amyl (155c), idyl (114d), noyl (87c), odyl (59d,79c), oxyl (112c), teyl (92b,c,168c)
- **Y - - L** yarl (40d,107d), yawl (136b,171d,175d), yell (145c), yowl, ypil (117a,168c)
- **YM - -** Ymer (67a,131c), Ymir (67a,131c)
- **- YM -** cyma (101a,b), cyme (58d,69c), hymn (150c), ryme (178d), tymp (20c), zyme (55c)
- **- - YM** clym (12b), etym (133d), onym (162c)
- **YN - -** Ynca (193)
- **- YN -** dyna (34c), dyne (59d,173b), gyne (34b,55b,183c), jynx (78a), Jynx (184a), lynx (26c,181d), Lynx (36b), myna (19a,c,70b), rynd (100a), syne (140b,147a), tyne, Tyne (108a), wynn (165d)
- **- - YN** coyn (37a), Gwyn (40c,50b), llyn (120d,140a)
- **Y - - N** yarn (154b,161b,184b), yawn, yean (88a), yuan (190), Yuan (30b, 101d)
- **YO - -** Yobi, yodh (91d), yoga (10b,13c,77a), yogh (10c,185a), yogi (76d), yoke (85b,92d,173c), yolk, yond (164d), yoop, yore (10b,69d,93c, 110b,165d), york (38c), York (50b,c), youp (185d), your (124c), yowl, yowt (139c)
- **- YO -** eyot (82d), ryot (115c)
- **- - YO** buyo (18b), cayo, coyo (15a,30c), Enyo (12c,69c,178a), Idye (191), kayo (87c), Mayo (193), whyo (59d,65a)
- **Y - - O** Yedo (166d), yeso (72d)
- **YP - -** ypil (117a,168c)
- **- YP -** gyps, Gyps (71d), hype (185a), hypo (117b), hyps, rype (19b,125a), sype (110c), type (31d,115a,155a), typo (35c,51b), typp (185b), typy
- **- - YP** tryp (114a)
- **Y - - P** Yapp (22a), yaup, yawp, yelp, yoop, youp (185d)
- **- YR -** Byrd (9c,120b), byre (38a), eyra (181d), eyre (23c,31b,85c), Eyre, eyry (47b,106c), fyrd (110a), gyre (31b,171b), gyri (22d,

131b), **gyro** (34d), **Lyra** (36b,74a), **lyre** (11c,81c,105a,111c), **Myra** (10a,31b,183c), **pyre** (64c), **pyro**, **Syra**, **tyre** (15a), **Tyre** (31b,90d, 117b), **tyro** (9b,17d,108c), **Tyrr** (68c,109c,163d,178a), **Wyrd** (107d)

- -YR   **skyr** (21d,151a)

Y - -R   **yarr** (72a), **year**, **Ymer** (67a,131c), **Ymir** (67a,131c), **your** (124c), **Yser**

YS - -   **Yser**

- YS -   **cyst**, **lyse**, **myst** (71c,123b)

- -YS   **Alys** (183c), **Emys** (167c,171b), **days**, **Itys** (163b), **ways**

Y - -S   **yeas** (177c)

- YT -   **myth** (8b,91a), **Tyto** (16c)

- -YT   **skyt** (138c,140b)

Y - -T   **yelt** (151b), **yowt** (139c), **yuft** (135c), **Yuit** (51c), **yurt** (101d)

YU - -   **yuan** (190), **Yuan** (30b,101d), **yuca** (27a), **yuft** (135c), **Yuga** (76d), **Yuit** (51c), **Yule** (30d), **Yuma**, **Yunx** (184a), **yurt** (101d), **yutu** (19b,166a)

- YU -   **syud** (103b)

- -YU   **Vayu** (68c,182a)

Y - -U   **Yaou** (30c), **Yaru** (48d), **yutu** (19b,166a)

- YV -   **gyve** (55d,143b)

- YX -   **myxa** (168c,169a), **myxo**

- -YX   **Ceyx** (73b), **eryx** (137a), **onyx** (25d,28d,65d,142b), **oryx** (11a), **Pnyx** (71c), **Styx** (29b,73a,105c)

Y - -X   **Yunx** (184a)

- -YZ   **hayz**

ZA - -   **Zach** (96b), **zaim** (170d), **zain** (41a), **Zama** (73d,141d), **zany** (24a, 32d,59c), **zarf** (39c,155a), **zarp** (120c), **zati** (21d)

- ZA -   **Azam** (166c), **azan** (102d), **czar** (42d,49d,60b,135c), **izar** (65b, 103b), **Izar** (155b), **tzar** (42d,49d,60b,135c), **Uzan** (189)

- -ZA   **boza** (12a), **caza**, **Daza** (191), **Gaza** (117a), **Itza** (192), **Juza** (155b), **onza** (189), **tiza** (172a), **tuza** (119d), **vaza** (114a), **zuza** (189)

Z - -A   **Zama** (73d,141d), **zeta** (71b,91c), **Zipa** (29d), **zira** (188), **Zola** (63a), **zona** (144c,186d), **zuza** (189), **zyga** (134b)

- ZB -   **ezba** (188)

Z - -B   **Zimb** (6c)

Z - -C   **zinc** (21a)

Z - -D   **Zend**, **zoid**

ZE - -   **zeal** (12c,55d), **zebu** (22d,80d,112c), **zein**, **Zeke** (96b), **zeme** (55d,161b,180b), **zemi** (55d,161b,180b), **Zend**, **Zeno** (71b), **zenu** (143d), **zero** (31a,84c,108c), **Zero** (118d), **zest** (55d,72d), **zeta** (71b,91c), **Zeus** (135a)

- ZE -   **ezel** (47a,85d)

- -ZE   **adze** (40c,167a), **bize** (182a), **coze** (29b), **daze** (157d), **doze** (148a), **faze** (43d), **fuze** (98c), **gaze**, **guze** (128d), **haze** (100c,174d), **laze** (79b), **Laze** (191), **maze** (87b,157d), **naze** (26b,124b), **noze** (75a), ooze (53c,104b,116a), raze (42b,d,91d), size, unze (189)

Z--E   Zeke (96b), zeme (55d,161b,180b), zone (44c,50a,160a), zyme (55c)

Z--F   zarf (39c,155a)

Z--G   zing

-ZH-   Azha (155b)

Z--H   Zach (96b)

ZI--   Zimb (6c), zinc (21a), zing, Zion (75b,c,83a,157d), Zipa (29d), zipp, Zips (40c), zira (188), zizz (181a)

--ZI   cazi (103a), gazi, kazi (103a), Lazi (191), Nazi

Z--I   zati (21d), zemi (55d,161b,180b), Zuni (125b)

Z--L   zeal (12c,55d)

Z--M   zaim (170d), zoom

Z--N   zain (41a), zein, Zion (75b,c,83a,157d), zoon (43a)

ZO--   Zoar, Zoas (20b), zobo (186b), zodi, zogo (136a), zoid, Zola (63a), zona (144c,186d), zone (44c,50a,160a), zoom, zoon (43a)

-ZO-   Azof (20b,135d), azon (127b), Azov (20b,135d), mozo (152b), Muzo (192)

--ZO   bozo (55b), Idzo (191), kozo (113d,168c), lazo (88d,128b,133d)

Z--O   Zeno (71b), zero (31a,84c,108c), Zero (118d), zobo (186b), zogo (136a)

Z--P   zarp (120c), zipp

-ZR-   Ezra (96a)

Z--R   Zoar

Z--S   Zeus (135a), Zips (40c), Zoas (20b)

Z--T   zest (55d,72d)

ZU--   zulu (171d,175d), Zulu (86a), Zuni (125b), zuza (189)

-ZU-   azul (151d)

--ZU   anzu (11d), auzu (168c,180b), Enzu (102b), wuzu (102d)

Z--U   zebu (22d,80d,112c), zenu (143d), zulu (171d,175d), Zulu (86a)

ZY--   zyga (134b), zyme (55c)

--ZY   cazy (103a), cozy (149c), dazy, dozy, gazy, hazy (174b), Jozy, kazy (103a), lazy, oozy (148b), sizy (176d)

Z--Y   zany (24a,32d,59c)

--ZZ   bizz, buzz, fuzz (45d), huzz, jazz, razz (131b), sizz, zizz (181a)

Z--Z   zizz (181a)